20th Century® Bookkeeping and Accounting

First-Year Course

23d Edition

LEWIS D. BOYNTON
Chairman, Department of Business Education
Central Connecticut State College, New Britain, Connecticut

PAUL A. CARLSON
Professor Emeritus
Formerly Director, Division of Business Education
Wisconsin State College, Whitewater, Wisconsin

HAMDEN L. FORKNER
Professor Emeritus
Formerly Chairman, Department of Business Education
Teachers College, Columbia University, New York, New York

ROBERT M. SWANSON
Professor of Business Education and Office Administration
College of Business
Ball State University, Muncie, Indiana

SOUTH-WESTERN PUBLISHING COMPANY

Cincinnati • Chicago
Dallas
Burlingame, Calif.
New Rochelle, N.Y.

B85

Library of Congress Catalog Card No.: 67-12528

K367

Printed in the United States of America

PREFACE

BOOKKEEPING AND ACCOUNTING IN TODAY'S WORLD

A universal need exists today for a knowledge of the principles of bookkeeping and accounting. A knowledge of bookkeeping contributes to: (a) a person's ability to earn a living; (b) a person's understanding of the economic activities of the business world; and (c) a person's competence in managing his personal business affairs.

Bookkeeping and vocational competence

The study of bookkeeping prepares one for a business occupation. Full-time bookkeepers in both large and small businesses are needed in the successful operation of a business. Machine operators and other clerical workers who perform only one part of the bookkeeping process need an understanding of the total bookkeeping cycle in order to appreciate the part their particular task plays in the operation of the business.

A typist prepares statements and other reports dealing with bookkeeping work. A secretary takes dictation dealing with bookkeeping terms, business transactions, and financial records. She may also keep some bookkeeping records for her employer. A salesperson records cash and charge transactions and is often required to assist in inventory and other work related to bookkeeping. The study of bookkeeping, therefore, helps to prepare young people for successful participation in a variety of office and business occupations.

Bookkeeping and economic decisions

Business activities touch the lives of everyone. Economic decisions have to be made. Everyone who earns an income faces the problem of managing his income wisely and of providing for the future of his family. Intelligent decisions about buying a car or a home, participating in a pension plan, or voting on economic issues should be based on a knowledge of financial information and on the ability to interpret this information correctly. A knowledge of bookkeeping and accounting assists a person in making wise economic decisions.

Bookkeeping and automation

This is an era of automation. Early man used a chisel to record business transactions on stone tablets. Over the years he came to use, first, pen and ink; then, manually operated machines; and now automated machines activated by punched cards, punched paper tape, and magnetic tape. The automated machine, in spite of its magical ability and impressive appearance, is but a tool. The machine does not know what a man's mind will require of it. Nor could the chisel alone put the numbers where they belonged on the stone tablets. The chisel needed a hand and a mind to guide it. Similarly, the automated machine needs a hand and a mind to guide it. From the chisel of the earlier civilizations to the automated machines of this highly complicated era, the use of tools has been governed by principles. The study of bookkeeping is the study of principles that are basic to both hand-kept and machine-kept records.

Before automation can be applied to bookkeeping records, it is necessary to plan the kinds of records that will be needed. When the automated equipment produces records, it is necessary to interpret the records. Each of these steps requires a thorough knowledge of the total bookkeeping process. Whether a business owns its own data processing equipment or whether it uses the services of agencies that process bookkeeping data, a knowledge of bookkeeping is necessary in order to know what the records mean.

Over 98 percent of the more than four million firms in the United States employ less than 100 employees. Many small business firms have found that automated equipment is either too expensive to own or that it is not practical to convert their records from hand bookkeeping to automated bookkeeping. Similarly, departments within big businesses sometimes find that automated equipment is either too expensive or not practical.

In addition to being an era of automation, this is an age of records. It requires bookkeeping and accounting specialists with the appropriate education and experience to handle the accounts of the businesses and organizations serving the people of the world. In addition, it requires that each individual understand and use bookkeeping principles in the management of his personal economic affairs.

FEATURES OF THIS TEXTBOOK

A good textbook is an aid to the teacher and the student. Teachers know best what features in a textbook have aided them in helping students to learn. Therefore, bookkeeping teachers were consulted and they helped determine the contents of this edition.

This 23d Edition retains those features that have made *20th Century Bookkeeping and Accounting* the most widely used textbook in its field. This latest edition also includes new features that will keep it in the forefront of modern bookkeeping and modern bookkeeping teaching.

New features added

1. ***Bookkeeping terms and bookkeeping practices have been updated.*** For example, automation has brought to all offices the term *source document* to replace the older term *immediate record.* Similarly, *cycle billing*, a new procedure that is a product of automated data processing, is now found in many non-automated offices. The introduction in 1966 of payroll deductions for Medicare means that payroll procedures as outlined in earlier texts have been updated.
2. ***Increased attention is given to helping students understand debit and credit.*** Chapter 4 deals with the effect of business transactions upon balance sheet accounts. Chapter 5 deals with the effect of business transactions upon income and expense accounts. In these two chapters, and throughout the textbook, T accounts are extensively used in the debit and credit analysis of business transactions.
3. ***Automated data processing is treated more extensively.*** Special attention is given in Chapters 21 and 22 to the application of automation to the processing of bookkeeping data. In other chapters where applicable, automated equipment and processes are described.
4. ***Balance-column ruling of the general ledger accounts is introduced in Part 4.*** The use of general ledger accounts with balance-column ruling familiarizes first-year students with account forms commonly used in machine bookkeeping. Students learn how the use of such forms eliminates the need for ruling and balancing general ledger accounts at the close of a fiscal period.
5. ***Illustrations are made more effective by use of a fifth color.*** The addition of a fifth color in the 23d Edition makes it possible to show illustrations on up-to-date bookkeeping forms. Divider sheets that precede the parts of the textbook are introduced for the first time. The illustrations on the divider sheets, printed in five colors, invite the students' attention to important bookkeeping concepts in the chapters that follow.
6. ***A teacher's edition of the workbook is available.*** The teacher's edition is a self-contained workbook and key, consisting of the student's edition with solutions and answers overprinted in script form. By means of a photocopying machine, any page in the teacher's edition of the workbook may be used to make a transparency for use with an overhead projector.

Proven features retained

The proven step-by-step procedures and the expanding spiral development of bookkeeping learning are retained. The text material proceeds from a simple treatment of a small service business in the first learning cycle to ever-expanding learning cycles of larger and different kinds of businesses.

The provisions introduced in the preceding edition for students of different abilities have been expanded. The optional problems continue to help the teacher provide for individual differences. Close attention to short sentences and to reading difficulties also allows for the varying abilities of students in the bookkeeping class.

The 23d Edition continues to provide balance in bookkeeping theory, drill on principles, and application problems.

Acknowledgments

The publication of this 23d Edition of *20th Century Bookkeeping and Accounting*, like the publication of previous editions, reflects the combined efforts of many people. Teachers of bookkeeping and accounting have answered a questionnaire, and others have taken the time to write and offer suggestions for improvement. Professional accountants and specialists in the area of automated data processing have been consulted. Students, too, have contributed many worthwhile suggestions.

We are grateful to all of those who have participated in this revision and we wish to express our sincere appreciation for their help and suggestions.

Lewis D. Boynton
Paul A. Carlson
Hamden L. Forkner
Robert M. Swanson

CONTENTS

Part 1 The bookkeeping cycle in its simplest form

Part 6 Partnerships, corporations, and cooperatives

COMPLETE BOOKKEEPING RECORDS FOLLOW THE SAME PATTERN FOR ALL BUSINESSES

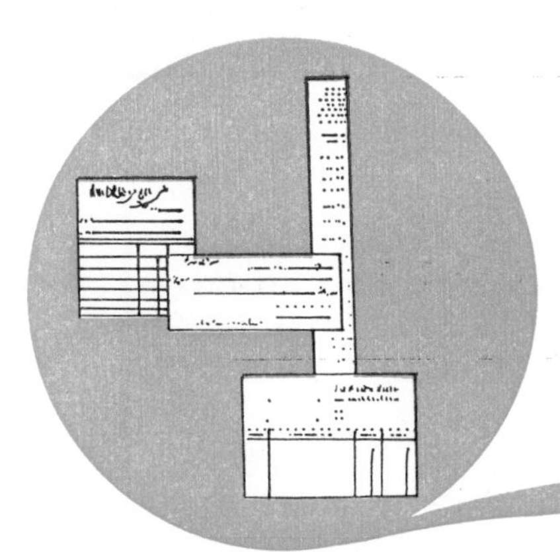

Every business transaction is recorded on some kind of source document.

The source documents are used for recording in a journal the business transactions in the order in which they occurred.

The entries in the journal are sorted and summarized in accounts in a ledger.

The accuracy of the accounts in the ledger is proven by taking a trial balance, which is often prepared as part of the work sheet.

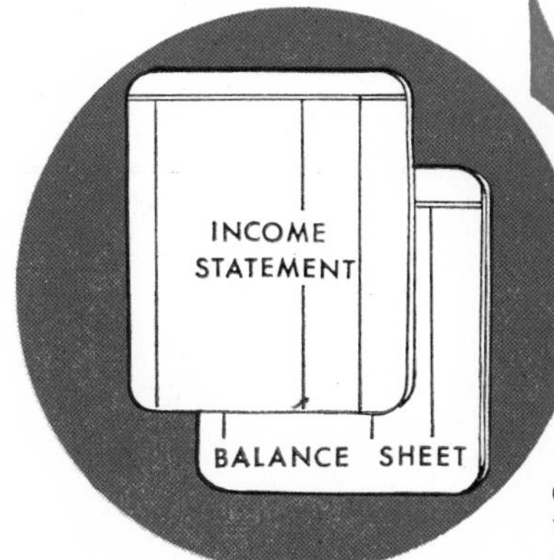

Financial statements are prepared periodically from the work sheet to show (a) what the business is worth, and (b) how well the business is doing.

HILL-TOP MOTEL

CHART OF ACCOUNTS

(1) ASSETS	Account Number	(4) INCOME	Account Number
Cash............	11	Room Sales......	41
Housekeeping Supplies.......	12		
		(5) EXPENSES	
Furniture and Fixtures.......	13	Advertising Expense........	51
Office Equipment.	14	Laundry Expense..	52
		Miscellaneous Expense........	53
(2) LIABILITIES		Rent Expense.....	54
Apex Plumbing Company........	21	Utilities Expense	55
Motel Equipment Company........	22		
(3) PROPRIETORSHIP			
Charles Martin, Capital.......	31		
Income and Expense Summary	32		

The chart of accounts for the Hill-Top Motel is illustrated above for ready reference in your study of Part 1 of this book.

CHAPTER 1 STARTING A BOOKKEEPING SYSTEM

The systematic recording of the financial operations of a business or of an individual is called *bookkeeping*. Bookkeeping records aid a business or an individual in planning for the future. Bookkeeping records are also needed for tax purposes and for government reports.

Bookkeeping records deal with such business operations as:

1. Purchasing and selling goods and services on credit.
2. Receiving and paying cash for goods and services.
3. Determining profits or losses that result from the operations of a business.
4. Determining the financial condition of the business.

The person who records the financial operations of a business in a systematic manner is called a *bookkeeper*. The person who plans, summarizes, and analyzes bookkeeping records is called an *accountant*. In some businesses, the work of the bookkeeper and the accountant is done by the same person.

BEGINNING A BOOKKEEPING SYSTEM FOR A BUSINESS

Before a bookkeeping system can be started, the owner of a business must find:

1. What the business owns.
2. What the business owes.
3. What the business is worth.

Charles Martin, with help from his wife, operates a 10-unit motel called the Hill-Top Motel. He pays a monthly rent for its use, and he provides the equipment and housekeeping supplies, such as bed linens and towels.

Mr. Martin has decided to set up a bookkeeping system that will give him complete information about the operation of his business. In order to start his bookkeeping system, Mr. Martin lists and totals in one column what his business owns. He lists and totals in another column what his business owes. These lists are shown on the next page.

What is owned:		What is owed:	
Cash on hand and in the bank...	$ 565.00	Apex Plumbing Company.......	$ 200.00
Housekeeping supplies......	550.00	Motel Equipment Company.......	1,300.00
Motel furniture and fixtures..	5,600.00	Total owed......	$1,500.00
Office equipment	485.00		
Total owned.....	$7,200.00		

Mr. Martin finds out how much his motel business is worth by subtracting the total that his business owes from the total of what it owns as follows:

Total owned..	$7,200.00
Less total owed......................................	1,500.00
What the business is worth...........................	$5,700.00

THE BALANCE SHEET

After a business finds out what it owns, what it owes, and what it is worth, the next step in starting a bookkeeping system is to make a balance sheet. In bookkeeping, a business form that lists (1) what is owned, (2) what is owed, and (3) what a business is worth on a specific date is called a *balance sheet.*

The beginning balance sheet for the Hill-Top Motel that Mr. Martin prepared from the information he has listed is shown below.

Hill-Top Motel
Balance Sheet
August 1, 1967

Assets		Liabilities	
Cash	565 00	Apex Plumbing Co.	200 00
Housekeeping Supplies	550 00	Motel Equipment Co.	1300 00
Furniture and Fixtures	5600 00	Total Liabilities	1500 00
Office Equipment	485 00		
		Proprietorship	
		Charles Martin, Capital	5700 00
Total Assets	7200 00	Total Liab. and Prop.	7200 00

Beginning balance sheet of the Hill-Top Motel

Heading of a balance sheet

The heading of a balance sheet contains three items: (1) the name of the business for which the balance sheet is prepared; (2) the name of the form; and (3) the date of the form. On the balance sheet of the Hill-Top Motel, these items are listed in the heading as follows:

Line 1. Who? — The name of the business: *Hill-Top Motel*

Line 2. What? — The name of the form: *Balance Sheet*

Line 3. When? — The date of the form: *August 1, 1967*

Body of a balance sheet

The body of a balance sheet has three sections that show: (1) what is owned, (2) what is owed, and (3) what the business is worth. A special business term is used to describe each of the three sections of a balance sheet as follows:

*1. **Assets.*** Anything of value that is owned is called an *asset*. Assets are listed on the left-hand side of the balance sheet, as shown in the diagram at the right.

BALANCE SHEET	
1. Assets	2. Liabilities and 3. Proprietorship
(Left-hand side)	(Right-hand side)

*2. **Liabilities.*** An amount that is owed is called a *liability*. The one to whom an amount is owed is called a *creditor*. Liabilities are listed on the right-hand side of the balance sheet.

*3. **Proprietorship.*** The owner of a business is called the *proprietor*. The amount that remains after the total liabilities are subtracted from the total assets is called *proprietorship*. For example:

Total assets on the balance sheet of the Hill-Top Motel....	$7,200.00
Less total liabilities on the balance sheet of the Hill-Top Motel....	1,500.00
Equals the amount of the owner's (Charles Martin's) proprietorship....	$5,700.00

The amount of proprietorship is shown beneath the liabilities on the right-hand side of the balance sheet.

Separating business records and personal records

Everyone who owns and operates a business has personal assets as well as business assets. He may also have personal liabilities as well as business liabilities. When he makes a balance sheet for the business, he includes only the assets and the liabilities of the business.

Why a balance sheet has two sides

The left-hand side of the balance sheet is used to list the assets. The right-hand side is used to list the claims against these assets. Thus, as shown at the right, a balance sheet has two sides in order to separate the assets from the claims against the assets.

BALANCE SHEET	
Assets	**Liabilities and proprietorship are claims against the assets.**
(Left-hand side)	(Right-hand side)

Equities

The claims against assets are sometimes called *equities*. There are two types of equities shown on every balance sheet: (1) the equity of the creditors and (2) the equity of the owner. Because creditors have first claim against the assets of the business, their claims are listed first on the right-hand side of the balance sheet.

The two sides of a balance sheet must be "in balance."

When a balance sheet is complete and accurate, the total of the left-hand side is always equal to the total of the right-hand side. When the totals of the two sides are equal, the balance sheet is said to be "in balance." When the two totals are not equal, the error or errors must be found and corrected so that the two sides will balance.

Note that the total of the left-hand side of the balance sheet of the Hill-Top Motel, $7,200.00, is equal to the total of the right-hand side, $7,200.00.

STEPS IN PREPARING A BALANCE SHEET

The steps listed below should be followed when preparing a balance sheet. As you study these steps, check each one with the illustration of the balance sheet of the Hill-Top Motel shown on the opposite page.

Step 1

Write the heading on three lines; center each item in the heading.

Step 2

Prepare the assets section on the left-hand side, as follows:

a Write the word *Assets* in the center of the first line of the wide column.

b List the name and amount of each asset, using a brief title to describe it.

Hill-Top Motel
Balance Sheet
August 1, 1967

(STEP 1)

Assets		Liabilities	
Cash	565 00	Apex Plumbing Co.	200 00
Housekeeping Supplies	550 00	Motel Equipment Co.	1 300 00
Furniture and Fixtures	5 600 00	Total Liabilities	1 500 00
Office Equipment	485 00		
		Proprietorship	
		Charles Martin, Capital	5 700 00
Total Assets	7 200 00	Total Liab. and Prop.	7 200 00

(STEP 2) (STEP 3) (STEP 4) (STEP 5)

A balance sheet showing the steps in its preparation

Step 3

Prepare the liabilities section on the right-hand side, as follows:

a Write the word *Liabilities* in the center of the first line of the wide column.

b List the name and amount of each liability, using a brief title to describe it.

c Rule a single line across the amount column directly under the last amount.

d Write the total of the liabilities in the amount column and label this amount *Total Liabilities.*

Step 4

Prepare the proprietorship section on the right-hand side, beneath the liabilities, as follows:

a Skip one line and write the word *Proprietorship* in the center of the wide column.

b Write the name of the proprietor and the word *Capital* on the next line.

In some bookkeeping systems the word written after the proprietor's name on the balance sheet may be *Investment*, or *Net Worth*, or *Proprietor*, or *Capital.* In this textbook the word *Capital* is used.

c On a separate sheet of paper, find the amount of the proprietorship by subtracting the total liabilities from the total assets.

d Write the amount of the proprietorship in the amount column on the same line as the name of the proprietor.

Step 5

Determine if the balance sheet is "in balance" and complete its preparation as follows:

a Rule a single line across the amount column on the right-hand side directly under the amount of the proprietorship. Rule a single line across the amount column on the left-hand side on the same line as the single line on the right-hand side.

b Add each column and compare the totals. The two totals should be the same. If the two totals are the same, this proves that the total of the assets equals the combined total of the liabilities and the proprietorship. (If the final totals are not the same, the error or errors must be found and corrected.)

c Record the totals directly under the addition line on each side. Do not skip a space.

d Write the words *Total Assets* on the same line as the left-hand total. Write the words *Total Liabilities and Proprietorship* on the same line as the right-hand total.

If necessary, the words on this line may be abbreviated to *Total Liab. and Prop.*

e Rule double lines across both amount columns directly under each total. The double lines show that the work is completed and that the balance sheet is "in balance."

COMMON BOOKKEEPING PRACTICES

The following illustration of the right-hand section of the Hill-Top Motel's balance sheet is used to point out five common bookkeeping practices. Each of these practices is described below.

1. Dollar signs, cent signs, and decimal points are not used when amounts are written in ruled columns of bookkeeping paper. A heavy vertical ruling in an amount column separates dollars from cents and serves as the decimal point.

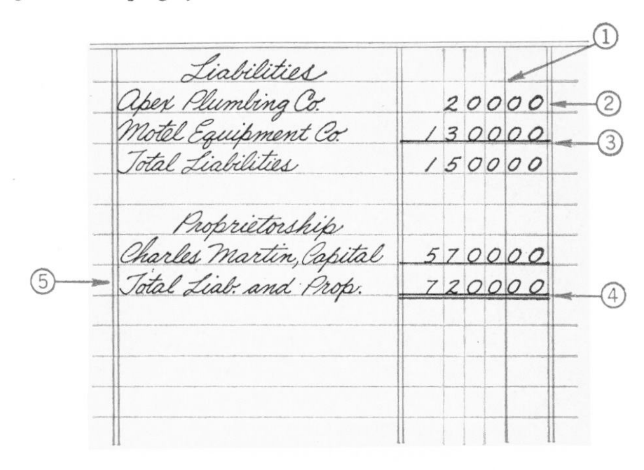

Some common bookkeeping practices

2. Two zeros are written in the cents column when an amount is in even dollars. This is the way a bookkeeping machine or an adding machine prints "no cents." If the cents column were left blank, there might be some doubt later as to whether the amount of the cents was recorded.
3. When the bookkeeper rules a single line beneath an amount, this single line indicates that either a total or a remainder will follow.
4. A double ruling across an amount column indicates that the work above the double lines is complete and accurate.

   The use of a ruler or other straight edge is essential for neat bookkeeping work.

5. Words are written in full when space is adequate. Words may be abbreviated when space is inadequate, as shown in the illustration above in the labeling of the *Total Liab. and Prop.*

THE BOOKKEEPING EQUATION

On any balance sheet, the total amount of the assets should be equal to the total amount of the liabilities plus the amount of the proprietorship. This important principle of bookkeeping may be stated in the form of a simple equation as follows:

ASSETS = LIABILITIES + PROPRIETORSHIP

The statement, Assets = Liabilities + Proprietorship, is known as the *bookkeeping equation.* This equation is true of all completed balance sheets. For example, the bookkeeping equation for the balance sheet illustrated on page 7 is:

ASSETS of $7,200.00 = LIABILITIES of $1,500.00
+ PROPRIETORSHIP of $5,700.00

Increasing Your Business Vocabulary

What is the meaning of each of the following:

a bookkeeping
b bookkeeper
c accountant
d balance sheet
e asset
f liability
g creditor
h proprietor
i proprietorship
j equities
k bookkeeping equation

Study Questions

1. How can the owner of a business find out how much his business is worth?
2. Name the three items in the heading of a balance sheet.
3. What special business term is used to describe each of the three sections of a balance sheet?
4. Why does a balance sheet have two sides?
5. What is meant when it is said that a balance sheet is "in balance"?
6. What are the five steps in preparing a balance sheet?
7. Why are dollar signs, cent signs, and decimal points omitted when recording amounts in ruled columns of bookkeeping paper?
8. Why should the cents column of ruled bookkeeping paper be filled in with zeros when an amount in even dollars is recorded?
9. State the bookkeeping equation that is true of all completed balance sheets.

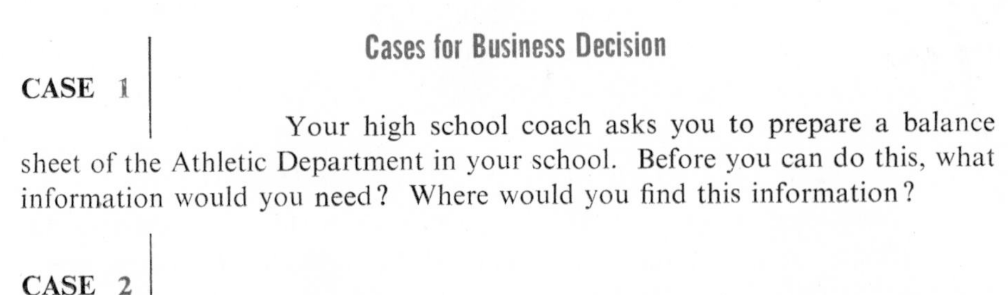

Cases for Business Decision

CASE 1

Your high school coach asks you to prepare a balance sheet of the Athletic Department in your school. Before you can do this, what information would you need? Where would you find this information?

CASE 2

The balance sheet of the Hill-Top Motel illustrated on page 7 shows that the business owes $1,500.00 to creditors. However, there is only $565.00 in cash to pay these bills. From what sources might Mr. Martin obtain additional cash to pay his creditors?

CASE 3

John Bannon is the proprietor of a rug-cleaning business. His balance sheet for the year just ended shows that his proprietorship is less than it was when he made his balance sheet a year ago. What are some of the reasons that may have caused this decrease in proprietorship?

CASE 4

When a person prepares a balance sheet for a business he owns, he must separate his personal assets and his personal liabilities from his business assets and his business liabilities. Give some examples of personal assets that should not be included in a business balance sheet. Give some examples of personal liabilities that should not be included in a business balance sheet.

Drills for Understanding

DRILL 1-A Classifying assets, liabilities, and proprietorship

In preparing a balance sheet, it is necessary to classify each item as an asset, a liability, or proprietorship. This drill is planned to give you practice in classifying and locating items on balance sheets.

If you do not have a workbook, prepare a form similar to the one illustrated below.

Instructions: Classify each of the following items by writing the word *asset*, *liability*, or *proprietorship* in the proper column. For example, the first item, Cash, is an asset. Because assets appear on the left-hand side of the balance sheet, the word *asset* is written in the left-hand column.

Items to be Classified	Balance Sheet	
	Left-hand side	Right-hand side
1. Cash	*Asset*	
2. Delivery equipment		
3. Amount owed to Apex Garage		
4. Office furniture		
5. Amount a business is worth		
6. Factory building		
7. Unpaid telephone bill		
8. Office equipment		
9. Any amount owned		
10. Any amount owed		
11. Machinery		
12. Difference between total assets and total liabilities		

DRILL 1-B | Using the bookkeeping equation

Instructions: Find the missing amount in the bookkeeping equation for each of the businesses listed below. If you do not have a workbook, write your answers on a separate piece of paper. The answer to Business No. 1 is given as an example.

Business No.	Assets	=	Liabilities	+	Proprietorship	Answers
1.	$10,000.00	=	$ 4,000.00	+	?	*$6,000.00*
2.	12,000.00	=	8,000.00	+	?	
3.	6,000.00	=	?	+	$ 4,500.00	
4.	7,555.75	=	1,450.30	+	?	
5.	?	=	6,880.00	+	4,120.00	
6.	7,421.20	=	2,312.00	+	?	
7.	141,633.50	=	23,164.25	+	?	

Application Problems

PROBLEM 1-1 | Balance sheet for a dry cleaning business

The following are the assets and the liabilities of the Premium Dry Cleaners, owned and operated by James Collins:

Assets		Liabilities	
Cash	$ 844.00	Five-Star Garage	$ 110.00
Delivery Equipment	2,266.00	Holt Equipment Company	785.00
Office Equipment	480.00		
Dry Cleaning Equipment	1,660.00		

Instructions: Prepare a balance sheet for the Premium Dry Cleaners. Use the date September 1 of the current year. Follow the steps for preparing a balance sheet given on pages 6 to 8. Use as your model the balance sheet illustrated on page 7. Be neat and accurate.

Self-checking: Check the accuracy and the completeness of your work by asking yourself the following questions:

1. Is each of the three items in the heading centered on each line?
2. Is the heading of each section centered within the body of the balance sheet?
3. Are the assets, liabilities, and proprietorship listed immediately below the appropriate heading without skipping a line?

4. Is there a blank line between the Liabilities section and the Proprietorship section to separate these two sections?
5. Is the amount of the total assets at the bottom of the left-hand side of the balance sheet on the same line as the amount of the total liabilities and proprietorship at the bottom of the right-hand side?
6. Are the two totals at the bottom of the balance sheet the same amount?
7. Are the single and double lines drawn across the amount columns only?

PROBLEM 1-2 | Balance sheet for a high school athletic department

The Hudson High School Athletic Department has the following assets and liabilities on June 1 of the current year:

Assets		Liabilities	
Cash	$ 864.00	City Printing Company	$ 28.00
Baseball Equipment	980.00	Harris Athletic Company	93.00
Basketball Equipment	650.00	Johnson Sports Store	187.00
Football Equipment	2,110.00		
Track Equipment	215.00		

Instructions: Prepare a balance sheet for the Hudson High School Athletic Department. Use the date June 1 of the current year. Use as your model the balance sheet illustrated on page 7. The amount of the proprietorship should be labeled, *Hudson H. S. Athletic Dept., Capital.*

Self-checking: Check your work with the questions listed under Problem 1-1.

Optional Problems

Ordinarily each student will be expected to solve no more than one of the optional problems at the end of the chapter. Your teacher will indicate which of the problems you should complete.

★SUPPLEMENTARY PROBLEM 1-S

Balance sheet for a repair service business

The following are the assets and the liabilities of the Appliance Repair Service, owned and operated by Charles Hart:

Assets		Liabilities	
Cash	$ 635.10	Atlas Supply Company	$ 214.00
Electrical Supplies	312.40	Auto Finance Company	860.00
Truck	2,250.00	Majestic Equipment Company	160.50
Equipment	840.40		

Instructions: Prepare a balance sheet for the Appliance Repair Service dated June 1 of the current year. Use the illustration of the balance sheet on page 7 as your model.

Self-checking: Check your work with the questions listed under Problem 1-1.

★ BONUS PROBLEM 1-B

Balance sheet for an individual

Mr. Richard Carlton, a high school graduate of a year ago, decides to start a bookkeeping system for his personal financial records. As the first step, he prepares a balance sheet showing how much he is worth. Mr. Carlton supplies the following information:

Has cash on hand and in the bank amounting to $140.00.

Owns U.S. Savings Bonds worth $56.25.

Owes his father, James Carlton, $8.00.

Owes Community Junior College, $10.00.

Owns a boat worth $240.00, but $60.00 of this amount is owed to the Easy-Payment Finance Company.

Owns a secondhand outboard motor worth $45.00.

Owns clothing valued at $280.00.

Recently bought his own TV set for $180.00, but $80.00 of this amount is still owed to the seller, Ward Sales Company.

Instructions: Prepare a balance sheet for Richard Carlton dated August 1 of the current year. Use as your model the illustration of the balance sheet on page 7.

Self-checking: Check your work with the questions listed under Problem 1-1.

CHAPTER 2 RECORDING THE OPENING ENTRY

A new bookkeeping system should begin with a balance sheet that shows the financial condition of the business at the time the new system is started. A balance sheet, however, is written on a piece of paper, which may be misfiled or lost. Therefore, the information shown on the balance sheet should be recorded in a permanent record book.

A book in which the records of a business are *first* written is called a *journal*. Each record in a journal is called an *entry*. The entry that records the information shown on a beginning balance sheet is called an *opening entry*.

The source of a journal entry

The entry that the bookkeeper makes in a journal is usually taken from some business paper. The business paper from which a journal entry is made is called a *source document*. The source document for making an opening entry is the beginning balance sheet.

Types of journals

Businesses use different kinds of journals. Some journals are used to record only one type of entry such as entries for sales or entries for purchases. A journal that is used to record only one type of entry is called a *special journal*. A journal that is used to record entries that cannot be recorded in special journals is called a *general journal*.

The general journal

The two-column general journal, shown below, is used by the Hill-Top Motel to record its beginning balance sheet.

GENERAL JOURNAL PAGE

	DATE	ACCOUNT TITLE	POST. REF.	DEBIT	CREDIT	
1						1
2						2
3						3
4						4

Two-column general journal

When a beginning balance sheet is recorded in a two-column general journal, the amounts on the left-hand side of the balance sheet are recorded in the left-hand amount column of the journal. The left-hand amount column of a two-column general journal is called the *debit column.* The amounts on the right-hand side of the balance sheet are recorded in the right-hand amount column of the journal. The right-hand amount column of a two-column general journal is called the *credit column.*

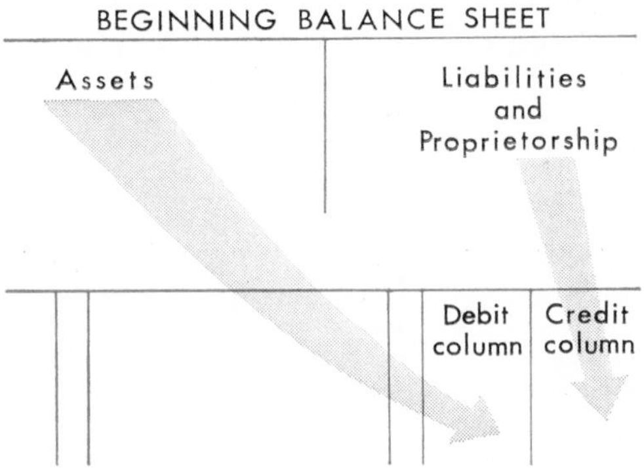

BEGINNING BALANCE SHEET

Assets	Liabilities and Proprietorship

			Debit column	Credit column

The source document for the opening entry

The beginning balance sheet of the Hill-Top Motel, shown below, is the source document from which the opening entry is made in the general journal.

Hill-Top Motel
Balance Sheet
August 1, 1967

Assets		Liabilities	
Cash	565 00	Apex Plumbing Co.	200 00
Housekeeping Supplies	550 00	Motel Equipment Co.	1,300 00
Furniture and Fixtures	5,600 00	Total Liabilities	1,500 00
Office Equipment	485 00		
		Proprietorship	
		Charles Martin, Capital	5,700 00
Total Assets	7,200 00	Total Liab. and Prop.	7,200 00

Beginning balance sheet of the Hill-Top Motel

Parts of a journal entry

Every journal entry has four parts: (1) a date, (2) a debit part, (3) a credit part, and (4) a brief description of the source document.

The meaning of "debit" and "credit" and the meaning and use of the Post. Ref. column in the journal will be explained in Chapter 3.

STEPS IN RECORDING THE OPENING ENTRY

The steps in recording the opening entry on page 1 of the general journal of the Hill-Top Motel are as follows:

Step 1

Date of entry. Write the date of the opening entry in the Date column as shown below.

GENERAL JOURNAL PAGE 1

	DATE		ACCOUNT TITLE	POST. REF.	DEBIT	CREDIT	
STEP 1 → 1	1967 Aug.	1					1
2							2
3							3
4							4
5							5
6							6

a Write the *year* in small figures at the top of the column.

b Write the *month* below the year on the first line in the first column.

Because the Date column is narrow, the name of the month may be abbreviated.

c Write the *day* of the month on the first line in the second column immediately after the name of the month.

The date is written once and only once for each entry, regardless of how many lines are used for the entry.

Step 2

Debit part of the entry. Write the debit part of the entry as shown below.

GENERAL JOURNAL PAGE 1

	DATE		ACCOUNT TITLE	POST. REF.	DEBIT	CREDIT	
STEP 1 → 1	1967 Aug.	1	Cash		565 00		1
STEP 2 → 2			Housekeeping Supplies		550 00		2
3			Furniture and Fixtures		5600 00		3
4			Office Equipment		485 00		4
5							5
6							6
7							7

a Write the name of each asset at the extreme left edge of the Account Title column.

b Write the amount of each asset in the Debit column.

Step 3

Credit part of the entry. Write the credit part of the entry as shown below.

GENERAL JOURNAL PAGE 1

		DATE		ACCOUNT TITLE	POST. REF.	DEBIT	CREDIT	
STEP 1	1	1967 Aug.	1	Cash		565 00		1
STEP 2	2			Housekeeping Supplies		550 00		2
	3			Furniture and Fixtures		5600 00		3
	4			Office Equipment		485 00		4
	5			Apex Plumbing Company			200 00	5
STEP 3	6			Motel Equipment Company			1300 00	6
	7			Charles Martin, Capital			5700 00	7
	8							8

a Write the name of each liability and the name of the proprietor, followed by the word Capital, in the Account Title column. Indent each name about one-half inch from the left edge of the Account Title column. Indenting these items helps to separate the debit part of the entry from the credit part.

b Write the amount of each credit item in the Credit column.

Step 4

Source of the entry. Write a brief description of the source document as shown below.

GENERAL JOURNAL PAGE 1

		DATE		ACCOUNT TITLE	POST. REF.	DEBIT	CREDIT	
STEP 1	1	1967 Aug.	1	Cash		565 00		1
STEP 2	2			Housekeeping Supplies		550 00		2
	3			Furniture and Fixtures		5600 00		3
	4			Office Equipment		485 00		4
	5			Apex Plumbing Company			200 00	5
STEP 3	6			Motel Equipment Company			1300 00	6
	7			Charles Martin, Capital			5700 00	7
STEP 4	8			August 1 balance sheet.				8
	9							9
	10							10

a Write a brief description of the source document in the Account Title column immediately below the last credit item.

b Indent each line of the description about one inch from the left edge of the Account Title column.

The purpose of the description is to identify the source of the journal entry in case reference must be made to the source document.

The complete opening entry

The complete opening entry in the general journal of the Hill-Top Motel is shown below.

GENERAL JOURNAL — PAGE 1

	DATE		ACCOUNT TITLE	POST. REF.	DEBIT	CREDIT	
1	1967 Aug.	1	Cash		565 00		1
2			Housekeeping Supplies		550 00		2
3			Furniture and Fixtures		5600 00		3
4			Office Equipment		485 00		4
5			Apex Plumbing Company			200 00	5
6			Motel Equipment Company			1300 00	6
7			Charles Martin, Capital			5700 00	7
8			August 1 balance sheet.				8
9							9
10							10
11							11

Opening entry of the Hill-Top Motel

PROOF OF ACCURACY

In the opening entry of the Hill-Top Motel, the amount of each asset is recorded in the Debit column of the general journal. The amount of each liability and the proprietorship is recorded in the Credit column. In every journal entry, the sum of the amounts in the debit part of the entry must equal the sum of the amounts in the credit part.

Whenever the sum of the debit amounts of an entry does not equal the sum of the credit amounts of the entry, the error or errors must be found and corrected. If an error is made in writing an amount, the incorrect amount should be canceled by drawing a line through it. The correct amount should then be written immediately above the canceled amount. If an error is made in any other part of the entry, the entry is corrected by drawing a line through the incorrect part and writing the correction immediately above.

Increasing Your Business Vocabulary

What is the meaning of each of the following:

a journal
b entry
c opening entry
d source document
e special journal
f general journal
g debit column
h credit column

Study Questions

1. Why should the information on the beginning balance sheet be recorded in a permanent record book?
2. What is the source document for making an opening entry?
3. What are the four parts of every entry in a general journal?
4. Where are the month, the day, and the year of the date of the opening entry written?
5. When an opening entry is recorded, what kinds of balance sheet items have their amounts recorded in the Debit column of the general journal?
6. When an opening entry is recorded, what kinds of balance sheet items have their amounts recorded in the Credit column of the general journal?
7. Why is the credit part of the opening entry indented?
8. What is the purpose of writing a brief description of the source document in the opening entry?
9. If the sum of the debit amounts of a journal entry does not equal the sum of the credit amounts of the entry, what should the bookkeeper do?
10. How is an error in writing an amount corrected?

Cases for Business Decision

CASE 1

In starting his bookkeeping system, Mr. Miles, owner of a motorcycle repair shop, prepares a list of his assets for the bookkeeper. The list contains 32 items having a total value of $1,800. In this list there are 10 items of office furniture and 22 items of shop equipment. Mr. Miles decides that the opening entry should show the total value of the office furniture separate from the total value of the shop equipment. What must the bookkeeper do before he can record the opening entry?

CASE 2

The Walker family decides to start a bookkeeping system that will give a complete record of the financial operations of the family. A balance sheet is prepared as the first step in starting their new bookkeeping system.

Mr. Walker bought the family home for $23,000, but he still owes the Capitol Building and Loan Association $10,000 on the house. One member of the family who has never studied bookkeeping thinks that the value of the house should be listed on the balance sheet as $13,000 ($23,000 minus $10,000).

Do you agree with this person's thinking on how to show the value of the house on the balance sheet? If not, what is the correct way of showing the value on the balance sheet?

Drill for Understanding

DRILL 2-A | Determining the debit and the credit of balance sheet items when recorded in an opening entry

This drill is planned to give you practice in (a) classifying balance sheet items, and (b) in determining which kinds of balance sheet items are recorded as debits and which kinds are recorded as credits in an opening entry. A form listing the balance sheet items is provided in your workbook for this drill.

Instructions: 1. Classify each item by writing the word *asset*, *liability*, or *proprietorship* in one of the Balance Sheet columns to indicate on which side of the balance sheet it should be listed.

2. If the amount of the item is written in the Debit column of the general journal when making an opening entry, make a check mark in the Debit column of the form. If the amount of the item is written in the Credit column of the journal when making an opening entry, make a check mark in the Credit column of the form. The first item, Delivery Truck, is given as an example.

Balance Sheet Items	Balance Sheet		General Journal: Column in which amount in opening entry is recorded	
	Left-hand side	Right-hand side	Debit column	Credit column
1. Delivery Truck..........	*Asset*		√	

If you do not have a workbook, copy the form above on a sheet of paper and use the following list of balance sheet items:

(1) Delivery Truck
(2) George Hollis (creditor)
(3) Office Furniture
(4) Marvin Chain, Capital
(5) Dry Cleaning Equipment
(6) Supplies
(7) Star Equipment Company (creditor)
(8) Cash
(9) Office Machines

Instructions: 3. Now cover your answers and see how rapidly you can do this drill mentally without looking at your answers. Repeat this drill several times for increased speed and accuracy.

Application Problems

PROBLEM 2-1 | Opening entry for a beauty shop

Instructions: 1. Prepare page 1 of a general journal by writing the proper heading at the top of each column. Use the same headings as shown in the general journal on page 19.

2. Record the opening entry in this general journal from the following balance sheet. Use September 1 of the current year as the date of the entry.

Suburban Beauty Shop
Balance Sheet
September 1, 19—

Assets		Liabilities	
Cash	240 00	Beauty Products Co.	80 00
Supplies	180 00	Delco Equipment Co.	865 00
Furniture	1 045 00	Total Liabilities	945 00
Equipment	2 914 00		
		Proprietorship	
		Janice Wiley, Capital	3 434 00
Total Assets	4 379 00	Total Liab. and Prop.	4 379 00

Self-checking: Compare your opening entry with the illustration on page 19 and check the accuracy of your work by asking yourself the following questions:

1. Are the year, the month, and the day written at the top of the Date column?
2. Is each debit item written at the extreme left edge of the Account Title column?
3. Is each credit item in the Account Title column indented about one-half inch?
4. Is a brief description of the source of the entry written and is it indented about one inch?

PROBLEM 2-2 | Opening entry for a professional man — a dentist

Instructions: Record an opening entry on page 1 of a general journal from the balance sheet shown on page 23. Use October 1 of the current year as the date of this entry.

Self-checking: Check the accuracy of your opening entry by asking yourself the questions given at the end of Problem 2-1.

Richard Newton
Balance Sheet
October 1, 19—

Assets			Liabilities		
Cash	780	00	Acme Equipment Co.	650	00
Supplies	745	90	Dental Supply Co.	112	40
Office Furniture	425	00			
Dental Equipment	3 114	00	Total Liabilities	762	40
			Proprietorship		
			Richard Newton, Capital	4 302	50
Total Assets	5 064	90	Total Liab. and Prop.	5 064	90

Optional Problems

★SUPPLEMENTARY PROBLEM 2-S

Balance sheet and opening entry for a garage

The Three-Corners Garage is owned and operated by Arthur Bolton. His records show the following assets:

Cash	$ 567.00
Supplies	300.00
Garage Equipment	3,861.00
Office Equipment	740.00

The garage owes the Stanley Motor Company $641.00 and the Miller Equipment Company $217.00.

The amount of Mr. Bolton's proprietorship is $4,610.00.

Instructions: 1. Prepare a balance sheet for the Three-Corners Garage dated July 1 of the current year.

2. Record the opening entry on page 1 of a general journal.

Self-checking: Check your balance sheet with the questions that are listed under Problem 1-1 on pages 12 and 13. Check your opening entry with the questions that are listed under Problem 2-1 on page 22.

★ BONUS PROBLEM 2-B

Balance sheet and opening entry; separating business records from personal records

The McHenry Trucking Company is owned and operated by Joseph McHenry. He asks you to prepare a balance sheet and an opening entry for his business records. He gives you the following information, which you will note is a mixture of business assets and business liabilities and personal assets and personal liabilities.

Assets: Cash in his personal checking account, $361.23; cash in the checking account of the McHenry Trucking Company, $784.00; office furniture, $231.00; office machines, $322.00; furniture in Mr. McHenry's home, $3,644.00; family automobile, $2,600.00; trucking equipment, $4,460.00; house in which he lives, $17,500; building used for storage of his trucking equipment and freight, $3,800.00.

Liabilities: Auto Finance Company, for payments yet to be made on trucking equipment, $1,850.00; Eastman Furniture Company, $120.00, for furniture purchased for Mr. McHenry's home; County Transfer Company, $430.00, for delivering freight shipments out of state for the McHenry Trucking Company; Reliance Equipment Company, $85.00, for second-hand adding machine used in the office of the McHenry Trucking Company.

Instructions: 1. Prepare a balance sheet for the McHenry Trucking Company. Use September 1 of the current year as the date.

2. Record the opening entry on page 1 of a general journal.

Self-checking: Check your balance sheet with the questions listed under Problem 1-1 on pages 12 and 13. Check your opening entry with the questions that are listed under Problem 2-1 on page 22.

CHAPTER 3 POSTING THE OPENING ENTRY

The opening entry in a journal is a complete record of the assets, the liabilities, and the proprietorship *at the time a bookkeeping system is installed.* The bookkeeping system, however, should show not only what a business has — assets, liabilities, and proprietorship — but also the changes that occur in these items.

As a business carries on its day-to-day operations, changes occur in the value of its assets, liabilities, and proprietorship. Goods and services are bought and sold. Cash is received and paid out. Debts are owed and paid. When the business makes a profit, the amount of the proprietorship increases. When the business has a loss, the amount of the proprietorship decreases. Bookkeeping records are kept to show these changes.

THE LEDGER

A bookkeeping form that is used to sort and summarize the changes caused by business operations is called an *account.* A group of accounts is called a *ledger.* In manual bookkeeping, the ledger is usually a looseleaf book. In machine bookkeeping, the ledger may consist of ledger sheets or ledger cards kept in a tray or a file.

Standard form of account

There are several forms of account. The standard form of account is shown below.

ACCOUNT NO.

DATE	ITEMS	POST. REF.	DEBIT	DATE	ITEMS	POST. REF.	CREDIT

Standard form of account

The standard form of account is divided into a left half and a right half. Each half of an account is ruled alike. The left-hand side of an account is called the *debit side*. The right-hand side of an account is called the *credit side*.

The amount column on the left-hand side has the heading *Debit*. The amount column on the right-hand side has the heading *Credit*. The headings of all the other columns are the same on each side of an account.

When amounts are recorded in the Debit column of an account, the account is said to be *debited*. When amounts are recorded in the Credit column of an account, the account is said to be *credited.*

Chart of accounts

There is an account in the ledger for each item on the beginning balance sheet. The name given to an account is called the *account title*. The account title is written at the top of the account. The number given to an account to show its location in the ledger is called an *account number*. Since the accounts are arranged in the ledger in numerical order, they can be located quickly. A list of account titles that shows the arrangement of the accounts in the ledger and the number assigned to each account is called a *chart of accounts*. The part of the chart of accounts of the Hill-Top Motel needed for the work in this chapter is shown below.

Hill-Top Motel
Chart of Accounts

(1) Assets	Account Number	(2) Liabilities	Account Number
Cash	11	Apex Plumbing Company	21
Housekeeping Supplies	12	Motel Equipment Company	22
Furniture and Fixtures	13	(3) Proprietorship	
Office Equipment	14	Charles Martin, Capital	31

Partial chart of accounts for the Hill-Top Motel

The complete chart of accounts used by the Hill-Top Motel is shown on page 2.

The first digit of each account number tells in which *division* of the ledger the account is placed. In the partial chart of accounts given above, all asset account numbers begin with 1; all liability account numbers begin with 2; the proprietorship account number begins with 3.

The second digit of each account number tells the *position* of the account within its *division* of the ledger. For example, the account number for Office Equipment is 14. This number shows that the office equipment account is in the *first* division of the ledger, the assets division, and that it is the *fourth* account in that division.

For various reasons that will be explained in later chapters, some businesses use a three-digit numbering system for their charts of account and some use a four-digit system. For example, a business larger than the Hill-Top Motel might assign the number 114 to the office equipment account.

Opening accounts in the ledger

Writing the account title and the account number on the first line of a ledger account form is called *opening an account.* An account needs to be opened in the ledger for each account listed on the chart of accounts. As additional accounts are needed, they are listed on the chart of accounts and are opened in the ledger.

Cash is the first account to be opened in the ledger of the Hill-Top Motel because it is the first account in the chart of accounts. The cash account is opened by (a) writing the name of the account, *Cash,* at the center of the first line of the first page of the ledger, and (b) writing the number of the cash account, *11,* in the upper right-hand corner of the ledger page.

The cash account, after it has been opened, appears in the ledger as follows:

Cash ACCOUNT NO. *11*

DATE	ITEMS	POST. REF.	DEBIT	DATE	ITEMS	POST. REF.	CREDIT

The cash account after it has been opened

The procedure in opening each of the remaining accounts is the same as that followed in opening the cash account.

POSTING THE OPENING ENTRY TO THE LEDGER

The opening entry of the Hill-Top Motel, developed in Chapter 2, is shown on the next page. Each of the amounts in the opening entry is transferred to the proper account in the ledger. Transferring the entries in a journal to the accounts in a ledger is called *posting.*

Steps in posting the opening entry

The first three steps in posting Line 1 of the journal are diagrammed and explained below. The final two steps are diagrammed and explained on the next page.

GENERAL JOURNAL PAGE 1

	DATE	ACCOUNT TITLE	POST. REF.	DEBIT	CREDIT	
1	1967 Aug. 1	Cash		565 00		1
2		Housekeeping Supplies		550 00		2
3		Furniture and Fixtures		5600 00		3
4		Office Equipment		485 00		4
5		Apex Plumbing Company			200 00	5
6	STEP 2	Motel Equipment Company			1300 00	6
7		Charles Martin, Capital			5700 00	7
8		August 1 balance sheet.				8
9						9
10			STEP 1			10
11						11

Cash ACCOUNT NO. 11

DATE	ITEMS	POST. REF.	DEBIT	DATE	ITEMS	POST. REF.	CREDIT
1967 Aug. 1	Balance		565 00				
	STEP 3						

Diagram of the first three steps in posting a debit item

Step 1

Write the *amount* of the cash debit, *$565.00*, in the Debit column of the cash account in the ledger as shown above.

In manual bookkeeping, the amount is written first because it is the most important part of the entry. In machine bookkeeping, however, a posting machine may proceed from left to right across the account form and print the date first and the amount last.

Step 2

Write the *date* of the journal entry, *1967, Aug. 1,* in the Date column of the ledger account as follows:

a Write the year, *1967*, at the top of the Date column.

b Write the month, *Aug.*, in the first column under the heading *Date* on the same line as the amount.

The year and the name of the month are written only once on the side of the account that is used.

c Write the day of the month, *1*, in the column immediately after the name of the month.

Step 3

Write the word *Balance* in the Items column of the account.

Bookkeepers distinguish between the beginning amount in an account and the amounts recorded later as a result of normal business operations. The beginning amount or balance in the cash account is therefore labeled with the single word *Balance* in the Items column.

Cross referencing — the final two steps in posting

The posting of an entry is not complete until a cross reference is made between the journal and the ledger. This cross referencing is diagrammed and explained in Steps 4 and 5 below.

GENERAL JOURNAL PAGE 1

	DATE		ACCOUNT TITLE	POST. REF.	DEBIT	CREDIT	
1	1967 Aug.	1	Cash	11	565 00		1
2			Housekeeping Supplies		550 00		2
3			Furniture and Fixtures		5600 00		3
4							4
5							5
6							6

STEP 4 STEP 5

Cash ACCOUNT NO. 11

DATE		ITEMS	POST. REF.	DEBIT	DATE		ITEMS	POST. REF.	CREDIT
1967 Aug.	1	Balance	J1	565 00					

Diagram of the final two steps in posting — cross referencing

Step 4

Write *J1* in the Post. Ref. column of the cash account. *J1* is written in the Post. Ref. column of the account to show that this debit to Cash came from page 1 of the general journal.

J is the abbreviation for general journal. *Post. Ref.* is the abbreviation for Posting Reference.

Step 5

Return to the journal and write in the Post Ref. column of the journal the account number of the account, *11*, to which the item was posted.

Writing the number 11 in the Post Ref. column of the general journal shows that this item was posted to account number 11 and that all the details of the posting of this line have been completed. For this reason the Post. Ref. figure in the journal is written as the *last* step in posting. When the bookkeeper is interrupted in posting, the proper use of Post. Ref. numbers enables him to resume his posting quickly at the right place.

Posting the remaining debit items of the opening entry

The same steps used in posting the first debit item of the opening entry are followed in posting the remaining debit items. The accounts to which all debit items have been posted are shown below. Each account is a separate page of the ledger.

Cash — ACCOUNT NO. 11

DATE		ITEMS	POST. REF.	DEBIT	DATE	ITEMS	POST. REF.	CREDIT
1967 Aug.	1	Balance	J1	565 00				

Housekeeping Supplies — ACCOUNT NO. 12

DATE		ITEMS	POST. REF.	DEBIT	DATE	ITEMS	POST. REF.	CREDIT
1967 Aug.	1	Balance	J1	550 00				

Furniture and Fixtures — ACCOUNT NO. 13

DATE		ITEMS	POST. REF.	DEBIT	DATE	ITEMS	POST. REF.	CREDIT
1967 Aug.	1	Balance	J1	5600 00				

Office Equipment — ACCOUNT NO. 14

DATE		ITEMS	POST. REF.	DEBIT	DATE	ITEMS	POST. REF.	CREDIT
1967 Aug.	1	Balance	J1	485 00				

Asset accounts with all debit items posted

Posting the credit items of the opening entry

The credit items in the general journal are posted in the same manner as the debit items, except that the credit items are posted to the *credit side* of the accounts. The five steps in posting the first credit item are illustrated in the diagram at the top of the next page.

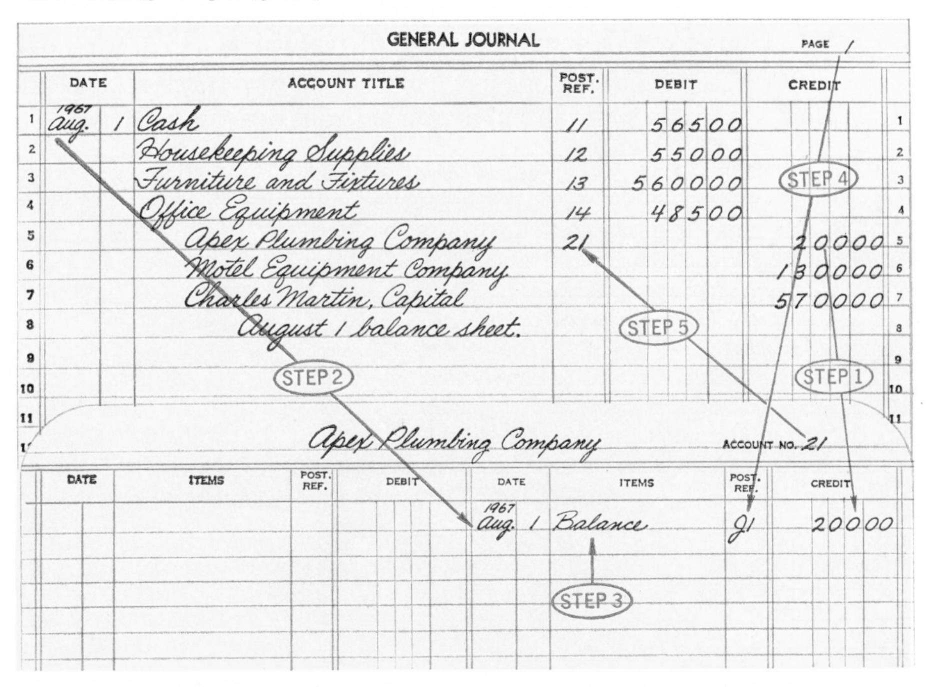

GENERAL JOURNAL PAGE 1

	DATE		ACCOUNT TITLE	POST. REF.	DEBIT	CREDIT	
1	1967 Aug.	1	Cash	11	565 00		1
2			Housekeeping Supplies	12	550 00		2
3			Furniture and Fixtures	13	5600 00		3
4			Office Equipment	14	485 00		4
5			Apex Plumbing Company	21		200 00	5
6			Motel Equipment Company			1300 00	6
7			Charles Martin, Capital			5700 00	7
8			August 1 balance sheet.				8

Apex Plumbing Company ACCOUNT NO. 21

DATE	ITEMS	POST. REF.	DEBIT	DATE	ITEMS	POST. REF.	CREDIT
				1967 Aug. 1	Balance	J1	200 00

Diagram of the posting of a credit item

The accounts to which all the credit items have been posted are shown below.

Apex Plumbing Company ACCOUNT NO. 21

DATE	ITEMS	POST. REF.	DEBIT	DATE	ITEMS	POST. REF.	CREDIT
				1967 Aug. 1	Balance	J1	200 00

Motel Equipment Company ACCOUNT NO. 22

DATE	ITEMS	POST. REF.	DEBIT	DATE	ITEMS	POST. REF.	CREDIT
				1967 Aug. 1	Balance	J1	1300 00

Charles Martin, Capital ACCOUNT NO. 31

DATE	ITEMS	POST. REF.	DEBIT	DATE	ITEMS	POST. REF.	CREDIT
				1967 Aug. 1	Balance	J1	5700 00

Liability and proprietorship accounts with all credit items posted

Post. Ref. column of the general journal after posting

After all the posting of the opening entry has been completed, the Post. Ref. column in the general journal appears as follows:

GENERAL JOURNAL — PAGE 1

	DATE		ACCOUNT TITLE	POST. REF.	DEBIT	CREDIT	
1	1967 Aug.	1	Cash	11	565 00		1
2			Housekeeping Supplies	12	550 00		2
3			Furniture and Fixtures	13	5600 00		3
4			Office Equipment	14	485 00		4
5			Apex Plumbing Company	21		200 00	5
6			Motel Equipment Company	22		1300 00	6
7			Charles Martin, Capital	31		5700 00	7
8			August 1 balance sheet.				8
9							9
10							10
11							11
12							12
13							13
14							14

Opening entry of Hill-Top Motel after posting

Use of Post. Ref. numbers

The numbers in the posting reference columns in the journal and in the ledger are useful for cross reference. Anyone looking at an entry in the journal can find the number of the account to which the journal entry was posted. With this information, the bookkeeper can quickly locate the account in the ledger. Also, anyone looking at an item in the ledger can find the number of the journal page from which the posting was made. With this information, the bookkeeper can quickly locate the entry in the journal. This cross reference information is useful if the accuracy of the posting is being checked.

THE NATURE OF ACCOUNT BALANCES

Each asset account opened in this chapter has a single amount posted to its debit side. Each liability account has a single amount posted to its credit side. The proprietorship account has a single amount posted to its credit side. As the balance of an account is increased or decreased, postings may be found on both sides of an account. The difference between the totals of the amounts posted to the two sides of an account is called the *account balance*. When an account contains only one posting, as illustrated in this chapter, this single amount is the account balance.

A balance on the left-hand side of an account is called a *debit balance*. A balance on the right-hand side of an account is called a *credit balance*. Note on page 30 that the balance of each asset account is a *debit balance*. Note on page 31 that the balance of each liability account is a *credit balance*. The balance of the proprietor's capital account is also a *credit balance*.

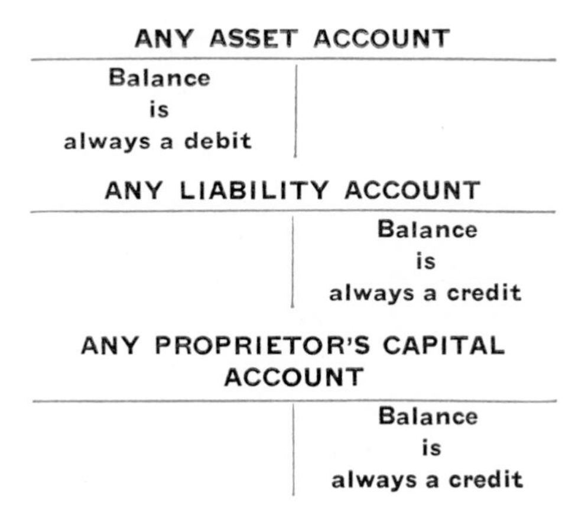

SUMMARIZING THE START OF A BOOKKEEPING SYSTEM

A diagram that shows all the steps involved in a particular activity or procedure is called a *flow chart*. The flow chart below summarizes the following activities involved in starting a bookkeeping system:

First, a beginning balance sheet is prepared listing the assets, the liabilities, and the proprietorship of the business as of the day the bookkeeping system is started.

Second, the information on the beginning balance sheet is recorded as an opening entry in a book of permanent record — a journal. The assets are recorded as debits; the liabilities and the proprietorship are recorded as credits.

Third, the items recorded in the opening entry in the journal are posted to individual accounts in the ledger.

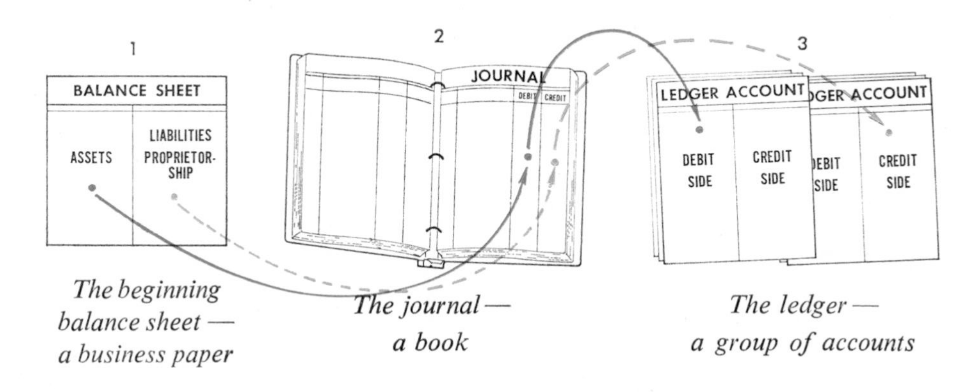

Flow chart showing the start of a bookkeeping system

Increasing Your Business Vocabulary

What is the meaning of each of the following:

a account
b ledger
c debit side
d credit side
e debited
f credited
g account title
h account number
i chart of accounts
j opening an account
k posting
l account balance
m debit balance
n credit balance
o flow chart

Study Questions

1. For what reasons does a business need a bookkeeping system?
2. What columnar headings on the two sides of a standard form of account are the same?
3. What columnar headings on the two sides of a standard form of account are not the same?
4. In the partial chart of accounts of the Hill-Top Motel on page 26, what is the first digit of (a) all asset account numbers, (b) all liability account numbers, (c) the proprietorship account number?
5. What does a bookkeeper write as the heading of an account when he opens an account?
6. What are the five steps in posting each amount of the opening entry?
7. Why is the word *Balance* written in the Items column of the ledger account when posting each item of the opening entry?
8. What is the purpose of writing a journal page number in the Post. Ref. column of the ledger account?
9. What are the two purposes of writing a ledger account number in the Post. Ref. column of the general journal?
10. After an opening entry has been posted, what kind of balance has (a) each asset account, (b) each liability account, (c) the proprietor's capital account?

Cases for Business Decision

CASE 1

The owner of Klein's Clothing Store notices that his bookkeeper has neglected to record in the Post. Ref. column of the general journal the ledger account numbers to which the various items in the opening entry were posted. How can this omission of cross references cause trouble for the bookkeeper?

CASE 2

Robert Cornell is interrupted by a telephone call while in the midst of posting his general journal. If he has been following correct bookkeeping procedure in his posting, how can he tell quickly where he left off in the journal at the time his work was interrupted?

Drills for Understanding

DRILL 3-A | Numbering accounts

Sunnybrook Tailors, a small custom tailoring business, uses the same two-digit numbering system for its chart of accounts as that of the Hill-Top Motel described on page 26. Sunnybrook Tailors, however, has eight asset accounts, six liability accounts, and one proprietorship account.

Instructions: 1. The location of different accounts in the ledger is given in the form below. Write the account number that would be assigned each of these accounts. Use the Account Number column for your answers. "The second asset account" is given as an example.

If you do not have a workbook, prepare your own form on a sheet of paper. Use a form similar to the one shown below.

Location of the account in the ledger	Account number
1. The second asset account	*12*
2. The third liability account	
3. The eighth asset account	
4. The proprietor's capital account	
5. The first asset account	
6. The fifth asset account	
7. The fifth liability account	
8. The first liability account	
9. The seventh asset account	
10. The second liability account	

Instructions: 2. Now cover the Account Number column and see how accurately you can recall the correct account numbers.

DRILL 3-B | Indicating accounts with debit balances and accounts with credit balances

The skeleton outline of an account, as illustrated at the right, is frequently used for purposes of drill and analysis. This form is commonly called a T account because it looks like a capital T.

Cash	

Cash	
Balance	

Instructions: A list of ten accounts in T-account form is provided in your workbook. Write the word *Balance* on the proper side of each account to show where the balance will always appear in that account. The first account in the list, Cash, is given above as an example.

If you do not have a workbook, prepare separate T accounts on a sheet of paper for the following accounts:

(1) Cash
(2) Delivery Truck
(3) Office Equipment Company (creditor)
(4) Office Supplies
(5) W. R. McConnell, Capital
(6) Office Machines
(7) Five-Star Garage (creditor)
(8) Office Furniture
(9) A. R. Singleton (creditor)
(10) R. Richards (creditor)

Application Problem

PROBLEM 3-1 | Recording and posting the opening entry for a plumber

The balance sheet on July 1 of Croll's Plumbing and Heating, owned by Leon Croll, is as follows:

Croll's Plumbing and Heating
Balance Sheet
July 1, 19--

Assets			Liabilities		
Cash	1 140	00	Hawkes Heating Company	550	50
Plumbing Supplies	1 360	50	Plumbing Service Company	141	35
Office Equipment	280	10	Total Liabilities	691	85
Plumbing Equipment	1 445	90			
Truck	2 895	00	**Proprietorship**		
			Leon Croll, Capital	6 429	65
Total Assets	7 121	50	Total Liab. and Prop.	7 121	50

Instructions: 1. Record the opening entry for Croll's Plumbing and Heating on page 1 of a general journal. Use July 1 of the current year as the date.

2. Open accounts in a ledger for all the account titles listed on the balance sheet. Allow one fourth of a page in your ledger for each account. Number the accounts as follows: asset accounts, 11 to 15; liability accounts, 21 and 22; and the proprietor's capital account, 31.

3. Post the opening entry.

Self-checking: Compare your accounts with the model accounts on pages 30 and 31. Check the accuracy of your posting by asking yourself the following questions:

1. Are the year, month, and day written at the top of the Date column on the side of the account that is used?
2. Are all the debits in the journal posted to the debit side of the five asset accounts?
3. Are all the credits in the journal posted to the credit side of the liability and the proprietorship accounts?
4. Is the number of the journal page written in the Post. Ref. column of each account?
5. Is an account number written in the Post. Ref. column of the journal for each line of the journal that was posted? Was this your last step in posting?

Optional Problems

⋆SUPPLEMENTARY PROBLEM 3-S

Preparing a chart of accounts; recording and posting an opening entry

The balance sheet of the Harper Insurance Agency is shown below. The owner, Harvey H. Harper, has employed you to set up a new bookkeeping system for him.

Harper Insurance Agency
Balance Sheet
August 1, 19—

Assets			Liabilities		
Cash..................	1 695	00	Allied Service Station	23	00
Automobile............	2 800	00	Arrow Auto Company...	1 200	00
Office Furniture.....	700	00	Office Supply Company	85	00
Office Machines......	890	00	Plaza Equipment Company..............	168	00
			Total Liabilities....	1 476	00
			Proprietorship		
			Harvey H. Harper, Capital...........	4 609	00
Total Assets.........	6 085	00	Total Liab. and Prop.	6 085	00

Instructions: 1. Prepare a partial chart of accounts similar to the one illustrated on page 26.

2. Open accounts in a ledger for all the accounts listed on the partial chart of accounts. Allow one fourth of a page in your ledger for each account.

3. Record the opening entry on page 1 of a general journal. Use August 1 of the current year as the date.

4. Post the opening entry.

Self-checking: Check the completeness of your work by using the questions listed under Problem 3-1.

★BONUS PROBLEM 3-B

Preparing a chart of accounts and a beginning balance sheet; recording and posting an opening entry

Mrs. Jerry T. Rolf owns the Rolf Beauty Shop. She has never kept a formal set of books. On September 1 of the current year she decides to start a bookkeeping system for the beauty shop. She has gathered the following information:

Cash: currency and coins in the cash register, $48.75; checks on hand that were received from customers, $34.20; and bank balance according to the checkbook, $1,741.05.

Office equipment: cash register, $450.00. Mrs. Rolf owes the Acme Office Machine Company $140.00 for this office equipment.

Office furniture: desk, $120.00; filing cabinet, $56.00; chair, $40.00. She owes the Otis Furniture Company $96.00 for this office furniture.

Beauty shop equipment: driers, mirrors, chairs, tables, storage cabinets, coat racks, and miscellaneous equipment, $1,380.00. She owes the Beauty Supply Company $230.00 for this equipment.

Mrs. Rolf owes the City Gas Company $34.00 for heat and light and she owes the Porter Realty Agency $120.00 for rent.

Instructions: 1. Prepare a partial chart of accounts for the Rolf Beauty Shop.

2. Open a ledger account for each account title listed in the chart of accounts. Allow one fourth of a page in your ledger for each account. Number the accounts as shown on your chart.

3. Prepare a balance sheet dated September 1 of the current year.

4. Record the opening entry on page 1 of a general journal.

5. Post the opening entry.

Self-checking: Check the completeness of your work by using the questions listed under Problem 3-1.

CHAPTER 4

DEBIT AND CREDIT OF BUSINESS TRANSACTIONS AFFECTING BALANCE SHEET ACCOUNTS

After the opening entry is posted, all the accounts appear in the ledger with beginning balances. In this chapter you will learn how these account balances are changed as a result of business operations.

Effect of business transactions on account balances

An exchange of one value for another value is known as a *business transaction.* Every business transaction, when recorded in a journal and then posted, increases or decreases the balance of each of two or more accounts in the ledger. For example, if the Hill-Top Motel receives $20.00 in cash from the sale of an old adding machine, the balances of both the cash account and the office equipment account in the ledger are changed. The balance of the cash account is *increased* $20.00 because the Hill-Top Motel now has $20.00 more cash. The balance of the office equipment account is *decreased* $20.00 because the Hill-Top Motel now owns less office equipment.

Why a ledger account has two sides

A ledger account has two sides in order to make it easier to show the changes that occur in account balances. The illustration below at the left shows how increases and decreases in the cash account would be recorded if they were listed in one amount column. The illustration below at the right shows how increases and decreases in cash are recorded in the cash account when it has two sides.

Cash		
Beginning balance		3,000.00
Increase	+	1,000.00
Decrease	−	100.00
Decrease	−	1,200.00
Increase	+	800.00
Decrease	−	700.00
Increase	+	200.00

The cash account as it would appear if it had only one amount column

Cash			
Balance	3,000.00	Decrease	100.00
Increase	1,000.00	Decrease	1,200.00
Increase	800.00	Decrease	700.00
Increase	200.00		

The cash account with two amount columns

The process of adding to or subtracting from the balance of an account is simplified when each account in the ledger has two sides. All increases are recorded on the balance side of the account. All decreases are recorded on the side opposite the balance of the account. This arrangement makes it easy to find the total of each column and to subtract the smaller total from the larger total to find the new balance of the account.

Analyzing business transactions with T accounts

Every business transaction is always recorded in a journal before showing the effect of the transaction in the ledger. Before a business transaction can be recorded in a journal, it is necessary to analyze the transaction and determine the debit part and the credit part of the entry. When analyzing the effect of a transaction on accounts, the following steps are taken:

Step 1

Determine the names of the accounts affected.

Step 2

Determine the classification of each account affected.

Step 3

Determine how the balance of each of these accounts is changed in terms of increases and decreases, the debits and the credits.

In the following pages, several transactions that affect the asset, liability, and proprietorship accounts of the Hill-Top Motel are analyzed into their debit and credit parts. In doing so, use is made of an outline form of ledger account that looks like a capital T. A skeleton form of ledger account that shows only the account title and the debit and credit sides is called a *T account.*

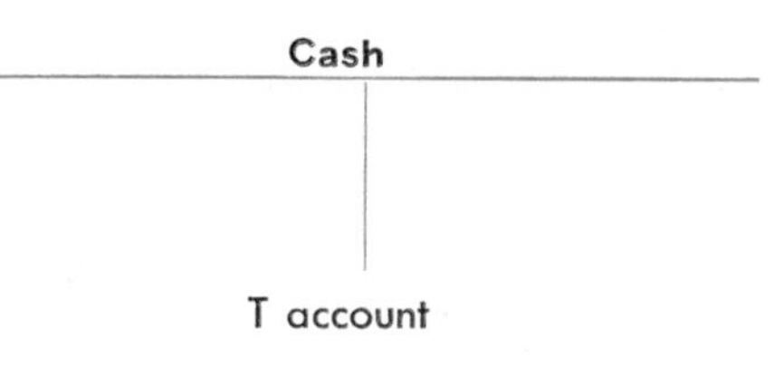

T account

TRANSACTION NO. 1 — SALE OF AN ASSET FOR CASH

August 1, 1967. Received cash, $20.00, from the sale of an old adding machine.

Analyzing Transaction No. 1

The steps in analyzing Transaction No. 1 are:

Step 1

Determine the names of the accounts affected.

a Cash

b Office Equipment

Step 2

Determine the classification of each account affected.

a Cash is an asset account.

b Office Equipment is an asset account.

Step 3

Determine how the balance of each of these accounts is changed.

a The Hill-Top Motel now has $20.00 more cash as a result of receiving $20.00 for the old adding machine. The balance of the cash account, an asset account, is *increased* $20.00. The *balance side* of every asset account is the *debit side*. All increases in any account balance are always recorded on the *balance side* of the account. The cash account is therefore *debited* for the amount of the increase.

The cash account at the right shows that a debit balance of $565.00 was in the account before this transaction took place. The $20.00 increase in the cash balance is recorded as a debit so that it can be added to this balance.

Cash

	(DEBIT)		(CREDIT)
Balance	565.00		
Increase	20.00		

b The Hill-Top Motel owns less office equipment as a result of selling its old adding machine. The balance of the office equipment account, an asset account, is *decreased* $20.00. The *balance side* of every asset account is the *debit side*. All decreases in any account balance are always recorded on the side *opposite* the balance side. The office equipment account is therefore *credited* for the amount of the decrease.

The office equipment account shows that a debit balance of $485.00 was in the account before this transaction took place. The decrease of $20.00 is recorded as a credit to show a decrease in this balance.

Office Equipment

	(DEBIT)		(CREDIT)
Balance	485.00	Decrease	20.00

T-account analysis of business transactions is used as the basis for making journal entries. The recording of the business transactions that are analyzed in Chapters 4 and 5 is presented in Chapter 6.

The debit amount equals the credit amount in each transaction

There are two parts in each business transaction — a debit part and a credit part. The debit part must always equal the credit part. When Transaction No. 1 is recorded in a journal and the journal entry is posted, the debit of $20.00 to the cash account is equal to the credit of $20.00 to the office equipment account. One asset account balance is increased and another asset account balance is decreased by the same amount.

Summary of increases and decreases in asset accounts

Increases in assets are recorded as debits. The balance of any asset account is always recorded on the *left-hand side* of the account as a *debit*. All increases in any account balance are always recorded on the *balance side* of the account. An increase in any asset account is therefore recorded on the *debit side* so that the amount can be added conveniently to the balance of the asset account.

ANY ASSET ACCOUNT	
Debit side is balance side and increase side	Credit side is decrease side

Decreases in assets are recorded as credits. All decreases in any account balance are always recorded on the side *opposite* the balance side of the account. Decreases in any asset account are therefore recorded on the *credit side* of the account.

TRANSACTION NO. 2 — PART PAYMENT OF A LIABILITY

August 1, 1967. Paid cash, $300.00, to the Motel Equipment Company in part payment of the amount owed.

Analyzing Transaction No. 2

The steps in analyzing Transaction No. 2 are:

Step 1

Determine the names of the accounts affected.

a Motel Equipment Company
b Cash

Step 2

Determine the classification of each account affected.

a Motel Equipment Company is a liability account.
b Cash is an asset account.

Step 3

Determine how the balance of each of these accounts is changed.

a The Hill-Top Motel decreases its liability to the Motel Equipment Company by $300.00 as a result of this part payment of an amount owed. The balance of the Motel Equipment Company account, a liability account, is *decreased* $300.00. The *balance side* of every liability account is the *credit side.* All decreases in any account balance are always recorded on the side *opposite* the balance side of the account. The Motel Equipment Company account is therefore *debited* for the amount of the decrease.

The Motel Equipment Company account shows that a credit balance of $1,300.00 was in the account before this transaction took place. The $300.00 decrease is recorded as a debit to show a decrease in this balance.

Motel Equipment Company

	(DEBIT)		(CREDIT)
Decrease	300.00	Balance	1,300.00

b The Hill-Top Motel has less cash as a result of having paid $300.00 to the Motel Equipment Company. The balance of the cash account, an asset account, is *decreased* $300.00. All decreases in any account balance are always recorded on the side *opposite* the balance side. The cash account is therefore *credited* for the amount of the decrease. The cash account shows this $300.00 decrease on the credit side of the account.

Cash

	(DEBIT)		(CREDIT)
Balance	565.00	Decrease	300.00
Increase	20.00		

When Transaction No. 2 is recorded in a journal and the journal entry is posted, the debit of $300.00 to the Motel Equipment Company account is equal to the credit of $300.00 to the cash account. A liability account balance is decreased and an asset account balance is decreased by the same amount.

Summary of increases and decreases in liability accounts

Increases in liabilities are recorded as credits. The balance of any liability account is always recorded on the *right-hand side* of the account as a *credit*. All increases in any account balance are always recorded on the *balance side* of the account. An increase in any liability account is therefore recorded on the *credit side* so that the amount can be added to the balance of the liability account.

ANY LIABILITY ACCOUNT

Debit side	Credit side
Debit side is decrease side	Credit side is balance side and increase side

Decreases in liabilities are recorded as debits. All decreases in any account balance are always recorded on the side *opposite* the balance side of the account. Decreases in any liability account are therefore recorded on the debit side of the account.

TRANSACTION NO. 3 — ADDITIONAL INVESTMENT BY PROPRIETOR

August 1, 1967. Received from the proprietor, Mr. Martin, a personal check for $1,000.00 as an additional investment in the business.

It is customary for one who operates his own business to have a personal bank account separate from his business bank account. A check received by the business from the proprietor is recorded like any other cash receipt transaction.

Analyzing Transaction No. 3

The steps in analyzing Transaction No. 3 are:

Step 1

Determine the names of the accounts affected.

a Cash

b Charles Martin, Capital

Step 2

Determine the classification of each account affected.

a Cash is an asset account.

b Charles Martin, Capital, is the proprietor's capital account.

Step 3

Determine how the balance of each of these accounts is changed.

a The Hill-Top Motel has $1,000.00 more cash as a result of receiving this additional investment. The balance of the cash account, an asset account, is *increased* $1,000.00. The *balance side* of every asset account is the *debit side*. All increases in any account balance are always recorded on the *balance side* of the account. The cash account is therefore *debited* for the amount of the increase. The cash account at the right shows this $1,000.00 increase.

Cash			
	(DEBIT)		(CREDIT)
Balance	565.00	Decrease	300.00
Increase	20.00		
Increase	1,000.00		

b Mr. Martin has increased his investment in the Hill-Top Motel as a result of this transaction. The balance of the Charles Martin, Capital, account, the proprietor's capital account, is *increased* $1,000.00. The balance side of any proprietor's capital account is the *credit side*. All increases in any account balance are always recorded on the *balance side* of the account. The proprietorship account, Charles Martin, Capital, is therefore *credited* for the amount of the increase in investment.

The Charles Martin, Capital, account shows that a balance of $5,700.00 was in the account before this transaction took place. The additional investment of $1,000.00 is recorded as a credit to show an increase in this balance.

Charles Martin, Capital

(DEBIT)	(CREDIT)	
	Balance	5,700.00
	Increase	1,000.00

When Transaction No. 3 is recorded in a journal and the journal entry is posted, the debit of $1,000.00 to the cash account is equal to the credit of $1,000.00 to the Charles Martin, Capital, account. An asset account balance is increased and a proprietorship account balance is increased by the same amount.

Summary of increases and decreases in the proprietor's capital account

Increases in proprietorship are recorded as credits. The balance of any proprietor's capital account is always recorded on the *right-hand side* of the account as a *credit*. All increases in any account balance are always recorded on the *balance side* of the account. An increase in the proprietor's capital account is therefore recorded on the *credit side* so that the amount of the increase can be added conveniently to the balance of the account.

ANY PROPRIETOR'S CAPITAL ACCOUNT

Debit side is decrease side	Credit side is balance side and increase side

Decreases in proprietorship are recorded as debits. All decreases in any account balance are always recorded on the side *opposite* the balance side of the account. Decreases in the proprietor's capital account are therefore recorded on the *debit side* of the account.

SUMMARY OF THE PRINCIPLES OF DEBIT AND CREDIT FOR BALANCE SHEET ACCOUNTS

Asset accounts always have *debit* balances. Therefore, an increase in an asset is always recorded on the *debit* side of the asset account. Decreases are recorded on the side opposite the balance side.

ANY ASSET ACCOUNT

+	–
Debit side is balance side and increase side	**Credit side is decrease side**

Liability accounts always have *credit* balances. Therefore, an increase in a liability is always recorded on the *credit* side of the liability account. Decreases are recorded on the side opposite the balance side.

ANY LIABILITY ACCOUNT

–	+
Debit side is decrease side	**Credit side is balance side and increase side**

The proprietor's capital account always has a *credit* balance. Therefore, an increase in proprietorship is always recorded on the *credit* side of the proprietor's capital account. Decreases are recorded on the side opposite the balance side.

ANY PROPRIETOR'S CAPITAL ACCOUNT

–	+
Debit side is decrease side	**Credit side is balance side and increase side**

Increases in any account balance are always recorded on the *balance side* of an account. Decreases in any account balance are always recorded on the side *opposite the balance side.*

Increasing Your Business Vocabulary

What is the meaning of each of the following:

a business transaction

b T account

Study Questions

1. Why does a ledger account have two sides?
2. What three steps are used to analyze each business transaction?
3. On which side of an account are increases always recorded?
4. Why is an increase in an asset account recorded as a debit?
5. On which side of an account are decreases always recorded?

6. Why is a decrease in an asset account recorded as a credit?
7. Why is an increase in a liability account recorded as a credit?
8. Why is a decrease in a liability account recorded as a debit?
9. Why is an increase in the proprietor's capital account recorded as a credit?
10. Why is a decrease in the proprietor's capital account recorded as a debit?

Cases for Business Decision

CASE 1

The bookkeeper for Lucille's Candy Store analyzes the payment of $180.00 to the U. S. Sugar Company as shown in the T accounts at the right.

What principles of bookkeeping has the bookkeeper failed to follow in analyzing the effect of the transaction upon the cash account? upon the U. S. Sugar Company account?

Cash	
180.00	

U. S. Sugar Company	
	180.00

CASE 2

The owner of Comisky's Tire Shop has never studied bookkeeping and he employs you to keep books for him. He does not understand why you debit the asset account, Office Equipment, and credit the asset account, Cash, when you record the purchase of a typewriter for cash. What explanation can you give him?

Drills for Understanding

DRILL 4-A | **The debit side, the credit side, and the balance side of accounts**

Instructions: 1. Make a T account for each of the account titles listed below and write the proper account title on each T account. The automobile account is shown at the right as an example.

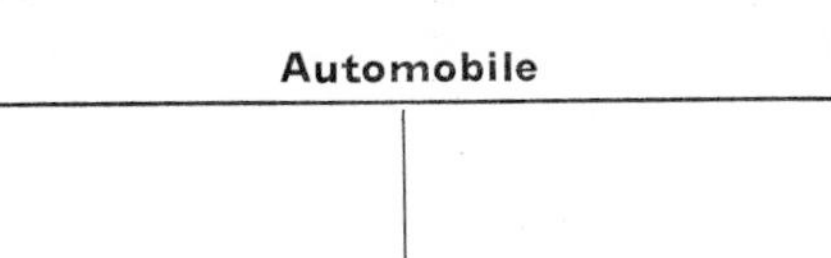

List of Account Titles

Cash	Office Furniture
Automobile	Land
C. R. Miller, Capital	Office Equipment Company (creditor)
Building	Office Supplies
Federal Savings Bank (creditor)	Office Machines

Instructions: 2. Write the words *Debit side* on the debit side of each T account and write the words *Credit side* on the credit side of each T account. The automobile account is shown as an example.

Automobile	
Debit side	**Credit side**

3. Write the words *Balance side* on the debit side of each account that usually has a debit balance. Write the words *Balance side* on the credit side of each account that usually has a credit balance. The automobile account is shown as an example.

Automobile	
Debit side **Balance side**	**Credit side**

DRILL 4-B | The increase side and the decrease side of accounts

Instructions: 1. Use the same T accounts that were prepared in Drill 4-A. In each T account make a plus sign (+) on the side of the account that is the increase side. Make a minus sign (−) on the side that is the decrease side. The automobile account is shown as an example.

Automobile	
Debit side **Balance side** +	**Credit side** −

DRILL 4-C | Self-checking oral drill on debit and credit

Instructions: Without looking at your written answers to the two drills above, check your understanding of debit and credit by seeing how fast and accurately you can answer the following questions:

1. What classification of account has its balance side on the debit side?
2. What classifications of accounts have their balance side on the credit side?
3. What classification of account has all increases written on the debit side?
4. What classifications of accounts have all increases written on the credit side?
5. What classifications of accounts have all decreases written on the debit side?
6. What classification of account has all decreases written on the credit side?

Application Problems

PROBLEM 4-1 | Analyzing the effect of transactions on accounts

Mr. James Carlton operates a real estate business. His ledger contains the following balance sheet accounts:

Cash
Office Supplies
Office Furniture
Office Machines
Automobile
Elm Street Garage (creditor)
Hart Stationery Store (creditor)
Olympic Equipment Company (creditor)
James Carlton, Capital

Instructions: 1. Prepare a form with the headings shown below for use in checking your understanding of how business transactions affect account balances. Allow two lines for each transaction.

Trans. No.	(a) Account Titles Affected	(b) Classification of Account	(c) Effect of Transaction on Balance of Account		(d) Recorded on which Side of the Account?	
			Increase	Decrease	Debit	Credit
1.	*Cash*	*Asset*	√		√	
	Office Furniture	*Asset*		√		√
2.						

Instructions: 2. For each of the following transactions: (a) Write the account titles affected. (b) Identify the classification of each account affected. (c) Indicate whether the balance of each of these accounts is increased or decreased. (d) Indicate on which side of the account the amount is to be recorded. Copy the analysis of Transaction No. 1, which is given as an example on the form above.

Transaction Number — *Transactions*

1. Received cash, $28.00, from sale of old office desk.
2. Paid cash, $320.00, for an electric typewriter.
3. Paid cash, $120.00, to Olympic Equipment Company in payment of amount owed.
4. Paid cash, $15.00, for office supplies.
5. Received cash, $20.00, from sale of old typewriter.
6. Paid cash, $50.00, to Elm Street Garage in part payment of amount owed.
7. Paid cash, $220.00, for a new office desk.
8. Received cash, $10.00, from the sale of an old adding machine.
9. Paid cash, $20.00, to Hart Stationery Store in payment of amount owed.
10. Paid cash, $18.00, for office supplies.
11. Received cash, $850.00, from sale of old automobile.
12. Paid cash, $3,200.00, for new automobile.
13. Received cash, $2,000.00, from James Carlton, the proprietor, as an additional investment in the business.

PROBLEM 4-2 Analyzing transactions into their debit and credit parts

Instructions: Use a pair of T accounts to analyze each of the transactions listed in Problem 4-1. Analyze each transaction into its debit and credit parts as follows:

(a) Write the account title and the debit amount in the first T account.

(b) Write the account title and the credit amount in the second T account.

The analysis of Transaction No. 1 is given at the right.

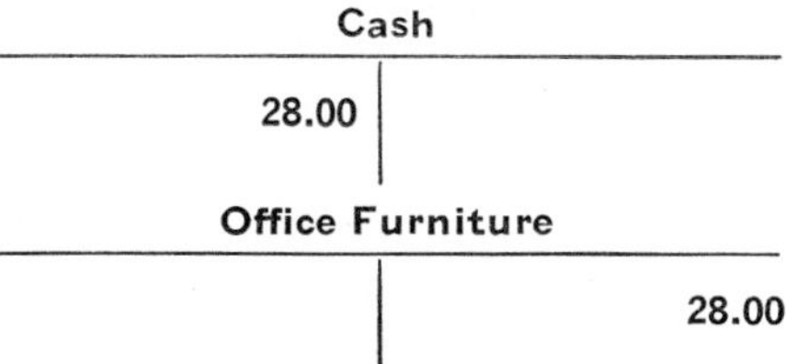

PROBLEM 4-3 | Analyzing transactions into their debit and credit parts

Mr. Clifford Chase operates an accounting business. On May 1, his ledger contains the following balance sheet accounts with balances as shown in the T accounts below.

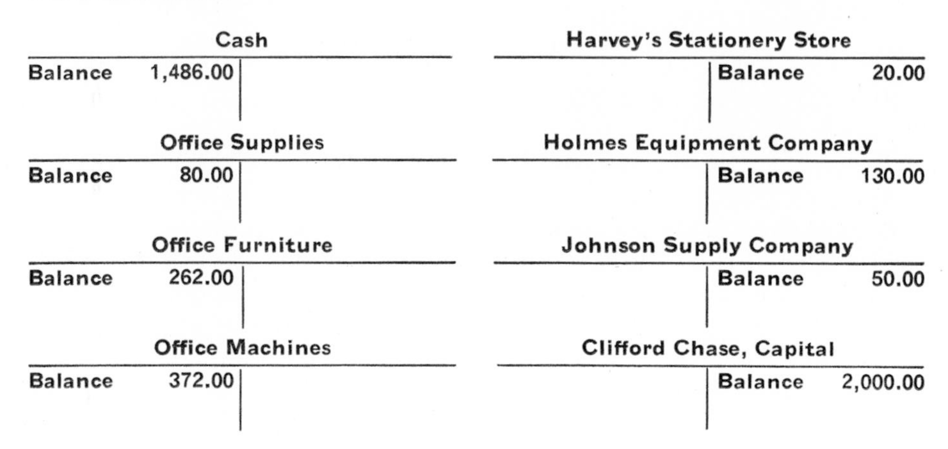

Account	Debit		Credit	
Cash	Balance	1,486.00		
Office Supplies	Balance	80.00		
Office Furniture	Balance	262.00		
Office Machines	Balance	372.00		
Harvey's Stationery Store			Balance	20.00
Holmes Equipment Company			Balance	130.00
Johnson Supply Company			Balance	50.00
Clifford Chase, Capital			Balance	2,000.00

Instructions: 1. On a sheet of paper, copy the T accounts as shown above with their balances. Allow seven lines for the cash account and three lines for each of the other accounts.

2. Analyze each of the following transactions into its debit and credit parts. Write the debit amount and the transaction number on the proper side of the account. Write the credit amount and the transaction number on the proper side of the account.

The analysis of the first two transactions and their effect on the accounts is shown at the right.

Cash

Debit		Credit	
Balance	1,486.00	(2)	50.00
(1)	37.00		

Office Furniture

Debit		Credit	
Balance	262.00	(1)	37.00

Johnson Supply Company

Debit		Credit	
(2)	50.00	Balance	50.00

Transaction Number — *Transactions*

1. Received cash, $37.00, from sale of old office furniture.
2. Paid cash, $50.00, to Johnson Supply Company in payment of amount owed.
3. Paid cash, $350.00, for new electric typewriter.
4. Paid cash, $12.00, for office supplies.
5. Received cash, $35.00, from sale of old office desk.
6. Paid cash, $235.00, for new office desk.
7. Paid cash, $100.00, to Holmes Equipment Company in part payment of amount owed.

8. Received cash, $10.00, from sale of old office chair.
9. Paid cash, $60.00, for new office chair.
10. Received cash, $500.00, from Mr. Chase, the proprietor, as an additional investment in the business.
11. Paid cash, $20.00, to Harvey's Stationery Store in payment of amount owed.

Optional Problems

★ SUPPLEMENTARY PROBLEM 4-S

Analyzing transactions into their debit and credit parts

Mr. John Todd operates an insurance agency. On August 1, his ledger contains the following balance sheet accounts with balances as shown in the T accounts below.

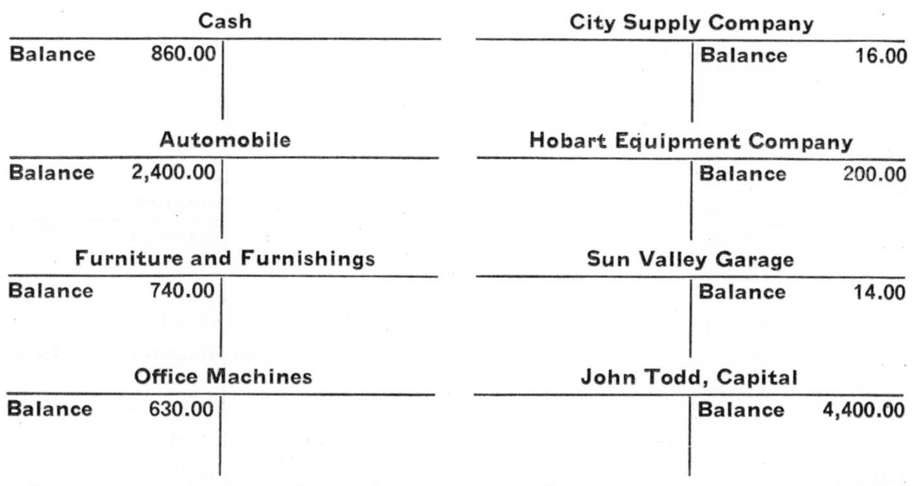

Instructions: 1. On a sheet of paper, copy the T accounts as shown above with their balances. Allow seven lines for the cash account and four lines for each of the other accounts.

2. Analyze each of the following transactions into its debit and credit parts. Write the debit amount and the transaction number on the proper side of the account. Write the credit amount and the transaction number on the proper side of the account.

Transaction
Number *Transactions*

1. Paid cash, $14.00, to Sun Valley Garage in payment of amount owed.
2. Received cash, $8.00, from sale of old rug.
3. Paid cash, $65.00, for new rug.
4. Paid cash, $100.00, to Hobart Equipment Company in part payment of amount owed.
5. Paid cash, $38.00, for a check-writing machine.
6. Paid cash, $60.00, for two new chairs.

7. Received cash, $18.00, from sale of old desk.
8. Received cash, $600.00, from Mr. Todd, the proprietor, as an additional investment in the business.
9. Received cash, $5.00, from sale of old desk chair.
10. Paid cash, $215.00, for new desk.
11. Paid cash, $16.00, to City Supply Company in payment of amount owed.

★ BONUS PROBLEM 4-B

Analyzing T accounts

The eight T accounts of Petri Business Consultants are shown below. Each T account shows the account balance and one or more increases or decreases in the account balance as the result of the first ten transactions for the month.

Cash

	Debit		Credit
Balance	4,960.50	(1)	17.80
(2)	15.00	(3)	149.50
(7)	85.00	(4)	72.60
(8)	2,000.00	(5)	235.00
		(6)	102.62
		(9)	2,950.00
		(10)	300.00

Automobile

	Debit		Credit
Balance	3,300.00		
(9)	2,950.00		

Supplies

	Debit		Credit
Balance	205.40		
(1)	17.80		

Merrill Supplies

	Debit		Credit
(6)	102.62	Balance	402.62
(10)	300.00		

Office Furniture

	Debit		Credit
Balance	2,400.00	(2)	15.00
(5)	235.00		

Staley Business Forms

	Debit		Credit
(4)	72.60	Balance	72.60

Office Equipment

	Debit		Credit
Balance	600.00	(7)	85.00
(3)	149.50		

Jeff Petri, Capital

	Debit		Credit
		Balance	10,990.68
		(8)	2,000.00

Instructions: 1. Prepare a form with the headings shown below for use in analyzing the T accounts. Allow two lines for each transaction.

(a) Transaction	(b) Account Debited	(c) Effect of Debit	(d) Account Credited	(e) Effect of Credit
1. *Paid cash, $17.80, for supplies.*	*Supplies*	*Increased an asset*	*Cash*	*Decreased an asset*
2.				

Instructions: 2. For each of the analyses numbered 1 through 10, write: (a) the transaction that took place, (b) the name of the account debited, (c) the effect of the debit upon the account balance, (d) the name of the account credited, and (e) the effect of the credit upon the account balance. The analysis of Transaction No. 1 is given as a sample on the form above.

CHAPTER 5

DEBIT AND CREDIT OF BUSINESS TRANSACTIONS AFFECTING INCOME ACCOUNTS AND EXPENSE ACCOUNTS

Most businesses are in operation for the purpose of earning a profit. To make a profit, a business must engage in business transactions that increase its proprietorship. For example, owners of motels receive cash for renting rooms; physicians receive fees for services performed; farmers sell their products. An increase in proprietorship that results from the operation of the business is called *income*. Income is sometimes called revenue.

INCOME TRANSACTIONS

Need for income accounts

All income transactions cause an increase in proprietorship. A business may have several kinds of income. For example, in addition to receiving income from room sales, some motels may have income from restaurant operations, from vending machines, and from a gift shop or newsstand. All income transactions could be recorded on the credit side of the proprietor's capital account, as shown in the one T account below.

Proprietor's Capital Account

Debit	Credit	Amount
	Room Sales	196.00
	Restaurant Sales	249.00
	Newsstand Sales	18.00
	Gift Shop Sales	33.00
	Room Sales	208.00
	Restaurant Sales	364.00
	Newsstand Sales	25.00
	Gift Shop Sales	87.00
	Investment by Owner	2,000.00
	Vending Machine Sales	42.00
	Room Sales	233.00
	Restaurant Sales	286.00
	Newsstand Sales	21.00
	Gift Shop Sales	67.00

All income transactions recorded in the proprietor's capital account

If the preceding plan were used, however, it would be difficult to determine quickly the total amount of each kind of income. Therefore, a separate account is kept in the ledger for each kind of income, as shown in the six T accounts below.

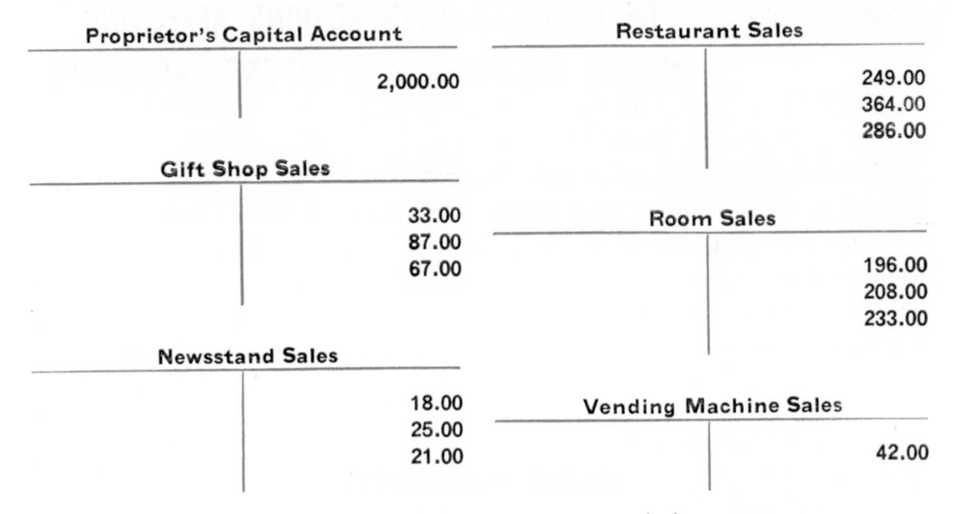

Each kind of income recorded in a separate ledger account

TRANSACTION NO. 4 — AN INCOME TRANSACTION

August 1, 1967. Received cash, $72.00, from room sales for one day.

Analyzing Transaction No. 4

The Hill-Top Motel records all income received from the use of its rooms in an income account called *Room Sales.* The room sales account is placed in the fourth division of the ledger, as shown in the chart of accounts on page 2. If the Hill-Top Motel had other sources of income, a separate account would be opened for each kind of income and placed in the income division of the ledger.

The same steps that are used in analyzing transactions affecting assets, liabilities, and proprietorship are taken in analyzing income transactions. The steps in analyzing Transaction No. 4 are:

Step 1

Determine the names of the accounts affected.

a Cash

b Room Sales

Step 2

Determine the classification of each account affected.

a Cash is an asset account.

b Room Sales is an income account.

Step 3

Determine how the balance of each of these accounts is changed.

a The Hill-Top Motel has more cash as a result of receiving $72.00 from its room sales for one day. The balance of the cash account, an asset account, is *increased* $72.00. The *balance side* of every asset account is the *debit side*. All increases in any account balance are always recorded on the *balance side* of the account. The cash account is therefore *debited* for the amount of the increase, $72.00.

Cash			
	(DEBIT)		(CREDIT)
Balance	565.00	Decrease	300.00
Increase	20.00		
Increase	1,000.00		
Increase	72.00		

b The income of the Hill-Top Motel has been *increased* $72.00 as a result of receiving cash for the use of rooms. The *balance side* of every income account is the *credit side*. All increases in any account are recorded on the *balance side* of the account. Therefore, the income account, Room Sales, is *credited* for the amount of the increase, $72.00.

Room Sales			
	(DEBIT)		(CREDIT)
		Increase	72.00

EXPENSE TRANSACTIONS

All businesses have operating costs. For example, a business pays for electricity, rent, telephone service, and other costs. Operating costs decrease proprietorship. A decrease in proprietorship that results from the operation of the business is called an *expense.*

Need for expense accounts

All expense transactions cause a decrease in proprietorship. A business may have a variety of expenses. For example, most motels have several kinds of expenses, such as laundry, advertising, telephone, water, electricity, and repairs. All expense transactions could be recorded on the debit side of the proprietor's capital account, as shown in the one T account on the next page.

Proprietor's Capital Account

Rent Expense	300.00	
Miscellaneous Expense	47.00	
Telephone Expense	32.00	
Laundry Expense	26.00	
Electricity Expense	84.00	
Laundry Expense	19.00	
Advertising Expense	15.00	
Laundry Expense	33.00	
Advertising Expense	24.00	
Laundry Expense	27.00	
Miscellaneous Expense	38.00	
Laundry Expense	29.00	
Advertising Expense	12.00	

All expense transactions recorded in the proprietor's capital account

If the plan above were used, however, it would be difficult to tell quickly the total amount of each kind of expense. Thus, a separate account is kept in the ledger for each kind of expense, as shown in the six T accounts below.

Advertising Expense

15.00	
24.00	
12.00	

Miscellaneous Expense

47.00	
38.00	

Electricity Expense

84.00	

Rent Expense

300.00	

Laundry Expense

26.00	
19.00	
33.00	
27.00	
29.00	

Telephone Expense

32.00	

Each kind of expense recorded in a separate ledger account

The Hill-Top Motel uses several expense accounts, all placed in alphabetic order in the fifth division of the ledger. These expense account titles are shown in the chart of accounts on page 2. Later, if the Hill-Top Motel has other types of expenses, a separate account will be opened for each of these expenses.

TRANSACTION NO. 5 — AN EXPENSE TRANSACTION

August 2, 1967. Paid cash, $200.00, for rent of the motel for August.

Analyzing Transaction No. 5

The steps in analyzing Transaction No. 5 are:

Step 1

Determine the names of the accounts affected.

a Rent Expense

b Cash

Step 2

Determine the classification of each account affected.

a Rent Expense is an expense account.

b Cash is an asset account.

Step 3

Determine how the balance of each of these accounts is changed.

a The operating expenses of the Hill-Top Motel have been *increased* $200.00 as a result of paying the monthly rent for the motel. The *balance side* of any expense account is the *debit side*. All increases in any account balance are always recorded on the *balance side* of the account. Therefore, the expense account, Rent Expense, is *debited* for the amount of the increase, $200.00, as shown in the T account above.

Rent Expense

	(DEBIT)		(CREDIT)
Increase	200.00		

b The Hill-Top Motel has $200.00 less cash as a result of having paid the monthly rent. The balance of the cash account, an asset account, is *decreased* $200.00. All decreases in any account balance are always recorded on the side *opposite* the balance side. The cash account is therefore *credited* for the amount of the decrease, $200.00, as shown in the T account above.

Cash

	(DEBIT)		(CREDIT)
Balance	565.00	Decrease	300.00
Increase	20.00	Decrease	200.00
Increase	1,000.00		
Increase	72.00		

SUMMARY OF THE PRINCIPLES OF DEBIT AND CREDIT FOR INCOME ACCOUNTS AND EXPENSE ACCOUNTS

Every income transaction and every expense transaction has a debit part and a credit part. The debit part should always equal the credit part.

Income accounts always have *credit* balances. Increases in the balance of any account are recorded on the *balance side* of the account. Therefore, an increase in the balance of any income account is always recorded on the *credit side* of the income account. Decreases in the balance of any account are always recorded on the side *opposite* the balance. Therefore, decreases in the balance of any income account are always recorded on the *debit side* of the income account.

ANY INCOME ACCOUNT	
−	+
Debit side is decrease side	Credit side is balance side and increase side

Expense accounts always have *debit* balances. Increases in the balance of any account are recorded on the *balance side* of the account. Therefore, an increase in the balance of any expense account is always recorded on the *debit side* of the expense account. Decreases in the balance of any account are always recorded on the side *opposite* the balance. Therefore, decreases in the balance of any expense account are always recorded on the *credit side* of the expense account.

ANY EXPENSE ACCOUNT	
+	−
Debit side is balance side and increase side	Credit side is decrease side

Increasing Your Business Vocabulary

What is the meaning of each of the following:

a income b expense

Study Questions

1. Give three examples of business transactions that increase proprietorship.
2. Give three examples of operating costs that decrease proprietorship.
3. What effect does an income transaction have on proprietorship?

4. Why is a separate ledger account kept for each kind of income?
5. Which side of an income account is the balance side?
6. Which side of an income account is used to record an increase in its balance?
7. Why is a separate ledger account kept for each kind of expense?
8. What effect does an expense transaction have on proprietorship?
9. Why is it undesirable to record all expense transactions on the debit side of the proprietor's capital account?
10. Which side of an expense account is the balance side?
11. Which side of an expense account is used to record an increase in its balance?

Cases for Business Decision

CASE 1

Mr. Adler has the following three expense accounts in his ledger: Advertising Expense, Miscellaneous Expense, and Rent Expense. When Mr. Adler reports his expenses on his federal income tax forms, he is required to report separately his expenses for salaries and wages paid, contributions, interest, and insurance. He has been recording all of these in the one miscellaneous expense account.

What suggestions might you make to Mr. Adler about recording his expenses so that he can more easily complete his income tax forms?

CASE 2

Mrs. Jason is the owner of a shoe store. She has never studied bookkeeping and does not understand why the receipt of cash from the sale of an old cash register should not be recorded as income. How would you explain to her that all cash received is not necessarily income?

CASE 3

Mr. Masters bought a typewriter for use in his office. He told the bookkeeper to record the cost of the typewriter as an expense. Is Mr. Masters following correct bookkeeping principles in giving these instructions to his bookkeeper? If the instructions are not correct, what reasons would you give Mr. Masters for doing otherwise?

CASE 4

Mary Polson owns and operates a beauty shop. She receives income from services rendered to customers and from the sale of cosmetics. In the past she has recorded all income in one account with the title, Income. She has decided that she would like to know how much income she receives from services rendered customers and how much income she receives from the sale of cosmetics. What changes should she make in her bookkeeping procedures?

Drills for Understanding

DRILL 5-A | The debit side, the credit side, and the balance side of accounts

Instructions: 1. Make a T account for each of the account titles listed below and write the proper account title on each T account.

List of Account Titles

Cash	Vending Machines Income
Automobile	J. C. King (creditor)
Simmons Company (creditor)	Furniture and Fixtures
R. J. Trout, Capital	Room Sales
Rent Expense	Laundry Expense
Advertising Expense	Miscellaneous Expense

Instructions: 2. Write the words *Debit side* on the debit side of each T account and write the words *Credit side* on the credit side of each T account.

3. Write the words *Balance side* on the debit side of each account that usually has a debit balance. Write the words *Balance side* on the credit side of each account that usually has a credit balance.

4. Make a plus sign (+) on the side of each T account that is the increase side. Make a minus sign (–) on the side of each T account that is the decrease side.

The cash account is shown at the right as an example.

Cash	
Debit side **Balance side** +	**Credit side** –

DRILL 5-B | Self-checking oral drill on debit and credit

Instructions: Without looking at your written answers to the drill above, check your understanding of debit and credit by seeing how fast and accurately you can answer the following questions:

1. What two classifications of accounts have their balances on the debit side?
2. What three classifications of accounts have their balances on the credit side?
3. What two classifications of accounts have each increase recorded on the debit side?
4. What three classifications of accounts have each increase recorded on the credit side?

Application Problems

PROBLEM 5-1 | Analyzing the effect of transactions on accounts

Before employing you to record transactions in his journal, Mr. J. G. Chapman, who manages a tourist inn, wants to check upon your present knowledge of debits and credits. His chart of accounts is shown below.

Chapman Tourist Inn
Chart of Accounts

(1) Assets	Account Number	(4) Income	Account Number
Cash	11	Room Sales	41
Housekeeping Supplies	12		
Office Equipment	13	**(5) Expenses**	
Furniture and Fixtures	14	Advertising Expense	51
(2) Liabilities		Electricity Expense	52
Atlas Company	21	Laundry Expense	53
		Rent Expense	54
(3) Proprietorship		Telephone Expense	55
J. G. Chapman, Capital	31		

Instructions: 1. Prepare a form with the headings shown below for use in checking your understanding of how business transactions affect account balances. Allow two lines for each transaction.

Trans. No.	(a) Account Titles Affected	(b) Classification of Account	(c) Effect of Transaction on Balance of Account		(d) Recorded on which Side of the Account?	
			Increase	Decrease	Debit	Credit
1.	*Rent Expense*	*Expense*	√		√	
	Cash	*Asset*		√		√
2.						

Instructions: 2. For each of the following transactions: (a) Write the account titles affected. (b) Identify the classification of each account affected. (c) Indicate whether the balance of each of these accounts is increased or decreased. (d) Indicate on which side of the account the amount is to be recorded. Copy the analysis of Transaction No. 1, which is given as an example on the form above.

Transaction Number	*Transactions*
1.	Paid cash, $150.00, for June rent.
2.	Received cash, $25.00, from sale of old bedroom furniture.
3.	Received cash, $46.00, from room sales.
4.	Paid cash, $73.00, to Atlas Company in payment of amount owed.
5.	Paid cash, $8.00, for laundry.
6.	Received cash, $34.00, from room sales.
7.	Received cash, $10.00, from sale of old office desk.
8.	Received cash, $40.00, from room sales.
9.	Paid cash, $6.00, for installing an outdoor sign advertising the tourist inn.
10.	Received cash, $28.00, from room sales.
11.	Paid cash, $12.00, for telephone bill.
12.	Paid cash, $6.00, for laundry.
13.	Paid cash, $32.00, for electric bill.
14.	Paid cash, $15.00, for advertisement in tourist magazine.
15.	Received cash, $750.00, from Mr. Chapman, the proprietor, as an additional investment in the business.

PROBLEM 5-2 | Analyzing transactions into their debit and credit parts

Instructions: Use a pair of T accounts to analyze each of the transactions listed in Problem 5-1. Analyze each transaction into its debit and credit parts as follows:

(a) Write the account title and the debit amount in the first T account.

(b) Write the account title and the credit amount in the second T account.

The analysis of Transaction No. 1 is given at the right.

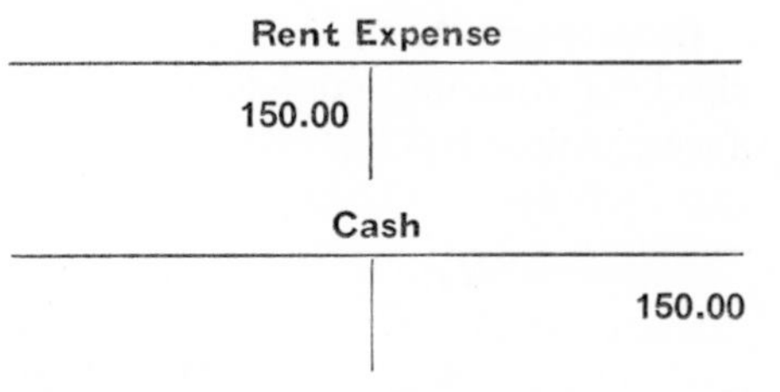

PROBLEM 5-3 | Analyzing transactions into their debit and credit parts

Duncan Ellis owns and operates the Suburban Delivery Service. On October 1 his ledger contains the following account balances: Cash, $450.00; Delivery Equipment, $4,200.00; Office Equipment, $650.00; Center City Motors (creditor), $2,300.00; and Duncan Ellis, Capital, $3,000.00.

Instructions: 1. On a sheet of paper prepare a T account for each of the accounts above and record the account balance. Also prepare a T account for each of the following accounts: Delivery Income, Advertising Expense, Delivery Truck Expense, Miscellaneous Expense, and Telephone Expense. There is no account balance on October 1 in the income account and the four expense accounts. Allow eight lines for the cash account and three lines for each of the other accounts.

2. Analyze each of the following transactions into its debit and credit parts. Write the debit amount and the transaction number on the proper side of the account. Write the credit amount and the transaction number on the proper side of the account.

Transaction
Number *Transactions*

1. Paid cash, $13.00, for telephone expense.
2. Paid cash, $9.50, for gas and oil for delivery truck.
3. Received cash, $243.00, from delivery income.
4. Paid cash, $128.00, for office desk and chair.
5. Received cash, $18.00, from sale of old office desk and chair.
6. Paid cash, $11.40, for gas and oil for delivery truck.
7. Paid cash, $12.50, for advertising expense.
8. Received cash, $385.00, from delivery income.
9. Paid cash, $2.00, for washing the delivery truck. (Delivery Truck Expense)
10. Paid cash, $3.50, for leather work gloves. (Miscellaneous Expense)
11. Paid cash, $500.00, to Center City Motors in part payment of amount owed.

Optional Problems

★SUPPLEMENTARY PROBLEM 5-S

Analyzing transactions into their debit and credit parts

John M. Compton operates the Compton Roller Skating Rink. On January 1, his ledger contains the following account balances: Cash, $700.00; Office Equipment, $500.00; Skating Equipment, $1,500.00; Plymouth Repair Company (creditor), $50.00; and John M. Compton, Capital, $2,650.00.

Instructions: 1. On a sheet of paper, prepare a T account for each of the accounts above and record the account balance. Also prepare a T account for each of the following accounts: Admissions Income, Advertising Expense, Miscellaneous Expense, Rent Expense, and Utilities Expense. There is no account balance on January 1 in the income account and the four expense accounts. Allow eight lines for the cash account and three lines for each of the other accounts.

2. Analyze each of the following transactions into its debit and credit parts. Write the debit amount and the transaction number on the proper side of the account. Write the credit amount and the transaction number on the proper side of the account.

Transaction
Number *Transactions*

1. Paid cash, $165.00, for rent of skating rink.
2. Received cash, $85.00, from admissions income.
3. Paid cash, $14.00, for telephone expense.

4. Paid cash, $50.00, to Plymouth Repair Company in payment of amount owed.
5. Received cash, $75.00, from admissions income.
6. Paid cash, $8.50, for repair of floor. (Miscellaneous Expense)
7. Received cash, $110.00, from admissions income.
8. Paid cash, $18.50, for electricity expense.
9. Paid cash, $12.00, for advertisements in newspaper.
10. Paid cash, $90.00, for new skating equipment.

★ BONUS PROBLEM 5-B

Analyzing T accounts

The nine accounts of the Texas Freight Company, owned and operated by D. R. Tracy, are shown below. Each T account shows the account balance and one or more increases or decreases in the account balance as the result of the first ten transactions for the month.

Cash

	Debit		Credit
Balance	18,760.40	(1)	237.80
(3)	25.00	(2)	4,970.00
(4)	2,735.90	(5)	4,800.20
(6)	3,850.00	(7)	87.00
(9)	3,012.65	(8)	196.30
		(10)	475.00

D. R. Tracy, Capital

	Debit		Credit
		Balance	35,070.20

Delivery Income

	Debit		Credit
		(4)	2,735.90
		(9)	3,012.65

Delivery Trucks

	Debit		Credit
Balance	24,750.00	(6)	3,850.00
(2)	4,970.00		

Advertising Expense

	Debit		Credit
(7)	87.00		

Office Equipment

	Debit		Credit
Balance	1,360.00	(3)	25.00

Delivery Truck Expense

	Debit		Credit
(1)	237.80		
(8)	196.30		

Lone Star Motors, Inc.

	Debit		Credit
(5)	4,800.20	Balance	9,800.20

Rent Expense

	Debit		Credit
(10)	475.00		

Instructions: 1. Prepare a form with the headings shown below for use in analyzing the T accounts. Allow two lines for each transaction.

(a) Transaction	(b) Account Debited	(c) Effect of Debit	(d) Account Credited	(e) Effect of Credit
1. *Paid cash, $237.80, for truck expense.*	*Delivery Truck Exp.*	*Increased an expense*	*Cash*	*Decreased an asset*

Instructions: 2. For each of the analyses numbered 1 through 10, write: (a) the transaction that took place, (b) the name of the account debited, (c) the effect of the debit upon the account balance, (d) the name of the account credited, and (e) the effect of the credit upon the account balance. The analysis of Transaction No. 1 is given as a sample on the form above.

CHAPTER 6 | JOURNALIZING BUSINESS TRANSACTIONS

After each business transaction is analyzed, the debit part and the credit part of the transaction are recorded in a journal. Separating a transaction into its debit and credit parts and recording each part in a journal is called *journalizing*.

Double-entry bookkeeping

The recording of the debit part and the credit part of each transaction is called *double-entry bookkeeping*. Double-entry bookkeeping is used in practically all well-organized businesses because it is the only method that provides a complete record of the effect of each business transaction on the ledger accounts. Recording only the debit part or only the credit part of a transaction is called *single-entry bookkeeping*. Because single-entry bookkeeping is incomplete bookkeeping, it is not commonly used by persons who have learned double-entry bookkeeping.

Journalizing transactions increases accuracy

When a transaction is journalized, both the debit part and the credit part are recorded together on the same page. Thus, if only a part of the transaction is recorded, the omission is seen readily and the error can be corrected immediately. When the debit and the credit parts are recorded together, it is easy to recognize that the debit part equals the credit part.

If transactions were recorded directly in ledger accounts, interruption in the work might cause the bookkeeper to record only part of the transaction and to forget to record the other part. An error of this kind would be very difficult to locate.

The cash journal used by the Hill-Top Motel

It would be possible to journalize all the transactions of a business in a two-column general journal similar to the one used by the Hill-Top Motel in recording the opening entry. If the Hill-Top Motel continued to use this general journal for recording cash transactions, the entries for the first five transactions in August, which were analyzed in Chapters 4 and 5, would appear as shown on the next page.

GENERAL JOURNAL PAGE 1

	DATE	ACCOUNT TITLE	POST. REF.	DEBIT	CREDIT	
9	1	Cash		20 00		9
10		Office Equipment			20 00	10
11		R1				11
12	1	Motel Equipment Company		300 00		12
13		Cash			300 00	13
14		Ck1				14
15	1	Cash		1000 00		15
16		Charles Martin, Capital			1000 00	16
17		R2				17
18	1	Cash		72 00		18
19		Room Sales			72 00	19
20		R3-8				20
21	2	Rent Expense		200 00		21
22		Cash			200 00	22
23		Ck2				23
24						24
25						25
26						26
27						27
28						28
29						29
30						30
31						31

Cash transactions recorded in a two-column general journal

Mr. Martin, the proprietor of the Hill-Top Motel, finds that he can journalize and post cash transactions more easily if he uses a special journal. A journal in which all cash transactions and only cash transactions are recorded is called a *cash journal.*

> The two-column general journal was once commonly used by small businesses for journalizing all business transactions. Today it is generally used only for special entries such as the opening entry illustrated in Chapter 2. The use of the two-column general journal for other special entries is presented in later chapters.

The cash journal used by the Hill-Top Motel is shown at the top of the next page. The transactions journalized in it are the same as those illustrated in the two-column general journal above.

Although the form of the cash journal is different from that of the general journal, the entry for each transaction is still divided into two equal parts — a debit part and a credit part. For example, on Line 1 of the cash journal, the $20.00 debit to Cash is equal to the $20.00 credit to Office Equipment.

CASH JOURNAL PAGE 1

	1	2					3	4	5	
	CASH DEBIT	GENERAL DEBIT	DATE	ACCOUNT TITLE	NO.	POST. REF.	GENERAL CREDIT	ROOM SALES CREDIT	CASH CREDIT	
1	20 00		1967 Aug. 1	Office Equipment	R1		20 00			1
2		300 00	1	Motel Equipment Company	Ck1				300 00	2
3	1000 00		1	Charles Martin, Capital	R2		1000 00			3
4	72 00		1	✓	R3-8			72 00		4
5		200 00	2	Rent Expense	Ck2				200 00	5
6										6
7										7
8										8
9										9
10										10
11										11
12										12
13										13
14										14
15										15

Cash transactions recorded in a cash journal

Advantages of using a cash journal

The advantages of using a cash journal with special amount columns with the headings Cash Debit, Cash Credit, and Room Sales Credit are:

1. In a cash journal, a special column is provided for each account that is debited or credited frequently during the month. For the Hill-Top Motel, these accounts are Cash and Room Sales. The cash account requires two special columns, one column for cash receipts and the other for cash payments. The amounts entered in special columns are not posted separately. Only the total of a special column is posted.

   If a two-column general journal were used to record the transactions that occur frequently, each amount would have to be posted separately. Therefore, special columns in a cash journal save labor and time in the later posting of the cash journal.

2. When both the debit amount and the credit amount of a transaction are recorded in special columns, it is not necessary to write any account title in the Account Title column. For example, in Transaction No. 4 on Line 4 of the cash journal illustrated above, both the debit amount and the credit amount are recorded in special columns. Therefore, a check mark (√) is placed in the Account Title column to show that no account title needs to be written in this wide column and that the writing of an account title has not been overlooked.

   If a two-column general journal were used for these transactions, time and labor would be required to write an account title for each part of every transaction.

3. In a cash journal, a General Debit column and a General Credit column are provided for accounts that are not debited or credited very often. It is not helpful to have a special column for an account that is debited or credited only once each month. For example, neither the rent nor the electricity bill would be paid more than once a month.

   When part of a transaction cannot be recorded in a special column, the amount is recorded in the proper General column and the account is identified in the Account Title column. However, the cash received part or the cash payment part of the transaction is recorded in the proper Cash column and the entire entry is completed on a single line of the cash journal. If such a transaction were recorded in a two-column general journal, at least three lines would be required for the complete entry.
4. When a cash journal is used, the number of the receipt for each cash receipt and the number of the check for each cash payment are written in the No. column. Thus, it is unnecessary to use a separate line for describing the source document as is done in a two-column general journal.
5. In the cash journal of the Hill-Top Motel, shown on page 67, the complete entry of each transaction is recorded on a single line. In the general journal shown on page 66, at least three lines are used to record each transaction. If a two-column general journal were used to record all transactions, the general journal would be bulkier than a cash journal.

Each kind of business plans its cash journal to fit its needs. One type of business might provide special columns in its cash journal for those expense items that occur frequently, such as Advertising Expense Debit, Automobile Expense Debit, and Miscellaneous Expense Debit. Examples of cash journals with many special columns are given in later chapters.

JOURNALIZING TRANSACTION NO. 1 — SALE OF AN ASSET FOR CASH

August 1, 1967. Received cash, $20.00, from the sale of an old adding machine. Issued Receipt No. 1.

The source document for cash received

A machine that is used to record in handwritten form the information about a transaction is called an *autographic register*. Mr. Martin, the proprietor of the Hill-Top Motel, uses an autographic register on which to record all receipts of cash.

The register contains two printed rolls of paper with a carbon sheet between the rolls. Thus, a carbon copy is made of each receipt that is written. The original receipt is given to the person from whom the cash is received. The carbon copy, kept by Mr. Martin, is the source document of the transaction.

An illustration of an autographic register and the carbon copy of the first receipt issued by the Hill-Top Motel are shown below.

Other common ways of recording receipts of cash are to write a receipt in a receipt book or to record the transaction on a cash register.

The Hamilton Autographic Register Co

Autographic register

OFFICE COPY
HILL-TOP MOTEL
3442 Oak Ridge Road
Hopkins, Minnesota 55343

1

Date August 1 1967

Name J. R. Cobb
Street 9508 Windsor Road
City Hopkins, Minnesota 55345

From sale of adding machine	20 00

Rec'd by Charles Martin

Carbon copy of a receipt
from the autographic register

The journal entry for Transaction No. 1

After this transaction is analyzed into its debit and credit parts, as explained on pages 40 to 42, the following entry is made on Line 1 of the Hill-Top Motel's cash journal:

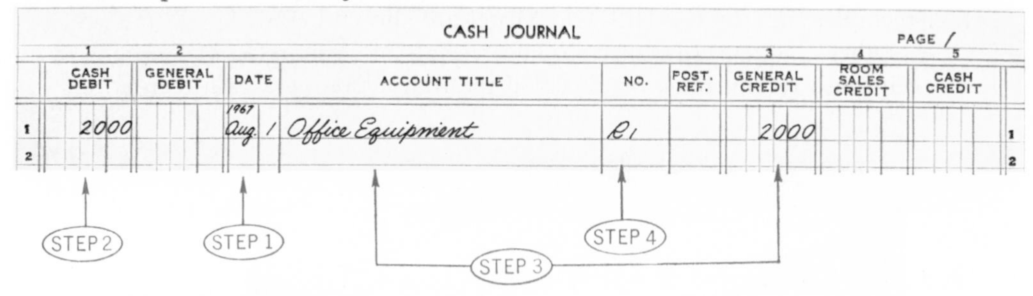

CASH JOURNAL — PAGE 1

	1 CASH DEBIT	2 GENERAL DEBIT	DATE	ACCOUNT TITLE	NO.	POST. REF.	3 GENERAL CREDIT	4 ROOM SALES CREDIT	5 CASH CREDIT	
1	20 00		1967 Aug. 1	Office Equipment	R1		20 00			1
2										2

The same four steps taken in journalizing the opening entry in the general journal are followed when journalizing business transactions in the cash journal. For Transaction No. 1, these four steps are:

Step 1

Date of entry. Write the year, month, and day — *1967, Aug. 1* — at the top of the Date column as shown above.

Step 2

Debit part of entry. Debit the cash account for $20.00 by writing *$20.00* in the Cash Debit column on Line 1. The cash account is identified by the heading of the column, *Cash Debit*. It is not necessary to write the account title *Cash* because the column heading, *Cash Debit*, identifies this column as the one in which to record all amounts debited to the cash account. The cash account is debited because the balance of the asset account Cash is increased.

Step 3

Credit part of entry. Credit the office equipment account for $20.00 (a) by writing *$20.00* in the General Credit column and (b) by writing the account title *Office Equipment* in the Account Title column. The office equipment account is credited because the sale of an old adding machine decreases the balance of the asset account Office Equipment.

Step 4

Brief description of source document. Write *R1* in the No. column to show that Receipt No. 1 is issued in this transaction. The letter *R* in the No. column stands for *receipt* and is followed by the number of the receipt. The number is obtained from the carbon copy of the receipt.

The journal entry does not show what item of office equipment was sold or to whom it was sold. *R1* in the No. column of the cash journal shows that detailed information about this transaction may be obtained quickly from the carbon copy of this receipt. Therefore, it is not necessary to repeat these details in the cash journal entry.

JOURNALIZING TRANSACTION NO. 2 — PART PAYMENT OF A LIABILITY

August 1, 1967. Paid cash, $300.00, to the Motel Equipment Company in part payment of the amount owed. Issued Check No. 1.

The source document of a cash payment

Each time cash is paid by the Hill-Top Motel, Mr. Martin, the proprietor, writes a check for the amount. Before writing the check, he fills out the stub of the check. The check stub shown at the right is the source document of this cash payment.

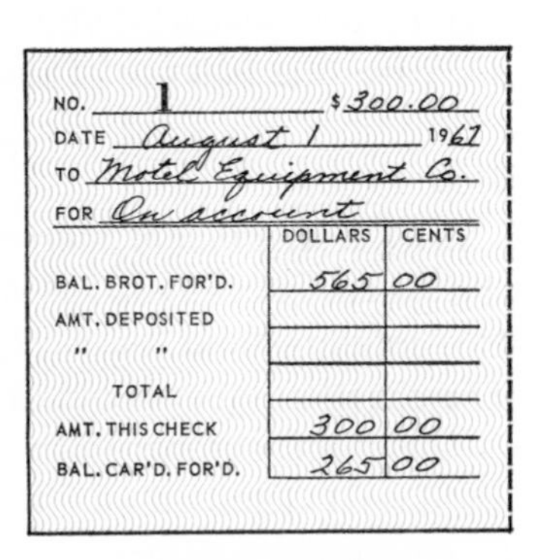

NO. 1 $300.00
DATE August 1 1967
TO Motel Equipment Co.
FOR On account

	DOLLARS	CENTS
BAL. BROT. FOR'D.	565	00
AMT. DEPOSITED		
" "		
TOTAL		
AMT. THIS CHECK	300	00
BAL. CAR'D. FOR'D.	265	00

Check stub for Transaction No. 2

The journal entry for Transaction No. 2

After this transaction is analyzed into its debit and credit parts, as explained on pages 42 and 43, the following entry is made on Line 2 of the cash journal:

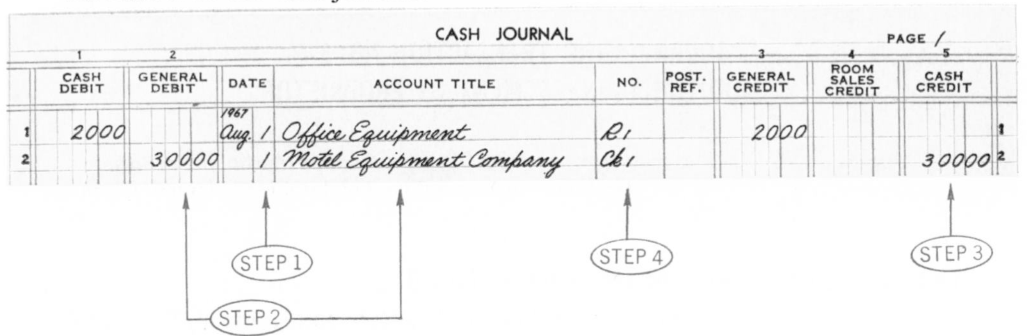

CASH JOURNAL PAGE 1

	1 CASH DEBIT	2 GENERAL DEBIT	DATE	ACCOUNT TITLE	NO.	POST. REF.	3 GENERAL CREDIT	4 ROOM SALES CREDIT	5 CASH CREDIT	
1	20 00		1967 Aug. 1	Office Equipment	R1		20 00			1
2		300 00	1	Motel Equipment Company	Ck1				300 00	2

The four steps in journalizing this transaction are:

Step 1

Date of entry. Write the day of the month, *1*, in the Date column.

The year and the month are written only once on each page of the cash journal, but the day of the month is recorded for each transaction.

Step 2

Debit part of entry. Debit the Motel Equipment Company account for $300.00 (a) by writing *$300.00* in the General Debit column and (b) by writing the account title *Motel Equipment Company* in the Account Title column. The Motel Equipment Company account is debited because the balance of this liability account is decreased.

Step 3

Credit part of entry. Credit Cash for $300.00 by writing *$300.00* in the Cash Credit column. The column heading, *Cash Credit*, identifies this column as the one in which to record all amounts credited to the cash account. The cash account is credited because this cash payment transaction decreases the balance of the asset account Cash.

Step 4

Brief description of source document. Write *Ck1* in the No. column to show that Check No. 1 is issued in this transaction. The letters *Ck* in the No. column stand for *check* and are followed by the number of the check. The check number is obtained from the check stub.

The check number in the No. column shows which check stub contains additional details about the transaction. Since this information can be located quickly when needed, it is not necessary to record any of these details in the cash journal.

JOURNALIZING TRANSACTION NO. 3— ADDITIONAL INVESTMENT BY PROPRIETOR

August 1, 1967. *Received cash, $1,000.00, from Charles Martin, the proprietor, as an additional investment in the business. Issued Receipt No. 2.*

The source document for Transaction No. 3

When Mr. Martin took $1,000.00 out of his personal funds and invested it in his business, he issued Receipt No. 2 to himself. The carbon copy of Receipt No. 2 furnishes all the information needed for the journal entry to record Transaction No. 3.

The journal entry for Transaction No. 3

After this transaction is analyzed into its debit and credit parts, as explained on pages 44 and 45, the following entry is made on Line 3 of the cash journal.

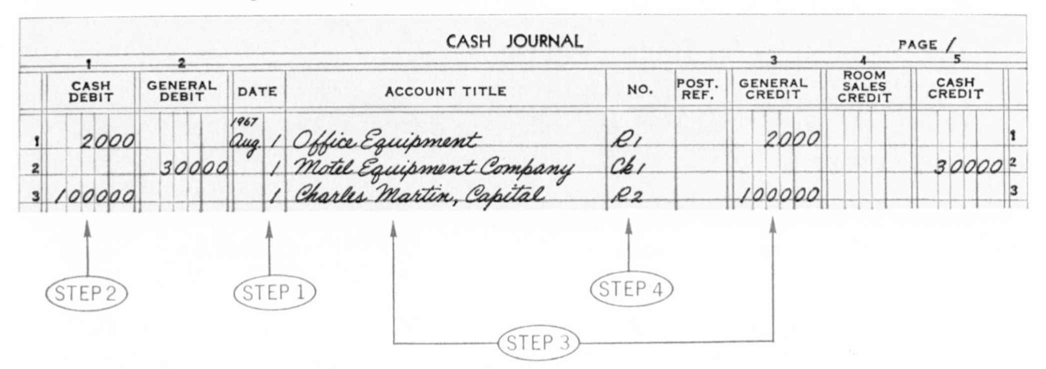

CASH JOURNAL PAGE 1

	1	2					3	4	5	
	CASH DEBIT	GENERAL DEBIT	DATE	ACCOUNT TITLE	NO.	POST. REF.	GENERAL CREDIT	ROOM SALES CREDIT	CASH CREDIT	
1	2000		1967 Aug. 1	Office Equipment	R1		2000			1
2		30000	1	Motel Equipment Company	Ck1				30000	2
3	100000		1	Charles Martin, Capital	R2		100000			3

The four steps in journalizing this transaction are:

Step 1

Date of entry. Write the day of the month, *1*, in the Date column.

Step 2

Debit part of entry. Debit the cash account for $1,000.00 by writing *$1,000.00* in the Cash Debit column. The cash account is debited because the balance of the asset account Cash is increased.

Step 3

Credit part of entry. Credit the proprietor's capital account for $1,000.00 (a) by writing *$1,000.00* in the General Credit column and (b) by writing the account title *Charles Martin, Capital,* in the Account Title column. The proprietor's capital account is credited because the additional investment in the business increases the balance of the proprietorship account.

Step 4

Brief description of source document. Write *R2* in the No. column to show that Receipt No. 2 is the source document for this transaction.

JOURNALIZING TRANSACTION NO. 4— AN INCOME TRANSACTION

August 1, 1967. Received cash, $72.00, from room sales. Issued Receipts Nos. 3–8.

The source documents for Transaction No. 4

At the end of each day, Mr. Martin totals all the receipts that have been written for cash received from room sales. The total cash received is recorded in the cash journal each day, along with the receipt numbers.

The journal entry for Transaction No. 4

After this transaction is analyzed into its debit and credit parts, as explained on pages 54 and 55, the following entry is made on Line 4 of the cash journal:

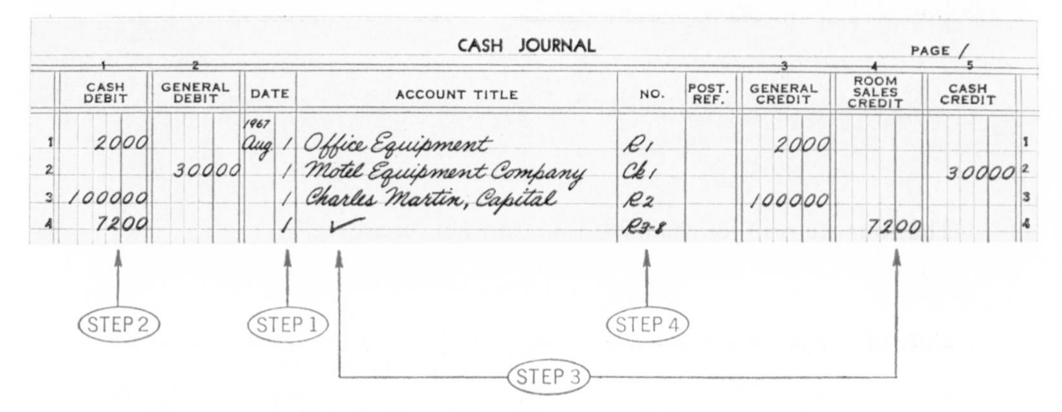

CASH JOURNAL — PAGE 1

	1 CASH DEBIT	2 GENERAL DEBIT	DATE		ACCOUNT TITLE	NO.	POST. REF.	3 GENERAL CREDIT	4 ROOM SALES CREDIT	5 CASH CREDIT	
			1967								
1	20 00		Aug.	1	Office Equipment	R1		20 00			1
2		300 00		1	Motel Equipment Company	Ck1				300 00	2
3	1000 00			1	Charles Martin, Capital	R2		1000 00			3
4	72 00			1	✓	R3-8			72 00		4

The four steps in recording an income transaction in the cash journal are the same as those in recording other kinds of transactions:

Step 1

Date of entry. Write the day of the month, *1*, in the Date column.

Step 2

Debit part of entry. Debit the cash account for $72.00 by writing *$72.00* in the Cash Debit column. The cash account is debited because the balance of the asset account Cash is increased.

Step 3

Credit part of entry. Credit the room sales account for $72.00 by writing *$72.00* in the Room Sales Credit column. It is not necessary to write the words *Room Sales* in the Account Title column because the heading of the special column, Room Sales Credit, shows clearly that the room sales account is credited for $72.00. Place a check mark (√) in the Account Title column to indicate that no account title needs to be written for this entry. The room sales account is credited because this income transaction increases the balance of the income account Room Sales.

Step 4

Brief description of source document. Write *R3-8* in the No. column to show that Receipts Nos. 3 through 8 are the source documents being totaled to obtain the amount for this entry.

The use of a special column for the room sales account

Whenever an income account in the ledger is credited frequently, the use of a special column in the journal for such an account saves time in both recording and posting. Income from room sales occurs almost daily at the Hill-Top Motel. Thus, a special column labeled *Room Sales Credit* is provided in the cash journal for recording this frequent source of income. This special column saves time in posting to the ledger because it is not necessary to post each amount separately. Only the total of a special column needs to be posted.

JOURNALIZING TRANSACTION NO. 5— AN EXPENSE TRANSACTION

August 2, 1967. Paid cash, $200.00, for rent of motel for August. Issued Check No. 2.

The journal entry for Transaction No. 5

After this transaction is analyzed into its debit and credit parts, as explained on page 57, the following entry is made on Line 5 of the cash journal:

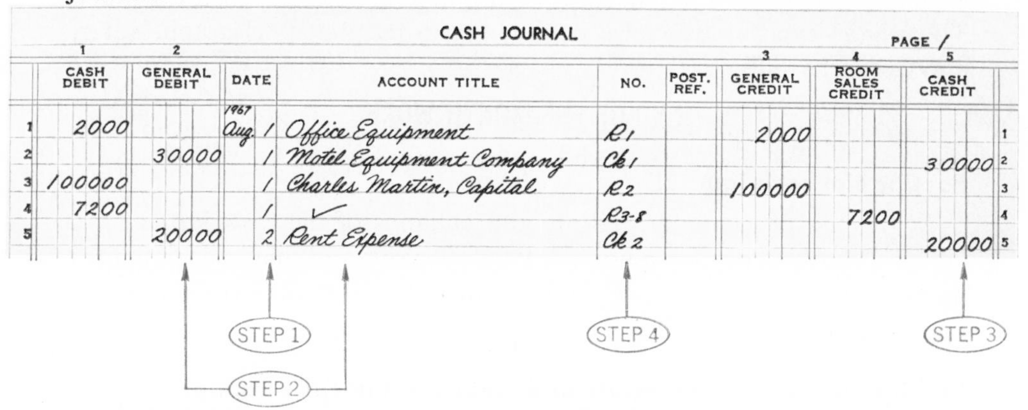

CASH JOURNAL — PAGE 1

	1 Cash Debit	2 General Debit	Date	Account Title	No.	Post. Ref.	3 General Credit	4 Room Sales Credit	5 Cash Credit	
1	20 00		1967 Aug. 1	Office Equipment	R1		20 00			1
2		300 00	1	Motel Equipment Company	Ck1				300 00	2
3	1000 00		1	Charles Martin, Capital	R2		1000 00			3
4	72 00		1	✓	R3-8			72 00		4
5		200 00	2	Rent Expense	Ck2				200 00	5

The four steps in recording an expense transaction in the cash journal are the same as those in recording other transactions:

Step 1

Date of entry. Write the day of the month, *2*, in the Date column.

Step 2

Debit part of entry. Debit the rent expense account for $200.00 (a) by writing *$200.00* in the General Debit column and (b) by writing the account title *Rent Expense* in the Account Title column. The rent expense account is debited because this expense transaction increases the balance of the expense account Rent Expense. The balance of every expense account is always a debit balance.

Step 3

Credit part of entry. Credit the cash account for $200.00 by writing *$200.00* in the Cash Credit column. The cash account is credited because the balance of the asset account Cash is decreased.

Step 4

Brief description of source document. Write *Ck2* in the No. column to show that Check No. 2 is issued in this transaction.

JOURNALIZING TRANSACTIONS NOS. 6 THROUGH 35

The transactions for the remainder of August are similar to those that have been discussed. The complete cash journal of the Hill-Top Motel for August is shown on page 77.

The Hill-Top Motel maintains five expense accounts: Advertising Expense, Laundry Expense, Miscellaneous Expense, Rent Expense, and Utilities Expense. The miscellaneous expense account is debited for all expenses that cannot be charged to any of the other expense accounts. The utilities expense account is debited for all telephone, telegraph, water, and electricity bills.

END-OF-THE-MONTH WORK

Footing the cash journal

At the end of the month all amount columns of the cash journal are added. The total of each amount column is written in small pencil figures immediately below the line of the last entry. Pencil totals written in small figures are commonly called *footings*.

Proving the equality of debits and credits in the cash journal

The footings of the debit columns are listed and added on a separate sheet of paper. The footings of the credit columns are also listed and added. The calculations are shown below:

Cash Debit footing.......	$2,684.00	General Credit footing....	$1,063.00
General Debit footing....	762.00	Room Sales Credit footing.	1,621.00
		Cash Credit footing......	762.00
Total debits.............	$3,446.00	Total credits.............	$3,446.00

The sum of the totals of all *debit* columns should equal the sum of the totals of all *credit* columns. If the sum of all debit totals does not equal the sum of all credit totals, one or more errors have been made. The error or errors should be located and corrected.

CASH JOURNAL — PAGE 1

	1 CASH DEBIT	2 GENERAL DEBIT	DATE	ACCOUNT TITLE	NO.	POST. REF.	3 GENERAL CREDIT	4 ROOM SALES CREDIT	5 CASH CREDIT	
1	20 00		1967 Aug. 1	Office Equipment	R1		20 00			1
2		300 00	1	Motel Equipment Company	Ck1				300 00	2
3	1000 00		1	Charles Martin, Capital	R2		1000 00			3
4	72 00		1	✓	R3-8			72 00		4
5		200 00	2	Rent Expense	Ck2				200 00	5
6	64 00		2	✓	R9-15			64 00		6
7	52 00		3	✓	R16-21			52 00		7
8		35 00	4	Advertising Expense	Ck3				35 00	8
9	78 00		4	✓	R22-29			78 00		9
10	84 00		5	✓	R30-37			84 00		10
11		17 50	7	Miscellaneous Expense	Ck4				17 50	11
12	38 00		8	✓	R38-40			38 00		12
13	77 00		9	✓	R41-48			77 00		13
14	64 00		10	✓	R49-55			64 00		14
15	78 00		11	✓	R56-62			78 00		15
16	97 00		12	✓	R63-72			97 00		16
17	43 00		14	Furniture and Fixtures	R73		43 00			17
18		44 50	14	Laundry Expense	Ck5				44 50	18
19	44 00		15	✓	R74-78			44 00		19
20	48 00		16	✓	R79-83			48 00		20
21	77 00		17	✓	R84-91			77 00		21
22	104 00		18	✓	R92-101			104 00		22
23	87 00		19	✓	R102-110			87 00		23
24		61 15	21	Utilities Expense	Ck6				61 15	24
25	20 00		22	✓	R111-112			20 00		25
26	7 00		23	✓	R113			7 00		26
27	78 00		24	✓	R114-120			78 00		27
28	100 00		25	✓	R121-128			100 00		28
29		41 45	26	Laundry Expense	Ck7				41 45	29
30	84 00		26	✓	R129-136			84 00		30
31		14 00	28	Housekeeping Supplies	Ck8				14 00	31
32	67 00		29	✓	R137-143			67 00		32
33	97 00		30	✓	R144-150			97 00		33
34	104 00		31	✓	R151-160			104 00		34
35		48 40	31	Utilities Expense	Ck9				48 40	35
	2684 00	762 00					1063 00	1621 00	762 00	
36	2684 00	762 00	31	Totals			1063 00	1621 00	762 00	36
37										37
38										38
39										39

Cash journal of Hill-Top Motel for August

Proving cash

Determining that the amount of cash on hand agrees with the bookkeeping records is known as *proving cash.* Cash on hand is the bank balance plus all cash not deposited. Cash is proved daily in most businesses. Cash should always be proved when the cash journal is footed at the end of a month.

The following calculations are made to prove cash after the cash journal of the Hill-Top Motel is footed at the end of August:

Cash balance at the beginning of the month as shown by the cash account in the ledger.	$ 565.00
Plus cash received during the month (footing of Cash Debit column of the cash journal).	2,684.00
Total of beginning balance plus cash received.	$3,249.00
Less cash paid during the month (footing of Cash Credit column of the cash journal).	762.00
Amount of cash that should be on hand.	$2,487.00

The Hill-Top Motel deposits all cash as it is received. The last check stub in the checkbook of the Hill-Top Motel shows a bank balance of $2,487.00. This proves that the cash on hand agrees with the cash journal record.

Ruling the cash journal

After the equality of debits and credits is proved and cash is proved, a single line is drawn across all amount columns under the last entry. The totals of the columns are written in ink. The last day of the month is written in the Date column on the line with the totals. The word *Totals* is written in the Account Title column. A double line is drawn across all amount columns. A ruler and pen should always be used in drawing lines.

Another method of ruling the cash journal is shown in the illustration below. If a page that is almost full is totaled, the printed rulings at the bottom of the page may be used. In this case the spaces between the last entry and the printed rulings are canceled by drawing a diagonal line across the Account Title column from the Date column to the No. column.

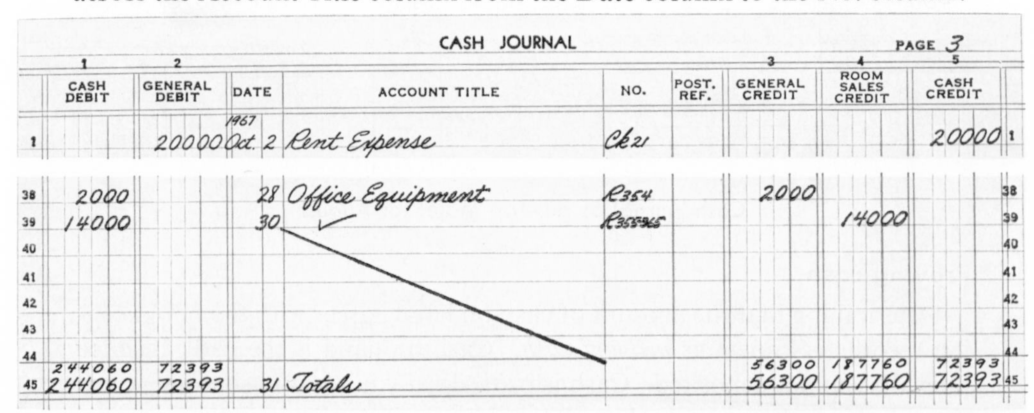

CASH JOURNAL PAGE 3

	1 CASH DEBIT	2 GENERAL DEBIT	DATE	ACCOUNT TITLE	NO.	POST. REF.	3 GENERAL CREDIT	4 ROOM SALES CREDIT	5 CASH CREDIT	
1		20000	1967 Oct. 2	Rent Expense	Ck21				20000	1
38	2000		28	Office Equipment	R354		2000			38
39	14000		30	✓	R355-365			14000		39
40										40
41										41
42										42
43										43
44	244060	72393					56300	187760	72393	44
45	244060	72393	31	Totals			56300	187760	72393	45

A cash journal with totals at the bottom of the page

Increasing Your Business Vocabulary

What is the meaning of each of the following:

a journalizing
b double-entry bookkeeping
c single-entry bookkeeping
d cash journal
e autographic register
f footings
g proving cash

Study Questions

1. Why should every transaction be recorded in a journal instead of directly in ledger accounts?
2. What are the advantages of using a cash journal with special amount columns?
3. What business paper does the Hill-Top Motel use for the source document of each cash received transaction?
4. What is the meaning of *R1* in the No. column on Line 1 in the cash journal on page 77?
5. What business paper does the Hill-Top Motel use for the source document of each cash payment?
6. What is the meaning of *Ck1* in the No. column on Line 2 in the cash journal on page 77?
7. Why is a check mark (√) placed in the Account Title column when journalizing a transaction showing income from room sales?
8. Why does the cash journal of the Hill-Top Motel have a special column labeled Room Sales Credit?
9. How is the equality of debits and credits in the cash journal proved?
10. How is cash proved?

Cases for Business Decision

CASE 1

Roger Miles uses a receipt book that has a receipt stub record for each receipt issued. Jack Doyle uses a receipt book that has a carbon copy for each receipt issued and no stub record. What are the advantages of Doyle's plan of using a carbon copy of each receipt issued instead of a receipt stub record?

CASE 2

Mr. Hudson uses a cash register to record all his cash receipt transactions. As each cash receipt transaction occurs, the amount of cash received is automatically recorded on a tape inside the register. At the end of the day, Mr. Hudson presses the total bar of the cash register and the total receipts for the day are recorded on the tape. At the end of the day, the amount of cash in the register should equal the total shown on the tape. If there is more cash in the register than the amount shown on the tape, what kinds of errors might have been made?

CASE 3

Both Elden Rankin and Clyde Norman use cash journals similar to the one illustrated on page 77. When Rankin records each receipt of income, he writes the amount in the Cash Debit column and in the Fees Income Credit column and makes a check mark in the Account Title column. Norman follows the same procedure, except that he writes the account title, Fees Income, in the Account Title column. Which person do you believe follows the better plan? Why?

Drills for Understanding

The following drills are planned to give you additional skill, accuracy, and speed in selecting proper account titles for business transactions and in analyzing the effect of the transaction.

DRILL 6-A Analyzing the entries of journalized transactions

Instructions: 1. Turn to the completed cash journal on page 77. On a form similar to the one shown below, prepare an analysis of the first entry in that cash journal. Allow two lines for each analysis. Copy the first analysis, which is given as an example.

Line No.	(a) Account Titles Affected	(b) Classification of Account	(c) Is Account Debited?	(c) Is Account Credited?	(d) Effect of Transaction on Balance of Account Increase	(d) Effect of Transaction on Balance of Account Decrease
1	*Cash*	*Asset*	√		√	
	Office Equipment	*Asset*		√		√

Instructions: 2. Write a similar analysis of each of the entries recorded on Lines 2 through 10 of the cash journal on page 77.

DRILL 6-B | Analyzing transactions

Instructions: 1. On a form similar to the one shown below, copy the analysis of Transaction No. 1, which is given as an example. The 11 transactions to be analyzed are listed below.

Trans. No.	(a) Account Titles Affected	(b) Classification of Account	(c) Is Account		(d) Effect of Transaction on Balance of Account	
			Debited?	Credited?	Increase	Decrease
1	*Rent Expense*	*Expense*	√		√	
	Cash	*Asset*		√		√

Instructions: 2. Write a similar analysis of Transactions Nos. 2 to 11, using the following account titles in Column (a) of your form.

List of Account Titles

Cash
Office Equipment
Furniture and Fixtures
Cooper Company (creditor)
Room Sales
Advertising Expense
Laundry Expense
Rent Expense
Utilities Expense

Transaction Number	*Transactions*
1.	Paid cash for June rent. (You copied this answer when you completed Instruction 1.)
2.	Received cash from sale of old furniture.
3.	Received cash from room sales.
4.	Paid cash to Cooper Company in partial payment of amount owed.
5.	Paid cash for laundry.
6.	Received cash from sale of old adding machine.
7.	Paid cash for having advertising folders printed.
8.	Paid cash to Cooper Company for remainder of amount owed.
9.	Paid cash for telephone bill. This is a utilities expense.
10.	Paid cash for electric bill. This is a utilities expense.
11.	Paid cash for advertisement in magazine.

Application Problems

PROBLEM 6-1 | Journalizing cash transactions of a hunting lodge

After being closed for the summer, the Far North Lodge reopened for the season on October 15 of the current year.

Instructions: 1. Prepare a cash journal similar to the one on page 77 by writing the proper headings at the top of each column. Number the page 8.

2. Journalize the following transactions of the Far North Lodge. In the Account Title column of your journal, use the account titles listed in Drill 6-B.

Transactions

Oct. 15. Paid cash, $75.00, for rent of lodge for remainder of October. (Check No. 1)
16. Received cash, $18.50, from sale of old furniture. (Receipt No. 1)
17. Received cash, $42.00, from room sales. (Receipts Nos. 2–5)
19. Paid cash, $40.00, to Cooper Company in payment of amount owed. (Check No. 2)
20. Paid cash, $18.00, for laundry. (Check No. 3)
21. Received cash, $15.50, from sale of old office desk. (Receipt No. 6)
22. Received cash, $126.00, from room sales. (Receipts Nos. 7–17)
23. Paid cash, $60.00, for installing road signs advertising the lodge. (Check No. 4)
26. Received cash, $88.00, from room sales. (Receipts Nos. 18–27)
27. Paid cash, $8.00, for telephone bill. (Check No. 5)
28. Paid cash, $12.00, for laundry. (Check No. 6)
29. Paid cash, $12.50, for electric bill. (Check No. 7)
30. Received cash, $120.00, from room sales. (Receipts Nos. 28–41)
31. Paid cash, $18.00, for advertisement in magazine. (Check No. 8)

Instructions: 3. Foot each of the five columns of your cash journal, using small pencil figures. Place these tiny pencil figures close to the line above so that they seem to hang from it. Study the model journal on page 77.

4. Prove the equality of debits and credits in your cash journal by finding the sum of all the debit totals and the sum of all the credit totals. The sum of the totals of the two debit columns should equal the sum of the totals of the three credit columns.

5. Prove cash. The cash balance on hand on October 15 was $864.50. The last check stub shows a bank balance of $1,031.00. All cash received has been deposited.

6. If the sum of the totals of the debits in your cash journal is equal to the sum of the totals of the credits, rule a single line across all amount columns of your cash journal. Compare your work with the cash journal on page 77.

7. Write the totals of each column in ink. Write the date on the line with the totals. Label the totals by writing the word *Totals* in the Account Title column. All of the totals should be on the same line.

8. Rule double lines across all amount columns immediately below the totals. Use as your model the cash journal on page 77.

PROBLEM 6-2 | Journalizing cash transactions of a real estate business

John Upton is a real estate agent and obtains his income from commissions that he earns on property sold and property rented. The title that he uses for his income account is Commissions Income.

Instructions: 1. Record on page 15 of a five-column cash journal the October transactions of the Upton Realty Agency given below. Use the current year in recording the date. Use the account titles shown in the following chart of accounts.

Upton Realty Agency
Chart of Accounts

(1) Assets	Account Number	(3) Proprietorship	Account Number
Cash	11	John Upton, Capital	31
Automobile	12	**(4) Income**	
Office Furniture	13	Commissions Income	41
Office Machines	14	**(5) Expenses**	
		Advertising Expense	51
(2) Liabilities		Automobile Expense	52
Olympic Company	21	Miscellaneous Expense	53
Peerless Garage	22	Rent Expense	54

Instructions: 2. Debit the account Miscellaneous Expense for all expenses that cannot be charged to any other expense account.

3. Number all receipts, beginning with No. 51.

4. Number all checks, beginning with No. 114.

Transactions

Oct. 2. Received cash, $450.00, as commission from sale of a house.
3. Paid cash, $90.00, for rent of office for October.
3. Received cash, $18.00, from sale of old office furniture.
4. Paid cash, $5.75, for gas and oil for automobile.
5. Received cash, $80.00, as commission from renting a house.
7. Paid cash, $85.00, to Olympic Company in part payment of account.
10. Paid cash, $144.00, for new office furniture.
12. Paid cash, $42.50, to Peerless Garage in payment of amount owed.
15. Paid cash, $225.00, for a new office machine.
17. Received cash, $220.00, as commission from sale of a house.
19. Paid cash, $6.00, for office stationery.

23. Paid cash, $4.25, for advertisement in newspaper.
25. Received cash, $65.00, as commission from renting a house.
27. Paid cash, $12.00, for telephone bill.
30. Paid cash, $6.50, for electric bill.
31. Received cash, $160.00, as commission from sale of two house lots.

Instructions: 5. Foot each of the five columns of your cash journal. Use small pencil figures.

6. Prove the equality of debits and credits in your cash journal.

7. Prove cash. The cash balance at the beginning of the month was $350.50. The last check stub shows a bank balance at the end of the month of $722.50. All cash received has been deposited.

8. Write the column totals and the date. Write the word *Totals* in the Account Title column.

9. Rule the cash journal.

This problem will be continued in the next chapter. If it is collected by your teacher at this time, it will be returned to you before it is needed in Problem 7-1.

Optional Problems

*SUPPLEMENTARY PROBLEM 6-S

Journalizing cash transactions of a certified public accountant

Walter Manning is a certified public accountant and obtains his income from fees for professional accounting services. The title he uses for his income account is Fees Income.

Instructions: 1. Record on page 10 of a five-column cash journal the selected transactions given on page 85. Use the current year in recording the date. Use the account titles shown in the following chart of accounts.

Manning Accounting Services
Chart of Accounts

(1) Assets	Account Number	(3) Proprietorship	Account Number
Cash	11	Walter Manning, Capital	31
Automobile	12	**(4) Income**	
Office Furniture	13	Fees Income	41
Professional Library	14	**(5) Expenses**	
(2) Liabilities		Automobile Expense	51
Edison Company	21	Miscellaneous Expense	52
Shaw Company	22	Rent Expense	53

Instructions: 2. Number all checks, beginning with No. 601.

3. Number all receipts, beginning with No. 248.

Transactions

May 1. Paid cash, $110.00, for rent of the office for May.
1. Paid cash, $15.00, for parking space for the automobile for May. This is automobile expense.
2. Received cash, $25.00, from sale of old office desk.
2. Received cash, $200.00, for accounting services. This is fees income.
2. Paid cash, $5.85, for gas and oil for automobile.
3. Paid cash, $240.00, for a new desk and a bookcase.
4. Received cash, $270.00, for accounting services.
10. Received cash, $175.00, for accounting services.
14. Paid cash, $10.50, for a new book on accounting. This is professional library.
15. Received cash, $250.00, for accounting services.
19. Received cash, $110.00, for accounting services.
22. Paid cash, $160.00, to the Shaw Company for amount owed on account.
25. Paid cash, $31.25, to the Edison Company for amount owed on account.
29. Received cash, $190.00, for accounting services.
31. Paid cash, $15.20, for the electric bill for May. This is miscellaneous expense.
31. Paid cash, $9.50, for the telephone bill for May. This is miscellaneous expense.

Instructions: 4. Foot each of the amount columns of your cash journal. Use small pencil figures.

5. Prove the equality of debits and credits in your cash journal.

6. Prove cash. The cash balance at the beginning of the month was $544.44. The last check stub shows a bank balance at the end of the month of $1,167.14. All cash received has been deposited.

7. Write the column totals on the Totals line of your cash journal. Write the word *Totals* in the Account Title column.

8. Rule the cash journal.

★ BONUS PROBLEM 6-B

Journalizing cash transactions of a realtor

The Owens Realty Agency is owned and operated by J. L. Owens. Mr. Owens uses a cash journal that has the same columnar headings as the cash journal illustrated in this chapter, but the arrangement of the columns is not the same. The amount columns in Mr. Owens' cash journal are as follows:

CASH JOURNAL Page 15

Cash		Date	Account Title	No.	P. R.	General		Commissions Income Credit
Debit	Credit					Debit	Credit	

Some of the account titles in his ledger are listed below. These are not all the accounts in his ledger, but they are all that you will need in this problem.

Cash	Advertising Expense
Office Equipment	Automobile Expense
Office Furniture	Miscellaneous Expense
Commissions Income	Rent Expense

Instructions: 1. Record the following selected transactions in a cash journal ruled like the form above. Use the current year in recording the date. Use the account titles listed above.

2. Number all receipts, beginning with No. 71.

3. Number all checks, beginning with No. 92.

Transactions

Dec. 1. Received $240.00 as commission on sale of a vacant lot.
1. Paid $60.50 for repairs to the automobile.
2. Paid $185.00 for rent for December.
4. Received $250.00 as commission for renting property.
5. Received $10.00 as refund from Lamont Equipment Company for overcharge on office equipment bought from them last month. This refund decreases the cost of the equipment.
5. Paid $25.00 as a refund to a customer of a part of the commission received from him last month.
7. Paid $9.25 for advertising.
9. Paid $15.00 to have the office cleaned.
11. Paid $18.30 for gas and oil for the automobile.
15. Received $575.00 as commission on the sale of a house.
18. Received $60.00 as commission for renting a house.
19. Received $42.00 from sale of old furniture.
22. Paid $9.50 for entertaining a customer. (Miscellaneous Expense)
25. Paid $16.50 for advertising.
28. Received $3,800.00 as commission for sale of a farm.

Instructions: 4. Foot each of the amount columns of your cash journal. Use small pencil figures.

5. Prove the equality of debits and credits in your cash journal.

6. Prove cash. The cash balance at the beginning of the month was $1,420.00. The last check stub shows a bank balance at the end of the month of $6,057.95. All cash received has been deposited.

7. Write the column totals on the Totals line of your cash journal. Write the word *Totals* in the Account Title column.

8. Rule the cash journal.

CHAPTER 7 | POSTING

The cash journal of the Hill-Top Motel on page 77 shows all the business transactions for the month of August recorded in the order in which they occurred. The cash journal, however, does not sort the entries into accounts and summarize the effect of the transactions on account balances. For example, the cash journal does not show in one place the total amount spent for Laundry Expense.

Need for posting

In order that Mr. Martin, the proprietor of the Hill-Top Motel, may have a clear picture of what has happened to the balance of each account in the ledger, it is necessary to complete all posting from the cash journal. Posting sorts the journal entries into the proper ledger accounts so that the contents of each account may be summarized. New balances may then be determined easily and quickly.

Each business transaction has its debit part and its credit part recorded together on one page in a journal.

The debit amount and the credit amount of each journal entry are sorted into the proper accounts in a ledger.

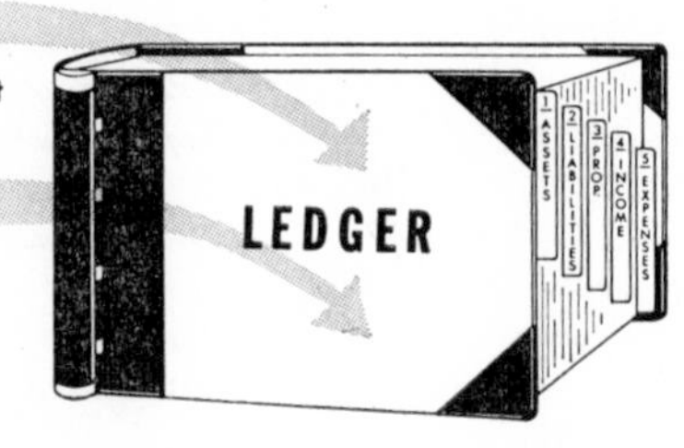

The order for arranging accounts in the ledger

Accounts in the ledger should be arranged in the same order as they appear on reports prepared at the end of the month. The first group of accounts to be listed on a balance sheet is the assets, followed by the liabilities, and then the proprietorship. In the ledger, the asset accounts appear first, followed by the liability accounts, and then the proprietorship account. Each of these groups of accounts is called a division of the ledger. In addition to these three groups of balance sheet accounts, the ledger of the Hill-Top Motel has a division for income accounts and a division for expense accounts. These five divisions are arranged in the ledger in the order shown at the right.

(1) **Assets**
(2) **Liabilities**
(3) **Proprietorship**
(4) **Income**
(5) **Expenses**

Chart of accounts of the Hill-Top Motel

The chart of accounts of a business outlines the plan of its ledger. It also serves as a guide in journalizing by showing the exact account titles that must be used when recording a transaction. The five-division chart of accounts of the Hill-Top Motel is shown on page 2. In this chart of accounts, the rent expense account is number 54. The first digit, 5, is the number of the ledger division in which the rent expense account is located. The second digit, 4, shows that Rent Expense is the fourth account in the expense division of the ledger.

Some businesses have more than five divisions in their ledgers. For example, the chart of accounts on page 166 outlines the plan of a ledger with six divisions.

POSTING THE GENERAL COLUMNS OF THE CASH JOURNAL

A portion of the cash journal of the Hill-Top Motel, showing the August 1–5 transactions ready for posting, is shown below. (The complete page of the cash journal is shown on page 77.)

CASH JOURNAL — PAGE 1

	1 CASH DEBIT	2 GENERAL DEBIT	DATE	ACCOUNT TITLE	NO.	POST. REF.	3 GENERAL CREDIT	4 ROOM SALES CREDIT	5 CASH CREDIT	
			1967							
1	20 00		Aug. 1	Office Equipment	R1		20 00			1
2		300 00	1	Motel Equipment Company	Ck1				300 00	2
3	1000 00		1	Charles Martin, Capital	R2		1000 00			3
4	72 00		1	✓	R3-8			72 00		4
5		200 00	2	Rent Expense	Ck2				200 00	5
6	64 00		2	✓	R9-15			64 00		6
7	52 00		3	✓	R16-21			52 00		7
8		35 00	4	Advertising Expense	Ck3				35 00	8
9	78 00		4	✓	R22-29			78 00		9
10	84 00		5	✓	R30-37			84 00		10

Each individual amount in the General Debit column of the cash journal must be posted separately to the *debit* side of the account named in the Account Title column. Each individual amount in the General Credit column must be posted separately to the *credit* side of the account named in the Account Title column.

The special columns in the cash journal of the Hill-Top Motel are Cash Debit, Room Sales Credit, and Cash Credit. Only the totals of these three special columns are posted. This plan saves much time and labor in posting. For example, the total of all the debits in the Cash Debit column of the cash journal is transferred to the cash account in the ledger in a single posting at the end of the month.

Steps in posting Line 1 of the cash journal

The entry on Line 1 of the cash journal shows a debit to Cash and a credit to Office Equipment. The debit to Cash is not posted separately because it will be included when the total of this column is posted to the cash account. The steps in posting the credit to Office Equipment are diagrammed and explained below.

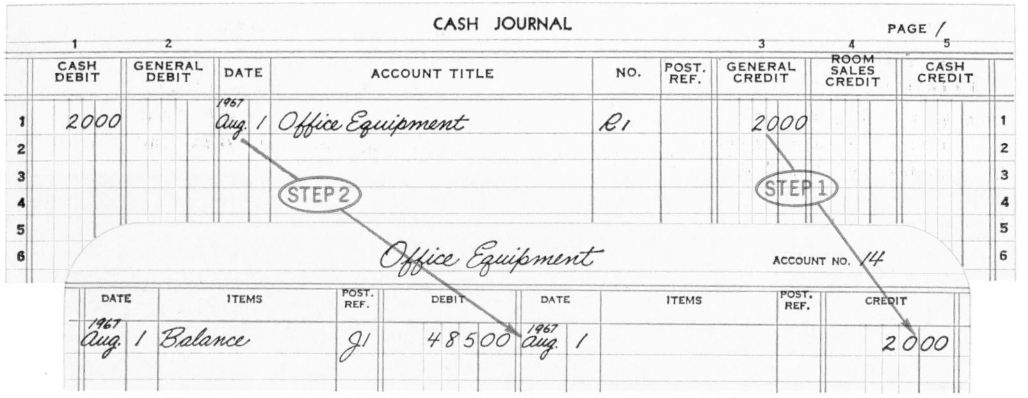

Diagram of first two steps in posting from General Credit column of the cash journal

Step 1

Write the *amount* of the credit, *$20.00*, in the Credit amount column of the office equipment account as shown above.

Step 2

Write the *date* of this journal entry in the Date column on the credit side of the office equipment account.

Since this is the first entry on the credit side of the office equipment account, it is necessary to write the complete date: *1967, Aug. 1.*

Step 3

Write *C1* in the Post. Ref. column of the account in the ledger to show that this entry was posted from page 1 of the cash journal.

C is the abbreviation for cash journal.

Step 4

Return to the cash journal and write in the Post. Ref. column the number of the ledger account, *14*, to which this General Credit amount was posted. This shows that this item was posted to account number 14 and that all the details of the posting of this line have been completed. For this reason the Post. Ref. figure in the journal is written as the last step in posting.

The posting of an entry is not complete until a cross reference is made between the journal and the ledger, as explained in Steps 3 and 4. This cross referencing is diagrammed below.

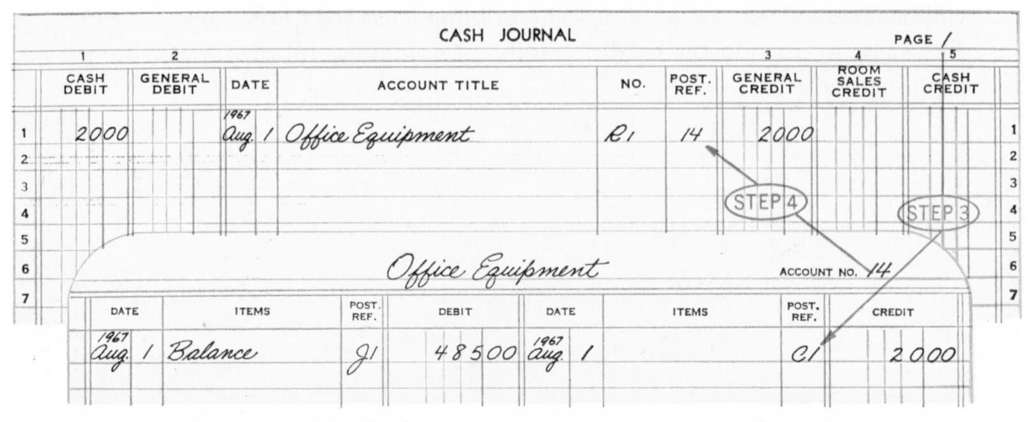

Diagram of the final two steps in posting — cross referencing

Steps in posting Line 2 of the cash journal

The entry on Line 2 of the cash journal shows a debit to Motel Equipment Company and a credit to Cash. The credit to Cash is not posted separately because it will be included when the total of the Cash Credit column is posted to the cash account at the end of the month. The steps in posting the debit to Motel Equipment Company are diagrammed and explained below.

CASH JOURNAL — PAGE 1

	Cash Debit	General Debit	Date	Account Title	No.	Post. Ref.	General Credit	Room Sales Credit	Cash Credit	
1	20 00		1967 Aug. 1	Office Equipment	R1	14	20 00			1
2		300 00	1	Motel Equipment Company	Ck1				300 00	2

STEP 2 STEP 1

Motel Equipment Company — ACCOUNT NO. 22

Date	Items	Post. Ref.	Debit	Date	Items	Post. Ref.	Credit
1967 Aug. 1			300 00	1967 Aug. 1	Balance	J1	1,300 00

Diagram of first two steps in posting from General Debit column of the cash journal

Step 1

Write the *amount* of the debit, *$300.00*, in the Debit amount column of the Motel Equipment Company account as shown above.

Step 2

Write the *date* of this journal entry in the Date column on the debit side of the Motel Equipment Company account.

Since this is the first entry on the debit side of the Motel Equipment Company account, it is necessary to write the complete date: *1967, Aug. 1.*

Step 3

Write *C1* in the Post. Ref. column of the account in the ledger to show that this entry was posted from page 1 of the cash journal.

Step 4

Return to the cash journal and write in the Post. Ref. column the number of the ledger account, *22*, to which the entry was posted.

The final two steps in posting, indicating the cross referencing between the journal and the ledger, are diagrammed below.

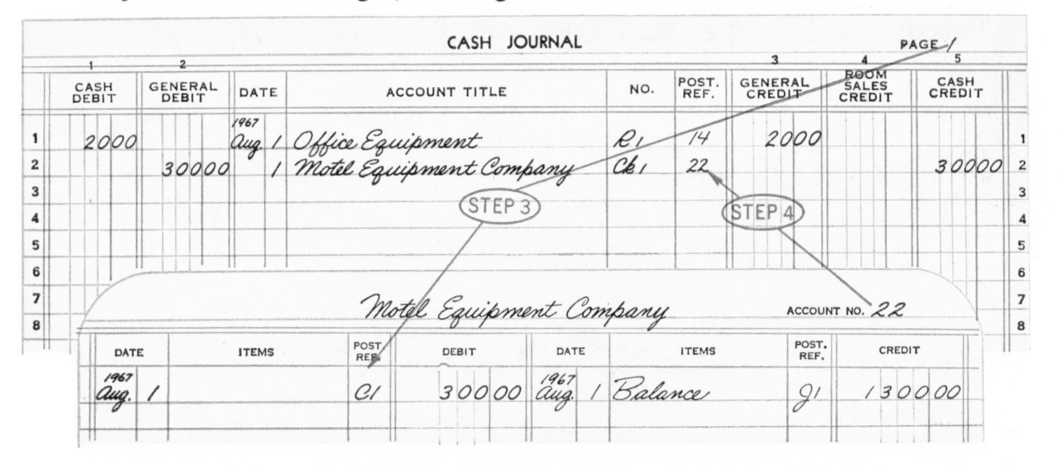

Diagram of the final two steps in posting — cross referencing

Completing the posting of the two General columns

Each amount in the General Debit column of the cash journal is posted to the debit side of the account named in the Account Title column. Each amount in the General Credit column of the cash journal is posted to the credit side of the account named in the Account Title column.

The amounts recorded in the General Debit and the General Credit columns of the cash journal are usually posted at frequent intervals during the month so that there will not be too much work at the end of the month.

Since the individual amounts that make up the total of each General column are posted separately, the total itself is not posted. The total of a column is posted only when the heading of the column is the name of an account.

A check mark in parentheses is placed below the total of each of the two General columns to show that these totals are not to be posted. (See the following illustration which shows a check mark below the total of each of the two General columns of the cash journal.)

POSTING THE SPECIAL COLUMNS OF THE CASH JOURNAL

The bottom portion of the cash journal of the Hill-Top Motel indicating the necessary posting of column totals is shown below.

CASH JOURNAL — PAGE 1

	1 CASH DEBIT	2 GENERAL DEBIT	DATE	ACCOUNT TITLE	NO.	POST. REF.	3 GENERAL CREDIT	4 ROOM SALES CREDIT	5 CASH CREDIT	
1	2000		1967 Aug. 1	Office Equipment	R1	14	2000			1
34	10400		31	✓	R151-160	✓		10400		34
35	268400	4840 76200	31	Utilities Expense	Ck9	55	106300	162100	4840 76200	35
36	268400	76200	31	Totals			106300	162100	76200	36
37		(✓)					(✓)			37

Column Totals NOT Posted

Column Totals Posted at End of Month

In the cash journal of the Hill-Top Motel, the Cash Debit column, the Cash Credit column, and the Room Sales Credit column are special columns. The individual items in these special columns are *not* posted. Only the totals of these special columns are posted.

The total of each special column is posted to the account named in the heading of the column. For example, the total of the Cash Debit column of the cash journal is posted to the debit side of the cash account. The total of the Cash Credit column is posted to the credit side of the cash account. The total of the Room Sales Credit column is posted to the credit side of the room sales account.

Posting the total of the Cash Debit column

The steps in posting the total of the Cash Debit column are explained on the next page.

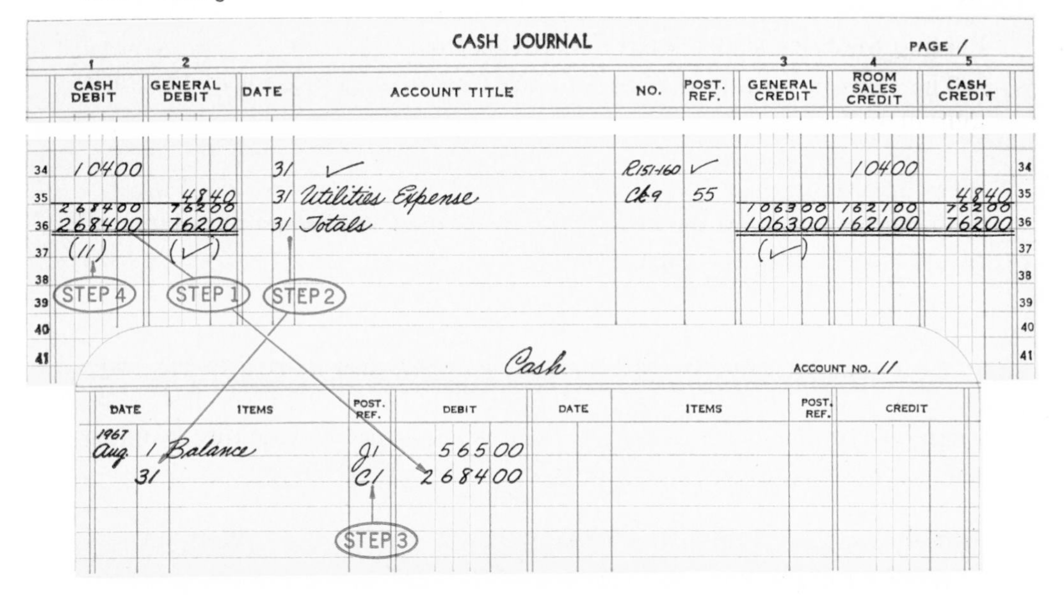

Diagram of first two steps in posting the total of Cash Debit column

Step 1

Write the *amount* of the debit, *$2,684.00*, in the Debit amount column of the cash account in the ledger.

Step 2

Write the *day* found on the Totals line of the cash journal, *31*, in the Date column on the debit side of the cash account.

> This is the second entry on the debit side of the cash account. The date of the first entry in the cash account is 1967, Aug. 1. The date of the second entry is also the same year and the same month; therefore, it is not necessary to repeat 1967 and Aug. on the debit side of the cash account.

Step 3

Write *C1* in the Post. Ref. column of the cash account in the ledger to show that this entry was posted from page 1 of the cash journal.

Step 4

Return to the cash journal and write the account number of the cash account in parentheses (*11*) immediately under the total of the Cash Debit column.

Posting the total of the Cash Credit column

The steps in posting the total of the Cash Credit column of the cash journal are:

Step 1

Write the *amount* of the total, *$762.00*, in the Credit amount column of the cash account in the ledger.

Step 2

Write the *day* found on the Totals line of the cash journal in the Date column on the credit side of the cash account. Since this is the first entry on the credit side of the cash account, it is necessary to write the complete date: *1967, Aug. 31.*

Step 3

Write *C1* in the Post. Ref. column of the cash account in the ledger to show that this entry was posted from page 1 of the cash journal.

Step 4

Return to the cash journal and write the account number of the cash account in parentheses, *(11)*, immediately under the total of the Cash Credit column. (See the completed cash journal on page 96 showing this final step in the posting of the Cash Credit column.)

After the totals of the Cash Debit column and the Cash Credit column of the cash journal are posted, the cash account in the ledger appears as follows:

Cash — ACCOUNT NO. 11

DATE		ITEMS	POST. REF.	DEBIT	DATE		ITEMS	POST. REF.	CREDIT
1967 Aug.	1	Balance	J1	565 00	1967 Aug.	31		C1	762 00
	31		C1	2 684 00					
						STEP 2		STEP 3	STEP 1

Posting the total of the Room Sales Credit column

The steps in posting the total of the Room Sales Credit column of the cash journal are:

Step 1

Write the *amount* of the total, *$1,621.00*, in the Credit amount column of the room sales account in the ledger.

Step 2

Write the *day* found on the Totals line of the cash journal in the Date column on the credit side of the room sales account. Since this is the first entry on the credit side of the room sales account, it is necessary to write the complete date: *1967, Aug. 31.*

Step 3

Write *C1* in the Post. Ref. column of the room sales account in the ledger to show that this entry was posted from page 1 of the cash journal.

Step 4

Return to the cash journal and write the account number of the room sales account in parentheses, *(41)*, immediately under the total of the Room Sales Credit column. (See the completed cash journal on page 96 showing this final step in the posting of the Room Sales Credit column.)

The room sales account in the ledger after posting appears as follows:

Room Sales — ACCOUNT NO. 41

DATE	ITEMS	POST. REF.	DEBIT	DATE	ITEMS	POST. REF.	CREDIT
				1967 Aug. 31		C1	1621 00
				STEP 2		STEP 3	STEP 1

A check mark is placed in the Post. Ref. column of the cash journal for each entry in the Room Sales Credit column to show that no posting is required for the item on this line. (See illustration on page 96.) Many experienced bookkeepers prefer to insert a check mark in the Post. Ref. column at the time each amount in the Room Sales Credit column is recorded. Such a procedure indicates in advance of posting that each of these amounts will not be posted individually.

THE COMPLETED CASH JOURNAL AND LEDGER

The cash journal after posting

The cash journal of the Hill-Top Motel after posting has been completed is shown on the next page. The Post. Ref. column of the cash journal contains an account number or a check mark on each line, except the Totals line. Each *account number* in the Post. Ref. column shows that an amount in one of the General columns on that line was posted individually. Each *check mark* in the Post. Ref. column shows that the amount is not to be posted individually.

CASH JOURNAL — PAGE 1

	1	2					3	4	5	
	CASH DEBIT	GENERAL DEBIT	DATE	ACCOUNT TITLE	NO.	POST. REF.	GENERAL CREDIT	ROOM SALES CREDIT	CASH CREDIT	
1	2000		1967 Aug. 1	Office Equipment	R1	14	2000			1
2		30000	1	Motel Equipment Company	Ck 1	22			30000	2
3	100000		1	Charles Martin, Capital	R2	31	100000			3
4	7200		1	✓	R3-8	✓		7200		4
5		20000	2	Rent Expense	Ck 2	54			20000	5
6	6400		2	✓	R9-15	✓		6400		6
7	5200		3	✓	R16-21	✓		5200		7
8		3500	4	Advertising Expense	Ck 3	51			3500	8
9	7800		4	✓	R22-29	✓		7800		9
10	8400		5	✓	R30-37	✓		8400		10
11		1750	7	Miscellaneous Expense	Ck 4	53			1750	11
12	3800		8	✓	R38-40	✓		3800		12
13	7700		9	✓	R41-48	✓		7700		13
14	6400		10	✓	R49-55	✓		6400		14
15	7800		11	✓	R56-62	✓		7800		15
16	9700		12	✓	R63-72	✓		9700		16
17	4300		14	Furniture and Fixtures	R73	13	4300			17
18		4450	14	Laundry Expense	Ck 5	52			4450	18
19	4400		15	✓	R74-78	✓		4400		19
20	4800		16	✓	R79-83	✓		4800		20
21	7700		17	✓	R84-91	✓		7700		21
22	10400		18	✓	R92-101	✓		10400		22
23	8700		19	✓	R102-110	✓		8700		23
24		6115	21	Utilities Expense	Ck 6	55			6115	24
25	2000		22	✓	R111-112	✓		2000		25
26	700		23	✓	R113	✓		700		26
27	7800		24	✓	R114-120	✓		7800		27
28	10000		25	✓	R121-128	✓		10000		28
29		4145	26	Laundry Expense	Ck 7	52			4145	29
30	8400		26	✓	R129-136	✓		8400		30
31		1400	28	Housekeeping Supplies	Ck 8	12			1400	31
32	6700		29	✓	R137-143	✓		6700		32
33	9700		30	✓	R144-150	✓		9700		33
34	10400		31	✓	R151-160	✓		10400		34
35	268400	4840 76200	31	Utilities Expense	Ck 9	55	106300	162100	4840 76200	35
36	268400	76200	31	Totals			106300	162100	76200	36
37	(11)	(✓)					(✓)	(41)	(11)	37
38										38

Cash journal of the Hill-Top Motel for August after posting is completed

An account number appears below each special column total. This shows that the total of each of the special columns was posted. A check mark below the General Debit and the General Credit totals shows that the totals of these columns are not to be posted.

The ledger after posting

The ledger of the Hill-Top Motel after all posting for the month of August has been completed is shown on pages 97 and 98.

Cash — Account No. 11

Date	Items	Post. Ref.	Debit	Date	Items	Post. Ref.	Credit
1967				1967			
Aug. 1	Balance	J1	565 00	Aug. 31		C1	762 00
31		C1	2 684 00				

Housekeeping Supplies — Account No. 12

Date	Items	Post. Ref.	Debit	Date	Items	Post. Ref.	Credit
1967							
Aug. 1	Balance	J1	550 00				
28		C1	14 00				

Furniture and Fixtures — Account No. 13

Date	Items	Post. Ref.	Debit	Date	Items	Post. Ref.	Credit
1967				1967			
Aug. 1	Balance	J1	5 600 00	Aug. 14		C1	43 00

Office Equipment — Account No. 14

Date	Items	Post. Ref.	Debit	Date	Items	Post. Ref.	Credit
1967				1967			
Aug. 1	Balance	J1	485 00	Aug. 1		C1	20 00

Apex Plumbing Company — Account No. 21

Date	Items	Post. Ref.	Debit	Date	Items	Post. Ref.	Credit
				1967			
				Aug. 1	Balance	J1	200 00

Motel Equipment Company — Account No. 22

Date	Items	Post. Ref.	Debit	Date	Items	Post. Ref.	Credit
1967				1967			
Aug. 1		C1	300 00	Aug. 1	Balance	J1	1 300 00

Charles Martin, Capital — Account No. 31

Date	Items	Post. Ref.	Debit	Date	Items	Post. Ref.	Credit
				1967			
				Aug. 1	Balance	J1	5 700 00
				1		C1	1 000 00

Ledger of the Hill-Top Motel after posting all transactions for August

Room Sales — ACCOUNT NO. 41

DATE	ITEMS	POST. REF.	DEBIT	DATE	ITEMS	POST. REF.	CREDIT
				1967 Aug. 31		C1	1621 00

Advertising Expense — ACCOUNT NO. 51

DATE	ITEMS	POST. REF.	DEBIT	DATE	ITEMS	POST. REF.	CREDIT
1967 Aug. 4		C1	35 00				

Laundry Expense — ACCOUNT NO. 52

DATE	ITEMS	POST. REF.	DEBIT	DATE	ITEMS	POST. REF.	CREDIT
1967 Aug. 14		C1	44 50				
26		C1	41 45				

Miscellaneous Expense — ACCOUNT NO. 53

DATE	ITEMS	POST. REF.	DEBIT	DATE	ITEMS	POST. REF.	CREDIT
1967 Aug. 7		C1	17 50				

Rent Expense — ACCOUNT NO. 54

DATE	ITEMS	POST. REF.	DEBIT	DATE	ITEMS	POST. REF.	CREDIT
1967 Aug. 2		C1	200 00				

Utilities Expense — ACCOUNT NO. 55

DATE	ITEMS	POST. REF.	DEBIT	DATE	ITEMS	POST. REF.	CREDIT
1967 Aug. 21		C1	61 15				
31		C1	48 40				

Ledger of the Hill-Top Motel after posting all transactions for August (concluded)

Study Questions

1. Why is it necessary to post the entries in the cash journal of the Hill-Top Motel?
2. What are the five divisions in the ledger of the Hill-Top Motel?
3. What meaning does each of the two digits have in the account number 54, which is assigned to Rent Expense in the chart of accounts on page 2?
4. Why is the amount in the Cash Debit column on Line 1 of the cash journal not posted as a separate amount to the cash account?
5. What are the four steps in posting an amount in the General Credit column of the cash journal?
6. What are the four steps in posting an amount in the General Debit amount column of the cash journal?
7. How do you show in the cash journal that the total of each of the two General columns is not to be posted?
8. What are the four steps in posting the total of the Cash Debit column of the cash journal?
9. What are the four steps in posting the total of the Cash Credit column of the cash journal?
10. What are the four steps in posting the total of the Room Sales Credit column of the cash journal?

Cases for Business Decision

CASE 1

Mr. May arranges all his ledger accounts in alphabetical order. Mr. Franks arranges his ledger accounts as shown in the chart of accounts on page 2. What are the disadvantages of the plan used by Mr. May?

CASE 2

Mr. Arthur Cline posts from both General columns of the cash journal in the order in which the transactions appear. Mr. Henry O'Dell posts all the amounts in the General Debit column first and then posts all the amounts in the General Credit column. Which plan do you prefer? Why?

Drills for Understanding

DRILL 7-A | Analyzing the cash journal after posting

Instructions: Turn to page 96 in your text showing the cash journal of the Hill-Top Motel for August after posting. Answer the following questions:

1. How many postings were made to Account No. 52? to Account No. 11?
2. On what days were laundry bills paid?

3. How could you find out for what kind of utilities expense the $48.40 was spent on August 31?
4. How could you find out the exact kind of furniture or fixtures that was sold on August 14?
5. How many checks were written in August? How many receipts?
6. Was more cash received than paid out in August? If so, how much more?
7. On how many days in August was income received from room sales?

DRILL 7-B | Analyzing the ledger

Instructions: Turn to pages 97 and 98 in your text showing the ledger of the Hill-Top Motel after all transactions for August have been posted. Answer the following questions:

1. How much laundry expense did the Hill-Top Motel have in August?
2. What is the balance of the office equipment account at the end of August?
3. From what journal page was the $1,300.00 credit to Motel Equipment Company posted on August 1?
4. How much is owed to the Motel Equipment Company on August 31?
5. From what journal page was the $35.00 debit to Advertising Expense posted?
6. Mr. Martin has asked you, the bookkeeper, why the miscellaneous expense account was debited for $17.50 on August 7. What orderly steps should you take to find the answer to his question?

Application Problem

PROBLEM 7-1 | Posting the cash journal of a real estate business

The cash journal completed in Problem 6-2 of Chapter 6 is required for this problem. If Problem 6-2 has not been returned to you, complete Appendix Problem 7-A.

Instructions: 1. Prepare the Upton ledger by opening the accounts listed on the chart of accounts on page 83. Place six accounts on each page of the ledger.

2. The asset accounts have *debit* balances as follows:

Cash................	$ 350.50	Office Furniture........	$760.00
Automobile..........	1,750.00	Office Machines........	550.00

Copy these balances in the ledger that you have just prepared. Use the date October 1 of the current year. Whenever a balance is copied in a ledger account, write the word *Balance* in the Items column and place a check mark in the posting reference column.

Instructions: 3. The liability accounts and the proprietorship account have *credit* balances as follows:

Olympic Company......	$185.00	John Upton, Capital...	$3,183.00
Peerless Garage........	42.50		

Copy these balances in the ledger. Use the date October 1 of the current year.

Instructions: 4. Turn to the cash journal you completed for Problem 6-2. Post each amount recorded in the General Debit and the General Credit columns.

5. Place a check mark in the Post. Ref. column for each entry crediting Commissions Income. This check mark shows that this entry is not posted individually.

6. Post the totals of the three special columns of your cash journal to the proper accounts in your ledger. Place a check mark under the General Debit and General Credit columns to indicate that these totals are not to be posted.

Optional Problems

★SUPPLEMENTARY PROBLEM 7-S

Journalizing and posting the transactions of a theater

Scott Tupper is the owner and operator of the Webb City Theater.

Instructions: 1. Open the twelve accounts in the ledger that will be needed for this problem. Place six accounts on each page of your ledger. Mr. Tupper's chart of accounts is given below.

Webb City Theater
Chart of Accounts

(1) ASSETS	Acct. No.	(4) INCOME	Acct. No.
Cash..................	11	Admissions Income.....	41
Equipment............	12		
		(5) EXPENSES	
(2) LIABILITIES			
		Advertising Expense...	51
Clark Optical Company	21	Film Rental Expense...	52
Stein's Sound Service	22	Miscellaneous Expense.	53
		Rent Expense..........	54
(3) PROPRIETORSHIP		Salary Expense........	55
		Utilities Expense.....	56
Scott Tupper, Capital	31		

Instructions: 2. Copy the following balances in the proper accounts in your ledger, using July 1 of the current year as the date. Whenever a balance is copied in a ledger account, write the word *Balance* in the Items column and place a check mark in the posting reference column.

	Debit Balance	*Credit Balance*
Cash	1,350.00	
Equipment	10,250.00	
Clark Optical Company		345.00
Stein's Sound Service		180.00
Scott Tupper, Capital		11,075.00

Instructions: 3. On page 14 of a cash journal similar to the model journal on page 96, record the following transactions for July. Number all checks, beginning with No. 183. Number all receipts, beginning with No. 24.

Transactions

July 2. Paid cash, $200.00, for rent for July.
3. Paid cash, $54.85, for advertising.
5. Paid cash, $255.00, for projection equipment.
7. Received cash, $501.50, from admissions income for the week.
11. Paid cash, $165.00, to Clark Optical Company on account.
12. Received cash, $25.00, from sale of old equipment.
13. Received cash, $481.50, from admissions income for the week.
14. Paid cash, $18.50, for admission tickets. (Miscellaneous Expense)
16. Paid cash, $100.00, to Stein's Sound Service on account.
18. Paid cash, $8.75, for telephone bill. (Miscellaneous Expense)
20. Received cash, $603.20, from admissions income for the week.
24. Paid cash, $47.50, for advertising.
27. Received cash, $588.00, from admissions income for the week.
30. Paid cash, $1,000.00, for film rentals.
31. Paid cash, $522.50, for salaries.
31. Paid cash, $101.85, for electricity expense. (Utilities Expense)
31. Received cash, $281.50, from admissions income.

Instructions: 4. Post the individual amounts in the General Debit and General Credit columns to the accounts in the ledger.

5. Place a check mark in the Post. Ref. column for each entry crediting Admissions Income to show that this entry is not posted individually.

6. Foot each amount column with small pencil figures.

7. Prove the equality of debits and credits in your cash journal.

8. Prove cash. The cash balance is $1,356.75. All cash receipts have been deposited.

9. Total and rule the cash journal.

10. Post the totals of the three special columns. Place a check mark under the General Debit and General Credit columns to indicate that these totals are not to be posted.

★BONUS PROBLEM 7-B

Journalizing and posting the transactions of a physician

The chart of accounts of Dr. L. W. Austin, a physician, is given below.

Instructions: 1. Open the twelve accounts in the ledger that will be needed for this problem. Place six accounts on each page of your ledger.

Dr. L. W. Austin
Chart of Accounts

(1) ASSETS	Acct. No.	(4) INCOME	Acct. No.
Cash	11	Professional Fees	41
Automobile	12		
Office Furniture	13	(5) EXPENSES	
Medical Equipment	14		
		Automobile Expense	51
(2) LIABILITIES		Miscellaneous Expense	52
		Rent Expense	53
Arrow Furniture Co.	21	Salary Expense	54
Medical Supply Co.	22		
(3) PROPRIETORSHIP			
L. W. Austin, Capital	31		

Instructions: 2. Copy the following account balances in the proper accounts in the ledger, using October 1 of the current year as the date. Whenever a balance is copied in a ledger account, write the word *Balance* in the Items column and place a check mark in the posting reference column.

Cash, $10,210.00; Automobile, $4,200.00; Office Furniture, $3,360.00; Medical Equipment, $8,680.00; Arrow Furniture Company, $1,465.00; Medical Supply Company, $3,420.00; L. W. Austin, Capital, $11,690.00; Professional Fees, $17,410.00; Automobile Expense, $540.00; Miscellaneous Expense, $125.00; Rent Expense, $3,240.00; Salary Expense, $3,630.00.

Instructions: 3. On page 12 of a cash journal like the one illustrated in Bonus Problem 6-B on page 85, record the following transactions for October of the current year. The income column should be headed "Professional Fees Credit." Number all checks, beginning with No. 431. The receipt numbers are given after each cash receipt transaction.

Transactions

Oct. 1. Paid cash, $350.00, for October rent.
2. Received cash, $135.00, from fees. (Receipt No. 264)
3. Paid cash, $180.00, for office furniture.
4. Paid cash, $30.50, for stationery.
9. Received cash, $680.00, from fees. (Receipts Nos. 265–269)
10. Paid cash, $460.00, to Arrow Furniture Company on account.
15. Paid cash, $200.00, for salary expense.
16. Paid cash, $80.00, for automobile expense.
19. Received cash, $620.00, from fees. (Receipts Nos. 270–276)
20. Received cash, $80.50, from sale of old office furniture. (Receipt No. 277)
21. Paid cash, $710.00, to Medical Supply Company on account.
23. Paid cash, $14.60, for postage.
24. Received cash, $710.00, from fees. (Receipts Nos. 278–285)
30. Received cash, $616.00, from fees. (Receipts Nos. 286–294)
30. Paid cash, $230.00, for salary expense.
30. Paid cash, $24.60, for telephone.
30. Paid cash, $49.80, for automobile expense.

Instructions: 4. Post the individual amounts in the General Debit and General Credit columns to the accounts in the ledger.

5. Place a check mark in the Post. Ref. column for each entry crediting Professional Fees to show that this entry is not posted individually.

6. Foot each amount column with small pencil figures.

7. Prove the equality of debits and credits in your cash journal.

8. Prove cash. The cash balance is $10,722.00. All cash receipts have been deposited.

9. Total and rule the cash journal.

10. Post the totals of the three special columns. Place a check mark under the General Debit and General Credit columns to indicate that these totals are not to be posted.

CHAPTER 8 PROVING THE ACCURACY OF POSTING

The bookkeeper must be sure that his records are accurate. A single error in a ledger account can cause a balance sheet to be out of balance. A single error can cause the bookkeeper to overstate or to understate the profit of a business. A business may overpay or underpay its federal taxes as a result of bookkeeping errors. The bookkeeper, therefore, must be careful to avoid errors, know how to find errors, and correct errrors properly as soon as they are found.

Two methods of checking the accuracy of bookkeeping records are presented in this chapter:

1. *Proving the accuracy of the cash account* in the ledger by comparing its balance with the amount of cash on hand.
2. *Proving the accuracy of the ledger* by testing whether the debits in the ledger equal the credits in the ledger.

PROVING THE ACCURACY OF THE CASH ACCOUNT

Finding the balance of the cash account

The cash account of the Hill-Top Motel after the balance has been found and recorded is shown below.

Cash ACCOUNT NO. 11

DATE		ITEMS	POST. REF.	DEBIT	DATE		ITEMS	POST. REF.	CREDIT
1967 Aug.	1	Balance	J1	565 00	1967 Aug.	31		C1	762 00
	31	2487.00	C1	2684 00					
				3249 00					

The steps in finding the balance of the cash account are:

Step 1

Add the amounts in the Debit column; write the total in small pencil figures immediately under the last amount in that column. The footing is written very small so that the next line can be used for another entry.

Add the amounts in the Credit column and record the footing as you did in the Debit column. Since there is only one entry on the credit side of the cash account above, it is not necessary to make a pencil footing on the credit side of this account.

Step 2

Subtract the total of the credit side from the total of the debit side on a separate sheet of paper as follows:

Total of debit side of cash account......................	$3,249.00
Total of credit side of cash account......................	762.00
Difference between two sides of account..................	$2,487.00

The difference between the totals of the amounts posted to the two sides of an account is the account balance. The cash account balance is $2,487.00.

Step 3

Write the account balance in small pencil figures in the Items column of the account on the side with the larger total. Write this amount in line with the small pencil footing of the Debit column.

In the cash account on page 105, the account balance, $2,487.00, is written on the debit side of the account.

Comparing the cash account balance with the cash on hand

On August 31, the last check stub of the Hill-Top Motel shows a balance of $2,487.00. Since all cash receipts have been deposited, the check-stub balance shows the actual amount of cash on hand. The balance of the cash account in the ledger is also $2,487.00. When the cash on hand is found to agree with the balance of the cash account, the cash account is said to be proved.

A disagreement between the cash account balance and the amount of cash on hand may indicate that one or more errors have been made either in posting to the cash account or in calculating its balance.

PROVING THE ACCURACY OF THE LEDGER

The trial balance

The sum of the debits in the cash journal in Chapter 6 was found to be equal to the sum of the credits. It follows then that if no errors are made in posting, the total of the debit amounts in the ledger should equal the total of the credit amounts in the ledger. Therefore, a method of testing the accuracy of posting is to prove the equality of the debits and the credits in the ledger.

The proof of the equality of the debits and the credits in the ledger is called a *trial balance.* The trial balance consists of a list of account titles with the balances arranged in a debit amount column and a credit amount column and each amount column totaled. (See the illustration of a trial balance on page 110.)

Footing the accounts and finding their balances

The accounts in the ledger should be footed and the account balances should be calculated before preparing the trial balance.

When an account has several entries on each side, both the Debit column and the Credit column are footed. The footing of the smaller side is subtracted from that of the larger side. The difference between the two footings is written in the Items column on the side of the account that has the larger total. This amount is the account balance. Account No. 11, Cash, in the ledger on page 108 shows this method of footing and calculating the account balance.

When an account has two or more entries on one side only, that side is footed. The balance is not written in the Items column because the footing is the balance. Account No. 12, Housekeeping Supplies, in the ledger on page 108 shows this method of footing.

When an account has only one debit entry and one credit entry, footings are not needed in the Debit and the Credit columns. The account balance is written in the Items column on the side that has the larger amount. Account No. 13, Furniture and Fixtures, in the ledger on page 108 shows this method.

When an account has only one entry, it is not necessary to write a footing or a balance. The one amount in the account serves as the footing and the balance. Such an account is Account No. 21, Apex Plumbing Company, shown in the ledger on page 108.

A complete ledger showing account balances

The complete ledger of the Hill-Top Motel containing the necessary footings and balances for all accounts is shown on pages 108 and 109.

Cash ACCOUNT NO. 11

DATE		ITEMS	POST. REF.	DEBIT	DATE		ITEMS	POST. REF.	CREDIT
1967 Aug.	1	Balance	J1	565 00	1967 Aug.	31		C1	762 00
	31	2487.00	C1	2684 00					
				3249 00					

Housekeeping Supplies ACCOUNT NO. 12

DATE		ITEMS	POST. REF.	DEBIT	DATE		ITEMS	POST. REF.	CREDIT
1967 Aug.	1	Balance	J1	550 00					
	28		C1	14 00					
				564 00					

Furniture and Fixtures ACCOUNT NO. 13

DATE		ITEMS	POST. REF.	DEBIT	DATE		ITEMS	POST. REF.	CREDIT
1967 Aug.	1	Balance 5557.00	J1	5600 00	1967 Aug.	14		C1	43 00

Office Equipment ACCOUNT NO. 14

DATE		ITEMS	POST. REF.	DEBIT	DATE		ITEMS	POST. REF.	CREDIT
1967 Aug.	1	Balance 465.00	J1	485 00	1967 Aug.	1		C1	20 00

Apex Plumbing Company ACCOUNT NO. 21

DATE		ITEMS	POST. REF.	DEBIT	DATE		ITEMS	POST. REF.	CREDIT
					1967 Aug.	1	Balance	J1	200 00

Motel Equipment Company ACCOUNT NO. 22

DATE		ITEMS	POST. REF.	DEBIT	DATE		ITEMS	POST. REF.	CREDIT
1967 Aug.	1		C1	300 00	1967 Aug.	1	Balance 1000.00	J1	1300 00

Charles Martin, Capital ACCOUNT NO. 31

DATE		ITEMS	POST. REF.	DEBIT	DATE		ITEMS	POST. REF.	CREDIT
					1967 Aug.	1	Balance	J1	5700 00
						1		C1	1000 00
									6700 00

A ledger with the accounts footed

Room Sales — ACCOUNT NO. 41

DATE	ITEMS	POST. REF.	DEBIT	DATE	ITEMS	POST. REF.	CREDIT
				1967 Aug. 31		C1	1621 00

Advertising Expense — ACCOUNT NO. 51

DATE	ITEMS	POST. REF.	DEBIT	DATE	ITEMS	POST. REF.	CREDIT
1967 Aug. 4		C1	35 00				

Laundry Expense — ACCOUNT NO. 52

DATE	ITEMS	POST. REF.	DEBIT	DATE	ITEMS	POST. REF.	CREDIT
1967 Aug. 14		C1	44 50				
26		C1	41 45 85 95				

Miscellaneous Expense — ACCOUNT NO. 53

DATE	ITEMS	POST. REF.	DEBIT	DATE	ITEMS	POST. REF.	CREDIT
1967 Aug. 7		C1	17 50				

Rent Expense — ACCOUNT NO. 54

DATE	ITEMS	POST. REF.	DEBIT	DATE	ITEMS	POST. REF.	CREDIT
1967 Aug. 2		C1	200 00				

Utilities Expense — ACCOUNT NO. 55

DATE	ITEMS	POST. REF.	DEBIT	DATE	ITEMS	POST. REF.	CREDIT
1967 Aug. 21		C1	61 15				
31		C1	48 40 109 55				

A ledger with the accounts footed (concluded)

Steps in preparing a trial balance

Step 1

Write the trial balance heading at the top of a sheet of paper that has two amount columns. The heading consists of three lines: (1) the name of the business, (2) the words "Trial Balance," and (3) the date. The date is the month, the day, and the year for which the trial balance is prepared.

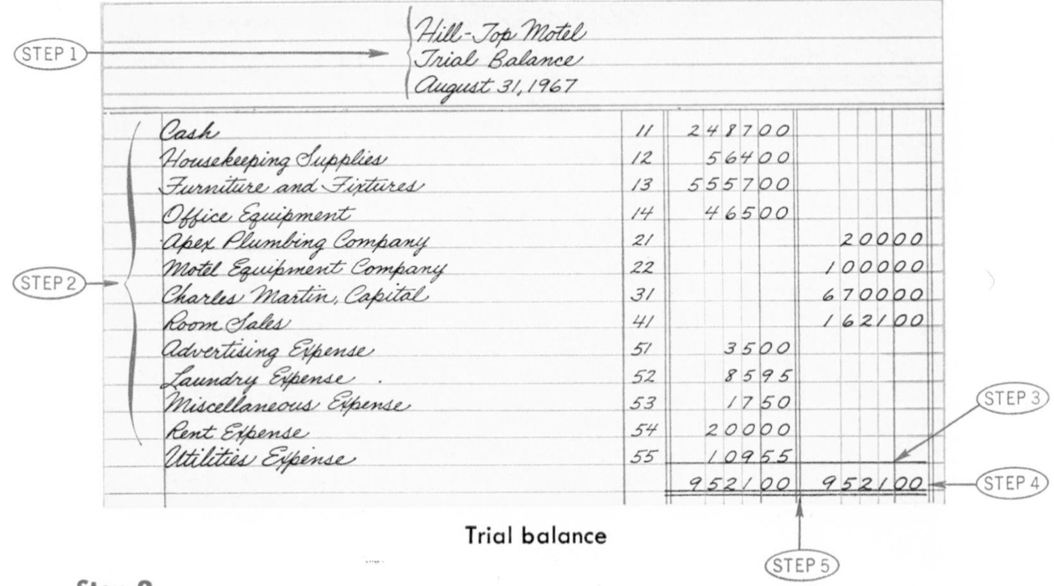

Hill-Top Motel
Trial Balance
August 31, 1967

Account	No.	Debit	Credit
Cash	11	2487 00	
Housekeeping Supplies	12	564 00	
Furniture and Fixtures	13	5557 00	
Office Equipment	14	465 00	
Apex Plumbing Company	21		200 00
Motel Equipment Company	22		1000 00
Charles Martin, Capital	31		6700 00
Room Sales	41		1621 00
Advertising Expense	51	35 00	
Laundry Expense	52	85 95	
Miscellaneous Expense	53	17 50	
Rent Expense	54	200 00	
Utilities Expense	55	109 55	
		9521 00	9521 00

Trial balance

Step 2

Enter on the trial balance each account in the ledger and its balance. In each case record the account title, the account number, and the balance. If the balance is a debit, enter it in the left-hand or debit amount column; if the balance is a credit, enter it in the right-hand or credit amount column.

Step 3

Rule a single line across both amount columns of the trial balance under the last amount listed.

Step 4

Add each amount column and compare the totals. If the two totals are the same, write the totals on the first line below the single ruling. (If the totals are not the same, the error or errors must be found and corrected.)

Step 5

Rule a double line under the totals across the amount columns. Note how the totals have been entered and the trial balance has been ruled in the illustration.

Since a double ruling indicates that the work has been completed, the double line should not be drawn until the trial balance is in balance.

Proof provided by the trial balance

If the two totals of the trial balance are equal, the trial balance is said to be in balance. When the trial balance is in balance, the bookkeeper can assume that the posting has been completed accurately.

FINDING AND CORRECTING ERRORS

Errors not detected by a trial balance

A trial balance that is in balance does not *always* prove the complete accuracy of the bookkeeping records. The following kinds of errors in journalizing and posting are not detected by a trial balance:

1. If the journalizing of a transaction is omitted, the ledger will still be in balance. But the error will not be indicated by the trial balance. If, however, the omitted transaction affects cash, the error will be found when cash is proved. Until the error is corrected, the balance of the cash account will not agree with the cash on hand.
2. If an amount is posted to the correct side, but to the wrong account, the trial balance will still be in balance. For example, if the $48.40 debited to the Utilities Expense account on August 31 had been posted by mistake to the debit side of the Rent Expense account, the trial balance would still be in balance. If an error of this kind is not found at the time the trial balance is prepared, it should be discovered when the financial reports are prepared.

Finding errors when a trial balance does not balance

In checking a trial balance that does not balance, proceed as follows:

Step 1

Prove the addition of each trial balance column by adding again in the opposite direction from that previously followed. Find the amount of the difference between the debit total and the credit total of the trial balance. A difference of 10, 100, or 1,000 is probably the result of an error in addition.

Step 2

Look in the ledger for the amount of the difference between the debit total and the credit total of the trial balance. The amount of the difference may be an account balance that was omitted from the trial balance. Also, look in the journal for this amount. Perhaps this amount was not posted when it should have been.

Step 3

Divide the amount of the difference between the two totals of the trial balance by 2. Look through the accounts to see if this amount has been recorded on the wrong side of an account. Also, check to see if this amount has been written in the wrong column of the trial balance. For example, if the difference between the two columns of the trial balance is $80.00, look for $40.00 on the wrong side of an account or in the wrong column of the trial balance.

Step 4

Divide the amount of the difference between the two totals of the trial balance by 9. If this difference is evenly divisible by 9, look for an amount in the trial balance in which the digits have been transposed in copying the balance from the ledger. Also, look through the accounts for an amount in which the digits have been transposed when posted from the journal. For example, if the trial balance is out of balance $27.00, this amount is evenly divisible by 9, with a quotient of 3.00. The amount of the quotient indicates that there is a difference of 3 between the two digits that have been transposed. Look, therefore, for amounts containing at least four digits with the transposition between the third and the fourth digits from the right, such as $14.55 written as $41.55, or $25.40 written as $52.40, or $136.84 written as $163.84.

The amount of a difference that is evenly divisible by 9 may indicate that the decimal point has been incorrectly moved one or more spaces to the right or the left, such as writing $768.00 as $76.80 or $7,680.00.

Step 5

Compare the balances on the trial balance with the balances in the ledger accounts. An error may have been made in copying an account balance on the trial balance.

Step 6

Verify the pencil footings and the account balances in the ledger. An error may have been made in footing an account or in calculating the balance.

Step 7

Verify the posting of each item in the journal. As each posting is verified, place a small check mark (√) on the double vertical line at the left of the corresponding amount in both the journal and the ledger. An item may have been posted twice, not posted at all, entered on the wrong side of an account, or copied incorrectly. Examine first the journal and then the ledger to find items not checked or items that have been checked twice.

The error or errors should now be found because all the work has been retraced.

Correcting errors in the ledger

If an item has been posted to the wrong side of an account, a line should be drawn through the incorrect posting. The item should then be posted correctly, as shown below.

Office Machines ACCOUNT NO. 14

DATE		ITEMS	POST. REF.	DEBIT	DATE		ITEMS	POST. REF.	CREDIT
1967					1967				
Jan.	1	Balance	J11	1254 40	Jan.	2		C12	215 00
	13		C12	176 00		~~13~~		~~C12~~	~~176 00~~

Correction of the posting to the wrong side of an account

If an incorrect amount has been posted to the right account, a line should be drawn through the incorrect amount. The correct amount should then be written above it, as shown below.

McDaniels Company ACCOUNT NO. 24

DATE		ITEMS	POST. REF.	DEBIT	DATE		ITEMS	POST. REF.	CREDIT
1967				125 00	1967				
Jan.	1		C2	~~12 50~~	Jan.	1	Balance	J1	391 00

Correction of the posting of an incorrect amount

If an item has been posted to the wrong account, a line should be drawn through the incorrect posting and the item should be posted correctly. If the posting of an item has been omitted, the amount should be posted at once. If an item has been posted twice, a line should be drawn through the second posting in the account.

An error in a pencil footing in the ledger should be erased and replaced by the correct pencil footing.

Correcting errors in the trial balance

If an account balance has been omitted from the trial balance, it should be inserted in its proper position. If an account balance has been placed in the wrong column of the trial balance, the amount should be canceled with a line and the same amount should be written in the correct column. A similar correction should be made for a balance copied incorrectly. The trial balance totals should also be corrected.

Increasing Your Business Vocabulary

What is the meaning of the following:

trial balance

Study Questions

1. What steps are used in finding the balance of the cash account?
2. Where is the pencil footing of each side of an account written?
3. Why should the pencil footings of an account be written very small?
4. When can it be said that the cash account is proved?
5. What is the purpose of the trial balance?
6. What are the three parts of the heading of a trial balance?
7. What are the steps in preparing a trial balance?
8. What kind of errors in journalizing and posting are not detected by a trial balance even though it is in balance?
9. How is the posting of an amount to the wrong side of an account corrected?
10. How is the posting of an incorrect amount to the right account corrected?

Cases for Business Decision

CASE 1

Throughout the month the bookkeeper for Alice's Dress Shop makes several errors in her work. At the end of the month, a trial balance is prepared. Which of the following errors in posting will not be indicated by the trial balance?

(a) A debit of $42.00 was posted to the debit side of the wrong account.

(b) A debit of $4.50 to the miscellaneous expense account was posted to the credit side of that account.

CASE 2

The bookkeeper for the Barker Clothing Store posts the individual items in his cash journal frequently. He posts the totals of the special columns at the end of each month. But he takes a trial balance only after he has completed twelve months of posting. What are the disadvantages of taking a trial balance only once a year?

CASE 3

The bookkeeper for Mr. Aaron, owner of a jewelry store, has prepared a trial balance at the end of November. When Mr. Aaron examines the trial balance, he notices that the Jewelry Supply Company's account has a credit balance of $150.00. Mr. Aaron distinctly recalls writing a check to pay this creditor. He asks the bookkeeper why the account still has a credit balance when the amount was paid. What probable error should the bookkeeper try to locate and correct?

Drill for Understanding

DRILL 8-A | Classifying accounts on a trial balance

Instructions: 1. On the left-hand side of a sheet of paper, copy in one column the ledger account titles given below.

1. Automobile
2. Automobile Expense
3. Bloomfield Garage (creditor)
4. Cash
5. Commissions Income
6. Furniture and Fixtures
7. Insurance Expense
8. John Kurth, Capital
9. Miscellaneous Expense
10. Office Machines
11. Office Supplies
12. Rent Expense
13. Richmond Company (creditor)
14. Utilities Expense

Instructions: 2. Rule three columns at the right of your list of accounts and write in the headings shown in the form below.

Account Titles	Classifi-cation	Trial Balance	
		Debit	Credit
1. Automobile	*A*	√	

Instructions: 3. Classify each account on your list as an asset, a liability, proprietorship, an income, or an expense by writing in the Classification column:

A for Asset L for Liability I for Income
P for Proprietorship E for Expense

Instructions: 4. Indicate whether the balance of each account will appear in the Debit column or the Credit column of the trial balance by making a check mark in the appropriate column. The first account is given as an example.

5. Now cover your answers and see how rapidly you can classify these accounts mentally without looking at your answers. Repeat this drill several times for increased speed and accuracy.

Application Problems

PROBLEM 8-1 | Taking a trial balance

If you are not using the workbook correlating with this textbook, complete Appendix Problem 8-A instead of this problem.

The ledger accounts of the Archer Realty Agency are in your workbook.

Instructions: 1. Foot the ledger accounts. Write the footings in very small figures with a sharp pencil and place each footing close to the last item. If an account has entries on both sides, write the balance in small pencil figures in the Items column of the larger side.

2. Prove the cash account. The bank balance according to the checkbook on October 31 is $698.37. All cash receipts have been deposited. The bank balance should agree with the balance of the cash account in the ledger.

3. Prepare a trial balance dated October 31 of the current year. If the two totals of the trial balance are equal, rule double lines as shown on the model trial balance on page 110.

Self-checking: Compare your ledger with the illustrations on pages 108 and 109 and ask yourself the following questions:

1. Are the pencil footings written in the ledger in small figures with a sharp, firm pencil?
2. Is each amount column of an account footed when, and only when, it contains two or more entries?
3. For each account having one or more entries on both the debit and the credit sides, is the balance of the account written in small pencil figures in the Items column of the larger side?

PROBLEM 8-2 | Finding and correcting errors indicated by a trial balance

If you are not using the workbook correlating with this textbook, complete Appendix Problem 8-B instead of this problem.

The journal and the ledger of Lewis Thornton, after the posting of the entries for November of the current year, are given in the workbook.

Instructions: 1. Foot the ledger accounts. Write the footings in very small figures with a sharp pencil and place each footing close to the last item. If an account has entries on both sides, write the balance in small pencil figures in the Items column of the larger side.

2. Prove the cash account. The bank balance according to the checkbook on November 30 is $2,003.37. All cash receipts have been deposited.

3. Prepare a trial balance dated November 30 of the current year. In the heading, use the name of the business, Thornton's Tax Service. If the totals of the trial balance are not equal, proceed as you were directed in Steps 1–7, pages 111 and 112, to find the error or errors. Correct any errors in the journal or the ledger, using the methods explained and illustrated on page 113. Then complete the trial balance.

PROJECT 1 — JOURNALIZING, POSTING, AND TAKING A TRIAL BALANCE

Bookkeeping work to be completed in Project 1

This project makes use of all the steps in the bookkeeping process that have been developed in the preceding eight chapters. These steps are:

1. Opening accounts in the ledger.
2. Recording and posting the opening entry.
3. Journalizing business transactions.
4. Footing, proving, and ruling the cash journal.
5. Posting to ledger accounts.
6. Preparing a trial balance.

Sterling Realty Agency

Frank Sterling is the owner of the Sterling Realty Agency. The agency earns commissions on houses and other real estate that it sells or rents for customers.

The chart of accounts used by the Sterling Realty Agency is shown below.

Sterling Realty Agency
Chart of Accounts

	Acct. No.		Acct. No.
(1) Assets		(4) Income	
Cash..................	11	Commissions Income...	41
Automobile...........	12		
Office Furniture.....	13	(5) Expenses	
Office Machines......	14	Advertising Expense..	51
		Automobile Expense...	52
(2) Liabilities		Entertainment Expense	53
Lenox Furniture Co...	21	Miscellaneous Expense	54
Woodland Garage......	22	Rent Expense.........	55
(3) Proprietorship			
Frank Sterling, Capital...........	31		

Use made of expense accounts

Expense transactions are to be charged to expense accounts as follows:

Advertising Expense is debited for all advertising for the business.

Automobile Expense is debited for the cost of operating the automobile for business purposes.

Entertainment Expense is debited for the cost of entertaining prospective customers.

Miscellaneous Expense is debited for expenses such as postage, stationery, electricity, telephone service, and any expense item not covered by other expense accounts.

Rent Expense is debited for rent.

Opening accounts in the ledger

Mr. Sterling decides to open a new set of books.

Instructions: 1. Open accounts in the new ledger in the order in which they are listed in the chart of accounts on the preceding page. Allow five lines for each account. Number the accounts with the account numbers given in the chart of accounts.

Recording and posting the opening entry

The balance sheet of Sterling Realty Agency as of the close of business on June 30 is shown below.

Sterling Realty Agency
Balance Sheet
June 30, 19—

Assets		Liabilities	
Cash	860 00	Lenox Furniture Company	490 00
Automobile	3 200 00	Woodland Garage	1 200 00
		Total Liabilities	1 690 00
Office Furniture	888 00		
Office Machines	542 00		
		Proprietorship	
		Frank Sterling, Capital	3 800 00
Total Assets	5 490 00	Total Liab. and Prop.	5 490 00

Instructions: 2. Record the opening entry in the new set of books from the balance sheet illustrated above. Record the opening entry on page 1 of the two-column general journal. Date the opening entry July 1 of the current year.

3. Post the opening entry. Remember to indicate in the Items column of the ledger accounts that each of these amounts is a "Balance."

Journalizing business transactions

Instructions: 4. Record the following transactions on page 1 of a cash journal similar to the one illustrated on page 96, except that the heading of the special income column should be "Commissions Income Credit" instead of "Room Sales Credit." The check numbers begin with No. 121. The receipt numbers begin with No. 71.

July 1. Paid $175.00 for rent for July.
1. Received $725.00 as commission on the sale of a house.
3. Paid $125.00 for additional office furniture.
4. Paid $300.00 to Woodland Garage on account.
6. Received $80.00 as commission for the rental of a house.
7. Paid $320.00 for a new typewriter.
7. Paid $42.00 for advertising in local newspaper.
8. Received $20.00 as commission for renting a garage.
10. Paid $16.80 for gas and oil for automobile.
11. Received $180.00 as commission on the sale of a lot.
13. Paid $23.00 for advertising handbills.
13. Received $860.00 as commission on the sale of a house.
14. Paid $11.00 for dinner for prospective customers.
17. Received $45.00 as commission on the rental of an apartment.
19. Paid $40.00 for a new chair for the office.
21. Paid $12.50 for newspaper advertisements.
24. Paid $13.50 for dinner for prospective customers.
24. Paid $11.60 for gas and oil for automobile.
26. Received $18.00 from the sale of old office furniture.
26. Received $80.00 as commission on the sale of a lot.
27. Paid $15.00 for postage stamps.
27. Received $70.00 as commission for the rental of a house.
28. Paid $8.75 for repairs to automobile.
29. Received $130.00 as commission for the rental of a store building.
31. Paid $18.75 for the electric light bill for the month of July.
31. Paid $16.60 for telephone service for the month.
31. Paid $200.00 to Lenox Furniture Company on account.

Footing, proving, and ruling the cash journal

Instructions: 5. Foot all columns of the cash journal.

6. Prove the equality of debits and credits in the cash journal. The sum of the totals of the two debit columns should equal the sum of the totals of the three credit columns.

7. Prove cash. The bank balance according to the checkbook is $1,718.50. All cash receipts have been deposited.

8. Total and rule the cash journal. (See model on page 96.)

Posting to ledger accounts

Instructions: 9. Post each amount in the General Debit column and in the General Credit column. Place a check mark in parentheses under the total of the General Debit column and the General Credit column to show that the totals of these columns are not to be posted. (See model on page 96.)

10. Post the total of each of the three special columns of the cash journal: Cash Debit, Cash Credit, and Commissions Income Credit. Write the proper account number in parentheses under each total after the posting is completed. (See model on page 96.)

Preparing a trial balance

Instructions: 11. Foot the accounts in the ledger that have more than one entry on either side of the account. If an account has entries on both sides of the account, write the balance in small pencil figures in the Items column on the side that has the larger total. (Use as your guide the models on pages 108 and 109.)

12. Prepare a trial balance. (See model on page 110.)

CHAPTER 9 | THE SIX-COLUMN WORK SHEET

The owner of every business wants to know from time to time how well the business is doing. Is it operating at a profit or at a loss? How much is the profit? How much is the loss?

The information that Mr. Martin, proprietor of the Hill-Top Motel, needs in order to answer these questions is in the accounts in the ledger. However, the information in the ledger accounts needs to be summarized and analyzed. A trial balance summarizes the information in the accounts, but a trial balance does not indicate the amount of the profit or the loss.

Analysis paper and the work sheet

The analysis to determine the profit or the loss of a business is made on a single sheet of paper with six or more amount columns. Accounting paper with a number of amount columns that are used for analysis purposes is known as *analysis paper*. Analysis paper on which the financial condition of a business is summarized is called a *work sheet*. The work sheet is a bookkeeper's working paper and is not a part of the permanent records of the business. It may therefore be prepared in pencil.

The fiscal period

The length of time for which an analysis of business operations is made is called a *fiscal period*. The fiscal period may be any length of time desired, such as four weeks, a month, three months, six months, or one year.

THE WORK SHEET OF THE HILL-TOP MOTEL

The work sheet of the Hill-Top Motel for the month ended August 31, 1967, is shown on the next page.

The six amount columns of this work sheet are composed of pairs of Debit and Credit columns under the major section headings of *Trial Balance*, *Income Statement*, and *Balance Sheet*.

All the ledger account balances are sorted and summarized in the trial balance section.

A trial balance may be taken at any time to prove the accuracy of the ledger. When a work sheet is prepared, a trial balance is always taken and recorded directly on the analysis paper used for preparing the work sheet.

Hill-Top Motel
Work Sheet
For Month Ended August 31, 1967

	Account Titles	Acct. No.	Trial Balance (1) Debit	Trial Balance (2) Credit	Income Statement (3) Debit	Income Statement (4) Credit	Balance Sheet (5) Debit	Balance Sheet (6) Credit	
1	Cash	11	2487 00				2487 00		1
2	Housekeeping Supplies	12	564 00				564 00		2
3	Furniture and Fixtures	13	5557 00				5557 00		3
4	Office Equipment	14	465 00				465 00		4
5	Apex Plumbing Company	21		200 00				200 00	5
6	Motel Equipment Company	22		1000 00				1000 00	6
7	Charles Martin, Capital	31		6700 00				6700 00	7
8	Room Sales	41		1621 00		1621 00			8
9	Advertising Expense	51	35 00		35 00				9
10	Laundry Expense	52	85 95		85 95				10
11	Miscellaneous Expense	53	17 50		17 50				11
12	Rent Expense	54	200 00		200 00				12
13	Utilities Expense	55	109 55		109 55				13
14			9521 00	9521 00	448 00	1621 00	9073 00	7900 00	14
15	Net Income				1173 00			1173 00	15
16					1621 00	1621 00	9073 00	9073 00	16
17									17
18									18
19									19
20									20
21									21
22									22
23									23
24									24
25									25

STEP 1 STEP 2 STEP 3 STEP 4 STEP 5 STEP 6 STEP 7 STEP 8 STEP 9

Six-column work sheet

In the Income Statement section, the amount of each expense is listed in the Debit column, and the amount of each income in the Credit column.

The Balance Sheet section shows the amount of each asset in the Debit column, and the amount of each liability and the amount of the proprietorship in the Credit column.

USE OF THE WORK SHEET

The completed work sheet is used in preparing the financial reports at the end of the fiscal period.

The information in the Balance Sheet section of the work sheet is used to prepare a new balance sheet. This new balance sheet shows the assets, the liabilities, and the proprietorship on the last day of the fiscal period for which the work sheet is made.

The information in the Income Statement section of the work sheet is used to prepare a financial report showing the income earned and the expenses incurred during the period. When the income is larger than the expenses, the amount of the difference is called *net income.* When the expenses are larger than the income, the difference is called *net loss.* The report showing the income, the expenses, and the net income or the net loss is called the *income statement.* The preparation of the balance sheet and the income statement from the information on the work sheet is explained in Chapter 10.

Business is increasingly using the term *income statement* in preference to the older term *profit and loss statement.* Therefore, this textbook uses the term *income statement.*

PREPARING A SIX-COLUMN WORK SHEET

The steps listed below should be followed when preparing a work sheet. As you study the steps, compare each one with the illustration of the work sheet of the Hill-Top Motel shown on the opposite page.

Step 1

Write the heading on three lines; center each item in the heading.

a Write the name of the business, *Hill-Top Motel*, on the first line.

b Write the name of the form, *Work Sheet*, on the second line.

c Write the length and the closing date of the fiscal period for which the analysis is made, *For Month Ended August 31, 1967*, on the third line.

Step 2

Write the column headings (if they are not preprinted on the analysis paper). The column headings, reading from left to right on the illustrated work sheet, are Account Titles, Account Number, Trial Balance Debit and Credit, Income Statement Debit and Credit, and Balance Sheet Debit and Credit.

Step 3

Record the trial balance. When a work sheet is prepared at the same time a trial balance is taken, the trial balance is recorded directly on the work sheet. The steps used in recording the trial balance on the work sheet are the same as Steps 2 to 5 on page 110.

Step 4

Extend the balance sheet items into the Balance Sheet section, as follows:

a Extend the amount of each asset from the Trial Balance Debit column (Column 1) into the Balance Sheet Debit column (Column 5).

b Extend the amount of each liability and the amount of the proprietorship from the Trial Balance Credit column (Column 2) into the Balance Sheet Credit column (Column 6).

Step 5

Extend the income and expense items into the Income Statement section, as follows:

a Extend the amount of each income from the Trial Balance Credit column (Column 2) into the Income Statement Credit column (Column 4).

b Extend the amount of each expense from the Trial Balance Debit column (Column 1) into the Income Statement Debit column (Column 3).

Step 6

Total the Income Statement columns and the Balance Sheet columns.

a Rule a single line across the Income Statement columns and the Balance Sheet columns to indicate addition.

b Add each column and write the totals on the same line as the Trial Balance totals.

Step 7

Calculate and record the net income (or the net loss).

a Subtract the smaller total in the Income Statement columns from the larger total, as follows:

Total of Income Statement Credit column (income).....	$1,621.00
Total of Income Statement Debit column (expenses)....	448.00
Net Income (income minus expenses).................	$1,173.00

When the total of the Income Statement Debit column is larger than the total of the Income Statement Credit column, subtract the total of the credit column from the total of the debit column to find the amount of the net loss.

b Write the amount of the net income, *$1,173.00*, immediately below the smaller of the two totals in the Income Statement columns.

c Write the words *Net Income* in the Account Titles column on the same line as the amount of the net income.

d Rule a single line across the Income Statement columns and add these columns.

When these two proving totals of the Income Statement columns are equal, the amount of the net income (or the net loss) from these two columns is assumed to be correct.

Step 8

Extend the net income into the Balance Sheet Credit column.

a Extend the amount of the net income, *$1,173.00*, into the Balance Sheet Credit column to show the increase in proprietorship as a result of the net income earned by the business during August.

If there is a net loss for the month, the proprietorship is decreased. The amount of a net loss is therefore extended into the Balance Sheet Debit column because this is the column in which deductions in proprietorship must be shown.

b Rule a single line across the Balance Sheet columns and add these columns.

When these two proving totals of the Balance Sheet columns are equal, the amount of the net income (or the net loss) as extended from the Income Statement columns is assumed to be correct.

Step 9

Rule double lines below the final totals of the Income Statement columns and the Balance Sheet columns. The double lines show that all work has been completed and is assumed to be correct.

Increasing Your Business Vocabulary

What is the meaning of each of the following:

a analysis paper
b work sheet
c fiscal period
d net income
e net loss
f income statement

Study Questions

1. Why may a work sheet be prepared in pencil?
2. For what purpose is the completed work sheet used?
3. What are the three items in the heading of the work sheet?
4. What is the columnar heading of each of the amount columns of the six-column work sheet?
5. To what columns in the six-column work sheet illustrated on page 122 are the debit amounts in the trial balance extended?
6. To what columns in the six-column work sheet illustrated on page 122 are the credit amounts in the trial balance extended?
7. When the total of the Income Statement Credit column is larger than the total of the Income Statement Debit column, what is the amount of the difference called?
8. When the total of the Income Statement Debit column is larger than the total of the Income Statement Credit column, what is the amount of the difference called?
9. Why is the amount of the net income obtained from the Income Statement columns of the work sheet extended to the Balance Sheet Credit column?
10. Why is the amount of the net loss that is obtained from the Income Statement columns of the work sheet extended to the Balance Sheet Debit column?

Cases for Business Decision

CASE 1

The bookkeeper for the Economy Car Rental Company transfers in error the balance of the automobile expense account to the Balance Sheet Debit column of the work sheet.

a Will this error be discovered when the net income is calculated on the work sheet?

b What is the effect of this error on the net income as calculated on the work sheet?

c When is an error of this type likely to be discovered?

CASE 2

The beginning balance sheet of the Hill-Top Motel for August 1, 1967, shown on page 16, lists the liability account, Motel Equipment Company, and the amount owed, $1,300.00. The Balance Sheet Credit column of the work sheet at the end of August, shown on page 122, lists the same liability account, but the amount is different. What kind of transaction caused the difference in this account balance?

CASE 3

The beginning balance sheet of the Hill-Top Motel for August 1, 1967, shown on page 16, lists the balance of Housekeeping Supplies as $550.00, the balance of Furniture and Fixtures as $5,600.00, and the balance of Office Equipment as $485.00. However, the Balance Sheet Debit column of the work sheet at the end of August, illustrated on page 122, shows that these account balances are different from those on the beginning balance sheet. What kinds of transactions could have caused the differences in these account balances?

Drill for Understanding

DRILL 9-A Sorting account balances on the work sheet

Drill 8-A on page 115 gave you practice in determining in which column of the trial balance the balances of different kinds of accounts would appear. This drill is a continuation of Drill 8-A. It is planned to give you additional skill in determining the kind of ledger accounts whose balances are found in the Balance Sheet Debit and Credit columns and the Income Statement Debit and Credit columns.

Instructions: 1. On a sheet of paper, rule a form similar to the one illustrated below. Fill in the headings as shown in the illustration. In the Account Titles column, copy the list of account titles given below.

	3	4	5	6
Account Titles	Income Statement		Balance Sheet	
	Debit	Credit	Debit	Credit
1. *Automobile*			√	

List of Account Titles

1. Automobile
2. Automobile Expense
3. Bloomfield Garage (creditor)
4. Cash
5. Commissions Income
6. Furniture and Fixtures
7. Insurance Expense
8. John Kurth, Capital
9. Miscellaneous Expense
10. Office Machines
11. Office Supplies
12. Rent Expense
13. Richmond Company (creditor)
14. Utilities Expense

Instructions: 2. Determine whether the balance of each of these accounts would be extended to the Income Statement columns or to the Balance Sheet columns. Then, after each account title, place a check mark in the appropriate debit or credit column of either the Income Statement columns or the Balance Sheet columns of the work sheet. The first item is given as an example.

Application Problem

PROBLEM 9-1 | Work sheet for an insurance agency

On October 31 of the current year, the end of a fiscal period of one month, the account balances in the ledger of the Bradley Insurance Agency are:

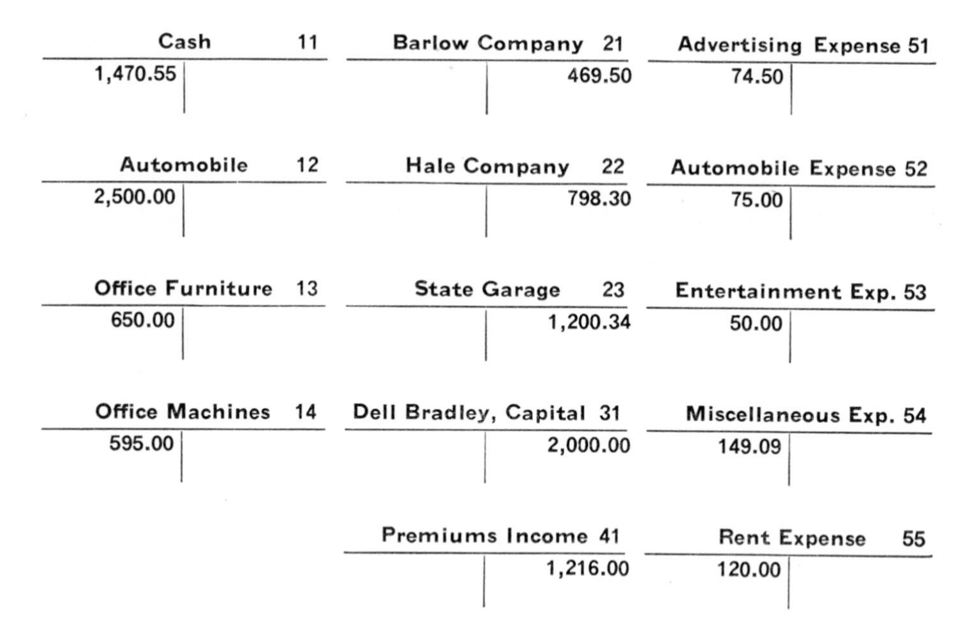

Account	No.	Debit	Credit
Cash	11	1,470.55	
Automobile	12	2,500.00	
Office Furniture	13	650.00	
Office Machines	14	595.00	
Barlow Company	21		469.50
Hale Company	22		798.30
State Garage	23		1,200.34
Dell Bradley, Capital	31		2,000.00
Premiums Income	41		1,216.00
Advertising Expense	51	74.50	
Automobile Expense	52	75.00	
Entertainment Exp.	53	50.00	
Miscellaneous Exp.	54	149.09	
Rent Expense	55	120.00	

Instructions: Prepare a six-column work sheet for the Bradley Insurance Agency dated October 31 of the current year. Write the proper heading at the top of each column of the analysis paper. Use the account titles, account numbers, and account balances shown above. Use as your model the work sheet illustrated on page 122.

Self-checking: Compare your completed work sheet with the model work sheet on page 122 and check the accuracy of your work by asking yourself the following questions:

1. Did you rule a single line across all six amount columns on the line immediately above the trial balance totals?
2. Do the two totals of your trial balance agree?
3. Did you rule a double line under both trial balance totals across two amount columns only?
4. Did you write a total for each of the two Income Statement columns and for each of the two Balance Sheet columns? Did you place all four of these totals on the same line?

5. Did you write the amount of the net income in the Income Statement Debit column and also in the Balance Sheet Credit column?

6. Did you rule a single line across the last four amount columns immediately under the amount of the net income?

7. Do the two proving totals of the Income Statement columns of your work sheet agree?

8. Do the two proving totals of the Balance Sheet columns of your work sheet agree?

9. Are the proving totals of the last four amount columns of your work sheet all written on the same line?

10. Did you rule a double line across the last four amount columns immediately under the proving totals to show that all of your work sheet has been completed?

This problem will be continued in the next chapter. If it is collected by your teacher at this time, it will be returned to you before it is needed in Problem 10-1.

Optional Problems

★SUPPLEMENTARY PROBLEM 9-S

Work sheet for an optometrist

The account balances in the ledger of R. W. Bruce, an optometrist, on November 30 of the current year, the end of a fiscal period of one month, are:

Account	Balance	Account	Balance
Cash	$1,444.80	R. W. Bruce, Capital	$8,638.85
Automobile	2,800.00	Professional Fees	1,501.00
Equipment	4,110.00	Insurance Expense	30.00
Office Furniture	987.10	Miscellaneous Expense	34.80
Office Machines	714.10	Rent Expense	210.00
Bellows Company (creditor)	40.00	Salary Expense	275.00
Sawyer Optical Supplies (creditor)	349.25	Utilities Expense	18.80
Wilson Company (creditor)	95.50		

Instructions: Prepare a six-column work sheet for Dr. R. W. Bruce. Use the account titles and the account balances given above.

Self-checking: Except for the omission of account numbers, is your work sheet similar in all respects to the model on page 122?

★ BONUS PROBLEM 9-B

Work sheet for a theater

The account balances in the ledger of James Moore, proprietor of the Strand Theater, on November 30 of the current year, the end of a fiscal period of one month, are:

Cash	$2,144.50	James Moore, Capital	$14,180.70
Air Conditioning Equip.	2,750.00	Admissions Income	1,069.00
Projection Equipment	8,000.00	Advertising Expense	209.10
Sound Equipment	1,542.00	Electricity Expense	74.25
Film Producers, Inc. (creditor)	279.60	Film Rental Expense	802.90
		Maintenance Expense	37.50
International Studios (creditor)	138.40	Projection Expense	36.00
		Rent Expense	225.00
Majestic Films (creditor)	117.20	Water Expense	34.50
Midwest Sound Service (creditor)	46.00		
National Supply Co. (creditor)	24.85		

Instructions: Prepare a six-column work sheet for the Strand Theater, using the account titles and account balances given above.

Self-checking: 1. Did you write the amount of the net loss in the Income Statement Credit column and in the Balance Sheet Debit column?

2. Did you write the words *Net Loss* in the Account Titles column on the same line with the amount of the net loss?

CHAPTER 10 THE INCOME STATEMENT AND THE BALANCE SHEET

Two important financial statements are prepared from the information on the work sheet: the income statement and the balance sheet. The income statement shows the financial *progress* of a business over a *period of time*, as illustrated in the diagram below. The balance sheet shows the financial *condition* of a business *on a specific date*.

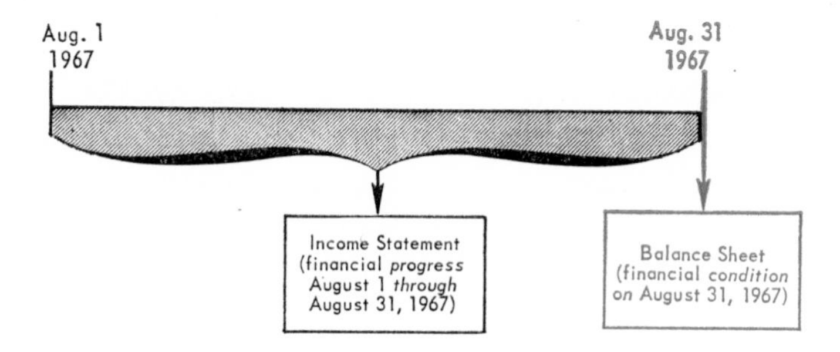

Financial statements are used primarily as an aid in the proper management of a business. They also provide information to those outside the business who are entitled to it. For example, a bank that is asked to lend money to a business is entitled to know something about the financial condition of the business.

PREPARING THE INCOME STATEMENT

The information needed to prepare an income statement is found in three parts of the work sheet: (1) the heading, (2) the Account Titles column, and (3) the Income Statement columns. The heading of the work sheet supplies the name of the business and the period of time for which the income statement is being prepared. The Account Titles column supplies the names of the accounts listed on the income statement. The Income Statement columns contain all the amounts needed in preparing the income statement.

The parts of the work sheet for the Hill-Top Motel that are needed in the preparation of the income statement are shown on the next page.

Hill-Top Motel
Work Sheet
For Month Ended August 31, 1967

	ACCOUNT TITLES	ACCT. NO.	INCOME STATEMENT (3) DEBIT	INCOME STATEMENT (4) CREDIT
8	Room Sales	41		1621 00
9	Advertising Expense	51	35 00	
10	Laundry Expense	52	85 95	
11	Miscellaneous Expense	53	17 50	
12	Rent Expense	54	200 00	
13	Utilities Expense	55	109 55	
14			448 00	1621 00
15	Net Income		1173 00	
16			1621 00	1621 00
17				
18				
19				
20				

Parts of work sheet used for preparing an income statement

The income statement of the Hill-Top Motel for the month of August shown below was prepared from the Income Statement columns of the work sheet.

Hill-Top Motel
Income Statement
For Month Ended August 31, 1967

Income:		
Room Sales		1621 00
Expenses:		
Advertising Expense	35 00	
Laundry Expense	85 95	
Miscellaneous Expense	17 50	
Rent Expense	200 00	
Utilities Expense	109 55	
Total Expenses		448 00
Net Income		1173 00

Income statement

Heading of an income statement

Each income statement covers a definite fiscal period. The fiscal period is the same as that shown on the work sheet from which the statement is prepared.

The heading of the income statement of the Hill-Top Motel includes:

Line 1 — Name of the business: *Hill-Top Motel*
Line 2 — Name of the form: *Income Statement*
Line 3 — { Length of the accounting period: *For Month*
Date: *Ended August 31, 1967*

Income section of an income statement

The information for preparing the income section of the income statement is obtained directly from the Income Statement Credit column of the work sheet (Column 4).

The heading of the income section of the income statement is the single word "Income." This heading is written on the first line, beginning at the vertical line at the left. The title of the income account, Room Sales, is written on the second line, indented about one-half inch. Since the Hill-Top Motel receives income from room sales only, the amount of the room sales is also the total income. The amount of room sales, $1,621.00, is therefore written in the *second* amount column, which is used for totals.

Expense section of an income statement

The information for preparing the expense section of the income statement is obtained directly from the Income Statement Debit column of the work sheet (Column 3).

The heading of the second section of the income statement is "Expenses." This heading is written at the left margin. The titles of the individual expense accounts are listed in the same order in which they are given on the work sheet. Each account title is indented one-half inch from the vertical red line. The amount of each expense account is written in the first amount column of the income statement. The total of the expenses is written in the totals column, the second amount column. The total expenses, $448.00, can then be subtracted easily from the total income, $1,621.00, because both totals are in the same column.

Net income

The amount of the net income has already been calculated on the work sheet. The net income is calculated also on the income statement by subtracting the total expenses from the total income. The amount of the net income shown on the income statement should, of course, agree with the amount of the net income shown on the work sheet.

Ruling the income statement

In all bookkeeping forms, a single line is ruled across an amount column to indicate either addition or subtraction. In the illustration of the income statement on page 132, a single line is ruled across the first amount column to indicate addition of all the expense amounts. A single line is ruled across the second amount column to indicate subtraction of the total expenses from the total income to find the net income.

Double lines are ruled across the amount columns to show that all work has been completed and is assumed to be correct.

PREPARING THE BALANCE SHEET

The information needed to prepare a balance sheet is found in three parts of the work sheet: (1) the heading, (2) the Account Titles column, and (3) the Balance Sheet columns. The heading of the work sheet contains the name of the business and the date for which the balance sheet is prepared. The Account Titles column supplies the names of the accounts listed on the balance sheet. The Balance Sheet columns of the work sheet contain all the amounts needed in preparing the balance sheet.

The parts of the work sheet of the Hill-Top Motel that are needed in the preparation of the balance sheet are shown below.

Hill-Top Motel
Work Sheet
For Month Ended August 31, 1967

	ACCOUNT TITLES	ACCT. NO.	5 BALANCE SHEET DEBIT	6 BALANCE SHEET CREDIT
1	Cash	11	2487 00	
2	Housekeeping Supplies	12	564 00	
3	Furniture and Fixtures	13	5557 00	
4	Office Equipment	14	465 00	
5	Apex Plumbing Company	21		200 00
6	Motel Equipment Company	22		1000 00
7	Charles Martin, Capital	31		6700 00
14			9073 00	7900 00
15	Net Income			1173 00
16			9073 00	9073 00
17				

Parts of work sheet used for preparing a balance sheet

The Balance Sheet columns of the work sheet are used to prepare the balance sheet of the Hill-Top Motel for the month of August shown below.

Hill-Top Motel
Balance Sheet
August 31, 1967

Assets		Liabilities	
Cash	2487 00	Apex Plumbing Co.	200 00
Housekeeping Supplies	564 00	Motel Equipment Co.	1000 00
Furniture and Fixtures	5557 00	Total Liabilities	1200 00
Office Equipment	465 00		
		Proprietorship	
		Charles Martin, Capital	7873 00
Total Assets	9073 00	Total Liab. and Prop.	9073 00

Balance sheet

Heading of a balance sheet

The heading of a balance sheet consists of three items: (1) the name of the business, (2) the name of the form, and (3) the specific date for which the balance sheet is prepared. Each item is written on a separate line.

Assets section of a balance sheet

The information for the assets section of a balance sheet is obtained from the Balance Sheet Debit column of the work sheet (Column 5). The titles of the asset accounts are written on the left-hand side of the balance sheet in the same order as shown on the work sheet. The total of the left-hand side of the balance sheet is written on the same line as the final total on the right-hand side. Therefore, the "Total Assets" line and the amount of the total cannot be written until after the "Total Liabilities and Proprietorship" line has been determined.

Liabilities section of a balance sheet

The information for the liabilities section of the balance sheet is obtained from the Balance Sheet Credit column of the work sheet (Column 6). The liability accounts are written on the right-hand side of the balance sheet in the same order as shown on the work sheet. A single line is ruled across the amount column under the amount of the last liability. The amount of the total and the words "Total Liabilities" are written as shown in the illustration.

Proprietorship section of a balance sheet

The information for the proprietorship section of the balance sheet is obtained from the Balance Sheet Credit column of the work sheet (Column 6). Mr. Martin's proprietorship at the close of business on August 31, 1967, as shown on the work sheet consists of two items: (1) the balance in his capital account, and (2) the net income that his business has earned. These amounts are totaled as follows:

The balance in the proprietor's capital account (as shown on Line 7 of the work sheet)........................	$6,700.00
Plus the net income for August (as shown on Line 15 of the work sheet)................................	1,173.00
Amount of present capital to be shown on balance sheet..	$7,873.00

The amount of the present capital, $7,873.00, is written in the right-hand amount column of the balance sheet. The present capital is then added to the total liabilities to obtain the "Total Liabilities and Proprietorship," $9,073.00.

To prove the accuracy of these calculations, the Total Liabilities and Proprietorship is compared with the Total Assets on the balance sheet. If these two amounts agree, all calculations on the balance sheet are assumed to be correct.

In some businesses, the calculation of the present capital is shown on the balance sheet. When this is done, the proprietorship section of a balance sheet showing a net income would appear as follows:

Proprietorship

Arthur Jones, Capital.........................	3,400.00	
Add Net Income..............................	512.00	
Arthur Jones, Present Capital..................		3,912.00
Total Liabilities and Proprietorship.............		6,166.00

Ruling the balance sheet

A single line is ruled across an amount column of the balance sheet to indicate addition. Double lines are ruled to indicate that the balance sheet has been completed and found to be in balance. Double lines are ruled under the final totals of each side of the balance sheet.

In the balance sheet of the Hill-Top Motel, the two proving totals are $9,073.00. Double lines are ruled under the two proving totals across both amount columns.

Study Questions

1. What is the purpose of the income statement?
2. What is the purpose of a balance sheet?
3. What is the primary use of financial statements?
4. What three parts of a work sheet supply all the information needed for preparing an income statement?
5. What are the three parts of the heading of an income statement?
6. What are the two main sections of the body of the income statement?
7. How is the net income calculated from the information on the income statement?
8. How do you prove the accuracy of the amount of the net income shown on the income statement?
9. What three parts of a work sheet supply all the information needed for preparing a balance sheet?
10. How does the heading of the balance sheet differ from the heading of the income statement?
11. What are the three main sections of the body of the balance sheet?
12. On the partial work sheet shown on page 134, what two items are totaled to determine the amount of the present capital?

Cases for Business Decision

CASE 1

Mr. Martin, who operates the Hill-Top Motel, finds that his net income for the month of August is $1,173.00, as shown on the income statement on page 132. Mr. Martin is offered $1,200.00 a month to manage a motel for one of the big chains. What decisions must he make in order to determine whether to continue to rent and operate the Hill-Top Motel or to become a manager of a large chain motel?

CASE 2

Mr. T. W. Kirk, the owner of the Hill-Top Motel, has been renting the motel to Mr. Martin for several years. Mr. Kirk and Mr. Martin have been talking about expanding the motel by adding five units. What factors should the two men take into account before making a decision?

Drills for Understanding

DRILL 10-A | Using the bookkeeping equation for figuring net income and net loss

At the time a work sheet is completed, the total proprietorship consists of two amounts: (1) the balance in the proprietor's capital account, and (2) either the net income or the net loss for the period.

The data below show the total assets, the total liabilities, and the balance in the capital account as shown on the work sheets of seven different businesses.

Instructions: 1. Use the information shown below to figure the net income or the net loss of each business for the period. The answers for Businesses A and B are given as examples.

2. List the total amount of proprietorship that will be reported on the balance sheet of each business at the close of this fiscal period. Business A, for example, will report a total of $6,000 — the balance in the capital account, $5,000, plus the net income for the period, $1,000. Business B will report a total of $11,000 — the balance in the capital account, $11,500, less the net loss for the period, $500.

Business	A	B	C	D	E	F	G
Total Assets.....	$10,000	$15,000	$6,000	$33,650	$21,600	$81,750	$33,890
Total Liabilities..	4,000	4,000	1,000	4,325	11,500	21,050	4,540
Balance in Capital Account........	5,000	11,500	3,500	24,000	11,000	55,000	30,000
Net Income.....	*1,000*	...	____	____	____	____	____
or							
Net Loss........	...	*500*	____	____	____	____	____
Total Proprietorship............	*$6,000*	*$11,000*	____	____	____	____	____

DRILL 10-B | Classifying accounts

This drill is planned to give you additional skill in determining which ledger account balances are found on the balance sheet and which ledger account balances are found on the income statement.

Instructions: 1. On a sheet of paper, rule a form similar to the one illustrated on the next page. Fill in the headings as shown in the illustration. Then, in the Account Titles column (Column 1), copy the list of account titles given below the form.

1	2	3
Account Titles	**Income Statement**	**Balance Sheet**
1. *Archer Company (Creditor)*		√

List of Account Titles

1. Archer Company (creditor)
2. Admissions Income
3. Advertising Expense
4. Martha Blair, Capital
5. Automobile
6. Automobile Expense
7. Cash
8. Commissions Income
9. Utilities Expense
10. Entertainment Expense
11. William Metz, Capital
12. Kitchen Equipment
13. McIntyre Company (creditor)
14. Miscellaneous Expense
15. Office Equipment

Instructions: 2. If the account title appears on the income statement, place a check mark in Column 2, Income Statement column. If the account title appears on the balance sheet, place a check mark in Column 3, Balance Sheet column.

The first item, Archer Company (creditor), is given as an example. Since this is a liability account, it appears on the balance sheet. A check mark is placed in Column 3.

Application Problems

PROBLEM 10-1 | Financial reports for an insurance agency

The work sheet prepared in Problem 9-1 of Chapter 9 is required for this problem. If it has not been returned to you, complete Appendix Problem 10-A.

Instructions: 1. Prepare an income statement from the Income Statement columns of the work sheet that you completed in Problem 9-1. Use as your model the income statement on page 132.

2. Prepare a balance sheet from the Balance Sheet columns of the work sheet that you completed in Problem 9-1. Use as your model the balance sheet on page 135.

Self-checking: Ask yourself the following questions:

1. Did you center each line of the heading of your income statement?
2. Did you place the headings of the two sections of the income statement, Income and Expenses, close to the vertical red line at the left of the wide column?
3. Did you keep an even indention for all the account titles listed on your income statement?
4. Did you rule a double line under the amount of the net income to show completion of all work?
5. Did you center each of the three lines of the heading of your balance sheet?
6. Did you center the heading of each of the three main sections of the balance sheet: Assets, Liabilities, and Proprietorship?
7. Is the amount of the total assets at the bottom of the left-hand side of the balance sheet on the same line as the amount of the total liabilities and proprietorship at the bottom of the right-hand side?
8. Did you neatly rule the double lines across the amount columns only, under the two proving totals of your balance sheet?

PROBLEM 10-2 | Work sheet and financial reports for a physician

The account balances in the ledger of Dr. Harold Miner on May 31 of the current year, at the end of a fiscal period of one month, are as follows:

Cash	$1,772.70	Harold Miner, Capital	$8,900.00
Automobile	3,600.00	Fees Income	1,345.00
Equipment	3,621.75	Automobile Expense	65.80
Office Furniture	1,462.50	Miscellaneous Expense	23.45
Medical Supply Co. (creditor)	163.00	Rent Expense	150.00
Parker Company (creditor)	225.00	Salary Expense	350.00
Swift Equipment Co. (creditor)	450.00	Utilities Expense	36.80

Instructions: 1. Prepare a six-column work sheet for Dr. Harold Miner, using the account balances given above. Use as your model the work sheet on page 122.

2. Prepare an income statement from the Income Statement columns of the work sheet. Use as your model the income statement on page 132.

3. Prepare a balance sheet from the Balance Sheet columns of the work sheet. Use as your model the balance sheet on page 135.

Self-checking: 1. Except for the omission of account numbers, is your work sheet similar in all respects to the model on page 122?

2. Check the accuracy of your financial reports by asking yourself the questions listed under Problem 10-1.

Optional Problems

★ SUPPLEMENTARY PROBLEM 10-S

Financial reports for a bowling center

The work sheet for the Simpson Bowling Lanes for the month of December of the current year is given below.

Simpson Bowling Lanes
Work Sheet
For Month Ended December 31, 19--

Account Titles	Acct. No.	Trial Balance		Income Statement		Balance Sheet	
		Debit	Credit	Debit	Credit	Debit	Credit
Cash...............	11	2,196 00				2,196 00	
Bowling Supplies...	12	1,112 50				1,112 50	
Office Supplies....	13	210 20				210 20	
Bowling Equipment..	14	21,000 00				21,000 00	
Office Equipment...	15	1,860 20				1,860 20	
Anders Shoe Co.....	21		1,000 00				1,000 00
Daniel Co..........	22		350 00				350 00
Mohawk Repair Co...	23		125 90				125 90
Puritan Cleaners...	24		40 30				40 30
United Supply Co...	25		210 00				210 00
Hal Simpson, Cap...	31		23,650 00				23,650 00
Bowling Income.....	41		1,750 50		1,750 50		
Advertising Expense	51	71 50		71 50			
Electricity Expense	52	84 00		84 00			
Maintenance Expense	53	121 50		121 50			
Miscellaneous Exp..	54	26 40		26 40			
Rent Expense.......	55	400 00		400 00			
Telephone Expense..	56	23 40		23 40			
Water Expense......	57	21 00		21 00			
		27,126 70	27,126 70	747 80	1,750 50	26,378 90	25,376 20
Net Income.........				1,002 70			1,002 70
				1,750 50	1,750 50	26,378 90	26,378 90

Instructions: 1. Prepare an income statement.

2. Prepare a balance sheet.

Self-checking: Check your work by asking yourself the questions that are listed under Problem 10-1.

★BONUS PROBLEM 10-B

Financial reports for an architect

The work sheet for J. R. Lawson for the month of March of the current year is given below.

J. R. Lawson
Work Sheet
For Month Ended March 31, 19--

Account Titles	Acct. No.	Trial Balance		Income Statement		Balance Sheet	
		Debit	Credit	Debit	Credit	Debit	Credit
Cash...............	11	4,929 60				4,929 60	
Automobile.........	12	4,200 00				4,200 00	
Office Furniture...	13	2,820 00				2,820 00	
Office Equipment...	14	4,290 00				4,290 00	
Arrow Company......	21		300 00				300 00
Carew Supplies.....	22		910 00				910 00
J. R. Lawson, Cap..	31		15,360 32				15,360 32
Fees Income........	41		1,200 00		1,200 00		
Automobile Expense.	51	80 32		80 32			
Miscellaneous Exp..	52	360 40		360 40			
Rent Expense.......	53	150 00		150 00			
Salary Expense.....	54	940 00		940 00			
		17,770 32	17,770 32	1,530 72	1,200 00	16,239 60	16,570 32
Net Loss...........					330 72	330 72	
				1,530 72	1,530 72	16,570 32	16,570 32

Instructions: 1. Prepare an income statement.

2. Prepare a balance sheet.

Self-checking: 1. Compare your income statement with the model on page 132. Did you use the words "Net Loss" instead of "Net Income" in your solution to this problem?

2. Compare your balance sheet with the model on page 135. In calculating the present capital, did you subtract the net loss from the balance of the proprietor's capital account?

CHAPTER 11 CLOSING THE LEDGER

The changes in Mr. Martin's proprietorship that result from operating the Hill-Top Motel during the fiscal period are recorded in separate income and expense accounts. Separate income accounts and separate expense accounts are maintained in order to provide the proprietor with detailed information about the amount of each income and the amount of each expense.

After the income statement is completed, the income and expense accounts have served their purpose for the fiscal period. In order to get the income and expense accounts ready for the next fiscal period, it is necessary (1) to close and rule the income and expense accounts, and (2) to transfer the amount of net income or net loss to the proprietor's capital account.

CLOSING ENTRIES

Need for an income and expense summary account

In order to complete the two steps indicated above, the balance of each income and each expense account is first transferred to a summary account. The account to which the balance of each income and each expense account is transferred at the end of the fiscal period is called *Income and Expense Summary.* The income and expense summary account is placed in the proprietorship division of the ledger because it shows the net increase or the net decrease in proprietorship.

Journal entries are made to transfer the balances from the income and the expense accounts to Income and Expense Summary. An entry that transfers the balance from one account to another is called a *closing entry.* An account that has had its balance transferred to another account is called a *closed account.*

After the balances are transferred, the income and expense summary account shows the total expenses on the debit side and the total income on the credit side. The difference between the two sides of the account shows the net increase or the net decrease in proprietorship. The balance of the income and expense summary account is transferred to the proprietor's capital account. The process of transferring the balances of the income and the expense accounts through a summary account to the proprietor's capital account is called *closing the ledger.*

Procedure for closing the ledger

Three steps are taken in closing the ledger of the Hill-Top Motel. The chart below diagrams these three steps.

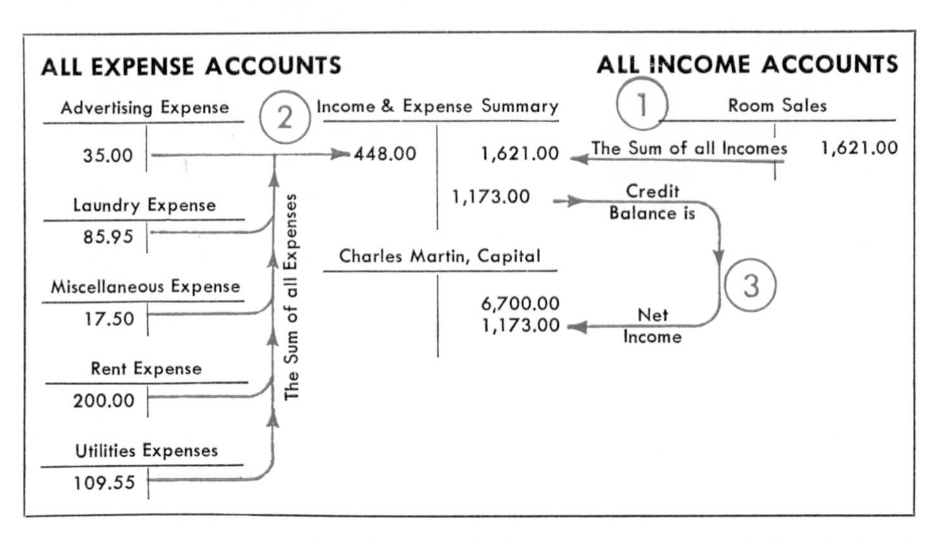

Diagram showing the transfer of account balances at the time the ledger is closed

Step 1

Transfer the credit balance of the income account to the credit side of the income and expense summary account.

Step 2

Transfer the sum of the debit balances of the expense accounts *as a single amount* to the debit side of the income and expense summary account.

Step 3

Transfer the credit balance of the income and expense summary account to the credit side of the proprietor's capital account.

After these transfers of account balances have been completed, Mr. Martin's capital account shows the net increase in proprietorship for the fiscal period. As a result, his proprietorship account in the ledger now agrees with the amount shown in the proprietorship section of the balance sheet.

Closing Entry No. 1 — closing the income account

The information necessary for closing the income account is found in the Income Statement Credit column of the work sheet. The balance of the room sales income account, $1,621.00, is shown in the Income Statement Credit column of the work sheet below. The balance of the income account is transferred to the income and expense summary account.

	ACCOUNT TITLES	ACCT. NO.	1 TRIAL BALANCE DEBIT	2 TRIAL BALANCE CREDIT	3 INCOME STATEMENT DEBIT	4 INCOME STATEMENT CREDIT
8	Room Sales	41		1621 00		1621 00

Before any closing entry is made, the room sales account and the income and expense summary account appear as shown below.

Income and Expense Summary — ACCOUNT NO. 32

DATE	ITEMS	POST. REF.	DEBIT	DATE	ITEMS	POST. REF.	CREDIT

Room Sales — ACCOUNT NO. 41

DATE	ITEMS	POST. REF.	DEBIT	DATE	ITEMS	POST. REF.	CREDIT
				1967 Aug. 31		C1	1621 00

The balance of the room sales account is a *credit* before the transfer. After the transfer, the balance will be a *credit* item in the income and expense summary account. The amount to be credited to Income and Expense Summary is $1,621.00.

The general journal entry to transfer the credit balance of the room sales account to the credit side of the income and expense summary account is shown below.

GENERAL JOURNAL — PAGE 1

	DATE	ACCOUNT TITLE	POST. REF.	DEBIT	CREDIT	
10		Closing Entries				10
11	31	Room Sales	41	1621 00		11
12		Income and Expense Summary	32		1621 00	12

Closing Entry No. 1 — closing the income account

The form of general journal used was illustrated in Chapter 2 when the opening entry was discussed. Mr. Martin also uses his general journal for recording his closing entries.

The words "Closing Entries" are written in the Account Title column before the first closing entry is made. Since this heading explains the nature of the three closing entries, a separate explanation for each closing entry is unnecessary.

The procedure of using a journal entry to transfer an account balance in the ledger is desirable because (1) it helps the bookkeeper avoid errors and (2) it is easier to audit the work of the bookkeeper if all transfers of account balances are first recorded together in the journal.

After Closing Entry No. 1 has been posted, the two accounts affected appear as follows:

Income and Expense Summary ACCOUNT NO. 32

DATE	ITEMS	POST. REF.	DEBIT	DATE	ITEMS	POST. REF.	CREDIT
				1967 Aug. 31		J1	1621 00

Room Sales ACCOUNT NO. 41

DATE	ITEMS	POST. REF.	DEBIT	DATE	ITEMS	POST. REF.	CREDIT
1967 Aug. 31		J1	1621 00	1967 Aug. 31		C1	1621 00

The room sales account illustrated above is now closed. The original *credit* balance of the room sales account, $1,621.00, has now been transferred to the *credit* side of the income and expense summary account.

If there were other income accounts, their balances would be transferred to Income and Expense Summary in the same manner.

Closing Entry No. 2 — closing the expense accounts

The information necessary for closing the expense accounts is found in the Income Statement Debit column of the work sheet. The balances of the expense accounts are shown in the Income Statement Debit column of the work sheet below. The balances of the expense accounts are transferred to the income and expense summary account as a single amount.

	ACCOUNT TITLES	ACCT. NO.	TRIAL BALANCE (1) DEBIT	TRIAL BALANCE (2) CREDIT	INCOME STATEMENT (3) DEBIT	INCOME STATEMENT (4) CREDIT
9	Advertising Expense	51	35 00		35 00	
10	Laundry Expense	52	85 95		85 95	
11	Miscellaneous Expense	53	17 50		17 50	
12	Rent Expense	54	200 00		200 00	
13	Utilities Expense	55	109 55		109 55	
14			9521 00	9521 00	448 00	1621 00
15	Net Income				1173 00	
16					1621 00	1621 00
17						

The expense accounts are closed in the order in which they appear on the work sheet. All the expense account balances are transferred to the income and expense summary account in one entry. An entry that contains two or more debits or two or more credits is known as a *combined entry*. All the expense account balances are *debits* before the transfer is made. After the transfer, the total of all the expense account balances will be a *debit* item in the income and expense summary account. The sum of the expense account balances is $448.00. The amount to be *debited* to Income and Expense Summary is therefore $448.00.

The general journal entry to transfer the debit balances of the expense accounts to the debit side of the income and expense summary account is shown below.

GENERAL JOURNAL — PAGE 1

	DATE	ACCOUNT TITLE	POST. REF.	DEBIT	CREDIT	
13	31	Income and Expense Summary	32	448 00		13
14		Advertising Expense	51		35 00	14
15		Laundry Expense	52		85 95	15
16		Miscellaneous Expense	53		17 50	16
17		Rent Expense	54		200 00	17
18		Utilities Expense	55		109 55	18

Closing Entry No. 2 — closing the expense accounts

After Closing Entry No. 2 has been posted, the income and expense summary account and the first of the expense accounts appear as follows:

Income and Expense Summary — ACCOUNT NO. 32

DATE	ITEMS	POST. REF.	DEBIT	DATE	ITEMS	POST. REF.	CREDIT
1967 Aug. 31		J1	448 00	1967 Aug. 31		J1	1621 00

Advertising Expense — ACCOUNT NO. 51

DATE	ITEMS	POST. REF.	DEBIT	DATE	ITEMS	POST. REF.	CREDIT
1967 Aug. 4		C1	35 00	1967 Aug. 31		J1	35 00

The credits to the other expense accounts are posted in the same manner as the credit to Advertising Expense. All expense accounts are shown in the complete ledger on pages 153 and 154.

Closing Entry No. 3 — closing the income and expense summary account

The net income shown on the work sheet of the Hill-Top Motel is $1,173.00. (See page 132.) This amount is the same as the balance in the income and expense summary account after all income and expense accounts were closed into this summary account. (A credit of $1,621.00 minus a debit of $448.00 equals $1,173.00.) The next step in closing the ledger is to transfer the credit balance of the income and expense summary account to the credit side of the proprietor's capital account.

The general journal entry to transfer the credit balance of the income and expense summary account to the credit side of the proprietor's capital account is shown below.

GENERAL JOURNAL — PAGE 1

	DATE		ACCOUNT TITLE	POST. REF.	DEBIT	CREDIT	
19		31	Income and Expense Summary	32	1173 00		19
20			Charles Martin, Capital	31		1173 00	20

Closing Entry No. 3 — closing the income and expense summary account

After Closing Entry No. 3 has been posted, the income and expense summary account and the proprietor's capital account appear as follows:

Charles Martin, Capital — ACCOUNT NO. 31

DATE		ITEMS	POST. REF.	DEBIT	DATE		ITEMS	POST. REF.	CREDIT
					1967 Aug.	1	Balance	J1	5700 00
						1		C1	1000 00 (6700 00)
						31		J1	1173 00 (7873 00)

Income and Expense Summary — ACCOUNT NO. 32

DATE		ITEMS	POST. REF.	DEBIT	DATE		ITEMS	POST. REF.	CREDIT
1967 Aug.	31		J1	448 00	1967 Aug.	31		J1	1621 00
	31		J1	1173 00					

The income and expense summary account now has a zero balance. As a result, it is said to be in balance and therefore closed. Mr. Martin's capital account now shows: (1) the amount of capital at the start of this fiscal period, $5,700.00, (2) the additional investment by Mr. Martin,

$1,000.00, and (3) the net increase in proprietorship that came from operating the motel during this fiscal period, $1,173.00. The sum of these three amounts now equals his present capital, $7,873.00. Since the present capital shown on the balance sheet is also $7,873.00, Mr. Martin's capital account in the ledger now agrees with the proprietorship section of the balance sheet.

Summary of closing entries

This chapter has explained step by step the three journal entries that are needed to close the ledger. The three journal entries as they appear in the general journal of the Hill-Top Motel after being posted are:

GENERAL JOURNAL — PAGE 1

		DATE	ACCOUNT TITLE	POST. REF.	DEBIT	CREDIT	
	10		Closing Entries				10
Closing Entry No. 1	11	31	Room Sales	41	1621 00		11
	12		Income and Expense Summary	32		1621 00	12
Closing Entry No. 2	13	31	Income and Expense Summary	32	448 00		13
	14		Advertising Expense	51		35 00	14
	15		Laundry Expense	52		85 95	15
	16		Miscellaneous Expense	53		17 50	16
	17		Rent Expense	54		200 00	17
	18		Utilities Expense	55		109 55	18
Closing Entry No. 3	19	31	Income and Expense Summary	32	1173 00		19
	20		Charles Martin, Capital	31		1173 00	20

Closing entries for Hill-Top Motel after posting

The three closing entries are made from the work sheet illustrated on page 132 in the following order:

Closing Entry No. 1. Income and Expense Summary is credited for the total of the Income Statement Credit column. Each income account is debited for its balance to show the decrease in the balance of the income account.

Closing Entry No. 2. Income and Expense Summary is debited for the total of the Income Statement Debit column. Each expense account is credited for its balance to show the decrease in the balance of the expense account.

Closing Entry No. 3. Income and Expense Summary is debited for the amount of the net income. The proprietor's capital account is credited for the same amount to show the increase in proprietorship.

After the three closing entries in the journal are posted, the accounts in the income and expense divisions of the ledger appear as follows:

1. Each income account is now in balance because its credit balance has been transferred to the credit side of Income and Expense Summary.
2. Each expense account is now in balance because its debit balance has been transferred to the debit side of Income and Expense Summary.
3. The account Income and Expense Summary is in balance because its credit balance has been transferred to the credit side of the proprietor's capital account.

    In case of a net loss, the balance of the income and expense summary account is a debit balance and is transferred to the debit side of the proprietor's capital account.

4. The proprietor's capital account now shows on its credit side the increase in proprietorship due to the addition of the net income.

    In case of a net loss, the proprietor's capital account will show the decrease in proprietorship on its debit side.

RULING AND BALANCING ACCOUNTS

Ruling accounts that are closed

As a result of posting the closing entries, each income account, each expense account, and the income and expense summary account are in balance and are said to be closed. In order to show that these accounts are closed, the accounts are ruled. This ruling will prevent the amounts now recorded in these accounts from being confused with the amounts that are entered during the following fiscal period. The laundry expense account after ruling is shown below.

Laundry Expense ACCOUNT NO. 52

DATE		ITEMS	POST. REF.	DEBIT	DATE		ITEMS	POST. REF.	CREDIT
1967 Aug.	14		C1	44 50	1967 Aug.	31		J1	85 95
	26		C1	41 45					
				85 95					85 95

STEP 1 STEP 2 STEP 3

The following steps are usually taken in ruling an income or an expense account:

Step 1

Write the totals of the debit side and the credit side of the account on the same line.

Step 2

Rule a single line across the amount columns on the line above each total. This single line indicates addition.

Step 3

Rule double lines on the line under the totals across all columns except the Items column to show that the account is closed.

When an account that is closed has only one debit and one credit, it is clear that the debit equals the credit. It is therefore unnecessary to total the amount columns. The account is ruled with double lines across all columns except the Items columns as shown below.

Miscellaneous Expense — ACCOUNT NO. 53

DATE	ITEMS	POST. REF.	DEBIT	DATE	ITEMS	POST. REF.	CREDIT
1967 Aug. 7		C1	17 50	1967 Aug. 31		J1	17 50

Balancing accounts that are open

After the closing entries are posted, the only accounts that are open are the balance sheet accounts. When a balance sheet account contains more than one entry on each side, the account should be ruled and the balance recorded on the proper side of the account. After the account is ruled and balanced, the entries of a new fiscal period are clearly separated from those of the previous period. The process of determining the balance of an account, writing it on the smaller side, totaling and ruling the account, and bringing the balance into the new section of the account below the double lines is known as *balancing an account.*

When an asset, a liability, or a proprietorship account has one or more entries on each side, the account may be balanced as follows:

Step 1

Write the balance of the account on the side having the smaller total. Write the last day of the fiscal period in the Date column and the word "Balance" in the Items column. Place a check mark in the Post. Ref. column to show that this item was not posted from a journal. (See the cash account on page 152.)

Step 2

Total and rule the account in the manner in which an income or an expense account is totaled and ruled when it is closed.

Step 3

Write the balance again, this time below the double ruling on the side originally having the larger footing. Write the complete date (year, month, and day) of the new balance, using the first day of the new fiscal period. Write the word "Balance" in the Items column, and place a check mark in the Post. Ref. column.

On the following pages the asset and the liability accounts that are balanced are Cash, Furniture and Fixtures, Office Equipment, and Motel Equipment Company.

The asset account Housekeeping Supplies, the liability account Apex Plumbing Company, and the proprietorship account Charles Martin, Capital, are not balanced because they have entries on one side of the account only.

Ledger that has been closed, balanced, and ruled

The ledger of the Hill-Top Motel, after the closing entries have been posted and the accounts have been balanced and ruled, is shown below and on pages 153 and 154.

Cash ACCOUNT NO. 11

DATE		ITEMS	POST. REF.	DEBIT	DATE		ITEMS	POST. REF.	CREDIT
1967 Aug.	1	Balance	J1	565 00	1967 Aug.	31		C1	762 00
	31	2487.00	C1	2684 00 / 3249 00		31	Balance	✓	2487 00
				3249 00					3249 00
1967 Sept.	1	Balance	✓	2487 00					

Housekeeping Supplies ACCOUNT NO. 12

DATE		ITEMS	POST. REF.	DEBIT	DATE		ITEMS	POST. REF.	CREDIT
1967 Aug.	1	Balance	J1	550 00					
	28		C1	14 00 / 564 00					

Furniture and Fixtures ACCOUNT NO. 13

DATE		ITEMS	POST. REF.	DEBIT	DATE		ITEMS	POST. REF.	CREDIT
1967 Aug.	1	Balance 5557.00	J1	5600 00	1967 Aug.	14		C1	43 00
						31	Balance	✓	5557 00
				5600 00					5600 00
1967 Sept.	1	Balance	✓	5557 00					

Ledger of Hill-Top Motel closed, balanced, and ruled

Office Equipment — ACCOUNT NO. 14

DATE		ITEMS	POST. REF.	DEBIT	DATE		ITEMS	POST. REF.	CREDIT
1967 Aug.	1	Balance 465.00	J1	485 00	1967 Aug.	1		C1	20 00
						31	Balance	✓	465 00
				485 00					485 00
1967 Sept.	1	Balance	✓	465 00					

Apex Plumbing Company — ACCOUNT NO. 21

DATE		ITEMS	POST. REF.	DEBIT	DATE		ITEMS	POST. REF.	CREDIT
					1967 Aug.	1	Balance	J1	200 00

Motel Equipment Company — ACCOUNT NO. 22

DATE		ITEMS	POST. REF.	DEBIT	DATE		ITEMS	POST. REF.	CREDIT
1967 Aug.	1		C1	300 00	1967 Aug.	1	Balance 1000.00	J1	1 300 00
	31	Balance	✓	1 000 00					
				1 300 00					1 300 00
					1967 Sept.	1	Balance	✓	1 000 00

Charles Martin, Capital — ACCOUNT NO. 31

DATE		ITEMS	POST. REF.	DEBIT	DATE		ITEMS	POST. REF.	CREDIT
					1967 Aug.	1	Balance	J1	5 700 00
						1		C1	1 000 00 (6 700 00)
						31		J1	1 173 00 (7 873 00)

Income and Expense Summary — ACCOUNT NO. 32

DATE		ITEMS	POST. REF.	DEBIT	DATE		ITEMS	POST. REF.	CREDIT
1967 Aug.	31		J1	448 00	1967 Aug.	31		J1	1 621 00
	31		J1	1 173 00					
				1 621 00					1 621 00

Room Sales — ACCOUNT NO. 41

DATE		ITEMS	POST. REF.	DEBIT	DATE		ITEMS	POST. REF.	CREDIT
1967 Aug.	31		J1	1 621 00	1967 Aug.	31		C1	1 621 00

Ledger of Hill-Top Motel closed, balanced, and ruled (continued)

Advertising Expense — ACCOUNT NO. 51

DATE	ITEMS	POST. REF.	DEBIT	DATE	ITEMS	POST. REF.	CREDIT
1967 Aug. 4		C1	35 00	1967 Aug. 31		J1	35 00

Laundry Expense — ACCOUNT NO. 52

DATE	ITEMS	POST. REF.	DEBIT	DATE	ITEMS	POST. REF.	CREDIT
1967 Aug. 14		C1	44 50	1967 Aug. 31		J1	85 95
26		C1	41 45				
			85 95				
			85 95				85 95

Miscellaneous Expense — ACCOUNT NO. 53

DATE	ITEMS	POST. REF.	DEBIT	DATE	ITEMS	POST. REF.	CREDIT
1967 Aug. 7		C1	17 50	1967 Aug. 31		J1	17 50

Rent Expense — ACCOUNT NO. 54

DATE	ITEMS	POST. REF.	DEBIT	DATE	ITEMS	POST. REF.	CREDIT
1967 Aug. 2		C1	200 00	1967 Aug. 31		J1	200 00

Utilities Expense — ACCOUNT NO. 55

DATE	ITEMS	POST. REF.	DEBIT	DATE	ITEMS	POST. REF.	CREDIT
1967 Aug. 21		C1	61 15	1967 Aug. 31		J1	109 55
31		C1	48 40				
			109 55				
			109 55				109 55

Ledger of Hill-Top Motel closed, balanced, and ruled (concluded)

POST-CLOSING TRIAL BALANCE

After the closing entries have been posted and the accounts have been ruled and balanced, it is customary to take a trial balance to test the equality of debits and credits in the ledger. The trial balance taken after the closing entries have been posted and the accounts have been ruled and balanced is called a *post-closing trial balance*. The post-closing trial balance of the Hill-Top Motel appears on the next page.

No income or expense account appears on the post-closing trial balance because each of these accounts has been closed. The asset, liability, and proprietorship accounts that have balances are the only accounts appearing on a post-closing trial balance. The post-closing trial balance is used as a final means of checking to see that the ledger is in balance and ready for use in the new fiscal period.

Hill-Top Motel
Post-Closing Trial Balance
August 31, 1967

Account	No.	Debit	Credit
Cash	11	2487 00	
Housekeeping Supplies	12	564 00	
Furniture and Fixtures	13	5557 00	
Office Equipment	14	465 00	
Apex Plumbing Company	21		200 00
Motel Equipment Company	22		1000 00
Charles Martin, Capital	31		7873 00
		9073 00	9073 00

Post-closing trial balance of the Hill-Top Motel

SUMMARY OF THE STEPS IN THE BOOKKEEPING CYCLE

The complete series of activities involved in double-entry bookkeeping during a fiscal period is called the *bookkeeping cycle*. The flow chart below shows all the steps in the bookkeeping cycle.

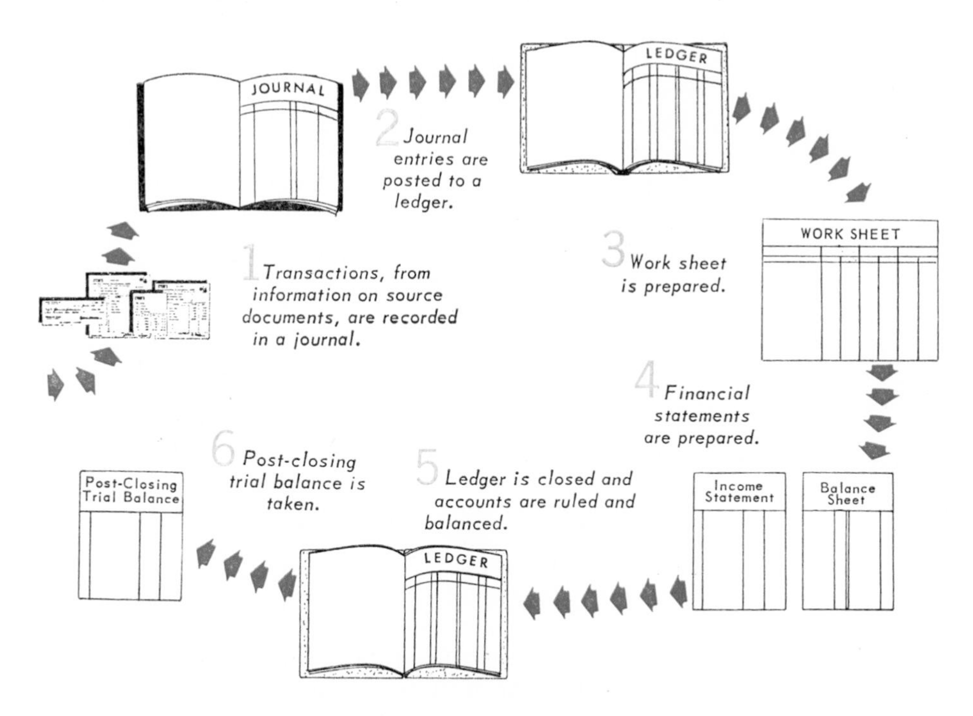

Flow chart of the steps in the bookkeeping cycle

Increasing Your Business Vocabulary

What is the meaning of each of the following:

a closing entry
b closed account
c closing the ledger
d combined entry
e balancing an account
f post-closing trial balance
g bookkeeping cycle

Study Questions

1. What must be done to get the income accounts and the expense accounts ready for the next fiscal period?
2. What account is used for the purpose of summarizing the income account and the expense accounts?
3. After the balances of the income accounts and the expense accounts are transferred, what items are shown (a) on the debit side of the income and expense summary account? (b) on the credit side of the income and expense summary account?
4. What are the three steps in the procedure of closing the ledger?
5. What two columns of the work sheet are used as a guide for preparing the closing entries in the general journal?
6. Why is it desirable to use a general journal entry to transfer an account balance in the ledger?
7. After the first two closing entries have been posted, what kinds of accounts in the ledger have been closed?
8. Why is the income and expense summary account in balance after Closing Entry No. 3 has been posted?
9. What kinds of accounts remain open in the ledger after the closing entries have been posted?
10. What are the three steps usually taken in balancing a balance sheet account?
11. What is the purpose of the post-closing trial balance?
12. What are the six steps for completing the bookkeeping cycle?

Cases for Business Decision

CASE 1

The Hartford Legal Service has the following account in the proprietorship division of its ledger:

Income and Expense Summary

Date	Debit	Date	Credit
1967		1967	
Dec. 31	2,100.00	Dec. 31	4,600.00
31	2,500.00		

a What does the amount on the credit side of the account represent?
b What does the first amount on the debit side represent?
c What does the second amount on the debit side represent?

CASE 2

John P. Knowles, florist, closes all his income and expense accounts directly into his capital account. He does not make use of the income and expense summary account. Why is his method of closing the ledger considered poor bookkeeping practice?

CASE 3

The post-closing trial balance of the Hill-Top Motel on page 155 shows Mr. Martin's capital to be $7,873.00. The trial balance of the Hill-Top Motel on page 110 shows Mr. Martin's capital to be $6,700.00. How do you account for this difference?

CASE 4

Mr. Catlin, owner of the Hi-View Motel, does not rule and balance his accounts at the end of each fiscal period as Mr. Martin does. What are the disadvantages of not ruling and balancing the ledger accounts?

Drills for Understanding

DRILL 11-A **Analyzing amounts that affect total proprietorship**

The following information is available for eight businesses:

Business	Balance in Capital Account at Start of Period	Additional Investment by Owner during Period	Net Income (+) or Net Loss (−) during Period	Balance in Capital Account after Ledger is Closed
1.	$10,000	None	+$ 6,450	*$16,450*
2.	45,000	None	− 4,211	?
3.	22,500	$2,000	+ 8,450	?
4.	18,400	None	?	$21,965
5.	?	None	− 7,500	21,500
6.	54,400	3,500	+ 12,450	?
7.	48,600	4,600	?	58,000
8.	24,880	None	+ 11,400	?

Instructions: On a separate sheet of paper, supply the missing amount for each of the businesses listed above. The answer to Business No. 1 is given as an example.

DRILL 11-B | Identification of accounts as open or closed

Instructions: 1. On the left side of a sheet of paper, write the heading *Account Titles.* Then copy the ledger account titles given below. Rule a one-inch wide column at the right of the list. Head this column *Answers.*

1. Arlington Company (creditor)
2. Automobile
3. Automobile Expense
4. Barker's Garage (creditor)
5. Cash
6. Fees Income
7. Furniture and Fixtures
8. Income and Expense Summary
9. Insurance Expense
10. Medical Equipment
11. Miscellaneous Expense
12. Office Equipment
13. Rent Expense
14. Richard Rowland, Capital
15. Upton Medical Company (creditor)
16. Utilities Expense

Instructions: 2. If the account is closed after the closing entries are posted, write capital C (for "Closed") in the Answers column. If the account remains open after all closing entries are posted, write capital O (for "Open"). The first item is given as an example.

Account Titles	Answers
1. *Arlington Company*	*O*

3. Now cover your answers and see how rapidly you can do this drill mentally without looking at your answers. Repeat this drill several times for increased speed and accuracy.

Application Problems

PROBLEM 11-1 | Recording closing entries in a general journal

Those parts of the work sheet for Britton's Hardware Store needed to record the closing entries for the month ended March 31 of the current year are shown at the top of the next page.

Instructions: Record in a two-column general journal the three closing entries required at the end of the fiscal period.

Self-checking: Compare your work with the model closing entries on page 149.

PROBLEM 11-2 | Recording closing entries in a general journal

Those parts of the work sheet of Hunter's Beauty Salon needed to record the closing entries for the month ended May 31 of the current year are shown at the bottom of the next page.

Instructions: Record in a two-column general journal the three closing entries required at the end of the fiscal period.

Self-checking: Compare your work with the model closing entries on page 149.

Britton's Hardware Store
Work Sheet
For Month Ended March 31, 19--

Account Titles	Acct. No.	Income Statement Debit		Income Statement Credit	
Walter Britton, Capital	31	......	...	......	...
Sales	41	......	...	1,350	50
Advertising Expense	51	16	50	......	...
Delivery Expense	52	23	45	......	...
Electricity Expense	53	8	90	......	...
Rent Expense	54	130	00	......	...
Salary Expense	55	375	00	......	...
Water Expense	56	3	95	......	...
		557	80	1,350	50
Net Income	......	792	70	......	...
		1,350	50	1,350	50

Partial work sheet for Problem 11-1

Hunter's Beauty Salon
Work Sheet
For Month Ended May 31, 19--

Account Titles	Acct. No.	Income Statement Debit		Income Statement Credit	
Gladys Hunter, Capital	31	......	...	......	...
Sales Income	41	......	...	661	75
Advertising Expense	51	85	00	......	...
Electricity Expense	52	32	40	......	...
Miscellaneous Expense	53	78	70	......	...
Rent Expense	54	150	00	......	...
Salary Expense	55	320	00	......	...
Telephone Expense	56	16	90	......	...
Water Expense	57	14	00	......	...
		697	00	661	75
Net Loss	......			35	25
		697	00	697	00

Partial work sheet for Problem 11-2

Compare the expense account numbers on Hunter's work sheet with those on Britton's work sheet. Note that each business has its own set of account numbers and that they vary from business to business.

PROBLEM 11-3 | Closing the ledger

If you are not using the workbook correlating with this textbook, complete Appendix Problem 11-A instead of this problem.

Instructions: 1. Foot the ledger accounts of George Tilden provided for this problem in the workbook. If an account has entries on both sides, write the balance in small pencil figures in the proper Items column.

2. Prove cash. The checkbook balance on November 30, 19--, is $1,597.80. This amount should agree with the balance in the cash account in the ledger. All cash receipts have been deposited.

3. Prepare a work sheet on six-column analysis paper for the monthly fiscal period ended November 30.

4. Prepare an income statement.

5. Prepare a balance sheet.

6. Record the closing entries on page 2 of a general journal.

7. Post the closing entries.

8. Rule the income and expense summary account, the income account, and the expense accounts.

9. Balance all asset, liability, and proprietorship accounts that need to be balanced.

10. Prepare a post-closing trial balance.

Self-checking: 1. Were the footings written in your ledger in small figures with a sharp, firm pencil?

2. Was each amount column of an account footed when, and only when, it contained two or more entries?

3. Is your work sheet similar to the model on page 122?

4. Is your income statement similar to the model on page 132?

5. Is your balance sheet similar to the model on page 135?

6. Are your closing entries similar to the model on page 149?

7. After you have closed, ruled, and balanced your ledger, is it similar to the model ledger on pages 152 to 154?

8. Is your post-closing trial balance similar to the model on page 155?

PROJECT 2 THE COMPLETE BOOKKEEPING CYCLE

Bookkeeping work to be completed in Project 2

This project provides an opportunity for you to perform all the steps found in a complete bookkeeping cycle: (1) journalizing; (2) posting; (3) preparing a work sheet; (4) preparing financial statements; (5) closing the ledger, and (6) preparing a post-closing trial balance.

Center Theater

The Center Theater is a motion picture theater owned and operated by Paul Greer. It is open on Friday and Saturday evenings and on most holidays. In the operation of his bookkeeping system, Mr. Greer uses the following chart of accounts:

Center Theater
Chart of Accounts

(1) Assets	Acct. No.	(4) Income	Acct. No.
Cash.................	11	Admissions Income....	41
Air Conditioning Equipment..........	12	(5) Expenses	
Projection Equipment.	13	Advertising Expense..	51
Sound Equipment......	14	Film Rental Expense..	52
		Fuel Expense.........	53
(2) Liabilities		Maintenance Expense..	54
Film Distributors, Inc................	21	Projection Expense...	55
		Rent Expense.........	56
Metro Sound Service..	22	Utilities Expense....	57
(3) Proprietorship			
Paul Greer, Capital..	31		
Income and Expense Summary............	32		

Opening accounts in the ledger

Instructions: 1. Open accounts in the ledger in the order in which they are listed in the chart of accounts. Allow five lines for each account. Number the accounts with the account numbers given in the chart of accounts.

2. Copy the following balances in your ledger, using the date May 1 of the current year. As you copy these balances, write the word "Balance" in the Items column of each account and place a check mark (√) in the Post. Ref. column.

	Debit Balance	*Credit Balance*
Cash	1,560.00	
Air Conditioning Equipment	3,575.00	
Projection Equipment	9,070.00	
Sound Equipment	1,385.00	
Film Distributors, Inc.		200.00
Metro Sound Service		390.00
Paul Greer, Capital		15,000.00

Using a seven-column cash journal

A businessman may have as many amount columns in his journal as he desires. Amount columns should be added in the journal only when they will bring about a saving in time and effort in posting. The best test as to whether or not a special amount column should be provided in a journal is the number of times that the column will be used.

The Center Theater uses a cash journal with seven amount columns as illustrated below.

CASH JOURNAL — PAGE 4

	1 Cash Debit	2 Advertising Expense Debit	3 Film Rental Expense Debit	4 General Debit	Date	Account Title	Ck. No.	Post. Ref.	5 General Credit	6 Admissions Income Credit	7 Cash Credit	
1	312 50				1967 Apr. 1	✓		✓		312 50		1
2				300 00	3	Rent Expense	86	56			300 00	2
3			120 00		3	✓	87	✓			120 00	3
4		15 00			4	✓	88	✓			15 00	4
22				12 20	29	Maintenance Expense	97	54			12 20	22
23	163 50				29	✓		✓		163 50		23
24	1481 70	98 00	465 00	365 75	30	Totals			36 85	1371 80	1002 60	24
25	(11)	(51)	(52)	(✓)					(✓)	(41)	(11)	25
26												26
27												27
28												28
29												29
30												30
31												31
32												32
33												33
34												34
35												35

Analyzing the seven-column cash journal of the Center Theater

The cash journal of the Center Theater differs from the one used in Project 1 in the following respects:

Advertising Expense Debit. Advertising expenses occur often. Each payment for an advertising expense is recorded in the Advertising Expense Debit column and in the Cash Credit column.

Film Rental Expense Debit. Payments for film rentals are made frequently each month; thus, a special column is provided for Film Rental Expense. Each payment for film rental is recorded as a debit in the Film Rental Expense column and as a credit in the Cash Credit column.

Check No. column. The Check No. column replaces the No. column used in Project 1. The Center Theater receives its income from admissions and does not issue receipts. The Check No. column is used only to record the number of each check written.

Admissions Income Credit. The Center Theater receives its income from the sale of tickets. Each day's total receipts are recorded in the Cash Debit column and in the Admissions Income Credit column.

Journalizing transactions in a seven-column cash journal

Instructions: 3. Record the following transactions on page 5 of a seven-column cash journal similar to the one illustrated on page 162. Number all checks, beginning with No. 98. (Note the instructions given in the workbook for carrying forward the totals of a completed journal page.)

May 1. Paid $110.00 for film rental.
1. Paid $300.00 for rent for May.
4. Paid $80.00 to Metro Sound Service on account.
5. Received $160.50 from admissions.
6. Received $211.00 from admissions.
8. Paid $33.00 for advertising.
11. Paid $100.00 to Film Distributors, Inc., on account.
12. Received $188.00 from admissions.
13. Paid $140.00 for film rental.
13. Received $234.50 from admissions.
15. Paid $43.00 for fuel.
16. Received $23.00 from sale of old sound equipment.
17. Paid $16.00 for repairs to seats. (Maintenance Expense)
18. Paid $6.90 for repairs to projector. (Projection Expense)
18. Paid $28.00 for advertising.
19. Received $168.00 from admissions.
20. Received $188.00 from admissions.
22. Paid $90.00 for film rental.
23. Paid $100.00 to Film Distributors, Inc., on account.
24. Paid $56.00 for new projection equipment.
25. Received $18.00 from sale of old sound equipment.
26. Paid $33.00 for advertising.
26. Received $143.50 from admissions.
27. Received $158.50 from admissions.
29. Paid $85.00 for film rental.
29. Paid $28.00 for advertising.
29. Paid $14.50 for repair of carpet. (Maintenance Expense)

May 30. Received $225.00 from admissions.
31. Paid $58.60 for electricity. (Utilities Expense)
31. Received $24.00 from sale of old projection equipment.
31. Paid $13.30 for water. (Utilities Expense)

Footing, proving, and ruling the cash journal

Instructions: 4. Foot all columns of the cash journal.

5. Prove the equality of debits and credits in the cash journal.

6. Prove cash. The checkbook balance is $1,966.70. All cash receipts have been deposited.

7. Total and rule the cash journal. (See model on page 162.)

Posting to ledger accounts

8. Post each amount in the General Debit column and in the General Credit column. Place a check mark in the posting reference column opposite each amount entered in a special column. Place a check mark in parentheses under the total of each General column to show that the total is not to be posted.

9. Post the total of each of the five special columns in the cash journal. Write the proper account number in parentheses under each total.

Preparing a work sheet

10. Foot the accounts in the ledger that have more than one entry on either side. If an account has entries on both sides, write the balance in small pencil figures in the Items column.

11. Prepare a trial balance on six-column analysis paper, using the first two amount columns for the trial balance.

12. Complete the work sheet. (See model on page 122.)

Preparing financial statements

13. Prepare the income statement. (See model on page 132.)

14. Prepare the balance sheet. (See model on page 135.)

Closing the ledger

15. Record the closing entries on page 3 of a two-column general journal. (Use as your guide the illustration of closing entries on page 149.)

16. Post the closing entries.

17. Rule the income and expense summary account, the income account, and the expense accounts. (Use as your guide the model accounts on pages 153 and 154.)

18. Balance and rule all asset, liability, and proprietorship accounts that need to be balanced. (Use as your guide the model accounts on pages 152 and 153.)

Preparing a post-closing trial balance

19. Prepare a post-closing trial balance. (See model on page 155.)

A SERVICE BUSINESS SELLS SERVICE

Real estate agencies, insurance agencies, motels, physicians, and theaters sell services.

A MERCHANDISING BUSINESS SELLS GOODS

Grocery stores, hardwares, furniture stores, book stores, and department stores sell goods.

A business that buys and sells goods often finds that it can save time by using more than one journal and more than one ledger. In Part 2 of this textbook we shall learn:

1. How a merchandising business accounts for merchandise it buys and sells by using the following journals:

   Purchases Journal
   Cash Payments Journal
   Sales Journal
   Cash Receipts Journal
   General Journal

2. How a merchandising business accounts for merchandise it buys and sells by using the following ledgers:

   General Ledger
   Accounts Payable Ledger
   Accounts Receivable Ledger

McCANN OFFICE FURNITURE

CHART OF ACCOUNTS

Classification	*Account Number*	*Account Title*
		Balance Sheet Accounts
(1) Assets	11	Cash
	12	Accounts Receivable
	13	Merchandise Inventory
	14	Supplies
	15	Prepaid Insurance
(2) Liabilities	21	Accounts Payable
(3) Proprietorship	31	John McCann, Capital
	32	John McCann, Drawing
	33	Income and Expense Summary
		Income Statement Accounts
(4) Income	41	Sales
(5) Cost of Merchandise	51	Purchases
(6) Expenses	61	Delivery Expense
	62	Insurance Expense
	63	Miscellaneous Expense
	64	Rent Expense
	65	Salary Expense
	66	Supplies Expense

The chart of accounts for McCann Office Furniture is illustrated above for ready reference in your study of Part 2 of this book.

CHAPTER 12 RECORDING THE BUYING OF MERCHANDISE ON ACCOUNT

Mr. John McCann owns and operates a retail store known as McCann Office Furniture. The store carries in stock for resale such items as office supplies and furniture. A firm that buys and sells goods is called a *merchandising business.* Goods that a merchandising business buys for resale are known as *merchandise.*

The purchase order

A business form prepared by a buyer on which is described the merchandise he desires to buy is called a *purchase order.* McCann Office Furniture prepares all purchase orders in duplicate. The original copy is sent to the firm from which the merchandise is to be purchased. The carbon copy of the purchase order is kept for the records of McCann Office Furniture.

The invoice

When McCann Office Furniture buys merchandise, the store receives from the supplier a form describing the goods shipped and giving the cost of the items. A business form furnished to the purchaser by the seller on which are listed the goods sold, the method of shipment, and the cost of the items is called an *invoice.*

An invoice received by McCann Office Furniture for a purchase of merchandise from the Dunham Manufacturing Company is shown on the next page.

Invoices often differ in appearance from one business to another. Each business firm uses an invoice form that is best suited to its purposes. However, a complete invoice for any business should contain the following information:

1. Name and address of the seller.
2. Name and address of the buyer.
3. Date of the invoice.
4. Method of shipment.
5. Seller's invoice number.
6. Buyer's purchase order number.
7. Terms of the sale.
8. Quantity, description, and unit price of the items shipped.
9. Total amount for each item and the total amount of the invoice.

RECD NOV 6 1967

TO McCann Office Furniture
640 Central Avenue
Portland, Oregon 97227

DUNHAM MANUFACTURING COMPANY
P.O. Box 78
Salem, Oregon 97301

DATE November 3, 1967 SALESMAN Bonner SHIPPED VIA Lyons Truck Company

OUR NO. 3318 CUST. ORDER NO. 2060 TERMS Net 30 days

QUANTITY	CAT. NO.	DESCRIPTION	PRICE	TOTAL
3 ✓	106L	4-drawer, letter-size file	55.00	165.00 ✓
4 ✓	108L	4-drawer, letter-size file	52.00	208.00 ✓
6 ✓	3306L	4-drawer, visible-card file	18.00	108.00 ✓
10 ✓	22	3-tier, desk-top file, walnut	5.30	53.00 ✓
2 doz. ✓	33	Folder guides, metal tab	3.00 doz.	6.00 ✓
		Total		540.00 ✓ RCL

Invoice

When an invoice is received by McCann Office Furniture, it is stamped with the current date. The invoice shown above has been stamped in the left-hand corner with the date, *Nov. 6, 1967.*

It is important for the buyer to know that he has received the items he ordered and that they are priced correctly. The check marks on the invoice above indicate that the invoice has been checked and is correct. The person who checked the invoice wrote his initials, *RCL*, near the total.

JOURNALIZING PURCHASES ON ACCOUNT

Most of the merchandise bought by McCann Office Furniture is paid for at a later date. A transaction in which merchandise is bought with an agreement that it is to be paid for at a later date is called a *purchase on account.*

Sometimes a business pays cash at the time the merchandise is purchased. The journalizing of cash purchases will be described in Chapter 13.

The purchases journal

When a business makes many purchases of merchandise on account, time is saved in journalizing and posting by recording all the invoices in a separate journal. A special journal for recording purchases of merchandise on account is called a *purchases journal.*

The purchases journal used by McCann Office Furniture is shown below. Each page of the purchases journal provides columns in which all the information needed about a transaction can be summarized on a single line. Detailed information of any kind is called *data.* The data for recording a purchase-on-account transaction are obtained from the invoice received from the seller.

Purchase-on-account transaction No. 1

November 6, 1967. Purchased merchandise on account from the Dunham Manufacturing Company, $540.00.

After each invoice for a purchase on account has been verified, the data are summarized on a single line in the purchases journal. The source document for this purchase-on-account transaction is the invoice shown on page 168. The steps in journalizing this transaction in the purchases journal are:

Step 1

Write the date the invoice was received, *1967, Nov. 6,* in the Date column. This is the date stamped on the invoice when it was received.

Step 2

Write the name of the business firm from which the purchase was made, *Dunham Manufacturing Company,* in the Account Credited column.

Step 3

Write the amount of the invoice, *$540.00,* in the amount column.

Step 4

Place a check mark on the invoice at the right of the seller's name to show that the invoice has been recorded.

PURCHASES JOURNAL PAGE 10

	DATE		ACCOUNT CREDITED	POST. REF.	PURCHASES, DR. ACCTS. PAY., CR.	
1	1967 Nov.	6	Dunham Manufacturing Company		540 00	1
2						2
3						3
4						4
5						5
6						6
7						7

STEP 1 STEP 2 STEP 3

Journalizing purchase-on-account transaction No. 1

In the purchases journal all that is needed to describe the source document is the date the invoice was received, the name of the creditor, and the amount of the invoice. Any additional data can be obtained from the invoice in the file.

All the invoices received during the month are recorded in the purchases journal in the manner described for purchase-on-account transaction No. 1. The purchases journal of McCann Office Furniture for November, showing all entries for the invoices received, is given below.

PURCHASES JOURNAL — PAGE 10

	DATE		ACCOUNT CREDITED	POST. REF.	PURCHASES, DR. ACCTS. PAY., CR.	
1	1967 Nov.	6	Dunham Manufacturing Company		540 00	1
2		9	Swartz Supply Company		120 00	2
3		10	Alfred Boyd & Sons		470 00	3
4		14	Filing Systems, Inc.		430 00	4
5		17	Swartz Supply Company		96 00	5
6		21	Willis Paper Suppliers		646 00	6
7		24	Filing Systems, Inc.		480 00	7
8		27	Martin Equipment, Inc.		397 00	8
9		30	Alden Typewriter Company		81 00	9

Purchases journal with all purchases on account recorded for the month

Totaling and ruling the purchases journal

After all the invoices for purchases on account have been recorded during the month, a single line is drawn across the amount column under the last amount. Next, the amount column is totaled immediately below the single line. The date of the last day of the month is written in the Date column, and the word *Total* is written in the Account Credited column. Double lines are then ruled across the amount column. The totaling and ruling of the purchases journal is shown below.

PURCHASES JOURNAL — PAGE 10

	DATE		ACCOUNT CREDITED	POST. REF.	PURCHASES, DR. ACCTS. PAY., CR.	
1	1967 Nov.	6	Dunham Manufacturing Company		540 00	1
9		30	Alden Typewriter Company		81 00	9
10		30	Total		3260 00	10
11						11

Purchases journal, totaled and ruled

Analyzing the total of the purchases journal

In a merchandising business the cost of merchandise sold, along with the total operating expenses, is deducted from the total income to determine the net income. Part of the data needed to determine the cost of merchandise sold is the total purchases. The account provided in the ledger to record the cost of all the merchandise purchased is called *Purchases.*

A ledger that contains all the accounts needed to prepare the income statement and the balance sheet is called a *general ledger*. In a merchandising business a separate division of the general ledger is provided for accounts that represent the cost of goods. This division of the general ledger is called *Cost of Merchandise*, as shown in the chart of accounts on page 166.

Purchases	51
3,260.00	

The total of the amount column of the purchases journal is the total purchases on account for the month. This total is an increase in the balance of the account Purchases. Since the balance side of the purchases account is the debit side, the purchases account in the general ledger of McCann Office Furniture is debited for the total purchases, $3,260.00, as shown above at the right.

When a business purchases on account from many business firms, the general ledger might contain a great many accounts with creditors. In order to avoid a bulky general ledger, it is customary to summarize the total amount owed all creditors in a single general ledger account. The account in the general ledger used to summarize all amounts owed to creditors is called *Accounts Payable.* This account is classified as a liability, as shown in the chart of accounts on page 166.

Accounts Payable	21
	3,260.00

The total of the purchases journal shows the total amount owed to creditors for the purchase of merchandise on account. The total of the amount column of the purchases journal is an increase in the balance of the accounts payable account. The liability, Accounts Payable, has a credit balance. Increases are recorded on the balance side, which is the credit side. Therefore, the accounts payable account in the general ledger of McCann Office Furniture is credited for the total purchases, $3,260.00, as shown above at the right.

POSTING THE TOTAL OF THE PURCHASES JOURNAL

The illustrations below show the Total line of the purchases journal and the two accounts in the general ledger, Accounts Payable and Purchases. The two accounts are shown as they appear after the total of the amount column in the purchases journal has been posted.

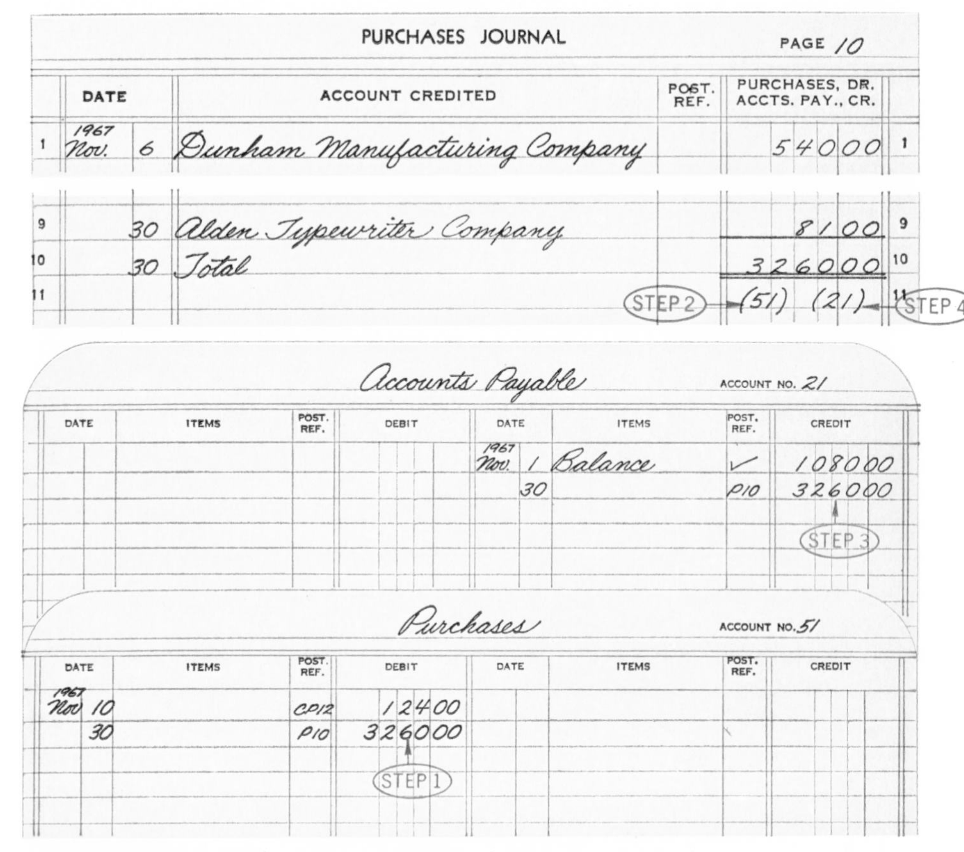

PURCHASES JOURNAL — PAGE 10

	DATE		ACCOUNT CREDITED	POST. REF.	PURCHASES, DR. ACCTS. PAY., CR.	
1	1967 Nov.	6	Dunham Manufacturing Company		540 00	1
9		30	Alden Typewriter Company		81 00	9
10		30	Total		3260 00	10
11					(51) (21)	11

Accounts Payable — ACCOUNT NO. 21

DATE		ITEMS	POST. REF.	DEBIT	DATE		ITEMS	POST. REF.	CREDIT
					1967 Nov.	1	Balance	✓	1080 00
						30		P10	3260 00

Purchases — ACCOUNT NO. 51

DATE		ITEMS	POST. REF.	DEBIT	DATE		ITEMS	POST. REF.	CREDIT
1967 Nov.	10		CP12	124 00					
	30		P10	3260 00					

The heading of the amount column in the purchases journal shows that the total purchases is debited to Purchases and credited to Accounts Payable. The steps in posting the total of the amount column in the purchases journal to the two accounts in the general ledger are:

Step 1

Post the amount, *$3,260.00*, to the debit side of the purchases account. Write the date, *30*, in the Date column. Write the page number of the purchases journal, *P10*, in the Post. Ref. column of the account.

> *P* is the abbreviation for Purchases Journal. The previous debit of $124.00 on November 10 to the purchases account is explained in Chapter 13.

Step 2

Write the number of the purchases account in parentheses, *(51)*, below the double lines under the total of the amount column in the purchases journal.

Step 3

Post the amount, *$3,260.00*, to the credit side of the accounts payable account. Write the date, *30*, in the Date column. Write the page number of the purchases journal, *P10*, in the Post. Ref. column of the account.

Step 4

Write the number of the accounts payable account in parentheses, *(21)*, below the double lines under the total of the amount column in the purchases journal.

> Writing the numbers of the two general ledger accounts in parentheses below the total of the amount column in the purchases journal shows that the posting of the total has been completed.

The posting of the one total of the purchases journal as a *debit* to Purchases and a *credit* to Accounts Payable maintains an equality of debits and credits in the general ledger. Maintaining an equality of debits and credits in the general ledger at all times is a very important principle of double-entry bookkeeping.

ACCOUNTS PAYABLE LEDGER

The accounts payable account in the general ledger shows the total amount owed to all creditors, but it does not show the amount owed each creditor. Therefore, it is common practice to have a separate ledger in which an account is kept for each creditor. A ledger that contains accounts with creditors only is called an *accounts payable ledger*.

When an accounts payable ledger is used, the sum of the balances of all the accounts with creditors is the same as the balance of the accounts payable account in the general ledger. Each time the accounts payable account in the general ledger is increased, a creditor's account in the accounts payable ledger must also be increased by the same amount. Each time the accounts payable account in the general ledger is decreased, a creditor's account in the accounts payable ledger must also be decreased by the same amount.

> When an accounts payable account is used in the general ledger to summarize the total amount owed to creditors, only the one account, Accounts Payable, needs to be listed on the trial balance and on the balance sheet.

The controlling account for the accounts payable ledger

A ledger that is summarized in a single account in the general ledger is called a *subsidiary ledger.* An account in the general ledger that summarizes all the account balances in a subsidiary ledger is called a *controlling account.* The accounts payable account in the general ledger is the controlling account for the accounts payable ledger. The relationship between the accounts payable ledger and the accounts payable account in the general ledger is shown in the illustration below.

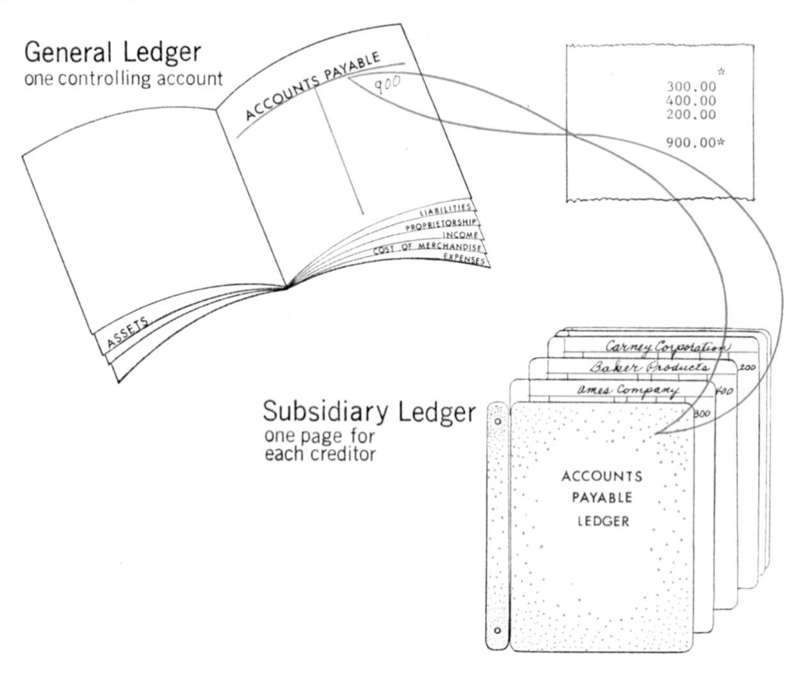

The balances of the individual accounts in the accounts payable ledger (a subsidiary ledger) are brought together and summarized in Accounts Payable (a controlling account in the general ledger).

Accounts payable ledger form

McCann Office Furniture keeps all accounts with creditors in an accounts payable ledger. The accounts in this ledger have balance-column ruling as shown below.

NAME

ADDRESS

DATE	ITEMS	POST. REF.	DEBIT	CREDIT	CREDIT BALANCE

Accounts payable ledger form with balance-column ruling

Each account in the accounts payable ledger is opened by writing the name and the address of the creditor on the first two lines of the account page. The name and address of each new creditor are obtained from the invoice. The Debit column is used to record all debit amounts. The Credit column is used to record all credit amounts. The Credit Balance column is used to record the balance of the creditor's account. The Credit Balance column readily shows the amount owed each creditor.

POSTING FROM THE PURCHASES JOURNAL TO THE ACCOUNTS PAYABLE LEDGER

Each entry in the purchases journal is an amount owed to a creditor named in the Account Credited column. Therefore, each entry in the purchases journal is posted as a credit to the account named.

In order to keep all accounts with creditors up-to-date, individual entries in the purchases journal are posted frequently during the month. The total is posted only at the end of the month.

Posting to a creditor's account having a zero balance

The illustration below shows the purchases journal and the account for Dunham Manufacturing Company in the accounts payable ledger after the entry on Line 1 of the purchases journal has been posted.

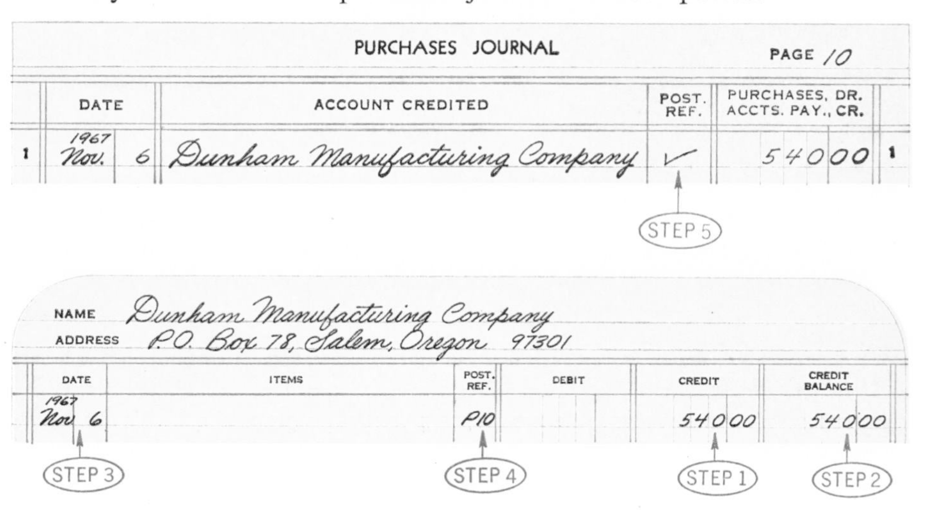

PURCHASES JOURNAL PAGE 10

	DATE		ACCOUNT CREDITED	POST. REF.	PURCHASES, DR. ACCTS. PAY., CR.	
	1967					
1	Nov.	6	Dunham Manufacturing Company	✓	540 00	1

NAME Dunham Manufacturing Company
ADDRESS P.O. Box 78, Salem, Oregon 97301

DATE		ITEMS	POST. REF.	DEBIT	CREDIT	CREDIT BALANCE
1967						
Nov	6		P10		540 00	540 00

The steps in posting the entry on Line 1 of the purchases journal are:

Step 1

Write the amount, *$540.00*, in the Credit column of the account for Dunham Manufacturing Company.

Step 2

Add the amount in the Credit column to the amount of the previous balance shown in the Credit Balance column, and write the new balance, *$540.00*, in the Credit Balance column.

Before this entry was posted, the Dunham Manufacturing Company account had a zero balance. Therefore, the amount written in the Credit Balance column is the new balance, *$540.00*.

Step 3

Write the year, month, and day, *1967, Nov. 6*, in the Date column.

Step 4

Write the page number of the purchases journal, *P10*, in the Post. Ref. column of the account.

Step 5

Place a check mark in the Post. Ref. column of the purchases journal to show that the posting of the item on the first line of the journal has been completed.

Accounts with creditors are placed in alphabetic order in the accounts payable ledger. When records are kept by hand, usually the accounts are not given account numbers. Thus, a check mark is used instead of an account number to show that the posting has been completed.

Recording a creditor's balance on a new page in the accounts payable ledger

On November 1, 1967, McCann Office Furniture prepared a new page in the accounts payable ledger for Swartz Supply Company. At that time the account balance was $80.00. This amount is recorded on the new page as shown below.

NAME *Swartz Supply Company*
ADDRESS *120 South Turner Avenue, Portland, Oregon 97203*

DATE		ITEMS	POST. REF.	DEBIT	CREDIT	CREDIT BALANCE
1967 Nov.	*1*	*Balance*	✓			*80 00*

The name and address of the creditor are written on the lines provided at the top of the account page. The account balance is written in the Credit Balance column. The date is recorded in the Date column, and the word *Balance* is written in the Items column. A check mark is placed in the Post. Ref. column to show that this entry was not posted from a journal. The same procedure is followed in opening a new page for any account that has a balance.

Posting to a creditor's account having a previous balance

The illustration below shows the purchases journal and the account for Swartz Supply Company after the entry on Line 2 of the purchases journal is posted.

PURCHASES JOURNAL — PAGE 10

	DATE		ACCOUNT CREDITED	POST. REF.	PURCHASES, DR. ACCTS. PAY., CR.	
1	1967 Nov.	6	Dunham Manufacturing Company	✓	540 00	1
2		9	Swartz Supply Company	✓	120 00	2

NAME Swartz Supply Company
ADDRESS 120 South Turner Avenue, Portland, Oregon 97203

DATE		ITEMS	POST. REF.	DEBIT	CREDIT	CREDIT BALANCE
1967 Nov.	1	Balance	✓			80 00
	9		P10		120 00	200 00

The same steps are followed in posting the entry on Line 2 of the purchases journal as are used for posting the entry on Line 1. In Step 2, however, the amount in the Credit column, $120.00, is added to the previous balance, $80.00, and the new balance, *$200.00*, is written in the Credit Balance column.

THE COMPLETED PURCHASES JOURNAL

The purchases journal of McCann Office Furniture for November, 1967, after all the posting has been completed, is shown below.

PURCHASES JOURNAL — PAGE 10

	DATE		ACCOUNT CREDITED	POST. REF.	PURCHASES, DR. ACCTS. PAY., CR.	
1	1967 Nov.	6	Dunham Manufacturing Company	✓	540 00	1
2		9	Swartz Supply Company	✓	120 00	2
3		10	Alfred Boyd & Sons	✓	470 00	3
4		14	Filing Systems, Inc.	✓	430 00	4
5		17	Swartz Supply Company	✓	96 00	5
6		21	Willis Paper Suppliers	✓	646 00	6
7		24	Filing Systems, Inc.	✓	480 00	7
8		27	Martin Equipment, Inc.	✓	397 00	8
9		30	Alden Typewriter Company	✓	81 00	9
10		30	Total		3,260 00	10
11					(51) (21)	11

Purchases journal after all posting has been completed

A FLOW CHART OF RECORDING THE BUYING OF MERCHANDISE ON ACCOUNT

A summary of the procedure followed in recording the buying of merchandise on account is shown below in chart form.

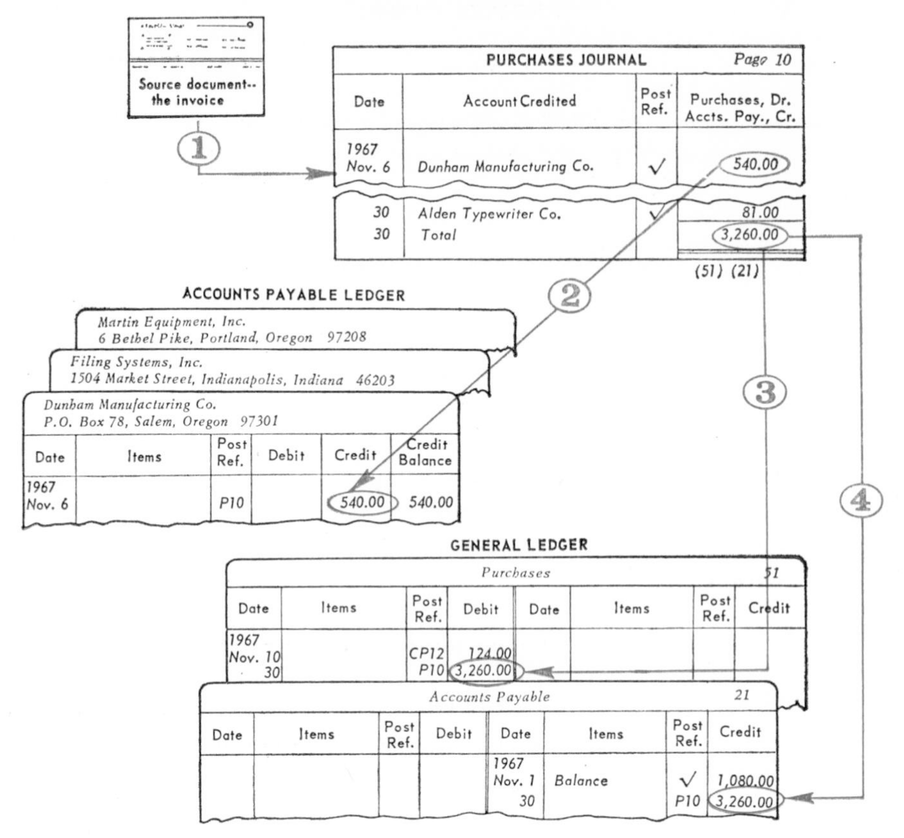

A flow chart of recording the buying of merchandise on account

This procedure may be summarized as follows:

1. After the invoice has been verified, it is recorded in the purchases journal.
2. Each item in the amount column of the purchases journal is posted as a credit to the individual creditor's account in the accounts payable ledger. This posting is done frequently during the month.
3. The total of the amount column in the purchases journal is posted as a debit to the purchases account in the general ledger. This is done at the end of the month.
4. The total of the amount column in the purchases journal is also posted as a credit to the accounts payable account in the general ledger. This is done at the end of the month.

ANOTHER METHOD OF RECORDING PURCHASES ON ACCOUNT— USING INVOICES AS A PURCHASES JOURNAL

Some businesses file all their invoices together and use the file of invoices as a purchases journal. These businesses post directly from the invoices to the creditors' accounts in the accounts payable ledger.

When invoices are used as a purchases journal, the steps are:

Step 1

Verify the accuracy of each invoice.

Step 2

Post the total of each invoice directly to the proper creditor's account in the accounts payable ledger.

Step 3

Place a check mark at the right of the creditor's name on the invoice to show that it has been posted.

Step 4

File all invoices received during the month in a special file for the current month's purchases only.

Step 5

At the end of the month, add the totals of all invoices in the special file to obtain the total amount of merchandise purchased on account during the month. The invoices in the illustration below have been totaled on an adding machine.

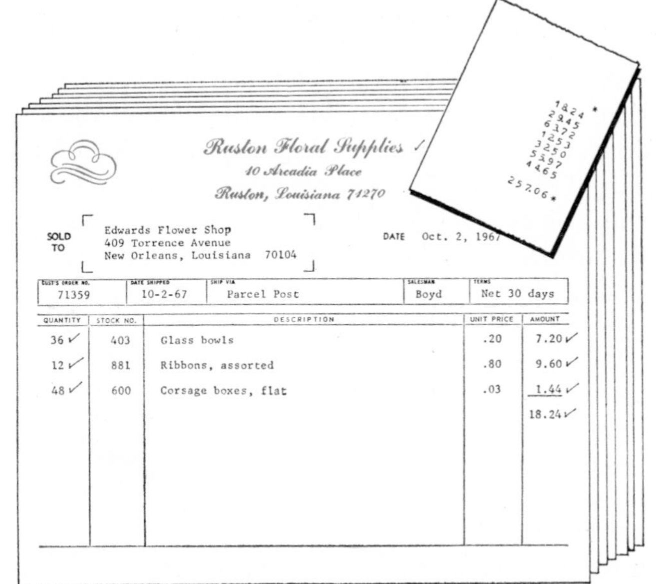

Ruston Floral Supplies ✓
10 Arcadia Place
Ruston, Louisiana 71270

SOLD TO: Edwards Flower Shop
409 Torrence Avenue
New Orleans, Louisiana 70104

DATE Oct. 2, 1967

CUST'S ORDER NO.	DATE SHIPPED	SHIP VIA	SALESMAN	TERMS
71359	10-2-67	Parcel Post	Boyd	Net 30 days

QUANTITY	STOCK NO.	DESCRIPTION	UNIT PRICE	AMOUNT
36 ✓	403	Glass bowls	.20	7.20 ✓
12 ✓	881	Ribbons, assorted	.80	9.60 ✓
48 ✓	600	Corsage boxes, flat	.03	1.44 ✓
				18.24 ✓

Invoices with an adding machine tape showing the total purchases for the month

Step 6

Record in the general journal the total of all invoices for purchases on account received during the month. Debit Purchases and credit Accounts Payable for the same amount, $257.06, as shown below.

GENERAL JOURNAL — PAGE 15

	DATE		ACCOUNT TITLE	POST. REF.	DEBIT	CREDIT	
1	1967 Oct.	31	Purchases		257 06		1
2			Accounts Payable			257 06	2
3			Invoices for October purchases				3
4			on account.				4
5							5
6							6
7							7
8							8
9							9
10							10
11							11
12							12
13							13
14							14

Step 7

Post the journal entry to the general ledger accounts, Purchases and Accounts Payable.

TRANSPORTATION CHARGES ON MERCHANDISE PURCHASED

As a convenience to the customer, the seller often pays the transportation charges on merchandise at the time of the shipment. When this is done, the transportation charges are included on the invoice and become part of the total of the invoice. If the seller pays the transportation charges and includes them on the invoice, the buyer debits the entire amount of the invoice, including the transportation charges, to the purchases account. Transportation charges on incoming shipments are a part of the total cost of merchandise purchased.

In other instances, the transportation charges on merchandise purchased are paid by the buyer directly to the transportation company. When the buyer pays the transportation agency, he debits the purchases account for the amount of the transportation charges. Some businesses prefer to record the transportation charges in a separate account with a title such as *Transportation on Purchases* or *Freight In.* When either of these accounts is used, it is classified as a Cost of Merchandise account.

Increasing Your Business Vocabulary

What is the meaning of each of the following:

a merchandising business
b merchandise
c purchase order
d invoice
e purchase on account
f purchases journal
g data
h general ledger
i accounts payable ledger
j subsidiary ledger
k controlling account

Study Questions

1. What information should a complete invoice contain?
2. What are the columnar headings of the purchases journal used by McCann Office Furniture?
3. What are the steps in recording a purchase-on-account transaction in the purchases journal?
4. Why is no explanation written in the purchases journal for each entry?
5. Why is the total of the amount column of the purchases journal recorded as a debit to the purchases account in the general ledger?
6. Why is the total of the amount column of the purchases journal recorded as a credit to the accounts payable account in the general ledger?
7. Why is it common practice to have a separate ledger in which an account is kept for each creditor?
8. What are the steps in posting from the purchases journal to a creditor's account that has a previous balance?
9. Why are the individual entries in the purchases journal posted frequently during the month?
10. When a business uses its invoices as a purchases journal, what entry is made in the general journal at the end of the month?

Cases for Business Decision

CASE 1

Mr. Holt has five creditors from whom he makes all of his purchases on account. Mr. Morton purchases from 15 creditors. Both Mr. Holt and Mr. Morton keep all accounts with creditors in a general ledger. If you were the bookkeeper for Mr. Morton, what recommendations might you offer to improve his bookkeeping system?

CASE 2

The total of the purchases journal of Ayres Animal Hospital is $76.00. At the end of the month, the accounts payable account in the general ledger does not agree with the sum of the balances of all creditors' accounts in the accounts payable ledger. The total of the balances of the creditors' accounts is $76.00 more than the balance of the accounts payable account. What is the probable cause of the difference?

Drill for Understanding

DRILL 12-A | Using an accounts payable ledger

This drill is planned to give you practice in opening accounts with creditors and posting entries to accounts in an accounts payable ledger with balance-column ruling.

Instructions: 1. Open an account for each of the nine creditors listed below in the column at the left. Use a balance-column account form similar to the one on page 174. Allow four lines for each account. Arrange the accounts in alphabetical order.

2. Post each entry shown below in the column at the right as you would if you were posting from a purchases journal. All of these transactions were journalized on page 7 of the purchases journal; therefore, record P7 in the Post. Ref. column of the account for each entry.

Accounts to Be Opened

R. B. Fox, 2063 Main St.
Sherman, Texas 75090

J. M. Miller, 4379 Hoyt Avenue
Lafayette, Louisiana 70501

L. W. Polk, 1324 Riverside Avenue
Port Arthur, Texas 77640

Albert Beck, 100 N. Beckett Drive
New Orleans, Louisiana 70127

W. L. Grant, 2496 Lilly Street
Odessa, Texas 79760

James Visser, 19 Circle Drive
Le Blanc, Louisiana 70651

R. H. Black, 7 Winslow Circle
Beaumont, Texas 77704

Lee Bonslow, 5143 North Wells St.
Killeen, Texas 76540

Robert Bowen, Inc., Box 103
San Juan, Texas 78589

Entries

Date (*Current year*)		Creditor	Amount of Invoice
Feb.	1	R. B. Fox	$ 85.00
	1	L. W. Polk	870.00
	1	Lee Bonslow	260.00
	2	Albert Beck	18.00
	3	J. M. Miller	260.00
	4	James Visser	110.00
	5	Robert Bowen, Inc.	40.00
	9	R. B. Fox	100.00
	10	Albert Beck	42.00
	10	R. H. Black	300.00
	10	Robert Bowen, Inc.	21.00
	12	L. W. Polk	200.00
	12	Lee Bonslow	174.00
	16	James Visser	440.00
	16	W. L. Grant	400.00
	17	Albert Beck	107.00
	17	Robert Bowen, Inc.	33.00
	18	J. M. Miller	190.00
	19	L. W. Polk	80.00
	20	W. L. Grant	320.00
	20	Lee Bonslow	230.00
	22	J. M. Miller	110.00
	22	W. L. Grant	50.00
	23	James Visser	60.00
	23	R. H. Black	166.00
	24	R. B. Fox	90.00
	24	R. H. Black	75.00
	26	Robert Bowen, Inc.	9.00
	27	Albert Beck	35.00
	27	W. L. Grant	160.00

Application Problems

PROBLEM 12-1 | Journalizing purchases on account

The following purchases on account were made by Steck's Men's Shop during June of the current year.

June 3.	Holden and Hodge	$462.00
6.	Gooden Men's Suits, Inc	631.25
9.	Bryan Hat Company	730.50
14.	Sherman Clothing Company	358.00
16.	Long and Clark	440.00
19.	Gooden Men's Suits, Inc	607.90
22.	Holden and Hodge	420.00
23.	Sherman Clothing Company	593.75
27.	Long and Clark	981.00
29.	Holden and Hodge	125.00

Instructions: 1. Prepare page 4 of a purchases journal by writing the proper heading at the top of each column. Use the same headings as shown in the purchases journal on page 169.

2. Journalize each of the transactions above.

3. Total and rule the purchases journal.

The purchases journal prepared in this problem will be used in Problem 12-2.

PROBLEM 12-2 | Posting from the purchases journal to two ledgers

Steck's Men's Shop has the following accounts in the accounts payable ledger:

Creditor	*Account Balance on June 1 of Current Year*
Bryan Hat Company, 1347 Alameda Drive Lancaster, New York 14086	$ 686.00
Gooden Men's Suits, Inc., 2649 Moore Avenue Rochester, New York 14603	594.00
Holden and Hodge, 340 Washington Street Newark, New Jersey 07130	——
Long and Clark, 1922 Morris Street Chester, Pennsylvania 19013	1,264.40
Sherman Clothing Company, P. O. Box 284 Long Branch, New Jersey 07740	——

Instructions: 1. Open an account for each of the creditors listed above. Use an accounts payable ledger with balance-column ruling as shown on page 174. Allow five lines for each account. Record the balance of each acccount that has a balance.

2. Post the entries in the purchases journal prepared in Problem 12-1 to the proper accounts in the accounts payable ledger.

3. Open the following accounts in the general ledger of Steck's Men's Shop. Allow four lines for each account. Record the balance of each account that has a balance.

Account Number	*Account Title*	*Account Balance on June 1 of Current Year*
11	Cash	$8,090.00
21	Accounts Payable	2,544.40
32	Harold Steck, Drawing	——
51	Purchases	——
63	Miscellaneous Expense	——
64	Rent Expense	——
65	Salary Expense	——

This is not a complete general ledger. Only those accounts needed for Problem 12-2 and for Problem 13-2 in the next chapter are included. The drawing account will be discussed and used in Chapter 13.

Instructions: 4. Post the total of the purchases journal prepared in Problem 12-1 to the proper accounts in the general ledger.

The ledgers prepared in this problem will be used in Problem 13-2.

Optional Problems

⋆SUPPLEMENTARY PROBLEM 12-S

Journalizing and posting purchases on account

Velma Gaines owns and operates a small gift shop. She sells greeting cards, small gifts, costume jewelry, and school supplies. During the month of August of the current year, the following purchases on account were made:

Aug.	1. York Book Company.	$150.00
	3. Swift Publishing Company.	290.00
	3. Erie Card Company.	45.00
	7. York Book Company.	52.00
	8. Wilder Jewelry Company.	93.00
	12. Swift Publishing Company.	356.00
	19. Erie Card Company.	79.00
	23. York Book Company.	257.00
	25. Wilder Jewelry Company.	68.00
	29. Swift Publishing Company.	27.00

Instructions: 1. Journalize each transaction on page 3 of a purchases journal similar to the one shown on page 169.

2. Total and rule the purchases journal.

3. Open an account in the accounts payable ledger for each of the following creditors. Allow four lines for each account. Record the balance of each account that has a balance.

Creditor	*Account Balance on August 1 of Current Year*
Erie Card Company, 957 Eighth Street Erie, Pennsylvania 16501	$142.00
Swift Publishing Company, 54 South Kilgore Avenue Harrisburg, Pennsylvania 17101	——
Wilder Jewelry Company, 197 Central Avenue Harrisburg, Pennsylvania 17101	80.00
York Book Company, 324 Central Avenue New York, New York 11215	——

Instructions: 4. Post the entries in the purchases journal to the proper accounts in the accounts payable ledger.

5. Open the following two accounts in the general ledger. Allow four lines for each account. Record the balance of each account that has a balance.

Account Number	*Account Title*	*Account Balance on August 1 of Current Year*
21	Accounts Payable	$222.00
51	Purchases	——

Instructions: 6. Post the total of the purchases journal to the proper accounts in the general ledger.

⋆ BONUS PROBLEM 12-B

Journalizing and posting purchases on account

The Fulton Store uses several books of original entry. One of these books is a purchases journal similar to the one illustrated on page 169. In this journal, only purchases of merchandise on account are recorded. All other transactions are recorded in other journals. During the month of October, the Fulton Store completed the transactions given below.

Instructions: 1. From the following transactions, select only those that are purchases of merchandise on account and record them on page 7 of the purchases journal.

Oct. 1. Paid cash, $400.00, for rent for October.
3. Purchased merchandise on account from Alden Brothers, $375.00.
6. Sold merchandise on account to E. T. Landon, $250.00.
8. Received $100.00 from R. T. Kelly on account.
9. Purchased merchandise on account from Alden Brothers, $650.00.
9. Purchased a typewriter on account for use in the office from Rayburn Office Supplies, $375.00.

10. Purchased merchandise on account from Stokes and Company, $432.00.
13. Paid cash, $14.80, for the telephone bill for September.
16. Sold merchandise on account to H. O. Morgan, $68.40.
20. Purchased merchandise on account from Miles Anderson, $130.00.
20. Purchased a display case for the salesroom on account from Rayburn Office Supplies, $425.00.
20. Received $250.00 from E. T. Landon on account.
22. Paid $375.00 to Alden Brothers on account.
23. Purchased merchandise on account from Miles Anderson, $295.00.
27. Sold merchandise on account to B. J. Cutler, $165.50.
29. Purchased office supplies on account from Rayburn Office Supplies, $25.40.
31. Received $3,650.00 from cash sales for the month.
31. Purchased merchandise on account from Alden Brothers, $135.00.

Instructions: 2. Total and rule the purchases journal.

3. Open accounts in an accounts payable ledger for the following creditors. Allow four lines for each account. Record the balances as of October 1 of the current year.

Alden Brothers, 27 East Fifth Street, Peoria, Illinois 61617.....	$515.00
Miles Anderson, 2901 Mound Street, St. Louis, Missouri 63155.	——
Rayburn Office Supplies, 397 Main Street, Muncie, Indiana 47301.	87.60
Stokes and Company, 819 Westfield Boulevard, Indianapolis, Indiana 46209..	——

Instructions: 4. Post the entries from the purchases journal to the proper accounts in the accounts payable ledger.

5. Open accounts in the general ledger for Account No. 21, Accounts Payable, and Account No. 51, Purchases. Allow four lines for each account. Record the credit balance of the accounts payable account.

6. Post the total of the purchases journal to the proper accounts in the general ledger.

CHAPTER 13 RECORDING CASH PAYMENTS

The receipt and the payment of cash are among the most frequent business transactions. The owner of a business should know the total amount of cash received and cash paid as well as the balance of cash on hand. A bookkeeping system must provide procedures for handling and recording cash transactions. This chapter will describe how cash payments are handled.

THE SOURCE DOCUMENT FOR RECORDING CASH PAYMENTS

The payment of cash for any reason is known as a *cash payments transaction*. Most businesses use checks to make all major cash payments. An order in writing, signed by the depositor, ordering the bank to pay cash from the depositor's account is known as a *check*. Checks are safer than money to send through the mail. After a check has been cashed, the bank returns it to the business that wrote it. The returned check is good evidence that payment has been made. The returned check also serves as a receipt for the payment. McCann Office Furniture makes all major cash payments by check.

The source document for recording a cash payment is the check stub that is prepared when each check is written. Each check stub should be filled out completely so that the bookkeeper will have all the information needed for making the journal entry. An illustration of a check stub and a check prepared by McCann Office Furniture is shown below.

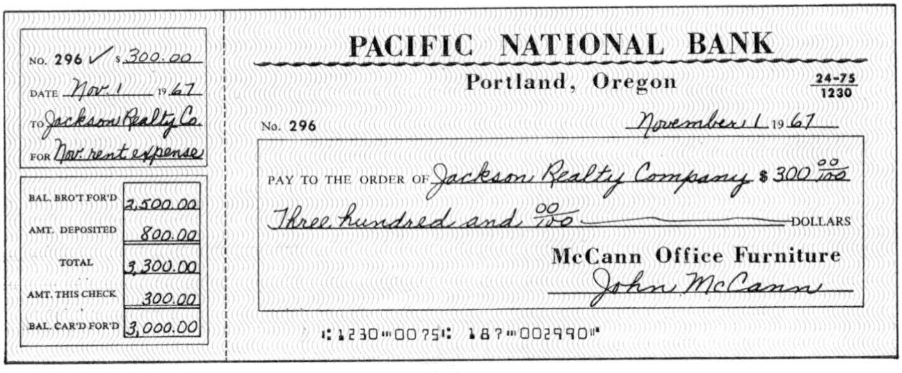

NO. 296 ✓ $ 300.00
DATE Nov. 1 19 67
TO Jackson Realty Co.
FOR Nov. rent expense

BAL. BRO'T FOR'D	2,500.00
AMT. DEPOSITED	800.00
TOTAL	3,300.00
AMT. THIS CHECK	300.00
BAL. CAR'D FOR'D	3,000.00

PACIFIC NATIONAL BANK
Portland, Oregon 24-75/1230

No. 296 November 1 19 67

PAY TO THE ORDER OF Jackson Realty Company $ 300 00/100

Three hundred and 00/100 DOLLARS

McCann Office Furniture
John McCann

⑆1230⑈0075⑆ 187⑈002990⑈

Check stub and check

THE THREE-COLUMN CASH PAYMENTS JOURNAL

A special journal in which only cash payments are recorded is called a *cash payments journal.* In the three-column cash payments journal, each payment is recorded on a single line.

CASH PAYMENTS JOURNAL — PAGE

	DATE	ACCOUNT DEBITED	CK. NO.	POST. REF.	1 GENERAL DEBIT	2 ACCOUNTS PAY. DEBIT	3 CASH CREDIT	
1								1
2								2
3								3

Three-column cash payments journal

Special amount columns are provided in the cash payments journal for those types of transactions that occur frequently. For example, there is a special amount column for Accounts Payable Debit because McCann Office Furniture makes frequent payments to creditors. Cash payments that do not occur frequently, such as the monthly payment for rent, are recorded in the General Debit column.

JOURNALIZING CASH PAYMENTS

Cash payments transaction No. 1: Paying rent expense

November 1, 1967. Paid cash, $300.00, for November rent. Issued check No. 296.

Check Stub No. 296, shown on page 187, is the source document for recording the entry in the cash payments journal.

Analyzing cash payments transaction No. 1. In this transaction the expense account, Rent Expense, is debited for $300.00 and the cash account is credited for $300.00. (See page 57 for the T-account analysis of a similar transaction.)

Journalizing cash payments transaction No. 1. The entry to record this transaction is shown below.

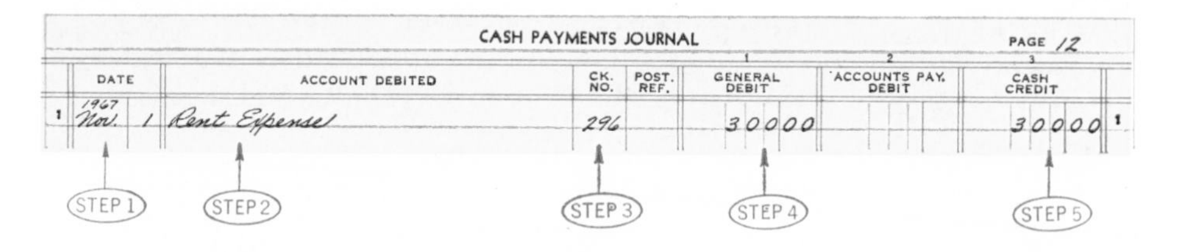

CASH PAYMENTS JOURNAL — PAGE 12

	DATE		ACCOUNT DEBITED	CK. NO.	POST. REF.	1 GENERAL DEBIT	2 ACCOUNTS PAY. DEBIT	3 CASH CREDIT	
1	1967 Nov.	1	Rent Expense	296		300 00		300 00	1

The steps in recording this entry are:

Step 1

Write the date, *1967, Nov. 1,* on the first line in the Date column.

Step 2

Write the account debited, *Rent Expense,* in the Account Debited column.

Step 3

Write the check number, *296,* in the Ck. No. column.

Step 4

Write the amount of the cash payment, *$300.00,* in the General Debit column.

Step 5

Write the amount, *$300.00,* in the Cash Credit column. The account title, Cash, is not written because a special amount column is provided for all cash payments.

Step 6

Place a check mark on Check Stub No. 296 after the number of the check. The check mark shows that the transaction has been recorded in the cash payments journal. (See the check stub illustration on page 187.)

Cash payments transaction No. 2: Paying cash on account to a creditor

November 9, 1967. Paid cash, $540.00, to the Dunham Manufacturing Company on account. Issued Check No. 297.

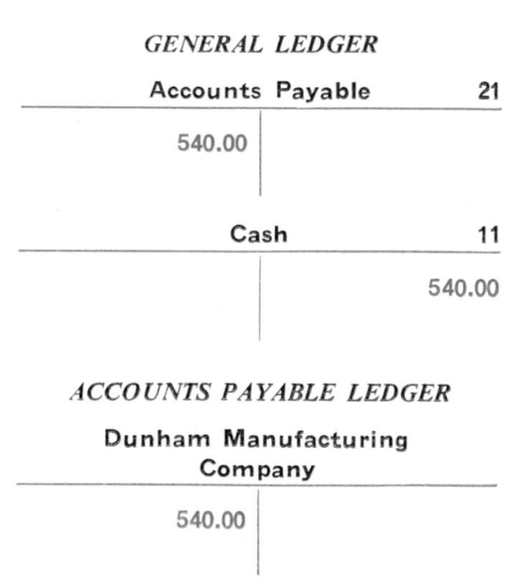

Analyzing cash payments transaction No. 2. In this transaction the liability account in the general ledger, Accounts Payable, is debited for $540.00 because the balance of this liability account is decreased. Cash is credited for $540.00 because the balance of this asset account is decreased. Each time the accounts payable account in the general ledger is debited, the proper creditor's account in the accounts payable ledger must also be debited for the same amount. Thus, the creditor's account, Dunham Manufacturing Company, in the accounts payable ledger is debited for $540.00.

Journalizing cash payments transaction No. 2. The entry to record this transaction is shown below.

CASH PAYMENTS JOURNAL — PAGE 12

	Date		Account Debited	Ck. No.	Post. Ref.	1 General Debit	2 Accounts Pay. Debit	3 Cash Credit	
1	1967 Nov.	1	Rent Expense	296		300 00		300 00	1
2		9	Dunham Manufacturing Company	297			540 00	540 00	2

STEP 1 STEP 2 STEP 3 STEP 4 STEP 5

The steps in recording this entry are:

Step 1

Write the day, *9*, in the Date column. It is not necessary to repeat the year and the month on the same page.

Step 2

Write the account debited, *Dunham Manufacturing Company*, in the Account Debited column to indicate the name of the creditor whose account is debited in the accounts payable ledger.

Step 3

Write the check number, *297*, in the Ck. No. column.

Step 4

Write the amount of the cash payment, *$540.00*, in the Accounts Payable Debit column.

Step 5

Write the amount of the cash payment, *$540.00*, in the Cash Credit column.

Step 6

Place a check mark on Check Stub No. 297 to show that the information has been recorded in the cash payments journal.

Cash payments transaction No. 3: Cash withdrawal by the proprietor

November 9, 1967. Paid cash, $100.00, to Mr. John McCann, owner, for his personal use. Issued Check No. 298.

Assets taken out of the business by the proprietor are called *withdrawals*. The proprietor may withdraw assets such as cash, merchandise, supplies, and equipment. Withdrawals are not recorded in the proprietor's capital account but in a separate account. The proprietorship account in which all withdrawals of assets by the proprietor are recorded is called a *drawing account*. The entries in the proprietor's drawing account show him how much his withdrawals are for each fiscal period.

The title of the proprietorship account in which all withdrawals by Mr. McCann are recorded is *John McCann, Drawing*. The account is assigned number 32, which shows that it is the second account in the proprietorship division of the general ledger.

Analyzing cash payments transaction No. 3. The proprietor's capital account has a credit balance. Because withdrawals decrease proprietorship, a proprietorship account is debited for all withdrawals. Therefore, the amount of the withdrawal, $100.00, is debited to the proprietorship account, John McCann, Drawing. Cash is credited for $100.00 to show a decrease in the balance of this asset account.

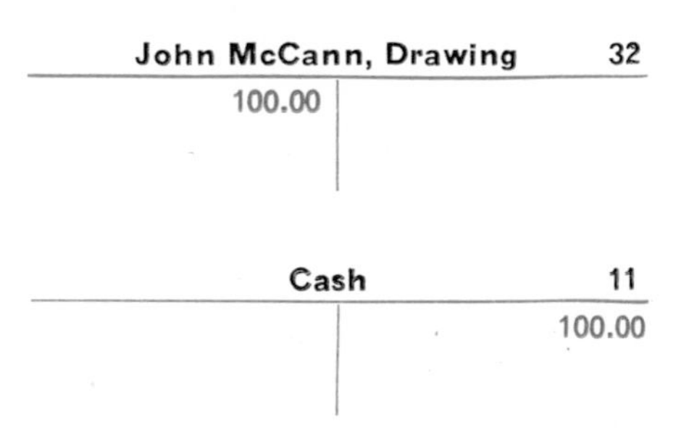

Journalizing cash payments transaction No. 3. The entry to record this transaction is shown below.

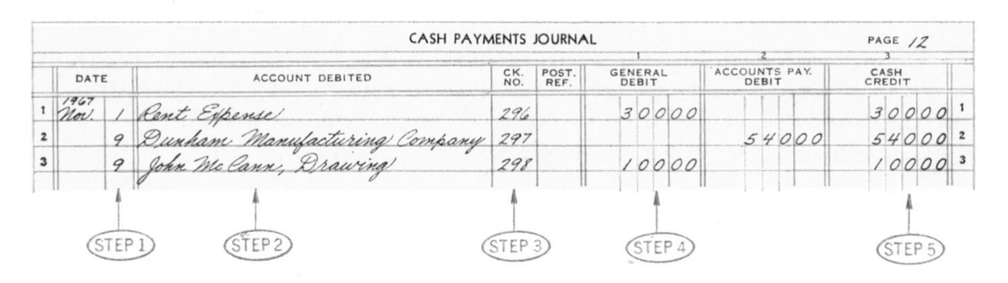
CASH PAYMENTS JOURNAL PAGE 12

	DATE		ACCOUNT DEBITED	CK. NO.	POST. REF.	GENERAL DEBIT (1)	ACCOUNTS PAY. DEBIT (2)	CASH CREDIT (3)	
1	1967 Nov.	1	Rent Expense	296		300 00		300 00	1
2		9	Dunham Manufacturing Company	297			540 00	540 00	2
3		9	John McCann, Drawing	298		100 00		100 00	3

The steps in recording this entry are:

Step 1

Write the day, 9, in the Date column.

Step 2

Write the account debited, *John McCann, Drawing*, in the Account Debited column.

Step 3

Write the check number, *298,* in the Ck. No. column.

Step 4

Write the amount of the withdrawal, *$100.00,* in the General Debit column.

Withdrawals are not common enough to justify a special amount column in the cash payments journal.

Step 5

Write the amount of the cash payment, *$100.00,* in the Cash Credit column.

Step 6

Place a check mark on Check Stub No. 298 to show that the information has been recorded in the cash payments journal.

Cash payments transaction No. 4: Cash purchase of merchandise

November 10, 1967. Paid cash, $124.00, to the City Book Store for the purchase of merchandise. Issued Check No. 299.

A cash purchase of merchandise is recorded in the cash payments journal. Only purchases of merchandise on account are recorded in the purchases journal.

McCann Office Furniture makes very few cash purchases. Because cash purchases do not occur often, there is no advantage in providing a special amount column for purchases in the cash payments journal.

Analyzing cash payments transaction No. 4. A purchase of merchandise increases the balance of the purchases account. The balance side of the purchases account is the debit side. Therefore, this increase in purchases, $124.00, is debited to the purchases account. Cash is credited for $124.00 to show a decrease in the balance of this asset account.

Purchases	51
124.00	

Cash	11
	124.00

Journalizing cash payments transaction No. 4. The entry to record this transaction is shown at the top of the next page.

CASH PAYMENTS JOURNAL — PAGE 12

	DATE		ACCOUNT DEBITED	CK. NO.	POST. REF.	1 GENERAL DEBIT	2 ACCOUNTS PAY. DEBIT	3 CASH CREDIT	
1	1967 Nov.	1	Rent Expense	296		300 00		300 00	1
2		9	Dunham Manufacturing Company	297			540 00	540 00	2
3		9	John McCann, Drawing	298		100 00		100 00	3
4		10	Purchases	299		124 00		124 00	4
5									5
6									6
7									7
8									8
9									9

The account title, *Purchases,* is written in the Account Debited column. The amount of the debit to Purchases is written in the General Debit column. The amount of the credit to Cash is written in the Cash Credit column. The date of the transaction and the check number are recorded in the proper columns.

During the month of November, McCann Office Furniture makes other cash payments by check. Each cash payment is journalized in the manner described for Entries Nos. 1 to 4. The completed cash payments journal of McCann Office Furniture for the month of November is shown on page 196.

POSTING INDIVIDUAL ITEMS FROM THE CASH PAYMENTS JOURNAL

Posting from the General Debit column

Each amount recorded in the General Debit column is posted to the general ledger account named in the Account Debited column. The posting of the entry on Line 1 of the cash payments journal to the rent expense account in the general ledger is shown in the illustration below.

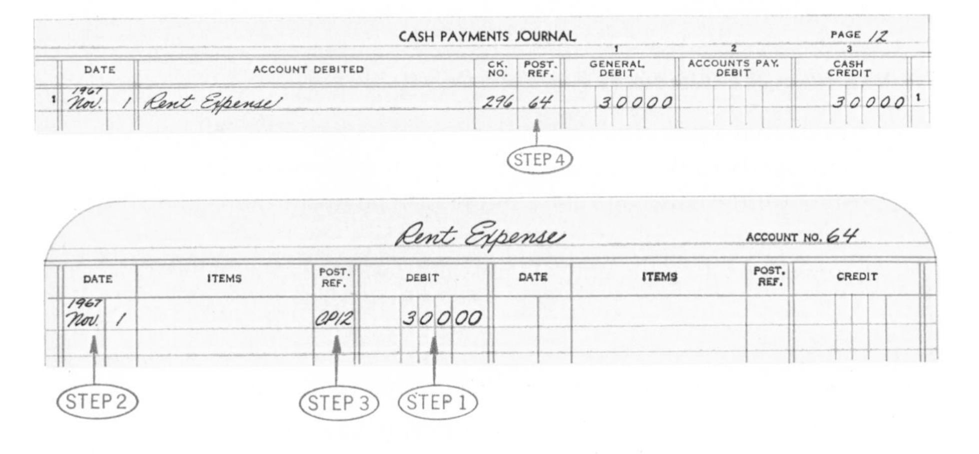

CASH PAYMENTS JOURNAL — PAGE 12

	DATE		ACCOUNT DEBITED	CK. NO.	POST. REF.	1 GENERAL DEBIT	2 ACCOUNTS PAY. DEBIT	3 CASH CREDIT	
1	1967 Nov.	1	Rent Expense	296	64	300 00		300 00	1

Rent Expense — ACCOUNT NO. 64

DATE		ITEMS	POST. REF.	DEBIT	DATE	ITEMS	POST. REF.	CREDIT
1967 Nov.	1		CP12	300 00				

The steps in posting the debit part of this entry to the rent expense account are:

Step 1

Post the amount, *$300.00*, to the debit side of the rent expense account in the general ledger.

Step 2

Write the date, *1967, Nov. 1*, at the top of the Date column in the general ledger account.

Step 3

Write *CP12* in the Post. Ref. column of the general ledger account to show that the entry is posted from page 12 of the cash payments journal.

CP is the abbreviation for Cash Payments Journal.

Step 4

Write the account number of Rent Expense, *64*, in the Post. Ref. column of the cash payments journal to show that the posting of this item is completed.

The chart of accounts used by McCann Office Furniture is given on page 166.

Each amount in the General Debit column of the cash payments journal is posted separately to the debit side of the account named in the Account Debited column. The amounts in the General Debit column are posted frequently during the month. In this way the bookkeeper keeps his work up-to-date and avoids a large amount of posting at the end of the month.

The credit to Cash for the entry on Line 1 of the cash payments journal is posted as part of the total at the end of the month. The posting of the totals of the cash payments journal will be described later in this chapter.

Posting from the Accounts Payable Debit column

The individual amounts listed in the Accounts Payable Debit column are posted frequently to the creditors' accounts in the accounts payable ledger. The posting for the entry on Line 2 of the cash payments journal is shown in the illustration at the top of the next page.

The steps in posting the entry from Line 2 of the cash payments journal are:

Step 1

Post the amount, *$540.00*, to the debit column of the Dunham Manufacturing Company account in the accounts payable ledger.

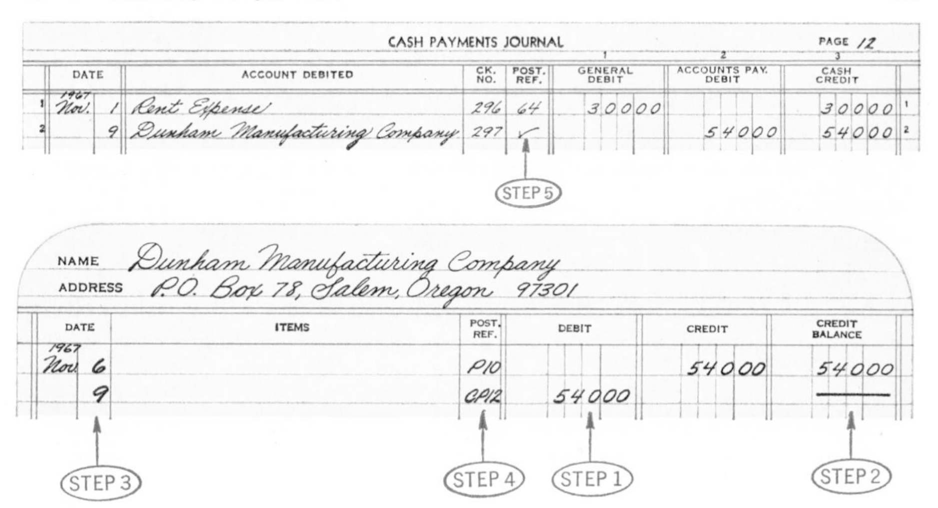

CASH PAYMENTS JOURNAL — PAGE 12

	DATE		ACCOUNT DEBITED	CK. NO.	POST. REF.	1 GENERAL DEBIT	2 ACCOUNTS PAY. DEBIT	3 CASH CREDIT	
1	1967 Nov.	1	Rent Expense	296	64	300 00		300 00	1
2		9	Dunham Manufacturing Company	297	✓		540 00	540 00	2

NAME Dunham Manufacturing Company
ADDRESS P.O. Box 78, Salem, Oregon 97301

DATE		ITEMS	POST. REF.	DEBIT	CREDIT	CREDIT BALANCE
1967 Nov.	6		P10		540 00	540 00
	9		CP12	540 00		——

Step 2

Subtract the debit amount, *$540.00*, from the previous credit balance. The new balance is written in the Credit Balance column. As shown in the illustration above, the account for the Dunham Manufacturing Company has a zero balance after this entry is posted. To show that there is no balance, a short line is drawn in the Credit Balance column.

Step 3

Write the day, *9*, in the Date column of the account.

Step 4

Write *CP12* in the Post. Ref. column of the account to show that the entry is posted from page 12 of the cash payments journal.

Step 5

Place a check mark in the Post. Ref. column of the cash payments journal to show completion of the posting.

Each entry in the Accounts Payable Debit column is posted in the same way as the entry on Line 2.

PROVING, TOTALING, AND POSTING THE CASH PAYMENTS JOURNAL

At the end of the fiscal period, the amount columns of the cash payments journal are proved and totaled, and the totals of the special amount columns are posted. The illustration on the next page shows the cash payments journal for McCann Office Furniture after all the entries have been posted.

CASH PAYMENTS JOURNAL — PAGE 12

	DATE		ACCOUNT DEBITED	CK. NO.	POST. REF.	1 GENERAL DEBIT	2 ACCOUNTS PAY. DEBIT	3 CASH CREDIT	
1	1967 Nov.	1	Rent Expense	296	64	300 00		300 00	1
2		9	Dunham Manufacturing Company	297	✓		540 00	540 00	2
3		9	John McCann, Drawing	298	32	100 00		100 00	3
4		10	Purchases	299	51	124 00		124 00	4
5		13	Willis Paper Suppliers	300	✓		104 00	104 00	5
6		14	Miscellaneous Expense	301	63	11 00		11 00	6
7		16	Swartz Supply Company	302	✓		200 00	200 00	7
8		17	Delivery Expense	303	61	25 00		25 00	8
9		17	Salary Expense	304	65	200 00		200 00	9
10		20	Filing Systems, Inc.	305	✓		430 00	430 00	10
11		21	Miscellaneous Expense	306	63	12 00		12 00	11
12		27	Alfred Boyd & Sons	307	✓		406 00	406 00	12
13		28	Delivery Expense	308	61	28 00		28 00	13
14		29	Martin Equipment, Inc.	309	✓		490 00	490 00	14
15		29	John McCann, Drawing	310	32	100 00		100 00	15
16		30	Salary Expense	311	65	200 00 1100 00	2170 00	200 00 3270 00	16
17		30	Totals			1100 00	2170 00	3270 00	17
18									18
19									19
20									20
21									21
22									22

Completed cash payments journal — McCann Office Furniture

Withholding taxes and social security taxes are not shown in the cash payments journal illustrated above. The recording of these payroll taxes will be described in a later chapter.

Proving the totals of the cash payments journal

The steps in proving the totals of the amount columns in the cash payments journal are:

Step 1

Foot each column of the cash payments journal in small pencil figures.

Step 2

Add the debit column totals, $1,100.00 and $2,170.00, on a separate sheet of paper. The sum of the debit column totals, $3,270.00, is the same as the total of the Cash Credit column. Therefore, the equality of debits and credits in the cash payments journal is proved.

When there are many daily cash payments, it is customary to pencil foot the columns of the cash payments journal at frequent intervals during the month and to prove the equality of debits and credits. Because McCann Office Furniture has few cash payments, frequent pencil footings are not made.

Totaling and ruling the cash payments journal

After the equality of debits and credits in the cash payments journal is proved, a single line is ruled across all amount columns below the last amount in the Cash Credit column. The date of the last day of the month is written in the Date column, and the word *Totals* is written in the Account Debited column. The totals are recorded in ink below the single ruled line. A double line is then ruled across all amount columns. The illustration on page 196 shows the totals and the ruling for the cash payments journal of McCann Office Furniture for November.

Posting the totals of the cash payments journal

At the end of the month the total of the Accounts Payable Debit column and the total of the Cash Credit column are posted to the appropriate accounts in the general ledger. The total of the General Debit column is not posted because the individual items in this column have been posted previously to accounts in the general ledger.

The Totals line of the cash payments journal after posting and the two accounts in the general ledger to which the totals are posted are shown below.

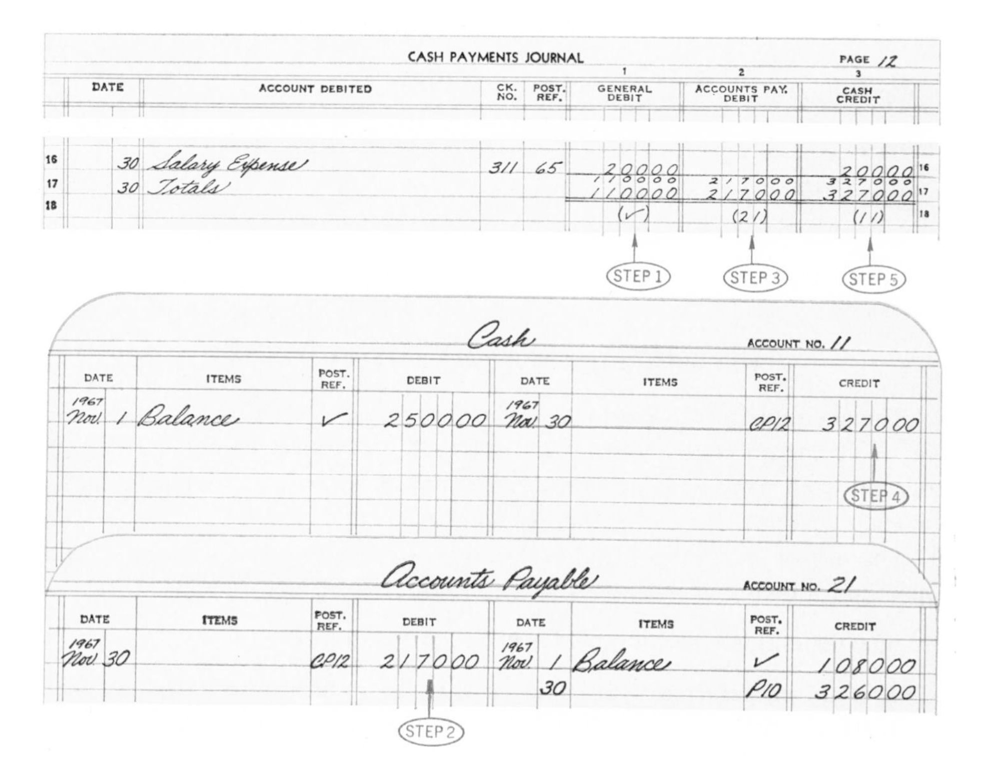

CASH PAYMENTS JOURNAL — PAGE 12

	DATE	ACCOUNT DEBITED	CK. NO.	POST. REF.	1 GENERAL DEBIT	2 ACCOUNTS PAY. DEBIT	3 CASH CREDIT	
16	30	Salary Expense	311	65	200 00		200 00	16
					1 100 00	2 170 00	3 270 00	
17	30	Totals			1 100 00	2 170 00	3 270 00	17
18					(✓)	(21)	(11)	18

Cash — ACCOUNT NO. 11

DATE	ITEMS	POST. REF.	DEBIT	DATE	ITEMS	POST. REF.	CREDIT
1967 Nov. 1	Balance	✓	2 500 00	1967 Nov. 30		CP12	3 270 00

Accounts Payable — ACCOUNT NO. 21

DATE	ITEMS	POST. REF.	DEBIT	DATE	ITEMS	POST. REF.	CREDIT
1967 Nov. 30		CP12	2 170 00	1967 Nov. 1	Balance	✓	1 080 00
				30		P10	3 260 00

The steps in posting the Totals line of the cash payments journal are:

Step 1

Place a check mark in parentheses on the first line below the total of the General Debit column. The check mark shows that the total of the column is not to be posted.

Step 2

Post the total of the Accounts Payable Debit column, *$2,170.00*, to the debit side of the accounts payable account in the general ledger. Write the date, *1967, Nov. 30*, in the Date column, and *CP12* in the Post. Ref. column of the account.

Step 3

Write the number of the accounts payable account in parentheses, (*21*), on the first line below the total of the Accounts Payable Debit column. Writing the account number shows that the posting of the total is completed.

Step 4

Post the total of the Cash Credit column, *$3,270.00*, to the credit side of the cash account in the general ledger. Write the date, *1967, Nov. 30*, in the Date column, and *CP12* in the Post. Ref. column of the account.

Step 5

Write the number of the cash account in parentheses, (*11*), on the first line below the total of the Cash Credit column to show completion of the posting.

THE COMPLETED ACCOUNTS PAYABLE LEDGER

The accounts payable ledger of McCann Office Furniture after the posting from the purchases journal and the cash payments journal for November has been completed is shown on the opposite page. The credit balance in each account shows the amount still owed each creditor.

The use of an accounts payable ledger for the accounts of all creditors has the following advantages:

1. The general ledger contains fewer accounts and, thus, is reduced in size.
2. It is not necessary to list the name of each creditor on the trial balance. Instead, only one account, the accounts payable account, is shown on the trial balance.

NAME Alden Typewriter Company
ADDRESS 64 Harbor Avenue, Toledo, Ohio 43601

DATE		ITEMS	POST. REF.	DEBIT	CREDIT	CREDIT BALANCE
1967 Nov.	30		P10		81 00	81 00

NAME Alfred Boyd & Sons
ADDRESS 1258 East Jackson Street, Portland, Oregon 97227

DATE		ITEMS	POST. REF.	DEBIT	CREDIT	CREDIT BALANCE
1967 Nov.	1	Balance	✓			406 00
	10		P10		470 00	876 00
	27		CP12	406 00		470 00

NAME Dunham Manufacturing Company
ADDRESS P.O. Box 78, Salem, Oregon 97301

DATE		ITEMS	POST. REF.	DEBIT	CREDIT	CREDIT BALANCE
1967 Nov.	6		P10		540 00	540 00
	9		CP12	540 00		—

NAME Filing Systems, Inc.
ADDRESS 1504 Market Street, Indianapolis, Indiana 46203

DATE		ITEMS	POST. REF.	DEBIT	CREDIT	CREDIT BALANCE
1967 Nov.	14		P10		430 00	430 00
	20		CP12	430 00		—
	24		P10		480 00	480 00

NAME Martin Equipment, Inc.
ADDRESS 6 Bethel Pike, Portland, Oregon 97208

DATE		ITEMS	POST. REF.	DEBIT	CREDIT	CREDIT BALANCE
1967 Nov.	1	Balance	✓			490 00
	27		P10		397 00	887 00
	29		CP12	490 00		397 00

NAME Swartz Supply Company
ADDRESS 120 South Turner Avenue, Portland, Oregon 97203

DATE		ITEMS	POST. REF.	DEBIT	CREDIT	CREDIT BALANCE
1967 Nov.	1	Balance	✓			80 00
	9		P10		120 00	200 00
	16		CP12	200 00		—
	17		P10		96 00	96 00
	30		J4		112 00	208 00

NAME Willis Paper Suppliers
ADDRESS 830 Broadway, Grand Rapids, Michigan 49521

DATE		ITEMS	POST. REF.	DEBIT	CREDIT	CREDIT BALANCE
1967 Nov.	1	Balance	✓			104 00
	13		CP12	104 00		—
	21		P10		646 00	646 00

Accounts payable ledger — McCann Office Furniture

3. The work of posting can be divided between two or more persons. While one person is posting to the general ledger accounts, another person can post to the accounts payable ledger accounts.

4. The balance of the accounts payable account is used to prove the accuracy of all the postings made from both the purchases journal and the cash payments journal. This type of proof is explained in detail below.

SCHEDULE OF ACCOUNTS PAYABLE

The balance of the controlling account, Accounts Payable, in the general ledger should be the same as the sum of the balances of the creditors' accounts in the accounts payable ledger. If the two amounts are the same, it proves that all posting from both the purchases journal and the cash payments journal has been completed accurately. In preparing proof of the posting to the accounts payable ledger, all balances of the creditors' accounts are listed and totaled. A list of all creditors that shows the balance owed to each creditor and the total amount owed to all creditors is called a *schedule of accounts payable.*

The schedule of accounts payable prepared from the accounts payable ledger illustrated on page 199 is shown below.

McCann Office Furniture
Schedule of Accounts Payable
November 30, 1967

Alden Typewriter Company	81 00	
Alfred Boyd & Sons	470 00	
Filing Systems, Inc.	480 00	
Martin Equipment, Inc.	397 00	
Swartz Supply Company	208 00	
Willis Paper Suppliers	646 00	
Total Accounts Payable		2,282 00

Schedule of accounts payable

The steps in preparing the schedule of accounts payable are:

Step 1

Write the heading on three lines; center each item in the heading.

Step 2

List the name of each creditor and the amount of his balance at the time the schedule of accounts payable is prepared.

Step 3

Add the balances listed on the schedule to find the total amount owed all creditors.

Step 4

Foot the controlling account in the general ledger, Accounts Payable, and determine the account balance. The account balance is the total amount owed all creditors. The accounts payable account with its footing and balance is shown below.

Accounts Payable ACCOUNT NO. 21

DATE	ITEMS	POST. REF.	DEBIT	DATE	ITEMS	POST. REF.	CREDIT
1967 Nov. 30		CP12	2,170 00	1967 Nov. 1	Balance	✓	1,080 00
				30		P10	3,260 00
				30	2,282.00	J4	112 00
							4,452 00

Accounts payable account in the general ledger

The November 30 posting of $112.00 from the general journal will be explained in Chapter 16.

Step 5

Compare the total of the schedule of accounts payable, *$2,282.00*, with the balance of the accounts payable account in the general ledger, *$2,282.00*. Since the two amounts agree, it is assumed that all posting affecting creditors' accounts and Accounts Payable is accurate.

If the total of the schedule of accounts payable and the balance of the accounts payable account do not agree, the error must be found and corrected before the bookkeeper continues his work.

A FLOW CHART FOR POSTING

A summary of the steps followed in posting from the purchases journal and the cash payments journal to the accounts payable ledger and the accounts payable account in the general ledger is shown in the flow chart on the next page.

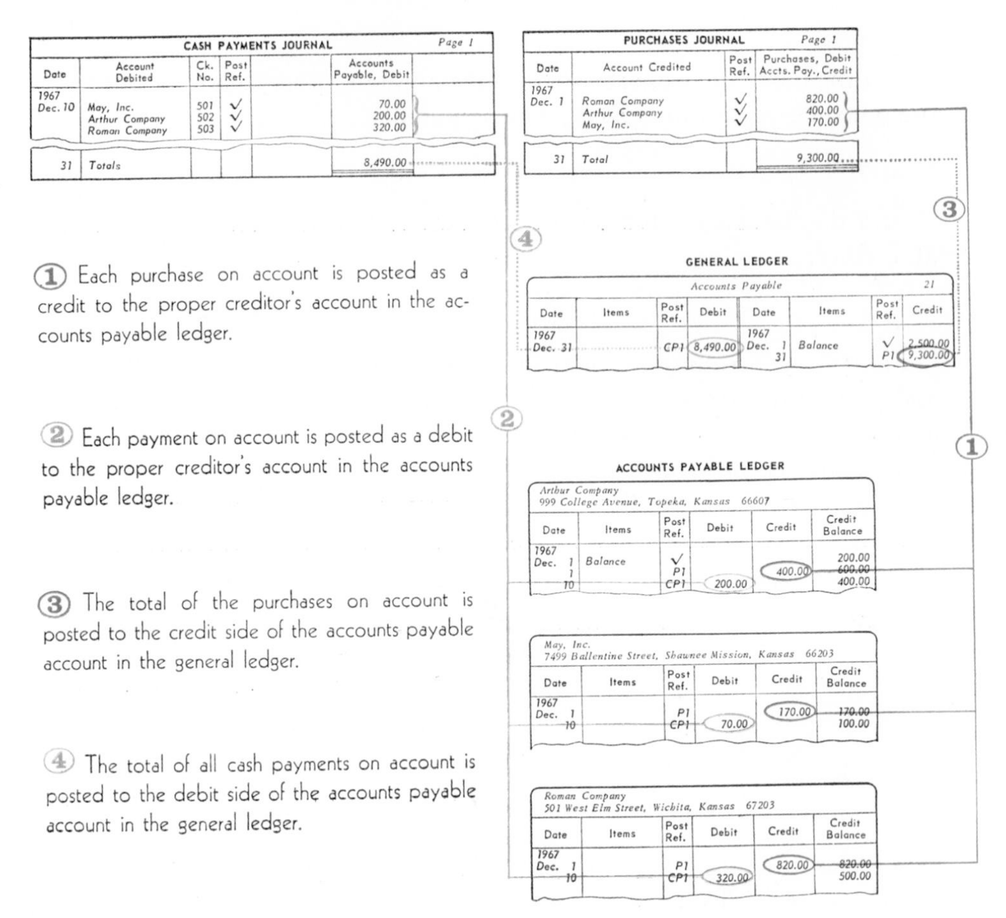

CASH PAYMENTS JOURNAL Page 1

Date	Account Debited	Ck. No.	Post Ref.		Accounts Payable, Debit	
1967 Dec. 10	May, Inc.	501	✓		70.00	
	Arthur Company	502	✓		200.00	
	Roman Company	503	✓		320.00	
31	Totals				8,490.00	

PURCHASES JOURNAL Page 1

Date	Account Credited	Post Ref.	Purchases, Debit Accts. Pay., Credit
1967 Dec. 1	Roman Company	✓	820.00
	Arthur Company	✓	400.00
	May, Inc.	✓	170.00
31	Total		9,300.00

GENERAL LEDGER

Accounts Payable 21

Date	Items	Post Ref.	Debit	Date	Items	Post Ref.	Credit
1967 Dec. 31		CP1	8,490.00	1967 Dec. 1	Balance	✓	2,500.00
				31		P1	9,300.00

ACCOUNTS PAYABLE LEDGER

Arthur Company
999 College Avenue, Topeka, Kansas 66607

Date	Items	Post Ref.	Debit	Credit	Credit Balance
1967 Dec. 1	Balance	✓			200.00
1		P1		400.00	~~600.00~~
10		CP1	200.00		400.00

May, Inc.
7499 Ballentine Street, Shawnee Mission, Kansas 66203

Date	Items	Post Ref.	Debit	Credit	Credit Balance
1967 Dec. 1		P1		170.00	~~170.00~~
10		CP1	70.00		100.00

Roman Company
501 West Elm Street, Wichita, Kansas 67203

Date	Items	Post Ref.	Debit	Credit	Credit Balance
1967 Dec. 1		P1		820.00	~~820.00~~
10		CP1	320.00		500.00

(1) Each purchase on account is posted as a credit to the proper creditor's account in the accounts payable ledger.

(2) Each payment on account is posted as a debit to the proper creditor's account in the accounts payable ledger.

(3) The total of the purchases on account is posted to the credit side of the accounts payable account in the general ledger.

(4) The total of all cash payments on account is posted to the debit side of the accounts payable account in the general ledger.

A flow chart of posting to the accounts payable ledger and the accounts payable account in the general ledger

CASH METHOD OF HANDLING PURCHASES ON ACCOUNT

Some businesses prefer to handle all purchases on account as though they were cash purchases. This is done by recording each purchase transaction only at the time the invoice is paid. This method makes it unnecessary to maintain a purchases journal, accounts with creditors, or an accounts payable controlling account in the general ledger.

The steps in the cash method of handling purchases on account are:

Step 1

Verify each purchase invoice and then file it under the date it is to be paid.

Step 2

Examine the file each day and issue checks to creditors in payment of the invoices due on that day.

Step 3

Record the amount of the check in the cash payments journal as a debit in a new special amount column, Purchases Debit, and as a credit in the Cash Credit column.

Step 4

Post the total of the Purchases Debit column of the cash payments journal to the purchases account in the general ledger at the end of the month.

When the financial statements are prepared, the balance sheet must show the total amount of liabilities. The income statement must show the cost of all goods purchased for sale. Therefore, at the end of the fiscal period, the total of all the unpaid invoices is shown as Accounts Payable on the balance sheet. The total of all the unpaid invoices is included as part of Purchases on the income statement.

Increasing Your Business Vocabulary

What is the meaning of each of the following:

a cash payments transaction
b check
c cash payments journal
d withdrawals
e drawing account
f schedule of accounts payable

Study Questions

1. Why does a business use checks to make major cash payments?
2. What source document is used as a basis for recording cash payments?
3. How many lines of the cash payments journal are needed to record a cash payments transaction?
4. What account is debited and what account is credited for the payment of rent?
5. Why is a check mark placed on the stub of the check after the entry has been recorded in the cash payments journal?
6. What accounts are debited and what account is credited when a payment on account is made to a creditor?
7. What effect do withdrawals have upon proprietorship?
8. Why is there no special column for purchases in the cash payments journal illustrated on page 196?
9. To what accounts are the amounts in the General Debit column of the cash payments journal posted?

10. Why is the amount of each cash payment not posted individually as a credit to the cash account?

11. To what accounts are the amounts in the Accounts Payable Debit column of the cash payments journal posted?

12. Why is the total of the General Debit column of the cash payments journal not posted at the end of the month?

13. What is the relationship between the accounts payable account in the general ledger and the creditors' accounts in the accounts payable ledger after all the posting has been completed?

14. Why is a schedule of accounts payable prepared after all the posting has been completed?

Cases for Business Decision

CASE 1

Terry Robbins, manager of Robbins Pet Shop, has never studied bookkeeping. When he records a cash payment in the cash payments journal, he does not understand why both the account title debited and the account title credited are not written. How would you explain to him why both account titles are not written?

CASE 2

The bookkeeper for the Household Appliance Company is preparing a schedule of accounts payable. He finds that the total of the schedule is $240.00 less than the balance of the accounts payable account in the general ledger. What kinds of errors might he have made to cause this difference?

CASE 3

The Gardner Feed Store has a special column in its cash payments journal for rent expense. In this chapter you have seen that no special column is provided in the cash payments journal for rent expense. How would you explain to Mr. Gardner that there is no need for a special rent expense column in his cash payments journal?

CASE 4

Mr. Morris of the Morris Dairy Farm is checking over his monthly schedule of accounts payable. He notices that the total amount owed all creditors is $1,780.60. He wants to find out when payment is due each of his creditors. Where can he get this information?

Drill for Understanding

DRILL 13-A | Analyzing transactions affecting purchases and cash payments

Instructions: For each of the transactions listed below, prepare two T accounts to show which account in the *general ledger* is debited and which account is credited. If the transaction also affects an account in the *accounts payable ledger*, prepare a third T account to show whether the creditor's account is debited or credited. The first transaction is given as an example.

General Ledger				*Accounts Payable Ledger*	
Purchases		**Accounts Payable**		**Hale Company**	
300.00			300.00		300.00

1. Purchased merchandise on account from Hale Company, $300.00.
2. Paid cash, $100.00, to Bell, Inc., on account.
3. The owner, Tom Allen, withdrew cash, $150.00, for his personal use.
4. Paid cash, $230.00, for one month's rent.
5. Paid cash, $300.00, for weekly salaries.
6. Purchased merchandise on account from Retz, Inc., $500.00.
7. Paid cash, $50.00, to Downtown Supply Company, for merchandise.
8. Paid cash, $30.00, to Millers Delivery Service, for delivering merchandise sold. (Miscellaneous Expense)
9. Paid cash, $200.00, to Hale Company, on account.

Application Problems

PROBLEM 13-1 | Recording cash payments

The following cash payments were made by Steck's Men's Shop during June of the current year. All checks were numbered consecutively, beginning with No. 901.

Instructions: 1. Prepare page 6 of a cash payments journal by writing the proper heading at the top of each column. Use the same headings as shown in the cash payments journal on page 196.

2. Journalize each of the following transactions:

June 1. Paid $200.00 to B. J. Burham for the June rent.
2. Paid $300.00 to the owner, Harold Steck, as a withdrawal for personal use.
5. Paid $462.00 to Holden and Hodge on account.
9. Paid $24.60 to Bell Telephone Company for the June telephone bill. (Miscellaneous Expense)
13. Paid $594.00 to Gooden Men's Suits, Inc., on account.
15. Paid $686.00 to Bryan Hat Company on account.
16. Paid $280.00 for semimonthly salaries.
19. Paid $305.00 for cash purchase of merchandise.
19. Paid $358.00 to Sherman Clothing Company on account.
21. Paid $1,264.40 to Long and Clark on account.
23. Paid $220.00 to Holden and Hodge on account.
26. Paid $225.50 for cash purchase of merchandise.
29. Paid $300.00 to the owner, Harold Steck, as a withdrawal for personal use.
29. Paid $75.50 for cash purchase of merchandise.
30. Paid $280.00 for semimonthly salaries.
30. Paid $45.00 to Midway Electric Company for the June electric bill. (Miscellaneous Expense)

Instructions: 3. Foot, prove, total, and rule the cash payments journal.

The cash payments journal completed in this problem will be used in Problem 13-2.

PROBLEM 13-2 | Posting from a cash payments journal; preparing a schedule of accounts payable

The accounts payable ledger and the general ledger prepared in Problem 12-2 and the cash payments journal prepared in Problem 13-1 are needed to complete this problem. If these are not available, complete Appendix Problem 13-A.

Instructions: 1. Post the amounts in the General Debit column of the cash payments journal to the general ledger.

2. Post the amounts in the Accounts Payable Debit column of the cash payments journal to the creditors' accounts in the accounts payable ledger.

3. Post the totals of the special amount columns in the cash payments journal to the general ledger.

4. Prepare a schedule of accounts payable from the accounts payable ledger. (Use the illustration on page 200 as a guide.)

If the total of the schedule of accounts payable and the balance of the accounts payable account in the general ledger do not agree, recheck your work until you find the error.

Optional Problems

★ SUPPLEMENTARY PROBLEM 13-S

Recording and posting cash payments

Donald McVean owns Don's Gift Shop. During the month of August of the current year, he completed the cash payments transactions listed below. All payments were made by check, beginning with No. 250.

Instructions: 1. Record the cash payments transactions on page 8 of a cash payments journal similar to the one shown on page 196.

Aug. 1. Paid $125.00 for August rent.
2. Paid $300.00 to Perry Dodd on account.
3. Paid $163.75 to Moore Products on account.
4. Paid $180.00 for weekly salaries.
8. Paid $119.80 to Paul Evans on account.
11. Paid $180.00 for weekly salaries.
15. Paid $75.00 for cash purchase of merchandise.
16. Paid $110.00 to Beck Stores, Inc., on account.
18. Paid $180.00 for weekly salaries.
19. Paid $32.90 for telephone bill. (Miscellaneous Expense)
21. Paid $250.00 to R. D. Lee Company on account.
23. Paid $165.40 for cash purchase of merchandise.
25. Paid $180.00 for weekly salaries.
25. Paid $300.00 to Mr. McVean for withdrawal of cash for personal use.
28. Paid $75.00 to Perry Dodd on account.
29. Paid $53.00 for electric bill. (Miscellaneous Expense)
30. Paid $127.00 to Byers & Black Company on account.
31. Paid $42.50 to R. D. Lee Company on account.
31. Paid $39.50 for cash purchase of merchandise.

Instructions: 2. Foot, prove, total, and rule the cash payments journal.

3. Open the following accounts in a general ledger. For those accounts with a balance, record the balance as of August 1 of the current year. Allow four lines for each account.

Acct. No.	*Account Title*	*Account Balance*
11	Cash	$3,960.00
21	Accounts Payable	1,514.30
32	Donald McVean, Drawing	—
51	Purchases	—
61	Miscellaneous Expense	—
62	Rent Expense	—
63	Salary Expense	—

Instructions: 4. Open the following accounts for creditors in the accounts payable ledger. Allow four lines for each account. Record the balance for each account as of August 1 of the current year.

Creditor	*Account Balance on August 1 of Current Year*
Beck Stores, Inc., 204 Clifton Avenue Clearwater, Florida 33515	$211.25
Byers & Black Company, 16 W. Ninth Street Panama City, Florida 32407	127.00
Perry Dodd, 860 Grove Blvd. Ookala, Hawaii 96774	450.00
Paul Evans, 554 Kennedy Avenue Lake Worth, Florida 33460	219.80
R. D. Lee Company, 7204 Miami Road Baltimore, Maryland 21230	342.50
Moore Products, 1547 Kenova Street Grundy, Virginia 24614	163.75

Instructions: 5. Post the individual amounts in the General Debit column and the Accounts Payable Debit column of the cash payments journal.

6. Post the totals of the special amount columns of the cash payments journal.

7. Prepare a schedule of accounts payable.

★ BONUS PROBLEM 13-B

Recording and posting cash payments

B. R. Polson is the owner of Polsons Gift Shop. He finds he can save time in posting by using a cash payments journal with a special column for Purchases Debit and a special column for Miscellaneous Expense Debit. The cash payments journal he uses is shown below.

CASH PAYMENTS JOURNAL PAGE

Date	Account Debited	Ck. No.	Post. Ref.	General Debit	Accounts Payable Debit	Purchases Debit	Misc. Expense Debit	Cash Credit

During the month of October of the current year, Mr. Polson had the following cash payments transactions, all of which were paid by check, beginning with No. 351. All expense items other than rent and salary are classified as Miscellaneous Expense.

Instructions: 1. Record each of the transactions on page 30 of a cash payments journal with five amount columns as shown on page 208.

Oct. 1. Paid $400.00 for October rent.
2. Paid $24.80 for telephone bill.
3. Paid $16.80 for electric bill.
3. Paid $747.20 to J. O. Mills Company on account.
4. Paid $128.20 to Globe Company for cash purchase of merchandise.
5. Paid $38.60 to T. M. Jory on account.
8. Paid $14.80 for water bill.
10. Paid $200.00 to Fox & Sons on account.
12. Paid $350.00 to Happy Greeting Cards on account.
16. Paid $39.80 to J. O. Mills Company for cash purchase of merchandise.
22. Paid $103.60 to Jason Company on account.
26. Paid $294.20 to Morris Company for cash purchase of merchandise.
26. Paid $4.90 to Fast Freight, Inc., for transportation charges on October 16 purchase from J. O. Mills Company. (Mr. Polson debits the purchases account for all transportation charges on merchandise bought.)
26. Paid $27.50 for neon lighting tubes.
29. Paid $237.00 to T. M. Jory on account.
30. Paid $37.18 to Acme Truck Company for transportation charges on October 26 purchase from Morris Company.
30. Paid $295.00 for salary of clerk.
30. Paid $189.90 to Sacramento Gift House on account.
30. Withdrew $400.00 for personal use.

Instructions: 2. Foot, prove, total, and rule the cash payments journal.

3. Open the following accounts in a general ledger. Record the balances as of October 1 of the current year.

Acct. No.	*Account Title*	*Account Balance*
11	Cash	$5,750.00
21	Accounts Payable	2,450.20
32	B. R. Polson, Drawing	—
51	Purchases	—
61	Miscellaneous Expense	—
62	Rent Expense	—
63	Salary Expense	—

Instructions: 4. Open the following creditors' accounts in the accounts payable ledger. Record the balances as of October 1 of the current year.

Creditor	*Account Balance on October 1 of Current Year*
Fox & Sons, 4040 Sonora Santa Ana, Calif. 92706	$228.00
Happy Greeting Cards, 830 Archer Lane Madison, Wisconsin 53730	375.60
Jason Company, 6 Terra Linda Riverside, Calif. 92508	300.00
T. M. Jory, 90 Martin Road Weston, Ontario	390.40
J. O. Mills Company, Valley Road Santa Ana, Calif. 92730	747.20
Sacramento Gift House, 874 Arden Street Sacramento, Calif. 95807	409.00

5. Post the individual amounts in the General Debit column and the Accounts Payable Debit column of the cash payments journal.

6. Post the totals of the special columns of the cash payments journal.

7. Prepare a schedule of accounts payable.

CHAPTER 14 RECORDING THE SALE OF MERCHANDISE ON ACCOUNT

A transaction in which merchandise is sold with an agreement that the amount is to be paid at a later date is known as a *sale on account.* A sale on account is sometimes called a *charge sale* or a *sale on credit.* Those to whom a business sells merchandise are known as *customers.* A customer to whom a sale on account is made is called a *charge customer.*

McCann Office Furniture sells merchandise both for cash and on account. The recording of cash sales will be described in Chapter 15.

THE SALES SLIP — THE SOURCE DOCUMENT

A business form that shows all the details about a sale is known as a *sales slip.* A sales slip is sometimes called a *sales ticket.* McCann Office Furniture uses sales slips as the source documents from which information is obtained for recording sales on account.

In many stores each salesman has his own sales slip book in which he records each charge sale as it is completed. Each sales slip is numbered, and the salesman must account for each number. One copy of the sales slip is used by the bookkeeper in making the journal entry for each sale on account. Another copy of the sales slip is handed to the customer or is wrapped with the merchandise when it is given or delivered to him. Before the sales slip is given to the customer, he may be required to sign it to show that he approves the charge to his account.

McCann Office Furniture
640 Central Avenue, Portland, Oregon 97227

No. 262 Date Nov. 2 19 67

Sold to:
Frank Wright ✓
1240 Short Street
Portland, Oregon 97208

Terms: 30 days

Quantity	Description	Unit Price	Amount
1	452 Desk	128.00	128.00
2	452C Chairs	13.00	26.00
		Total	154.00

Frank Wright — Customer's Signature
R.L.S. — Salesman

Sales slip

Analyzing a sales slip

The form and the arrangement of items on the sales slip vary with the particular needs of each business. The sales slip on page 211 shows the following information:

1. Name and address of the seller.
2. Sales slip number.
3. Date of the sale.
4. Name and address of the customer.
5. Terms of the sale.
6. Quantity, description, and unit price of each item sold.
7. Total amount for each item and the total amount of the sale.
8. Customer's signature.
9. Salesman's name, initials, or number.

If a business needs to record other information on its sales slip, additional space is provided. For example, a business with more than one selling department may provide space for the department name or number.

Charge-a-plates and sales on account

An embossed metal or plastic plate that is used to identify a customer who has a charge account is called a *charge-a-plate*. A charge-a-plate is sometimes known as a *credit card*. A common form of charge-a-plate is shown at the right.

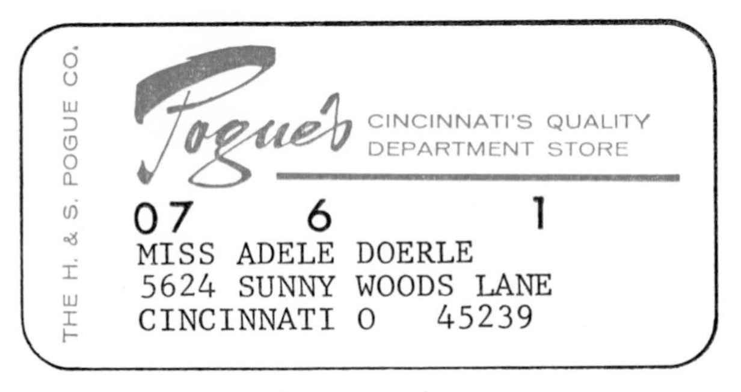

Charge-a-plate

When the sales slip is prepared, the salesperson places the customer's charge-a-plate and the sales slip in a special imprinting device. This device records the customer's name, address, and account number on all copies of the sales slip. The use of a charge-a-plate eliminates the time-consuming process of writing on the sales slip this type of information about a charge customer. The charge-a-plate also serves to identify the customer as one to whom the business has granted the privilege of buying merchandise and services on account. Before a charge-a-plate is issued to a customer, his credit rating is carefully checked by the business.

JOURNALIZING SALES ON ACCOUNT

A special journal in which all sales of merchandise on account are recorded is called a *sales journal*. A sales journal is sometimes called a *sales book* or a *sales register*.

The sales journal

McCann Office Furniture records all sales of merchandise on account in a sales journal such as the one shown below. Only sales on account are recorded in the sales journal. Each page of the sales journal provides columns in which all the data needed about a sale on account can be summarized on a single line.

SALES JOURNAL					PAGE	
	DATE	SALE NO.	ACCOUNT DEBITED	POST. REF.	ACCTS. REC., DR. SALES, CR.	
1						1
2						2

Sales journal

Sale-on-account transaction No. 1

November 2, 1967. Sold merchandise on account to Frank Wright, $154.00. Sales Slip No. 262.

After the information on the sales slip has been verified, the data are summarized on a single line in the sales journal. The sales slip used as the source document for sale-on-account transaction No. 1 is shown on page 211. The steps in journalizing this transaction in the sales journal are:

Step 1

Write the date of the sale, *1967, Nov. 2,* in the Date column.

Step 2

Record the number of the sales slip, *262,* in the Sale No. column.

Step 3

Write the name of the customer to whom the sale was made, *Frank Wright,* in the Account Debited column.

SALES JOURNAL						PAGE 9	
	DATE		SALE NO.	ACCOUNT DEBITED	POST. REF.	ACCTS. REC., DR. SALES, CR.	
1	1967 Nov.	2	262	Frank Wright		154 00	1
2							2
3	STEP 1		STEP 2	STEP 3		STEP 4	3
4							4

Journalizing sale-on-account transaction No. 1

Step 4

Record the amount of the sale on account, *$154.00*, in the amount column.

Step 5

Place a check mark on the sales slip at the right of the customer's name to show that the sales slip has been recorded.

In the sales journal all that is needed to describe each transaction is the date, the sale number, the name of the customer, and the amount of the sale. Any additional data can be obtained from the sales slip.

All sales slips for sales on account made during the month are recorded in the sales journal in the same manner as described for sale-on-account transaction No. 1. The sales journal of McCann Office Furniture for the month of November, showing all entries for sales on account, is illustrated below.

SALES JOURNAL — PAGE 9

	DATE		SALE NO.	ACCOUNT DEBITED	POST. REF.	ACCTS. REC., DR. SALES, CR.	
1	1967 Nov.	2	262	Frank Wright		154 00	1
2		3	263	W. R. Johns		300 00	2
3		6	264	William Poole		124 00	3
4		9	265	John Shreves		251 00	4
5		9	266	Raymond Holland		298 00	5
6		13	267	Wayne Hunter		352 00	6
7		14	268	Donald Carter		125 00	7
8		16	269	John Shreves		74 00	8
9		20	270	William Poole		285 00	9
10		24	271	Donald Carter		70 00	10
11		27	272	John Shreves		101 00	11
12		30	273	W. R. Johns		176 00	12

Sales journal with all sales on account recorded for the month

On many items sold by retailers, the retailer must collect sales taxes. The method of journalizing taxes collected from the customer and the method of paying these taxes to the government is not discussed in this chapter.

Totaling and ruling the sales journal

After all the sales slips for sales on account have been journalized for the month, a single line is ruled across the amount column and the column is totaled. The date of the last day of the month is written in the Date column, and the word *Total* is written in the Account Debited column. Double lines are then ruled across the amount column. The totaling and ruling of the sales journal of McCann Office Furniture is shown below.

SALES JOURNAL — PAGE 9

	DATE		SALE NO.	ACCOUNT DEBITED	POST. REF.	ACCTS. REC., DR. SALES, CR.	
1	1967 Nov.	2	262	Frank Wright		154 00	1
2		3	263	W. R. Johns		300 00	2
11		27	272	John Shreves		101 00	11
12		30	273	W. R. Johns		176 00	12
13		30		Total		2 310 00	13

Sales journal, totaled and ruled

Analyzing the total of the sales journal

The total of the amount column in the sales journal is the total amount of the sales of merchandise on account. A separate account, Sales, is kept in the income division of the general ledger in which all sales of merchandise are summarized. See the chart of accounts on page 166.

When a business sells to many customers on account, the general ledger might contain a great many accounts with customers. In order to avoid a bulky general ledger, it is customary to summarize the total amount to be collected from all customers in a single general ledger account. The account in the general ledger that summarizes all the amounts to be collected from charge customers is called *Accounts Receivable.* This account is classified as an asset, as shown in the chart of accounts on page 166.

The total of the amount column in the sales journal is the sum of amounts to be collected from charge customers for sales on account during the month. The total of the amount column is an increase in the balance of the accounts receivable account. The asset account, Accounts Receivable, has a debit balance. Increases are recorded on the balance side, which is the debit side. Therefore, the accounts receivable account in the general ledger of McCann Office Furniture is debited for $2,310.00, the total amount to be collected from customers.

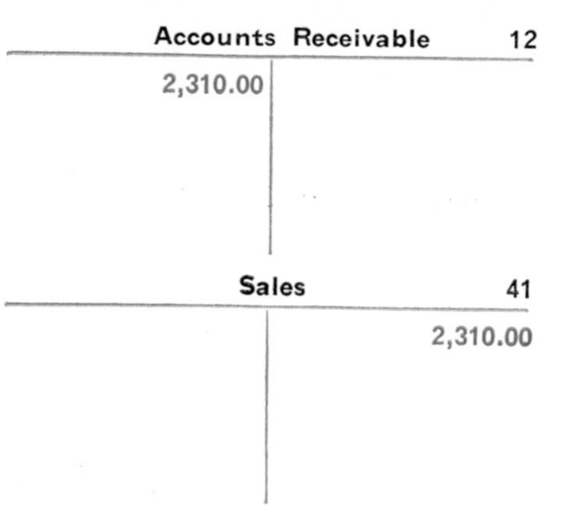

The total of the amount column of the sales journal is also the total amount of charge sales during the month. The total charge sales represent an increase in income. Income accounts always have a credit balance, and increases in income are recorded on the balance side, the credit side. Therefore, the sales account in the general ledger is credited for $2,310.00 to show an increase in income.

POSTING THE TOTAL OF THE SALES JOURNAL

After the sales slips for the month have been recorded in the sales journal, and the sales journal has been totaled and ruled, the total of the amount column is posted to the accounts in the general ledger.

The illustrations below show the Total line of the sales journal and the two accounts in the general ledger, Accounts Receivable and Sales. The two accounts are shown as they appear after the total of the amount column of the sales journal has been posted.

SALES JOURNAL — PAGE 9

	DATE		SALE NO.	ACCOUNT DEBITED	POST. REF.	ACCTS. REC., DR. SALES, CR.	
1	1967 Nov.	2	262	Frank Wright		154 00	1
2		3	263	W. R. Johns		300 00	2
12		30	273	W. R. Johns		176 00	12
13		30		Total		2310 00	13
14					STEP 2 →	(12) (41) ← STEP 4	14

Accounts Receivable — ACCOUNT NO. 12

DATE		ITEMS	POST. REF.	DEBIT	DATE	ITEMS	POST. REF.	CREDIT
1967 Nov.	1	Balance	✓	1102 00				
STEP 1 →	30		S9	2310 00				

Sales — ACCOUNT NO. 41

DATE	ITEMS	POST. REF.	DEBIT	DATE		ITEMS	POST. REF.	CREDIT
				1967 Nov.	30		S9	2310 00 ← STEP 3

In the sales journal, the heading of the amount column indicates that the total sales is debited to Accounts Receivable and credited to Sales. The steps in posting the total of the amount column in the sales journal to the two accounts in the general ledger are:

Step 1

Post the amount, *$2,310.00*, to the debit side of the accounts receivable account. Write the date, *30*, in the Date column. Write the page number of the sales journal, *S9*, in the Post. Ref. column of the account.

S is the abbreviation for Sales Journal.

Step 2

Write the number of the accounts receivable account in parentheses, (*12*), below the double lines under the total of the amount column in the sales journal.

Step 3

Post the amount, *$2,310.00*, to the credit side of the sales account. Write the date, *1967, Nov. 30*, in the Date column. Write the page number of the sales journal, *S9*, in the Post. Ref. column of the account.

Step 4

Write the number of the sales account in parentheses, (*41*), below the double lines under the total of the amount column in the sales journal.

Placing the numbers of the two general ledger accounts in parentheses below the total of the amount column in the sales journal shows that the posting of the total has been completed.

The posting of the one total of the sales journal as a *debit* to Accounts Receivable and a *credit* to Sales maintains the equality of debits and credits in the general ledger. Maintaining an equality of debits and credits in the general ledger at all times is a very important principle of double-entry bookkeeping.

ACCOUNTS RECEIVABLE LEDGER

The accounts receivable account in the general ledger shows the total amount to be collected from all charge customers. But it does not show the amount to be collected from each customer. Therefore, it is common practice to have a separate ledger in which an account is kept for each charge customer. A ledger that contains accounts with charge customers only is called an *accounts receivable ledger*.

The sum of the balances of all the accounts in the accounts receivable ledger is the same as the balance of the accounts receivable account in the general ledger. Each time the accounts receivable account in the general ledger is increased, a charge customer's account in the accounts receivable ledger must also be increased by the same amount. Each time the accounts receivable account in the general ledger is decreased, a charge customer's account in the accounts receivable ledger must also be decreased by the same amount.

When an accounts receivable account is used in the general ledger to summarize the total amount to be collected from all charge customers, only one account, Accounts Receivable, needs to be listed on the trial balance and on the balance sheet.

Relationship between the accounts receivable account and the accounts receivable ledger

The accounts receivable account in the general ledger is the controlling account for the accounts receivable ledger. The accounts receivable ledger is also called a subsidiary ledger. The relationship between the accounts receivable ledger and the accounts receivable account in the general ledger is shown in the chart below.

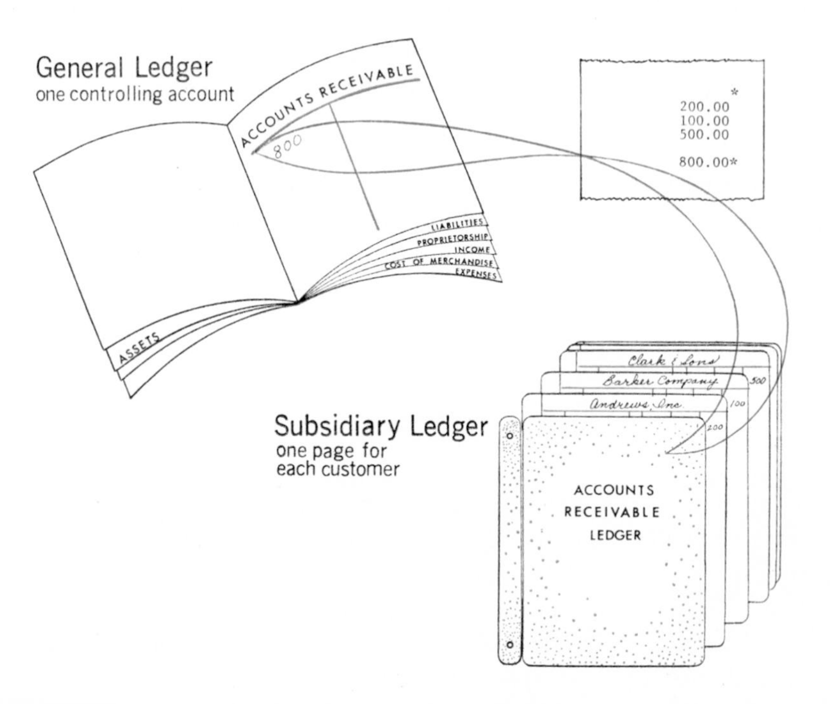

The balances of the individual accounts in the accounts receivable ledger (a subsidiary ledger) are brought together and summarized in Accounts Receivable (a controlling account in the general ledger.)

Accounts receivable ledger form

McCann Office Furniture keeps all accounts with charge customers in an accounts receivable ledger. The accounts receivable ledger form, illustrated below, has a balance-column ruling similar to that used for the accounts payable ledger described in Chapter 12. The difference is that for the customers' accounts, the balance column is headed Debit Balance instead of Credit Balance.

NAME

ADDRESS

DATE	ITEMS	POST. REF.	DEBIT	CREDIT	DEBIT BALANCE

Each account in the accounts receivable ledger is opened by writing the name and the address of the customer on the first two lines of the account page. The name and address of each new customer are obtained from the first sales slip issued to the customer. The Debit Balance column is used to record the balance of the customer's account after each debit or each credit amount has been posted to the account. The Debit Balance column shows the current amount to be collected from each charge customer.

POSTING FROM THE SALES JOURNAL TO THE ACCOUNTS RECEIVABLE LEDGER

Each entry in the sales journal is an amount to be collected from a charge customer named in the Account Debited column. Therefore, each entry in the sales journal is posted individually to the charge customer's account in the accounts receivable ledger.

Steps in posting to a customer's account

The illustration on the next page shows the sales journal and the account for Frank Wright in the accounts receivable ledger after the entry on Line 1 of the sales journal has been posted.

The steps in posting the entry on Line 1 of the sales journal are:

Step 1

Write the amount of the sale, *$154.00,* in the Debit column of the account for Frank Wright.

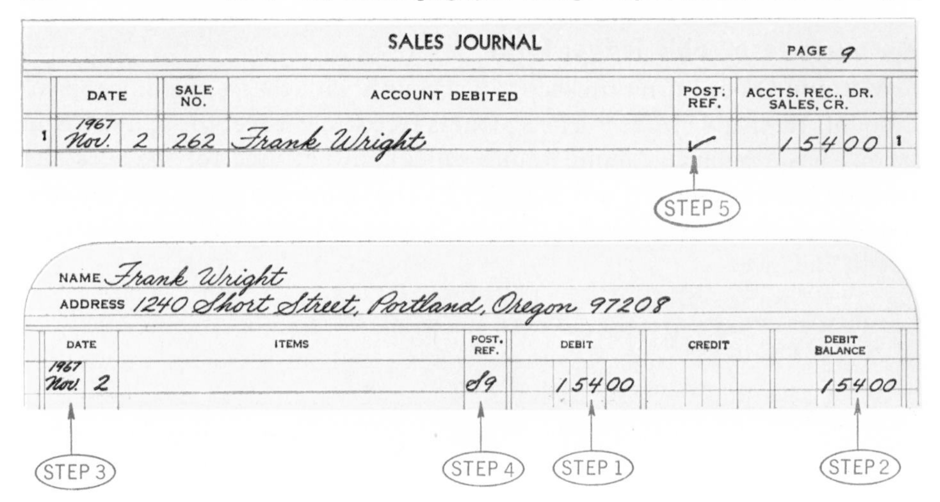
SALES JOURNAL PAGE 9

	DATE		SALE NO.	ACCOUNT DEBITED	POST. REF.	ACCTS. REC., DR. SALES, CR.	
1	1967 Nov.	2	262	Frank Wright	✓	154 00	1

NAME Frank Wright
ADDRESS 1240 Short Street, Portland, Oregon 97208

DATE		ITEMS	POST. REF.	DEBIT	CREDIT	DEBIT BALANCE
1967 Nov.	2		S9	154 00		154 00

Step 2

Add the amount in the Debit column to the amount of the previous balance shown in the Debit Balance column. Write the new balance, *$154.00*, in the Debit Balance column.

> Before this entry was posted, the Frank Wright account had a zero balance. Therefore, the amount written in the Debit Balance column is the new balance, *$154.00.*

Step 3

Write the year, month, and day, *1967, Nov. 2,* in the Date column of the account.

Step 4

Write the page number of the sales journal, *S9*, in the Post. Ref. column of the account.

Step 5

Place a check mark in the Post. Ref. column of the sales journal to show that the posting of the item on Line 1 of the sales journal has been completed.

> Accounts with charge customers are placed in alphabetic order in the accounts receivable ledger. When records are kept by hand, usually the accounts are not given account numbers. Thus, a check mark is used instead of an account number to show that the posting has been completed.

Recording a customer's balance on a new page in the accounts receivable ledger

On November 1, 1967, McCann Office Furniture prepared a new page in the accounts receivable ledger for W. R. Johns. At that time the account balance for W. R. Johns was $79.00. This amount is recorded on the new page as shown below.

NAME W. R. Johns
ADDRESS 2609 West Jackson Street, Portland, Oregon 97203

DATE		ITEMS	POST. REF.	DEBIT	CREDIT	DEBIT BALANCE
1967 Nov.	1	Balance	✓			79 00

The name and address of the customer are written on the lines provided at the top of the account page. The account balance is written in the Debit Balance column. The date is recorded in the Date column, and the word *Balance* is written in the Items column. A check mark is placed in the Post. Ref. column to show that the entry was not posted from a journal. The same procedure is followed in opening a new page for any account that has a balance.

Posting to a customer's account having a previous balance

The illustration below shows the sales journal and the account for W. R. Johns after the entry on Line 2 of the sales journal has been posted.

SALES JOURNAL PAGE 9

	DATE		SALE NO.	ACCOUNT DEBITED	POST. REF.	ACCTS. REC., DR. SALES, CR.	
1	1967 Nov.	2	262	Frank Wright	✓	154 00	1
2		3	263	W. R. Johns	✓	300 00	2

NAME W. R. Johns
ADDRESS 2609 West Jackson Street, Portland, Oregon 97203

DATE		ITEMS	POST. REF.	DEBIT	CREDIT	DEBIT BALANCE
1967 Nov.	1	Balance	✓			79 00
	3		S9	300 00		379 00

The same steps are followed in posting the entry on Line 2 of the sales journal as are used for posting the entry on Line 1. In Step 2, however, the amount in the Debit column, *$300.00*, is added to the previous balance, $79.00, and the new balance of the account, *$379.00*, is written in the Debit Balance column.

THE COMPLETED SALES JOURNAL

The completed sales journal of McCann Office Furniture for the month of November, 1967, after all the posting has been completed, is shown below.

SALES JOURNAL — PAGE 9

	DATE		SALE NO.	ACCOUNT DEBITED	POST. REF.	ACCTS. REC., DR. SALES, CR.	
1	1967 Nov.	2	262	Frank Wright	✓	154 00	1
2		3	263	W. R. Johns	✓	300 00	2
3		6	264	William Poole	✓	124 00	3
4		9	265	John Shreves	✓	251 00	4
5		9	266	Raymond Holland	✓	298 00	5
6		13	267	Wayne Hunter	✓	352 00	6
7		14	268	Donald Carter	✓	125 00	7
8		16	269	John Shreves	✓	74 00	8
9		20	270	William Poole	✓	285 00	9
10		24	271	Donald Carter	✓	70 00	10
11		27	272	John Shreves	✓	101 00	11
12		30	273	W. R. Johns	✓	176 00	12
13		30		Total		2310 00	13
14						(12) (41)	14
15							15
16							16
17							17

Sales journal after all posting has been completed

In order to keep all accounts with charge customers up-to-date, the individual entries in the sales journal are posted frequently during the month. The total of the sales journal is posted only at the end of the month.

A FLOW CHART OF RECORDING THE SALE OF MERCHANDISE ON ACCOUNT

A summary of the procedure followed in recording the sales of merchandise on account is shown in the flow chart on page 223. This procedure may be summarized as follows:

1. After the sales slip has been verified, it is recorded in the sales journal.
2. Each item in the amount column of the sales journal is posted as a debit to the individual customer's account in the accounts receivable ledger. This posting is done frequently during the month.

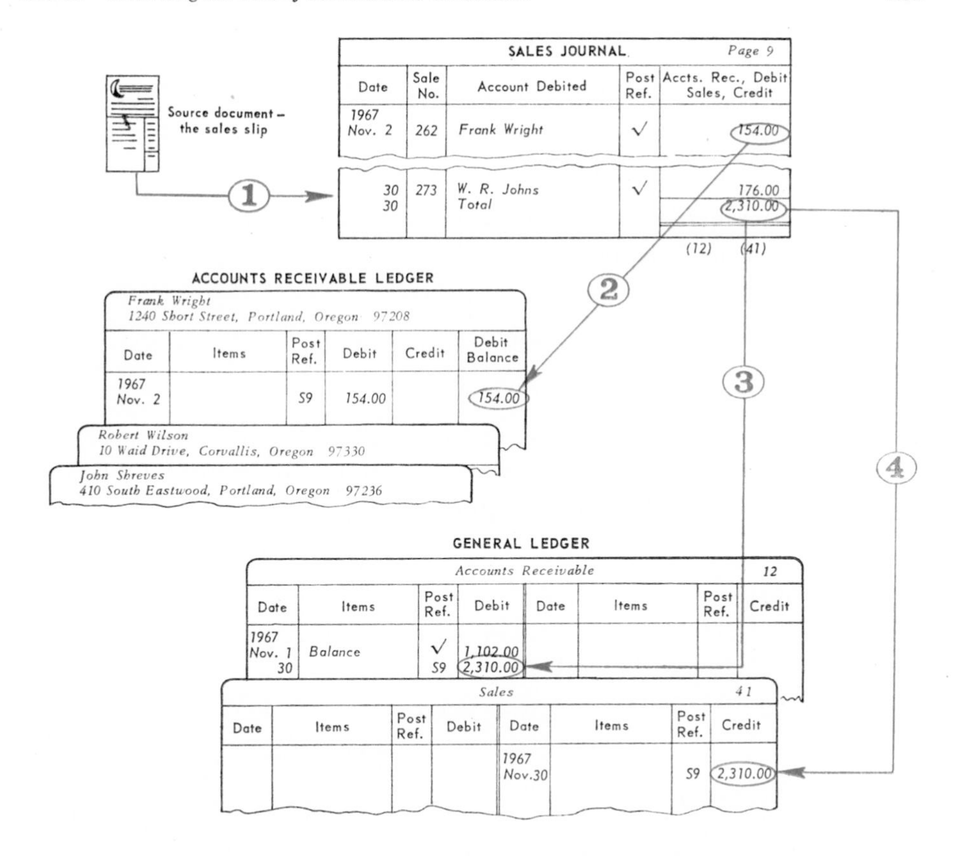

A flow chart of recording the sale of merchandise on account

3. The total of the amount column in the sales journal is posted as a debit to the accounts receivable account in the general ledger. This posting is done at the end of the month.

4. The total of the amount column in the sales journal is also posted as a credit to the sales account in the general ledger. This posting is done at the end of the month.

ANOTHER METHOD OF RECORDING SALES ON ACCOUNT— USING SALES SLIPS AS A SALES JOURNAL

Some businesses file all their sales slips together and use them as a sales journal. These businesses post directly from the sales slips to the customers' accounts in the accounts receivable ledger. At the end of the month, the total of all the sales slips for the month is recorded in the general journal in one entry.

When sales slips are used as a sales journal, the steps are:

Step 1

Post the total of each sales slip directly to the debit side of the proper customer's account in the accounts receivable ledger.

Step 2

Place a check mark at the right of the customer's name on the sales slip to show that it has been posted.

Step 3

File all sales slips for the month in a special file.

Step 4

At the end of the month, add the totals of all sales slips in the special file to obtain the total amount of sales on account for the month. Ordinarily an adding machine is used for this purpose.

Step 5

Record in the general journal the total of all sales slips prepared during the month. Debit Accounts Receivable and credit Sales for the same amount, *$4,870.00*, as shown below.

GENERAL JOURNAL — PAGE 4

	DATE		ACCOUNT TITLE	POST. REF.	DEBIT	CREDIT	
1	1967 Apr.	30	Accounts Receivable		4870 00		1
2			Sales			4870 00	2
3			Sales slips Nos. 490 to 612				3
4			for April.				4
5							5

Step 6

Post the general journal entry to the two general ledger accounts, Accounts Receivable and Sales.

TRANSPORTATION CHARGES ON MERCHANDISE SOLD

Transportation charges for delivering merchandise sold may be paid by the seller. When the seller agrees to pay the transportation charges, the shipping terms are *f.o.b. destination.* The letters *f.o.b.* stand for *free on board.* The cost of delivering the merchandise is debited to an account with a title such as *Delivery Expense* or *Freight Out.* When McCann Office Furniture pays a transportation company for delivering merchandise, the delivery expense account is debited and the cash account is credited. When the buyer agrees to pay the transportation charges, the shipping terms are *f.o.b. shipping point.* In most instances, the customers of McCann Office Furniture pay the transportation charges.

Increasing Your Business Vocabulary

What is the meaning of each of the following:

a sale on account
b customers
c charge customer
d sales slip
e charge-a-plate
f sales journal
g accounts receivable ledger
h f.o.b. destination
i f.o.b. shipping point

Study Questions

1. What is the source document from which information is obtained for recording a sale of merchandise on account?
2. What kind of sales transactions are recorded in a sales journal?
3. What information is summarized on a single line in the sales journal for each sale recorded?
4. Why is a check mark placed on the sales slip after the information on it has been summarized in the sales journal?
5. What general ledger account is debited and what general ledger account is credited when the total of the sales journal is posted?
6. Why are the account numbers placed below the total of the sales journal shown on page 216?
7. Why is S9 written in the Post. Ref. column of the account for Frank Wright shown on page 220?
8. What is the relationship between the accounts receivable account in the general ledger and the separate accounts for customers in the accounts receivable ledger?
9. Why are individual entries in the sales journal posted frequently to customers' accounts in the accounts receivable ledger?

Cases for Business Decision

CASE 1

The College Clothing Store employs three salespeople. Each salesperson uses a separate autographic register to record sales of merchandise on account. The sales slips are consecutively numbered in each autographic register. In one autographic register, the numbers begin with 1001; in the second register, the numbers begin with 2001; in the third, the numbers begin with 3001. How will the use of the Sale No. column in the sales journal for the College Clothing Store differ from that of the Sale No. column in the sales journal shown on page 222?

CASE 2

The owner of Tom's Radio and TV Shop is concerned that his total sales for the past six months have been considerably lower than for the previous months. What are some of the factors that the owner should investigate regarding this decrease in sales?

CASE 3

A grocer sells for cash a typewriter that he has used in the store. He records this transaction in his sales journal. Is this procedure correct? Why?

CASE 4

Mark Peterson makes 450 sales on account in an average month. He records each sale in the sales journal, from which he posts to the subsidiary and the general ledgers.

(a) How much work might be saved by posting directly from the sales slips to the customers' accounts in the subsidiary ledger?

(b) If this method were followed, how should he record the total sales for the month?

Drills for Understanding

DRILL 14-A | Accounts receivable

Fischer Electronics keeps its customers' accounts in a general ledger. A portion of the debit column from the trial balance for the month ended November 30 of the current year is shown at the right.

Instructions: Answer the following questions:

1. What is the total amount due from all charge customers?
2. If Fischer Electronics were to use an accounts receivable ledger:
   (a) What should be the name of the controlling account to be used?
   (b) What would be the balance of the controlling account on the November 30 trial balance?
   (c) How many lines would be saved on the trial balance?
   (d) How many customers' accounts would appear in the accounts receivable ledger?

Portion of Debit Column of Trial Balance

Cash	$4,000.00
Merchandise Inventory	6,000.00
Robert Bogart	150.00
James Bowen	170.00
Ansel Brown	75.00
George Green	65.00
Robert Martin	240.00
Rose Moore	90.00
Donald Scott	75.00
Albert Topping	125.00
William Wallace	90.00
John Walsh	180.00
Supplies	100.00
Prepaid Insurance	80.00

DRILL 14-B | Analyzing purchases and sales transactions

The business transactions given below are similar to those described in Chapters 12, 13, and 14.

Transactions

1. Sold merchandise on account to A. J. Peters.
2. Purchased merchandise on account from J. W. Sells.
3. Paid cash to Marion Company on account.
4. Purchased merchandise on account from Mills, Inc.
5. Sold merchandise on account to C. Sampson.
6. Purchased merchandise on account from Lee Knox.
7. Paid cash to Showers Brothers on account.
8. Sold merchandise on account to Dell Products.
9. Paid cash to Bard Company for merchandise purchased.

Instructions: 1. Use a form similar to the one shown below for analyzing each of the transactions above. The first transaction is given as an example.

	Name of general ledger account to be		Name of account in accounts receivable ledger			Name of account in accounts payable ledger		
	Debited	Credited		Dr.	Cr.		Dr.	Cr.
1.	*Accounts Receivable*	*Sales*	*A. J. Peters*	√				
2.								
3.								

Instructions: 2. For each of the transactions indicate which account in the general ledger is debited and which account is credited.

3. Indicate also the name of the account in the accounts receivable ledger or the accounts payable ledger that is debited or credited.

Application Problems

PROBLEM 14-1 | Journalizing sales on account

The following sales of merchandise on account were made by Carr Company, wholesale grocers, during the month of November of the current year.

Date		*Customer*	*Amount of Sale*
Nov.	1	E. M. Alexander	$140.00
	3	Hogan Drugs	302.50
	6	J. B. Bonnett	90.40
	8	S. W. Hull	120.00
	10	Ross Brothers	345.75
	14	Shoemaker & Company	260.10
	17	H & H Company	140.20
	17	S. W. Hull	230.20
	20	E. M. Alexander	190.40
	21	Ross Brothers	110.50
	22	Hogan Drugs	225.80
	27	J. B. Bonnett	150.50
	28	Shoemaker & Company	75.00
	28	H & H Company	260.40
	30	S. W. Hull	130.25

Instructions: 1. Prepare page 11 of a sales journal by writing the proper heading at the top of each column. Use the same headings as shown in the sales journal on page 214.

2. Journalize each of the transactions above. Number all sales slips consecutively, beginning with No. 911.

The sales journal prepared in this problem will be used in Problem 14-2.

PROBLEM 14-2 | Posting from the sales journal to two ledgers

Carr Company has the following accounts in the accounts receivable ledger:

Customer	*Account Balance on Nov. 1 of Current Year*
E. M. Alexander, 3301 Memorial Drive Pueblo, Colorado 81003	$400.20
J. B. Bonnett, 905 South Walnut Golden, Colorado 80401	310.30
H & H Company, 312 North Broadway Prescott, Arizona 86301	240.20
Hogan Drugs, 131 South Madison Sterling, Colorado 80751	125.00
S. W. Hull, 204 Jackson Street Tucson, Arizona 85727	350.60
Ross Brothers, Dixie Plaza Denver, Colorado 80208	320.40
Shoemaker & Company, 425 North High Denver, Colorado 80206	120.30

Instructions: 1. Open an account for each of the customers. Use an accounts receivable ledger with balance-column ruling as shown on page 219. Allow five lines for each account. Record the balance of each account.

2. Post the entries in the sales journal prepared in Problem 14-1 to the proper accounts in the accounts receivable ledger.

3. Total and rule the sales journal.

4. Open the following accounts in the general ledger of Carr Company. Allow four lines for each account. Record the balance of each account that has one.

Account Number	*Account Title*	*Account Balance on Nov. 1 of Current Year*
11	Cash	$4,930.20
12	Accounts Receivable	1,867.00
31	R. J. Carr, Capital	6,797.20
41	Sales	—

This is not a complete general ledger. Only those accounts needed for Problem 14-2 and for Problem 15-2 in the next chapter are included.

Instructions: 5. Post the total of the sales journal prepared in Problem 14-1 to the proper accounts in the general ledger.

The ledgers prepared in this problem will be used in Problem 15-2.

Optional Problems

★SUPPLEMENTARY PROBLEM 14-S

Journalizing and posting sales on account

Lee Cross is the owner and manager of the Cross TV Store. During the month of August of the current year, the following sales on account were made:

Date		*Customer*	*Amount of Sale*
Aug.	3	W. E. Roberts	$274.80
	7	B. R. Shank	461.50
	10	Robert Newton	150.35
	14	Henry Steele	152.60
	21	B. R. Shank	85.40
	25	Henry Steele	53.90
	29	Vivian Brown	140.60
	31	B. R. Shank	63.95

Instructions: 1. Journalize each transaction on page 8 of a sales journal similar to the one shown on page 214. Number the sales slips consecutively, beginning with No. 220.

2. Open an account in the accounts receivable ledger for each of the following customers. Allow four lines for each account. Record the balance of each account that has one.

Customer	*Account Balance on Aug. 1 of Current Year*
Vivian Brown, 111 East Riverside Avenue, Medford, Oregon 97501	$110.00
Robert Newton, 231 East Willard, Medford, Oregon 97501	—
W. E. Roberts, 61 Main Street, Medford, Oregon 97501	165.00
B. R. Shank, 67 South York, Medford, Oregon 97502	35.00
Henry Steele, 2101 South Elm, Medford, Oregon 97502	300.00

Instructions: 3. Post the entries in the sales journal to the proper accounts in the accounts receivable ledger.

4. Total and rule the sales journal.

5. Open the following two accounts in the general ledger. Allow four lines for each account. Record the balance of each account that has one.

Account Number	*Account Title*	*Account Balance on Aug. 1 of Current Year*
12	Accounts Receivable	$610.00
41	Sales	—

Instructions: 6. Post the total of the sales journal to the proper accounts in the general ledger.

⋆BONUS PROBLEM 14-B

Journalizing and posting sales on account

The Cannon Manufacturing Company makes kitchen utensils and appliances. The company sells merchandise to customers on account and, as a convenience, it prepays the delivery costs. The delivery cost is stated as a separate item on the sales slip and is charged to the customer's account along with the sales price of the goods sold. The Cannon Manufacturing Company wants its sales journal to show both the amount of each sale and the delivery cost. It therefore uses a sales journal with the following headings:

SALES JOURNAL PAGE

Date	Sale No.	Account Debited	Post. Ref.	Accounts Receivable Debit	Sales Credit	Delivery Expense Credit

Each amount recorded in the Accounts Receivable Debit column and posted to a customer's account is the sum of the sale and the delivery costs that are prepaid by the company. At the time of recording each sale, the delivery expense account is credited for the amount of the transportation charges. When the Cannon Manufacturing Company pays a transportation company for delivering the goods, the delivery expense account is debited and the cash account is credited.

The sale-on-account transactions and the delivery costs for the month of March of the current year are:

Date	*Customer*	*Amount of Sale*	*Delivery Costs*
Mar. 1	J. K. Kohler Company	$ 324.90	$13.60
5	A. L. Brown Company	298.60	Called for by Brown truck
8	Holt Company	296.80	24.10
12	Merit Sales Company	1,920.00	62.40
15	J. K. Kohler Company	2,148.20	58.60
18	Holt Company	1,824.32	39.80
21	Merit Sales Company	2,126.90	61.50
26	A. L. Brown Company	610.30	Called for by Brown truck
30	E. J. Blue Company	1,479.48	41.10

Instructions: 1. Record the sales transactions on page 3 of a three-column sales journal like the one illustrated above. Number the sales in consecutive order, beginning with No. 238.

2. Foot, total, and rule the sales journal.

3. Open accounts for the customers and record their balances in an accounts receivable ledger that has balance-column ruling. Allow four lines for each customer's account. The customers' accounts and their balances are as follows:

Customer	*Account Balance on March 1 of Current Year*
E. J. Blue Company, 2318 Harvey Road, Omaha, Nebraska 68105	$1,924.20
A. L. Brown Company, 1417 Vine Street, Detroit, Michigan 48208	1,364.40
Holt Company, 472 Ninth Street, Madison, Wisconsin 53702	2,284.90
J. K. Kohler Company, 246 A Street, Ann Arbor, Michigan 48104	610.20
Merit Sales Company, 192 Main Street, Des Moines, Iowa 50303	1,874.60

Instructions: 4. Post each amount in the Accounts Receivable column of the sales journal to the proper customer's account in the accounts receivable ledger.

5. Open the three general ledger accounts that are needed in this problem: Accounts Receivable, 12; Sales, 41; and Delivery Expense, 61. Record the debit balance in the accounts receivable account as of March 1 of the current year.

6. Post the totals of the sales journal to the proper accounts in the general ledger.

CHAPTER 15 RECORDING CASH RECEIPTS

The receipt of cash for any reason is known as a *cash receipts transaction.* A business may receive cash from (1) customers on account, (2) cash sales, and (3) other sources. The checks received by McCann Office Furniture from customers as payment on account are used as the source documents for recording these cash receipts. When cash is received in the form of currency or coins, the cash register tape is used by McCann Office Furniture as the source document for recording these cash receipts. A transaction in which cash is received at the time of selling the merchandise is called a *cash sale.*

THE FOUR-COLUMN CASH RECEIPTS JOURNAL

A special journal in which all cash receipts and only cash receipts are recorded is called a *cash receipts journal.* Each cash receipts transaction is recorded on a single line of the cash receipts journal. The cash receipts transactions of McCann Office Furniture are recorded in a four-column cash receipts journal similar to that shown below.

CASH RECEIPTS JOURNAL — PAGE

	DATE	ACCOUNT CREDITED	POST. REF.	1 GENERAL CREDIT	2 SALES CREDIT	3 ACCOUNTS REC. CREDIT	4 CASH DEBIT	
1								1
2								2
3								3
4								4
5								5

Four-column cash receipts journal

Special amount columns are provided in the cash receipts journal for those types of transactions that occur frequently. For example, there is a special amount column for Accounts Receivable Credit because McCann Office Furniture often receives cash from charge customers. The Sales Credit column is used for recording all cash sales. Most cash receipts come from charge customers and from cash sales. However, cash may occasionally be received from several other sources. Cash receipts that do not occur frequently are recorded in the General Credit column.

JOURNALIZING CASH RECEIPTS

Recording the beginning cash balance

To avoid referring frequently to the general ledger to get the amount of cash on hand at the beginning of each month, the cash balance is written in the Account Credited column of the cash receipts journal. This entry is not posted. An entry to record information that is not to be posted is called a *memorandum entry.*

On November 1, 1967, McCann Office Furniture has a cash balance amounting to $2,500.00. The memorandum entry to record this beginning cash balance in the cash receipts journal is shown below.

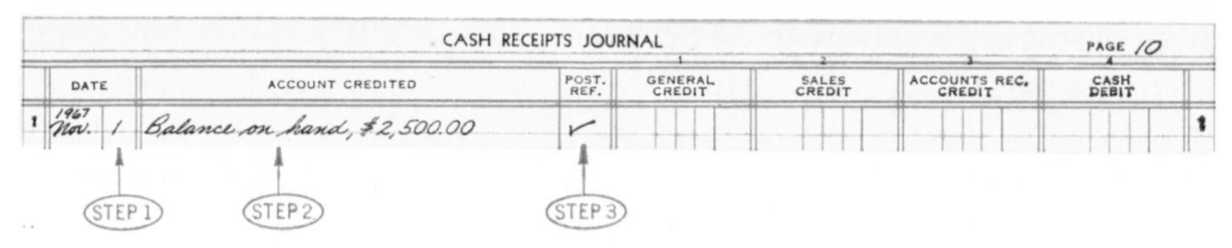

CASH RECEIPTS JOURNAL — PAGE 10

	DATE		ACCOUNT CREDITED	POST. REF.	1 GENERAL CREDIT	2 SALES CREDIT	3 ACCOUNTS REC. CREDIT	4 CASH DEBIT	
1	1967 Nov.	1	Balance on hand, $2,500.00	✓					1

Memorandum entry for recording the beginning cash balance

The steps in recording this memorandum entry are:

Step 1

Write the date, *1967, Nov. 1,* in the Date column.

Step 2

Record the memorandum entry for the cash balance, *Balance on hand, $2,500.00,* in the Account Credited column. Nothing is written in the amount columns.

Step 3

Place a check mark in the Post. Ref. column to show that nothing is to be posted from this line.

The memorandum entry is not posted because the cash balance on November 1, 1967, is already accounted for in the cash account in the general ledger. To prevent adding the cash balance to the current month's cash receipts, the amount of the cash balance does not appear in any amount column in the cash receipts journal.

Cash receipts transaction No. 1: Receipt of cash on account

November 2, 1967. Received a check for $290.00 from William Poole on account.

The check received from William Poole is the source document from which the bookkeeper for McCann Office Furniture obtains information for recording the entry in the cash receipts journal.

Analyzing cash receipts transaction No. 1. The cash received from William Poole increases the balance of the asset account, Cash. Therefore, Cash is debited for the amount of the receipt, $290.00, as shown in the T account at the right.

The transaction also results in a decrease in the balance of the asset account, Accounts Receivable. Therefore, the accounts receivable account in the general ledger is credited for $290.00. Each time the accounts receivable account in the general ledger is credited, the proper customer's account in the accounts receivable ledger must also be credited for the same amount. Thus, the customer's account, William Poole, in the accounts receivable ledger is credited for $290.00.

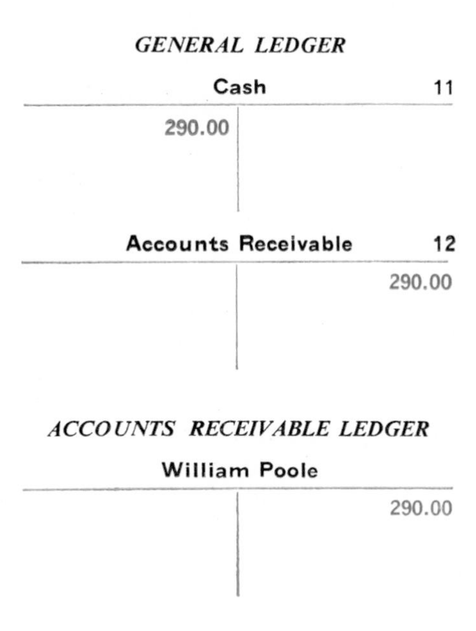

Journalizing cash receipts transaction No. 1. The entry to record this transaction is shown below.

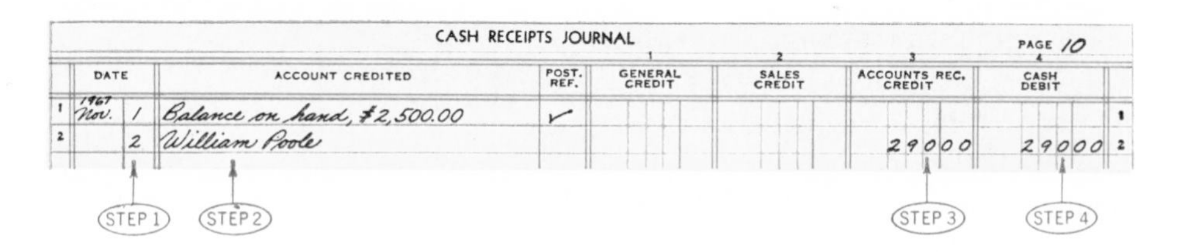

CASH RECEIPTS JOURNAL — PAGE 10

	DATE		ACCOUNT CREDITED	POST. REF.	1 GENERAL CREDIT	2 SALES CREDIT	3 ACCOUNTS REC. CREDIT	4 CASH DEBIT	
1	1967 Nov.	1	Balance on hand, $2,500.00	✓					1
2		2	William Poole				290 00	290 00	2

Entry for receipt of cash on account

The steps in recording the receipt of cash from William Poole to apply on his account are:

Step 1

Record the date, *2*, in the Date column.

Step 2

Write the account credited, *William Poole,* in the Account Credited column to indicate the name of the customer whose account is credited in the accounts receivable ledger.

Step 3

Record the amount of the cash receipt, *$290.00*, in the Accounts Receivable Credit column.

Step 4

Record the amount, *$290.00*, in the Cash Debit column.

The source document for this receipt of cash on account is the check received in payment. The transaction is described sufficiently by writing the date, the name of the account credited, and the amount. Therefore, no further description need be written in the cash receipts journal.

Cash receipts transaction No. 2: Cash sales of merchandise for the day

November 3, 1967. Cash sales shown by the cash register tape are $564.00.

Cash sales are recorded in the cash receipts journal only. *Sales on account* are recorded in the sales journal only. The cash register tape is the source document for recording the daily cash sales in the cash receipts journal.

Analyzing cash receipts transaction No. 2. The cash receipt of $564.00 is recorded as a debit to Cash since the balance of this asset account is being increased.

The amount of income from the sale of merchandise has been increased. Since income accounts have credit balances, each increase in an income account is recorded as a credit. Therefore, the sales account is credited for the amount of this transaction, $564.00.

Cash	11
564.00	

Sales	41
	564.00

Journalizing cash receipts transaction No. 2. The entry to record this transaction is shown at the top of the next page.

The steps in recording the entry for cash sales are:

Step 1

Record the date, *3*, in the Date column.

Step 2

Place a check mark (√) in the Account Credited column to indicate that no account title needs to be written for this entry. It is not necessary to

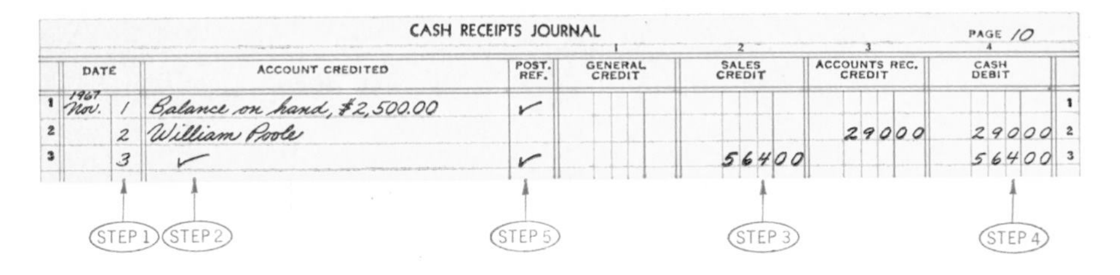

CASH RECEIPTS JOURNAL — PAGE 10

	DATE		ACCOUNT CREDITED	POST. REF.	GENERAL CREDIT (1)	SALES CREDIT (2)	ACCOUNTS REC. CREDIT (3)	CASH DEBIT (4)	
1	1967 Nov.	1	Balance on hand, $2,500.00	✓					1
2		2	William Poole				290 00	290 00	2
3		3	✓	✓		564 00		564 00	3

Entry for cash sales of merchandise

write the word *Sales* in the Account Credited column because the heading of the special column, Sales Credit, shows clearly that the sales account is credited for $564.00.

Step 3

Record the amount of the cash sales, *$564.00*, in the Sales Credit column.

Step 4

Record the amount, *$564.00*, in the Cash Debit column.

Step 5

Place a check mark in the Post. Ref. column to show that nothing on this line is to be posted separately. The debit to Cash is posted as part of the total of the Cash Debit column. The credit to Sales is posted as part of the total of the Sales Credit column.

Cash receipts transaction No. 3: Additional investment of cash

November 4, 1967. Received a personal check for $1,000.00, from John McCann, owner of McCann Office Furniture, as an additional investment in the business.

A person who owns and operates a business has a personal checking account that is kept separately from the checking account of the business. Thus, the owner does not become confused about how much of the money in the bank is for the use of the business and how much is for his personal use. When a personal check is received from the owner as described in this transaction, the check is handled in the same manner as any other cash receipt.

Analyzing cash receipts transaction No. 3. When the owner invests additional cash in the business, the balance of the cash account is increased. Thus, this increase of $1,000.00 is recorded as a debit to the cash account.

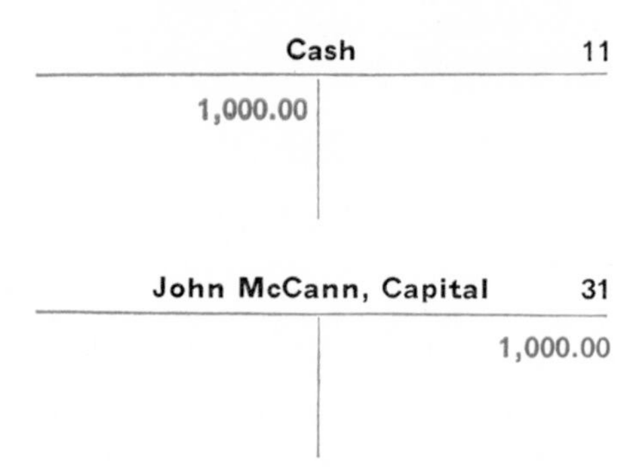

An additional investment in the business increases the balance of the proprietor's capital account. The proprietor's capital account is credited for $1,000.00 because all increases in proprietorship are recorded as credits.

Journalizing cash receipts transaction No. 3. The entry to record this transaction is shown below.

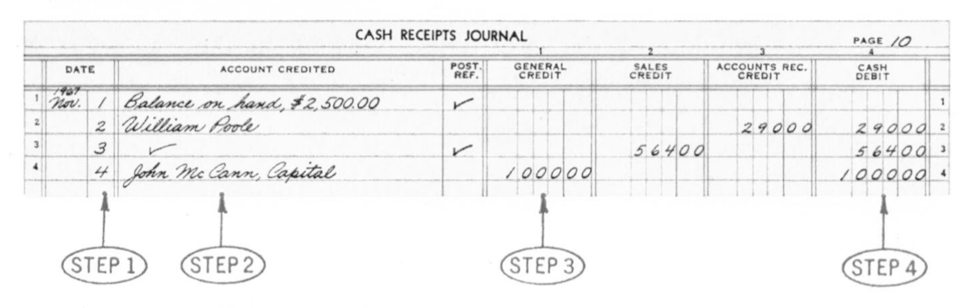

CASH RECEIPTS JOURNAL — PAGE 10

	DATE		ACCOUNT CREDITED	POST. REF.	1 GENERAL CREDIT	2 SALES CREDIT	3 ACCOUNTS REC. CREDIT	4 CASH DEBIT	
1	19— Nov.	1	Balance on hand, $2,500.00	✓					1
2		2	William Poole				290 00	290 00	2
3		3	✓	✓		564 00		564 00	3
4		4	John McCann, Capital		1000 00			1000 00	4

Entry for additional investment by the proprietor

The steps in recording the additional investment by Mr. McCann are:

Step 1

Record the date, *4*, in the Date column.

Step 2

Write the name of the account to be credited, *John McCann, Capital,* in the Account Credited column.

Step 3

Record the amount of the investment, *$1,000.00*, in the General Credit column. No special column is provided for credits to the proprietor's capital account. Therefore, this amount is recorded in the General Credit column.

Step 4

Record the amount of cash received, *$1,000.00*, in the Cash Debit column.

During the month of November, McCann Office Furniture records each cash receipt in the manner described for Entries Nos. 1 to 3. The completed cash receipts journal of McCann Office Furniture for the month of November is shown on page 241.

POSTING INDIVIDUAL ITEMS FROM THE CASH RECEIPTS JOURNAL

Posting from the Accounts Receivable Credit column

The owner of a business needs to know how much each customer owes the business. This information assists the owner in deciding whether to permit further sales on account to a particular customer. For this reason the amounts in the Accounts Receivable Credit column of the cash receipts journal are posted frequently to the customers' accounts in the accounts receivable ledger.

The illustration below shows the cash receipts journal and the account for William Poole after the entry on Line 2 of the cash receipts journal has been posted.

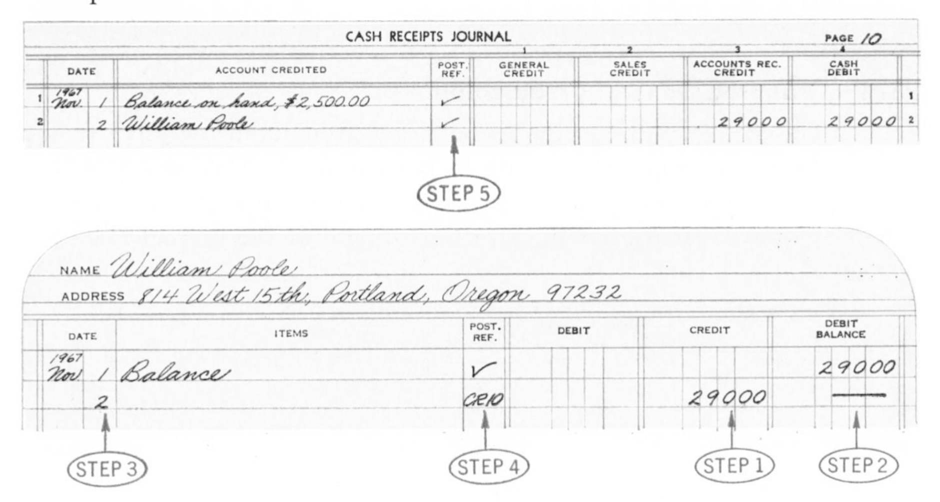

CASH RECEIPTS JOURNAL PAGE 10

	DATE		ACCOUNT CREDITED	POST. REF.	1 GENERAL CREDIT	2 SALES CREDIT	3 ACCOUNTS REC. CREDIT	4 CASH DEBIT	
1	1967 Nov.	1	Balance on hand, $2,500.00	✓					1
2		2	William Poole	✓			290 00	290 00	2

NAME William Poole

ADDRESS 814 West 15th, Portland, Oregon 97232

DATE		ITEMS	POST. REF.	DEBIT	CREDIT	DEBIT BALANCE
1967 Nov.	1	Balance	✓			290 00
	2		CR10		290 00	—

The steps in posting the entry on Line 2 of the cash receipts journal are:

Step 1

Post the amount, *$290.00*, shown in the Accounts Receivable Credit column, as a credit to the William Poole account in the accounts receivable ledger.

Step 2

Subtract the credit amount, *$290.00*, from the previous debit balance. The new balance is written in the Debit Balance column. As shown in the illustration above, the account for William Poole has a zero balance after this entry is posted. Since there is no balance, a short line is drawn in the Debit Balance column.

Step 3

Write the date, *2*, in the Date column of the account.

Step 4

Write *CR10* in the Post. Ref. column of the account to show that this entry was posted from page 10 of the cash receipts journal.

CR is the abbreviation for cash receipts journal.

Step 5

Place a check mark in the Post. Ref. column of the cash receipts journal to show the completion of the posting.

> The debit in the Cash Debit column on Line 2 of the cash receipts journal is not posted as a separate amount. Only the total of this column is posted. Posting the totals of the cash receipts journal will be explained later in this chapter.

Each entry in the Accounts Receivable Credit column is posted in the same way as the entry on Line 2.

Posting from the General Credit column

Each amount recorded in the General Credit column is posted to the general ledger account whose title is written in the Account Credited column. The illustration below shows the cash receipts journal and the general ledger account after the entry on Line 4 of the journal has been posted.

CASH RECEIPTS JOURNAL — PAGE 10

	Date		Account Credited	Post. Ref.	1 General Credit	2 Sales Credit	3 Accounts Rec. Credit	4 Cash Debit	
1	1967 Nov.	1	Balance on hand, $2,500.00	✓					1
2		2	William Poole	✓			290 00	290 00	2
3		3	✓	✓		564 00		564 00	3
4		4	John McCann, Capital	31	1,000 00			1,000 00	4

STEP 4

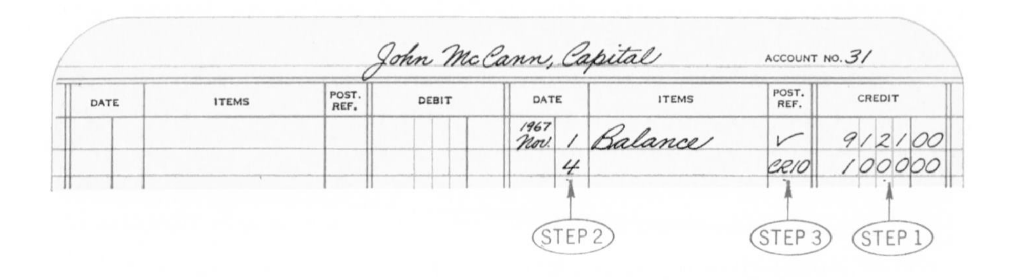

John McCann, Capital — ACCOUNT NO. 31

Date		Items	Post. Ref.	Debit	Date		Items	Post. Ref.	Credit
					1967 Nov.	1	Balance	✓	9,121 00
						4		CR10	1,000 00

The steps in posting the entry on Line 4 of the cash receipts journal are:

Step 1

Post the amount, *$1,000.00*, to the credit side of the general ledger account, John McCann, Capital.

Step 2

Write the date, *4*, in the Date column of the account.

Step 3

Write *CR10* in the Post. Ref. column of the general ledger account to show that the entry was posted from page 10 of the cash receipts journal.

Step 4

Write the number of the proprietorship account, *31*, in the Post. Ref. column of the cash receipts journal to show that the posting of Line 4 is completed.

PROVING, TOTALING, AND POSTING THE CASH RECEIPTS JOURNAL

At the end of the month, the amount columns of the cash receipts journal are proved and totaled, and the totals of the special amount columns are posted. The illustration below shows the cash receipts journal for McCann Office Furniture after all the entries have been recorded and after the individual items in the General Credit and the Accounts Receivable Credit columns have been posted.

CASH RECEIPTS JOURNAL PAGE 10

	Date		Account Credited	Post. Ref.	General Credit (1)	Sales Credit (2)	Accounts Rec. Credit (3)	Cash Debit (4)	
1	1967 Nov.	1	Balance on hand, $2,500.00	✓					1
2		2	William Poole	✓			290 00	290 00	2
3		3	✓	✓		564 00		564 00	3
4		4	John McCann, Capital	31	1,000 00			1,000 00	4
5		4	W. R. Johns	✓			79 00	79 00	5
6		5	Robert Wilson	✓			410 00	410 00	6
7		6	Wayne Hunter	✓			175 00	175 00	7
8		9	Donald Carter	✓			148 00	148 00	8
9		10	✓	✓		732 00		732 00	9
10		12	John Shreves	✓			251 00	251 00	10
11		14	W. R. Johns	✓			300 00	300 00	11
12		16	William Poole	✓			124 00	124 00	12
13		17	✓	✓		504 00		504 00	13
14		19	Donald Carter	✓			125 00	125 00	14
15		24	✓	✓		611 00		611 00	15
16		27	Frank Wright	✓			154 00	154 00	16
17		30	John Shreves	✓			74 00	74 00	17
18		30	Totals		1,000 00	2,411 00	2,130 00	5,541 00	18
19									19
20									20

Completed cash receipts journal — McCann Office Furniture

Proving the totals of the cash receipts journal

Before posting the totals of the cash receipts journal, the bookkeeper should prove the equality of debits and credits in the journal. The steps in proving the totals of the amount columns in the cash receipts journal are:

Step 1

Foot each column of the cash receipts journal in small pencil figures.

Step 2

Add the footings of the three credit columns, $1,000.00, $2,411.00, and $2,130.00, on a separate sheet of paper. The sum of the credit column totals, $5,541.00, is the same as the total of the Cash Debit column. Therefore, the equality of debits and credits in the cash receipts journal is proved.

When there are many daily cash receipts, it is customary to pencil foot the columns of the cash receipts journal and to prove the equality of debits and credits at frequent intervals during the month. Because McCann Office Furniture has few cash receipts, pencil footings are made only at the end of the month.

Proving cash on hand

Cash should be proved before the totals in the cash receipts journal and the cash payments journal are posted. The formula for proving cash on hand is:

Beginning balance + Cash receipts − Cash payments = Cash on hand

Using this formula, the bookkeeper for McCann Office Furniture proves cash as shown in the following calculation:

Beginning balance (Line 1 of the cash receipts journal, page 241)	$2,500.00
Plus cash receipts (total of Cash Debit column of cash receipts journal, page 241)	5,541.00
Total	$8,041.00
Minus cash payments (total of Cash Credit column of cash payments journal, page 196)	3,270.00
Cash on hand November 30 according to journals	$4,771.00
Cash on hand according to check stub	$4,771.00

If the business has some cash on hand that has not been deposited, this amount is added to the check-stub balance to find the "Cash on hand according to check stub."

When the amount of cash on hand according to the two cash journals and according to the check-stub balance is the same, the cash is said to be proved. This is proof that the amounts of the entries in the two cash journals and in the check stubs are correct.

Cash is usually proved each day. When this is done, both the cash receipts journal and the cash payments journal are footed by placing small footings in each amount column to show the cumulative total as of that date.

Cash short and over

Sometimes errors are made in making change at the time cash is received. If the cash on hand proves to be less than is shown by the records, the cash is said to be *short.* If the cash on hand is more than the records show, the cash is said to be *over.* If the error cannot be found, an entry is made in a cash journal to record the amount by which the cash is short or over.

The method of recording cash short or cash over is not described in this chapter. No entry is required in the records of McCann Office Furniture for November because the cash on hand was proved.

Totaling and ruling the cash receipts journal

The cash receipts journal is totaled and ruled in a manner similar to that described for the cash payments journal in Chapter 13. A single line is ruled across all amount columns below the last amount in the Cash Debit column. The date of the last day of the month is written in the Date column, and the word *Totals* is written in the Account Credited column. The totals are recorded in ink below the single ruled line. A double line is then ruled across all amount columns. The illustration on page 241 shows the totals and the ruling for the cash receipts journal of McCann Office Furniture for November.

Posting the totals of the cash receipts journal

The total of the General Credit column is not posted. The individual entries in this column have been posted previously to the general ledger accounts.

The totals of the Sales Credit column and the Cash Debit column are posted to the appropriate accounts in the general ledger. The individual amounts in these two columns are not posted separately.

The total of the Accounts Receivable Credit column is posted to the appropriate account in the general ledger. The individual items in this column have been posted previously to the customers' accounts in the accounts receivable ledger.

The Totals line of the cash receipts journal for McCann Office Furniture and the three accounts in the general ledger to which the totals are posted are shown below.

CASH RECEIPTS JOURNAL — PAGE 10

	Date		Account Credited	Post. Ref.	1 General Credit	2 Sales Credit	3 Accounts Rec. Credit	4 Cash Debit	
1	1967 Nov.	1	Balance on hand, $2,500.00	✓					1
17		30	John Shreves	✓			74 00	74 00	17
					1000 00	2411 00	2130 00	5541 00	
18		30	Totals		1000 00	2411 00	2130 00	5541 00	18
19					(✓)	(41)	(12)	(11)	19

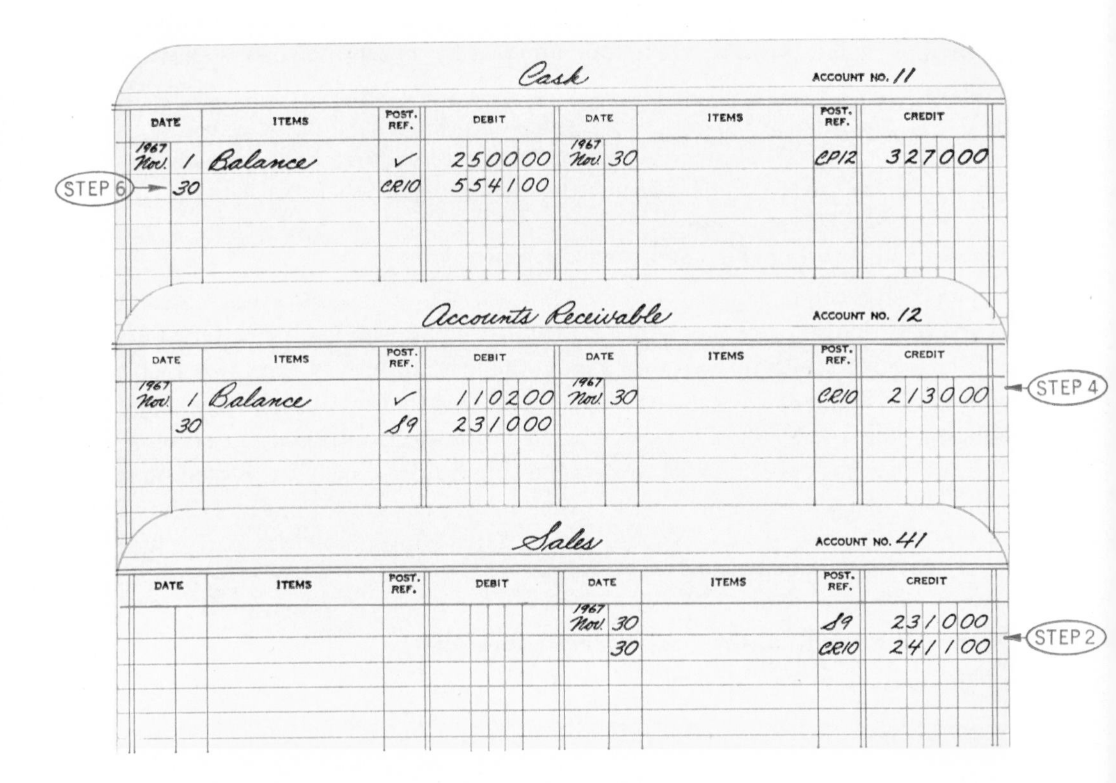

Cash — ACCOUNT NO. 11

Date		Items	Post. Ref.	Debit	Date		Items	Post. Ref.	Credit
1967 Nov.	1	Balance	✓	2500 00	1967 Nov.	30		CP12	3270 00
	30		CR10	5541 00					

Accounts Receivable — ACCOUNT NO. 12

Date		Items	Post. Ref.	Debit	Date		Items	Post. Ref.	Credit
1967 Nov.	1	Balance	✓	1102 00	1967 Nov.	30		CR10	2130 00
	30		S9	2310 00					

Sales — ACCOUNT NO. 41

Date		Items	Post. Ref.	Debit	Date		Items	Post. Ref.	Credit
					1967 Nov.	30		S9	2310 00
						30		CR10	2411 00

The steps in posting the Totals line of the cash receipts journal are:

Step 1

Place a check mark in parentheses on the first line below the total of the General Credit column. The check mark shows that the total of the column is not to be posted.

Step 2

Post the total of the Sales Credit column, *$2,411.00*, to the credit side of the sales account in the general ledger. Write the day, *30*, in the Date column, and CR10 in the Post. Ref. column of the account.

Step 3

Write the number of the sales account in parentheses, (*41*) on the first line below the total of the Sales Credit column in the cash receipts journal. Writing the account number shows that the posting of the total is completed.

Step 4

Post the total of the Accounts Receivable Credit column, *$2,130.00*, to the credit side of the accounts receivable account in the general ledger. Write the date, *1967, Nov. 30*, in the Date column, and CR10 in the Post. Ref. column of the account.

Step 5

Write the number of the accounts receivable account in parentheses, (*12*), on the first line below the total of the Accounts Receivable Credit column in the cash receipts journal. Writing the account number shows that the posting of the total is completed.

Step 6

Post the total of the Cash Debit column, *$5,541.00*, to the debit side of the cash account in the general ledger. Write the date, *30*, in the Date column, and CR10 in the Post. Ref. column of the account.

Step 7

Write the number of the cash account in parentheses, (*11*), on the first line below the total of the Cash Debit column in the cash receipts journal to show completion of the posting.

THE COMPLETED ACCOUNTS RECEIVABLE LEDGER

The accounts receivable ledger of McCann Office Furniture after the posting from the sales journal and the cash receipts journal for November has been completed is shown on pages 246 and 247. The debit balance in each account shows the amount still to be collected from each customer.

NAME Donald Carter
ADDRESS 1462 Ashland Avenue, Portland, Oregon 97230

DATE		ITEMS	POST. REF.	DEBIT	CREDIT	DEBIT BALANCE
1967 Nov.	1	Balance	✓			148 00
	9		CR10		148 00	—
	14		S9	125 00		125 00
	19		CR10		125 00	—
	24		S9	70 00		70 00

NAME Raymond Holland
ADDRESS 866 North Main Street, Portland, Oregon 97208

DATE		ITEMS	POST. REF.	DEBIT	CREDIT	DEBIT BALANCE
1967 Nov.	9		S9	298 00		298 00
	20		J4	352 00		650 00

NAME Wayne Hunter
ADDRESS 100 Plum, Eugene, Oregon 97401

DATE		ITEMS	POST. REF.	DEBIT	CREDIT	DEBIT BALANCE
1967 Nov.	1	Balance	✓			175 00
	6		CR10		175 00	—
	13		S9	352 00		352 00
	20		J4		352 00	—

NAME W. R. Johns
ADDRESS 2609 West Jackson Street, Portland, Oregon 97203

DATE		ITEMS	POST. REF.	DEBIT	CREDIT	DEBIT BALANCE
1967 Nov.	1	Balance	✓			79 00
	3		S9	300 00		379 00
	4		CR10		79 00	300 00
	14		CR10		300 00	—
	30		S9	176 00		176 00

Accounts receivable ledger — McCann Office Furniture

NAME *William Poole*
ADDRESS *814 West 15th, Portland, Oregon 97232*

DATE		ITEMS	POST. REF.	DEBIT	CREDIT	DEBIT BALANCE
1967 Nov.	1	Balance	✓			290 00
	2		CR10		290 00	———
	6		S9	124 00		124 00
	16		CR10		124 00	———
	20		S9	285 00		285 00

NAME *John Shreves*
ADDRESS *410 South Eastwood, Portland, Oregon 97236*

DATE		ITEMS	POST. REF.	DEBIT	CREDIT	DEBIT BALANCE
1967 Nov.	9		S9	251 00		251 00
	12		CR10		251 00	———
	16		S9	74 00		74 00
	27		S9	101 00		175 00
	30		CR10		74 00	101 00

NAME *Robert Wilson*
ADDRESS *10 Waid Drive, Corvallis, Oregon 97330*

DATE		ITEMS	POST. REF.	DEBIT	CREDIT	DEBIT BALANCE
1967 Nov.	1	Balance	✓			410 00
	5		CR10		410 00	———

NAME *Frank Wright*
ADDRESS *1240 Short Street, Portland, Oregon 97208*

DATE		ITEMS	POST. REF.	DEBIT	CREDIT	DEBIT BALANCE
1967 Nov.	2		S9	154 00		154 00
	27		CR10		154 00	———

Accounts receivable ledger — McCann Office Furniture (concluded)

SCHEDULE OF ACCOUNTS RECEIVABLE

If all the posting from the sales journal and the cash receipts journal is completed accurately, the balance of the controlling account, Accounts Receivable, in the general ledger will be the same as the sum of the balances of the customers' accounts in the accounts receivable ledger. In preparing proof of the posting to the accounts receivable ledger, all balances of the customers' accounts are listed and totaled. A list of all customers that shows the balance due from each customer and the total amount due from all customers is called a *schedule of accounts receivable.*

The schedule of accounts receivable prepared from the accounts receivable ledger illustrated on pages 246 and 247 is shown below.

McCann Office Furniture
Schedule of Accounts Receivable
November 30, 1967

Donald Carter	70 00	
Raymond Holland	650 00	
W.R. Johns	176 00	
William Poole	285 00	
John Shreves	101 00	
Total Accounts Receivable		1282 00

Schedule of accounts receivable

The steps in preparing the schedule of accounts receivable are:

Step 1

Write the heading on three lines; center each item in the heading.

Step 2

List the name of each customer and the amount of his balance at the time the schedule of accounts receivable is being prepared.

Step 3

Add the balances listed on the schedule to find the total amount due from all customers.

Step 4

Foot the controlling account in the general ledger, Accounts Receivable, and determine the account balance. The account balance is the total amount due from all customers. The accounts receivable account with its footings and balance is shown below.

Accounts Receivable ACCOUNT NO. 12

DATE		ITEMS	POST. REF.	DEBIT	DATE		ITEMS	POST. REF.	CREDIT
1967 Nov.	1	Balance	✓	1,102 00	1967 Nov.	30		CR10	2,130 00
	30	1,282.00	S9	2,310 00					
				3,412 00					

Step 5

Compare the total of the schedule of accounts receivable, *$1,282.00,* with the balance of the accounts receivable account in the general ledger, *$1,282.00.* Since the two amounts agree, it is assumed that all posting affecting customers' accounts and Accounts Receivable is accurate.

If the total of the schedule of accounts receivable and the balance of the accounts receivable account do not agree, the error must be found and corrected before the bookkeeper continues his work.

STATEMENT OF ACCOUNT

A business form that shows the charges to a customer's account, the amounts credited to his account, and the balance of his account is known as a *statement of account.* It is customary for a business to send each customer a statement of account at regular intervals. When a customer receives his statement of account, he should compare it with his own records. If his records do not agree with the statement he has received, he should notify the business from whom he received the statement.

An example of the statement of account sent to customers by McCann Office Furniture is shown on the next page.

Some businesses mail a statement of account to each customer at the end of the month. However, a business with many charge customers often distributes the preparation and mailing of statements over the month. Preparing and mailing statements of account to customers on specific days

IN ACCOUNT WITH

McCANN

Office Furniture

640 Central Avenue, Portland, Oregon 97227

Donald Carter
1462 Ashland Avenue
Portland, Oregon 97230

PAY LAST AMOUNT IN THIS COLUMN

PURCHASING DATE	INVOICE	CHARGES	CREDITS	BALANCE
Nov. 1, 1967		BALANCE FORWARD		148.00
9	1243		148.00	---
14		125.00		125.00

ALL ACCOUNTS DUE FIRST OF THE MONTH FOLLOWING PURCHASE

Statement of account

of each month is called *cycle billing*. When a business uses cycle billing, a schedule is prepared to show which customers' statements of account will be prepared and mailed at the different times each month. An example of such a schedule is shown below.

FOX PRODUCTS, INC.
CYCLE BILLING SCHEDULE

Initial of customer's last name	Day of month on which statement of account is prepared and mailed
A to D	4th
E to K	10th
L to P	16th
Q to S	22nd
T to Z	28th

Cycle billing schedule

If the mailing date falls on Sunday or a holiday, the statement of account is usually mailed on the next regular business day.

Because McCann Office Furniture has a small number of accounts receivable accounts, cycle billing is not used. However, statements of account are prepared and mailed at the middle of each month. Thus, preparing and mailing statements is done at a time of the month when the bookkeeper is not busy with end-of-month financial activities.

A FLOW CHART FOR POSTING

A summary of the steps followed in posting from the sales journal and the cash receipts journal to the accounts receivable ledger and the accounts receivable account in the general ledger is shown in the flow chart below.

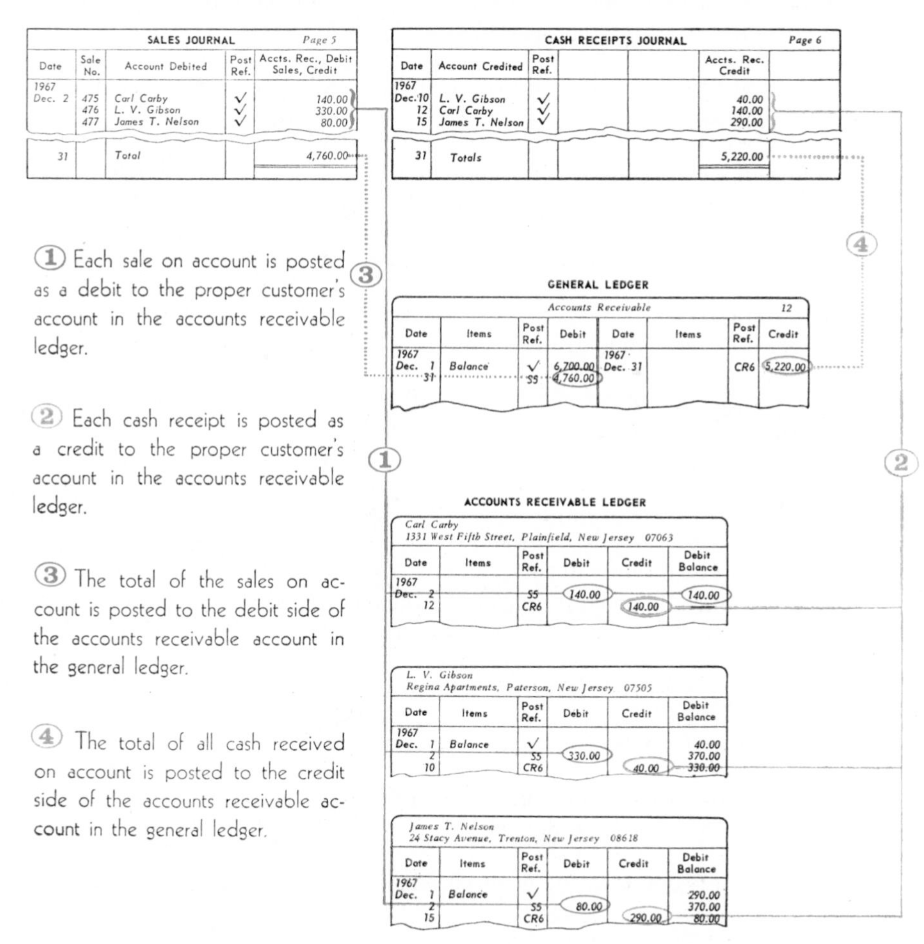

A flow chart of posting to the accounts receivable ledger and the accounts receivable account in the general ledger

Increasing Your Business Vocabulary

What is the meaning of each of the following:

a cash receipts transaction
b cash sale
c cash receipts journal
d memorandum entry
e cash short
f cash over
g schedule of accounts receivable
h statement of account
i cycle billing

Study Questions

1. What source documents are used by McCann Office Furniture for recording the receipt of cash from customers?
2. For what types of transactions are special amount columns provided in the cash receipts journal?
3. Why is a memorandum entry made in the cash receipts journal to record the beginning cash balance for each month?
4. Why is the memorandum entry in the cash receipts journal not posted?
5. What effect does the receipt of cash on account have upon (a) the general ledger accounts and (b) the accounts receivable ledger?
6. Why is a check mark placed in the Post. Ref. column of the cash receipts journal when each cash sale is recorded?
7. What effect does an additional investment of cash by the owner have upon the general ledger accounts?
8. Why are the amounts in the Accounts Receivable Credit column of the cash receipts journal posted frequently to the customers' accounts in the accounts receivable ledger?
9. What steps are taken in proving the totals of the cash receipts journal?
10. What is the formula for proving cash on hand?
11. When proving cash on hand, how should the bookkeeper handle the cash on hand that has not been deposited?
12. With what account in the general ledger should the total of the schedule of accounts receivable agree?
13. Why do some businesses use cycle billing in scheduling the preparation and mailing of their monthly statements of account?

Cases for Business Decision

CASE 1

The Cash and Carry Market sells for cash only. What change in the cash receipts journal used by McCann Office Furniture as shown on page 241 would you recommend for the market? Why?

CASE 2

At the end of the current month, the owner of Sand's Hardware looks at the accounts receivable account in his general ledger and notices that the debit balance of the account is almost twice as large as it was the previous month. For what reasons might the account balance have increased so greatly?

CASE 3

T. M. Brent operates a retail radio and television shop. He uses a cash receipts journal with columns similar to those used by McCann Office Furniture as shown on page 241. L. V. Hart, who operates the same kind of store, uses a cash receipts journal without a special column for Sales Credit. What are the advantages of Mr. Brent's plan?

CASE 4

Harvey Men's Shop proves cash only once a week. What are the disadvantages of this plan as compared with the plan of a store that proves cash every day?

Drills for Understanding

DRILL 15-A | **Cash receipts transactions**

The following are the cash receipts for the week of September 1–6:

Sept.	1. Balance on hand	$4,300.00
	2. Cash sales	290.00
	3. Accounts receivable	560.00
	Cash sales	470.00
	4. Accounts receivable	80.00
	Cash sales	135.00
	5. Accounts receivable	75.00
	Cash sales	690.00
	6. Accounts receivable	140.00
	Cash sales	660.00
	Sale of office furniture	50.00

Instructions: Answer each of the following questions:

1. In what journal should these transactions be recorded?
2. What is the total of cash sales for the week?
3. What is the total of cash received from charge customers?
4. Will Cash be debited or credited for each cash receipt? Why?
5. What was the total amount of cash received during the week?
6. Will Accounts Receivable be debited or credited? Why?
7. If the special column for Sales Credit were not used, how many entries would have to be posted to the Sales account?
8. How many postings are saved by recording the entries in a cash receipts journal that has a special column for Sales Credit?

DRILL 15-B Analyzing transactions affecting sales on account and cash receipts

Instructions: For each of the transactions listed below, prepare two T accounts to show which account in the *general ledger* is debited and which account is credited. If the transaction also affects an account in the *accounts receivable ledger*, prepare a third T account to show whether the account is debited or credited. The first transaction is given as an example.

General Ledger				Accounts Receivable Ledger	
Accounts Receivable		Sales		M. G. Terry	
100.00			100.00	100.00	

1. Sold merchandise on account to M. G. Terry, $100.00.
2. Cash sales as shown on the cash register tape, $500.00.
3. Received a personal check for $750.00 from Arnold Dye, the owner, as an additional investment in the business.
4. Received $50.00 from R. O. Mott on account.
5. Received $15.00 from the sale of old office desks.

Application Problems

PROBLEM 15-1 | Recording cash receipts

On November 1 of the current year the cash balance of the Carr Company was $4,630.20. During the month of November the cash receipts transactions listed below were completed.

Instructions: 1. Prepare page 12 of a cash receipts journal by writing the proper heading at the top of each column. Use the same headings as shown in the cash receipts journal on page 241.

2. Record the cash balance with a memorandum entry dated November 3.

3. Journalize each of the following transactions.

Nov. 3. Received $2,390.00 from cash sales.
3. Received $320.40 from Ross Brothers on account.
7. Received $310.30 from J. B. Bonnett on account.
10. Received $4,155.30 from cash sales.
14. Received $125.00 from Hogan Drugs on account.
17. Received $3,910.00 from cash sales.
20. Received $345.75 from Ross Brothers on account.
21. Received $120.30 from Shoemaker & Company on account.
24. Received $6,331.50 from cash sales.
27. Received $350.60 from S. W. Hull on account.
28. Received $400.20 from E. M. Alexander on account.
30. Received $335.10 from Shoemaker & Company on account.
30. Received $6,101.40 from cash sales.

Instructions: 4. Foot, prove, total, and rule the cash receipts journal.

The cash receipts journal completed in this problem will be used in Problem 15-2.

PROBLEM 15-2 | Posting from a cash receipts journal; preparing a schedule of accounts receivable

The accounts receivable ledger and the general ledger prepared in Problem 14-2 and the cash receipts journal prepared in Problem 15-1 are needed to complete this problem. If these are not available, complete Appendix Problem 15-A.

Instructions: 1. Post the amounts in the Accounts Receivable Credit column of the cash receipts journal prepared in Problem 15-1 to customers' accounts in the accounts receivable ledger used in Problem 14-2.

2. Post the totals of the special columns of the cash receipts journal to the general ledger used in Problem 14-2.

3. Prepare a schedule of accounts receivable from the accounts in the accounts receivable ledger in a form similar to the one illustrated on page 248.

4. Compare the total of the schedule of accounts receivable with the balance of the accounts receivable in the general ledger. If there is a difference, recheck your work until the error is found.

Optional Problems

★ SUPPLEMENTARY PROBLEM 15-S

Journalizing and posting cash receipts

Lee Cross, owner and manager of Cross TV Store, completed the cash receipts transactions during December of the current year as shown below. The cash balance as of December 1 was $1,390.00.

Instructions: 1. Record the cash balance with a memorandum entry dated December 1. Use a cash receipts journal similar to the one illustrated on page 241. Use page 10 as the journal page.

2. Record the following cash receipts transactions.

Dec. 5. Received $35.00 from B. R. Shank on account.
8. Received $504.60 from cash sales.
12. Received $165.00 from W. E. Roberts on account.
15. Received $840.20 from cash sales.
18. Received $15.00 from the sale of office supplies to a neighboring merchant.

Office supplies are not a part of the merchandise kept in stock for resale. For this reason, the sales account is not credited for this transaction. Instead, Office Supplies is credited.

19. Received $300.00 from Henry Steele on account.
22. Received $421.30 from cash sales.
26. Received $461.50 from B. R. Shank on account.
28. Received $692.25 from cash sales.
28. Received $152.60 from Henry Steele on account.
29. Received $250.60 from Vivian Brown on account.
29. Received $471.40 from cash sales.

Instructions: 3. Foot, prove, total, and rule the cash receipts journal.

4. Open the following accounts in a general ledger. For those accounts with a balance, record the balance as of December 1 of the current year. Allow four lines for each account.

Acct. No.	*Account Title*	*Account Balance*
11	Cash	$1,390.00
12	Accounts Receivable	2,093.10
13	Office Supplies	165.40
31	Lee Cross, Capital	4,130.50
41	Sales	—

Instructions: 5. Post the individual items in the General Credit column and the totals of the special columns to the accounts in the general ledger.

★BONUS PROBLEM 15-B

Journalizing and posting cash receipts

The Moss Equipment Company calls its cash receipts journal a cash received record. The form of the cash received record is shown below.

CASH RECEIVED RECORD — PAGE 14

CASH RECEIVED FOR THE MONTH OF ________ 19__

DEBITS			CREDITS					
						GENERAL LEDGER		
CASH	DAY	RECEIVED FROM	ACCOUNTS RECEIV-ABLE	√	SALES	ACCT. NO.	AMOUNT	√

Note that immediately after the Accounts Receivable column and the General Ledger Amount column there are columns headed with a check mark. These check mark columns are used in place of Post. Ref. columns. When items from the Accounts Receivable and the General Ledger Amount columns are posted, a check mark is placed after the amount to show completion of the posting.

Also note that there is an Account Number column immediately before the General Ledger Amount column. The account number, instead of the account title, is recorded at the time of the entry.

The numbers, titles, and balances of the accounts used in this problem are:

Acct. No.	*Account Title*	*Account Balance*
11	Cash	$ 5,624.00
12	Accounts Receivable	1,840.00
13	Store Equipment	960.00
14	Office Equipment	1,480.00
15	Delivery Equipment	4,280.00
31	M. L. Moss, Capital	14,200.00
41	Sales	——

The cash receipts transactions listed on the next page were completed by the Moss Equipment Company during the month of December of the current year.

Instructions: 1. Record the cash balance with a memorandum entry dated December 1. Use a cash received record similar to the one shown on page 257. Use page 14 as the page number of the cash received record.

2. Record the following cash receipts transactions.

Dec. 3. Received $640.00 from cash sales.
6. Received $195.00 from H. L. Foley on account.
8. Received $120.00 from the sale of an old display counter to A. L. Marks. (Store Equipment)
10. Received $480.00 from cash sales.
15. Received $360.00 from J. K. Stevens on account.
17. Received $420.00 from cash sales.
20. Received $35.00 from the sale of an old typewriter to J. C. Warren. (Office Equipment)
21. Received $2,000.00 from M. L. Moss as an additional investment.
24. Received $690.00 from cash sales.
27. Received $96.00 from J. D. Crane on account.
28. Received $980.00 from the sale of an old delivery truck to J. R. Bodie. (Delivery Equipment)
31. Received $760.00 from cash sales.

Instructions: 3. Foot, prove, total, and rule the amount columns.

4. Open the seven general ledger accounts listed on page 257 and record the balances. Allow four lines for each account.

5. Post to the general ledger accounts.

CHAPTER 16 RECORDING MISCELLANEOUS ENTRIES IN THE GENERAL JOURNAL

Most of the transactions of McCann Office Furniture are recorded in special journals: the purchases journal, the cash payments journal, the sales journal, and the cash receipts journal. Not all transactions, however, can be recorded in special journals. Transactions that cannot be recorded in special journals are called *miscellaneous entries.* Miscellaneous entries are recorded in a general journal.

KINDS OF MISCELLANEOUS ENTRIES

The kinds of miscellaneous entries recorded in the general journal are:

1. Entries to record withdrawals of merchandise by the proprietor.
2. Entries to correct errors.
3. Entries to record the buying on account or the selling on account of items other than merchandise.
4. Entries to adjust accounts at the end of the fiscal period.
5. Entries to close accounts at the end of the fiscal period.
6. Entry to record the beginning balance sheet of a business when a new bookkeeping system is installed.

The first three kinds of miscellaneous entries are discussed in this chapter. Entries 4 and 5, to adjust and to close accounts, are described in Chapter 20. Entry 6, to record the beginning balance sheet, was discussed in Chapter 2.

Miscellaneous entry No. 1: Withdrawal of merchandise by the proprietor

November 16, 1967. John McCann, the proprietor, withdrew merchandise for personal use, at cost, $150.00.

Mr. McCann needed a desk at home for personal use. Taking the desk out of stock for use at home is a withdrawal of merchandise for the personal use by the owner. The source document for this transaction is an office memorandum, signed by Mr. McCann, which shows the withdrawal of the desk at the cost price of $150.00.

Analyzing miscellaneous entry No. 1. The proprietor's capital account has a credit balance. Because withdrawals decrease proprietorship, a proprietorship account is debited for all withdrawals. Therefore, the amount of the withdrawal of the merchandise, $150.00, is debited to the proprietorship account, John McCann, Drawing, as shown in the T account at the right.

John McCann, Drawing	32
150.00	

The balance side of the purchases account is the debit side. When the desk taken by Mr. McCann was originally purchased and placed in stock for resale, its cost, $150.00, was debited to the Purchases account. When Mr. McCann withdrew the desk for personal use, he reduced the amount of merchandise that was purchased for resale. Decreases in the purchases account are recorded on the side opposite the balance side, the credit side. Therefore, this withdrawal of merchandise costing $150.00 is credited to the purchases account.

Purchases	51
	150.00

Journalizing miscellaneous entry No. 1. Miscellaneous entry No. 1 is recorded in the general journal as shown below.

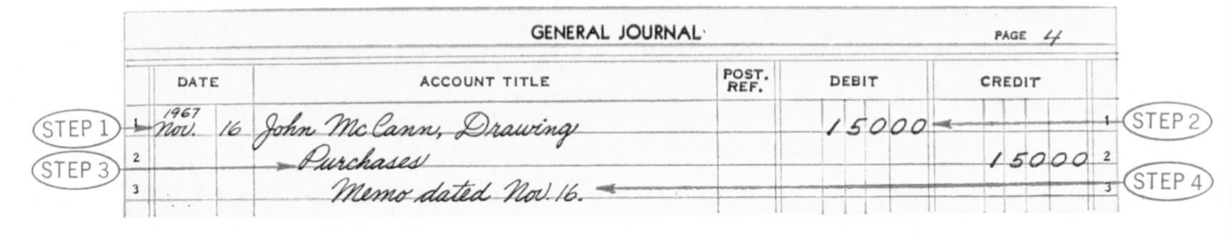

GENERAL JOURNAL PAGE 4

	DATE		ACCOUNT TITLE	POST. REF.	DEBIT	CREDIT	
1	1967 Nov.	16	John McCann, Drawing		150 00		1
2			Purchases			150 00	2
3			Memo dated Nov. 16.				3

Recording the withdrawal of merchandise by the proprietor

The steps in journalizing miscellaneous entry No. 1 are:

Step 1

Write the date, *1967, Nov. 16*, in the Date column.

Step 2

Write the account debited, *John McCann, Drawing*, in the Account Title column, and the amount, *$150.00*, in the Debit column.

Step 3

Write the account credited, *Purchases*, in the Account Title column, and the amount, *$150.00*, in the Credit column. The credit part of the entry is indented to show that the account is to be credited.

Step 4

Write a brief description of the source document, *Memo dated Nov. 16*, in the Account Title column. The description is indented twice as much as the credit part of the entry.

Posting miscellaneous entry No. 1. This entry is posted to the two accounts in the general ledger. John McCann, Drawing, is debited and Purchases is credited.

Miscellaneous entry No. 2: Correcting entry

November 20, 1967. Wayne Hunter, a customer, reported that on the statement he received, there is a $352.00 charge to his account for merchandise that he had not ordered and had not received.

An investigation of the report from Mr. Hunter reveals that Sale No. 267 on November 13 had been charged to Mr. Hunter when it should have been charged to Raymond Holland. An entry is needed to correct the error made in recording this sale. Entries made in the general journal to correct errors in two or more ledger accounts are known as *correcting entries.*

McCann Office Furniture sends Mr. Hunter a memorandum in which credit is given for the amount of the incorrect charge to his account. The carbon copy of this memorandum is the source document for recording this entry.

Analyzing miscellaneous entry No. 2. The amount of the sale, $352.00, was incorrectly debited to the account of Wayne Hunter, as shown in the first T account at the right. The amount of the sale should have been debited to the account of Raymond Holland.

To correct the error made in recording this sale, Mr. Holland's account is debited for $352.00. Mr. Hunter's account is credited for $352.00 to cancel the incorrect debit amount. See the T accounts at the right.

ACCOUNTS RECEIVABLE LEDGER

(Mr. Hunter's account before the correction)

Wayne Hunter	
352.00	

(Customers' accounts after the correction)

Raymond Holland	
(Correction) 352.00	

Wayne Hunter	
352.00	*(Correction)* 352.00

Journalizing miscellaneous entry No. 2. This entry is recorded in the general journal as shown at the top of the next page.

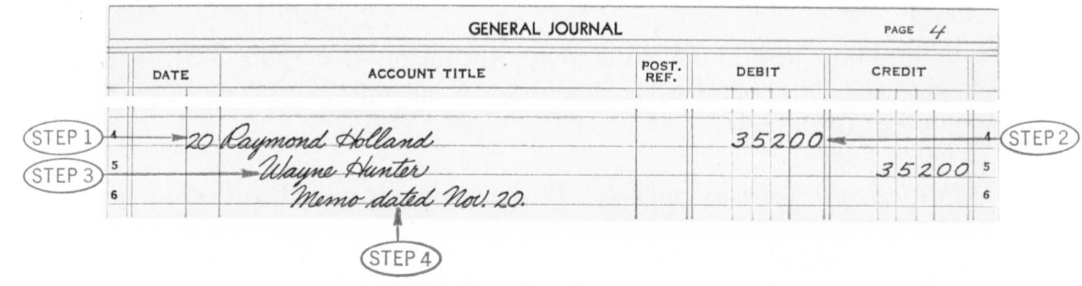

Recording a correcting entry

The steps in journalizing miscellaneous entry No. 2 are:

Step 1

Write the date, *20*, in the Date column.

Step 2

Write the account debited, *Raymond Holland*, in the Account Title column, and the amount, *$352.00*, in the Debit column.

Step 3

Write the account credited, *Wayne Hunter*, in the Account Title Column, and the amount *$352.00*, in the Credit column.

Step 4

Write a brief description of the source document, *Memo dated Nov. 20*, in the Account Title column.

Posting miscellaneous entry No. 2. Both customers' accounts are in the accounts receivable ledger. Mr. Holland's account is debited for $352.00 and Mr. Hunter's account is credited for the same amount. As there is no change in the total accounts receivable, this correcting entry does not affect the balance of the accounts receivable account in the general ledger. Therefore, no posting is made to Accounts Receivable in the general ledger.

Miscellaneous entry No. 3: Buying supplies on account

November 30, 1967. Bought store supplies on account from Swartz Supply Company, $112.00.

McCann Office Furniture buys supplies such as wrapping paper, sealing tape, twine, bags, cleaning supplies, and sales slip books for use in the store. Supplies are not bought for sale to customers. Therefore, supplies are not merchandise. Only merchandise purchased on account, which is to be sold, is recorded in the purchases journal. The buying on account of any item that is not merchandise is recorded in the general journal. The invoice from Swartz Supply Company is the source document for miscellaneous entry No. 3.

Analyzing miscellaneous entry No. 3. The balance of the asset account, Supplies, is increased $112.00. The increase side of an asset account is the debit side. Therefore, the asset account, Supplies, is debited for the amount of the increase, $112,00.

The balance of the liability account, Accounts Payable, is increased $112.00. The increase side of the accounts payable account is the credit side. Therefore, Accounts Payable, a controlling account in the general ledger, is credited for the amount of the increase, $112.00. The balance of the individual creditor's account, Swartz Supply Company, is also increased $112.00. Therefore, Swartz Supply Company, a creditor's account in the subsidiary accounts payable ledger, is credited for $112.00.

GENERAL LEDGER

Supplies 14

Debit	Credit
112.00	

Accounts Payable 21

Debit	Credit
	112.00

ACCOUNTS PAYABLE LEDGER

Swartz Supply Company

Debit	Credit
	112.00

Journalizing miscellaneous entry No. 3. This entry is recorded in the general journal as shown below.

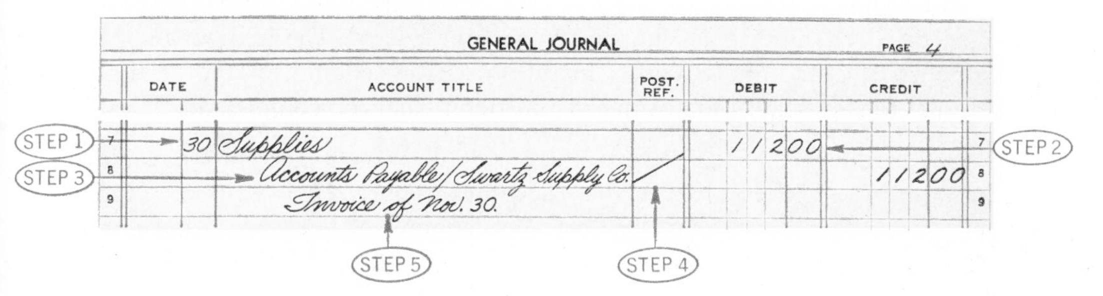

GENERAL JOURNAL PAGE 4

	DATE	ACCOUNT TITLE	POST. REF.	DEBIT	CREDIT	
7	30	Supplies		112 00		7
8		Accounts Payable/Swartz Supply Co.	✓		112 00	8
9		Invoice of Nov. 30.				9

Recording the buying of supplies on account

The steps in recording miscellaneous entry No. 3 are:

Step 1

Write the date, *30*, in the Date column.

Step 2

Write the account to be debited, *Supplies*, in the Account Title column, and the amount, *$112.00*, in the Debit column.

Step 3

Write the accounts to be credited, *Accounts Payable/Swartz Supply Company*, in the Account Title column, and the amount, *$112.00*, in the Credit column. The credit part of the entry is indented to show that both accounts are to be credited.

A diagonal line is placed between the two account titles to separate them clearly. Both the controlling account, Accounts Payable, and the name of the creditor, Swartz Supply Company, are written because the credit amount must be posted to both an account in the general ledger and an account in the accounts payable ledger.

Step 4

Place a diagonal line, /, in the Post. Ref. column to show that the credit amount is to be posted to two accounts.

Step 5

Write a brief description of the source document, *Invoice of Nov. 30*, in the Account Title column.

Posting miscellaneous entry No. 3. The debit part of the journal entry is posted to the supplies account in the general ledger. The number of the supplies account, *14*, is written in the Post. Ref. column of the general journal to show that the posting of this debit has been completed.

The credit part of the journal entry is posted to the accounts payable account in the general ledger. The account number, *21*, is written to the left of the diagonal line in the Post. Ref. column of the general journal. The credit part of the journal entry is also posted to the Swartz Supply Company account in the accounts payable ledger. A check mark is placed to the right of the diagonal line in the Post. Ref. column of the general journal. The account number and the check mark in the Post. Ref. column show that all posting of the credit part of the entry has been completed.

Transactions with creditors are not recorded frequently in the general journal of McCann Office Furniture. For this reason a special amount column for Accounts Payable is not provided in the general journal. When a balance in the accounts payable ledger is increased, the balance of the controlling account in the general ledger must also be increased the same amount. It is necessary, therefore, to post the credit amount in this entry to the accounts payable account in the general ledger and to the creditor's account in the accounts payable ledger.

GENERAL JOURNAL OF McCANN OFFICE FURNITURE

The general journal of McCann Office Furniture after the miscellaneous entries for November have been journalized and posted is shown below.

GENERAL JOURNAL PAGE 4

	DATE		ACCOUNT TITLE	POST. REF.	DEBIT	CREDIT	
1	1967 Nov.	16	John McCann, Drawing	32	150 00		1
2			Purchases	51		150 00	2
3			Memo dated Nov. 16.				3
4		20	Raymond Holland	✓	352 00		4
5			Wayne Hunter	✓		352 00	5
6			Memo dated Nov. 20.				6
7		30	Supplies	14	112 00		7
8			Accounts Payable/Swartz Supply Co.	21/✓		112 00	8
9			Invoice of Nov. 30.				9
10							10
11							11
12							12

General journal of McCann Office Furniture after miscellaneous entries for November have been journalized and posted

ORDER OF POSTING WHEN SEVERAL JOURNALS ARE USED

As a general rule, all items affecting customers' accounts and creditors' accounts are posted frequently so that the balances of these accounts in the customers' ledger and in the creditors' ledger will always be up-to-date. Items affecting accounts in the general ledger are posted less frequently during the month. But all items, including the totals of special columns, must be posted before a trial balance is taken.

It is usually found satisfactory to post the several journals in the following order: (1) purchases journal; (2) cash payments journal; (3) sales journal; (4) cash receipts journal; and (5) general journal. This order of posting will help to bring the debits and the credits to the accounts in the ledgers in the order in which the transactions occurred.

GENERAL LEDGER OF McCANN OFFICE FURNITURE

The general ledger of McCann Office Furniture on November 30 after the posting has been completed from the five journals and the accounts have been footed is shown on pages 266 and 267.

No postings appear in Account Nos. 33, 62, and 66 since no transactions during the month of November affect these accounts. The use of these accounts will be explained in Chapter 18.

Cash — ACCOUNT NO. 11

DATE	ITEMS	POST. REF.	DEBIT	DATE	ITEMS	POST. REF.	CREDIT
1967 Nov. 1	Balance	✓	2500 00	1967 Nov. 30		CP12	3270 00
30	4,771.00	CR10	5541 00				
			8041 00				

Accounts Receivable — ACCOUNT NO. 12

DATE	ITEMS	POST. REF.	DEBIT	DATE	ITEMS	POST. REF.	CREDIT
1967 Nov. 1	Balance	✓	1102 00	1967 Nov. 30		CR10	2130 00
30	1,282.00	S9	2310 00				
			3412 00				

Merchandise Inventory — ACCOUNT NO. 13

DATE	ITEMS	POST. REF.	DEBIT	DATE	ITEMS	POST. REF.	CREDIT
1967 Nov. 1	Balance	✓	6245 00				

Supplies — ACCOUNT NO. 14

DATE	ITEMS	POST. REF.	DEBIT	DATE	ITEMS	POST. REF.	CREDIT
1967 Nov. 1	Balance	✓	155 00				
30		J4	112 00				
			267 00				

Prepaid Insurance — ACCOUNT NO. 15

DATE	ITEMS	POST. REF.	DEBIT	DATE	ITEMS	POST. REF.	CREDIT
1967 Nov. 1	Balance	✓	199 00				

Accounts Payable — ACCOUNT NO. 21

DATE	ITEMS	POST. REF.	DEBIT	DATE	ITEMS	POST. REF.	CREDIT
1967 Nov. 30		CP12	2170 00	1967 Nov. 1	Balance	✓	1080 00
				30		P10	3260 00
				30	2,282.00	J4	112 00
							4452 00

John McCann, Capital — ACCOUNT NO. 31

DATE	ITEMS	POST. REF.	DEBIT	DATE	ITEMS	POST. REF.	CREDIT
				1967 Nov. 1	Balance	✓	9121 00
				4		CR10	1000 00
							10121 00

John McCann, Drawing — ACCOUNT NO. 32

DATE	ITEMS	POST. REF.	DEBIT	DATE	ITEMS	POST. REF.	CREDIT
1967 Nov. 9		CP12	100 00				
16		J4	150 00				
29		CP12	100 00				
			350 00				

General ledger after all journals have been posted

Income and Expense Summary ACCOUNT NO. 33

DATE		ITEMS	POST. REF.	DEBIT	DATE		ITEMS	POST. REF.	CREDIT

Sales ACCOUNT NO. 41

DATE		ITEMS	POST. REF.	DEBIT	DATE		ITEMS	POST. REF.	CREDIT
					1967				
					Nov.	30		S9	2310 00
						30		CR10	2411 00
									4721 00

Purchases ACCOUNT NO. 51

DATE		ITEMS	POST. REF.	DEBIT	DATE		ITEMS	POST. REF.	CREDIT
1967					1967				
Nov.	10		CP12	124 00	Nov.	16		J4	150 00
	30	3,234.00	P10	3260 00					
				3384 00					

Delivery Expense ACCOUNT NO. 61

DATE		ITEMS	POST. REF.	DEBIT	DATE		ITEMS	POST. REF.	CREDIT
1967									
Nov.	17		CP12	25 00					
	28		CP12	28 00					
				53 00					

Insurance Expense ACCOUNT NO. 62

DATE		ITEMS	POST. REF.	DEBIT	DATE		ITEMS	POST. REF.	CREDIT

Miscellaneous Expense ACCOUNT NO. 63

DATE		ITEMS	POST. REF.	DEBIT	DATE		ITEMS	POST. REF.	CREDIT
1967									
Nov.	14		CP12	11 00					
	21		CP12	12 00					
				23 00					

Rent Expense ACCOUNT NO. 64

DATE		ITEMS	POST. REF.	DEBIT	DATE		ITEMS	POST. REF.	CREDIT
1967									
Nov.	2		CP12	300 00					

Salary Expense ACCOUNT NO. 65

DATE		ITEMS	POST. REF.	DEBIT	DATE		ITEMS	POST. REF.	CREDIT
1967									
Nov.	17		CP12	200 00					
	30		CP12	200 00					
				400 00					

Supplies Expense ACCOUNT NO. 66

DATE		ITEMS	POST. REF.	DEBIT	DATE		ITEMS	POST. REF.	CREDIT

and the accounts have been footed

Proving the equality of debits and credits in the general ledger

The bookkeeper for McCann Office Furniture uses an adding machine to obtain a total of all debit balances and a total of all credit balances in the general ledger accounts. The adding machine tapes for November 30 are shown below. The total of the debit balances and the total of the credit balances are then compared. If the two totals are the same, the equality of debits and credits in the general ledger has been proved. If the totals do not agree, the error or errors must be found and corrected.

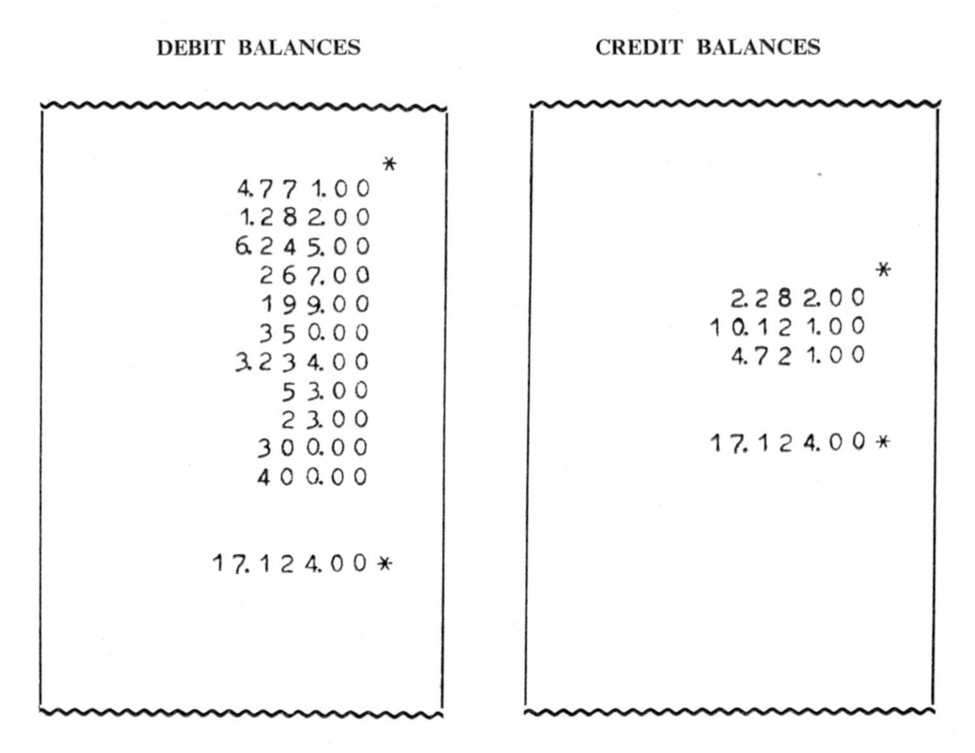

Adding machine tapes that prove the equality of debits and credits in the general ledger of McCann Office Furniture

Recording the trial balance on the work sheet

At the end of a fiscal period, the bookkeeper enters the trial balance in the appropriate columns of the work sheet, as shown on the next page. Every account in the general ledger is listed on the work sheet whether it has a balance or not. All accounts are listed in the Trial Balance section of the work sheet in the same order in which they appear in the ledger. The completion of this work sheet for McCann Office Furniture will be described in Chapter 18.

McCann Office Furniture
Work Sheet
For Month Ended November 30, 1967

	ACCOUNT TITLES	ACCT. NO.	TRIAL BALANCE DEBIT (1)	TRIAL BALANCE CREDIT (2)
1	Cash	11	4771 00	
2	Accounts Receivable	12	1282 00	
3	Merchandise Inventory	13	6245 00	
4	Supplies	14	267 00	
5	Prepaid Insurance	15	199 00	
6	Accounts Payable	21		2282 00
7	John McCann, Capital	31		10121 00
8	John McCann, Drawing	32	350 00	
9	Income & Expense Summary	33		
10	Sales	41		4721 00
11	Purchases	51	3234 00	
12	Delivery Expense	61	53 00	
13	Insurance Expense	62		
14	Miscellaneous Expense	63	23 00	
15	Rent Expense	64	300 00	
16	Salary Expense	65	400 00	
17	Supplies Expense	66		
18			17124 00	17124 00
19				
20				
21				
22				
23				
24				

Partial work sheet of McCann Office Furniture
showing completed trial balance section

Increasing Your Business Vocabulary

What is the meaning of each of the following:

a miscellaneous entries

b correcting entries

Study Questions

1. List the kinds of miscellaneous entries recorded in the general journal.
2. What account is debited and what account is credited to record the withdrawal of merchandise by the proprietor?

3. Why is the buying of supplies on account recorded in the general journal rather than in the purchases journal?
4. What two accounts in the general ledger are affected by the buying of supplies on account?
5. When recording a transaction in the general journal that affects Accounts Payable, why is it necessary to write the name of the creditor on the same line?
6. Why is it important to post items to customers' and creditors' accounts frequently?
7. In what order is it suggested that the special journals be posted?
8. How is the equality of debits and credits in the general ledger proved?

Cases for Business Decision

CASE 1

Mr. Wexler is the owner of a neighborhood grocery store. He withdraws groceries several times during the week for the use of his family. He keeps no record of these withdrawals. Mrs. Wexler has suggested that a record be kept of the cost of groceries used by the family so that this amount can be recorded as an expense of the business each month. Do you agree with the suggestion offered by Mrs. Wexler? Why?

CASE 2

Mr. Cohn recently purchased a jewelry store. A few days later his store was broken into and merchandise valued at $3,000 was stolen. Unfortunately, he had not yet purchased insurance covering burglary and theft. Should Mr. Cohn make a journal entry to record this loss? If so, what should the entry be?

CASE 3

Mr. Dobbs operates a garage. He repairs and services cars; sells gasoline, oil, tires, etc.; and also operates a tow service. Whenever the driver of the tow truck needs gasoline for the truck, he fills the tank from the garage service pump. No record is made of the amounts of gasoline taken. (a) If you were Mr. Dobbs' bookkeeper, what kinds of records would you want kept? (b) What journal entry would you make when the driver of the tow truck takes gasoline from the garage service pump?

CASE 4

The Breece Supply Company purchases eight desks from the Hi-Line Manufacturing Company. One of these desks is for use in the accounting department. The remaining seven are for resale to customers. The amount of the invoice is $800.00. The bookkeeper records the full amount of the invoice in the purchases journal. Is the bookkeeper making the correct entry? If not, what entry should he make?

Drill for Understanding

DRILL 16-A | Analyzing transactions of a merchandising business

Instructions: 1. For each transaction given below, indicate the journal in which the transaction would be recorded.

2. Prepare T accounts showing the names of the general ledger accounts and the subsidiary ledger account or accounts that are affected. Show the amount of the debit or credit to each account. Copy the analysis of transaction No. 1, which is given below as an example.

1. Journal to be used: *Purchases*

Subsidiary ledger to be used: *Accounts Payable*

GENERAL LEDGER

Purchases	
100.00	

Accounts Payable	
	100.00

SUBSIDIARY LEDGER

Leath's, Inc.	
	100.00

Transaction No. — *Transactions*

1. Purchased merchandise on account from Leath's, Inc., $100.00.
2. Paid cash for rent, $290.00.
3. Paid cash to Jackson & Smith on account, $150.00.
4. Received a check for $500.00 from John Anderson, the owner, as an additional investment in the business.
5. The bookkeeper discovers an error in which a cash purchase of supplies, $50.00, was debited to Purchases and credited to Cash.
6. Sold merchandise on account to John Carlson, $220.00.
7. John Anderson, the proprietor, withdrew merchandise for his personal use, $200.00.
8. Bought store supplies on account from Hines Company, $50.00.
9. Paid cash to Alt Company for the purchase of merchandise, $300.00.
10. Received cash from sales as shown by the cash register tape, $600.00.
11. Received a check from Albert Benson on account, $90.00.
12. The bookkeeper discovers an error in which a check for $30.00, received from Albert Brown, was recorded and posted to the account of Arnold Browne.

Application Problem

PROBLEM 16-1 | Analyzing and recording miscellaneous entries

The transactions listed below are some of those completed by John B. Kelly during the month of October of the current year. For his business records, Mr. Kelly uses a purchases journal, a sales journal, a cash receipts journal, a cash payments journal, and a general journal.

Instructions: 1. Select only those transactions that should be recorded in a general journal and record them on page 86 of two-column journal paper.

2. For each of the transactions not recorded in the general journal, state:

a The journal in which the transaction would be recorded.
b The account or accounts that would be debited.
c The account or accounts that would be credited.

Transactions

Oct. 2. Paid $300.00 for October rent. Check No. 110.
4. Received $156.95 from Richard Riggin on account.
5. Sold merchandise on account to Paul Evans, $248.25. Sales Slip No. 205.
6. Bought supplies on account from Smith, Inc., $56.00. Invoice of October 4.
10. Mr. Kelly withdrew merchandise for personal use, $119.00. Memo dated October 10.
11. Sold merchandise on account to Norman Bell, $142.75. Sales Slip No. 206.
12. Paid $195.50 to Smith, Inc., on account. Check No. 111.
12. Discovered that a September 27 sale of merchandise on account, $161.40, was charged to the account of S. A. Ward in error. The sale was made to S. M. Warden. Memo dated October 12.
13. Received $1,739.30 from cash sales for the period October 2 to 13.
16. Paid $179.20 to Hathaway Supply Company on account. Check No. 112.
18. Paid $300.00 to Mr. Kelly for his personal use. Check No. 113.
19. Bought office supplies on account from D. & H. Wholesale Company, $78.00. Invoice of October 18.
20. Purchased merchandise on account from S. Kenton, $599.70.
25. Bought office furniture on account from the Pierce Company, $450.00. Invoice of October 22.
31. Received $1,793.66 from cash sales for the period October 14 to 31.
31. Paid $500.00 for clerks' salaries for the month. Check No. 114.
31. Paid $56.00 to Smith, Inc., on account. Check No. 115.

Optional Problems

★ SUPPLEMENTARY PROBLEM 16-S

Analyzing and recording miscellaneous entries

Donald Jones owns and operates a paint store. During the first half of September of the current year he completed the selected transactions listed below. Mr. Jones uses a purchases journal, a sales journal, a cash receipts journal, a cash payments journal, and a general journal.

Instructions: 1. Select only those transactions that should be recorded in a general journal and record them on page 33 of two-column journal paper.

2. For each of the transactions not recorded in the general journal, state:
- **a** The journal in which the transaction would be recorded.
- **b** The account or accounts that would be debited.
- **c** The account or accounts that would be credited.

Transactions

Sept. 1. Paid $160.00 for September rent. Check No. 803.
2. Purchased merchandise on account from Fuller Paints, $78.80.
3. Sold merchandise on account to Bill Crawford, $9.83. Sales Slip No. 1839.
3. W. A. Lambert reported that he had been charged $5.50 for merchandise that he had not purchased. A check of the records shows that the sale was made to W. A. Lamb. Memo dated September 3.
4. Received $18.47 from Bill Crawford on account.
4. Bought new paint mixer on account from Tice Equipment Company, $124.90. Invoice of September 3.
5. Received $626.03 from cash sales for the period September 1 to 5.
8. Paid $75.00 to Mr. Jones for his personal use. Check No. 804.
8. Sold merchandise on account to Mrs. Ralph Hayes, $27.70. Sales Slip No. 1840.
9. Mr. Jones withdrew merchandise worth $51.75 for use in painting his home. Memo dated September 9.
10. Paid $50.00 to Fuller Paints on account. Check No. 805.
10. Paid $40.00 for salary of part-time clerk. Check No. 806.
10. Bought cleaning supplies on account from Valley Supply Company for use in the store, $69.40. Invoice of September 8.
10. Received $249.88 from cash sales for the period September 6 to 10.
13. Mr. Jones discovered that a $15.00 purchase of supplies on account in August had been debited to Purchases instead of to Supplies. Memo dated September 13.
14. Received a personal check for $450.00 from the owner, Mr. Jones, as an additional investment in the business.
15. Paid cash, $129.60, for a new display case. Check No. 807.

★ BONUS PROBLEM 16-B

Analyzing and recording miscellaneous entries

A. L. Howard owns and operates a retail clothing store. During the month of January of the current year he completed the transactions listed below.

Instructions: 1. Record the transactions for January 2 through 11 on page 64 of a general journal.

Transactions

Jan. 2. Bought a new display counter on account from the Johns Supply Company, $964.40. Invoice of January 2.

6. Agreed with a show card artist to exchange a suit of clothes that cost $60.00 for advertising display cards. Memo dated January 6.

9. Donated to the Salvation Army clothing that cost $85.00. Memo dated January 9. (The store has an account with the title Contributions.)

10. Withdrew from stock for personal use merchandise that cost $75.00. Memo dated January 10.

11. Sold an old display counter for $160.00 to Tark's Secondhand Store on account. Sales Slip No. 431.

Instructions: 2. For each of the transactions for January 15 through 27, state:

a The journal or journals in which the transaction would be recorded.

b The account or accounts that would be debited.

c The account or accounts that would be credited.

Transactions

Jan. 15. Purchased merchandise on account from Roberts Suit Company, $324.40.

16. Sold merchandise to J. H. Willis, $130.00, Sales Slip No. 466. Mr. Willis paid $30.00 in cash. He is to pay the remainder in 60 days.

17. Purchased merchandise for cash from the Ready Tie Company, $66.00. Check No. 655.

18. Received $360.00 from J. R. Moore on account.

19. Purchased an insurance policy from the Arcade Agency. Cost of policy, $180.00. Paid $90.00 in cash and agreed to pay the remainder in 60 days. Check No. 659.

20. Sold office supplies on account, $12.00, to B. F. Simms, a store owner next door. Sales Slip No. 512.

23. Bought a display counter for $390.00 from Modern Displays, Inc. Paid cash for one third of the purchase price, Check No. 662. The remainder of the January 23 invoice is to be paid in 30 days.

25. As a special one-day advertising offer, the store gave a free necktie to each customer who purchased more than $10.00 worth of merchandise. Thirty-two ties were given away. The ties cost the store 70¢ each. Memo dated January 25.

27. Mr. Howard withdrew $150.00 from the business for his personal use. Check No. 688.

CHAPTER 17 THE CHECKING ACCOUNT AND RECONCILIATION OF BANK STATEMENTS

Banks offer many services to business firms and individuals. Among these services are: (1) receiving cash for safekeeping; (2) paying out cash on the order of depositors; and (3) reporting to each depositor at regular intervals the amount of his deposits, withdrawals, and bank account balance.

Placing cash with a bank is called *making a deposit*. The one in whose name cash is deposited is called a *depositor*. The report the bank makes to a depositor showing his deposits, withdrawals, and bank account balance is called a *bank statement*.

Most banks provide at least two kinds of accounts for depositors: (1) accounts that permit depositors to withdraw cash by writing checks; and (2) accounts on which the bank pays interest to the depositor for cash left with it for a period of time. An account with a bank that permits the depositor to order payments to others from his bank balance is called a *checking account*. An account with a bank on which a bank pays interest to the depositor is called a *savings account*.

OPENING A CHECKING ACCOUNT

A business may receive cash from customers in the form of coins, bills, checks, and money orders. It is not safe to keep large amounts of cash at a store or an office, on one's person, or at home. Cash is safer in a bank because it is protected by the bank. In most banks each depositor's account is insured up to $15,000 by the Federal Deposit Insurance Corporation, an agency of the federal government. Businesses therefore usually deposit all cash receipts in a bank checking account and withdraw amounts of cash as needed. Withdrawals are made by writing a check. A check is an order in writing, signed by the depositor, ordering the bank to pay cash from his account.

The signature card

Each new depositor is required to sign his name on a card so that the bank may verify his signature on all of his business papers that come to the bank. The card a depositor signs to provide the bank with a copy of his authorized signature is called a *signature card.*

PACIFIC NATIONAL BANK
Portland, Oregon

Date Mo. JAN | Day 15 | Year 1965

This bank is authorized to recognize any of the signatures subscribed below in payment of Funds or the transaction of any business for this account.

Type of Account INDIVIDUAL ☐ JOINT ACCOUNT PAYABLE TO EITHER OR SURVIVOR ☑ PARTNERSHIP OR FIRM ☐ BUDGET ☑ REGULAR ☐

JOHN AND MARIE C. McCANN
(Name of Account)

(Signature) John McCann

(Signature) Marie C. McCann

(Signature)

(Signature)

one (Remarks — Number of Signatures Required) 621-8811 (Telephone)

708 ROBIN DR., PORTLAND, OREGON 97231 (Address) Opened By R.S.

This Account is opened and held subject to the Terms and Conditions on the reverse side.

Signature card for an individual

The signature card shown above was prepared by John McCann and his wife for their personal checking account. The bank is authorized to recognize only the signatures of Mr. or Mrs. McCann when transacting business for their personal checking account.

The signature card shown at the right is for McCann Office Furniture. Both Mr. McCann and his assistant manager, Mr. T. L. Blake, have signed this card. The bank is authorized to recognize either signature when transacting business for the McCann Office Furniture account.

Address 640 Central Avenue
Portland, Oregon 97227 Telephone 671-3934
Date opened March 1, 1966 Initial Deposit $1,500.00

Authorized Signatures of Checking ☒
McCANN OFFICE FURNITURE Savings ☐
No. 187-0029-90

PACIFIC NATIONAL BANK, PORTLAND, OREGON
(Subject to the terms and conditions on reverse side)

Print Name & Title	Specimen Signature
John McCann, Owner	John McCann
T. L. Blake, Asst. Mgr.	T. L. Blake

Any one to sign

Signature card for a business

The signature card is a safeguard established by the bank to protect against forgeries. The depositor must make certain he always signs his checks exactly as his signature appears on the signature card filed with the bank. If the signature on the check is not the same as that shown on the signature card, the bank may refuse to pay the check. If a business finds it necessary to appoint new or different persons to sign its checks, a new signature card is prepared and filed with the bank.

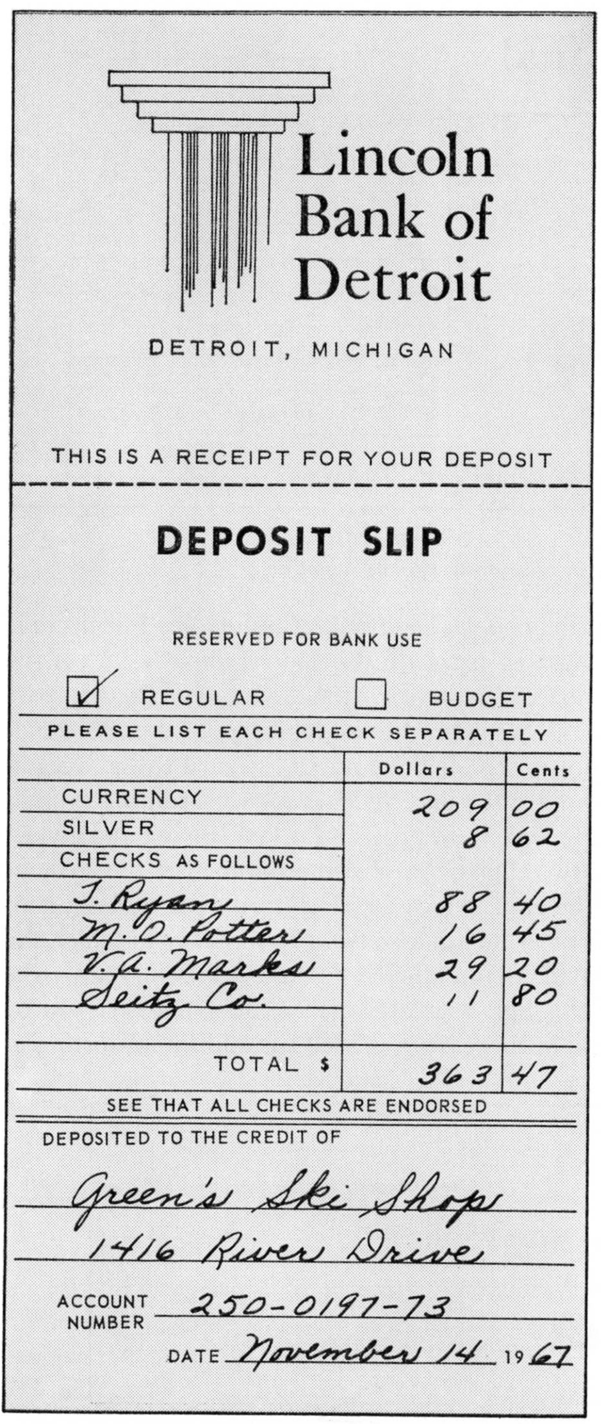
Lincoln Bank of Detroit

DETROIT, MICHIGAN

THIS IS A RECEIPT FOR YOUR DEPOSIT

DEPOSIT SLIP

RESERVED FOR BANK USE

☑ REGULAR ☐ BUDGET

PLEASE LIST EACH CHECK SEPARATELY

	Dollars	Cents
CURRENCY	209	00
SILVER	8	62
CHECKS AS FOLLOWS		
J. Ryan	88	40
M. O. Potter	16	45
V. A. Marks	29	20
Seitz Co.	11	80
TOTAL $	363	47

SEE THAT ALL CHECKS ARE ENDORSED

DEPOSITED TO THE CREDIT OF

Green's Ski Shop

1416 River Drive

ACCOUNT NUMBER 250-0197-73

DATE November 14 1967

Deposit slip
Checks identified by person from whom received

The deposit slip

The business form provided by the bank on which the depositor lists all cash and cash items to be deposited is called a *deposit slip.* The term *deposit ticket* is also used. The illustration at the left and the one on the next page show two common forms of deposit slips.

ABA numbers and magnetic ink characters

Checks may be listed on a deposit slip either (1) by the name of the person or company from whom each check was received, or (2) by the number of the bank against which each check was written. Identification numbers assigned to banks by the American Bankers Association are called *ABA numbers.* The ABA numbers are printed on the checks supplied by a bank for the use of its depositors.

Pacific National Bank

Portland, Oregon *Nov. 30* 19*67*

CASH	*611*	*00*
PLEASE LIST SEPARATELY CHECKS *24-220*	*154*	*00*
24-190	*74*	*00*
TOTAL	*839*	*00*

For deposit to account of:

McCann Office Furniture
Portland, Oregon

1230 0075 187 002990

Deposit slip
Checks identified by ABA number

The first check listed on the deposit slip for McCann Office Furniture is shown below. The bank number listed on the deposit slip, *24-220,* is the ABA number of the Oregon Trail Bank of Portland, Oregon. The first part of the number, *24,* is the number assigned to all banks located in Portland. The second part of the number, *220,* is the number assigned to the Oregon Trail Bank. The number under the line, *1230,* is a check routing symbol used by the Federal Reserve System to provide for fast sorting and collection of checks. The first two digits, *12,* give the number of the Federal Reserve District in which the bank is located. The third digit, *3,* designates the Federal Reserve Bank or branch that serves the territory in which the Oregon Trail Bank is located. If the digit is *1,* the bank is served by the Federal Reserve Bank; if the digit is greater than *1,* the bank is served by a branch. The fourth digit, in this case *0,* is used for additional sorting of checks.

Frank Wright
1240 Short Street
Portland, Oregon 97208

No. *421*

Portland, Oregon *November 24* 19*67* 24-220 / 1230 ← ABA Numbers

Pay to the Order of *McCann Office Furniture* $ *154 00/100*

One hundred fifty-four and 00/100 Dollars

Oregon Trail Bank *Frank Wright*

1230 0220 890 0093 49

Magnetic Ink Characters

Check with ABA numbers and magnetic ink characters

The numbers at the bottom of the check are specially printed so that they can be "read" by automatic machines that sort large numbers of checks according to the ABA routing number. Special number characters printed in magnetic ink that can be "read" by automatic machines are called *magnetic ink characters.* A machine that reads and processes data properly printed in magnetic ink is called a *magnetic ink character reader.*

In the check illustrated on page 278, the first number, *1230*, is the check routing symbol used by the Federal Reserve System. The second number, *0220*, is the number of the Oregon Trail Bank, prefaced by a zero to provide four digits for each bank number. The third number, *890 0093 49*, is the account number assigned by the bank to the checking account of Frank Wright. In many banks with a large volume of check activity, the checks are automatically sorted by magnetic ink character readers according to the accounts against which the checks are written.

Depositor's record of deposits

When cash is deposited in a bank, the teller provides the depositor with one of the following as a receipt for the amount deposited:

1. A copy of the deposit slip with the date and the name of the bank stamped on it.
2. A record of the deposit in a small book that the bank supplies to the depositor when his account is opened.
3. A receipt issued by the bank that shows the name of the depositor, the date, and the amount of the deposit.

The deposit slip for Green's Ski Shop, shown on page 277, has a receipt attached at the top. A special machine is used at the bank to record the deposit by stamping the amount and the date of the deposit on the receipt portion of the deposit slip. The receipt is detached from the deposit slip and returned to the depositor as his record of the deposit. The information on the deposit slip receipt should be recorded by the depositor on the next check stub to be used.

Endorsing checks

Before a bank will accept a check for deposit, the depositor must sign or stamp his name on the back of the check. The signature or the stamp of the depositor on the back of a check is called an *endorsement.* An endorsement is placed on the back of a check as shown in the illustration on the next page.

An endorsement transfers the ownership of the check. When a check is deposited, the ownership is transferred to the bank that credits the amount to the depositor's account. When the depositor endorses a check, he guarantees its payment.

FOR DEPOSIT AND CREDIT TO ACCOUNT OF McCANN OFFICE FURNITURE

No. 421

vember 24 1961

$154 00/100

Dollars

Wright

Endorsed check

Kinds of endorsements

Different kinds of endorsements serve different purposes. The principal forms of endorsements are described and illustrated below.

John McCann

Blank endorsement

Blank endorsement. An endorsement that consists only of the name of the endorser is called a *blank endorsement*. A lost or a stolen check with a blank endorsement can be cashed by the finder or a thief. Therefore, a blank endorsement should not be placed on the check until the depositor is at the bank ready to make his deposit or to cash the check.

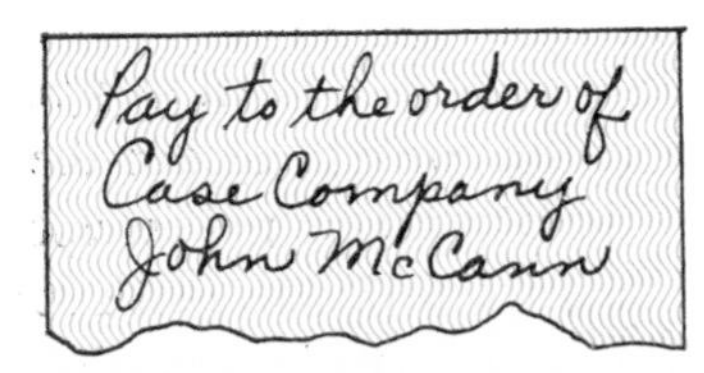

Endorsement in full

Endorsement in full. An endorsement that states to whom the check is to be paid, together with the name of the endorser, is called an *endorsement in full*. This kind of endorsement states that the check can be cashed or transferred only on the order of the person named in the endorsement.

Restrictive endorsement

Restrictive endorsement. An endorsement that limits the receiver of the check as to the use he can make of the funds collected is called a *restrictive endorsement*. Restrictive endorsements are commonly used when checks are prepared for deposit.

Bank service charges

Banks obtain some of their income by using part of the funds deposited with them to purchase interest-bearing securities, such as government bonds. Banks also lend part of the funds deposited and charge interest on the loans made. Some depositors have large bank balances and a considerable sum is thus available for investment by the bank. The bank receives more than enough interest from its investments to pay for all the clerical work and supplies used in handling the customers' accounts.

If a depositor's bank account balance is small, however, the expense of handling the depositor's funds may exceed the income received by the bank from the use of these funds. Also, many depositors do not leave cash in their checking account for a long enough period of time to permit the bank to use it for investment. For these reasons, banks usually make a monthly service charge whenever the depositor's account balance is small compared with the number of checks written. A charge made by a bank for servicing the checking account is called a *bank service charge*. Service charges vary in different communities and from bank to bank.

WRITING CHECKS

A check may be written in ink or by a machine. The check stub should always be completed before the check is written. The check stub should contain all the information about the transaction because the check stub is the source document for recording entries in the cash payments journal.

The one who orders the bank to pay cash from his account is called the *drawer*. The one to whom the bank is ordered to pay the cash is called the *payee*. The bank on which the check is drawn is called the *drawee*. In the illustration on page 278, Frank Wright is the drawer, McCann Office Furniture is the payee, and Oregon Trail Bank is the drawee.

Steps in writing a check

After completing the check stub, the following steps should be taken in writing the check:

Step 1

Date. Use the current date. Banks will not cash a check that is dated later than the day on which it is presented for payment. For example, if a check is dated November 20 and presented for payment on November 15, the bank will refuse to cash it.

Most checks used by businesses are prenumbered as part of the printing process. If the number has not been printed on the check, however, the number should be written in the space provided. The check number provides an easy means of identification and is used in filing the check for future reference.

Step 2

Name of payee. Write the name of the business — not the proprietor — if the check is being made out to a business firm. A check made payable to a married woman should be made out in her given name and her husband's last name.

Step 3

Amount. Write the amount both in figures and in words. For example, a check for $19.20 is written in figures as follows: $19^{\underline{20}}$. The figures are written very close to the printed dollar sign on the check so that it is impossible to write another number in front of them. The amount is also written in words as follows: Nineteen $\frac{20}{100}$. These words are written at the extreme left of the line provided so that nothing else can be written before the words.

Some businesses use a check-writing machine for writing the amounts on their checks. A check-writing machine usually perforates the amount of the check into the paper. This makes it almost impossible for anyone to change the amount of the check.

Step 4

Signature. The signature of the drawer of the check must be written exactly as it appears on the signature card.

Voiding a check

When the records of a business are audited by tax authorities or accountants, they expect the business to account for every check that has been written. Therefore, it is important to keep all canceled checks.

Banks usually refuse to cash a check that has been altered in any way. If an error is made in writing a check, a new check should be written. The check on which the error has been made should be filed. Before filing it, however, the word "Void" is written across the face of the check and across the corresponding check stub. Writing the word "Void" across the face of a check and the stub to indicate that the check and the stub are not to be used is called *voiding a check.*

So that each check number will be shown in the cash payments journal, a memorandum entry should be made for each check that is voided. The memorandum entry consists of: (1) the date in the Date column, (2) the words "Voided check" in the Account Debited column, (3) the number of the check in the Check No. column, (4) a check mark in the Post. Ref. column, and (5) a small dash in the Cash Credited column to show that no amount is recorded for the entry on this line in the cash payments journal.

RECONCILING THE BANK STATEMENT

Bank's record of each depositor's account

The bank keeps a ledger account for each depositor. The deposit slips and the checks are posted to the depositor's account each business day.

The balance that appears on the depositor's ledger account kept by the bank is known as the *bank balance*. At regular intervals, usually once each month, banks send each depositor a statement that shows all deposits, all withdrawals; the amount of the service charge and any other special charges; and the balance of his account at the bank. The bank statement is used by the depositor to check the accuracy of his own records as well as the accuracy of the statement itself.

Some banks mail their statements to depositors at the end of each month. Other banks follow a system similar to the cycle billing plan described in Chapter 15 so that a portion of the statements are prepared and mailed at different times each month.

Depositor's record of his bank account

A depositor who has a complete and accurate system of bookkeeping knows his bank balance at all times. The check stubs, if kept properly, can be referred to at any time and the last stub will show the bank balance. If a service charge is made by the bank, this amount should be deducted from the balance on the last check stub.

The records of a depositor, when all cash has been deposited, are proved as follows:

Beginning cash balance as shown in the cash receipts journal
plus
the total of the Cash Debit column of the cash receipts journal
minus
the total of the Cash Credit column of the cash payments journal
equals
the check-stub balance.

Checking the accuracy of the bank statement

It is uncommon for banks to make errors in their records. However, there are instances where errors do occur. For example, the bank may have accounts with more than one person with the same name. A check may be charged to the wrong account or a deposit may be credited to the wrong account. Another instance in which a bank may make a mistake is when it pays a check that has been forged. If a bank pays a forged check, the bank must stand the loss. When a depositor discovers that a bank made an error of any kind, he should notify the bank at once.

The depositor may make errors in addition or subtraction on his check stubs. He may locate the error when he proves cash or he may not locate it until he gets his bank statement.

In any of the cases above, the records of the bank and the records of the depositor would not agree. Good business practice, therefore, requires that the depositor compare his records with those of the bank immediately upon receipt of the bank statement.

The bank statement

The bank statement shows in detail: (1) the depositor's bank balance at the beginning of the period; (2) a listing of the checks paid by the bank; (3) the bank service charge, if any; (4) the amounts deposited; and (5) the depositor's bank balance at the end of the period.

When the bank statement is sent to the depositor, the bank also returns all checks that have been paid during the period. Checks that have been paid and returned to the depositor are called *canceled checks.* The bank cancels the checks by stamping or perforating the checks with the date on which they were paid. The canceled checks can be used as evidence that payment has been made. Thus, it is a good practice to keep all canceled checks as part of the records of an individual or a business.

The bank statement of McCann Office Furniture

On February 5, 1968, McCann Office Furniture received its bank statement for the month of January. The bank statement illustrated on page 285 shows:

1. The bank balance as of January 2, 1968, $4,059.02.
2. The checks paid by the bank during January.
3. The deposits made during January.
4. A service charge of $2.92 for January.
5. The bank balance as of January 31, 1968, $4,739.85.

Statement of account with:

Pacific National Bank

Portland, Oregon, 97201

187-0029-90
McCann Office Furniture
640 Central Avenue
Portland, Oregon 97227

CHECKS	CHECKS	DEPOSITS	DATE	BALANCE
Balance brought forward →			Jan 2 '68	4059.02
9.80			Jan 3 '68	4049.22
122.40	48.03		Jan 5 '68	3878.79
100.00	145.00	691.16	Jan 9 '68	4324.95
150.00	12.95		Jan 10 '68	4162.00
326.85	221.15	550.40	Jan 12 '68	4164.40
116.25			Jan 15 '68	4048.15
		401.95	Jan 16 '68	4450.10
15.80			Jan 17 '68	4434.30
27.80			Jan 18 '68	4406.50
15.00		695.75	Jan 22 '68	5087.25
410.33	100.00		Jan 24 '68	4576.92
326.85	10.00		Jan 26 '68	4240.07
		502.70	Jan 30 '68	4742.77
2.92SC			Jan 31 '68	4739.85

KEY

DM – Debit Memo
EC – Error Corrected
LS – List
CM – Credit Memo
RT – Returned Item
SC – Service Charge

↑ Last amount is your balance

PLEASE EXAMINE AT ONCE – IF NO ERROR IS REPORTED WITHIN TEN DAYS, THE ACCOUNT WILL BE CONSIDERED CORRECT. ALL ITEMS ARE CREDITED SUBJECT TO FINAL PAYMENT. KINDLY NOTIFY THIS BANK IMMEDIATELY OF CHANGE OF ADDRESS.

Bank statement for McCann Office Furniture

Outstanding deposits and outstanding checks

If a business deposits all the cash received during the month, the record of deposits shown on the bank statement should agree with the total cash received as shown in the cash receipts journal. Some businesses mail their deposits to the bank. Other firms may place their deposits at night in the bank's depository, a specially built safe to which the depositor has access from outside the bank building. Thus, there may be a delay on the part of the bank in recording a deposit that the business firm has already entered on its check stub. A deposit that has been made but which is not shown on the bank statement is called an *outstanding deposit.* An outstanding deposit is also called a *deposit in transit.*

If all payments are made by check and all the checks written during the month are cashed at the bank before the end of the month, the checks listed on the bank statement will agree with those in the cash payments journal. However, some checks may not be presented to the bank for payment in the same month in which they are written. A check that has been issued but not presented to the bank for payment is called an *outstanding check*.

Reconciling the bank statement of McCann Office Furniture

The process of bringing into agreement the bank balance as shown on the bank statement and the check-stub balance is called *reconciling the bank statement.*

The procedure followed by McCann Office Furniture in reconciling the bank statement is:

Step 1

Arrange the canceled checks received from the bank in order according to check number.

Step 2

Compare the checks with the check stubs and place a check mark on the stub of each check that has been returned.

Step 3

Prepare the reconciliation of the bank statement in the following form.

Reconciliation of Bank Statement
January 31, 1968

Balance on check stub		Balance on bank statement,	
No. 395, January 31, 1968	4712 02	January 31, 1968	4739 75
Deduct:		Add outstanding deposit	
Service charge for January	2 92	mailed January 31, 1968	213 61
		Total	4953 46
		Deduct outstanding checks:	
		Check No. Amount	
		391 141.25	
		394 50.00	
		395 53.11	
		Total outstanding checks	244 36
Adjusted check-stub balance,		Adjusted bank balance,	
January 31, 1968	4709 10	January 31, 1968	4709 10

Reconciliation of bank statement for McCann Office Furniture

a Record the balance, *$4,712.02*, shown on the last check stub written during the month of January.

b Deduct the bank service charge, *$2.92*, as shown on the bank statement. The difference is the adjusted check-stub balance, *$4,709.10*, at the end of the month.

c Record the balance at the end of the month, *$4,739.85*, as shown on the bank statement.

d Compare the deposits listed on the bank statement with whatever record of deposits is kept by the business. Add the amount of any deposit not listed on the bank statement to the bank balance.

> McCann Office Furniture mailed a deposit of $213.61 to the bank on the last day of the month and recorded this deposit on check stub No. 395 of January 31, 1968. Since this deposit is not listed on the bank statement, it is added to the bank statement balance.

e List the number and amount of each outstanding check, and total the column.

f Deduct the total of the outstanding checks, *$244.36*, to determine the adjusted bank balance, *$4,709.10*, at the end of the month.

The reconciliation of the bank statement for McCann Office Furniture shows that there is a balance of $4,709.10 against which checks may be written. Both the adjusted check-stub balance and the adjusted bank balance are the same. The bank statement is therefore said to be reconciled.

JOURNAL ENTRIES RELATED TO THE RECONCILED BANK STATEMENT

Recording the bank service charge

When a service charge is made by a bank, the amount is deducted from the balance on the check stub. It is also necessary to record the service charge in the cash payments journal. This is done by debiting Miscellaneous Expense in the General Debit column and crediting Cash in the Cash Credit column. The entry in the cash payments journal is shown below.

CASH PAYMENTS JOURNAL PAGE 15

	DATE		ACCOUNT DEBITED	CK. NO.	POST. REF.	1 GENERAL DEBIT	2 ACCOUNTS PAYABLE DEBIT	3 CASH CREDIT	
1	1968 Feb.	1	Misc. Exp.—bank service charge		✓	2 92		2 92	1
2									2
3									3
4									4
5									5

Entry to record the bank service charge

A check is not written for this entry; therefore, a check mark is placed in the Check No. column. Since there is no check stub to provide an explanation of this entry, the words "bank service charge" are written after the name of the account debited.

Recording a dishonored check

A check that the bank refuses to pay is known as a *dishonored check*. The bank may refuse to pay the check for a number of reasons. For example, the amount may have been altered, the signature of the drawer is not the same as that on the signature card, or there are insufficient funds in the drawer's checking account.

When a depositor is notified by his bank that a check he has deposited has been dishonored, he must pay the bank the amount of the check. The depositor may write his own check payable to the bank for the amount of the dishonored check, or the bank may deduct the amount from the depositor's account.

The amount of the dishonored check is recorded in the cash payments journal. The customer's account from whom the check was originally received is debited and Cash is credited. When this entry is posted, the customer's account will show that he still owes the depositor the amount of the dishonored check.

Increasing Your Business Vocabulary

What is the meaning of each of the following:

a making a deposit
b depositor
c bank statement
d checking account
e savings account
f signature card
g deposit slip
h ABA numbers
i magnetic ink characters
j magnetic ink character reader
k endorsement
l blank endorsement
m endorsement in full
n restrictive endorsement
o bank service charge
p drawer
q payee
r drawee
s voiding a check
t bank balance
u canceled checks
v outstanding deposit
w outstanding check
x reconciling the bank statement
y dishonored check

Study Questions

1. In what various forms does a business usually receive cash from customers?
2. Why is cash safer in a bank than in a store or an office?
3. Why is a depositor required to file a signature card with the bank?
4. Why should a depositor always sign his checks exactly as his signature appears on the signature card filed with the bank?
5. In what ways may checks be listed on a deposit slip?
6. Why must a depositor endorse a check that he is depositing in his account?
7. Why should a depositor not place a blank endorsement on his check until he is at the bank ready to make his deposit or cash the check?
8. What kind of endorsement is commonly used when checks are prepared for deposit?
9. Why do banks usually make a monthly service charge whenever a depositor's account balance is small compared with the number of checks written?
10. What information is contained in the memorandum entry in the cash payments journal for each check that is voided?
11. What use does the depositor make of the bank statement?
12. What information is shown on the bank statement?
13. What entry is made on a check stub to record a bank service charge?
14. What account is debited and what account is credited in the cash payments journal to record a bank service charge?
15. For what reasons may a bank refuse to pay a check?

Cases for Business Decision

CASE 1

Hank Bux, the manager of a service station, places a blank endorsement on each check at the time he receives it. He makes his deposit by mailing the checks and the deposit slip to the bank. What are the disadvantages of this practice?

CASE 2

When Mr. Orton deposited his business receipts for the day, he made an error and wrote his personal account number on the deposit slip instead of his business account number. The bank credited the deposit to his personal account. When will Mr. Orton discover this error and what should he do about it?

CASE 3

J. M. Bass receives his bank statement each month, but he reconciles his bank statement only once every three months. What are some of the problems that might arise from this practice?

Drills for Understanding

DRILL 17-A | Reconciling a bank statement

Jerome Emens has a checkbook balance of $196.45 at the end of March of the current year. His bank statement for March 31 shows the balance to be $209.35. When he compares the check stubs with the canceled checks, Mr. Emens discovers that the bank did not return Check No. 31 for $12.90, issued to the Welles Department Store on March 30. Reconcile Mr. Emens' bank statement.

DRILL 17-B | Reconciling a bank statement

Ralph Wiseman received his bank statement, which showed a balance of $319.60. Mr. Wiseman's check stub shows a balance of $320.80. When he compares the canceled checks with his check stubs, he discovers that all the checks he had written were returned with the bank statement. He also finds in comparing the check stubs with the bank statement that a bank service charge of $1.20 has not been recorded on the check stubs. Reconcile Mr. Wiseman's bank statement as of December 31 of the current year.

DRILL 17-C | Reconciling a bank statement

Ruth Grott has a check-stub balance of $436.20. The bank statement shows that Ruth's balance in the bank is $324.40. A comparison of the check stubs with the bank statement shows that all the checks written have been returned. However, a deposit of $110.00, made the day before and recorded on the check stub, is not shown on the bank statement. Also, a bank service charge of $1.80 shown on the bank statement has not been entered on the check stub. Reconcile Ruth's bank statement as of May 15 of the current year.

Application Problems

PROBLEM 17-1 | Preparing a deposit slip

On November 15 of the current year, George Short made a deposit consisting of the following items:

8 ten-dollar bills
12 one-dollar bills
4 half dollars
10 quarters
20 dimes
5 nickels

Checks from the following:

Peter Hansen, drawn on the First National Bank, Chicago, Illinois, ABA number 2-1	$ 75.00
Arthur Morgen, drawn on the Citizens Bank, Troy, New York, ABA number 50-65	20.00
James Downs, drawn on the Union Trust Bank, New York, ABA number 51-66	13.95
Duane Deal, drawn on the First State Bank, Buffalo, New York, ABA number 51-68	110.00

Instructions: Prepare a deposit slip for this deposit. Identify the checks by the ABA numbers. Mr. Short's account number is 203-00716.

PROBLEM 17-2 | Reconciling a bank statement for an individual

The following information relates to the bank account and the cash records of Paul Falcone for December of the current year:

Bank balance, December 31, as shown on the bank statement...... $982.20

Cash balance, December 31, as shown on the stub for the last check written in December 850.00

Checks outstanding:

No. 851 ...... $121.60
No. 858 ...... 12.00

Service charge by the bank as recorded on the December 31 bank statement 1.40

Instructions: Prepare the reconciliation of Mr. Falcone's bank statement in the same form as shown on page 286.

PROBLEM 17-3 | Reconciling a bank statement for a business

On December 1 of the current year, Catherine Thomas, owner of Thomas Candies, received her bank statement for November. Her check stubs, canceled checks, charge slips, and bank statement showed the following:

> The bank service charge was 90 cents. There was also a $2.00 charge against her account for collecting a note. A deposit of $130.00 made on the evening of November 30 was not shown on the bank statement. The following checks had been written but were not returned with the canceled checks: No. 105, $124.00; No. 109, $60.00; and No. 120, $22.50. The balance shown on the bank statement was $592.60.

The balance shown on the stub for the last check written in November was $519.00.

Instructions: 1. Record the two charge slips in the cash payments journal. In each case, debit Miscellaneous Expense. After the first, write the explanation "bank service charge"; after the second, "collection of note."

2. Prepare the reconciliation of the bank statement for Thomas Candies in the same form as shown on page 286.

PRACTICE SET 1 | SPENCER ATHLETIC GOODS

PART 1 RECORDING, POSTING, AND TRIAL BALANCE

Purpose of this practice set

This practice set illustrates the entire accounting cycle. It includes all the work of a fiscal period of one month for Spencer Athletic Goods, owned and operated by George Spencer. Although the records are those of a small wholesale athletic goods business, they illustrate the application of general principles of accounting that apply to all businesses.

Only Part 1 of the practice set is presented at this time. Part 2, the work at the end of the fiscal period, will be completed after the class has studied Chapters 18, 19, and 20.

Required materials

The transactions of this practice set may be recorded from the narrative of transactions given on pages 296 to 303 inclusive. The work may be completed in bound blank books that may be obtained from the publisher or on unbound sheets of ruled paper. If more realism is desired, a practice set using incoming and outgoing business papers and bound blank books may be obtained from the publisher.

Model illustrations

The journals and ledgers used in this practice set are listed below. Also listed are the pages of this textbook on which similar journals and ledgers are illustrated.

Journals and Ledgers	*Model Illustrations*
Purchases Journal........................	Page 177
Cash Payments Journal....................	Page 196
Sales Journal............................	Page 222
Cash Receipts Journal....................	Page 241
General Journal..........................	Page 265
General Ledger...........................	Pages 266 and 267
Accounts Receivable Ledger..............	Pages 246 and 247
Accounts Payable Ledger.................	Page 199

Chart of accounts

The accounts in the general ledger of Spencer Athletic Goods are listed in the following chart of accounts. This chart of accounts also appears on the inside front cover of the bound general ledger that is provided by the publisher for this practice set.

Spencer Athletic Goods
Chart of Accounts

(1) Assets	Account Number
Cash	11
Accounts Receivable	12
Merchandise Inventory	13
Supplies	14
Prepaid Insurance	15
Office Equipment	16
Warehouse Equipment	17
(2) Liabilities	
Accounts Payable	21
(3) Proprietorship	
George Spencer, Capital	31
George Spencer, Drawing	32
Income and Expense Summary	33

(4) Income	Account Number
Sales	41
(5) Cost of Merchandise	
Purchases	51
(6) Expenses	
Delivery Expense	61
Insurance Expense	62
Miscellaneous Expense	63
Rent Expense	64
Salary Expense	65
Supplies Expense	66

Opening a set of books for Spencer Athletic Goods

Note: If the blank books available from the publisher are used, omit Instructions Nos. 1 through 6. Turn to page 296 and commence recording the transactions for October. (In the blank books available from the publisher, all accounts in the general ledger, in the accounts receivable ledger, and in the accounts payable ledger have been opened and the beginning balances have been recorded for you. The journal pages are prenumbered and the beginning cash balance has been recorded for you in the cash receipts journal.

If unbound sheets of ruled paper (8½″ x 11″) are used, proceed with Instruction No. 1 given below.

Instructions: 1. If loose sheets are used for the journal pages, begin the numbering of each journal as follows: purchases journal, page 8; cash payments journal, page 11; sales journal, page 10; cash receipts journal, page 12; and general journal, page 19.

Instructions: 2. Open the accounts in the general ledger by writing the account titles and the account numbers in the order in which they are given in the chart of accounts. Place four accounts on each sheet.

Instructions: 3. Record in the general ledger the balance of each account listed below. Date each balance October 1 of the current year.

Balance Sheet Accounts	*Account Balances* Debit	Credit
Cash	$ 4,560.50	
Accounts Receivable	4,770.50	
Merchandise Inventory	60,150.00	
Supplies	824.00	
Prepaid Insurance	600.00	
Office Equipment	1,500.00	
Warehouse Equipment	4,200.00	
Accounts Payable		$ 4,660.50
George Spencer, Capital		71,944.50

Instructions: 4. Record the cash balance in the cash receipts journal as a memorandum entry in the manner shown in the illustration on page 234.

Instructions: 5. The names and addresses of the customers of Spencer Athletic Goods and their account balances are listed below.

a Open an account for each customer in the accounts receivable ledger. Three customers' accounts may be placed on each ledger sheet.

b Record each customer's balance in his account in the accounts receivable ledger, dating each balance October 1 of the current year.

Customers' Names and Addresses	*Account Balances*
All-Star Store, 694 Ellsmore Blvd., Laurel, Delaware 19956	$1,050.25
Astrosports, 661 Ault Street, Frankford, Delaware 19945	1,255.00
Dover Athletic Goods, 510 S. Main Street, Dover, Delaware 19901	950.00
The Goal Post, 12 N. McQuay Avenue, Hartly, Delaware 19953	155.00
Greer Hardware, 65 S. Woods Street, New Castle, Delaware 19720	——
Hobby Center, 83 Morningside Drive, Dover, Delaware 19901	——
Leisure Time Corner, 94 Michaels Street, Greenwood, Delaware 19950	420.25
Otts, 170 Marie Avenue, Camden, Delaware 19934	——
The Scoreboard, 2310 Cusher Place, Lewes, Delaware 19958	——
Sholes Sport Shop, 293 Richard Avenue, Wilmington, Delaware 19805	85.00
Varsity Shop, 221 Ronald Road, Clayton, Delaware 19938	855.00

Instructions: 6. The names and addresses of the creditors of Spencer Athletic Goods and their account balances are listed below.

a Open an account for each creditor in the accounts payable ledger. Three creditors' accounts may be placed on each ledger sheet.

b Record each creditor's balance in his account in the accounts payable ledger, dating each balance October 1 of the current year.

Creditors' Names and Addresses	*Account Balances*
American Athletics, 167 N. Parsons Avenue, Chicago, Illinois 60616	$1,450.50
Champion Products, 1401 Moss Street, Norman, Oklahoma 73072	860.00
J. D. Enterprises, P. O. Box 2000, Nashville, Tennessee 37214	———
Larsen Manufacturing, 446 W. Stewart Street, Atlanta, Georgia 30310	———
Letterman Goods, 2494 Myersville Road, Hartly, Delaware 19953	1,840.00
Outdoorsman, Inc., 16621 N. Rupert Street, Long Beach, California 90813	510.00
Ross Store Supplies, 92 Wheeler Street, Dover, Delaware 19901	———

Narrative of transactions for October

Instructions: Record the following transactions in the appropriate journals.

October 1

No. 1. Sold merchandise on account to All-Star Store, $2,400.00 (Sale No. 234).

No. 2. Purchased merchandise on account from Champion Products, $10,120.00.

No. 3. Paid $500.00 for rent for October (Check No. 378).

October 2

No. 4. Sold merchandise on account to Dover Athletic Goods, $3,240.00 (Sale No. 235).

No. 5. Sold merchandise on account to Astrosports, $1,159.50 (Sale No. 236).

No. 6. Paid $300.00 for new office equipment (Check No. 379).

October 3

No. 7. Received $1,255.00 from Astrosports on account.

No. 8. Purchased merchandise on account from Letterman Goods, $1,378.25.

No. 9. Sold merchandise on account to The Scoreboard, $2,675.00 (Sale No. 237).

October 4

No. 10. Sold merchandise on account to Otts, $4,850.25 (Sale No. 238).

No. 11. Paid $1,840.00 to Letterman Goods on account (Check No. 380).

No. 12. The cash sales for October 1 to 4 were $4,940.75.

Cash proof. Foot and prove the two cash journals and determine the cash balance. Use small pencil figures for the footings. See the discussion on pages 242 and 243. The cash balance is ascertained by counting the cash on hand and by adding to this amount the bank balance on the check stub. The cash balance is $8,116.25.

Posting. Post from each of the five journals the items that are to be posted individually. Do not post column totals at this time but at the end of the month only.

October 7

No. 13. Paid $1,450.50 to American Athletics on account (Check No. 381).

No. 14. Purchased merchandise on account from J. D. Enterprises, $9,230.00.

October 8

No. 15. Paid $510.00 to Outdoorsman, Inc., on account (Check No. 382).

No. 16. Sold merchandise on account to the Hobby Center, $2,890.00 (Sale No. 239).

No. 17. Sold merchandise on account to the Varsity Shop, $3,000.00 (Sale No. 240).

No. 18. Sold merchandise on account to The Goal Post, $2,800.00 (Sale No. 241).

October 9

No. 19. Paid $39.80 for telephone bill for September (Check No. 383).

No. 20. Purchased file folders, envelopes, and stationery on account from Ross Store Supplies, $121.40.

See pages 262 to 264 for a discussion of purchases of supplies on account and an illustration of a general journal entry of this type.

October 10

No. 21. Received $155.00 from The Goal Post on account.

No. 22. Purchased merchandise on account from J. D. Enterprises, $7,235.80.

No. 23. Sold merchandise on account to Sholes Sport Shop, $2,110.00 (Sale No. 242).

October 11

No. 24. Received $420.25 from Leisure Time Corner on account.

No. 25. An office memorandum from Mr. George Spencer indicates that on September 25, the Sholes Sport Shop was charged $85.00 for merchandise that they had not received. This sale should have been charged to the Varsity Shop.

See pages 261 and 262 for a discussion of correcting entries and an illustration of a general journal entry of this type.

No. 26. Cash sales for October 7 to 11 were $5,926.35.

Business Reports. The proprietor, George Spencer, requests reports on certain aspects of the business at various times during the month. Mr. Spencer has asked that you prepare a Cash Proof Report and a Purchases on Account and Sales on Account Report at this time.

Cash Proof Report. Foot and prove the two cash journals. Prove cash by completing the report form that is explained below. The cash balance, ascertained by counting the cash on hand and by adding this amount to the bank balance on the check stub, is $12,617.55.

Instructions: 1. On a blank sheet of paper (8½″ x 11″), copy the form shown below for the Cash Proof Report. If you are using the blank books available from the publisher, complete the reports on the special printed forms.

2. Use the date of October 11.

3. Enter the information required on the report.

4. Retain the report until instructed to submit it to your instructor.

Name________________

Spencer Athletic Goods
Cash Proof Report
October , 19—

1.	Beginning cash balance..............	$__________
2.	Plus cash receipts..................	__________
3.	Total...............................	$__________
4.	Minus cash payments.................	__________
5.	Cash balance according to journals..	$__________
6.	Cash balance according to check stub	$__________

Posting. Post the items that are to be posted individually from each of the five journals. Do not post column totals at this time but at the end of the month only.

Purchases on Account and Sales on Account Report. This is the second report requested at this time by Mr. Spencer. The report is illustrated below.

Instructions: 1. On the same sheet of paper used for the Cash Proof Report, copy the form given below.

2. Use your journals and ledgers to obtain the information required for the period October 1 to 11. Enter the information on your report for items 1 and 2.

3. Mr. Spencer has requested the amount of the account balance of several accounts as of October 11. For item 3 list the names and account balances for (a) All-Star Store, (b) Varsity Shop, and (c) Letterman Goods.

4. Submit both reports to your instructor.

```
                    Spencer Athletic Goods
     Purchases on Account and Sales on Account Report
                        October   , 19--

1. Number of purchases of                 Total
   merchandise on account ____            amount  $____________

2. Number of sales of                     Total
   merchandise on account ____            amount  $____________

3. Balances shown in the following accounts:

                                                Account
                  Accounts                      Balances

   (a) ________________________           $____________
   (b) ________________________           $____________
   (c) ________________________           $____________
```

October 14

No. 27. Received $940.00 from the Varsity Shop on account.

No. 28. Paid $9,230.00 to J. D. Enterprises on account (Check No. 384).

No. 29. Received $2,110.00 from Sholes Sport Shop on account.

No. 30. Purchased merchandise on account from Larsen Manufacturing, $10,780.50.

October 15

No. 31. Received $2,000.00 from Dover Athletic Goods on account.

No. 32. Sold merchandise on account to Greer Hardware, $1,925.30 (Sale No. 243).

No. 33. Paid $92.50 for repairs of warehouse equipment (Check No. 385). (Miscellaneous Expense)

October 16

No. 34. The proprietor, George Spencer, withdrew $400.00 for personal use (Check No. 386).

No. 35. Paid $1,500.00 for salaries for first half of month (Check No. 387).

No. 36. Received $3,450.25 from All-Star Store on account.

No. 37. Sold merchandise on account to Otts, $2,260.00 (Sale No. 244).

October 17

No. 38. Sold merchandise on account to The Goal Post, $574.10 (Sale No. 245).

No. 39. Paid $800.00 for new warehouse equipment (Check No. 388).

No. 40. Received $2,675.00 from The Scoreboard on account.

No. 41. Paid $340.00 to Lewis Transport Company for delivery service for the first half of the month (Check No. 389). (Delivery Expense)

October 18

No. 42. Received a check for $4,850.25 from Otts on account.

No. 43. Purchased supplies on account from Ross Store Supplies, $162.60.

No. 44. Cash sales for October 14 to 18 were $3,720.75.

Cash proof. Foot and prove the two cash journals and determine the cash balance. The cash balance, ascertained by counting the cash on hand and by adding to this amount the bank balance on the check stub, is $20,001.30.

Posting. Post the items that are to be posted individually from each of the five journals.

Reconciling the bank statement. On a blank sheet of paper, prepare a reconciliation of the bank statement of the Spencer Athletic Goods in the same form as that shown on page 286. If you are using the blank books available from the publisher, prepare your reconciliation of the bank statement on the special printed form. The data needed are:

a The October 15 balance on the bank statement is $16,214.85. A deposit of $2,000.00 made on the evening of October 15 is not shown on the bank statement. A charge slip is included for a service charge of $2.50, which is shown on the statement.

b When the canceled checks are compared with the check stubs, the following checks are found to be outstanding: No. 382, $510.00; No. 383, $39.80; No. 384, $9,230.00; No. 385, $92.50.

c The checkbook balance on October 15 is $8,345.05.

No. 45. Record the entry for the monthly bank service charge in the cash payments journal as shown on page 287.

October 21

No. 46. Paid $10,980.00 to Champion Products on account (Check No. 390).

No. 47. Received $2,890.00 from the Hobby Center on account.

No. 48. Received a refund of $10.00 on the repair bill paid on October 15. On the check received from the repair shop there was a note stating that a refund was being made because of an error in pricing one of the parts.

Record this transaction in the cash receipts journal as a credit to Miscellaneous Expense. Enter the amount in the General Credit column.

October 22

No. 49. Sold merchandise on account to Astrosports, $2,310.50 (Sale No. 246).

No. 50. Received a check for $2,800.00 from The Goal Post on account.

No. 51. Purchased merchandise on account from American Athletics, $6,715.00.

October 23

No. 52. Sold merchandise on account to the Varsity Shop, $1,245.00 (Sale No. 247).

No. 53. The proprietor, George Spencer, took golf clubs for personal use; original cost price was $130.00.

See the discussion of withdrawals by the proprietor on pages 259 to 261. Since this transaction is not a sale to a customer, credit the purchases account for the cost price of the merchandise. Record this transaction in the general journal.

No. 54. Purchased merchandise on account from Outdoorsman, Inc., $9,876.00.

October 24

No. 55. Paid $121.40 to Ross Store Supplies on account (Check No. 391).

No. 56. Purchased merchandise on account from Letterman Goods, $12,493.33.

October 25

No. 57. Sold merchandise on account to Sholes Sport Shop, $3,245.80 (Sale No. 248).

No. 58. Paid $10,780.50 to Larsen Manufacturing on account (Check No. 392).

No. 59. Cash sales for October 21 to 25 were $8,961.25.

Cash proof. Foot and prove the two cash journals and determine the cash balance. The cash balance, ascertained by counting the cash on hand and by adding this amount to the bank balance on the check stub, is $12,778.15.

Posting. Post the items that are to be posted individually from each of the five journals.

October 28

No. 60. Sold merchandise on account to Hobby Center, $3,159.60 (Sale No. 249).

No. 61. Paid $18.00 for gas utility bill for October (Check No. 393).

No. 62. Sold merchandise on account to Dover Athletic Goods, $1,546.20 (Sale No. 250).

No. 63. Received $1,159.50 from Astrosports on account.

October 29

No. 64. Received $1,000.00 from Sholes Sport Shop on account.

No. 65. Paid $52.10 for electricity bill for October (Check No. 394).

No. 66. Paid $8.30 for water bill for October (Check No. 395).

No. 67. Received $3,000.00 from the Varsity Shop on account.

No. 68. The proprietor, George Spencer, withdrew $400.00 for personal use (Check No. 396).

October 30

No. 69. Purchased merchandise on account from J. D. Enterprises, $5,248.12.

No. 70. Paid $13,871.58 to Letterman Goods on account (Check No. 397).

No. 71. Paid $1,025.70 for merchandise ordered and delivered today. Gave the check to the delivery truck driver (Check No. 398).

No. 72. Paid $1,500.00 for salaries for last half of month (Check No. 399).

October 31

No. 73. Paid $355.00 to Lewis Transit for delivery service (Check No. 400).

No. 74. Received $2,190.00 from Dover Athletic Goods on account.

No. 75. The cash sales for October 28 to 31 were $6,399.65.

Cash proof. Foot and prove the two cash journals. Prove cash by completing the Cash Proof Report, which is explained below. The cash balance, ascertained by counting the cash on hand and by adding to this amount the bank balance on the check stub, is $9,296.62.

Cash Proof Report. The proprietor, Mr. George Spencer, has asked you to prepare two reports at this time. The Cash Proof Report is similar to the one prepared on October 11.

Instructions: 1. On a blank sheet of paper (8½″ x 11″), prepare the Cash Proof Report in a form similar to that shown on page 298. If you are using the blank books available from the publisher, complete your reports on the special printed forms.

2. Use the date of October 31.

3. Enter the information required on your report.

4. Retain the report until instructed to submit it to your instructor.

Posting. Post the items that are to be posted individually from each of the five journals. Column totals are not to be posted at this time.

Purchases on Account and Sales on Account Report. This report is similar to the one prepared on October 11.

Instructions: 1. On the same sheet of paper used for the Cash Proof report, prepare the Purchases on Account and Sales on Account Report in a form similar to that given on page 299.

2. Use your journals and ledgers to obtain the information required for the period October 1 to 31. Enter the information on your report for items 1 and 2.

3. For item 3 list the names and account balances for (a) Dover Athletic Goods, (b) Sholes Sport Shop, and (c) J. D. Enterprises.

4. Submit both reports to your instructor.

Completing and posting the journals

Instructions: 1. Total and rule the purchases journal. Post the total. Compare your work with the purchases journal shown on page 172.

2. Total and rule the cash payments journal. Post the totals of the special columns. Compare your work with the cash payments journal on page 197.

3. Total and rule the sales journal. Post the total. Compare your work with the sales journal shown on page 216.

4. Total and rule the cash receipts journal. Post the totals of the special columns. Compare your work with the cash receipts journal shown on page 244.

Schedules and trial balance

Instructions: 1. Foot the general ledger accounts.

2. Prepare a schedule of accounts payable and a schedule of accounts receivable. Compare your work with the schedules on pages 200 and 248. Prove the accuracy of the subsidiary ledgers by comparing the schedule totals with the balances of the controlling accounts in the general ledger.

3. Prepare a trial balance on the work sheet. Use as your guide the model trial balance recorded on the work sheet on page 269.

a Write the heading for the monthly fiscal period ended October 31 of the current year.

> Only the Trial Balance columns are to be used at this time. The remaining amount columns will be used in Part 2 of the practice set, which will be completed after Chapters 18, 19, and 20 have been studied.

b Write in the Account Titles column each of the account titles given in the chart of accounts on page 294. Enter the account numbers in the Acct. No. column.

c Enter in the Trial Balance columns the balance of each account in the general ledger that has a balance.

d Total and rule the Trial Balance columns.

CHAPTER 18 EIGHT-COLUMN WORK SHEET WITH ADJUSTMENTS

NEED FOR ADJUSTING SOME ACCOUNTS

At the end of a fiscal period, some of the accounts of a business need to be brought up-to-date. In the general ledger of McCann Office Furniture, the accounts that need to be brought up-to-date at the end of a fiscal period are: Merchandise Inventory, Supplies, and Prepaid Insurance.

Need for adjusting the merchandise inventory account

An itemized list of goods on hand showing their value is called an *inventory*. The general ledger account that shows the value of the goods on hand at the beginning of the fiscal period is called Merchandise Inventory.

Merchandise Inventory	13
Nov. 1 Bal. 6,245.00	

On November 1, the start of the fiscal period, the merchandise inventory account of McCann Office Furniture shows the value of the goods on hand to be $6,245.00. On November 30, the end of the fiscal period, the account shows the same balance, $6,245.00. The merchandise inventory account does not show that the inventory has changed during the fiscal period as a result of purchases and sales.

Each purchase increases the amount of merchandise on hand, but all purchases are recorded in the purchases account. Each sale decreases the amount of merchandise on hand, but all sales are recorded in the sales account. This plan of recording purchases and sales in separate accounts is used in order to make it easier to determine quickly the total purchases and the total sales at the end of the fiscal period. However, if the value of the asset, Merchandise Inventory, is to be reported accurately on the balance sheet, the value of the merchandise on November 30 must be found and recorded properly in this account.

Need for adjusting the supplies account

The supplies account for McCann Office Furniture shows that there was a beginning balance of $155.00, that the supplies bought during the fiscal period amounted to $112.00, and that the debit balance at the end of the fiscal period was $267.00. Because it is not practical to credit the supplies account each time wrapping paper, twine, and other supplies are used during the period, the account balance is not up-to-date. Therefore, the asset account, Supplies, needs to be brought up-to-date so that its balance is the same as the actual value of the supplies on hand November 30.

Supplies		14
Nov. 1 Bal.	155.00	
30	112.00	
	267.00	

Need for adjusting the prepaid insurance account

The cost of insurance premiums paid in advance, and for which the benefits have not yet been received, is called *prepaid insurance.* The portion of the insurance premiums that has expired, or has been used up, during the fiscal period is an expense to the business. The prepaid insurance account shows that McCann Office Furniture owned $199.00 worth of insurance on November 1. For every day that passes since that date, the business owns insurance coverage for one less day. Thus, the value of this asset is decreasing constantly. It is not practical, however, to keep this account up-to-date by making daily entries that reduce the value of prepaid insurance. Instead, the prepaid insurance account is brought up-to-date before the balance sheet and the income statement are prepared at the end of the fiscal period.

Prepaid Insurance		15
Nov. 1 Bal.	199.00	

PLANNING THE ADJUSTMENTS ON THE WORK SHEET

Changes that are recorded in accounts at the end of a fiscal period so that the accounts will be brought up-to-date are called *adjustments.* All changes in ledger accounts must result from the posting of journal entries. The journal entries to record adjustments are called *adjusting entries.*

Work sheet with columns for adjustments

A six-column work sheet was presented in Chapter 9. Additional columns are required in the work sheet to plan the adjustments. Therefore, an eight-column work sheet is used by many businesses to plan their adjustments. Columns for planning the adjustments are immediately to the right of the Trial Balance columns, as shown in the illustration on the opposite page.

McCann Office Furniture
Work Sheet
For Month Ended November 30, 1967

	ACCOUNT TITLES	ACCT. NO.	1 TRIAL BALANCE DEBIT	2 TRIAL BALANCE CREDIT	3 ADJUSTMENTS DEBIT	4 ADJUSTMENTS CREDIT	5 INCOME STATEMENT DEBIT	6 INCOME STATEMENT CREDIT	7 BALANCE SHEET DEBIT	8 BALANCE SHEET CREDIT	
1	Cash	11	4771 00								1
2	Accounts Receivable	12	1282 00								2
3	Merchandise Inventory	13	6245 00								3
4	Supplies	14	267 00								4
5	Prepaid Insurance	15	199 00								5
6	Accounts Payable	21		2282 00							6
7	John McCann, Capital	31		10121 00							7
8	John McCann, Drawing	32	350 00								8
9	Income & Expense Summary	33									9
10	Sales	41		4721 00							10
11	Purchases	51	3234 00								11
12	Delivery Expense	61	53 00								12
13	Insurance Expense	62									13
14	Miscellaneous Expense	63	23 00								14
15	Rent Expense	64	300 00								15
16	Salary Expense	65	400 00								16
17	Supplies Expense	66									17
18			17124 00	17124 00							18
19											19
20											20
21											21
22											22
23											23
24											24

Eight-column work sheet with Trial Balance columns completed

The planning of the adjustments on the work sheet makes it possible to check the accuracy of the planning before the financial statements are prepared and before the adjusting entries are recorded in the journal. Every adjustment has a debit part and a credit part. Two accounts must therefore be used in each adjustment. The adjustment transfers part or all of the balance of one account to another account. This transfer is planned by writing the debit part of the adjustment in the Adjustments Debit column and the credit part of the adjustment in the Adjustments Credit column.

Recording the trial balance on the eight-column work sheet

When preparing the trial balance on an eight-column work sheet, every account listed in the chart of accounts is written in the Account Titles column regardless of whether the account has a balance. In the work sheet on page 307, note that the following accounts do not show a balance in the Trial Balance columns: Income and Expense Summary, Insurance Expense, and Supplies Expense.

ADJUSTING THE MERCHANDISE INVENTORY ACCOUNT

In order to determine the net income at the end of a fiscal period, up-to-date ledger accounts are needed to find out how much it cost to sell the merchandise. The elements needed to determine the cost of merchandise sold are the beginning merchandise inventory, purchases, and the ending merchandise inventory. The cost of merchandise sold is found as follows:

Beginning merchandise inventory + Purchases − Ending merchandise inventory = Cost of merchandise sold

To aid in calculating the cost of merchandise sold, all amounts needed are transferred and brought together in the income and expense summary account. The beginning inventory is the first of the amounts needed to find the cost of merchandise sold.

Analyzing the adjustment for the beginning merchandise inventory

The two accounts used in adjusting the beginning merchandise inventory account are: *Income and Expense Summary* and *Merchandise Inventory*. The T accounts at the right show the merchandise inventory account and the income and expense summary account before the adjustment is made.

BEFORE ADJUSTMENT

Merchandise Inventory 13	
Nov. 1 Bal. 6,245.00	

Income and Expense Summary 33	

The *beginning* merchandise inventory, as shown in the merchandise inventory account, is $6,245.00. The merchandise inventory account is not up-to-date, for the actual count of goods on November 30 shows that the inventory is valued at $6,310.00. In order to show the correct value of the inventory in the account, the amount of the beginning inventory is removed from the account and transferred to the income and expense summary account. The amount of the beginning merchandise inventory is removed from the account by crediting the account for $6,245.00, as shown in the T account at the right. The amount of the beginning inventory, $6,245.00, is transferred to the debit side of the income and expense summary account because it is a part of the cost of merchandise sold.

AFTER ADJUSTMENT

Merchandise Inventory 13	
Nov. 1 Bal. 6,245.00	Nov. 30 (a) 6,245.00

Income and Expense Summary 33	
Nov. 30 (a) 6,245.00	

The taking of an inventory is described on pages 321 and 322.

Adjusting the beginning merchandise inventory on the work sheet

The adjustment for the beginning merchandise inventory is shown in the Adjustments columns of the work sheet below.

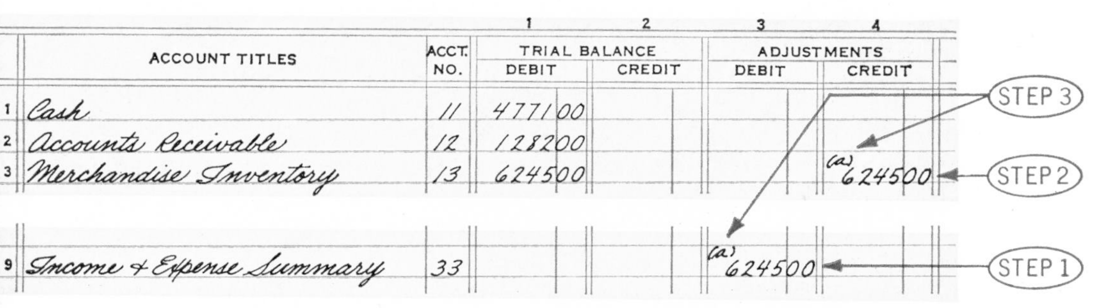

	ACCOUNT TITLES	ACCT. NO.	1 TRIAL BALANCE DEBIT	2 TRIAL BALANCE CREDIT	3 ADJUSTMENTS DEBIT	4 ADJUSTMENTS CREDIT
1	Cash	11	4771 00			
2	Accounts Receivable	12	1282 00			
3	Merchandise Inventory	13	6245 00			(a) 6245 00
9	Income & Expense Summary	33			(a) 6245 00	

Work sheet adjustment for beginning merchandise inventory

The steps in adjusting the beginning merchandise inventory on the work sheet are:

Step 1

Debit part of the adjustment. Write the amount of the beginning merchandise inventory, *$6,245.00*, in the Adjustments Debit column on the line with the account title *Income and Expense Summary.*

Step 2

Credit part of the adjustment. Write the amount of the beginning merchandise inventory, *$6,245.00*, in the Adjustments Credit column on the line with the account title *Merchandise Inventory.*

Step 3

Labeling the parts of the adjustment. Write the small letter "a" in parentheses, (*a*), before the amounts in the Adjustments columns.

A small letter is assigned each adjustment according to the order in which the adjustments are planned on the work sheet. This labeling helps to locate the two parts of the adjustment when the adjusting entries are later made in the journal.

Analyzing the adjustment for the ending merchandise inventory

The T accounts at the right show the merchandise inventory account and the income and expense summary account before and after the adjustment for the ending merchandise inventory.

BEFORE ADJUSTMENT

Merchandise Inventory	13
Nov. 1 Bal. 6,245.00	Nov. 30 (a) 6,245.00

Income and Expense Summary	33
Nov. 30 (a) 6,245.00	

AFTER ADJUSTMENT

Merchandise Inventory	13
Nov. 1 Bal. 6,245.00	Nov. 30 (a) 6,245.00
30 (b) 6,310.00	

Income and Expense Summary	33
Nov. 30 (a) 6,245.00	Nov. 30 (b) 6,310.00

The merchandise inventory account should be brought up-to-date to show the amount of the inventory at the end of the fiscal period. The merchandise inventory account is therefore debited for $6,310.00, the value of the ending inventory. The amount of the ending inventory is credited to the income and expense summary account. This is a credit because the ending inventory is a deduction from the cost of merchandise available for sale.

After the two adjustments of the merchandise inventory account are journalized and posted, the income and expense summary account shows two of the three amounts needed in calculating the cost of merchandise sold. The beginning inventory is a part of the cost of merchandise available for sale and is therefore shown on the debit side of the summary account. The ending inventory is a deduction from the cost of merchandise available for sale and is therefore shown on the credit side of the summary account. The merchandise inventory account is brought up-to-date and shows the asset value, $6,310.00, of merchandise inventory at the end of the fiscal period.

Adjusting the ending merchandise inventory on the work sheet

The adjustment for the ending merchandise inventory is shown in the Adjustments columns of the work sheet below.

	ACCOUNT TITLES	ACCT. NO.	1 TRIAL BALANCE DEBIT	2 TRIAL BALANCE CREDIT	3 ADJUSTMENTS DEBIT	4 ADJUSTMENTS CREDIT	
1	Cash	11	4771 00				
2	Accounts Receivable	12	1282 00				
3	Merchandise Inventory	13	6245 00		(b) 6310 00	(a) 6245 00	STEP 1, STEP 3
9	Income & Expense Summary	33			(a) 6245 00	(b) 6310 00	STEP 2, STEP 3
10							
11							

Work sheet adjustment for ending merchandise inventory

The steps in adjusting the ending merchandise inventory on the work sheet are:

Step 1

Debit part of the adjustment. Write the amount of the ending merchandise inventory, *$6,310.00*, in the Adjustments Debit column on the line with the account title *Merchandise Inventory.*

Step 2

Credit part of the adjustment. Write the amount of the ending merchandise inventory, *$6,310.00*, in the Adjustments Credit column on the line with the account title *Income and Expense Summary.*

Step 3

Labeling the parts of the adjustment. Write the small letter "b" in parentheses, (*b*), before the amounts in the Adjustments columns.

ADJUSTING THE SUPPLIES ACCOUNT AND THE SUPPLIES EXPENSE ACCOUNT

The two accounts used in the adjustment for supplies are *Supplies* and *Supplies Expense.* The supplies used during the fiscal period are an expense to the business.

Analyzing the adjustment for supplies used

The supplies account and the supplies expense account as they appear in the general ledger before and after the adjustment for supplies are shown in the T accounts at the right.

BEFORE ADJUSTMENT

Supplies 14

Debit		Credit	
Nov. 1 Bal.	155.00		
30	112.00		
	267.00		

Supplies Expense 66

Debit		Credit	

AFTER ADJUSTMENT

Supplies 14

Debit		Credit	
Nov. 1 Bal.	155.00	Nov. 30 (c)	125.00
30	112.00		
	267.00		

Supplies Expense 66

Debit		Credit	
Nov. 30 (c)	125.00		

The balance of the supplies account before the adjustment was $267.00. The inventory of supplies on hand, November 30, 1967, was $142.00. The difference between these two amounts, $125.00, is the cost of the supplies used during the month. The cost of the supplies used, $125.00, must be recorded as an expense of the business. Therefore, the cost of the supplies used is recorded as a debit to Supplies Expense to show an increase in the balance of this account.

The cost of supplies used is recorded as a credit to Supplies to show a decrease in the balance of this asset account. The total of the debit side, $267.00, less the total of the credit side, $125.00, equals the ending inventory of the supplies on hand, $142.00.

After this adjustment is journalized and posted, the balance of the supplies expense account is the cost of the supplies used during the fiscal period. The balance of the supplies account is the cost of supplies on hand at the end of the fiscal period.

Adjusting the supplies account and the supplies expense account on the work sheet

The adjustment for supplies is shown in the Adjustments columns of the work sheet on the next page.

The steps in adjusting the supplies account and the supplies expense account are:

Step 1

Debit part of the adjustment. Write the amount of the supplies expense, *$125.00*, in the Adjustments Debit column on the line with the account title, Supplies Expense.

			1	2	3	4	
	ACCOUNT TITLES	ACCT. NO.	TRIAL BALANCE DEBIT	TRIAL BALANCE CREDIT	ADJUSTMENTS DEBIT	ADJUSTMENTS CREDIT	
1	Cash	11	4771 00				
2	Accounts Receivable	12	1282 00				
3	Merchandise Inventory	13	6245 00		(b) 6310 00	(a) 6245 00	
4	Supplies	14	267 00			(c) 125 00	STEP 2
9	Income & Expense Summary	33			(a) 6245 00	(b) 6310 00	STEP 3
16	Salary Expense	65	400 00				
17	Supplies Expense	66			(c) 125 00		STEP 1

Work sheet adjustment for supplies used

Step 2

Credit part of the adjustment. Write the amount of the supplies expense, *$125.00*, in the Adjustments Credit column on the line with the account title, Supplies.

Step 3

Labeling the parts of the adjustment. Label the two parts of this adjustment with a small letter "c" in parentheses, (*c*).

ADJUSTING THE PREPAID INSURANCE ACCOUNT AND THE INSURANCE EXPENSE ACCOUNT

The two accounts used in the adjustment for expired insurance are *Prepaid Insurance* and *Insurance Expense.*

Analyzing the adjustment for expired insurance

The prepaid insurance account and the insurance expense account of McCann Office Furniture as they appear in the general ledger before the adjustment for expired insurance are shown in the T accounts at the right.

BEFORE ADJUSTMENT

Prepaid Insurance	15
Nov. 1 Bal. 199.00	

Insurance Expense	62

Before the adjustment, the prepaid insurance account has a debit balance of $199.00, dated November 1. This balance is the value of the asset Prepaid Insurance at the beginning of the fiscal period.

When the insurance policies were examined, it was found that $31.00 of the prepaid insurance had expired. Thus, the value of the prepaid insurance at the end of the fiscal period is $168.00. The prepaid insurance account must therefore be adjusted so that it will show its present asset value at the end of the fiscal period. At the same time, the insurance expense account must be adjusted to show the cost of the expired insurance for this fiscal period.

The amount of the expired insurance, $31.00, is recorded as a debit to Insurance Expense to show an increase in the balance of this expense account. The amount of the expired insurance, $31.00, is recorded as a credit to Prepaid Insurance to show a decrease in the balance of this asset account.

AFTER ADJUSTMENT

Prepaid Insurance		15	
Nov. 1 Bal.	199.00	Nov. 30 (d)	31.00

Insurance Expense		62	
Nov. 30 (d)	31.00		

After this adjustment is journalized and posted, the prepaid insurance account has a credit of $31.00, representing the deduction for expired insurance for this fiscal period. The new account balance is $168.00, the value of the asset Prepaid Insurance at the end of the fiscal period. The insurance expense account has a debit balance of $31.00, which is the insurance expense for the fiscal period.

Adjusting the prepaid insurance account and the insurance expense account on the work sheet

The adjustment for expired insurance is shown in the Adjustments columns of the work sheet below.

	ACCOUNT TITLES	ACCT. NO.	1 TRIAL BALANCE DEBIT	2 TRIAL BALANCE CREDIT	3 ADJUSTMENTS DEBIT	4 ADJUSTMENTS CREDIT	
1	Cash	11	4771 00				
2	Accounts Receivable	12	1282 00				
3	Merchandise Inventory	13	6245 00		(b) 6310 00	(a) 6245 00	
4	Supplies	14	267 00			(c) 125 00	
5	Prepaid Insurance	15	199 00			(d) 31 00	STEP 2
9	Income & Expense Summary	33			(a) 6245 00	(b) 6310 00	STEP 3
13	Insurance Expense	62			(d) 31 00		STEP 1
17	Supplies Expense	66			(c) 125 00		

Work sheet adjustment for expired insurance

The steps in adjusting the prepaid insurance account and the insurance expense account are:

Step 1

Debit part of the adjustment. Write the amount of the insurance expense, *$31.00,* in the Adjustments Debit column on the line with the account title, Insurance Expense.

Step 2

Credit part of the adjustment. Write the amount of the insurance expense, *$31.00,* in the Adjustments Credit column on the line with the account title, Prepaid Insurance.

Step 3

Labeling the parts of the adjustment. Label the two parts of this adjustment with a small letter "d" in parentheses, (*d*).

PROVING THE EQUALITY OF DEBITS AND CREDITS IN THE ADJUSTMENTS COLUMNS

After all the adjustments have been analyzed and recorded on the work sheet at the end of the fiscal period, the two Adjustments columns are totaled to prove the equality of debits and credits. The illustration of the partial work sheet on page 316 shows the first four amount columns after the adjustments have been recorded and the Adjustments columns have been totaled and ruled.

The total of the Adjustments Debit column, *$12,711.00*, is the same as the total of the Adjustments Credit column, *$12,711.00.* The two totals are written on the same line as the totals of the Trial Balance columns. Because the totals of the Adjustments columns are the same, the debits and credits in the Adjustments columns are assumed to be correct. Single and double lines are ruled across the Adjustments columns as shown in the illustration.

EXTENDING ACCOUNT BALANCES TO THE BALANCE SHEET AND THE INCOME STATEMENT COLUMNS OF THE WORK SHEET

At the end of the fiscal period, a balance sheet and an income statement are prepared to summarize all the facts about the operation of a business for a fiscal period. The balance sheet and the income statement are prepared directly from the work sheet. To assist in the preparation of these

McCann Office Furniture
Work Sheet
For Month Ended November 30, 1967

	ACCOUNT TITLES	ACCT. NO.	1 TRIAL BALANCE DEBIT	2 TRIAL BALANCE CREDIT	3 ADJUSTMENTS DEBIT	4 ADJUSTMENTS CREDIT
1	Cash	11	4771 00			
2	Accounts Receivable	12	1282 00			
3	Merchandise Inventory	13	6245 00		(b) 6310 00	(a) 6245 00
4	Supplies	14	267 00			(c) 125 00
5	Prepaid Insurance	15	199 00			(d) 31 00
6	Accounts Payable	21		2282 00		
7	John McCann, Capital	31		10121 00		
8	John McCann, Drawing	32	350 00			
9	Income & Expense Summary	33			(a) 6245 00	(b) 6310 00
10	Sales	41		4721 00		
11	Purchases	51	3234 00			
12	Delivery Expense	61	53 00			
13	Insurance Expense	62			(d) 31 00	
14	Miscellaneous Expense	63	23 00			
15	Rent Expense	64	300 00			
16	Salary Expense	65	400 00			
17	Supplies Expense	66			(c) 125 00	
18			17124 00	17124 00	12711 00	12711 00
19						
20						
21						
22						
23						
24						

Partial work sheet showing Trial Balance and Adjustments columns

reports, the balances of the accounts are extended to the Balance Sheet and to the Income Statement columns of the work sheet. The illustration of the completed work sheet on page 318 shows the account balances, after the necessary adjustments, extended to the appropriate columns.

Extending the balance sheet items to the Balance Sheet columns of the work sheet

The steps in extending the balance sheet items to the Balance Sheet columns of the work sheet are:

Step 1

Extend the cash account balance, *$4,771.00*, and the accounts receivable account balance, *$1,282.00*, as shown in the Trial Balance Debit column to the Balance Sheet Debit column.

Step 2

Extend the value of merchandise inventory at the end of the fiscal period, *$6,310.00*, to the Balance Sheet Debit column. The merchandise inventory account is debited for $6,245.00 in the Trial Balance Debit column and is credited for the same amount in the Adjustments Credit column. This debit and this credit cancel each other. Therefore, only the debit amount, $6,310.00, in the Adjustments Debit column is extended to the Balance Sheet Debit column.

Step 3

Extend the new balance of the supplies account, *$142.00*, to the Balance Sheet Debit column. The supplies account has a debit balance of $267.00 in the Trial Balance Debit column and a credit of $125.00 in the Adjustments Credit column. The credit is subtracted from the debit to get the new balance of this asset account, $142.00.

Step 4

Extend the new balance of the prepaid insurance account, *$168.00*, to the Balance Sheet Debit column. The prepaid insurance account has a debit balance of $199.00 in the Trial Balance Debit column and a credit of $31.00 in the Adjustments Credit column. The credit is subtracted from the debit to get the new balance of this asset account, $168.00.

Step 5

Extend the credit balance of Accounts Payable, *$2,282.00*, and the credit balance of John McCann, Capital, *$10,121.00*, from the Trial Balance Credit column to the Balance Sheet Credit column.

Step 6

Extend the balance of John McCann, Drawing, *$350.00*, from the Trial Balance Debit column to the Balance Sheet Debit column.

Extending the cost, income, and expense items to the Income Statement columns of the work sheet

The steps in extending the cost, income, and expense items to the Income Statement columns of the work sheet are:

Step 7

Extend both the debit amount and the credit amount of the income and expense summary account in the Adjustments columns to the Income Statement columns. The debit amount, *$6,245.00*, is the beginning inventory and is part of the cost of merchandise sold. This amount is extended

Mc Cann Office Furniture
Work Sheet
For Month Ended November 30, 1967

	ACCOUNT TITLES	ACCT. NO.	1 TRIAL BALANCE DEBIT	2 TRIAL BALANCE CREDIT	3 ADJUSTMENTS DEBIT	4 ADJUSTMENTS CREDIT	5 INCOME STATEMENT DEBIT	6 INCOME STATEMENT CREDIT	7 BALANCE SHEET DEBIT	8 BALANCE SHEET CREDIT	
1	Cash	11	4771 00						4771 00		1
2	Accounts Receivable	12	1282 00						1282 00		2
3	Merchandise Inventory	13	6245 00		(b) 6310 00	(a) 6245 00			6310 00		3
4	Supplies	14	267 00			(c) 125 00			142 00		4
5	Prepaid Insurance	15	199 00			(d) 31 00			168 00		5
6	Accounts Payable	21		2282 00						2282 00	6
7	John Mc Cann, Capital	31		10121 00						10121 00	7
8	John Mc Cann, Drawing	32	350 00						350 00		8
9	Income & Expense Summary	33			(a) 6245 00	(b) 6310 00	6245 00	6310 00			9
10	Sales	41		4721 00				4721 00			10
11	Purchases	51	3234 00				3234 00				11
12	Delivery Expense	61	53 00				53 00				12
13	Insurance Expense	62			(d) 31 00		31 00				13
14	Miscellaneous Expense	63	23 00				23 00				14
15	Rent Expense	64	300 00				300 00				15
16	Salary Expense	65	400 00				400 00				16
17	Supplies Expense	66			(c) 125 00		125 00				17
18			17124 00	17124 00	12711 00	12711 00	10411 00	11031 00	13023 00	12403 00	18
19	Net Income						620 00			620 00	19
20							11031 00	11031 00	13023 00	13023 00	20
21											21
22											22
23											23
24											24

Completed eight-column work sheet

to the Income Statement Debit column. The credit amount, *$6,310.00*, is the ending inventory and represents a deduction from the cost of merchandise sold. This amount is extended to the Income Statement Credit column.

The beginning inventory and the ending inventory will be needed in the preparation of the income statement. Both of these amounts, therefore, should be available in the Income Statement columns of the work sheet.

Step 8

Extend the credit balance of the sales account, *$4,721.00*, to the Income Statement Credit column. If there were other income accounts, the credit balances of these accounts also would be extended to this column.

Step 9

Extend the debit balance of the purchases account, *$3,234.00*, to the Income Statement Debit column. The amount of purchases, which makes up a part of the cost of merchandise sold, will be needed in preparing the income statement.

Step 10

Extend all expense account balances in the Trial Balance Debit column to the Income Statement Debit column. Also extend the adjustments of the insurance expense account and the supplies expense account in the Adjustments Debit column to the Income Statement Debit column.

Step 11

Rule a single line across the Income Statement and the Balance Sheet columns to indicate addition. Add each of these columns and write the totals on the same line as the Trial Balance totals.

CALCULATING NET INCOME ON THE WORK SHEET

The net income is found from the Income Statement columns on the work sheet. After the two columns are totaled as shown in the illustration on page 318, the net income is computed as follows:

Total of the Income Statement Credit column..........	$11,031.00
Less Total of the Income Statement Debit column.......	10,411.00
Net Income....................................	$ 620.00

The total of the Income Statement Credit column, $11,031.00, is the sum of (a) the income from sales and (b) the value of the ending inventory, which represents a deduction from the cost of merchandise available for sale. The total of the Income Statement Debit column, $10,411.00, is the sum of (a) the beginning inventory and purchases, which represent the cost of merchandise available for sale, and (b) the expense amounts. Since the total of the Credit column is larger than the total of the Debit column, the difference is net income.

Balancing and ruling the Income Statement columns

To complete the Income Statement columns, the amount of net income, $620.00, is written in the Income Statement Debit column on the line immediately under the Debit column total. The words *Net Income* are written in the Account Titles column on the line with the amount. The columns are then totaled and a double line is drawn below both totals to show that the debit total is the same as the credit total.

Balancing and ruling the Balance Sheet columns

The net income for the period, $620.00, represents an increase in proprietorship. The amount of the net income is therefore extended to the Balance Sheet Credit column so that it can be added to the amount of the proprietor's capital. The columns are then totaled and ruled. Since the Balance Sheet Debit total equals the Balance Sheet Credit total, the calculations on the work sheet are considered correct.

CALCULATING NET LOSS ON THE WORK SHEET

If the total of the Income Statement Debit column exceeds the total of the Income Statement Credit column, the difference is called net loss. For example, the footings of the Income Statement columns and the Balance Sheet columns of the work sheet for L. C. Barnett are shown below.

	ACCOUNT TITLES	5 INCOME STATEMENT DEBIT	6 INCOME STATEMENT CREDIT	7 BALANCE SHEET DEBIT	8 BALANCE SHEET CREDIT	
18		2364 00	2212 00	4586 00	4738 00	18
19	Net Loss		152 00	152 00		19
20		2364 00	2364 00	4738 00	4738 00	20
21						21

Showing net loss on a work sheet

The total of the Income Statement Debit column, $2,364.00, is larger than the total of the Income Statement Credit column, $2,212.00. This means that the cost of merchandise sold plus the expenses exceeds the total income. The amount of the difference between the two columns is always written under the smaller amount. Therefore, the amount of the net loss, $152.00, is written in the Income Statement Credit column.

The amount of the net loss, $152.00, is extended to the Balance Sheet Debit column because it represents a decrease in proprietorship. If the amount of the net loss is correct, it represents the difference between the totals of the Balance Sheet columns of the work sheet. Therefore, as proof of the accuracy of the work sheet, the net loss is added to the Balance Sheet Debit column.

TAKING AN INVENTORY

Before the adjustments for the ending merchandise inventory and the supplies used can be entered on the work sheet, the value of the merchandise and the supplies on hand at the end of the fiscal period must be determined.

Physical inventory

An actual count of the items on hand is called a *physical inventory*. A part of the form used by McCann Office Furniture in taking a physical inventory of the merchandise on November 30 is shown below.

MERCHANDISE INVENTORY
For Month Ended November 30, 1967

Items	Stock No.	Unit of Count	No. of Units on Hand	Unit Cost Price	Value
Cabinet, file, 2-drawer	F1067	each	10	35.00	350.00
Cabinet, file, 4-drawer	F1089	each	15	50.00	750.00
Chair, side-arm	C415	each	20	22.50	450.00
Ribbons, typewriter, black	R4453	doz.	3	14.40	43.20
Total					6,310.00

Inventory record sheet

Each column of the inventory form is filled out in the following manner:

Items. The name of each item on hand is listed in the Items column.

Stock number. When merchandise is ordered from a supplier, the items are usually ordered by stock number. The stock number is recorded in the Stock No. column as an additional means of identifying the item being listed on the inventory.

Unit of count. The Unit of Count column is used to record the way the goods are priced on the invoice received from the supplier. For example, file cabinets are priced for each cabinet; typewriter ribbons are priced by the dozen.

No. of units on hand. Each item is actually counted, and the total units on hand is recorded in the No. of Units on Hand column.

Unit cost price. The amounts in the Unit Cost Price column are taken from the invoices received from the suppliers. Sometimes when goods are placed on the shelves, they are marked with code numbers or letters that give the unit cost price. When this plan is followed, the cost can be recorded on the inventory record sheet at the same time the units are counted.

Value. The Value column is used to record the total value of each kind of item on hand. The quantity shown in the No. of Units on Hand column times the price shown in the Unit Cost Price column gives the total value of the item on hand.

After all the items have been counted and the inventory sheet filled out, the Value column is totaled. This total is the amount that appears on the work sheet as the ending merchandise inventory. In the illustration on page 321, the inventory record sheet shows that the ending merchandise inventory has a total value of $6,310.00.

A similar type of record sheet may be prepared for taking an inventory of the supplies on hand.

Perpetual inventory

An inventory record that shows changes in the amounts on hand as the changes occur is called a *perpetual inventory*. Other terms used are *running inventory* and *book inventory*. When a perpetual inventory is kept, a physical inventory should be taken at least once each year to make certain that items do not disappear from stock without a record being made of them.

Increasing Your Business Vocabulary

What is the meaning of each of the following:

a inventory

b prepaid insurance

c adjustments

d adjusting entries

e physical inventory

f perpetual inventory

Study Questions

1. Why is it necessary to adjust the merchandise inventory account at the end of the fiscal period?
2. Why must the supplies account be adjusted at the end of the fiscal period?
3. Why must the prepaid insurance account be adjusted at the end of the fiscal period?
4. Why are the Adjustments columns provided on the eight-column work sheet?
5. If the merchandise inventory account shows a beginning inventory at the end of the fiscal period, what account is debited and what account is credited in the first adjustment? Why?
6. What account is debited and what account is credited to record the ending merchandise inventory? Why?
7. Why is each adjustment in the Adjustments columns of the work sheet labeled with an identifying letter?
8. In adjusting the supplies account, what account is debited and what account is credited? Why?
9. In making the adjustment for expired insurance, what account is debited and what account is credited? Why?
10. In extending the two adjustments for merchandise inventory on the Income and Expense Summary line of the work sheet, why are both amounts recorded in the Income Statement columns?
11. When a physical inventory is taken, how is the total value of goods on hand determined?

Cases for Business Decision

CASE 1

After completing his work sheet at the end of a fiscal period, Henry Joslin finds that an error was made in taking the merchandise inventory. Goods valued at $200.00 were not entered as part of the ending inventory. What effect does this error have upon the amount of net income as calculated on the work sheet? What steps should Mr. Joslin take to correct this error?

CASE 2

Mr. Di Carlo, owner of a restaurant, purchased a fire insurance policy on his building and its contents. The policy, which cost $360.00, provides protection for a three-year period. When Mr. Di Carlo paid for the policy, he debited Prepaid Insurance for the entire purchase price, $360.00. Through an oversight, Mr. Di Carlo did not adjust the prepaid insurance account at the end of the fiscal period. What effect does the omission of this adjustment have upon the calculation of net income for the fiscal period? What should Mr. Di Carlo do to correct his error?

CASE 3

The Trial Balance columns of the work sheet of Donald Weiss on June 30 show that Merchandise Inventory has a balance of $1,460.00. Mr. Weiss has sold all of the beginning inventory and the merchandise purchased during the month. Since there is no stock of goods on hand, will Mr. Weiss have to make an adjustment for the beginning inventory? If so, how should this adjustment be planned on the work sheet?

Drills for Understanding

DRILL 18-A Adjusting the merchandise inventory account

Beginning and ending inventories for four business firms are given below.

Business Firm	Beginning Merchandise Inventory	Ending Merchandise Inventory
A	$9,500.00	$7,800.00
B	none	$6,100.00
C	$4,200.00	none
D	$7,900.00	$8,800.00

Instructions: For each business, state the adjustments needed to bring the merchandise inventory account up-to-date.

DRILL 18-B Adjustments columns of the work sheet

The data shown below are taken from the Adjustments columns of the work sheets of four business firms. The amounts given are those that appear on the line with the Income and Expense Summary account.

Business Firm	Adjustments	
	Debit	Credit
A	$5,000	$1,500
B	$2,500	$3,400
C	$ —	$5,100
D	$2,900	$ —

Instructions: For each business, answer the following questions:

a What amount represents the beginning inventory?

b What amount represents the ending inventory?

c What does the blank in the Adjustments Debit column for business C indicate?

d What does the blank in the Adjustments Credit column for business D indicate?

DRILL 18-C | Extensions on the work sheet

The following data are related to the preparation of work sheets for two business firms:

Business Firm	Trial Balance Debit Column		End-of-Period Information	
A	Supplies.............	$500.00	Supplies on hand......	$300.00
	Prepaid Insurance....	230.00	Insurance remaining...	140.00
B	Supplies.............	$800.00	Supplies on hand......	none
	Prepaid Insurance....	50.00	Insurance has expired at end of period	

Instructions: From the data given above, determine the following for each business firm:

a The amount of the adjustments needed to bring the supplies account and the prepaid insurance account up-to-date.

b The Adjustments column in which the amount should be recorded to show the change in the supplies account.

c The Adjustments column in which the amount should be recorded to show the change in the prepaid insurance account.

d The balance of the supplies account that will be extended to the Balance Sheet Debit column.

e The balance of the prepaid insurance account that will be extended to the Balance Sheet Debit column.

Application Problem

PROBLEM 18-1 | Work sheet for a hardware store

On December 31 of the current year, the end of a fiscal period of one year, the accounts and their balances in the general ledger of Watson Hardware and the list of inventories appear as shown below.

Account Titles	*Acct. No.*	*Balance*
Cash	11	$ 8,571.52
Accounts Receivable	12	8,010.75
Merchandise Inventory	13	25,257.68
Supplies	14	1,978.42
Prepaid Insurance	15	1,099.00
Accounts Payable	21	7,109.65
J. C. Watson, Capital	31	39,097.28
J. C. Watson, Drawing	32	6,751.00
Income and Expense Summary	33	—
Sales	41	96,705.34
Purchases	51	70,267.40
Delivery Expense	61	1,576.50
Insurance Expense	62	—
Miscellaneous Expense	63	600.00
Rent Expense	64	6,500.00
Salary Expense	65	12,300.00
Supplies Expense	66	—

Inventories, December 31

Merchandise inventory	$30,510.00
Supplies inventory	650.00
Value of insurance policies	825.00

Instructions: Prepare an eight-column work sheet for Watson Hardware. Use as your guide the eight-column work sheet illustrated on page 318.

The solution to Problem 18-1 will be needed for Problem 19-1 in the next chapter. If it is collected by your teacher at this time, it will be returned to you before it is needed in Chapter 19.

Optional Problems

★SUPPLEMENTARY PROBLEM 18-S

Work sheet for an apparel shop

On June 30 of the current year, the end of a fiscal period of one month, the accounts and their balances in the general ledger of Jeanne's Fashion Shop, and the list of inventories appear as shown below.

Account Titles	*Acct. No.*	*Balance*
Cash	11	$ 2,681.73
Accounts Receivable	12	5,201.75
Merchandise Inventory	13	22,548.65
Supplies	14	298.76
Prepaid Insurance	15	416.00
Accounts Payable	21	3,980.26
Jeanne Doyle, Capital	31	24,972.17
Jeanne Doyle, Drawing	32	624.00
Income and Expense Summary	33	—
Sales	41	8,864.91
Purchases	51	4,895.72
Delivery Expense	61	95.35
Insurance Expense	62	—
Miscellaneous Expense	63	155.38
Rent Expense	64	400.00
Salary Expense	65	500.00
Supplies Expense	66	—

Inventories, June 30

Merchandise inventory	$20,686.50
Supplies inventory	211.32
Value of insurance policies	315.00

Instructions: Prepare an eight-column work sheet for Jeanne's Fashion Shop. Use as your guide the eight-column work sheet illustrated on page 318.

★BONUS PROBLEM 18-B

Work sheet for a grocery store

Mr. A. L. Moss owns the Moss Grocery Store. He started this business on October 1 of the current year without any merchandise inventory. On December 31 of the current year, the end of a quarterly fiscal period, the accounts and their balances in the general ledger and the list of inventories appear as shown below.

Account Titles	*Acct. No.*	*Balance*
Cash	11	$ 7,030.80
Accounts Receivable	12	792.10
Merchandise Inventory	13	—
Supplies	14	142.80
Prepaid Insurance	15	85.00
Accounts Payable	21	4,750.25
A. L. Moss, Capital	31	6,856.61
A. L. Moss, Drawing	32	816.00
Income and Expense Summary	33	—
Sales	41	16,320.40
Purchases	51	15,910.56
Advertising Expense	61	622.40
Delivery Expense	62	739.20
Insurance Expense	63	—
Miscellaneous Expense	64	68.40
Rent Expense	65	700.00
Salary Expense	66	1,020.00
Supplies Expense	67	—

Inventories, December 31

Merchandise inventory	$ 2,300.00
Supplies inventory	94.20
Value of insurance policies	61.00

Instructions: Prepare an eight-column work sheet for the Moss Grocery Store. Use as your guide the eight-column work sheet illustrated on page 318.

CHAPTER 19 FINANCIAL REPORTS FOR A MERCHANDISING BUSINESS

Information about the operations of a business for a fiscal period is summarized on the work sheet. The work sheet does not show this information in its most convenient form, however. For this reason, financial reports are prepared in a form that gives more meaning to the information. The most commonly used financial reports are (1) the income statement, (2) the capital statement, and (3) the balance sheet.

THE INCOME STATEMENT

Uses of the income statement

At the end of a fiscal period, the owner may compare the income statement for that period with those prepared for previous fiscal periods. From this comparison, he learns whether his income is increasing or decreasing. He also learns whether the costs and the expenses are reasonable when compared with income, or whether some costs and expenses have been increasing more rapidly than they should. These comparisons assist him in making decisions about such items as: (1) how to increase income; (2) how to decrease costs; and (3) how to decrease expenses without reducing services.

Preparing the income statement from the work sheet

The part of the work sheet for McCann Office Furniture needed to prepare the income statement for the fiscal period ended November 30, 1967, is shown on the next page.

The income statement for a merchandising business has three main sections: (1) income, (2) cost of merchandise sold, and (3) expenses. The income statement for McCann Office Furniture, prepared from the data shown in the partial work sheet, is also shown on the next page.

Steps in preparing the income statement

The steps in preparing the income statement for McCann Office Furniture are:

	ACCOUNT TITLES	ACCT. NO.	5 INCOME STATEMENT DEBIT	6 INCOME STATEMENT CREDIT
9	Income & Expense Summary	33	6245 00	6310 00
10	Sales	41		4721 00
11	Purchases	51	3234 00	
12	Delivery Expense	61	53 00	
13	Insurance Expense	62	31 00	
14	Miscellaneous Expense	63	23 00	
15	Rent Expense	64	300 00	
16	Salary Expense	65	400 00	
17	Supplies Expense	66	125 00	
18			10411 00	11031 00
19	Net Income		620 00	
20			11031 00	11031 00
21				
22				
23				

Section of work sheet showing income statement columns

McCann Office Furniture
Income Statement
For Month Ended November 30, 1967

Income:		
Sales		4721 00
Cost of Merchandise Sold:		
Merchandise Inventory, Nov. 1, 1967	6245 00	
Purchases	3234 00	
Total Cost of Merchandise Available for Sale	9479 00	
Less Merchandise Inventory, Nov. 30, 1967	6310 00	
Cost of Merchandise Sold		3169 00
Gross Profit on Sales		1552 00
Expenses:		
Delivery Expense	53 00	
Insurance Expense	31 00	
Miscellaneous Expense	23 00	
Rent Expense	300 00	
Salary Expense	400 00	
Supplies Expense	125 00	
Total Expenses		932 00
Net Income		620 00

Income statement

Step 1

Write the heading on three lines:

a *Line 1*, the name of the business, *McCann Office Furniture.*

b *Line 2*, the name of the report, *Income Statement.*

c *Line 3*, the fiscal period that the income statement covers, *For Month Ended November 30, 1967.*

Step 2

Prepare the income section of the report.

a Write the name of this section, *Income*, at the extreme left of the wide column.

b Write the title of the income account, *Sales*, on the next line, indented about a half inch.

c Write the amount of sales, *$4,721.00*, in the second amount column so that the cost of merchandise sold can be subtracted from it.

If there is more than one source of income, the income account titles are listed at the left and the amounts are written in the first amount column. The amounts are totaled, the total income is extended to the second amount column, and the words "Total Income" are written below the last income account title.

Step 3

Prepare the cost of merchandise sold section of the report.

The original purchase price of the merchandise sold during the fiscal period is called the *cost of merchandise sold.* The cost of merchandise sold is computed as follows:

Beginning Inventory + Purchases − Ending Inventory = Cost of Merchandise Sold

Using the data shown in the Income Statement columns of the work sheet, the cost of merchandise sold is calculated as follows:

Beginning merchandise inventory, November 1	$6,245.00
(This amount is shown as a debit to Income and Expense Summary in the Income Statement Debit column of the work sheet.)	
Plus purchases made during November...........................	3,234.00
(This amount is shown as a debit to Purchases in the Income Statement Debit column of the work sheet.)	
Equals the total cost of merchandise available for sale during November..	$9,479.00
Less ending merchandise inventory, November 30	6,310.00
(This amount is shown as a credit to Income and Expense Summary in the Income Statement Credit column of the work sheet.)	
Equals the cost of merchandise sold................................	$3,169.00

The steps in preparing the cost of merchandise sold section are:

a Write the name of this section, *Cost of Merchandise Sold*, on the next line at the extreme left of the wide column.

b Indent about a half inch the items needed to calculate the cost of merchandise sold and write the amount of each item in the first amount column. Thus, the amounts will not interfere with the calculations to be made in the second amount column.

c Write the amount of the cost of merchandise sold, *$3,169.00*, in the second amount column.

Step 4

Calculate the gross profit on sales. The income that a merchandising business earns from operations before expenses are deducted is called *gross profit on sales.*

a Subtract the cost of merchandise sold, *$3,169.00*, from the total income, *$4,721.00*, to find the gross profit on sales.

b Write the amount of the gross profit on sales, *$1,552.00*, in the second amount column.

c Write the words, *Gross Profit on Sales*, in the wide column on the same line as the amount of the gross profit.

Step 5

Prepare the expenses section of the report.

a Write the name of this section, *Expenses*, at the extreme left of the wide column.

b List the expense account titles in the order that they appear on the work sheet, indenting the title of each expense account about a half inch.

c Write the amount of each expense account balance in the first amount column.

d Total the expenses and write the total, *$932.00*, in the second amount column on the first line below the last expense item listed.

e Write the words, *Total Expenses*, in the wide column on the same line as the total amount of the expenses.

Step 6

Calculate the net income.

a Subtract the total expenses, *$932.00*, from the amount of gross profit on sales, *$1,552.00*, to find the amount of net income.

b Write the net income, *$620.00*, in the second amount column.

c Write the words, *Net Income*, at the extreme left of the wide column.

d Rule double lines across both amount columns.

Income statement showing a net loss

When the expenses of a business are greater than the gross profit on sales, the difference is called *net loss.* For example, the partial work sheet for L. C. Barnett, page 320, shows a loss in one fiscal period. The final part of his income statement is prepared as shown below.

Gross Profit on Sales		593 00
Expenses:		
Miscellaneous Expense	47 00	
Postage Expense	75 00	
Rent Expense	200 00	
Salary Expense	400 00	
Supplies Expense	23 00	
Total Expenses		745 00
Net Loss		152 00

Section of income statement showing a net loss

THE CAPITAL STATEMENT

At the end of the fiscal period, the owner of a business is interested in learning what changes occurred in proprietorship. A financial report that summarizes the changes in the proprietor's capital that have occurred during the fiscal period is called a *capital statement.* The information needed to prepare the capital statement is taken from the proprietor's capital account in the general ledger and from the Balance Sheet columns of the work sheet. In preparing the capital statement, it is necessary to refer to the capital account to determine *the balance at the beginning of the period and the amount of any additional investments that may have been made during the period.*

The capital statement for McCann Office Furniture

The capital statement for McCann Office Furniture on November 30, 1967, is shown on the next page. The proprietor's capital account and the part of the work sheet for McCann Office Furniture needed to prepare the capital statement are also illustrated on the next page.

McCann Office Furniture
Capital Statement
For Month Ended November 30, 1967

John McCann, Capital, November 1, 1967	9,121 00	
Plus Additional Investment	1,000 00	
Total		10,121 00
Net Income for November, 1967	620 00	
Less Withdrawals for November, 1967	350 00	
Net Increase in Capital		270 00
John McCann, Capital, November 30, 1967		10,391 00

Capital statement

John McCann, Capital — ACCOUNT NO. 31

DATE	ITEMS	POST. REF.	DEBIT	DATE	ITEMS	POST. REF.	CREDIT
				1967 Nov. 1	Balance	✓	9,121 00
				4		CR10	1,000 00
							10,121 00

Proprietor's capital account

	ACCOUNT TITLES	ACCT. NO.	7 BALANCE SHEET DEBIT	8 BALANCE SHEET CREDIT	
1	Cash	11	4771 00		1
2	Accounts Receivable	12	1282 00		2
3	Merchandise Inventory	13	6310 00		3
4	Supplies	14	142 00		4
5	Prepaid Insurance	15	168 00		5
6	Accounts Payable	21		2282 00	6
7	John McCann, Capital	31		10121 00	7
8	John McCann, Drawing	32	350 00		8
18			13023 00	12403 00	18
19	Net Income			620 00	19
20			13023 00	13023 00	20
21					21
22					22
23					23
24					24

Section of work sheet showing balance sheet columns

Steps in preparing the capital statement

The steps in preparing the capital statement for McCann Office Furniture

Step 1

Write the heading on three lines:

a *Line 1*, the name of the business, *McCann Office Furniture.*

b *Line 2*, the name of the report, *Capital Statement.*

c *Line 3*, the fiscal period covered by the capital statement, *For Month Ended November 30, 1967.*

Step 2

a Write the words, *John McCann, Capital, November 1, 1967*, at the extreme left of the wide column.

b Write the amount of the capital, *$9,121.00*, in the first amount column. This amount is obtained from the proprietor's capital account in the general ledger.

Step 3

a Write the words *Plus Additional Investment* on the next line at the extreme left of the wide column to show that an amount is added to the beginning capital.

b Write the amount of the additional investment, *$1,000.00*, in the first amount column on the line immediately below the beginning capital. The amount of the additional investment made by Mr. McCann during the fiscal period is found by referring to the capital account in the general ledger.

Step 4

a Add the amount of the beginning capital, *$9,121.00*, and the amount of the additional investment, *$1,000.00*, and write the total, *$10,121.00*, in the second amount column.

b Write the word, *Total*, at the extreme left of the wide column.

Step 5

a Write the words *Net Income for November, 1967*, at the extreme left of the wide column.

b Write the amount of the net income, *$620.00*, in the first amount column. The amount of the net income is found in the Balance Sheet Credit column of the work sheet.

Step 6

a Write the words *Less Withdrawals for November, 1967,* in the wide column, indented about a half inch.

b Write the amount of the withdrawals *$350.00,* in the first amount column. The amount of the withdrawals is found in the Balance Sheet Debit column of the work sheet on the same line with the account title *John McCann, Drawing.*

Step 7

a Subtract the amount of the withdrawals, *$350.00,* from the amount of the net income, *$620.00,* and write the amount of the remainder *$270.00,* in the second amount column.

b Write the *Net Increase in Capital* on the same line with this amount, at the extreme left of the wide column.

Step 8

a Add the net increase, *$270.00,* to the total, *$10,121.00,* and write the sum, *$10,391.00,* in the second amount column.

b Write *John McCann, Capital, November 30, 1967,* at the extreme left of the wide column to identify the amount, $10,391.00.

c Rule double lines across both amount columns.

If the withdrawals exceed the net income, the difference is called net decrease in capital. The net decrease is subtracted from the total.

In some businesses, the information on the capital statement may be shown as a part of the balance sheet. An example of this method of reporting the changes in the proprietor's capital is illustrated on page 136.

THE BALANCE SHEET

Uses of the balance sheet

By studying the balance sheet, the owner can obtain useful information for managing his business. He can see whether he has sufficient cash on hand to pay his liabilities. By comparing the balance sheet for one fiscal period with those of previous fiscal periods, he can learn (1) whether his accounts receivable and his inventory are increasing more than they should; (2) whether his liabilities are decreasing or increasing; (3) whether his liabilities are increasing too rapidly when compared with the increase in his assets, and (4) whether his proprietorship is increasing or decreasing.

Two forms of balance sheet

The balance sheet may be prepared in either of two forms: (1) account form or (2) report form. In the account form, the assets are listed on the left and the liabilities and the proprietorship on the right. The account form of balance sheet is illustrated on page 135. A balance sheet with the assets, the liabilities, and the proprietorship in a vertical arrangement is called the *report form of balance sheet.* The report form of balance sheet is illustrated below.

Report form of balance sheet

The information in the Balance Sheet columns of the work sheet is used to prepare the balance sheet. The section of the work sheet for McCann Office Furniture needed to prepare the balance sheet on November 30, 1967, is shown on page 334.

McCann Office Furniture
Balance Sheet
November 30, 1967

Assets		
Cash	4771 00	
Accounts Receivable	1282 00	
Merchandise Inventory	6310 00	
Supplies	142 00	
Prepaid Insurance	168 00	
Total Assets		12673 00
Liabilities		
Accounts Payable		2282 00
Proprietorship		
John McCann, Capital		10391 00
Total Liabilities and Proprietorship		12673 00

Report form of balance sheet

Steps in preparing the balance sheet

The steps in preparing the balance sheet for McCann Office Furniture on November 30, 1967, are:

Step 1

Write the heading on three lines:

a *Line 1,* the name of the business, *McCann Office Furniture.*

b *Line 2,* the name of the report, *Balance Sheet.*

c *Line 3,* the date of the report, *November 30, 1967.*

Step 2

Prepare the assets section of the report.

a Write the title, *Assets*, in the middle of the wide column.

b Write the title of each asset account at the left of the wide column, and record the balance of each account in the first amount column.

c Write the total of the asset account balances, *$12,673.00*, in the second amount column; write *Total Assets* at the left of the wide column on the same line.

d Rule double lines across both amount columns.

Step 3

Prepare the liabilities section of the report.

a Skip a line and write the title of this section, *Liabilities*, in the middle of the wide column.

b Write the account title, *Accounts Payable*, at the left of the wide column on the next line. Since there is only one liability, the amount, *$2,282.00*, is written in the second amount column because it is also the total of this section of the balance sheet.

If there is more than one liability, each account title is listed, the balance of each account is written in the first amount column, and the total is extended to the second amount column. The total is labeled Total Liabilities.

Step 4

Prepare the proprietorship section of the report.

a Skip a line and write the title of this section, *Proprietorship*, in the middle of the wide column.

b Write the words *John McCann, Capital, November 30, 1967*, at the left of the wide column. Write the amount of Mr. McCann's capital *$10,391.00*, in the second amount column.

The amount of Mr. McCann's capital on November 30, 1967, is the same as that shown on the capital statement, page 334.

Step 5

Total the liabilities and the proprietorship sections of the report.

a Write the total amount, *$12,673.00*, in the second amount column, and write *Total Liabilities and Proprietorship* at the left of the wide column on the same line.

b Compare the total amount of the assets and the total amount of the liabilities and the proprietorship. Since these two amounts, *$12,673.00*, are the same, the balance sheet for McCann Office Furniture is in balance and is assumed to be correct.

c Rule double lines across both amount columns.

SUPPLEMENTARY FINANCIAL REPORTS

The three principal financial reports are the balance sheet, the capital statement, and the income statement. Additional reports may be prepared to give information about some of the items listed on the principal financial reports. A report prepared to supply details about items listed on a principal financial report is commonly called a *supporting schedule.* A supporting schedule is sometimes called a *supplementary report.* For example, the balance sheet shows the total amount of accounts receivable. It does not, however, show the account balance of each charge customer. When this information is desired, a supporting schedule is usually prepared. This supporting schedule is called a schedule of accounts receivable. A similar schedule is prepared for accounts payable. These supporting schedules for McCann Office Furniture are illustrated on pages 200 and 248.

REPORTING BUSINESS INCOME OR LOSS ON FEDERAL INCOME TAX RETURNS

Income tax laws require each individual who operates a single proprietorship, such as McCann Office Furniture, to report annually the details of the business operations as part of his personal income tax return. A special income tax form known as Schedule C, Form 1040, Profit (or Loss) From Business or Profession, is used for this purpose.

Schedule C, Form 1040, is prepared from the data on the income statement. A part of Schedule C, Form 1040, completed by Mr. McCann for McCann Office Furniture, is shown on page 340. This form was prepared from information on the income statement shown on page 341.

The procedure for filling out Schedule C, Form 1040 is outlined below.

The name and residence of the owner of McCann Office Furniture are written at the top of the schedule.

Line A. McCann Office Furniture is a retail business engaged in selling office supplies and furniture. Therefore, the word *Retail* is written on Line A to indicate the principal business activity. The product is described by writing the words *office supplies and furniture.*

Lines B and C. The name of the business, *McCann Office Furniture*, and the employer's identification number, *93-0764287*, are written on this line.

Every employer subject to social security taxes is assigned an identification number by the federal government. In the offices of the Internal Revenue Service, all records with McCann Office Furniture are filed under this identification number.

SCHEDULE C
(Form 1040)
U.S. Treasury Department
Internal Revenue Service

PROFIT (OR LOSS) FROM BUSINESS OR PROFESSION

(Sole Proprietorships)

(Compute social security self-employment tax on Schedule C-3 (Form 1040))

1967

Attach this schedule to your income tax return, Form 1040 — Partnerships, joint ventures, etc., must file on Form 1065

Name and address as shown on page 1, Form 1040

John McCann, 642 Central Ave., Portland, Oregon 97208

A. Principal business activity Retail; product Office Supplies & Furn.
(See separate instructions) (For example: retail—hardware; wholesale—tobacco; services—legal; manufacturing—furniture; etc.)

B. Business name McCann Office Furniture **C. Employer Identification Number** 93-0764287

D. Business location 640 Central Avenue (Number and street or rural route) Portland (City or post office) Oregon 97208 (State)

E. Indicate method of accounting: ☐ cash; ☒ accrual; ☐ other.

Line			
1.	Gross receipts or gross sales $ 60,774.00 Less: Returns and allowances $ 0		$ 60,774 00
2.	Inventory at beginning of year (If different than last year's closing inventory attach explanation)	6,419.00	
3.	Merchandise purchased $ 41,595.00, less cost of any items withdrawn from business for personal use $ 670.00	40,925.00	
4.	Cost of labor (do not include salary paid to yourself)		
5.	Material and supplies		
6.	Other costs (explain in Schedule C-1)		
7.	Total of lines 2 through 6	47,344.00	
8.	Inventory at end of this year	6,147.00	
9.	**Cost of goods sold** (line 7 less line 8)		41,197 00
10.	**Gross profit** (subtract line 9 from line 1)		19,577 00
	OTHER BUSINESS DEDUCTIONS		
11.	Depreciation (explain in Schedule C-2)		
12.	Taxes on business and business property (explain in Schedule C-1)		
13.	Rent on business property	3,600.00	
14.	Repairs (explain in Schedule C-1)		
15.	Salaries and wages not included on line 4 (exclude any paid to yourself)	4,800.00	
16.	Insurance	304.00	
17.	Legal and professional fees		
18.	Commissions		
19.	Amortization (attach statement)		
20.	Retirement plans, etc. (other than your share—see instructions)		
21.	Interest on business indebtedness		
22.	Bad debts arising from sales or services		
23.	Losses of business property (attach statement)		
24.	Depletion of mines, oil and gas wells, timber, etc. (attach schedule)		
25.	Other business expenses (explain in Schedule C-1)	2,683.00	
26.	Total of lines 11 through 25		11,387 00
27.	**Net profit (or loss)** (subtract line 26 from line 10). Enter here; on line 1, Schedule C-3; and on line 5, Part II, page 2, Form 1040		8,190 00

SCHEDULE C-1. EXPLANATION OF LINES 6, 12, 14, AND 25

Line No.	Explanation	Amount	Line No.	Explanation	Amount
25	Delivery Expense	$ 689.00			$
25	Misc. Expense	399.00			
25	Supplies Expense	1,595.00			
25	Total	2,683.00			

16—78364—1

Schedules C and C-1, Form 1040, from Internal Revenue Service

McCann Office Furniture
Income Statement
For Year Ended December 31, 1967

Income:		
Sales		$60,774.00
Cost of Merchandise Sold:		
Merchandise Inventory, January 1, 1967.	$ 6,419.00	
Purchases	40,925.00	
Total Cost of Merchandise Available for Sale. . .	$47,344.00	
Less Merchandise Inventory, December 31, 1967 . .	6,147.00	
Cost of Merchandise Sold.		41,197.00
Gross Profit on Sales.		$19,577.00
Expenses:		
Delivery Expense.	$ 689.00	
Insurance Expense	304.00	
Miscellaneous Expense	399.00	
Rent Expense.	3,600.00	
Salary Expense.	4,800.00	
Supplies Expense.	1,595.00	
Total Expenses.		11,387.00
Net Income		$ 8,190.00

Income statement

Line D. The business address of McCann Office Furniture is written on Line D.

Line E. On this line Mr. McCann indicates that the accrual method of accounting is used by his business.

The method of keeping records that shows (1) all income earned during a fiscal period even though the income is not yet received and (2) all expenses incurred during the fiscal period even though the expenses are not yet paid is known as the *accrual basis* of keeping records.

The method of keeping records that shows (1) only income actually received during a fiscal period and (2) only expenses paid during a fiscal period is known as the *cash basis* of keeping records.

Federal and state income tax laws permit the filing of income tax returns either on the accrual basis or the cash basis. These two accounting methods are further discussed in a later chapter.

Line 1. These amounts are copied directly from the income statement.

Line 2. The amount of the beginning inventory is obtained from the income statement.

Line 3. These two amounts must be obtained directly from the purchases account in the general ledger because these amounts are not shown on the income statement. The merchandise purchased, *$41,595.00,* is the total of the debit column of the purchases account in the general ledger. The withdrawal of merchandise by the proprietor, *$670.00,* is the total of the credit column of the purchases account. When the subtraction of the withdrawal is completed, the remainder, *$40,925.00*, should agree with the amount of purchases shown on the income statement.

Lines 4, 5, 6, and 7. McCann Office Furniture has no amounts for Lines 4, 5, and 6. The calculation for Line 7 is completed according to the instructions on the government form.

Line 8. The amount of the ending merchandise inventory is obtained from the income statement.

Lines 9 and 10. The calculations are completed as instructed on the form and the amounts are written in the proper spaces. The gross profit on sales recorded on the form is compared with the amount on the income statement. The two amounts should agree.

Lines 11 through 24. All of these amounts are taken directly from the income statement.

Line 25. "Other business expenses" are the business expenses that are not listed on Lines 11 through 24. These amounts are obtained from the income statement and are listed in Schedule C-1, as shown at the bottom of the filled-in form. The total of all the expenses listed in Schedule C-1 is written on Line 25.

Line 26. All the amounts on Lines 11 through 25 are added and the total, *$11,387.00*, is written on Line 26. This total should agree with the total expenses on the income statement.

Line 27. The net profit is obtained by subtracting the amount on Line 26 from the amount on Line 10. The amount of net profit on Schedule C, Form 1040, *$8,190.00*, should agree with the amount of net income shown on the income statement.

The terms "net profit" and "net income" are often used interchangeably. The term "net profit" is used on the government form. The term "net income" is generally preferred among accountants.

Increasing Your Business Vocabulary

What is the meaning of each of the following:

a cost of merchandise sold

b gross profit on sales

c net loss

d capital statement

e report form of balance sheet

f supporting schedule

Study Questions

1. What are the three most commonly used financial statements of a business?
2. What information can an owner obtain from a comparison of his income statements for two or more fiscal periods?
3. From what source does the proprietor obtain the information needed to prepare the income statement?
4. What are the three major sections of an income statement for a merchandising business?
5. How is the cost of merchandise sold calculated?
6. From what sources does the proprietor obtain the information needed to prepare the capital statement?
7. What information can the proprietor obtain from a comparison of his balance sheets for two or more fiscal periods?
8. How does the report form of balance sheet shown in this chapter differ from the account form of balance sheet shown in Chapter 10?
9. From what source does the proprietor obtain the information needed to prepare the balance sheet?
10. What information is shown on a schedule of accounts receivable that does not appear on the balance sheet?
11. From what sources does Mr. McCann obtain the data needed to complete Schedules C and C-1 of Form 1040?

Cases for Business Decision

CASE 1

Mr. K. D. Davis, owner of Davis Gift Shop, is analyzing his income statement for November and comparing it with his income statement for the same month a year ago. He notes that his sales this year are 25 percent higher than a year ago. He also notes that his expenses have increased almost 40 percent. What points should Mr. Davis consider in determining whether the increase in expenses is justified?

CASE 2

Albert Peters has been thinking about selling his business. However, he enjoys being his own boss and cannot make up his mind. He inspects his most recent financial statements and finds that he has a present capital of $9,851.00. He also finds that his net income for the fiscal year amounts to $591.00. What factors should Mr. Peters consider in connection with the amount of his net income in reaching a decision about selling the business?

CASE 3

Mr. John Marcus prepared a balance sheet for his business on June 30. The balance sheet showed that his total capital was $14,150.00. His balance sheet for May 31 showed that his total capital was $13,949.00. Discuss the probable causes of this change in capital.

Drills for Understanding

DRILL 19-A Computing the cost of merchandise sold

The data given below have been taken from the work sheets for three businesses.

	Income Statement	
	Debit	**Credit**
Business No. 1:		
Purchases	4,500.00	
Income and Expense Summary	5,000.00	3,500.00
Business No. 2:		
Purchases	4,900.00	
Income and Expense Summary	———	3,800.00
Business No. 3:		
Purchases	9,000.00	
Income and Expense Summary	10,000.00	

Instructions: Compute the cost of merchandise sold for each of the businesses listed above.

DRILL 19-B Computing the present capital

The data given below have been taken from the proprietors' capital accounts and the work sheets for four businesses.

	Business			
	No. 1	**No. 2**	**No. 3**	**No. 4**
Beginning Capital	$8,500.00	$11,600.00	$9,400.00	$6,000.00
Net Income	1,000.00	1,600.00	———	———
Net Loss	———	———	550.00	450.00
Additional Investment	———	———	1,500.00	———
Withdrawals	400.00	none	none	100.00

Instructions: Compute the present capital for each of the businesses listed above.

DRILL 19-C | Computing net income or net loss

The data given below have been taken from the work sheets for three businesses.

	Income Statement	
Business No. 1:	**Debit**	**Credit**
Income and Expense Summary	4,000.00	2,000.00
Income		6,000.00
Purchases	3,000.00	
Total Expenses	500.00	
Business No. 2:		
Income and Expense Sumary	9,000.00	3,000.00
Income		10,000.00
Purchases	3,500.00	
Total Expenses	1,500.00	
Business No. 3:		
Income and Expense Summary	2,000.00	1,500.00
Income		15,000.00
Purchases	8,500.00	
Total Expenses	3,500.00	

Instructions: For each of the businesses listed above, compute the following:

a Cost of merchandise sold

b Gross profit on sales

c Net income or net loss

Application Problem

PROBLEM 19-1 | Financial reports for a hardware store

The work sheet completed in Problem 18-1 of the preceding chapter is required for this problem. If Problem 18-1 has not been returned to you, complete Appendix Problem 19-A.

Instructions: 1. Prepare an income statement similar to the one illustrated on page 330.

2. Prepare a capital statement similar to the one illustrated on page 334. Mr. Watson made additional investments of $5,000.00 during the year.

3. Prepare a balance sheet in report form similar to the one illustrated on page 337.

Optional Problems

★ SUPPLEMENTARY PROBLEM 19-S

Eight-column work sheet and financial reports

The account balances and the inventory on June 30 of the current year, the end of a quarterly fiscal period, for Thomas Rossi, a neighborhood grocer, are:

Account Titles	*Acct. No.*	*Balances Debit*	*Balances Credit*
Cash	11	3,673.00	
Accounts Receivable	12	4,144.68	
Merchandise Inventory	13	9,745.11	
Supplies	14	212.46	
Prepaid Insurance	15	224.08	
Accounts Payable	21		5,246.18
Thomas Rossi, Capital	31		11,490.00
Thomas Rossi, Drawing	32	760.00	
Income and Expense Summary	33	—	—
Sales	41		16,908.25
Purchases	51	11,650.60	
Delivery Expense	61	259.85	
Insurance Expense	62	—	
Miscellaneous Expense	63	319.75	
Rent Expense	64	900.00	
Salary Expense	65	1,754.90	
Supplies Expense	66	—	

Inventories, June 30

Merchandise Inventory	$10,112.52
Supplies Inventory	$ 105.81
Value of insurance policies	$ 125.48

Instructions: 1: Prepare an eight-column work sheet similar to one illustrated on page 318.

2. From the Income Statement columns of the work sheet, prepare an income statement similar to the one illustrated on page 330.

3. From the Balance Sheet columns of the work sheet, prepare a capital statement similar to the one illustrated on page 334. Mr. Rossi made no additional investments during the quarter.

4. From the Balance Sheet columns of the work sheet, prepare a balance sheet in report form similar to the one illustrated on page 337.

★ **BONUS PROBLEM 19-B**

Eight-column work sheet and financial reports

The account balances and the inventories on February 28 of the current year, the end of a fiscal period of one month, for E. R. Caldwell, the owner of Caldwell Furniture, are shown below.

Account Titles	*Acct. No.*	*Balances* *Debit*	*Credit*
Cash	11	5,448.10	
Accounts Receivable	12	3,294.27	
Merchandise Inventory	13	20,632.76	
Supplies	14	280.00	
Prepaid Insurance	15	353.00	
Accounts Payable	21		4,017.00
E. R. Caldwell, Capital	31		23,684.73
E. R. Caldwell, Drawing	32	600.00	
Income and Expense Summary	33	———	———
Sales	41		7,839.45
Purchases	51	3,739.47	
Delivery Expense	61	271.38	
Insurance Expense	62	———	
Miscellaneous Expense	63	160.20	
Rent Expense	64	275.00	
Supplies Expense	65	———	
Wages Expense	66	487.00	

Inventories, February 28

Merchandise inventory	$17,630.00
Supplies inventory	$ 160.00
Value of insurance policies	$ 285.00

Instructions: 1. Prepare an eight-column work sheet similar to the one illustrated on page 318.

2. From the Income Statement columns of the work sheet, prepare an income statement similar to the one illustrated on page 330.

3. From the Balance Sheet columns of the work sheet, prepare a capital statement similar to the one illustrated on page 334. Mr. Caldwell made an additional investment of $2,500.00 on February 15 of the current year.

4. From the Balance Sheet columns of the work sheet, prepare a balance sheet in report form similar to the one illustrated on page 337.

McCann Office Furniture
Work Sheet
For Month Ended November 30, 1967

	ACCOUNT TITLES	ACCT. NO.	TRIAL BALANCE (1) DEBIT	TRIAL BALANCE (2) CREDIT	ADJUSTMENTS (3) DEBIT	ADJUSTMENTS (4) CREDIT	INCOME STATEMENT (5) DEBIT	INCOME STATEMENT (6) CREDIT	BALANCE SHEET (7) DEBIT	BALANCE SHEET (8) CREDIT	
1	Cash	11	477100						477100		1
2	Accounts Receivable	12	128200						128200		2
3	Merchandise Inventory	13	624500		(b) 631000	(a) 624500			631000		3
4	Supplies	14	26700			(c) 12500			14200		4
5	Prepaid Insurance	15	19900			(d) 3100			16800		5
6	Accounts Payable	21		228200						228200	6
7	John McCann, Capital	31		1012100						1012100	7
8	John McCann, Drawing	32	35000						35000		8
9	Income & Expense Summary	33			(a) 624500	(b) 631000	624500	631000			9
10	Sales	41		472100				472100			10
11	Purchases	51	323400				323400				11
12	Delivery Expense	61	5300				5300				12
13	Insurance Expense	62			(d) 3100		3100				13
14	Miscellaneous Expense	63	2300				2300				14
15	Rent Expense	64	30000				30000				15
16	Salary Expense	65	40000				40000				16
17	Supplies Expense	66			(c) 12500		12500				17
18			1712400	1712400	1271100	1271100	1041100	1103100	1302300	1240300	18
19	Net Income						62000			62000	19
20							1103100	1103100	1302300	1302300	20
21											21
22											22
23											23
24											24

Completed eight-column work sheet

CHAPTER 20 ADJUSTING AND CLOSING ENTRIES

ADJUSTING ENTRIES

The Adjustments columns of the work sheet are used to plan the changes that must be made in the general ledger accounts at the end of the fiscal period. It is necessary to record an adjustment in a journal for each adjustment on the work sheet because changes in the ledger should be made only as a result of posting journal entries. McCann Office Furniture records the adjusting entries in a two-column general journal.

Adjusting entry (a) — beginning merchandise inventory

The adjustments needed in the general ledger accounts of McCann Office Furniture were analyzed and planned on the work sheet described in Chapter 18. The portion of the work sheet illustrated below shows the adjustment for the beginning merchandise inventory at the end of the fiscal period, November 30, 1967.

	ACCOUNT TITLES	ACCT. NO.	1 TRIAL BALANCE DEBIT	2 TRIAL BALANCE CREDIT	3 ADJUSTMENTS DEBIT	4 ADJUSTMENTS CREDIT
3	Merchandise Inventory	13	6245 00			(a) 6245 00
9	Income & Expense Summary	33			(a) 6245 00	

Partial work sheet showing adjustment (a)

Adjusting entry (a) transfers the beginning balance of the merchandise inventory account to the debit side of the income and expense summary account where the amount is available for determining the cost of merchandise sold. In adjusting entry (a), the merchandise inventory account is credited in order to cancel the debit and thus show that the amount of the beginning inventory has been transferred to another account. The adjusting entry in the general journal for the beginning merchandise inventory and the accounts in the general ledger after this entry has been posted are shown on the next page.

GENERAL JOURNAL PAGE 5

	DATE		ACCOUNT TITLE	POST. REF.	DEBIT	CREDIT	
1			Adjusting Entries				1
2	1967 Nov.	30	Income and Expense Summary	33	6245 00		2
3			Merchandise Inventory	13		6245 00	3
4							4
5							5
6							6

Adjusting Entry (a)

Journal entry for the adjustment of beginning merchandise inventory

Merchandise Inventory ACCOUNT NO. 13

DATE		ITEMS	POST. REF.	DEBIT	DATE		ITEMS	POST. REF.	CREDIT
1967 Nov.	1	Balance	✓	6245 00	1967 Nov.	30		J5	6245 00

Income and Expense Summary ACCOUNT NO. 33

DATE		ITEMS	POST. REF.	DEBIT	DATE		ITEMS	POST. REF.	CREDIT
1967 Nov.	30		J5	6245 00					

General ledger accounts after posting of adjusting entry (a)

The adjusting entry is recorded in the usual general journal form with one exception. The explanation, "Adjusting Entries," is written above the first entry but is not repeated for the remaining adjusting entries. A separate explanation for each adjusting entry in the journal is not necessary.

Note in the accounts illustrated above that (1) the merchandise inventory account is in balance, and (2) the income and expense summary account now shows the amount of the beginning merchandise inventory.

Adjusting entry (b) — ending merchandise inventory

The ending merchandise inventory is an asset of the business. The amount of the ending inventory must be recorded as a debit to the merchandise inventory account so that this asset account will be up-to-date. The ending merchandise inventory is recorded as a credit to the income and expense summary account because the amount of the inventory is a deduction from the cost of merchandise available for sale. A portion of the work sheet for McCann Office Furniture showing the adjustment for the ending merchandise inventory is shown on the next page.

	ACCOUNT TITLES	ACCT. NO.	1 TRIAL BALANCE DEBIT	2 TRIAL BALANCE CREDIT	3 ADJUSTMENTS DEBIT	4 ADJUSTMENTS CREDIT
3	Merchandise Inventory	13	6245 00		(b) 6310 00	(a) 6245 00
9	Income & Expense Summary	33			(a) 6245 00	(b) 6310 00

Partial work sheet showing adjustment (b)

The adjusting entry in the general journal for the ending merchandise inventory and the accounts in the general ledger after this entry has been posted are shown below.

GENERAL JOURNAL PAGE 5

	DATE	ACCOUNT TITLE	POST. REF.	DEBIT	CREDIT	
4	30	Merchandise Inventory	13	6310 00		4
5		Income and Expense Summary	33		6310 00	5
6						6

Adjusting Entry (b)

Journal entry for the adjustment of ending merchandise inventory

Merchandise Inventory ACCOUNT NO. 13

DATE	ITEMS	POST. REF.	DEBIT	DATE	ITEMS	POST. REF.	CREDIT
1967 Nov. 1	Balance	✓	6245 00	1967 Nov. 30		J5	6245 00
30		J5	6310 00				

Income and Expense Summary ACCOUNT NO. 33

DATE	ITEMS	POST. REF.	DEBIT	DATE	ITEMS	POST. REF.	CREDIT
1967 Nov. 30		J5	6245 00	1967 Nov. 30		J5	6310 00

General ledger accounts after posting of adjusting entry (b)

The merchandise inventory account now has a debit balance of $6,310.00, the amount of the ending merchandise inventory. The income and expense summary account now has a debit of $6,245.00 (the amount of the beginning merchandise inventory) and a credit of $6,310.00 (the amount of the ending merchandise inventory).

Adjusting entry (c) — supplies used

Supplies Expense is debited to record the expense resulting from the use of supplies during the fiscal period. Supplies is credited to show the decrease in the balance of this asset account. A portion of the work sheet for McCann Office Furniture showing the adjustment for supplies used is shown below.

	ACCOUNT TITLES	ACCT. NO.	1 TRIAL BALANCE DEBIT	2 TRIAL BALANCE CREDIT	3 ADJUSTMENTS DEBIT	4 ADJUSTMENTS CREDIT
4	Supplies	14	267 00			(c) 125 00
17	Supplies Expense	66			(c) 125 00	

Partial work sheet showing adjustment (c)

The adjusting entry in the general journal for the supplies used and the two general ledger accounts after this entry has been posted are shown below.

GENERAL JOURNAL PAGE 5

	DATE	ACCOUNT TITLE	POST. REF.	DEBIT	CREDIT	
6	30	Supplies Expense	66	125 00		6
7		Supplies	14		125 00	7
8						8

Adjusting Entry (c)

Journal entry for the adjustment of supplies used

Supplies ACCOUNT NO. 14

DATE	ITEMS	POST. REF.	DEBIT	DATE	ITEMS	POST. REF.	CREDIT
1967 Nov. 1	Balance	✓	155 00	1967 Nov. 30		J5	125 00
30		J4	112 00 267 00				

Supplies Expense ACCOUNT NO. 66

DATE	ITEMS	POST. REF.	DEBIT	DATE	ITEMS	POST. REF.	CREDIT
1967 Nov. 30		J5	125 00				

General ledger accounts after posting of adjusting entry (c)

The balance of the supplies account, $142.00, is the amount of supplies on hand at the end of the fiscal period. The supplies expense account has a debit balance of $125.00, which is the amount of the supplies used during the current fiscal period ended November 30, 1967.

Adjusting entry (d) — expired insurance

Part of the value of the insurance premiums has expired during the fiscal period. The part that has expired is an expense. To record this expense, Insurance Expense is debited. Prepaid Insurance is credited to show the decrease in this asset account because of the expired insurance. A portion of the work sheet for McCann Office Furniture showing the adjustment for expired insurance is shown below.

	ACCOUNT TITLES	ACCT. NO.	1 TRIAL BALANCE DEBIT	2 TRIAL BALANCE CREDIT	3 ADJUSTMENTS DEBIT	4 ADJUSTMENTS CREDIT
5	Prepaid Insurance	15	199 00			(d) 31 00
13	Insurance Expense	62			(d) 31 00	

Partial work sheet showing adjustment (d)

The adjusting entry in the general journal for expired insurance and the two general ledger accounts after this entry has been posted are shown below.

GENERAL JOURNAL PAGE 5

	DATE		ACCOUNT TITLE	POST. REF.	DEBIT	CREDIT	
8		30	Insurance Expense	62	31 00		8
9			Prepaid Insurance	15		31 00	9
10							10

Adjusting Entry (d)

Journal entry for the adjustment of expired insurance

Prepaid Insurance ACCOUNT NO. 15

DATE		ITEMS	POST. REF.	DEBIT	DATE		ITEMS	POST. REF.	CREDIT
1967 Nov.	1	Balance	✓	199 00	1967 Nov.	30		J5	31 00

Insurance Expense ACCOUNT NO. 62

DATE		ITEMS	POST. REF.	DEBIT	DATE		ITEMS	POST. REF.	CREDIT
1967 Nov.	30		J5	31 00					

General ledger accounts after posting of adjusting entry (d)

The debit balance of the prepaid insurance account, $168.00, represents the value of the asset remaining at the end of the fiscal period. The insurance expense account has a debit balance of $31.00, which is the amount of the insurance premiums that expired during the fiscal period.

CLOSING ENTRIES

Closing entries are needed at the end of each fiscal period for the following reasons:

1. To clear the balances of all income accounts, all cost accounts, and all expense accounts by transferring their balances to the income and expense summary account.

   The clearing of these accounts causes the postings of the next fiscal period to be clearly separated from the entries of the past fiscal period. As a result of closing entries, each income account, each cost account, and each expense account begins a new fiscal period with a zero balance.

2. To bring the proprietor's capital account in the general ledger up-to-date.

   For this purpose two journal entries are required: (a) a journal entry to transfer the balance of the income and expense summary account to the proprietor's capital account, and (b) a journal entry to transfer the balance of the proprietor's drawing account to the proprietor's capital account.

All entries to close income, cost, and expense accounts are made from the information given in the Income Statement columns of the work sheet. No amount may be transferred from one account in the general ledger to another account unless the transfer results from the posting of a journal entry. Therefore, all closing entries are made in a journal and are posted to the accounts.

Closing entry No. 1 — closing the income statement accounts with credit balances

The portion of the work sheet for McCann Office Furniture that is needed in making the closing entries is shown at the top of the next page.

One journal entry is made to close all accounts whose balances are listed in the Income Statement Credit column of the work sheet. The only account with a balance in the Income Statement Credit column of the work sheet for McCann Office Furniture is the sales account.

	ACCOUNT TITLES	ACCT. NO.	INCOME STATEMENT 5 DEBIT	6 CREDIT
10	Sales	41		4721 00
11	Purchases	51	3234 00	
12	Delivery Expense	61	53 00	
13	Insurance Expense	62	31 00	
14	Miscellaneous Expense	63	23 00	
15	Rent Expense	64	300 00	
16	Salary Expense	65	400 00	
17	Supplies Expense	66	125 00	
18			10411 00	11031 00
19	Net Income		620 00	
20			11031 00	11031 00

Partial work sheet showing all income, cost, and expense account balances

The journal entry to close the sales account is shown below. The words "Closing Entries" are written in the Account Title column of the general journal immediately above the first closing entry. A separate explanation for each closing entry in the journal is not necessary.

GENERAL JOURNAL PAGE 5

	DATE		ACCOUNT TITLE	POST. REF.	DEBIT	CREDIT	
11			Closing Entries				11
12		30	Sales	41	4721 00		12
13			Income and Expense Summary	33		4721 00	13
14							14
15							15
16							16

Closing Entry No. 1 (lines 11–13)

Closing entry No. 1 — closing the income account

After closing entry No. 1 is posted, the sales account has a zero balance, as shown in the T account on the right. The amount of sales, $4,721.00, is posted as a credit to the income and expense summary account.

Sales 41

Closing	4,721.00	Balance	4,721.00

Income and Expense Summary 33

Beg. Inv.	6,245.00	End. Inv.	6,310.00
		Income	4,721.00

Closing entry No. 2 — closing the income statement accounts with debit balances

A combined entry is used to close all the accounts with balances listed in the Income Statement Debit column of the partial work sheet illustrated on page 355. The income and expense summary account is debited for the total of all the account balances listed in the Income Statement Debit column of the work sheet. Each of the accounts with a debit balance in the Income Statement Debit column is credited for the amount of its balance. The combined entry to close the cost account and the expense accounts of McCann Office Furniture is shown below.

GENERAL JOURNAL — PAGE 5

Closing Entry No. 2

	DATE	ACCOUNT TITLE	POST. REF.	DEBIT	CREDIT	
14	30	Income and Expense Summary	33	4166 00		14
15		Purchases	51		3234 00	15
16		Delivery Expense	61		53 00	16
17		Insurance Expense	62		31 00	17
18		Miscellaneous Expense	63		23 00	18
19		Rent Expense	64		300 00	19
20		Salary Expense	65		400 00	20
21		Supplies Expense	66		125 00	21
22						22

Closing entry No. 2 — closing the cost account and the expense accounts

After closing entry No. 2 is posted, the cost account and the expense accounts have zero balances, as shown in the T accounts below and on the next page. The total of these account balances, $4,166.00, is shown as a debit in the income and expense summary account.

The income and expense summary account now contains all the information that was used to calculate the net income for the fiscal period. In the income and expense summary account, the total

Income and Expense Summary			33
Beg. Inv.	6,245.00	End. Inv.	6,310.00
Cost & Expenses	4,166.00	Income	4,721.00

Purchases			51
Balance	3,234.00	Closing	3,234.00

Delivery Expense			61
Balance	53.00	Closing	53.00

Insurance Expense			62
Balance	31.00	Closing	31.00

Miscellaneous Expense			63
Balance	23.00	Closing	23.00

of the credit side, $11,031.00, minus the total of the debit side, $10,411.00, equals $620.00. This amount, $620.00, is the same as the amount of net income shown on the work sheet on page 355.

Rent Expense 64

Balance	300.00	Closing	300.00

Salary Expense 65

Balance	400.00	Closing	400.00

Supplies Expense 66

Balance	125.00	Closing	125.00

Closing entry No. 3 — closing the income and expense summary account

The balance of the income and expense summary account is closed into the proprietor's capital account. The information for this closing entry is obtained from the Net Income line of the work sheet illustrated on page 355. The closing entry as it appears in the general journal is shown below.

GENERAL JOURNAL PAGE 5

	DATE	ACCOUNT TITLE	POST. REF.	DEBIT	CREDIT	
22	30	Income and Expense Summary	33	620 00		22
23		John McCann, Capital	31		620 00	23
24						24
25						25

Closing Entry No. 3 (lines 22–23)

Closing entry No. 3 — closing the income and expense summary account

After closing entry No. 3 is posted, the income and expense summary account has a zero balance. The net income, $620.00, is shown as a credit in the proprietor's capital account.

Income and Expense Summary 33

Beg. Inv.	6,245.00	End. Inv.	6,310.00
Cost & Expenses	4,166.00	Income	4,721.00
Net Income	620.00		

John McCann, Capital 31

		Beg. Bal.	9,121.00
		Addnl. Investment	1,000.00
		Net Income	620.00

If business operations result in a net loss instead of a net income, the income and expense summary account is closed by debiting the proprietor's capital account and crediting the income and expense summary account.

Closing entry No. 4 — closing the proprietor's drawing account into the proprietor's capital account

Withdrawals by the proprietor decrease his capital. Therefore, at the end of the fiscal period, the total withdrawals shown in the proprietor's drawing account are closed into the proprietor's capital account. The work sheet for McCann Office Furniture, page 318, shows that Mr. McCann has withdrawn a total of $350.00 during the fiscal period.

The closing entry in the general journal to transfer the balance of the drawing account to the capital account is shown below.

GENERAL JOURNAL — PAGE 5

	DATE	ACCOUNT TITLE	POST. REF.	DEBIT	CREDIT	
24	30	John McCann, Capital	31	350 00		24
25		John McCann, Drawing	32		350 00	25
26						26

Closing Entry No. 4

Closing entry No. 4 — closing the drawing account

After closing entry No. 4 is posted, the drawing account has a zero balance. The debit of $350.00 to the John McCann, Capital, account shows the decrease in proprietorship resulting from withdrawals of assets from the business.

John McCann, Drawing — 32

Debit		Credit	
Balance	350.00	Closing	350.00

John McCann, Capital — 31

Debit		Credit	
Withdrawals	350.00	Beg. Bal.	9,121.00
		Addnl. Investment	1,000.00
		Net Income	620.00

After closing entry No. 4 is posted, the debit side of John McCann's capital account has only one entry. This debit of $350.00 shows the decrease in his proprietorship because of his total withdrawals of cash and merchandise for personal use during this fiscal period.

> Withdrawals are accumulated in the proprietor's drawing account during each fiscal period and are then closed into the proprietor's capital account at the end of each fiscal period.

The credit side of John McCann's capital account has three entries: (a) the balance of his capital account at the beginning of this fiscal period, $9,121.00; (b) the increase in his proprietorship because of his additional investment, $1,000.00; and (c) the increase in his proprietorship from the operations of the business for this fiscal period, $620.00.

The balance of John McCann's capital account on November 30 is his new net worth at the end of this fiscal period, $10,391.00. This amount is the same as that which appears in Mr. McCann's capital statement shown on page 334 and in the balance sheet on page 337.

THE COMPLETED GENERAL LEDGER

After the adjusting entries and the closing entries have been recorded in the general journal and posted to the general ledger accounts, the accounts are ruled and balanced. The steps in ruling and balancing general ledger accounts are described in Chapter 11, pages 150 to 152.

The general ledger for McCann Office Furniture, after all the work at the end of the fiscal period has been completed, is shown on pages 360 to 362. All the balance sheet accounts have been ruled and balanced. The new balance in each of these accounts has been brought down below the double ruled lines.

> The merchandise inventory account might have been balanced in the same manner as the cash account. The first debit is exactly equal to the credit and the second debit is the balance of the account. Thus, it is satisfactory to draw the double lines directly under the first debit and the first credit. The debit that remains below the double lines is the new account balance, the amount of the ending inventory.

All the income statement accounts are now in balance. They are all ruled with double lines to show that they are closed. Since their balances have been closed into the income and expense summary account, no balance is brought down below the double ruled lines.

POST-CLOSING TRIAL BALANCE

A post-closing trial balance is taken to prove that the sum of the debit balances is equal to the sum of the credit balances in the general ledger accounts. The post-closing trial balance for McCann Office Furniture, November 30, 1967, is shown on page 363.

All income, cost, and expense accounts as well as the proprietor's drawing account and the income and expense summary account have been closed. Only the balance sheet accounts remain open. The account balances listed on the post-closing trial balance agree with the account balances shown on the balance sheet on page 337. This is proof that the ledger has been brought up-to-date and is in balance.

Cash ACCOUNT NO. 11

DATE		ITEMS	POST. REF.	DEBIT	DATE		ITEMS	POST. REF.	CREDIT
1967 Nov.	1	Balance	✓	2500 00	1967 Nov.	30		CP12	3270 00
	30		CR10	5541 00		30	Balance	✓	4771 00
		4,771.00		8041 00					
				8041 00					8041 00
1967 Dec.	1	Balance	✓	4771 00					

Accounts Receivable ACCOUNT NO. 12

DATE		ITEMS	POST. REF.	DEBIT	DATE		ITEMS	POST. REF.	CREDIT
1967 Nov.	1	Balance	✓	1102 00	1967 Nov.	30		CR10	2130 00
	30		S9	2310 00		30	Balance	✓	1282 00
		1,282.00		3412 00					
				3412 00					3412 00
1967 Dec.	1	Balance	✓	1282 00					

Merchandise Inventory ACCOUNT NO. 13

DATE		ITEMS	POST. REF.	DEBIT	DATE		ITEMS	POST. REF.	CREDIT
1967 Nov.	1	Balance	✓	6245 00	1967 Nov.	30		J5	6245 00
	30		J5	6310 00					

Supplies ACCOUNT NO. 14

DATE		ITEMS	POST. REF.	DEBIT	DATE		ITEMS	POST. REF.	CREDIT
1967 Nov.	1	Balance	✓	155 00	1967 Nov.	30		J5	125 00
	30		J4	112 00		30	Balance	✓	142 00
		142.00		267 00					
				267 00					267 00
1967 Dec.	1	Balance	✓	142 00					

Prepaid Insurance ACCOUNT NO. 15

DATE		ITEMS	POST. REF.	DEBIT	DATE		ITEMS	POST. REF.	CREDIT
1967 Nov.	1	Balance	✓	199 00	1967 Nov.	30		J5	31 00
						30	Balance	✓	168 00
				199 00					199 00
1967 Dec.	1	Balance	✓	168 00					

General ledger closed, ruled, and balanced

Accounts Payable — ACCOUNT NO. 21

DATE		ITEMS	POST. REF.	DEBIT	DATE		ITEMS	POST. REF.	CREDIT
1967 Nov.	30		CP12	2170 00	1967 Nov.	1	Balance	✓	1080 00
	30	Balance	✓	2282 00		30		P10	3260 00
						30	2,282.00	J4	112 00
									4452 00
				4452 00					4452 00
					1967 Dec.	1	Balance	✓	2282 00

John McCann, Capital — ACCOUNT NO. 31

DATE		ITEMS	POST. REF.	DEBIT	DATE		ITEMS	POST. REF.	CREDIT
1967 Nov.	30		J5	350 00	1967 Nov.	1	Balance	✓	9121 00
	30	Balance	✓	10391 00		4	9,771.00	CR10	1000 00
									10121 00
						30		J5	620 00
				10741 00					10741 00
					1967 Dec.	1	Balance		10391 00

John McCann, Drawing — ACCOUNT NO. 32

DATE		ITEMS	POST. REF.	DEBIT	DATE		ITEMS	POST. REF.	CREDIT
1967 Nov.	9		CP12	100 00	1967 Nov.	30		J5	350 00
	16		J4	150 00					
	29		CP12	100 00					
				350 00					
				350 00					350 00

Income and Expense Summary — ACCOUNT NO. 33

DATE		ITEMS	POST. REF.	DEBIT	DATE		ITEMS	POST. REF.	CREDIT
1967 Nov.	30		J5	6245 00	1967 Nov.	30		J5	6310 00
	30		J5	4166 00		30		J5	4721 00
			J5	620 00					
				11031 00					11031 00

Sales — ACCOUNT NO. 41

DATE		ITEMS	POST. REF.	DEBIT	DATE		ITEMS	POST. REF.	CREDIT
1967 Nov.	30		J5	4721 00	1967 Nov.	30		S9	2310 00
						30		CR10	2411 00
									4721 00
				4721 00					4721 00

General ledger closed, ruled, and balanced (continued)

Purchases — ACCOUNT NO. 51

DATE		ITEMS	POST. REF.	DEBIT	DATE		ITEMS	POST. REF.	CREDIT
1967 Nov.	10		CP12	124 00	1967 Nov.	16		J4	150 00
	30	3,234.00	P10	3260 00		30		J5	3234 00
				3384 00					
				3384 00					3384 00

Delivery Expense — ACCOUNT NO. 61

DATE		ITEMS	POST. REF.	DEBIT	DATE		ITEMS	POST. REF.	CREDIT
1967 Nov.	17		CP12	25 00	1967 Nov.	30		J5	53 00
	28		CP12	28 00					
				53 00					
				53 00					53 00

Insurance Expense — ACCOUNT NO. 62

DATE		ITEMS	POST. REF.	DEBIT	DATE		ITEMS	POST. REF.	CREDIT
1967 Nov.	30		J5	31 00	1967 Nov.	30		J5	31 00

Miscellaneous Expense — ACCOUNT NO. 63

DATE		ITEMS	POST. REF.	DEBIT	DATE		ITEMS	POST. REF.	CREDIT
1967 Nov.	14		CP12	11 00	1967 Nov.	30		J5	23 00
	21		CP12	12 00					
				23 00					
				23 00					23 00

Rent Expense — ACCOUNT NO. 64

DATE		ITEMS	POST. REF.	DEBIT	DATE		ITEMS	POST. REF.	CREDIT
1967 Nov.	2		CP12	300 00	1967 Nov.	30		J5	300 00

Salary Expense — ACCOUNT NO. 65

DATE		ITEMS	POST. REF.	DEBIT	DATE		ITEMS	POST. REF.	CREDIT
1967 Nov.	17		CP12	200 00	1967 Nov.	30		J5	400 00
	30		CP12	200 00					
				400 00					
				400 00					400 00

Supplies Expense — ACCOUNT NO. 66

DATE		ITEMS	POST. REF.	DEBIT	DATE		ITEMS	POST. REF.	CREDIT
1967 Nov.	30		J5	125 00	1967 Nov.	30		J5	125 00

General ledger closed, ruled, and balanced (concluded)

McCann Office Furniture Post-Closing Trial Balance November 30, 1967		
Cash	4771 00	
Accounts Receivable	1282 00	
Merchandise Inventory	6310 00	
Supplies	142 00	
Prepaid Insurance	168 00	
Accounts Payable		2282 00
John McCann, Capital		10391 00
	12673 00	12673 00

Post-closing trial balance

Study Questions

1. Why are the adjustments that are planned on the work sheet recorded as entries in a journal?
2. What changes are made in the general ledger accounts by the adjustment for the beginning merchandise inventory?
3. Where is the explanation for the adjusting entries written in the general journal?
4. What changes in the general ledger accounts are made by the adjustment for the ending merchandise inventory?
5. After the adjustment for supplies used has been recorded in the general journal and posted to the general ledger accounts, what does the balance of the supplies account represent?
6. Why is it necessary to adjust the prepaid insurance account?
7. Why is it necessary to make closing entries at the end of the fiscal period?
8. From what columns of the work sheet is the information obtained for making the closing entries to close income accounts, cost accounts, and expense accounts?
9. To what account are the balances of all income accounts, cost accounts, and expense accounts transferred by the closing entries?
10. To what account is the balance of the income and expense summary account transferred by a closing entry?
11. Why is the proprietor's drawing account transferred to the proprietor's capital account by a closing entry?
12. Why should a post-closing trial balance be prepared after the adjusting and closing entries have been posted to the general ledger accounts?

Cases for Business Decision

CASE 1

After Mr. Crowley had studied his balance sheet and income statement, he decided that he did not need all of his $12,590.00 in capital to operate his business. He therefore decided to withdraw some of the capital and invest it in government bonds. What are some of the decisions he will have to make in order to determine how much he can safely withdraw?

CASE 2

When Mr. Farrell compared his November 30 post-closing trial balance with the post-closing trial balance for the previous month, he noticed that he had $2,100.00 more merchandise on hand at the end of November than he had at the end of October. What are some of the questions that Mr. Farrell should ask himself regarding this increase in the amount of merchandise inventory?

CASE 3

At the end of a fiscal period, Miss Cole prepares a trial balance and the financial statements. She does not, however, make any adjusting and closing entries. What effect will this omission of adjusting and closing entries have on her records at the end of the next fiscal period?

Drills for Understanding

DRILL 20-A **Adjusting entries**

A part of the Trial Balance columns and a part of the Adjustments columns of the work sheet for Sam Greenwood are shown below.

Account Titles	Trial Balance		Adjustments	
	Debit	Credit	Debit	Credit
Merchandise Inventory	9,000 00		(b) 5,000 00	(a) 9,000 00
Supplies	210 00			(c) 85 00
Prepaid Insurance	90 00			(d) 35 00
Income and Expense Summary			(a) 9,000 00	(b) 5,000 00
Insurance Expense			(d) 35 00	
Supplies Expense			(c) 85 00	

Instructions: 1. On a separate sheet of paper prepare a T account for each of the six accounts listed in the partial work sheet on page 364. If the account has a balance, record it on the proper side of the T account.

2. In the appropriate T accounts, record the debit amount and the credit amount for each of the following:

a The adjusting entry for the beginning merchandise inventory.
b The adjusting entry for the ending merchandise inventory.
c The adjusting entry for supplies used.
d The adjusting entry for expired insurance.

DRILL 20-B | Closing entries

A portion of the Income Statement columns and a part of the Balance Sheet columns of the work sheet for Sam Greenwood are shown below.

Account Titles	Income Statement		Balance Sheet	
	Debit	Credit	Debit	Credit
Sam Greenwood, Capital				17,000 00
Sam Greenwood, Drawing			400 00	
Income and Expense Summary	9,000 00	5,000 00		
Sales		8,700 00		
Purchases	2,000 00			
Insurance Expense	35 00			
Miscellaneous Expense	80 00			
Rent Expense	200 00			
Salary Expense	720 00			
Supplies Expense	85 00			
	12,120 00	13,700 00	23,580 00	22,000 00
Net Income	1,580 00			1,580 00
	13,700 00	13,700 00	23,580 00	23,580 00

Instructions: 1. On a separate sheet of paper prepare a T account for each of the ten account titles in the partial work sheet above. In each T account, record the amount that is given in the Income Statement columns or in the Balance Sheet columns.

2. In the appropriate T accounts, record the debit amount and the credit amount for each of the following:

a The closing entry to close the income account.
b The closing entry to close the cost account and the expense accounts.
c The closing entry to transfer the balance of the income and expense summary account to the capital account.
d The closing entry to transfer the balance of the drawing account to the capital account.

Application Problem

PROBLEM 20-1 | Work at the end of the fiscal period

If you are not using the workbook correlating with this textbook, complete Appendix Problem 20-A instead of this problem.

The ledger accounts of the Breece Electric Company as of April 30 of the current year, the end of the monthly fiscal period, are given in the workbook.

Instructions: 1. Foot the ledger accounts. Write the footings in very small figures with a sharp pencil and place each footing close to the last item.

2. Prove cash. The cash on hand and in the bank on April 30, 19—, is $4,587.50, which should agree with the balance in the cash account.

3. Prepare a trial balance in the Trial Balance columns of the work sheet. List each account title regardless of whether it has a balance.

4. Complete the work sheet, using the following additional data as of April 30:

Merchandise inventory..................	$11,290.30
Supplies inventory......................	264.00
Value of insurance policies...............	252.00

Compare your work with the work sheet illustrated on page 318.

5. Prepare an income statement from the information given on the work sheet. Compare your work with the income statement illustrated on page 330.

6. Prepare a capital statement from the information given on the work sheet and in the proprietor's capital account. Compare your work with the capital statement illustrated on page 334.

7. Prepare a balance sheet in report form from the information given on the work sheet. Compare your work with the balance sheet illustrated on page 337.

8. Record on page 2 of a general journal the adjusting entries shown in the Adjustments columns of the work sheet. Compare your work with the adjusting entries illustrated on pages 350 to 353.

9. Record in the general journal the closing entries from the information shown in the Income Statement columns and the Balance Sheet columns of the work sheet. Compare your work with the closing entries illustrated on pages 355 to 358.

10. Post the adjusting entries and the closing entries.

11. Rule the accounts that are closed. Balance and rule the open accounts. Compare your work with the general ledger accounts illustrated on pages 360 to 362.

12. Prepare a post-closing trial balance. Compare your work with the post-closing trial balance illustrated on page 363.

PRACTICE SET 1 | SPENCER ATHLETIC GOODS

PART 2 WORK AT THE END OF THE FISCAL PERIOD

At this time you are to complete the work at the end of a fiscal period for Spencer Athletic Goods. For this work you will need all the records that you completed for the month of October in Part 1 of this practice set.

Instructions: 1. Complete the eight-column work sheet, using the following data as of October 31 for adjustments. Compare your work with the work sheet on page 318.

Merchandise inventory..................	$68,845.00
Supplies inventory......................	850.00
Value of insurance policies...............	480.00

2. Prepare an income statement from the information given on the work sheet. Compare your work with the income statement illustrated on page 330.

3. Prepare a capital statement from the information given on the work sheet. Compare your work with the capital statement illustrated on page 334.

4. Prepare a balance sheet from the information given on the work sheet. Compare your work with the balance sheet illustrated on page 337.

5. Record in the general journal the adjusting entries for the adjustments shown in the Adjustments columns of the work sheet. Compare your work with the adjusting entries illustrated on pages 350 to 353.

6. Record in the general journal the closing entries from the information shown in the Income Statement columns and the Balance Sheet columns of the work sheet. Compare your work with the closing entries illustrated on pages 355 to 358.

7. Post the adjusting entries and the closing entries.

8. Rule the accounts in the general ledger that are closed. Rule and balance the open accounts. Compare your work with the general ledger accounts illustrated on pages 360 to 362.

9. Prepare a post-closing trial balance. Compare your work with the post-closing trial balance illustrated on page 363.

PROCESSING BOOKKEEPING DATA

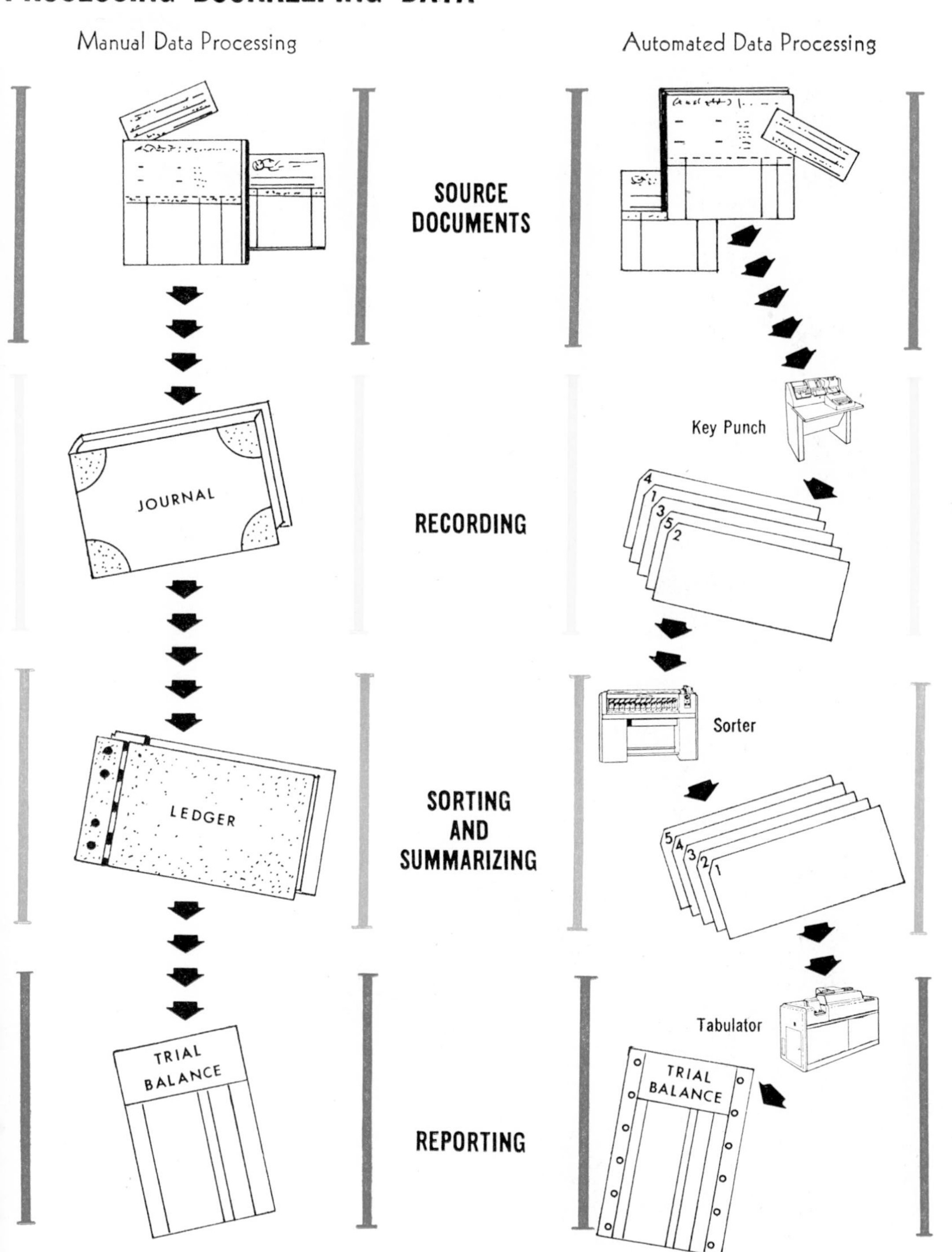

General Electric

Computer system including computer, magnetic tape handlers, tape reader/punch, console, card punches, card readers, and printer

CHAPTER 21 AUTOMATED DATA PROCESSING IN BOOKKEEPING

Recording, sorting, classifying, calculating, summarizing, and reporting the financial facts of a business are called *data processing*. A bookkeeper processes data when he journalizes, posts, takes a trial balance, and prepares a work sheet — in fact, whenever he handles detailed information.

Business is continually searching for more efficient means of processing financial information. As a result of this search, many new kinds of machines and equipment are being invented for use in processing bookkeeping data. The procedures described in this textbook are examples of some methods of data processing in bookkeeping. Data processing is done by hand, by bookkeeping machines, and by automated data processing equipment. A business processes its data by the method that best fits its needs.

MANUAL DATA PROCESSING

Keeping bookkeeping records by hand is called *manual data processing*. In the previous parts of this textbook, various procedures of manual data processing have been described. For example, in Part 1, the proprietor of the Hill-Top Motel used an autographic register for recording by hand each receipt of cash. Each day the cash receipts transactions were journalized by hand. At the end of the month, the total cash receipts were manually posted to the cash account and to the room sales account.

Write-it-once principle

The procedure of producing more than one copy of data in only one writing is called the *write-it-once principle*. Most businesses use the write-it-once principle to some extent in their bookkeeping systems. For example, when the Hill-Top Motel recorded a cash receipt on the autographic register, a carbon copy was made at the same time. More than one carbon copy could have been made if additional copies were needed.

Using the typewriter to process data

The typewriter is used to apply the write-it-once principle when a number of copies of the same data must be prepared. A set of forms assembled with carbon paper so that all the copies can be prepared at the same time is called a *carbon pack*. An illustration of a carbon pack for invoices is shown below.

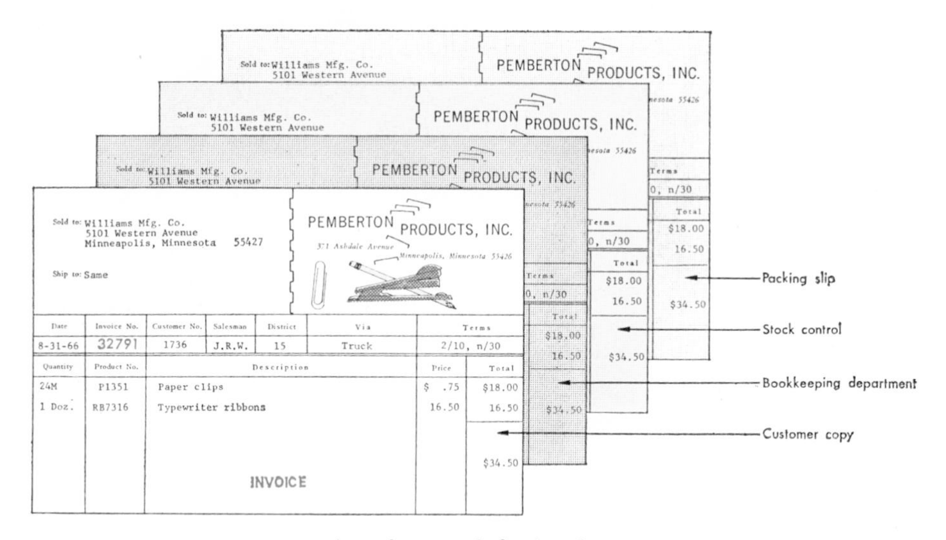

PEMBERTON PRODUCTS, INC.
371 Ashdale Avenue
Minneapolis, Minnesota 55426

Sold to: Williams Mfg. Co.
5101 Western Avenue
Minneapolis, Minnesota 55427

Ship to: Same

Date	Invoice No.	Customer No.	Salesman	District	Via	Terms
8-31-66	32791	1736	J.R.W.	15	Truck	2/10, n/30

Quantity	Product No.	Description	Price	Total
24M	P1351	Paper clips	$ .75	$18.00
1 Doz.	RB7316	Typewriter ribbons	16.50	16.50
				$34.50

INVOICE

A carbon pack for invoices

After the desired data have been typewritten on the carbon pack, the carbon paper is removed. The copies are separated and distributed to the persons who need the data. For example, as shown in the illustration above, the *original copy* of the invoice (white copy) is sent to the customer; the *second copy* (pink) is sent to the bookkeeping department for recording the data in the sales journal and for posting to the accounts receivable ledger; the *third copy* (yellow) is sent to the stock clerk, who makes the necessary entries on the stock records; and the *fourth copy* (blue) is sent to the shipping department to be packed with the shipment of merchandise.

Some business forms are printed on chemically coated paper that eliminates the need for using carbon paper. When "no carbon required" or "carbonless" paper is used, the writing or typing on the top sheet presses the chemical coatings together. This causes the data recorded on the top sheet to be reproduced instantly on the second and all following sheets.

Recording data on a pegboard

When data are recorded by hand, a specially designed writing board, such as that shown on the next page, may be used. A device used for writing the same information on several kinds of forms at the same time is called a *pegboard.* The pegboard is also known as an *accounting board* or a *writing board.*

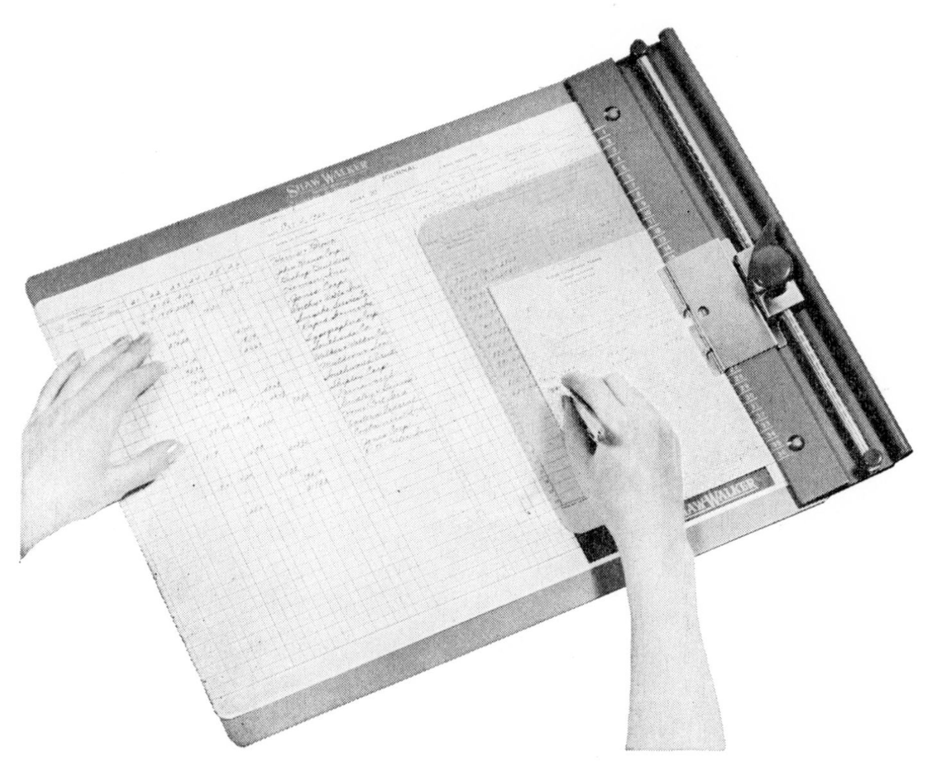

The Shaw-Walker Company

A pegboard

The pegboard has two major purposes: (1) to provide a solid writing base; and (2) to provide a means of holding several bookkeeping forms in proper alignment while data are being recorded. Carbon paper or carbonless paper is used so that the data written on the top form are reproduced on all other forms at the same time. For example, when a sale on account is to be recorded, a page of the sales journal is attached to the pegboard. Next, the customer's ledger sheet is properly positioned on top the sales journal page. Then, a monthly statement form for the customer is positioned on top both of these sheets. Thus, as the information about a charge sale is written on the monthly statement form, the same data are recorded on the customer's ledger sheet and on the sales journal page. The data are written only once, but they are recorded on three different bookkeeping records at the same time.

BOOKKEEPING MACHINES IN DATA PROCESSING

An office machine that carries forward balances, calculates, and prints the results on bookkeeping forms is called a *bookkeeping machine.* The bookkeeping machine has a movable carriage similar to that found on a typewriter. Thus, the carriage can move back and forth as data are being recorded on bookkeeping forms. A general-purpose bookkeeping machine is shown in the illustration below.

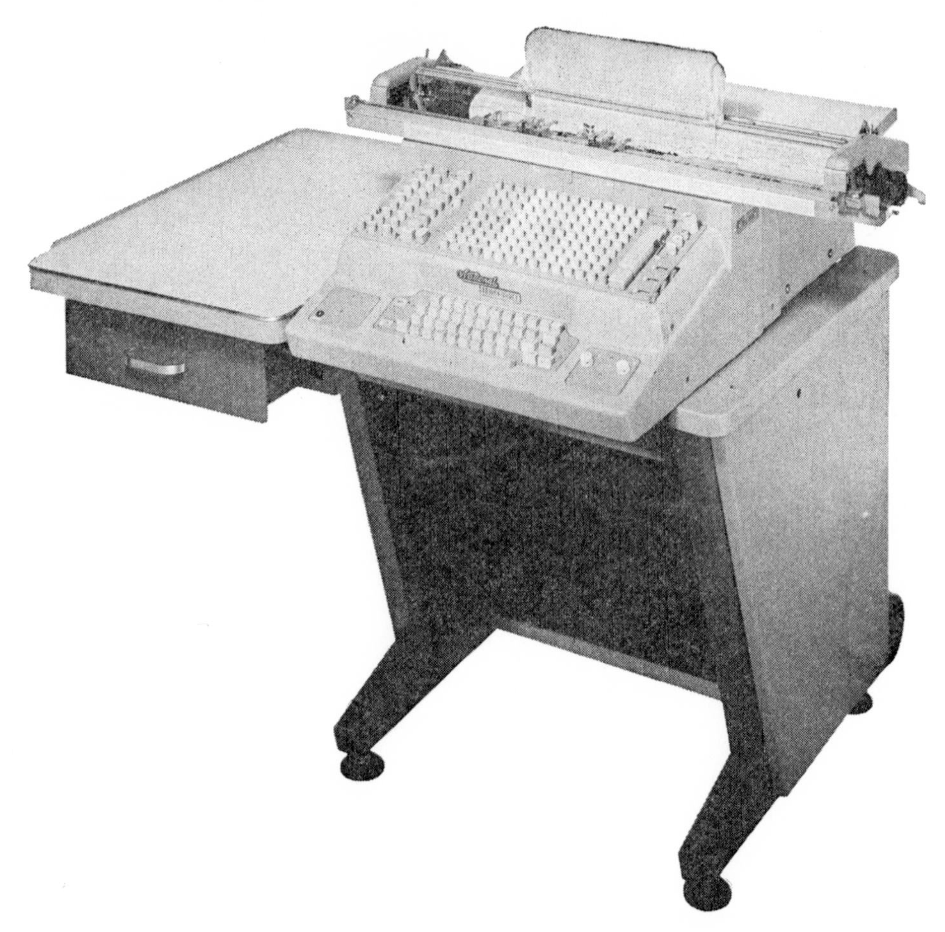

The National Cash Register Company

General-purpose bookkeeping machine

The principles followed when using a bookkeeping machine are the same as when recording data manually. The business forms used on bookkeeping machines may differ, however, from those used when recording data manually. For example, in manual data processing, the accounts receivable account may appear as shown at the top of the next page.

Accounts Receivable ACCOUNT NO. 12

DATE		ITEMS	POST. REF.	DEBIT	DATE	ITEMS	POST. REF.	CREDIT
1967 Nov.	1	Balance	✓	8600 00				
	30		S148	2700 00				
				11300 00				

General ledger account used for processing data manually

When a bookkeeping machine is used, the ledger card for the accounts receivable account may look like this:

LEDGER

ACCOUNT TITLE ACCOUNTS RECEIVABLE

ACCOUNT NO. 12

DATE	FOLIO	DEBITS	CREDITS	BALANCE
NOV 1'67			BALANCE FWD. →	8,600.00 •
NOV 30'67	148	2,700.00		11,300.00 •

General ledger card for processing data on a bookkeeping machine

The following steps show how a bookkeeping machine may be used in posting to the general ledger card illustrated above:

1. The ledger card is inserted into the carriage of the bookkeeping machine. The November 1 balance, $8,600.00, was prerecorded.
2. The carriage is moved so that the printing position is at the extreme left of the card, and the amount of the balance brought forward, *$8,600.00,* is entered by the operator on the keyboard of the machine.
3. The carriage moves to the Date column. The date, *Nov. 30, 1967,* is entered on the keyboard of the machine, which prints the information in the Date column.
4. The carriage moves to the Folio (Post. Ref.) column. The page number of the sales journal, *148,* is entered on the keyboard and the machine prints the number in the Folio column.

   The Folio column on the ledger card is used in the same way as the Posting Reference column. The Folio column shows the source of the data being recorded.

5. The carriage moves to the Debits column. The total amount of the debit, *$2,700.00*, as shown on page 148 of the sales journal, is entered on the keyboard and printed on the ledger card. When the bookkeeping machine is in this position on the ledger card, the amount entered in the Debits column, *$2,700.00*, is added to the balance brought forward, *$8,600.00*, which was entered on the keyboard in Step 2.
6. The carriage moves to the Balance column and prints the up-to-date balance of the account, *$11,300.00*.

The bookkeeping machine applies the write-it-once principle when it is used to prepare several bookkeeping records at the same time. For example, a page of the sales journal, a customer's ledger card, and a monthly statement form may be inserted in the machine. When the bookkeeping machine prints the data on the top form, the data are recorded on the other forms at the same time.

Similar procedures are followed when a bookkeeping machine is used to prepare ledger cards for creditors, payroll records, and other kinds of records where the same data must be recorded more than once on several forms. Because the data are recorded at the same time on more than one bookkeeping record, there is less chance that an error will be made than if the data were recorded separately on each form.

AUTOMATED DATA PROCESSING

The process by which work is done automatically with a minimum amount of human effort is called *automation*. Machines that handle data with little or no human help are used to do the work. Keeping bookkeeping records by means of machines and equipment that operate automatically is known as *automated data processing* (*ADP*). Automated data processing procedures eliminate the need for the rewriting of records. Thus, by making use of the write-it-once principle, the automated equipment reduces the possibility of errors caused by recopying the data in each record needed.

Punched cards

For most data processing machines and equipment, the bookkeeping data must be prepared in a form that can be "read" by the automated machines. One way to prepare data to be "read" by automated machines is to punch holes in a card so that each hole or combination of holes represents a number, or a letter, or a symbol. An example of a card *before* data have been punched into it is shown at the top of the next page.

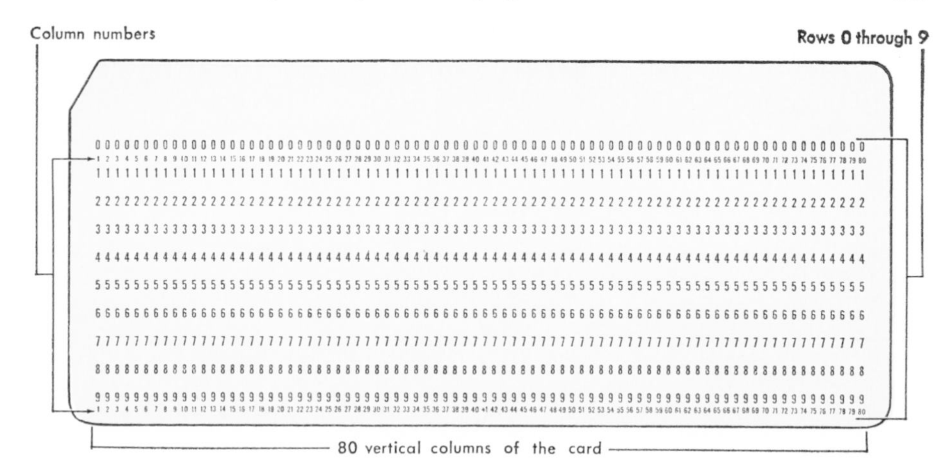

Blank card

The blank card shown above is divided into 80 vertical columns. The very small numbers at the top and the bottom of the card identify each of these 80 columns. Each of these columns is numbered 0 through 9. Each vertical column is divided into 10 rows. Each of the 80 columns on the card can be used for punching a hole or holes to represent a number, a letter, or a symbol.

Preparing punched cards

A machine used to make the holes in a card is called a *card-punch machine*. This machine is also called a *key-punch machine*. The illustration below shows one kind of card-punch machine.

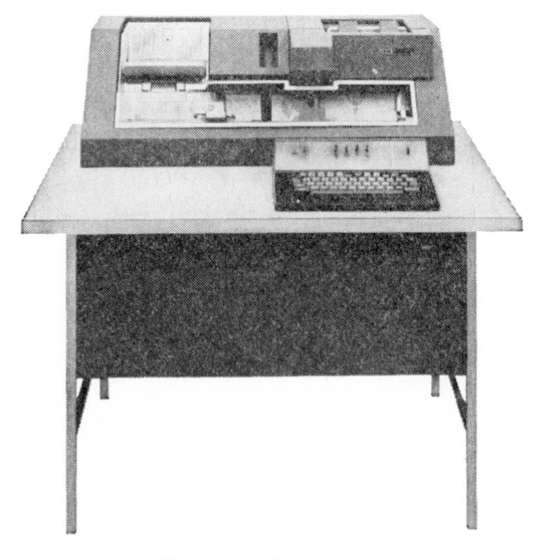

Card-punch machine

Recording numeric data. The card illustrated below shows how the holes are punched to record the digits 0 through 9. Only one digit can be punched in any one of the 80 columns. If a two-digit number, such as 10, is to be recorded, two columns of the card must be punched. While it is possible to punch both 1 and 0 in the same column, the machines that process the cards would be unable to "read" the amount as 10. The recording of numbers with more than one digit, such as 10, 456, and 7,040, is shown on the card below.

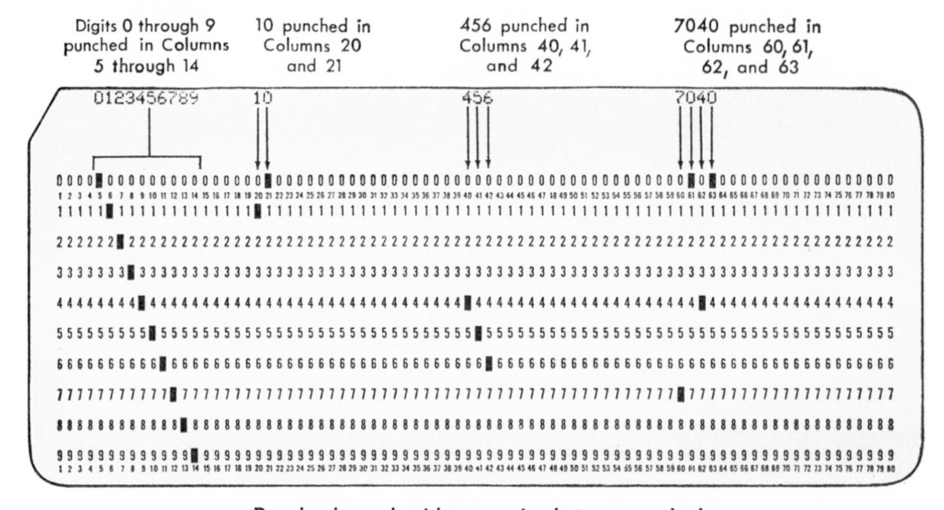

Punched card with numeric data recorded

Recording alphabetic data. To record a letter of the alphabet, two holes are punched in each column. The illustration at the right shows how each letter of the alphabet is recorded in a punched card.

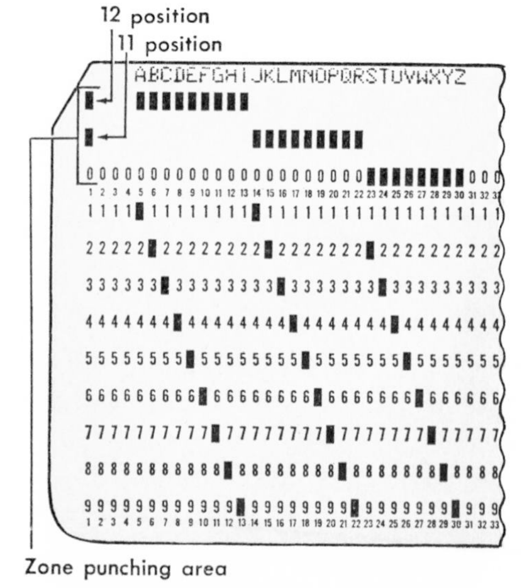

Alphabet recorded in a punched card

When alphabetic data are recorded in the card, two additional punching positions are used, as shown in the illustration at the right. The punching position nearest the top of a punched card is called the 12 position. The punching position immediately below is known as the 11 position. The 12 and 11 positions, along with the 0 row, make up the zone punching area of the card. Each letter of the alphabet is recorded by one zone punch and one digit punch in the same vertical column. For example, the letter A is recorded with one zone punch in the 12 position and one digit punch in the 1 row.

The names of individuals and businesses are usually abbreviated before such data are recorded in punched cards. This is done to save space so that a greater amount of information can be recorded in the 80 available columns. On the card shown at the right, the name of the business, Rogers Company, has been abbreviated and recorded as Rogers Co.

A column is left blank to separate words on a punched card. On the card at the right, column 7 has been left blank to show a space between the words *Rogers* and *Co.*

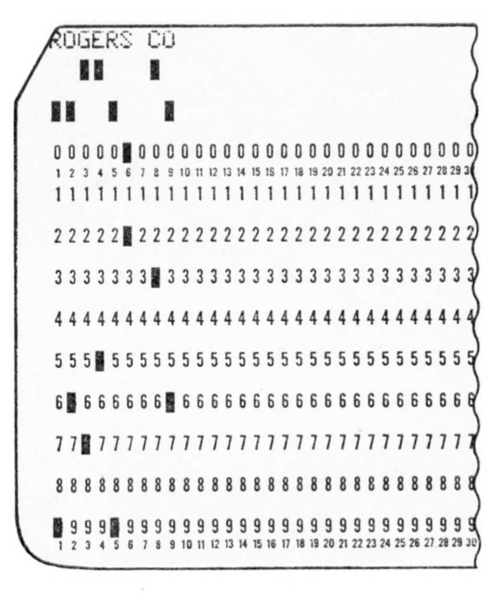

Name of business recorded in a punched card

To record a maximum amount of data in a punched card, a numeric code is often used. For example, instead of writing the complete name and address of a customer, a code number may be assigned to each customer. The number is punched into the card to identify the customer. In this way, all cards related to business dealings with the same customer can be identified by the customer's number. If, for example, Rogers Company were assigned the code number 29, this number rather than the company name would be punched into the card. Thus, by using this code number, seven columns on the punched card are saved and made available for the recording of additional data.

Recording special symbols. In addition to numeric and alphabetic data, certain special symbols can be recorded in a punched card as shown at the top of the next page. The special symbols (& # , $. - / @ % * ⌑) are made by one, two, and sometimes three punches in one card column.

In recording and processing bookkeeping data, special symbols are often omitted. For example, dollar signs and decimal points are not usually written in the amount columns of bookkeeping forms. The card at the

Special symbols recorded in a punched card

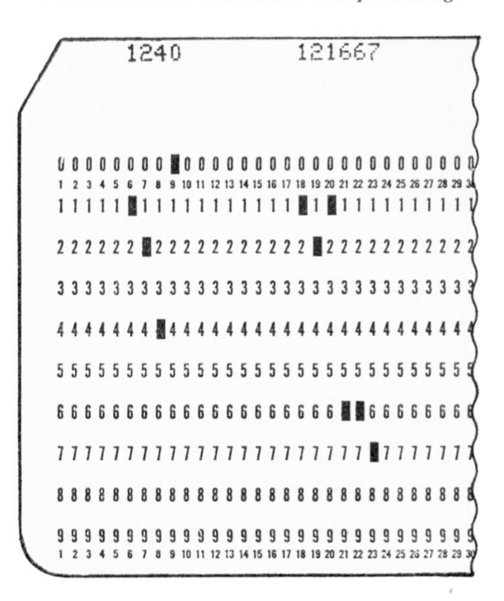

An amount of money and a date recorded in a punched card

above right shows the amount $12.40 punched in columns 6 to 9. The last two digits of the amount are understood to be cents. Therefore, it is not necessary to punch holes for either the dollar sign or the decimal point. If the dollar sign and the decimal point are not used, two columns on the card are saved and made available for additional data.

A date can be written in abbreviated form. For example, December 16, 1967, can be written as 12–16–67 or as 12/16/67. By omitting the symbols for the hyphen or the diagonal mark, the date can be punched as 121667 in six columns, as shown on the card at the above right.

The complete punched-card language

Only the punches for the numbers, the alphabet, and the special symbols can be "read" by the machines that process punched cards. Any other punches in any column on the card could not be interpreted by the data processing equipment. The card illustrated on the next page contains the complete punched-card language that is understood by machines used to process punched-card data.

Assuring the accuracy of punched cards

The business records and reports prepared from punched cards will be only as accurate as the data punched into the cards. Therefore, it is customary to verify the cards to make sure they have been correctly punched before they are used. The machine that is used to check the accuracy of punched cards is called a *verifier*. A verifier has much the same appearance

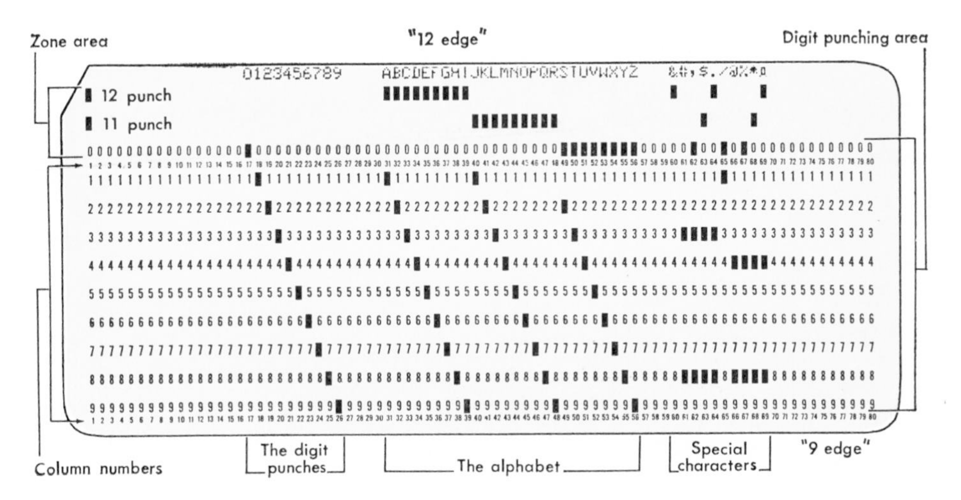

The complete language on a punched card

as a card-punch machine. After the cards have been prepared on the card-punch machine, the verifier is used to check that the data have been correctly punched in the proper position on the cards.

Uses of punched cards

The original punched cards containing complete bookkeeping data about a sale of merchandise on account can be reused for any of the following purposes:

1. To prepare multiple copies of the sales invoice.
2. To prepare the customer's statement of account.
3. To record the amount of the sale as a debit to the customer's account in the subsidiary ledger.
4. To record the amount of the sale as a debit to Accounts Receivable and as a credit to Sales in the general ledger.
5. To record items sold as deductions from stock in the inventory records.
6. To prepare various analyses of sales, such as sales by type of goods sold, sales by territory, and sales by name of salesman.

After the cards have been punched and verified, there is little danger of error in using and reusing the data recorded in the cards. Each data processing machine "reads" the holes and interprets them as letters, numbers, and symbols. The letter, number, or symbol will be "read" the same by all the machines each time the card is used.

THE AUTOMATED DATA PROCESSING CYCLE

In an automated data processing system, as well as in processing bookkeeping data by hand, the source documents are prepared manually. After the source documents have been prepared, however, the remainder of the work in the automated data processing cycle is done with little need for human help. The automated data processing cycle consists of three phases: (1) input, (2) processing and storage, and (3) output.

Input

The data to be processed in an automated data processing system are called *input*. The data are taken from source documents and recorded in a form that can be "read" by the data processing equipment. The special forms in which data are recorded for processing by automated equipment are called *input media*. Some common forms of input media are punched cards, punched paper tape, magnetic tape, and magnetic ink characters.

Punched cards. The punched card, described earlier in this chapter, is a widely used form of input media.

Punched paper tape. A special tape-punch machine is used to punch holes in a roll of narrow paper tape in much the same way holes are punched in cards. The location and position of the holes in the paper tape can be "read" by machines designed to process this kind of input media. The illustration below shows a strip of punched paper tape in which the numbers 0 through 9, the letters of the alphabet, and several symbols are punched.

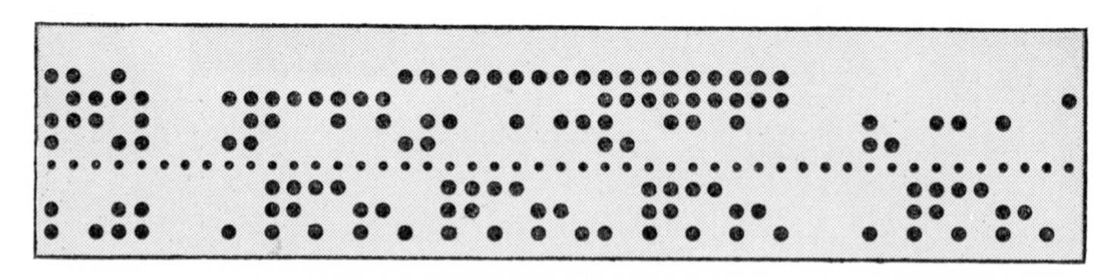

Punched paper tape

Magnetic tape. The magnetic tape used in data processing is similar to that used in tape recorders. The data are recorded on magnetic tape in the form of invisible magnetized spots that can be "read" by automatic machines. Magnetic tape can be "erased" and used again. Magnetic tape can be "read" much faster by automated data processing machines than is true of punched tape or punched cards.

Magnetic ink characters. The use of magnetic ink characters in the processing of data is called *magnetic ink character recognition* (*MICR*). As mentioned in Chapter 17, the magnetic ink character readers that "read" and process data are used principally by banks for sorting checks and other documents. The magnetic ink character reader senses the surface area of each character and recognizes its shape. The characters are printed in a style that is not exactly like ordinary numbers. Regular numbers, especially 2, 5, 6, and 9, are too much alike to be recognized accurately by the character reader.

The illustration below shows a check with magnetic ink characters printed along the lower margin of the check. The Federal Reserve check routing symbol, the bank's identification number, and the depositor's account number are printed in magnetic ink by the bank before the blank checks are issued to the depositor. The amount of the check, printed in the lower right-hand corner, is placed there later by a special machine used by the bank that is the first to handle the check.

Check with magnetic ink characters

The use of magnetic ink characters makes it possible for MICR machines to do any or all of the following operations:

1. Sort the checks by Federal Reserve bank number.
2. Sort the checks by the bank's identification number.
3. Sort the checks by the depositor's account number.
4. Feed check amounts and account numbers to accounting machines that prepare journals and post to depositors' accounts.

Processing and storage

Prior to the processing of data, during their processing, and sometimes after the data have been processed, it is necessary to store the data until they are needed again. Keeping the input media or data until needed is called *storage*.

In automated data processing, the work is planned so that the data may be sorted and accumulated according to the code used to prepare the input media. For example, the data on each sales invoice prepared during the day may be recorded on punched cards. The information about each item of merchandise sold is recorded on a separate card. A separate card containing all the information needed about each item is called a *unit record.*

Unit record cards may be sorted by many classifications. In the example given above, the unit record cards may be sorted by the amount of sales for each item of merchandise sold, by the amount of sales for each sales territory, or by the amount of sales made by each salesman. To sort the cards and accumulate data about the amount of sales for each item of merchandise the following steps are taken:

1. The unit record cards are sorted automatically to bring together all cards for each kind of merchandise. A machine that automatically groups all punched cards of a similar kind and arranges them in numeric or alphabetic order is called a *sorter.*
2. The amount on each unit record (punched card) is "read" and stored in a machine in much the same manner that an adding machine stores each amount added until a total is needed. A machine that selects the desired data from punched cards, temporarily stores the data, and prints the desired information is called a *tabulator.* The tabulator is also known as an *accounting machine.*
3. After all the unit records for each kind of merchandise have been "read" and the amounts accumulated, the total sales for this kind of merchandise is printed by the tabulating machine.

Prior to processing data as described above, the automated equipment must be given step-by-step instructions for doing each job. A set of instructions that directs a data processing machine is called a *program.* A person who plans the steps in the process and prepares the instructions is known as a *programmer.* To prepare a program for processing bookkeeping data, a person must have a good understanding of the principles of bookkeeping and accounting.

Output

The information produced by data processing systems is called *output.* The special forms on which the output is recorded are known as *output media.* The form of the output media will depend upon how the data are to be used. Some machines summarize and print the output directly onto business forms, such as schedules of accounts receivable, customers' monthly statements, or invoices. Sometimes the output media are punched cards. These newly punched cards may be used later for additional processing of the data.

The three phases of an automated data processing cycle that uses punched cards as the input media are summarized in the following chart.

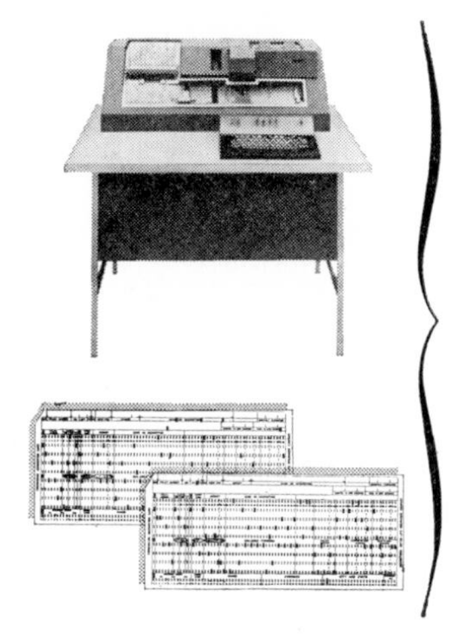

Input

Information on the source documents to be processed is punched into cards or tape in code form. Common office machines with card-punch or tape-punch attachments or a card-punch machine may be used. Ordinarily, a verifier is used to check the accuracy of the punched cards before they are processed.

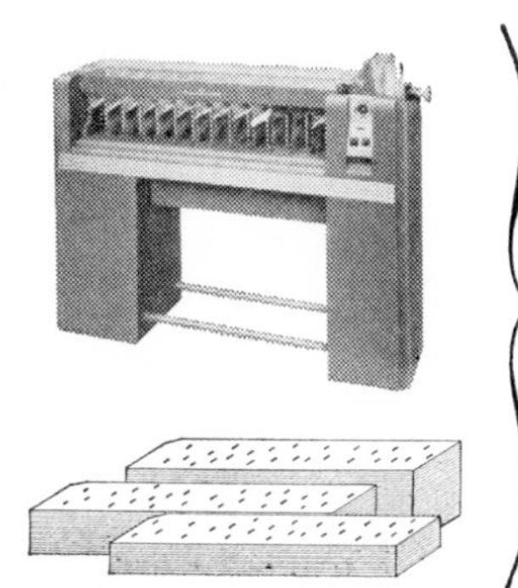

Processing and Storage

The cards are sorted and grouped according to the information desired. This is an automatic process handled by the sorter. The cards are then ready for further processing.

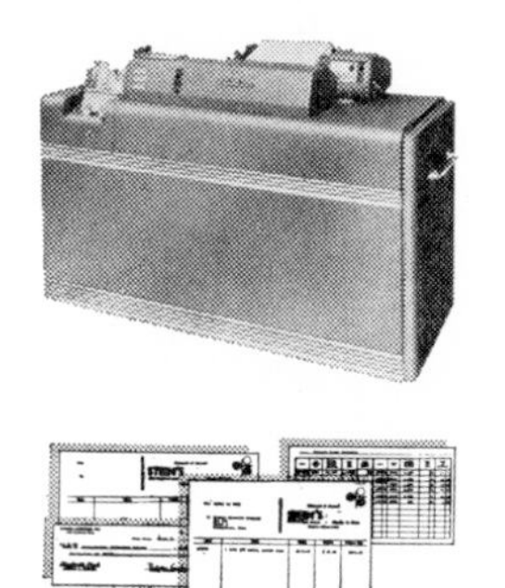

Output

The grouped cards are run through the tabulator. The tabulator selects the data desired from the punched cards and prints the information on output media such as sales reports, statements, and checks.

An automated data processing cycle that uses punched cards as the input media

Increasing Your Business Vocabulary

What is the meaning of each of the following:

- a data processing
- b manual data processing
- c write-it-once principle
- d carbon pack
- e pegboard
- f bookkeeping machine
- g automation
- h automated data processing (ADP)
- i card-punch machine
- j verifier
- k input
- l input media
- m magnetic ink character recognition (MICR)
- n storage
- o unit record
- p sorter
- q tabulator
- r program
- s programmer
- t output
- u output media

Study Questions

1. In what three ways may data be processed?
2. How is the write-it-once principle applied when a carbon pack is prepared on the typewriter?
3. When a bookkeeping machine is used to record a sale of merchandise on account, what three bookkeeping records may be prepared automatically by the machine at the same time in one operation?
4. Why are names of individuals and businesses usually abbreviated before such data are recorded in punched cards?
5. How many columns of a punched card are needed to record the amount $47.15?
6. After the punched cards have been verified, why is there little danger of error in reusing the data recorded in the cards?
7. What are the four common forms of input media?
8. After the amount of each check and the depositor's account number have been magnetically printed on checks, what kinds of operations may be performed by MICR machines as the result of the use of magnetic ink characters?
9. What are the three phases of the automated data processing cycle?

Case for Business Decision

CASE 1

The Bowen Company is a large wholesale drug business. In the last ten years, the number of customers has increased from 900 to 4,600. At the present time, the Bowen Company is processing its accounts receivable records on bookkeeping machines.

What factors should the Bowen Company consider in deciding whether to convert its present accounts receivable procedures to some form of punched-card data processing?

Application Problems

PROBLEM 21-1 | Interpreting data on punched cards

If you are not using the workbook correlating with this textbook, complete Appendix Problems 21-A and 21-B instead of Application Problems 21-1, 21-2, and 21-3.

Instructions: Use the three punched cards given in the workbook to record the information called for on the form below. The illustration of the punched card on page 381 will be helpful to you in reading the data punched in the cards. The data punched in Card No. 1 are given as an example on the form below.

Card No.	Customer's Name	Customer's Number	Date	Stock No. of Item Sold	Quantity	Unit Price	Amount
1	*Richard Smith*	*71610*	*10–10–67*	*185*	*8*	*100.00*	*800.00*
2							
3							

The punched cards used in this problem will be needed in Problem 21-3.

PROBLEM 21-2 | Recording data on punched cards

Instructions: Use the six blank punched cards given in the workbook. On each card use a pencil to darken the spaces where holes would be punched to record the following data:

Card No.	Customer's Name	Customer's Number	Date	Stock No. of Item Sold	Quantity	Unit Price	Amount
4	George Kent	45341	10–11–67	151	3	$125.00	$375.00
5	John Miller	51247	10–11–67	185	4	100.00	400.00
6	Richard Smith	71610	10–12–67	200	2	150.00	300.00
7	George Kent	45341	10–17–67	151	4	125.00	500.00
8	John Miller	51247	10–17–67	151	3	125.00	375.00
9	Richard Smith	71610	10–18–67	200	4	150.00	600.00

The punched cards prepared in this problem will be needed in Problem 21-3.

PROBLEM 21-3 | Using punched cards to prepare sales reports

For this problem you will need the three cards used in Problem 21-1 and the six cards prepared in Problem 21-2.

In this problem you will learn how punched cards can be sorted and classified in order to prepare two different types of sales reports.

Instructions: 1. Remove from the workbook and separate the nine punched cards used in Problems 21-1 and 21-2.

2. Sort the cards according to the customer's number, placing the lowest customer number on top the stack. When there is more than one punched card with the same customer's number, arrange the cards by date of sale, with the earliest date on top.

3. Find the total amount of sales made during October to each customer and record the information on a form similar to that at the right.

Total Sales by Customer		
Customer's Name	Customer's Number	Total Sales for October
	Total......	$

Instructions: 4. Resort the nine cards according to the stock number of the items sold. Arrange the stock numbers in their proper sequence, with the lowest number on top the stack.

5. Find the total amount of sales for each stock number and record the information on a form similar to that shown at the right.

Total Sales by Stock Number	
Stock Number of Items Sold	Total Sales for Each Stock Number
Total.........	$

Instructions: 6. Find the total sales by customer and the total sales by stock number. Compare the totals to see if they are the same. This provides you with a check that all cards have been included in your tabulations. If the totals are not the same, the error or errors should be located and corrected.

7. From the information you have recorded in the two sales reports, answer the following questions:

a To which customer was the largest amount of sales made during October?

b For which item of merchandise was the largest amount of sales made during October?

CHAPTER 22 AUTOMATED DATA PROCESSING SYSTEMS

The processing of data by automated machines requires that an orderly set of procedures be followed. If, in processing data manually, a bookkeeper omits the date when posting, his mind may recall the omission. He can return to the ledger and insert the date that was omitted. However, if an automated machine omits the recording of a date because this step was overlooked in planning the procedure, there is often no way for the machine to know that an omission has been made. Therefore, the steps or procedures to be followed in an automated data processing system must be logical, accurate, and complete. Automated equipment will do only what it has been programmed to do.

Flow charts in data processing

To assist in analyzing the logical order of the steps in a procedure, a flow chart is often prepared. In the flow chart shown below, the major steps in journalizing and posting are diagrammed.

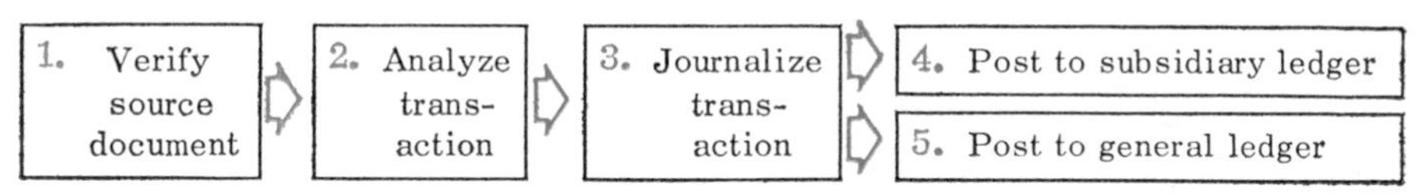

Flow chart showing major steps in journalizing and posting

The major steps within a procedure may be subdivided into smaller, more detailed steps. For instance, in manual bookkeeping, the posting to the general ledger, as shown above, may be further divided as follows:

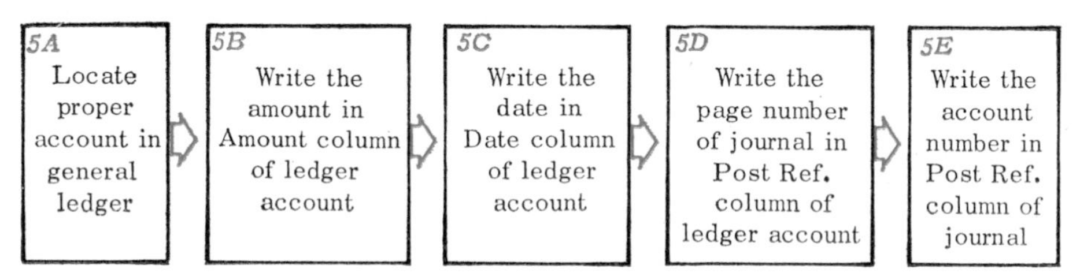

Flow chart showing posting to general ledger

Flow charts similar to those shown above are commonly used in analyzing the processing of bookkeeping data by automated machines.

THE TABULATING SYSTEM

One method commonly used in processing data automatically is the tabulating system. The system that uses separate automated machines to sort, calculate, and print data is called the *tabulating system.* In most tabulating systems, unit record cards are used as the input media. Since all the information needed about each item is contained on the unit record, the tabulating system is also known as the *unit-record system.*

Steps in the tabulating system

A flow chart showing the steps in the tabulating system of processing data is illustrated on the next page. These steps are:

Step 1

Check the accuracy of the source documents. The source documents may be checks, invoices, cash register tape, or any other business papers that serve as the original record of business transactions. The source documents are manually checked to make sure they are accurate and complete. The bookkeeper may use mechanical office equipment, such as an adding machine, in checking the accuracy of the source documents.

Step 2

Prepare the input media from the data on the source documents. In the flow chart on the next page, the input media are unit record cards prepared on a card-punch machine. Each unit record card contains all the information about each item on the source document.

Step 3

Verify the accuracy of the unit record cards. After the cards have been punched, the verifier is used to check that the card-punch machine operator correctly punched the information from the source documents.

Step 4

Sort and group the unit record cards according to the type of information desired in the final report. For example, the data in each card may represent the quantity of an item sold by a salesman in his sales territory. The cards may be sorted (1) in alphabetic order according to the name of the salesman, or (2) according to the sales territory, or (3) according to the quantity of each item sold.

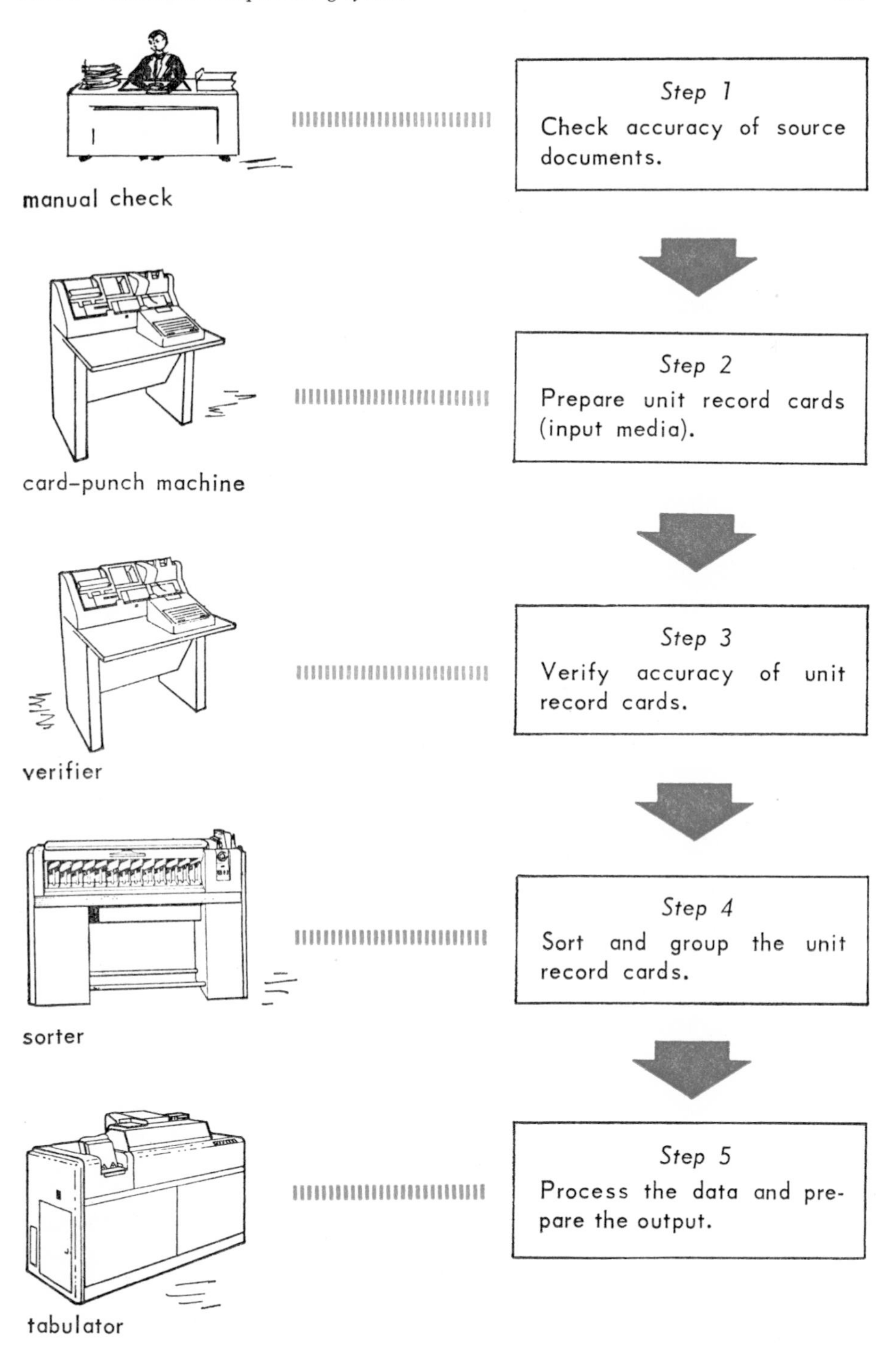

Flow chart showing the steps in the tabulating system

Sorting punched cards. A sorter is used to arrange the cards according to the order desired for additional processing. The same cards may be sorted many times to provide data in a different arrangement each time. For example, punched cards containing information about sales on account may be sorted according to the customers' names. From this arrangement, data can be obtained to show how much each customer owes. Next, the cards may be resorted according to the geographic location of customers. From this arrangement, information can be provided about the volume of sales in different states. A third sorting of cards may be made according to the item of merchandise sold. From this arrangement of the cards, data can be obtained showing the total sales of each item of merchandise and the quantity of each item remaining in inventory.

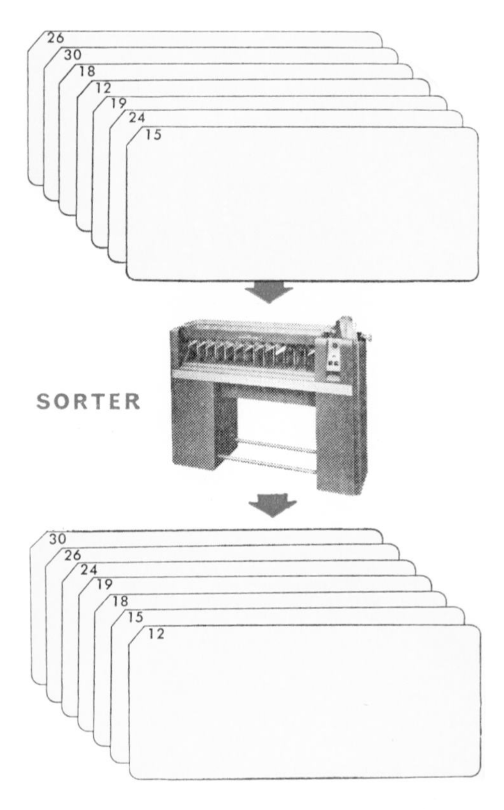

Using a sorter to arrange punched cards in numeric order

Merging punched-card files. As the result of each sorting operation, a card file is created in which the cards are arranged in the desired order. In some situations, it may be necessary to sort two card files in a desired order and then merge both files of cards into one new file. A machine that will merge two or more unit record card files into one file is called a *collator*. The illustration at the right shows one type of collator.

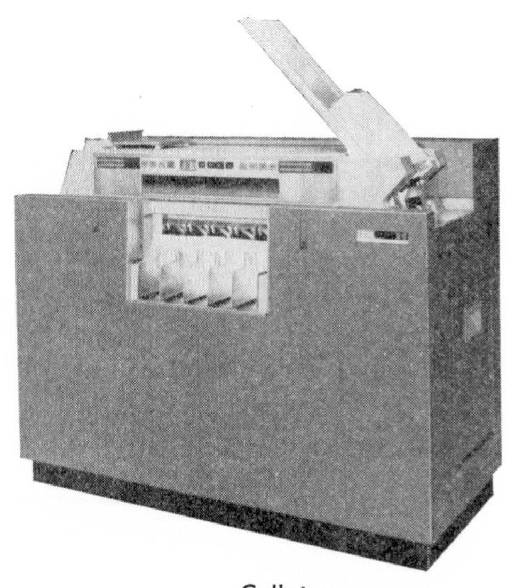

Collator

As an example, one card file may contain a punched card for each charge customer showing the balance of his account at the beginning of the month. A second card file may contain unit record cards representing sales on account made to customers during the first week of the month. These two files are merged so that the cards showing the beginning account balance and the sales data cards are brought together for each customer. The illustration below shows the merging of two files of punched cards to obtain a new file.

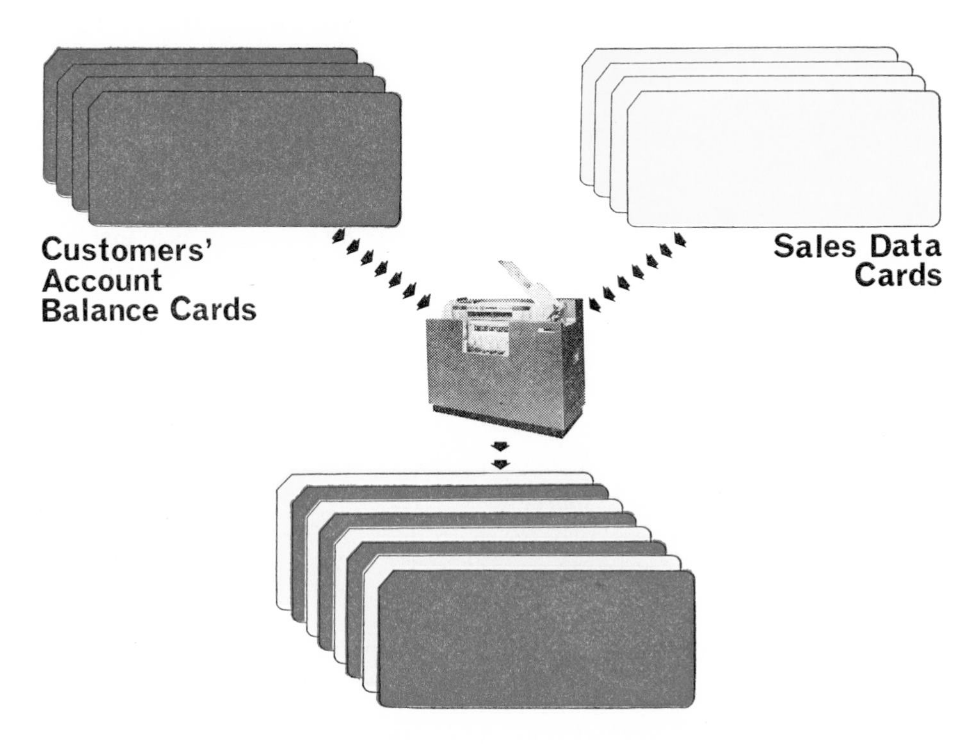

Using a collator to merge the customers' account balance cards and the sales data cards into a new file of cards

Step 5

Process the data in the punched cards and prepare the output. The tabulator, also called an accounting machine, summarizes the data on the cards, performs simple calculations, and prepares output in printed form.

When the calculations are very complex, an automatic machine that can multiply and divide is ordinarily used. The automated data processing machine that can multiply and divide as well as add and subtract is called a *calculator*.

APPLYING THE TABULATING SYSTEM TO THE PREPARATION OF SALES INVOICES

When an order is received from a customer, it is necessary to prepare an invoice, to ship the merchandise, and to record the sales transaction in the bookkeeping records. When the volume of orders becomes great, it is often not economical to process the invoices manually. It is possible to obtain greater efficiency, speed, and accuracy by using automated data processing equipment.

Processing customers' orders

Because of its volume of incoming orders, the Ames Company uses the tabulating system in processing its sales data. The flow chart at the right shows the plan followed in processing the customers' orders. These steps are:

Step 1

Check accuracy of source documents — customers' orders.

Step 2

Prepare a unit record card for each item on customer's order.

Step 3

Verify accuracy of unit record cards.

Step 4

Sort the unit record cards and merge the cards for the day's sales with the customer's master file.

Step 5

Process the data and prepare the invoices for the day's sales on account.

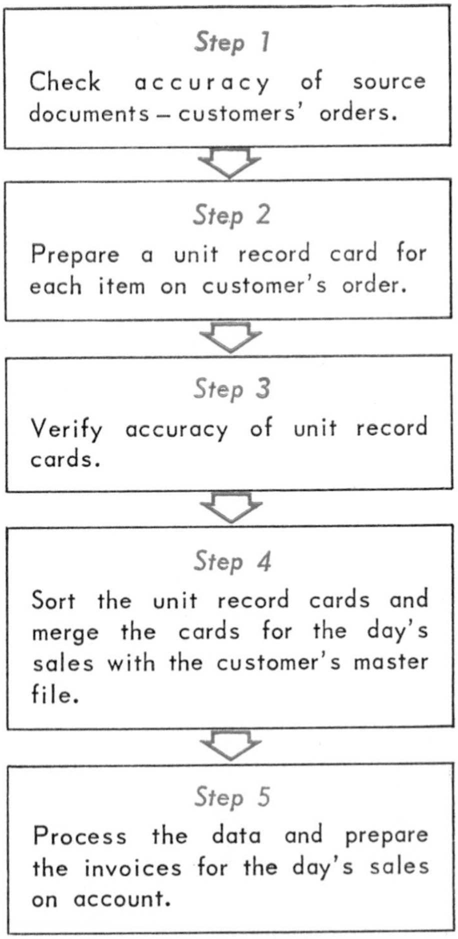

Flow chart showing the steps in processing invoices for sales on account

Step 1

Check accuracy of the source documents. The customers' orders are manually checked for accuracy.

Step 2

Prepare unit record cards for each sale-on-account transaction. A card is punched for each item ordered by a customer. The data punched into the card include the quantity, stock number, unit price, amount, customer's account number, sales number, and the date.

Step 3

Verify the accuracy of the unit record cards. Each card is verified to assure that it has been punched accurately.

Step 4

Sort the unit record cards and merge them with the customer's master file. After the sales data cards have been sorted by customer account number, the cards are merged with the customer's master file containing data about each charge customer. The cards in the customer's master file include the following data: (a) name and address, (b) account number, and (c) credit terms. After the two files are merged, a new file is created. As shown below, the sales data cards for Mr. Cooper are brought together with his master card to form a new file of cards.

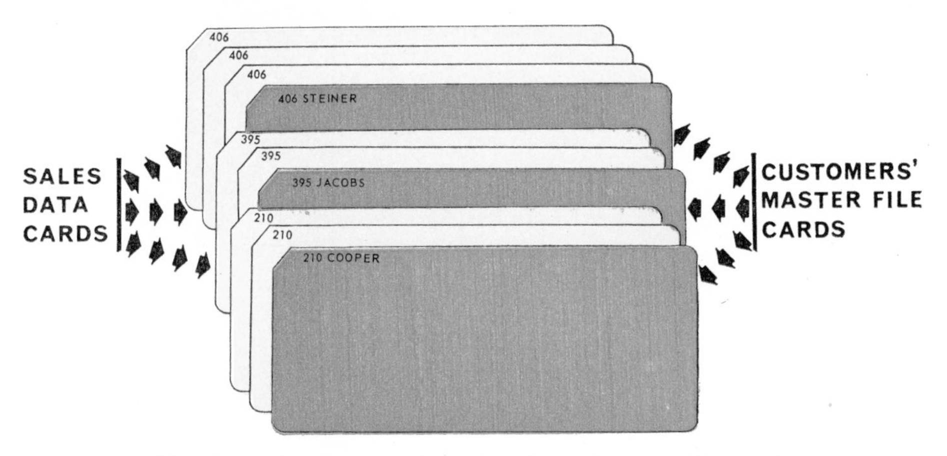

Merging sales data cards and customers' master file cards

Step 5

Prepare the customers' invoices for daily sales on account. The punched cards merged in Step 4 are fed into a tabulator. The tabulator "reads" the cards and prints an invoice for each customer. The illustration on the next page shows an invoice prepared by the tabulator. All the data commonly found on an invoice prepared manually are included on an invoice prepared by automated tabulating equipment.

Additional uses of the merged file

In addition to preparing multiple copies of the sales invoices, the Ames Company uses the file of customers' master cards and the sales data cards for the following purposes:

1. To bring the accounts receivable account and the sales account in the general ledger up-to-date.
2. To bring the customers' accounts in the accounts receivable ledger up-to-date.
3. To bring the perpetual inventory records up-to-date.
4. To prepare the customers' statements of account.

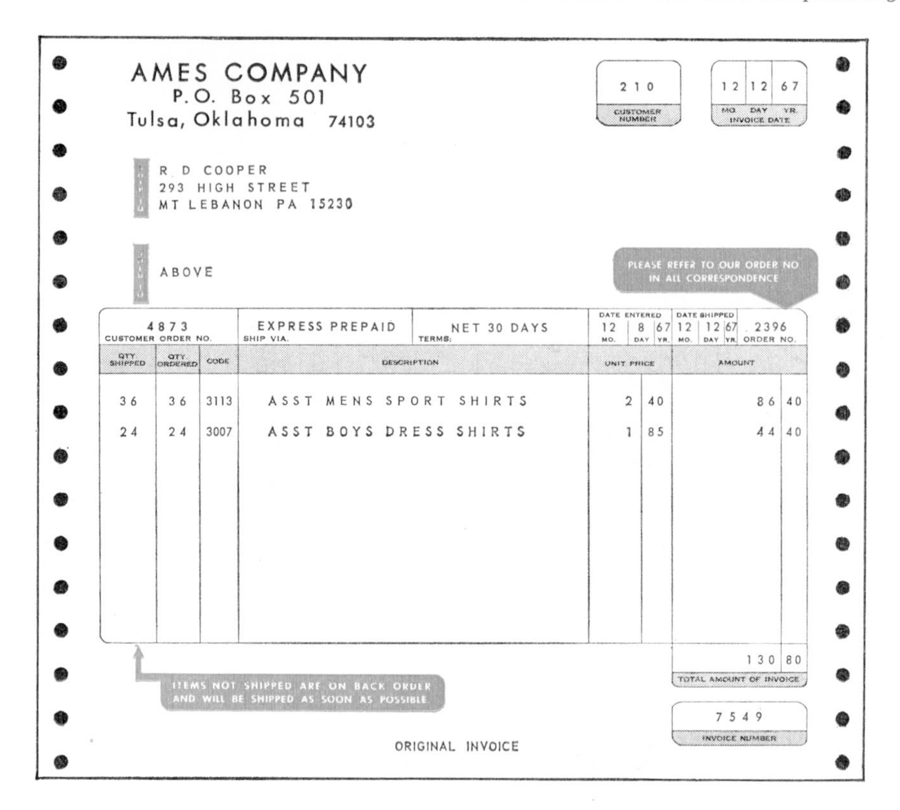

AMES COMPANY
P.O. Box 501
Tulsa, Oklahoma 74103

210
CUSTOMER NUMBER

12 | 12 | 67
MO. DAY YR.
INVOICE DATE

R D COOPER
293 HIGH STREET
MT LEBANON PA 15230

ABOVE

PLEASE REFER TO OUR ORDER NO IN ALL CORRESPONDENCE

CUSTOMER ORDER NO.	SHIP VIA.	TERMS:	DATE ENTERED MO. DAY YR.	DATE SHIPPED MO. DAY YR.	ORDER NO.
4873	EXPRESS PREPAID	NET 30 DAYS	12 8 67	12 12 67	2396

QTY. SHIPPED	QTY. ORDERED	CODE	DESCRIPTION	UNIT PRICE	AMOUNT
36	36	3113	ASST MENS SPORT SHIRTS	2 40	86 40
24	24	3007	ASST BOYS DRESS SHIRTS	1 85	44 40

130 80
TOTAL AMOUNT OF INVOICE

ITEMS NOT SHIPPED ARE ON BACK ORDER AND WILL BE SHIPPED AS SOON AS POSSIBLE

7549
INVOICE NUMBER

ORIGINAL INVOICE

Invoice prepared by the tabulator

THE ELECTRONIC COMPUTER SYSTEM

The tabulating system of processing data requires the use of several different data processing machines. The unit record cards must be transferred by hand from one machine to another. For instance, it is necessary to move manually a file of punched cards from the sorter to the next machine to be used, such as a tabulator. As the amount of data to be processed increases, equipment that will operate more rapidly than that used in the tabulating system may be needed.

A machine that handles data in the form of electrical impulses and performs all the functions of input, storage, processing, and output is called an *electronic computer*. A system that uses a computer to sort, calculate, and print data is called the *electronic computer system*.

Basic units of the electronic computer system

The electronic computer system includes five basic units of equipment: input, storage, arithmetic, output, and control.

Input unit. Data and the instructions to process the data are fed into the computer through the input unit. Some computers use an input unit that "reads" punched cards. Other computers may have input units that "read" punched paper tape, magnetic tape, or some form of magnetic ink characters. Where necessary, a computer may have more than one kind of input unit. In this way the computer can "read" data that are recorded in more than one form of input media.

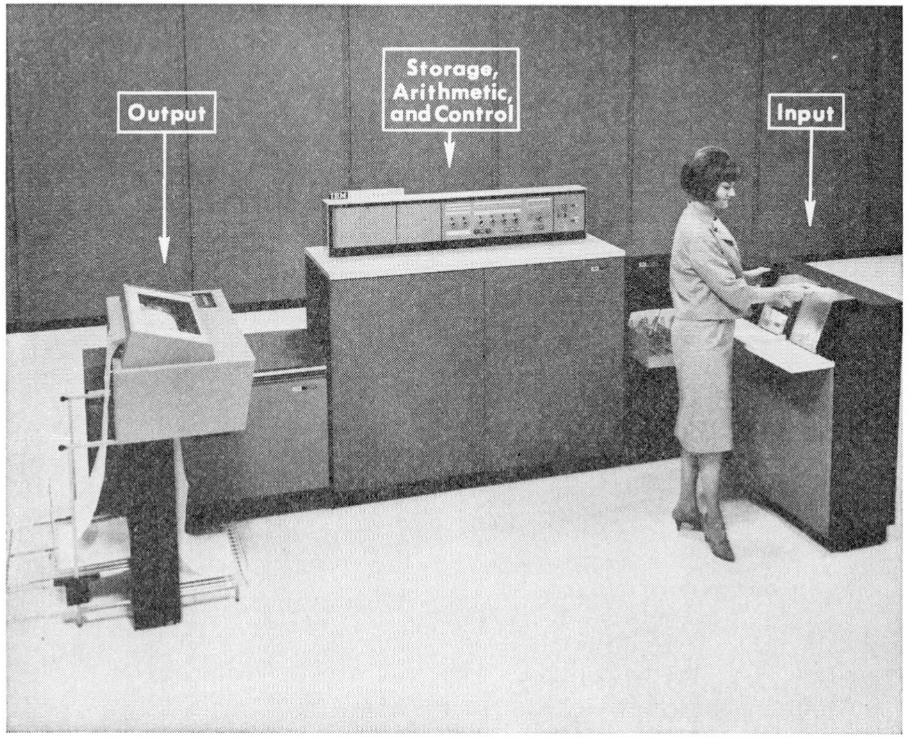

International Business Machines Corporation

An electronic computer system

Storage unit. Data and the program of instructions may be stored in the storage unit of the computer until they are needed for processing by other units of the computer. The storage unit of the computer is often called its "memory." The "memory" of a common adding machine is capable of storing a limited amount of data until a total or a subtotal is needed. Each time a number is added on the machine, a new total is accumulated in the machine where the number is added to the previous amount stored in the machine. When the total key is depressed, the total amount stored inside the machine is printed on the paper tape. The electronic computer also stores information. However, unlike the adding machine, the electronic computer has the capacity to store great quantities of data.

Arithmetic unit. The processing of bookkeeping data involves making computations or arranging data in a desired order. The arithmetic unit of the electronic computer system performs the basic arithmetic functions of adding, subtracting, multiplying, and dividing. The arithmetic unit is also capable of comparing data and preparing summaries according to the instructions given the computer.

Output unit. The output unit in the electronic computer system performs one of the functions of the tabulator in the tabulating system. For example, the output unit provides the processed data in a specific form, such as a printed invoice.

Control unit. One of the special features of the electronic computer system that distinguishes it from the tabulating system is its ability to receive and to follow a complete set of instructions for the processing of data. The set of instructions is called the program. By following the program, the electronic computer system performs all the desired steps from the initial input of data to the final output, with very little assistance from the computer operator.

The control unit links together the other four units of the electronic computer system. It causes each step in the processing of the data to be performed in the proper sequence by the proper unit in the system.

Electronic computer code

The units of an electronic computer system operate by means of electrical impulses. The electrical impulses become a code that represents data. Input–output units may have different codes. For example, the card code differs from punched paper tape code and these differ from magnetic tape code. However, the different codes are converted automatically to one identical code that the arithmetic unit and the control unit can process.

Binary number system. In an electronic computer, the electrical circuits are either on or off. A code consisting of two symbols is used to show when a circuit is turned on or off. A number system consisting of two symbols, such as 0 and 1, may be used. A number system with only two symbols is called a *binary number system.*

On

Some examples of values written in binary code form are shown at the top of the next page.

Off

Binary Positions				Binary Number	Value of the Binary Number
8 (4+4=8)	4 (2+2=4)	2 (1+1=2)	1 (1)		
0	0	0	1	0001	1
0	0	1	0	0010	2
0	0	1	1	0011	3
0	1	0	0	0100	4
0	1	0	1	0101	5
0	1	1	0	0110	6
0	1	1	1	0111	7
1	0	0	0	1000	8
1	0	0	1	1001	9
1	0	1	0	1010	10

Binary number system. The place value of a binary position doubles with each position from right to left.

The binary code and the computer. A circuit in the computer can be thought of as an electric light that is either on or off. A light that is on represents the symbol "1." A light that is off represents the symbol "0." A series of lights can be used to represent a series of binary numbers. For example, in the illustration at the right, the lights turned on in the top row represent the value of 9.

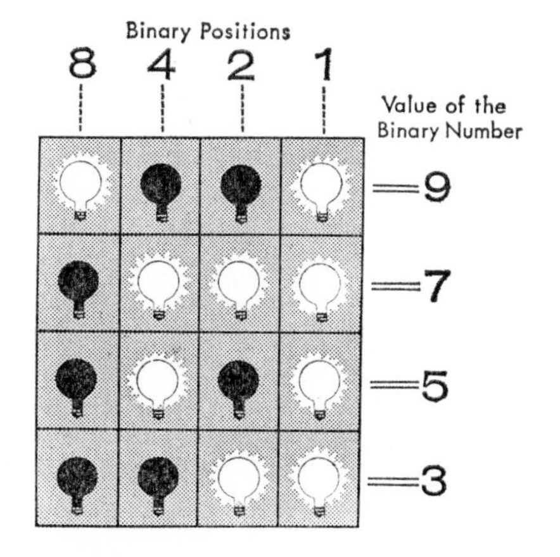

Using the on and off principle to express binary numbers

The input unit of the computer "reads" each hole in a punched card as a signal that turns circuits either on or off. Thus, a series of electrical circuits in the computer, turned either on or off, represents binary numbers in the same way as the lights in the illustration.

The binary numbers are used as a code to represent alphabetic and numeric data. The data stored as a binary number code in the computer are converted to alphabetic and numeric data by the output unit. The output is produced in such forms as punched cards, punched paper tape, magnetic tape, or printed business forms and reports.

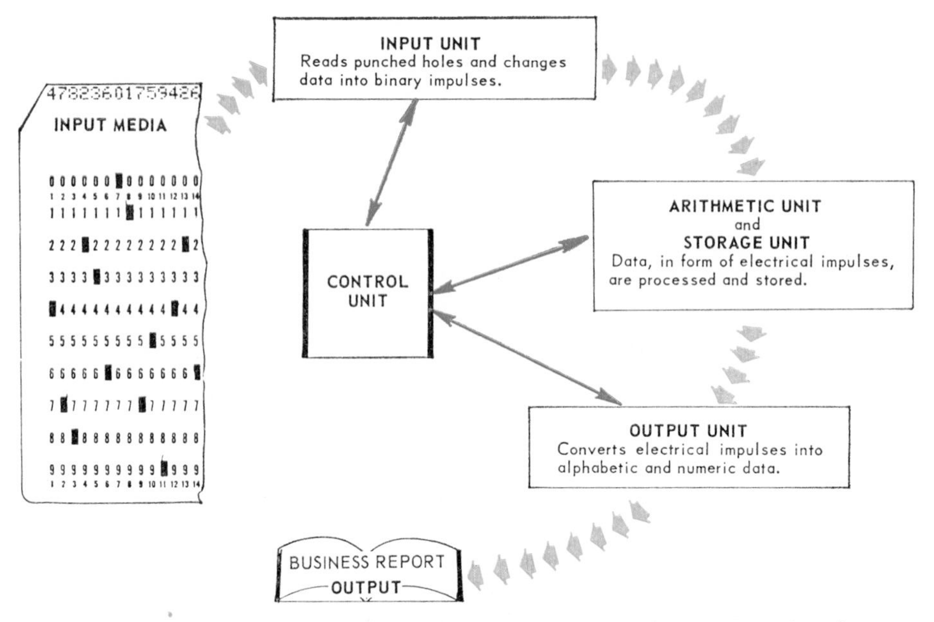

The electronic computer "reads" data punched into cards, converts the data to electrical impulses, processes and stores the data, and prints the results on forms and reports.

Steps in the electronic computer system

The steps in processing data with an electronic computer are:

Step 1

Check the accuracy of the source documents. This step is performed manually, as is done when the tabulating system is used.

Step 2

Provide the computer with instructions for processing the data. The program of instructions includes step-by-step directions for all the units of the electronic computer system. Because the computer cannot think for itself, the program must be carefully prepared by a programmer who outlines all the detailed steps to be taken by each of the units of the system.

Step 3

Provide the computer with the data to be processed. The data are fed into the computer by means of input media such as punched cards and magnetic tape.

Both the program of instructions and the data are "read" by the input unit of the electronic computer system and transferred to the storage unit. The data and the program are retained in the storage unit until needed.

Step 4

Process the data. The control unit "reads" the program in the storage unit. As the program is "read," the control unit directs the arithmetic unit to process the data. The processed data are temporarily returned to the storage unit until all the processing steps have been completed.

Step 5

Produce the output. When the processing has been completed, the control unit directs the output unit to provide the output.

Increasing Your Business Vocabulary

What is the meaning of each of the following:

a tabulating system
b collator
c calculator
d electronic computer
e electronic computer system
f binary number system

Study Questions

1. Why are flow charts important in planning a data processing system?
2. What are the steps in processing data with a tabulating system?
3. When a customer orders three different items of merchandise, how many sales data cards are prepared from the information on the source document?
4. What are the five basic units of equipment in an electronic computer system?
5. What is the purpose of the control unit in the electronic computer system?
6. What are the steps in processing data with an electronic computer system?
7. What manual bookkeeping operation is used in both the tabulating system and the electronic computer system?

Case for Business Decision

CASE 1

During a summer automobile tour of the East, the Mitchell family traveled on the New Jersey Turnpike, the New York Throughway, the Massachusetts Turnpike, and the Maine Turnpike. Each time the family entered one of the toll roads, their son Michael, who was driving the car, was given a punched card. Each time they left a toll road, the punched card was collected when the toll was paid. What kind of information do you believe that such punched cards supply to those who manage these state highways?

Application Problems

PROBLEM 22-1 | Preparing a flow chart for journalizing sales on account

In this problem the preparation of the flow chart is based on the sales journal described in Chapter 14.

Instructions: Prepare a flow chart to show the steps in journalizing a sale-on-account transaction in the sales journal.

PROBLEM 22-2 | Preparing a weekly sales report from data in punched cards

If you are not using the workbook correlating with this textbook, complete Appendix Problem 22-A instead of Application Problem 22-2.

In this problem you will read punched cards and manually prepare a sales report from information punched in the cards. If automated data processing equipment were available, it would be used to "read" the cards and print this report.

Instructions: 1. Remove from the workbook and separate the three punched cards representing the customers' master file cards.

(a) Use the illustration on page 381 as an aid in interpreting the punched holes in these cards. In the space provided at the top of each card, print the customer's name and the customer's account number.

(b) Sort the three cards into numeric order according to the customer's account number. (Note that this sorting also places the cards in alphabetic order.)

2. Remove from the workbook and separate the nine punched cards representing the sales on account to customers.

(a) Use the illustration on page 381 as an aid in interpreting the punched holes in the cards. In the space provided at the top of each card, print the customer's account number, date, quantity, stock number, unit price, and amount of sale.

(b) Sort the nine sales data cards according to the customer's account number.

(c) Sort the sales data cards for each customer according to date. Arrange each file of cards with the earliest date on top.

3. Merge the two files of cards prepared in Instructions 1 and 2. The sales data cards for each customer are to be placed behind the corresponding customer's master card.

4. Using the single file of cards you prepared in Instructions 3, prepare a summary report of sales on account for the week to the three customers. Use the form provided in the workbook for preparing your report.

A small business frequently uses a combination journal instead of special journals. A combination journal has special columns that take the place of special journals.

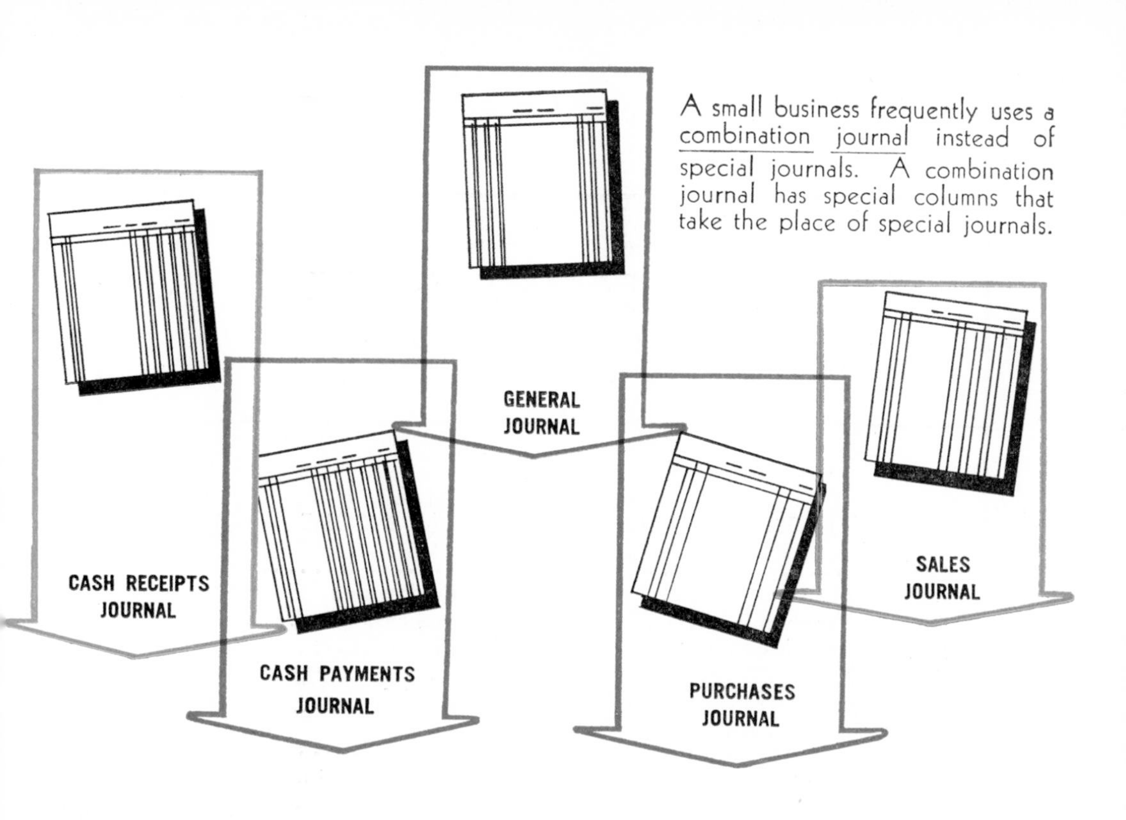

CASH		CK. NO.	DATE	ACCOUNT TITLE	POST. REF.	GENERAL		ACCOUNTS PAYABLE		PURCHASES DISCOUNT CR.	ACCOUNTS RECEIVABLE		SALES DISCOUNT DR.	PUR-CHASES DR.	SALES CR.
DR.	CR.					DR.	CR.	DR.	CR.		DR.	CR.			

THE COMBINATION JOURNAL

All business must keep detailed payroll records. Payroll records are needed not only to complete the picture of the expenses of a business, but also to complete special government forms and reports.

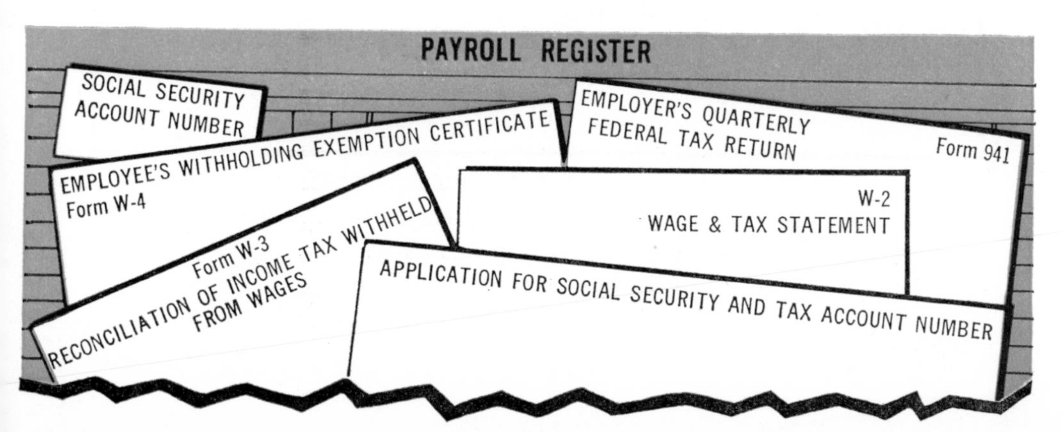

ATLAS PAPER COMPANY

CHART OF ACCOUNTS

(1) ASSETS	Account Number
Cash	11
Petty Cash	12
Accounts Receivable	13
Merchandise Inventory	14
Supplies	15
Prepaid Insurance	16
Equipment	17

(2) LIABILITIES	
Accounts Payable	21
FICA Taxes Payable	22
Employees Income Taxes Payable	23
State Unemployment Taxes Payable	24
Federal Unemployment Taxes Payable	25
Community Chest Donations Payable	26
Hospital Care Premiums Payable	27
U.S. Savings Bonds Payable	28

(3) PROPRIETORSHIP	
George Lind, Capital	31
George Lind, Drawing	32
Income and Expense Summary	33

(4) INCOME	Account Number
Sales	41
Sales Returns and Allowances	41.1
Sales Discount	41.2

(5) COST OF MERCHANDISE	
Purchases	51
Purchases Returns and Allowances	51.1
Purchases Discount	51.2

(6) EXPENSES	
Delivery Expense	61
Insurance Expense	62
Miscellaneous Expense	63
Payroll Tax Expense	64
Rent Expense	65
Salary Expense	66
Supplies Expense	67

The Chart of Accounts for Atlas Paper Company is illustrated above for ready reference in your study of Part 4 of this book.

CHAPTER 23 THE COMBINATION JOURNAL AND THE PETTY CASH FUND

When all the transactions of a business are recorded by one bookkeeper, all of the special journals and the general journal may be combined into a single journal that has several columns. A multicolumn journal that combines several journals into one book of original entry is called a *combination journal.* Some form of combination journal is very popular in most small businesses.

The manufacturers of loose-leaf journal pages and of bound journals offer a wide selection of multicolumn journals. These ready-made journals are available with or without printed headings, and a businessman may choose to have as many special columns in his combination journal as he needs. He may also choose the sequence in which the columns are to be placed on each page.

THE COMBINATION JOURNAL

The Atlas Paper Company is a wholesale paper business owned and operated by George Lind. Mr. Lind uses a combination journal that combines five journals into one book of original entry as shown below.

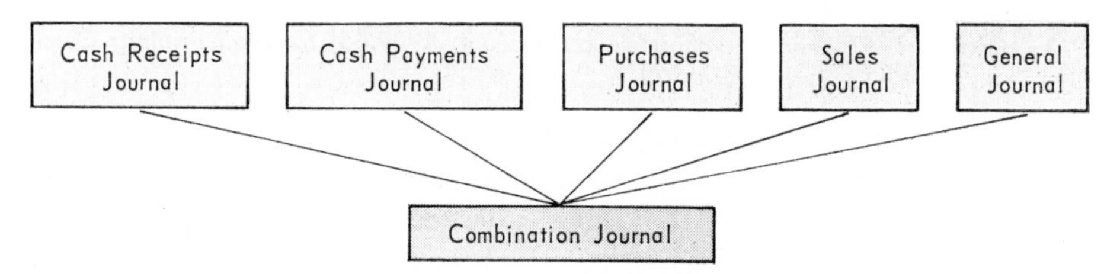

Recording the cash on hand in a combination journal

When cash is proved, it is necessary to know the cash on hand at the beginning of the month. The first line of the combination journal is used each month to record a memorandum entry of the cash on hand.

On May 1, 1967, Mr. Lind has $12,350.50 cash on hand. As shown in the combination journal on pages 406 and 407, the memorandum entry is written in the Account Title column on Line 1. Nothing is written in the amount columns. A check mark is placed in the Post. Ref. column to show that nothing is to be posted from Line 1.

PAGE 17 COMBINATION JOURNAL

	1	2					3	4	
	CASH						GENERAL		
	DEBIT	CREDIT	CK. NO.	DATE	ACCOUNT TITLE	POST. REF.	DEBIT	CREDIT	
1				1967 May 1	Balance on hand, $12,350.50	✓			1
2				1	Wall Printing Company	✓			2
3				1	Union Paper Company	✓			3
4		86975	127	1	Franklin Manufacturing Co.	✓			4
5		40000	128	1	Rent Expense	65	40000		5
6	57965			2	Norton Bindery, Inc.	✓			6
7				3	Equipment	16	12500		7
8					Allen Company	✓			8
9		64000	129	3	✓	✓			9
10	28977			4	✓	✓			10
35	35130			25	✓	✓			35
	1568483	1363517					250701	16910	
36	1568483	1363517		25	Carried Forward	✓	250701	16910	36

Combination journal (left page)

Recording transactions in a combination journal

The use of the combination journal may be readily understood from a study of the recording of a few typical transactions. The transactions recorded on Lines 2 through 10 of the combination journal illustrated above and on page 407 are discussed in the following paragraphs.

May 1, 1967. Sold merchandise on account, $929.65, to Wall Printing Company. (Line 2)

The debit to Accounts Receivable, $929.65, is written in the Accounts Receivable Debit column. As this amount must also be posted to the customer's account in the accounts receivable ledger, the name of the customer, Wall Printing Company, is written in the Account Title column. The credit to Sales, $929.65, is written in the Sales Credit column.

May 1, 1967. Purchased merchandise on account, $1,329.62, from Union Paper Company. (Line 3)

Purchases is debited by an entry in the Purchases Debit column, and Accounts Payable is credited by an entry in the Accounts Payable Credit column. In order that the credit may also be posted to the creditor's account in the accounts payable ledger, the name of the creditor, Union Paper Company, is written in the Account Title column.

FOR MONTH OF *May* 19 *67* PAGE *17*

	5	6	7	8	9	10	11	12	
	ACCOUNTS PAYABLE		PURCHASES DISCOUNT CREDIT	ACCOUNTS RECEIVABLE		SALES DISCOUNT DEBIT	PURCHASES DEBIT	SALES CREDIT	
	DEBIT	CREDIT		DEBIT	CREDIT				
1									1
2				929 65				929 65	2
3		1329 62					1329 62		3
4	869 75								4
5									5
6					579 65				6
7									7
8		125 00							8
9							640 00		9
10								289 77	10
35								351 30	35
36	8583 50 8583 50	11210 00 11210 00	200 43 200 43	15320 13 15320 13	13226 80 13226 80	140 20 140 20	13594 93 13594 93	17389 10 17389 10	36

Combination journal (right page)

May 1, 1967. Paid cash, $869.75, to Franklin Manufacturing Company in part payment of the amount owed. Issued Check No. 127. (Line 4)

The amount of the debit, $869.75, is recorded in the Accounts Payable Debit column. To indicate that this amount is also debited to the creditor's account in the accounts payable ledger, the name of the creditor, Franklin Manufacturing Company, is written in the Account Title column. The amount of the credit to Cash, $869.75, is written in the Cash Credit column. The check number, 127, is written in the Check No. column.

May 1, 1967. Paid cash, $400.00, for rent of building for May. Issued Check No. 128. (Line 5)

A special amount column is provided only when it will be used frequently. As Rent Expense is debited only once a month, a special column is not provided; instead, the debit is recorded in the General Debit column. The title of the account debited, Rent Expense, is written in the Account Title column. The amount credited to Cash is recorded in the Cash Credit column. The number of the check, 128, is written in the Check No. column.

May 2, 1967. Received a check for $579.65 from Norton Bindery, Inc., on account. (Line 6)

The amount of cash received, $579.65, is recorded in the Cash Debit column. The same amount is written in the Accounts Receivable Credit column. To show that the Norton Bindery account in the accounts receivable ledger is to be credited for the same amount, the company name is written in the Account Title column.

May 3, 1967. Purchased equipment on account, $125.00, from Allen Company. (Lines 7 and 8)

Since there is no special column for the equipment account, the debit amount must be recorded in the General Debit column. The title of the account to be debited, Equipment, is written in the Account Title column.

The accounts payable account in the general ledger must be credited for $125.00, and the creditor's account, Allen Company, in the accounts payable ledger must also be credited for $125.00. The amount, $125.00, is therefore written in the Accounts Payable Credit column and the name of the creditor is written in the Account Title column.

When the account titles for both the debit and the credit of a single transaction must be written, two lines are used. The account title for the debit is written on the first line. The account title for the credit is written on the next line and is indented about one-half inch. A brace ({) may be drawn to enclose the account titles to show that both account titles and both amounts pertain to the same transaction.

May 3, 1967. Purchased merchandise for cash, $640.00. Issued Check No. 129. (Line 9)

The amount of the debit to Purchases is entered in the Purchases Debit column, and the amount of the credit to Cash is entered in the Cash Credit column. A check mark is placed in the Account Title column because both the debit amount and the credit amount are recorded in special columns. The number of the check, 129, is written in the Ck. No. column.

Some bookkeepers may write the word Purchases, or draw a line, or write the account number of the purchases account in the Account Title column. Any one of these methods indicates that the bookkeeper did not overlook writing an account title in the Account Title column for each transaction. The bookkeeper for the Atlas Paper Company prefers, however, to place a check mark in the Account Title column. The Atlas Paper Company follows a similar procedure in recording cash sales.

May 4, 1967. Received cash, $289.77, from the May 1–4 cash sales. (Line 10)

The amount of the debit to Cash is entered in the Cash Debit column, and the amount of the credit to Sales is entered in the Sales Credit column. A check mark is placed in the Account Title column.

Forwarding the totals of the combination journal

When a page of the combination journal is filled before the end of a month, the totals of the first page are forwarded to the second page. The bottom line in the illustration on pages 406 and 407 shows how the "Totals" line is prepared for forwarding. The illustration on pages 410 and 411 shows how the first line on a new page indicates the totals brought forward. The procedure in forwarding totals of a filled page of the combination journal is:

Step 1

Add each column of the page and write small pencil footings for each column. (Note the placement of the small pencil footings in the combination journal illustrated on pages 406 and 407.)

Step 2

Prove that the sum of all debit footings equals the sum of all credit footings. If the debit footings do not equal the credit footings, find and correct the error or errors.

Step 3

Write the total of each column in ink. Draw a single line above the column totals to indicate addition. Draw a double line below the total of each amount column to indicate completion of all work.

Many printed forms provide single- and double-ruled lines at the bottom of each page. In such cases it is not necessary to rule lines.

Step 4

Write the day of the month in the Date column on the last line of the filled page; write "*Carried Forward*" in the Account Title column; and place a check mark in the Post. Ref. column to indicate that none of these totals is to be posted.

Step 5

Write the year, month, and day in the Date column, on the first line of the new page; write the words "*Brought Forward*" in the Account Title column; record the totals from the preceding page in the amount columns; and place a check mark in the Post. Ref. column. (Note how the "Brought Forward" line is written on Line 1 of the combination journal illustrated on pages 410 and 411.)

Proving the combination journal

At the end of each month, all columns of the combination journal are footed and proved. After the sum of the debit footings is proved equal to the sum of the credit footings, the column totals are written in ink. The combination journal is then ruled as shown on pages 410 and 411.

PAGE 18 COMBINATION JOURNAL

	1 CASH DEBIT	2 CASH CREDIT	CK. NO.	DATE	ACCOUNT TITLE	POST. REF.	3 GENERAL DEBIT	4 GENERAL CREDIT	
1	1568483	1363517		1967 May 25	Brought Forward	✓	250701	16910	1
2		8177	143	27	Reliable Tool Company	✓			2
3	29018			27	Stevens Printers	✓			3
12				31	Western Hardware Company	✓			12
13	1845000 1845000	1460050 1460050		31	Totals		262188 262188	26178 26178	13
14	(11)	(11)					(✓)	(✓)	14
15									15
16									16
17									17
18									18
19									19
20									20
21									21

Combination journal footed, totaled, ruled, and posted (left page)

Posting the individual items in the combination journal

Each amount in the General Debit column is posted individually to the debit of the account shown in the Account Title column. Each amount in the General Credit column is posted individually to the credit of the account shown in the Account Title column. The completion of the posting of each amount in the General columns is indicated by writing in the Post. Ref. column the number of the account to which the amount was posted.

Each amount in the Accounts Receivable columns is posted individually to a customer's account in the accounts receivable ledger. Each amount in the Accounts Payable columns is posted individually to a creditor's account in the accounts payable ledger. The titles of the customers' accounts and the creditors' accounts are given in the Account Title column. The completion of the posting of each item in the Accounts Receivable columns and the Accounts Payable columns is indicated by placing a check mark in the Post. Ref. column.

A check mark is also placed in the Post. Ref. column for each cash purchase entry and for each cash sale entry (see Lines 9, 10, and 35 on page 406). This check mark indicates that neither the debit nor the credit in these transactions is to be posted separately.

When a business uses a combination journal as its only book of original entry, only the page number from which the posting is made is shown in the Post. Ref. column of the ledger accounts. When a business uses two or more journals, letters are placed before the page number to show from which journal the posting was made. For example, S1 is used for page 1 of the sales journal, CP4 for page 4 of the cash payments journal, and J6 for page 6 of the general journal.

FOR MONTH OF *May* 19*67* PAGE *18*

	5	6	7	8	9	10	11	12	
	ACCOUNTS PAYABLE		PURCHASES DISCOUNT CREDIT	ACCOUNTS RECEIVABLE		SALES DISCOUNT DEBIT	PURCHASES DEBIT	SALES CREDIT	
	DEBIT	CREDIT		DEBIT	CREDIT				
1	858350	1121000	20043	1532013	1322680	14020	1359493	1738910	1
2	8177								2
3					29018				3
12		2550					2550		12
	1036527	1355000	30030	1743018	1545860	41000	1472530	1983145	
13	1036527	1355000	30030	1743018	1545860	41000	1472530	1983145	13
14	(21)	(21)	(51.2)	(13)	(13)	(412)	(51)	(41)	14
15									15
16									16
17									17
18									18
19									19
20									20
21									21

Combination journal footed, totaled, ruled, and posted (right page)

Posting the column totals of the combination journal

The total of each special column of the combination journal is posted to the account named in the column heading. The completion of the posting of each column total is indicated by writing the number of the account in parentheses below the column total.

> The use of the special columns, Purchases Discount Credit and Sales Discount Debit, is explained in the next chapter.

The totals of the General columns are not posted, since each amount in these columns is posted individually. To indicate that these totals are not to be posted, a check mark is placed in parentheses under each total.

Variations in the use of the combination journal

Some small businesses use a combination journal as their only book of original entry. Frequently, however, businesses that use a combination journal retain the general journal for recording miscellaneous entries such as adjusting, closing, and correcting entries. Some businesses also retain one or more of their special journals for recording sales, or purchases, or cash and then record only the summary totals from the special journals in the combination journal. For example, when invoices for one month are filed together and are used as a special sales journal, one entry is made in the combination journal at the end of the month; Accounts Receivable is debited and Sales is credited. This practice enables assistant bookkeepers to keep the subsidiary records, while the head bookkeeper controls the posting to the accounts in the general ledger.

THE FOUR-COLUMN GENERAL LEDGER ACCOUNT

The Atlas Paper Company uses a general ledger account form that has four amount columns: Debit, Credit, Debit Balance, and Credit Balance. The cash account, as it appears after the posting of the combination journal on May 31, 1967, is shown below.

Cash — ACCOUNT NO. 11

DATE	ITEMS	POST. REF.	DEBIT	CREDIT	BALANCE DEBIT	BALANCE CREDIT
1967 May 1	Balance	✓			12350 50	
31		18	18450 00		30800 50	
31		18		14600 50	16200 00	

Four-column general ledger account

The four-column general ledger account form shows clearly the amount of each debit and each credit that is posted to the account. The amount of the account balance is determined after each posting and is recorded in the appropriate Debit Balance or Credit Balance column. Thus, anyone looking at a four-column general ledger account can see the account balance easily and quickly.

In some businesses that use the four-column general ledger account, the account balance is not determined until after all the postings for the month have been made. When this procedure is followed, only the end-of-month balance is recorded in the appropriate balance column, usually at the time of preparing the trial balance.

THE PETTY CASH FUND

Most businesses have small expenses that are best paid in cash. For example, the postman presents a letter or a package on which a few cents are due; the expressman delivers a collect package; or a messenger is sent to the post office to mail a registered letter. An amount of cash kept on hand and used for making small payments is called a *petty cash fund.*

The use of a petty cash fund enables a business to follow the common practice of depositing *all* cash receipts in the bank and of making *all* withdrawals of such cash by writing checks. When this is done, the monthly bank statements may be used to prove the cash records of the business. This gives the bookkeeper a double check on the accuracy of his bookkeeping record of cash receipts and cash payments.

Establishing a petty cash fund

The petty cash fund is established by issuing a check payable to Petty Cash and by cashing this check. The petty cash money is kept separate from all other cash. The petty cash money is often kept in a small box in the office safe. One person is usually responsible for making all petty cash payments.

Mr. Lind decides that a petty cash fund of $50.00 is sufficient in the operation of his business. He issues a check in the amount of $50.00. When this check is recorded in his combination journal, Petty Cash is debited for $50.00 and Cash is credited for $50.00, as shown on Line 2 below.

PAGE 19 COMBINATION JOURNAL

	1	2					3	4	
	CASH		CK. NO.	DATE	ACCOUNT TITLE	POST. REF.	GENERAL		
	DEBIT	CREDIT					DEBIT	CREDIT	
1				1967 June 1	Balance on hand $16,200.00	✓			1
2		50 00	154	1	Petty Cash		50 00		2
3									3
4									4
5									5
6									6

Entry to establish a petty cash fund

The effect of this entry, when posted, is to transfer $50.00 from the cash account in the general ledger to a new asset account, Petty Cash. The petty cash account is placed immediately after the cash account in the general ledger, as shown in Mr. Lind's chart of accounts on page 404. After the debit part of the journal entry above is posted, the asset account, Petty Cash, appears as shown below.

Petty Cash ACCOUNT NO. 12

DATE	ITEMS	POST. REF.	DEBIT	CREDIT	BALANCE	
					DEBIT	CREDIT
1967 June 1		19	50 00		50 00	

The petty cash account

Making payments from the petty cash fund

When cash is paid from the petty cash fund, a form is filled out to show: (a) to whom the cash is paid, (b) what it is paid for, (c) the amount paid, (d) the general ledger account to be debited, (e) the signature of the person receiving the payment, and (f) the signature of the person making the payment. A form that provides written authority for a business transaction is known as a *voucher*. One form of petty cash voucher is shown above.

PETTY CASH VOUCHER

NO. 42 DATE June 9, 1967

PAID TO Clark Business Machines AMOUNT 8 85

FOR Servicing adding machine

CHARGE TO Miscellaneous Expense

ATLAS PAPER COMPANY

PAYMENT RECEIVED:

Ralph Smith APPROVED BY B. Jensen

Petty cash voucher

Each time a payment is made from the petty cash fund, a voucher for the payment is filled out and is placed in the petty cash box. At all times the sum of the petty cash vouchers plus the amount of money in the petty cash box should equal the original amount of the petty cash fund.

Replenishing the petty cash fund when the fund is low

At any time the amount of cash in the petty cash box is low, all the petty cash vouchers in the box are taken out and added. A check made payable to Petty Cash is written for the total of all the vouchers. The check is cashed and the money received for it is placed in the petty cash box. The total amount of money in the petty cash box is now the same as the original balance of the petty cash account at the time the fund was established. When all the vouchers in the petty cash box are replaced with money, the petty cash fund is said to be replenished.

A typical transaction to replenish the petty cash fund

June 16, 1967. Issued Check No. 165 for $48.53 to replenish the petty cash fund.

The steps to replenish the petty cash fund are:

Step 1

Count the money in the petty cash box. It is $1.47. Remove all the petty cash vouchers and sort them in stacks according to the accounts affected. According to the information on the vouchers, the accounts affected are: Supplies, Delivery Expense, and Miscellaneous Expense.

Step 2

Add each stack of petty cash vouchers. The totals are: Supplies, $14.75; Delivery Expense, $4.28; and Miscellaneous Expense, $29.50. Grand total, $48.53. Add this total to the cash remaining in the petty cash box, $1.47, to see whether it equals the original amount of the petty cash fund, $50.00.

Step 3

Write a check payable to Petty Cash for the total of all petty cash vouchers, $48.53. Cash the check and place the money in the petty cash box. The petty cash box now contains $50.00, the balance of the petty cash account in the general ledger.

Step 4

Write a summarizing entry in the combination journal for the total of each stack of petty cash vouchers and for the check issued to replenish the petty cash fund. Debit the proper account for the total of each stack of petty cash vouchers. Credit Cash for the total amount of the check written.

Recording the entry to replenish the petty cash fund

The summarizing entry for the petty cash payments made from June 1 to June 16 is recorded in the combination journal on June 16 as follows:

PAGE 19 — COMBINATION JOURNAL

	1	2					3	4	
	CASH		CK. NO.	DATE	ACCOUNT TITLE	POST. REF.	GENERAL		
	DEBIT	CREDIT					DEBIT	CREDIT	
22		48 53	165	16	Supplies		14 75		22
23					Delivery Expense		4 28		23
24					Miscellaneous Expense		29 50		24
25									25
26									26

Summarizing entry for petty cash payments made at time petty cash fund is replenished

Replenishing the petty cash fund at the end of each fiscal period

The petty cash fund should be replenished at the end of each fiscal period because the petty cash vouchers in the petty cash box represent transactions that have not been journalized and posted. If the petty cash fund is not replenished at the end of each fiscal period: (a) the balance of the petty cash account in the general ledger is not an accurate statement of cash on hand, (b) the balance sheet is not an accurate statement of assets, and (c) the income statement is not an accurate statement of expenses.

The procedure for replenishing the petty cash fund at the end of a fiscal period is the same as the procedure used each time the fund is low. (See the steps on pages 414 and 415 and the summarizing entry on page 415.)

It should be noted that no part of the summarizing entry to replenish the petty cash fund is posted to the petty cash account. Therefore, the check issued to replenish the petty cash fund does not change the balance of the petty cash account.

The balance of the petty cash fund in the general ledger never changes until the proprietor decides to increase or decrease the size of the fund. For example, Mr. Lind may find that a larger amount of currency and coin is often needed in the petty cash drawer. Thus, he may decide to increase the size of the petty cash fund from $50.00 to $75.00. If so, he would issue a check for $25.00 payable to Petty Cash. The journal entry to record this check would be: "Debit Petty Cash $25.00 and credit Cash $25.00." When this entry is posted, the balance of the petty cash account in the general ledger would be increased to $75.00.

Later, Mr. Lind may find that the petty cash payments of the business can be handled satisfactorily with only $60.00 in the petty cash box. If so, he would transfer $15.00 in money from the petty cash drawer to his other cash on hand by depositing the amount in the bank. The journal entry for this transaction would be: "Debit Cash $15.00 and credit Petty Cash $15.00." When this entry is posted, the balance of the petty cash account would become $60.00.

Increasing Your Business Vocabulary

What is the meaning of each of the following:

a combination journal b petty cash fund c voucher

Study Questions

1. Name the five journals that are combined to form the combination journal illustrated on pages 406 and 407.
2. Why is a memorandum entry of the cash on hand recorded on Line 1 of the combination journal illustrated on pages 406 and 407?
3. When is it necessary to use two lines, instead of one, in the Account Title column of a combination journal for recording a business transaction?
4. At what two times are the columns in a combination journal totaled?
5. How is the combination journal proved?
6. What amounts in the combination journal illustrated on pages 406 and 407 are posted individually during the month?
7. In the combination journal illustrated on pages 410 and 411, how is the posting of the column totals indicated?
8. Why do most businesses keep a petty cash fund?
9. At what two times should the petty cash fund be replenished?

Cases for Business Decision

CASE 1

Edward Kent, a furniture dealer, uses a cash receipts journal, a cash payments journal, a sales journal, a purchases journal, and a general journal. The bookkeeper, whom he has just employed, recommends that Mr. Kent should install a combination journal similar to the one illustrated on pages 406 and 407. What are some of the factors that might influence Mr. Kent's decision?

CASE 2

Walter Schmidt, a grocer, uses a combination journal that has the same 12 amount columns shown in this chapter on pages 406 and 407. Under what circumstances might Mr. Schmidt decide that some of these columns are not needed?

CASE 3

Mack Perkins, a motorcycle dealer, maintains a petty cash fund of $50.00. He replenishes the fund only when it gets below $5.00. If the fund is not below $5.00 at the end of the month, he does not replenish it. Why should Mr. Perkins replenish his petty cash fund regularly at the end of each month?

Application Problems

PROBLEM 23-1 Recording transactions in a combination journal

Mr. Paul B. Baker, a retail hardware dealer, completed the transactions on page 418 during the month of July of the current year. The cash balance on July 1 was $1,263.00.

Instructions: 1. Prepare page 8 of a combination journal by writing the heading at the top of each column. Use the same headings as shown in the combination journal on pages 406 and 407. (The use of Columns 7 and 10 is explained in the next chapter.)

2. Record the cash balance with a memorandum entry.

3. Record the transactions completed from July 1 through July 26.

Transactions

July 1. Issued Check No. 61 for $300.00 for the June rent.
2. Received $126.10 from Peter Potter on account.
3. Purchased merchandise on account from Starrett Bros., $409.33.
4. Sold merchandise on account to V. M. Moore, $88.20.

July 5. Received $220.48 from Henry Jackson on account.
5. Cash sales for July 1–5 were $293.85.
8. Issued Check No. 62 for $269.75 to Bailey Company on account.
9. Issued Check No. 63 for $73.88 for a cash purchase of merchandise.
10. Purchased merchandise on account from Moss & Menke, $612.21.
11. Received $15.00 for an old display case. (Store Equipment)
12. Cash sales for July 7–12 were $375.57.
14. Issued Check No. 64 for $168.90 to Starrett Bros. on account.
17. Sold merchandise on account to J. M. Handy, $28.50.
19. Cash sales for July 14–19 were $413.25.
21. Received $41.80 from T. B. Dent on account.
22. Issued Check No. 65 for $25.00 for advertising. (Advertising Expense)
24. Issued Check No. 66 for $303.67 for cash purchase of merchandise.
25. Issued Check No. 67 for $231.90 to the Hammitt Company on account.
26. Cash sales for July 21–26 were $408.17.

Instructions: 4. Assume that on July 26 you have filled page 8 of your combination journal. Total all columns and forward the totals to the next two pages of your combination journal. Then continue to record the transactions from July 27 to the end of the month.

July 27. Issued Check No. 68 for $300.00 to Mr. Baker for a withdrawal for personal use.
28. Sold merchandise on account to T. W. Baxter, $43.88.
29. Issued Check No. 69 for $66.19 for utility bills for the month. (Miscellaneous Expense)
30. Issued Check No. 70 for $31.85 to replenish the petty cash fund. The petty cash payments were as follows: Supplies, $9.80; Advertising Expense, $2.50; Delivery Expense, $2.25; and Miscellaneous Expense, $17.30.
30. Issued Check No. 71 for $440.00 for the monthly payroll. (Salary Expense)
30. Cash sales for July 28–31 were $227.13.

Instructions: 5. Foot all columns of the combination journal and prove the equality of debits and credits in the journal.

6. Total and rule the combination journal.

PROBLEM 23-2 | Establishing, proving, and replenishing the petty cash fund

E. J. Kinzer owns and operates a book store. On November 1 of the current year, Mr. Kinzer issued and cashed Check No. 83 for $75.00 to establish a petty cash fund. During the month of November, Mr. Kinzer paid cash from the petty cash fund and recorded the following information on the petty cash vouchers:

No. 101 — $1.65, telegram — Miscellaneous Expense
No. 102 — $1.25, special delivery — Delivery Expense
No. 103 — $ .85, ink and tape — Supplies
No. 104 — $7.00, office cleaned — Miscellaneous Expense
No. 105 — $2.50, newspaper advertisement — Advertising Expense
No. 106 — $3.95, wrapping materials — Supplies
No. 107 — $1.95, two telegrams — Miscellaneous Expense
No. 108 — $2.90, luncheon — Miscellaneous Expense
No. 109 — $7.00, office cleaned — Miscellaneous Expense
No. 110 — $8.00, postage stamps — Supplies
No. 111 — $1.45, special delivery — Delivery Expense
No. 112 — $9.25, typewriter repairs — Miscellaneous Expense

Instructions: 1. Record Check No. 83 on November 1 on page 11 of a combination journal like the model on page 415.

2. On a separate sheet of paper rule four columns with the headings Supplies, Advertising Expense, Delivery Expense, and Miscellaneous Expense. Since the actual petty cash vouchers are not available, use this sheet of paper with its four columns as a device for sorting the petty cash vouchers into four stacks.

3. Prove the petty cash fund. At the end of the month, the amount of money in the petty cash fund is $27.25.

4. Record in the combination journal the issuance of check No. 98 on November 30 to replenish the petty cash fund.

Optional Problems

★SUPPLEMENTARY PROBLEM 23-S

Recording transactions in a combination journal

Robert Rasmussen operates a children's clothing store. During the month of May of the current year he completed the following transactions. The cash balance on May 1 was $967.80.

Instructions: 1. Record the cash balance with a memorandum entry on page 15 of a combination journal like the one illustrated on pages 406 and 407.

2. Record the transactions for the month of May.

Transactions

May 1. Purchased merchandise on account from Atkins Bros., $430.00.
1. Issued Check No. 231 for $250.00 for May rent.
2. Sold merchandise on account to J. B. Dane, $35.75.
3. Received $60.00 from Michael Grey on account.
5. Issued Check No. 232 for $310.00 for cash purchase of merchandise.
6. Cash sales for May 1–6 were $620.70.
8. Issued Check No. 233 for $430.00 to Atkins Bros. on account.
9. Issued Check No. 234 for $33.50 for cash purchase of supplies.
9. Received $20.00 from sale of old typewriter. (Office Equipment)
10. Issued Check No. 235 for $63.80 to Office Supply Company on account.

May 12. Purchased merchandise on account from Lawton Wholesalers, $431.40.
13. Cash sales for May 8–13 were $770.14.
16. Purchased merchandise on account from Atkins Bros., $280.80.
18. Issued Check No. 236 for $50.00 to Office Supply Company on account.
19. Issued Check No. 237 for $23.50 for newspaper advertising. (Advertising Expense)
20. Received $83.75 from J. B. Dane on account.
20. Sold merchandise on account to M. M. Milton, $183.20.
20. Cash sales for May 15–20 were $610.40.
23. Sold merchandise on account to Ronald Carr, $23.90.
23. Issued Check No. 238 for $200.00 to Lawton Wholesalers on account.
27. Cash sales for May 22–27 were $590.63.
31. Issued Check No. 239 to replenish the petty cash fund. The summary of petty cash payments was as follows: Supplies, $6.20; Delivery Expense, $16.00; Advertising Expense, $14.80; and Miscellaneous Expense, $7.60.
31. Issued Check No. 240 for $410.25 for the monthly payroll. (Salary Expense)
31. Issued Check No. 241 for $250.00 to Mr. Rasmussen for a withdrawal for personal use.
31. Cash sales for May 29–31 were $280.10.

Instructions: 3. Foot all columns of the combination journal and prove the equality of debits and credits.

4. Total and rule the combination journal.

★BONUS PROBLEM 23-B

A combination journal with different rulings

Introductory remarks. The rulings of combination journals follow two common patterns. The journal illustrated on pages 406 and 407 is called a divided-column form. Its amount columns are divided by the Account Title column, some placed on the left and others on the right of this wide column. The other common pattern is for *all* the amount columns to be *on the right* of the wide column.

Instructions: 1. Use a 10-column combination journal with rulings and column headings as follows:

Date	Account Title	Ck. No.	Post. Ref.	General		Cash		Accounts Payable		Accounts Receivable		Purchases Dr.	Sales Cr.
				Dr.	Cr.	Dr.	Cr.	Dr.	Cr.	Dr.	Cr.		

Instructions: 2. Record the beginning cash balance and the transactions given in Supplementary Problem 23-S.

3. Foot all columns of the combination journal and prove the equality of debits and credits.

4. Total and rule the combination journal.

CHAPTER 24 PROBLEMS RELATING TO SALES AND PURCHASES

SALES RETURNS AND ALLOWANCES

Nearly all businesses, at one time or another, sell merchandise that proves unsatisfactory to the customer. The customer may change his mind about the purchase, he may have received the wrong style or size, or he may have received damaged goods. Often the customer returns the merchandise to the seller and asks that his account be credited or that he be given a cash refund. The return of goods previously sold to a customer for which the customer is allowed credit on account or is given a cash refund is called a *sales return.*

In some instances the seller may grant credit to a customer without requiring the customer to return the merchandise. Credit given to a customer for part of the sales price of goods, when these goods are not returned, is called a *sales allowance.* Sales allowances are generally the result of damaged or imperfect goods or a shortage in the shipment.

Sales returns and sales allowances represent a decrease in sales. As a result, some businesses debit the sales account for the amount of the sales returns and the sales allowances. It is recommended, however, that these amounts be debited to a separate account with the title *Sales Returns and Allowances.* Thus, a business can readily see how large the sales returns and allowances are and whether they are increasing or decreasing from year to year. If the amounts are very large, one account may be kept for sales returns and another account for sales allowances. Usually it is satisfactory to combine the two into the same account.

> The sales returns and allowances account is placed in the Income division of the general ledger because the amounts debited to this account represent a decrease in the balance of the income account. See the chart of accounts for the Atlas Paper Company on page 404.

The credit memorandum

A business form that contains a record of the amount of credit granted by the seller for returns, allowances, and similar items is called a *credit memorandum.* A typical credit memorandum is shown on the next page.

Credit Memorandum No. 41

ATLAS PAPER COMPANY
812 OAK STREET • LINCOLN, NEBRASKA 68527

To: Wall Printing Company
2016 State Street
Lincoln, Nebraska 68527

We have this day credited your account as follows:

Quantity	Description	Price	Total
5M	8½ x 14 - 20 White Duplicator	2.40	12.00

If the above is incorrect please return stating difference.

Credit memorandum

A sales returns and allowances transaction

June 2, 1967. Issued credit memorandum No. 41 for $12.00 to Wall Printing Company for merchandise returned.

The source document for this transaction is the carbon copy of the credit memorandum shown above.

Analyzing the sales returns and allowances transaction. The merchandise returned by Wall Printing Company represents a decrease in the sales of Atlas Paper Company. The Atlas Paper Company has a separate account in its general ledger, Sales Returns and Allowances, in which are recorded all decreases in sales as a result of credit granted to customers. Since the sales account always has a credit balance, the sales returns and allowances account is always debited to show a decrease in the income from sales. Therefore, in this transaction, the sales returns and allowances account is *debited* for the amount of the return, *$12.00*, as shown in the T account above.

GENERAL LEDGER

Sales Returns and Allowances 41.1

June 2	12.00		

Accounts Receivable 13

June 1 Balance	8,460.50	June 2	12.00

ACCOUNTS RECEIVABLE LEDGER

Wall Printing Company

June 1 Balance	929.65	June 2	12.00

The account number of the sales returns and allowances account, *41.1*, indicates that the balance of this account is deducted from the balance of the account with the number 41, *Sales*. Thus, the sales returns and allowances account is often called a *minus sales account*. In this book, the balance of any account whose number contains a decimal is a deduction from the balance of the account having the same number without the decimal. Many variations in the system of numbering accounts are used in business.

The amount due from a customer is decreased as a result of a sales return. Therefore, the customer's account in the accounts receivable ledger, Wall Printing Company, is *credited* for the amount of the return, *$12.00*. Also, the accounts receivable account in the general ledger is *credited* for the amount of the return, *$12.00*.

Recording the sales returns and allowances transaction. The entry to record this sales returns and allowances transaction is shown on Lines 3 and 4 of the combination journal on pages 424 and 425.

To record the debit part of the entry, the account title, *Sales Returns and Allowances*, is written in the Account Title column of the combination journal. The amount, *$12.00*, is written in the General Debit column. Because the Atlas Paper Company does not anticipate many sales returns and allowances transactions, a special column is not provided in the combination journal.

To record the credit to the customer's account and to Accounts Receivable, the name of the customer, *Wall Printing Company*, is written on the next line in the Account Title column. The name of the customer is indented to show that it is a credit entry. The amount of the credit, *$12.00*, is written in the Accounts Receivable Credit column.

PURCHASES RETURNS AND ALLOWANCES

The buyer of merchandise may be allowed credit for the return of part or all the merchandise purchased. Merchandise returned by a buyer for which he receives credit is called a *purchases return*. A buyer may also be allowed credit by the seller if the merchandise received was inferior in quality or was damaged in transit. In this situation the merchandise is usually retained by the buyer. Credit that is allowed for merchandise that is not completely satisfactory, but that is not returned, is called a *purchases allowance*.

The buyer usually receives a credit memorandum from the seller showing the amount of the purchases return or the purchases allowance. As purchases returns and purchases allowances are ordinarily few in number, they are usually recorded in the same account with the title *Purchases Returns and Allowances*.

PAGE 19 — COMBINATION JOURNAL

	1 CASH DEBIT	2 CASH CREDIT	CK. NO.	DATE	ACCOUNT TITLE	POST. REF.	3 GENERAL DEBIT	4 GENERAL CREDIT	
1				1967 June 1	Balance on hand, $16,200.00	✓			1
2		50 00	154	1	Petty Cash		50 00		2
3				2	Sales Returns and Allow.		12 00		3
4					Wall Printing Company				4
5				2	Krehbiel's Printers				5
6				2	Union Paper Company				6
7					Purchases Returns + Allow.			180 00	7
8		416 50	155	2	Weyman Paper Mill				8
9	294 00			3	Buckeye Printing Shop				9
10									10

Combination journal with entries for returns and allowances (left page)

The purchases returns and allowances account is placed in the Cost of Merchandise division of the general ledger. The purchases returns and allowances account is numbered 51.1 to show that the balance of this account is a deduction from the balance of the account numbered 51, *Purchases*. The purchases returns and allowances account is often called a *minus purchases account*.

A purchases returns and allowances transaction

June 2, 1967. Received a credit memorandum for $180.00 from Union Paper Company for merchandise returned to them.

The source document for this transaction is the credit memorandum received from Union Paper Company, the firm from whom the merchandise was originally purchased.

Analyzing the purchases returns and allowances transaction. The amount owed a creditor is decreased as the result of a purchases return. Therefore, the accounts payable account in the general ledger is *debited* for the amount of the return, *$180.00*, as shown in the T account at the right. The creditor's account, Union Paper Company, in the accounts payable ledger is also *debited* for for the amount of the return, *$180.00.*

GENERAL LEDGER

Accounts Payable 21

June 2	180.00	June 1 Balance	12,470.50

Purchases Returns and Allowances 51.1

		June 2	180.00

ACCOUNTS PAYABLE LEDGER

Union Paper Company

June 2	180.00	June 1 Balance	1,329.62

FOR MONTH OF *June* 19*67* PAGE *19*

	5	6	7	8	9	10	11	12	
	ACCOUNTS PAYABLE		PURCHASES DISCOUNT CREDIT	ACCOUNTS RECEIVABLE		SALES DISCOUNT DEBIT	PURCHASES DEBIT	SALES CREDIT	
	DEBIT	CREDIT		DEBIT	CREDIT				
1									1
2									2
3									3
4					1200				4
5				84000				84000	5
6	18000								6
7									7
8	42500		850						8
9					30000	600			9
10									10

Combination journal with entries for returns and allowances (right page)

The merchandise returned by Atlas Paper Company represents a decrease in the amount of goods purchased from Union Paper Company. The Atlas Paper Company has a separate account in its general ledger, Purchases Returns and Allowances, in which are recorded all decreases in purchases as a result of purchases returned. Since the purchases account always has a debit balance, Purchases Returns and Allowances is always credited to show a decrease in the amount of purchases. Therefore, in this transaction, the purchases returns and allowances account is *credited* for the amount of the return, *$180.00*, as shown in the T account on the opposite page.

Recording the purchases returns and allowances transaction. The entry to record this purchases returns and allowances transaction is shown on Lines 6 and 7 of the combination journal above.

To record the debit part of the entry, the creditor's name, *Union Paper Company*, is written in the Account Title column. The amount of the debit, *$180.00*, is written in the Accounts Payable Debit column.

To record the credit,the account title, *Purchases Returns and Allowances*, is written in the Account Title column on the next line. The amount, *$180.00*, is written in the General Credit column.

DISCOUNTS AND TERMS OF SALE

In many lines of business, manufacturers and wholesalers print price lists and catalogs that show prices greater than those the retailer will actually pay. A manufacturer's or a wholesaler's catalog price that is subject to a reduction is known as a *list price*. A reduction in the list price granted to customers is called a *trade discount*.

When a trade discount is granted, the seller's invoice shows the actual amount charged after the trade discount has been deducted from the list price. The invoice is recorded by both the seller and the buyer at the same amount. No journal entry is made to show the amount of the trade discount. Only the net amount of the invoice is used in the journal entry.

Terms of sale

The agreement between the buyer and the seller as to payment for merchandise is called the *terms of sale*. If payment is to be made immediately, the terms of sale are said to be "cash" or "net cash." When the buyer is allowed a period of time before payment must be made, the sale is called a "credit sale." The credit period of a sale usually begins with the date of the invoice. The credit period may extend for 30 days, 60 days, or for any agreed-upon length of time. The terms of a credit sale are usually stated on the invoice sent to the buyer by the seller.

Cash discount

When merchandise is bought on credit, the buyer is expected to pay the seller within the credit period agreed upon. To encourage the buyer to make payment before the end of this period, the seller may allow a deduction from the amount of the invoice. A deduction that the seller allows on the amount of the invoice to encourage the buyer to make prompt payment is called a *cash discount*.

When a cash discount is included in the terms of a credit sale, the discount is usually expressed as a percentage that can be deducted from the amount of the invoice. For example, on the invoice shown below, the terms of sale are written as *2/10, n/30*. These terms are commonly read

ATLAS PAPER COMPANY
Wholesale Papers and Twines
812 Oak Street, Lincoln, Nebraska 68527

Sold To SCHNEIDER PAPERS, INC.
719 POPLAR STREET
LINCOLN, NEBRASKA 68530

Date JUNE 4, 1967

Our No. 647

Terms: 2/10, N/30

Shipped Via ATLAS TRUCK

Quantity	Unit	Description	Weight	Price	Amount
34500	SHTS.	22 1/2 X 34 1/2 - 149M WHITE BUCKEYE COVER	5141#	26.45 CWT	1359.79

Invoice showing terms of payment

"two ten, net thirty." This means that the buyer may deduct 2 percent of the invoice amount if payment is made within 10 days from the date of the invoice. The term "net thirty" means that if the buyer does not pay the invoice within 10 days, he is required to pay the total amount of the invoice within 30 days.

Other businesses may offer different terms. For example, a business may indicate the date for full payment of the invoice as *EOM*. This means that full payment is expected not later than the "end of the month." If the terms are stated as *1/10, n/30 EOM*, a 1 percent discount may be taken if the invoice is paid within 10 days after the end of the month in which the invoice is dated. The full amount of the invoice must be paid on or before 30 days after the end of the month.

Purchases discount

A cash discount on purchases taken by the buyer is called a *purchases discount*. When the buyer takes advantage of a purchases discount, he pays less than the purchase price recorded on his books. Thus, a purchases discount is a deduction from purchases. Purchases discounts are recorded by the buyer in the general ledger account called *Purchases Discount*.

In the general ledger of Atlas Paper Company, Purchases Discount is given the account number 51.2 to show that the balance of this minus purchases account is a deduction from the balance of account number 51, Purchases. The purchases discount account is contained in the Cost of Merchandise division of the general ledger, as shown on page 404.

A purchases discount transaction

June 2, 1967. Issued Check No. 155 for $416.50 to Weyman Paper Mill in payment of our May 23 invoice of $425.00 less a 2 percent discount of $8.50.

Analyzing the purchases discount transaction. The amount of the invoice, *$425.00*, is *debited* to Accounts Payable in the general ledger and to the account of Weyman Paper Mill in the accounts payable ledger. The debit to both of these accounts shows a reduction in the amount owed this creditor.

Cash is *credited* for *$416.50*, the amount of the check.

GENERAL LEDGER

Accounts Payable 21

June 2	425.00	June 1 Balance	12,470.50

Cash 11

June 1 Balance	16,200.00	June 2	416.50

Purchases Discount 51.2

		June 2	8.50

ACCOUNTS PAYABLE LEDGER

Weyman Paper Mill

June 2	425.00	June 1 Balance	425.00

Purchases Discount is *credited* for $8.50 because it is a deduction on the income statement from the balance of the purchases account. The purchases account always has a debit balance.

Recording the purchases discount transaction. As shown on Line 8 of the combination journal, pages 424 and 425, the amount of the invoice, *$425.00*, is written in the Accounts Payable Debit column. The amount of cash paid, *$416.50*, is written in the Cash Credit column. The amount of the purchases discount, *$8.50*, is written in the Purchases Discount Credit column. The name of the creditor, *Weyman Paper Mill*, is written in the Account Title column.

Since purchases discounts are recorded frequently by the Atlas Paper Company, a special amount column, Purchases Discount Credit, is provided in the combination journal.

Sales discount

A cash discount on sales granted to a customer by a seller is called a *sales discount*. When a customer takes advantage of a sales discount, the seller receives a sum less than the sales price recorded on his books. Thus, a sales discount is a deduction from the income from sales. Sales discounts are recorded by the seller in the general ledger account called *Sales Discount*.

In the general ledger of Atlas Paper Company, Sales Discount is given the account number 41.2 to show that the balance of this minus sales account is a deduction from the balance of account number 41, Sales. The sales discount account is contained in the Income division of the general ledger, as shown on page 404.

A sales discount transaction

June 3, 1967. Received cash, $294.00, from Buckeye Printing Shop in payment of May 24 invoice for $300.00 less a 2 percent discount of $6.00.

Analyzing the sales discount transaction. Cash is *debited* for the amount received, *$294.00*, in payment of this invoice.

Sales Discount is *debited* for $6.00, the amount of the sales discount. The balance of the sales discount account is a deduction on the income statement from the balance of the sales account.

GENERAL LEDGER

Cash — 11

June 1	Balance	16,200.00		
3		294.00		

Sales Discount — 41.2

June 3		6.00		

Accounts Receivable — 13

June 1	Balance	8,460.50	June 3	300.00

ACCOUNTS RECEIVABLE LEDGER

Buckeye Printing Shop

June 1 Balance	300.00	June 3	300.00

Accounts Receivable is *credited* for $300.00, the amount of the invoice. This credit shows a decrease in the amount to be collected from charge customers. This amount, *$300.00,* is also credited to the account of Buckeye Printing Shop in the accounts receivable ledger to show that the May 24 invoice has been collected in full.

Recording the sales discount transaction. The entry on Line 9 of the combination journal, pages 424 and 425, shows the recording of this transaction. The amount of cash received, *$294.00,* is written in the Cash Debit column. The amount of the sales discount, *$6.00,* is written in the Sales Discount Debit column. The amount of the invoice, *$300.00,* is written in the Accounts Receivable Credit column. The name of the customer, *Buckeye Printing Shop,* is written in the Account Title column.

The Atlas Paper Company has frequent entries for the receipt of cash from customers who are allowed a cash discount. Therefore, a special amount column, Sales Discount Debit, is provided in the combination journal.

WORK SHEET SHOWING CASH DISCOUNTS AND RETURNS ON SALES AND PURCHASES

The work sheet for Atlas Paper Company for the month ended June 30, 1967, is shown on page 430. The work sheet includes the four new accounts discussed in this chapter: Sales Returns and Allowances, Sales Discount, Purchases Returns and Allowances, and Purchases Discount.

The balance of the sales returns and allowances account and the balance of the sales discount account are deductions from Sales; therefore, these two debit balances are extended to the Income Statement Debit column of the work sheet. The balance of the purchases returns and allowances account and the balance of the purchases discount account are deductions from Purchases; therefore, these two credit balances are extended to the Income Statement Credit column of the work sheet.

> The accounts that are used in connection with recording payroll taxes (Accounts Nos. 22 through 28 and No. 64) are not listed on the work sheet on page 430. The recording of payroll taxes will be described in the following two chapters.

Atlas Paper Company
Work Sheet
For Month Ended June 30, 1967

	ACCOUNT TITLES	ACCT. NO.	TRIAL BALANCE (1) DEBIT	TRIAL BALANCE (2) CREDIT	ADJUSTMENTS (3) DEBIT	ADJUSTMENTS (4) CREDIT	INCOME STATEMENT (5) DEBIT	INCOME STATEMENT (6) CREDIT	BALANCE SHEET (7) DEBIT	BALANCE SHEET (8) CREDIT	
1	Cash	11	10460 50						10460 50		1
2	Petty Cash	12	50 00						50 00		2
3	Accounts Receivable	13	9370 20						9370 20		3
4	Merchandise Inventory	14	13600 00		(b) 14950 00	(a) 13600 00			14950 00		4
5	Supplies	15	487 35			(c) 264 20			223 15		5
6	Prepaid Insurance	16	1100 00			(d) 48 00			1052 00		6
7	Equipment	17	4400 00						4400 00		7
8	Accounts Payable	21		14270 00						14270 00	8
9	George Lind, Capital	31		25543 45						25543 45	9
10	George Lind, Drawing	32	850 00						850 00		10
11	Income and Expense Summary	33			(a) 13600 00	(b) 14950 00	13600 00	14950 00			11
12	Sales	41		22455 10				22455 10			12
13	Sales Returns and Allowances	41.1	122 60				122 60				13
14	Sales Discount	41.2	464 30				464 30				14
15	Purchases	51	17550 25				17550 25				15
16	Purchases Returns + Allowances	51.1		310 80				310 80			16
17	Purchases Discount	51.2		393 00				393 00			17
18	Delivery Expense	61	642 00				642 00				18
19	Insurance Expense	62			(d) 48 00		48 00				19
20	Miscellaneous Expense	63	84 70				84 70				20
21	Rent Expense	65	400 00				400 00				21
22	Salary Expense	66	3390 45				3390 45				22
23	Supplies Expense	67			(c) 264 20		264 20				23
24			62972 35	62972 35	28862 20	28862 20	36566 50	38108 90	41355 85	39813 45	24
25	Net Income						1542 40			1542 40	25
26							38108 90	38108 90	41355 85	41355 85	26
27											27
28											28
29											29

INCOME STATEMENT SHOWING CASH DISCOUNTS AND RETURNS ON SALES AND PURCHASES

The income statement prepared from the work sheet on page 430 is shown below. This income statement includes the two accounts related to sales: Sales Returns and Allowances and Sales Discount. The balances of these accounts are totaled on the income statement and deducted from the total sales. The total sales less sales returns and allowances and sales discount is called *net sales.*

Atlas Paper Company
Income Statement
For Month Ended June 30, 1967

Income:				
Sales			22455 10	
Less: Sales Returns and Allowances		122 60		
Sales Discount		464 30	586 90	
Net Sales				21868 20
Cost of Merchandise Sold:				
Merchandise Inventory, June 1, 1967			13600 00	
Purchases		17550 25		
Less: Purchases Returns and Allow.	310.80			
Purchases Discount	393.00	703 80		
Net Purchases			16846 45	
Total Cost of Mdse. Available for Sale			30446 45	
Less Merchandise Inventory, June 30, 1967			14950 00	
Cost of Merchandise Sold				15496 45
Gross Profit on Sales				6371 75
Operating Expenses:				
Delivery Expense			642 00	
Insurance Expense			48 00	
Miscellaneous Expense			84 70	
Rent Expense			400 00	
Salary Expense			3390 45	
Supplies Expense			264 20	
Total Operating Expenses				4829 35
Net Income				1542 40

Income statement

The income statement above also includes the two accounts related to purchases: Purchases Returns and Allowances and Purchases Discount. The balances of these accounts are totaled on the income statement and deducted from the total purchases. The total purchases less purchases returns and allowances and purchases discount is called *net purchases.*

Each of the expenses is listed on the income statement under the heading Operating Expenses. Any expenses incurred in the normal operations of the business, other than the cost of merchandise sold, are called *operating expenses.*

Some businesses treat Sales Discount as an expense instead of as a deduction from sales. Sometimes Purchases Discount is treated as income instead of as a deduction from purchases. When this is done, Sales Discount is not considered to be a regular operating expense of the business. Neither is Purchases Discount considered to be a regular operating income of the business. These items are reported at the bottom of the income statement under the separate headings "Other Income" and "Other Expenses." This procedure is becoming less common, however.

CLOSING ENTRIES THAT INCLUDE CASH DISCOUNTS AND RETURNS ON SALES AND PURCHASES

The closing entries made from the work sheet shown on page 430 are similar to the closing entries described in earlier chapters. The four new accounts described in this chapter must also be closed. The closing entries shown below include these new accounts.

PAGE 20 — COMBINATION JOURNAL

	1	2					3	4	
	CASH		CK. NO.	DATE	ACCOUNT TITLE	POST. REF.	GENERAL		
	DEBIT	CREDIT					DEBIT	CREDIT	
1				1967	Closing Entries				1
2				June 30	Sales		22455 10		2
3					Purchases Returns and Allow.		310 80		3
4					Purchases Discount		393 00		4
5					Income + Expense Summary			23158 90	5
6				30	Income + Expense Summary		22966 50		6
7					Sales Returns + Allow.			122 60	7
8					Sales Discount			464 30	8
9					Purchases			17550 25	9
10					Delivery Expense			642 00	10
11					Insurance Expense			48 00	11
12					Miscellaneous Expense			84 70	12
13					Rent Expense			400 00	13
14					Salary Expense			3390 45	14
15					Supplies Expense			264 20	15
16				30	Income + Expense Summary		1542 40		16
17					George Lind, Capital			1542 40	17
18				30	George Lind, Capital		850 00		18
19					George Lind, Drawing			850 00	19
20									20
21									21
22									22

Closing entries in the combination journal

Increasing Your Business Vocabulary

What is the meaning of each of the following:

a sales return
b sales allowance
c credit memorandum
d purchases return
e purchases allowance
f list price
g trade discount
h terms of sale
i cash discount
j purchases discount
k sales discount
l net sales
m net purchases
n operating expenses

Study Questions

1. What is the difference between a sales return and a sales allowance?
2. What is the source document for recording a transaction related to sales returns and allowances?
3. What account is debited and what accounts are credited by the seller to record a transaction in which merchandise is returned by a charge customer?
4. Why does the Atlas Paper Company, described in this chapter, number the purchases returns and allowances account as 51.1?
5. What accounts are debited and what account is credited by the buyer to record a transaction in which credit is received for merchandise returned to a creditor?
6. Why is no journal entry made for a trade discount?
7. Why does a seller of merchandise often allow a cash discount?
8. What is meant by the terms of sale 2/10, n/30?
9. When a buyer issues a check to a creditor to pay an invoice, and a discount is allowed, what accounts are debited and what accounts are credited by the buyer to record the transaction?
10. When a seller receives cash on account from a charge customer, and a discount is allowed, what accounts are debited and what accounts are credited by the seller to record the transaction?
11. In which division of the general ledger of the Atlas Paper Company is each of the following accounts located?
    (a) Sales Returns and Allowances
    (b) Purchases Returns and Allowances
    (c) Sales Discount
    (d) Purchases Discount
12. How does a business that uses accounts for sales returns and allowances and for sales discount calculate its net sales on the income statement?

Cases for Business Decision

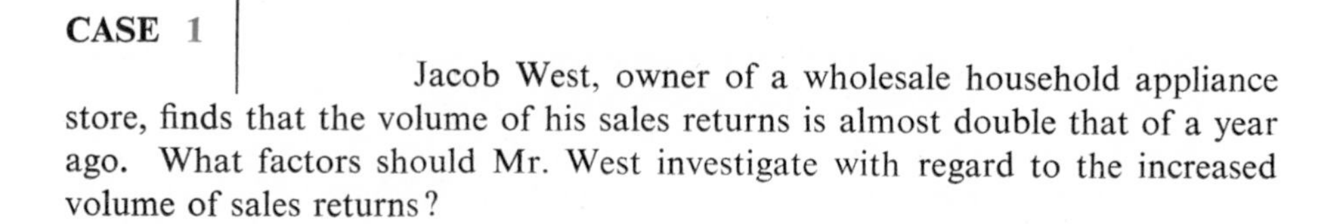

CASE 1

Jacob West, owner of a wholesale household appliance store, finds that the volume of his sales returns is almost double that of a year ago. What factors should Mr. West investigate with regard to the increased volume of sales returns?

CASE 2

Some of the customers of the Office Supply Company report that competing suppliers allow them a cash discount but that the Office Supply Company does not. What factors must the owner of the Office Supply Company investigate before he can decide if he should change his policy?

CASE 3

The Office Supply Company buys most of its merchandise subject to a 2 percent cash discount if the invoice amounts are paid within ten days. What factors should the owner consider in making a decision as to whether he should take advantage of these cash discounts?

CASE 4

On December 13 the bookkeeper for Robert Dove receives a check for $196.00 dated December 11. This is in payment of a $200 invoice dated December 1 with the terms 2/10, n/60. Thus, the payment has been received two days after the discount-taking period. The envelope in which the check was mailed shows a December 11 postmark. If you were the bookkeeper for Mr. Dove, how would you handle this situation?

Drill for Understanding

DRILL 24-A | **Calculating the terms of sale**

Instructions: 1. For each invoice listed below, calculate the selling price.

Invoice	Invoice Date	List Price	Trade Discount	Credit Terms	Date Paid
a	January 9	$100	10%	n/30	February 8
b	January 14	$250	none	2/10,n/30	February 9
c	January 22	$300	20%	2/10,n/30	January 30
d	January 25	$200	40%	1/10,n/30 EOM	February 9
e	January 31	$600	33⅓%	2/10,n/60	April 1

Instructions: 2. Find the amount of cash discount taken by each customer, assuming that the invoices were paid on the dates indicated.

3. Find the amount paid by each customer, assuming that the invoices were paid on the dates indicated.

Application Problems

PROBLEM 24-1 | **Recording in a combination journal transactions related to sales and purchases**

Instructions: 1. Record the following selected transactions, which were completed by Jack Winters during the month of December of the current year, on page 35 of a combination journal similar to the one on pages 424 and 425. All sales shown in these transactions were made on account.

Dec. 1. Issued Check No. 315 for $80.00 for cash purchase of merchandise.
1. Purchased merchandise on account, $500.00, from Murphy & Company.
1. Received a check for $643.50 from D. T. Smith for our invoice of November 22 for $650.00 less a 1% discount of $6.50.
4. Issued Check No. 316 for $124.41 to Harter and Company in payment of their invoice of November 26 for $125.67 less a 1% discount of $1.26.
5. Received a credit memorandum for $20.00 from Murphy & Company for defective merchandise returned to them.
8. Sold merchandise on account, $830.60, to B. F. Goodman.
8. Issued Check No. 320 for $470.40 to Murphy & Company in payment of the balance of $480.00 on their invoice of December 1 less a 2% discount of $9.60.

   The amount of the invoice of December 1 was $500.00, but a credit memorandum for $20.00 was received from Murphy & Company on December 5. The balance of the invoice to which the discount applied was $480.00.
13. Purchased merchandise on account, $1,122.80, from Donor Brothers.
15. Issued a credit memorandum for $30.00 to B. F. Goodman for merchandise returned.
19. Received a check for $792.59 from B. F. Goodman and gave him credit for that amount plus $8.01, a 1% discount.

   The amount of the invoice of December 8 was $830.60. A credit of $30.00 was given on December 15. The balance of the invoice to which the discount applied was $800.60.
20. Sold merchandise on account, $535.80, to John King.
22. Issued Check No. 324 for $1,100.34 to Donor Brothers in payment of their invoice of December 13 less a 2% discount of $22.46.
25. Received a credit memorandum for $13.00 from Mason Brothers for merchandise returned by us.
26. Sold merchandise on account, $450.00, to D. T. Smith.
29. Received a check for $530.44 from John King for our invoice of December 20 less a 1% discount of $5.36.
30. Issued Check No. 326 for $37.60 to replenish the petty cash fund. The summary of petty cash payments was as follows: Supplies, $6.10; Delivery Expense, $6.50; Miscellaneous Expense, $25.00.

Instructions: 2. Foot each column of the combination journal, prove the equality of debits and credits, and total and rule the journal.

PROBLEM 24-2 | Work at the end of a quarterly fiscal period

The accounts and the account balances in the general ledger of Neil Adams, a retail merchant, on June 30 of the current year, the end of the quarterly fiscal period, are given below.

Account Titles	Acct. No.	Balances	
		Debit	Credit
Cash	11	2,827.23	
Petty Cash	12	45.00	
Accounts Receivable	13	2,053.75	
Merchandise Inventory	14	6,274.50	
Supplies	15	589.63	
Prepaid Insurance	16	250.00	
Accounts Payable	21		1,935.45
Neil Adams, Capital	31		7,201.00
Neil Adams, Drawing	32	900.00	
Income and Expense Summary	33	———	
Sales	41		15,230.40
Sales Returns and Allowances	41.1	244.40	
Sales Discount	41.2	163.89	
Purchases	51	9,570.30	
Purchases Returns and Allowances	51.1		67.50
Purchases Discount	51.2		138.10
Insurance Expense	61	———	
Miscellaneous Expense	62	203.75	
Rent Expense	63	400.00	
Salary Expense	64	1,050.00	
Supplies Expense	65	———	

Instructions: 1. Prepare an eight-column work sheet for the quarterly fiscal period ended June 30 of the current year. The additional data needed at the end of the period are:

Merchandise inventory, June 30	$5,340.80
Supplies inventory, June 30	210.00
Value of insurance policies, June 30	154.00

2. Prepare an income statement, a capital statement, and a balance sheet.

3. Record the adjusting entries on page 24 of the combination journal.

4. Record the closing entries on page 24 of the combination journal.

Optional Problems

⋆SUPPLEMENTARY PROBLEM 24-S

Recording in a combination journal transactions related to sales and purchases

Instructions: 1. Record the following selected transactions, which were completed by John Dickson during the month of June of the current year, on page 49 of a combination journal similar to the one on pages 424 and 425. All purchases and sales shown in these transactions were made on account.

June 2. Received a check for $165.82 from B. C. Porter for our invoice of May 23 for $167.50 less a 1% discount of $1.68.
5. Purchased merchandise on account, $452.90, from McHenry Bros.
5. Sold merchandise on account, $112.55, to T. B. Baxter.
6. Received a credit memorandum for $11.50 from McHenry Bros. for defective merchandise returned to them.
6. Issued Check No. 891 for $463.69 to Peyton Company in payment of their invoice of May 29 for $473.15 less a 2% discount of $9.46.
9. Issued a credit memorandum for $7.95 to T. B. Baxter for merchandise returned.
9. Issued Check No. 892 for $432.57 to McHenry Bros. in payment of the balance of $441.40 on their invoice of June 5 less a 2% discount of $8.83.

The amount of the invoice of June 5 was $452.90, but a credit of $11.50 was received on June 6. The balance of the invoice to which the discount applied was $441.40.

12. Sold merchandise on account, $364.50, to A. D. King.
13. Issued Check No. 894 for $43.60 to Red Arrow Lines for delivery expense on merchandise sold.
14. Received a check for $103.55 from T. B. Baxter and gave him credit for this amount plus $1.05, a 1% discount.

The amount of the invoice of June 5 was $112.55. A credit of $7.95 was given on June 9. The balance of the invoice to which the discount applied was $104.60.

19. Purchased merchandise on account, $611.44, from the Clyde Company.
22. Received a check for $360.85 from A. D. King for our invoice of June 12 for $364.50 less a 1% discount of $3.65.
26. Sold merchandise on account, $183.25, to B. F. Vance.
26. Issued Check No. 897 for $599.21 to the Clyde Company in payment of their invoice of June 19 for $611.44 less a 2% discount of $12.23.
27. Purchased merchandise on account, $534.65, from Knight & Sons.
30. Issued Check No. 898 for $51.80 to Red Arrow Lines for delivery expense on merchandise sold.
30. Received a credit memorandum for $21.30 from Knight & Sons for merchandise returned by us.
30. Issued Check No. 899 for $46.87 to replenish the petty cash fund. The summary of petty cash payments is as follows: Supplies, $13.20; Delivery Expense, $6.10; Miscellaneous Expense, $15.32; and Postage Expense, $12.25.

Instructions: 2. Foot each column of the combination journal, prove the equality of debits and credits, and total and rule the journal.

★ BONUS PROBLEM 24-B

Recording in a combination journal transactions related to sales and purchases

Instructions: 1. Record the following selected transactions, which were completed by Frank Hobbs during the month of June of the current year, on page 19 of a combination journal similar to the one on pages 424 and 425. All customers who paid on account within the discount period deducted the cash discount to which they were entitled. Also, Mr. Hobbs deducted the cash discount to which he was entitled when he paid a creditor within the discount period.

June 3. Received a check from A. J. Fox in payment of our invoice of May 15. The terms of the sale were 1/20, n/30. The original amount of the invoice was $340.00.
4. Purchased merchandise on account, $630.20, from A. R. Wells. Terms, 2/10, n/30 EOM.
4. Sold merchandise on account, $130.20, to F. R. Rhodes. Terms, 2/10, 1/20, n/30 EOM.
6. Issued Check No. 682 to Acme Sales Company in payment of their May 24 invoice for $416.20. Terms, 2/10, n/30.
9. Received a credit memorandum for $30.20 from A. R. Wells for merchandise returned to them.
9. Issued a credit memorandum for $8.00 to F. R. Rhodes for merchandise returned by them on our invoice of June 4.
10. Issued Check No. 689 to A. R. Wells in payment of their June 4 invoice less the credit memorandum of June 9 and the cash discount.
12. Sold merchandise on account, $240.80, to L. D. Myers. Terms, 2/10, n/30.
13. Issued Check No. 694 for $60.80 for advertising expense.
14. Received a check for $119.76 from F. R. Rhodes in payment of our invoice of June 4 less the sales return of June 9 and the cash discount.
18. Purchased merchandise on account, $816.40, from C. A. Carlton Company. Terms, 2/10, n/30.
20. Received a check for $235.98 from L. D. Myers in payment of our invoice of June 12 less the cash discount.
20. Sold merchandise on account, $140.80, to R. J. Oakes. Terms, 2/10, n/30 EOM.
27. Issued Check No. 708 to C. A. Carlton Company in payment of invoice of June 18 less the cash discount.
27. Purchased merchandise on account, $730.10, from The Bell Company. Terms, 2/10, 1/20, n/30.
30. Issued Check No. 719 for $76.20 to Area Van Company for delivery expense on merchandise sold.
30. Received a check from R. J. Oakes for $137.98 in payment of our invoice of June 20 less the cash discount.
30. Issued Check No. 720 to replenish the petty cash fund. The summary of petty cash payments is as follows: Supplies, $19.30; Advertising Expense, $14.20; Delivery Expense, $7.60; Miscellaneous Expense, $42.20; and Postage Expense, $10.90.

Instructions: 2. Foot each amount column of the combination journal, prove the equality of debits and credits, and total and rule the journal.

CHAPTER 25 | PAYROLL RECORDS

A special business form showing the wage or salary payable to each employee for a certain period of time is called a *payroll.* In small businesses, the bookkeeper usually keeps the payroll records. In larger businesses, one or more payroll clerks may spend all or most of their time keeping payroll records.

Detailed and accurate payroll records are needed for determining the correct amount owed to employees on pay day. They are necessary because employers are required by federal laws to withhold certain taxes from each employee's earnings and to pay these taxes to the government. They are necessary because a business is also required to pay, out of its own income, certain federal and state taxes based upon the earnings of its employees. Finally, if the amount of taxes withheld is ever challenged by an employee or the government, complete payroll records may supply the necessary proof of accurate payment.

PAYROLL TAXES

Employees' income taxes

A business is required to collect for the government the federal income taxes levied upon the employees of that business. The employer does this by withholding for income tax purposes a part of his employees' wages.

The amount of income taxes that a person must pay depends upon the number of qualified persons, including himself, that he supports. For example, a married man earning $90 a week and supporting a wife and two children pays less income tax than a single person with the same weekly earnings.

Each person supported by the employee, including himself, entitles the employee to a reduction in the amount of tax he must pay. An amount of money on which a person does not have to pay income tax is called an *exemption.* Each person is allowed one exemption for himself, one exemption for his wife (or husband), and one exemption for each additional person who qualifies as his dependent.

The number of exemptions a worker declares and his marital status affect the amount that is deducted each pay period for his income tax. Whenever a business employs a new worker, that person must report the number of his exemptions and his marital status to the employer. He does this by filling out and signing Form W-4, Employee's Withholding Exemption Certificate, which is illustrated below.

FORM W-4
U.S. Treasury Department
Internal Revenue Service

EMPLOYEE'S WITHHOLDING EXEMPTION CERTIFICATE

Type or print full name Roy A. Tupper Social Security Number 194-08-0862
Home address 812 Oak Street City Lincoln State Nebraska ZIP code 68521

EMPLOYEE: File this form with your employer. Otherwise, he must withhold U.S. Income tax from your wages without exemption.

EMPLOYER: Keep this certificate with your records. If the employee is believed to have claimed too many exemptions, the District Director should be so advised.

HOW TO CLAIM YOUR WITHHOLDING EXEMPTIONS

1. If SINGLE (or if married and wish withholding as single person), write "1." If you claim no exemptions, write "0" . . . ______
2. If MARRIED, one exemption each is allowable for husband and wife if not claimed on another certificate.
   (a) If you claim both of these exemptions, write "2"; (b) If you claim one of these exemptions, write "1"; (c) If you claim neither of these exemptions, write "0" 2
3. Exemptions for age and blindness (applicable only to you and your wife but not to dependents):
   (a) If you or your wife will be 65 years of age or older at the end of the year, and you claim this exemption, write "1"; if both will be 65 or older, and you claim both of these exemptions, write "2" . . . . . ______
   (b) If you or your wife are blind, and you claim this exemption, write "1"; if both are blind, and you claim both of these exemptions, write "2" . . . . . ______
4. If you claim exemptions for one or more dependents, write the number of such exemptions. (Do not claim exemption for a dependent unless you are qualified under Instruction 4 on other side.) 1
5. If you claim additional withholding allowances for itemized deductions fill out and attach Schedule A (Form W-4), and enter the number of allowances claimed (if claimed file new Form W-4 each year) . . . . . ______
6. Add the exemptions and allowances (if any) which you have claimed above and write total 3
7. Additional withholding per pay period under agreement with employer. (See Instruction 1.) . . . . . $

I CERTIFY that the number of withholding exemptions claimed on this certificate does not exceed the number to which I am entitled. 048—16—79061—1

(Date) January 2, 1967 (Signed) Roy A. Tupper

Employee's Withholding Exemption Certificate, Form W-4

The law requires that each employer have on file for each employee a W-4 form properly filled out. If the number of exemptions or the marital status changes, a revised form should be filed with the employer. From the W-4 form for each employee, the bookkeeper determines the marital status and the number of exemptions to consider when figuring the income tax to be withheld each pay period.

Federal income taxes are withheld from employees' earnings in all 50 states. Some states and cities also levy income taxes that employers are required to withhold from their employees' pay.

The amounts withheld by the employer represent a liability for him until he makes payment to a district director of internal revenue or to a bank that is authorized to receive such funds.

Employees' and employers' social security taxes

The social security laws of our federal government provide:

1. Old-age, survivors, and disability insurance benefits for qualified employees and their wives or husbands, widows or widowers, dependent children, and parents.
2. Grants to states that provide benefits for persons temporarily unemployed and for certain relief and welfare purposes, such as aid to the blind.

3. Payments to the aged for the costs of certain hospital and related services. The federal health insurance program, designed for people who have reached age 65, is popularly known as *medicare.*

The general term that refers to all the taxes imposed under the social security laws is *social security taxes.*

FICA tax. The social security tax paid to the federal government by both employees and employers for use in paying old-age, survivors, and disability insurance benefits and hospital insurance benefits (medicare) is called *FICA tax.* FICA is the abbreviation for Federal Insurance Contributions Act. This tax is also known as *OAB* or *old-age benefits tax.* The FICA tax is based on the amount of wages paid to employees. The employee's tax is withheld from his wages by the employer. The amount deducted from the employee's wages, together with an equal amount that must be contributed by the employer, is paid to the government by the employer.

FUTA tax. The social security tax paid by the employer and used by the federal government to assist the states in paying persons temporarily unemployed is called *FUTA tax.* FUTA is the abbreviation for Federal Unemployment Tax Act.

State unemployment tax. The tax paid to the state, usually by employers only, for use in paying persons temporarily unemployed is called *state unemployment tax.*

Tax bases. At the time this book was published, FICA taxes were based on the first $6,600 paid to an employee during a calendar year. Federal and state unemployment taxes were based on the first $3,000 paid to an employee during a calendar year. These amounts may be changed by Congress, but the same principles of bookkeeping will apply regardless of changes in amounts.

Obtaining a social security card and an account number

Every employee in an occupation covered by the social security laws is required to have a social security card. The number on each person's social security card is not only his social security tax account number but also his federal income tax account number. Any person who files a federal income tax return must have a social security card. He must write his social security number on his tax return. Any person who receives

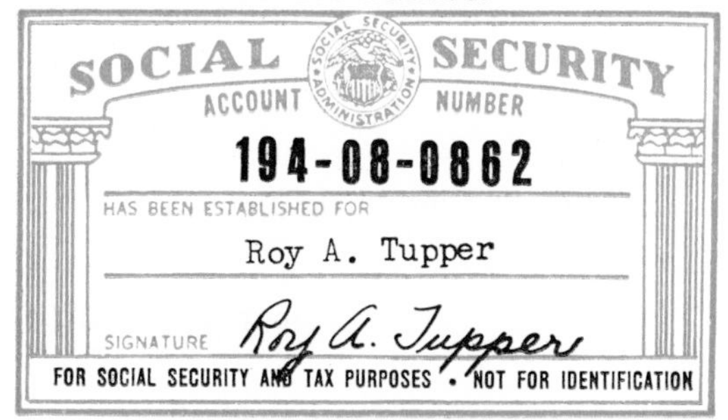
SOCIAL SECURITY
ACCOUNT NUMBER
194-08-0862
HAS BEEN ESTABLISHED FOR
Roy A. Tupper
SIGNATURE Roy A. Tupper
FOR SOCIAL SECURITY AND TAX PURPOSES • NOT FOR IDENTIFICATION

Social security card

any income other than wages must report his social security number to the person or persons from whom he receives this income. They in turn must report to the Internal Revenue Service any income payments and include the social security number of each payee.

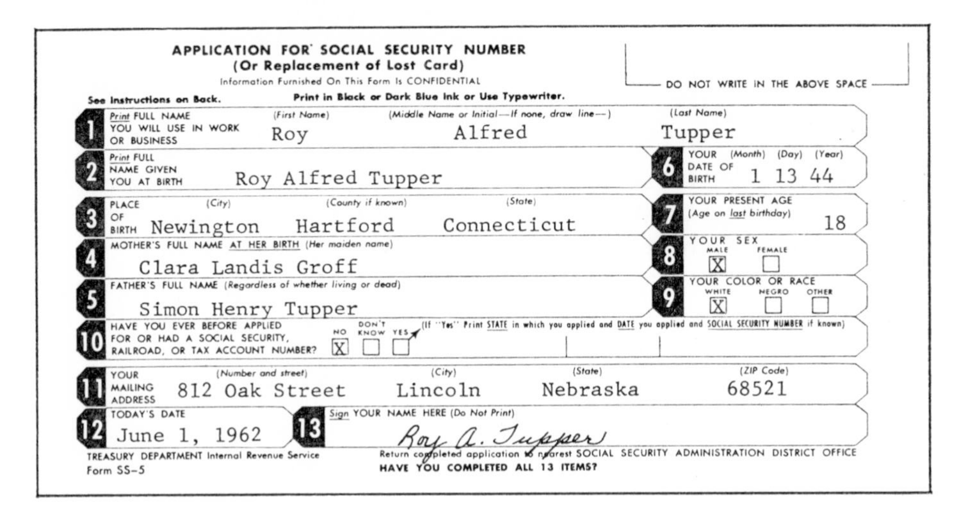

APPLICATION FOR SOCIAL SECURITY NUMBER
(Or Replacement of Lost Card)
Information Furnished On This Form Is CONFIDENTIAL

DO NOT WRITE IN THE ABOVE SPACE

See Instructions on Back. Print in Black or Dark Blue Ink or Use Typewriter.

1 Print FULL NAME YOU WILL USE IN WORK OR BUSINESS (First Name) Roy (Middle Name or Initial—If none, draw line—) Alfred (Last Name) Tupper

2 Print FULL NAME GIVEN YOU AT BIRTH Roy Alfred Tupper

6 YOUR DATE OF BIRTH (Month) 1 (Day) 13 (Year) 44

3 PLACE OF BIRTH (City) Newington (County if known) Hartford (State) Connecticut

7 YOUR PRESENT AGE (Age on last birthday) 18

4 MOTHER'S FULL NAME AT HER BIRTH (Her maiden name) Clara Landis Groff

8 YOUR SEX MALE [X] FEMALE [ ]

5 FATHER'S FULL NAME (Regardless of whether living or dead) Simon Henry Tupper

9 YOUR COLOR OR RACE WHITE [X] NEGRO [ ] OTHER [ ]

10 HAVE YOU EVER BEFORE APPLIED FOR OR HAD A SOCIAL SECURITY, RAILROAD, OR TAX ACCOUNT NUMBER? NO [X] DON'T KNOW [ ] YES [ ] (If "Yes" Print STATE in which you applied and DATE you applied and SOCIAL SECURITY NUMBER if known)

11 YOUR MAILING ADDRESS (Number and street) 812 Oak Street (City) Lincoln (State) Nebraska (ZIP Code) 68521

12 TODAY'S DATE June 1, 1962

13 Sign YOUR NAME HERE (Do Not Print) Roy A. Tupper

TREASURY DEPARTMENT Internal Revenue Service
Form SS-5

Return completed application to nearest SOCIAL SECURITY ADMINISTRATION DISTRICT OFFICE
HAVE YOU COMPLETED ALL 13 ITEMS?

Application for social security account number

A social security card is issued to anyone upon request, without charge, by the Social Security Administration. The application form may be obtained from any local office of the Social Security Administration and from some post offices. The application should be sent to the nearest field office of the Social Security Administration. Every person seeking a job should obtain a social security card in advance of employment because having a card simplifies making application for employment.

If a person loses his social security card, he may apply for a new card. In this case he uses the same application form as shown above, but supplies different answers to Item 10 than on his initial application.

If an employee changes her name by marriage, she should notify the Social Security Administration of the change. A form for reporting the change may be obtained from the Social Security field office.

PREPARING THE PAYROLL

The use of payroll time cards

The first requirement of an adequate payroll record system is an accurate record of the time each employee has worked. Time cards and a time clock are often used to obtain this information.

The Atlas Paper Company uses a time clock to record the time of arrival and departure of each employee each day. Each employee has a card with his name on it in a rack beside the time clock. He "rings in" each morning and after lunch, and he "rings out" at noon and when he leaves at night. Each time an employee "rings in" or "rings out," the clock records the time on the card. The bookkeeper uses the time cards in making the weekly payroll record for each employee.

Firms employing only a few persons usually do not find it economical to use a time clock. Employees are assumed to be present unless the bookkeeper is notified of absence. Executives and junior executives are not usually required to use a time clock because they are paid a certain salary each month and their pay is not affected by brief absences.

Analyzing the payroll time card

The time card for Roy A. Tupper, a shipping clerk of the Atlas Paper Company, for the week ended June 24, 1967, is shown at the right.

At the top of the card is the number 20, which is Mr. Tupper's payroll number. The use of the number makes it easier to place each time card in the rack in its proper place than it would be if the cards were filed alphabetically. On the next lines are Mr. Tupper's name and the payroll period.

PAY ROLL NO. 20

NAME Roy A. Tupper

WEEK ENDING June 24, 1967

MORNING IN	MORNING OUT	AFTERNOON IN	AFTERNOON OUT	OVERTIME IN	OVERTIME OUT	HOURS
M 7:56	M 12:00	M 12:55	M 5:02			8
TU 7:58	TU 12:02	TU 12:58	TU 5:05			8
W 7:59	W 12:03	W 12:57	W 5:01			8
TH 7:58	TH 12:00	TH 1:01	TH 5:03	TH 5:55	TH 9:01	3 8
FR 7:59	FR 12:01	FR 12:56	FR 5:03			8

	HOURS	RATE	EARNINGS
REGULAR	40	2.40	96.00
OVERTIME	3	3.60	10.80
TOTALS	43		106.80

Payroll time card

For recording the time, there are three sections — Morning, Afternoon, and Overtime — with an "In" and an "Out" under each section. When Mr. Tupper reported for work on Monday, he inserted the card in the slot in the time clock, which recorded his time of arrival as M 7:56. The other entries on this line indicate that he checked out for lunch at 12:00 and in at 12:55 and that he left for the day at 5:02. On Thursday he worked three hours overtime, as shown on the line for Thursday.

At the end of the week, the bookkeeper entered the number of hours worked each day in the right-hand column. Each firm has its own rules regarding deductions for tardiness. The bookkeeper must know these rules in order to make the proper deductions if employees are late.

Determining the employee's earnings

Each employee's hours of work and earnings are calculated as follows:

Step 1

Examine the time card for tardiness and early leaving and make the necessary notations.

Mr. Tupper reported to work one minute late on Thursday afternoon. Deductions are not made by the Atlas Paper Company for such short periods of tardiness.

Step 2

Extend the regular hours into the Hours column.

The regular hours for Mr. Tupper are 8 for Monday through Friday.

Step 3

Calculate the amount of overtime for each day and enter the amount above the regular hours for the day.

Mr. Tupper worked from 6:00 p.m. to 9:00 p.m. on Thursday; hence, the figure 3 is written above the figure 8 for that day.

Step 4

Add the regular hours and the overtime hours separately and enter the two totals in the spaces provided at the bottom of the card.

Step 5

Enter the rates for regular time and overtime and compute the earnings.

Step 6

Add the Hours and the Earnings columns to find the total hours and the total earnings.

After the payroll for the week is completed, the time cards are filed.

The payroll register

Each week information about the entire payroll is recorded on a special business form called a *payroll register*. The payroll register of the Atlas Paper Company for the week ended June 24 is shown on the next page.

Analyzing the payroll register

At the top of the payroll register the last day of the payroll week, June 24, and the date of payment, June 26, are entered.

A few days before the end of the payroll period, the time card numbers, the names of the employees, their marital status, and the number of their exemptions are listed in the register. The amount of total earnings from

PAYROLL REGISTER

WEEK ENDED June 24, 1967 DATE OF PAYMENT June 26, 1967

NO.	EMPLOYEE'S NAME	MARITAL STATUS	NO. OF EXEMPTIONS	TOTAL EARNINGS	DEDUCTIONS					NET PAY	
					FICA TAX	INCOME TAX	OTHER		TOTAL	AMOUNT	CK.NO.
1	John T. Archer	M	2	9600	422	970			1392	8208	643
4	Charles Austin	S	1	12000	528	1810	CC	150	2488	9512	644
2	Richard Brett	M	3	11650	513	1080	CC	50	1643	10007	645
6	Howard M. Caldwell	S	1	7440	327	930			1257	6183	646
19	Phillip Dalton	M	4	11080	488	800	CC	50	1338	9742	647
7	Paul Maxon	M	3	12000	528	1150			1678	10322	648
16	Harry Nixon	M	2	8900	392	850			1242	7658	649
8	William S. Parker	M	2	15000	660	1930	B	200	2790	12210	650
5	Howard Price	M	2	8900	392	850			1242	7658	651
18	James Randolph	S	1	6500	286	760	B	200	1246	5254	652
9	Allen J. Ross	M	3	9600	422	770			1192	8408	653
11	Henry Stahl	S	1	11650	513	1710	B CC	400 100	2723	8927	654
20	Roy A. Tupper	M	3	10680	470	930			1400	9280	655
10	Walter Wick	M	3	12000	528	1150			1678	10322	656
3	Russell Williams	M	2	6200	273	460			733	5467	657
17	Mary Zisk	S	1	7500	330	930	B	200	1460	6040	658
	Totals			160700	7072	17080	CC B	350 1000	25502	135198	

OTHER DEDUCTIONS: CC—COMMUNITY CHEST: GI—GROUP INSURANCE: HC—HOSPITAL CARE: B—U.S. SAVINGS BONDS: UD—UNION DUES

Payroll register

each time card is written in the Total Earnings column of the payroll register opposite the employee's name.

The Deductions section is used to record the various amounts deducted from the employees' earnings. The FICA Tax column is used to record the amount deducted for old-age, survivors, and disability benefit and hospital insurance benefit taxes. The amount of the FICA tax may be found by multiplying the total earnings by the tax rate. It may also be found from a social security and hospital insurance tax table. A section of such a table is illustrated on page 447.

The tax rates used in this chapter were taken from the laws in effect at the time this book was published. At that time, the FICA tax rate for each calendar year was as follows: 1967 and 1968, 4.4%; 1969–1972, 4.9%; and 1973–1975, 5.4%. These rates may be changed by Congress, but the same accounts will be debited and credited regardless of any changes in rates.

The Income Tax column is used to record the amount of income tax withheld from each employee's earnings. This amount is determined from tables furnished by the government that take into account the amount of wages earned, the marital status, and the number of exemptions claimed. Parts of two such tables showing the withholdings based on weekly wages for married and for single persons are illustrated on pages 448 and 449. To determine Roy A. Tupper's income tax on the $106.80 he earned during the week ended June 24, the proper wage bracket in the first two columns of the table for married persons on page 449 is found. This is the $105–$110 bracket. The income tax to be withheld is the amount shown on this line under the column for 3 withholding exemptions — $9.30.

In addition to withholding tax tables for weekly payroll periods, the government provides separate tables for daily, biweekly, semimonthly, and monthly payroll periods.

The Other column is used to list withholdings for which no special column is provided. The various deductions entered in this column are identified by initials, which are explained at the bottom of the payroll register. For example, withholdings for Community Chest are marked "CC" and the withholdings for U. S. Savings Bonds are marked "B." The different items in this column are sorted and classified and a separate total is shown for each class.

The Net Pay section is used to record the amount due each employee and the number of the payroll check issued to him. The net pay is calculated by subtracting the amount of each employee's total deductions from his total earnings.

After all the deductions have been computed and the net pay has been recorded for each employee, each of the amount columns is totaled. The accuracy of these additions is verified by comparing the total of the Total Earnings column with the sum of the totals of the Net Pay column and the Total Deductions columns.

Before the checks are written for the net pay amounts, the manager or some person designated by him examines the payroll computations and approves the payroll.

Keeping employees' earnings records

The detailed account of all items affecting the payments made to each employee is called an *employee's earnings record.* The Atlas Paper Company keeps all of the employee's earnings records on cards. A separate card is kept for each employee. The employee's earnings record for Mr. Tupper is shown on page 448.

Analyzing the employee's earnings record

The employee's earnings record provides information for 13 weeks, a quarter of a year. The record is made with quarterly divisions because the government requires the employer to file reports on special forms for each quarter.

Social Security and Hospital Insurance Tax Table

FOR USE IN 1967

This table applies to all payroll periods. The rate is 4.4% for employers and 4.4% for employees, so that the amounts shown below are the taxes for which each is liable. (Example: Tax on wages of at least $61.94 but less than $62.16 is $2.73.)

Wages			Wages			Wages			Wages			Wages		
At least	But less than	Tax	At least	But less than	Tax	At least	But less than	Tax	At least	But less than	Tax	At least	But less than	Tax
$61.94	$62.16	$2.73	$73.07	$73.30	$3.22	$84.89	$85.12	$3.74	$106.71	$106.94	$4.70	$116.03	$116.25	$5.11
62.16	62.39	2.74	73.30	73.53	3.23	85.12	85.35	3.75	106.94	107.16	4.71	116.25	116.48	5.12
62.39	62.62	2.75	73.53	73.75	3.24	85.35	85.57	3.76	107.16	107.39	4.72	116.48	116.71	5.13
62.62	62.85	2.76	73.75	73.98	3.25	85.57	85.80	3.77	107.39	107.62	4.73	116.71	116.94	5.14
62.85	63.07	2.77	73.98	74.21	3.26	85.80	86.03	3.78	107.62	107.85	4.74	116.94	117.16	5.15
63.07	63.30	2.78	74.21	74.44	3.27	86.03	86.25	3.79	107.85	108.07	4.75	117.16	117.39	5.16
63.30	63.53	2.79	74.44	74.66	3.28	86.25	86.48	3.80	108.07	108.30	4.76	117.39	117.62	5.17
63.53	63.75	2.80	74.66	74.89	3.29	86.48	86.71	3.81	108.30	108.53	4.77	117.62	117.85	5.18
63.75	63.98	2.81	74.89	75.12	3.30	86.71	86.94	3.82	108.53	108.75	4.78	117.85	118.07	5.19
63.98	64.21	2.82	75.12	75.35	3.31	86.94	87.16	3.83	108.75	108.98	4.79	118.07	118.30	5.20
64.21	64.44	2.83	75.35	75.57	3.32	87.16	87.39	3.84	110.35	110.57	4.86	118.30	118.53	5.21
64.44	64.66	2.84	75.57	75.80	3.33	87.39	87.62	3.85	110.57	110.80	4.87	118.53	118.75	5.22
64.66	64.89	2.85	75.80	76.03	3.34	87.62	87.85	3.86	110.80	111.03	4.88	118.75	118.98	5.23
64.89	65.12	2.86	76.03	76.25	3.35	87.85	88.07	3.87	111.03	111.25	4.89	118.98	119.21	5.24
65.12	65.35	2.87	76.25	76.48	3.36	88.07	88.30	3.88	111.25	111.48	4.90	119.21	119.44	5.25
65.35	65.57	2.88	76.48	76.71	3.37	88.30	88.53	3.89	111.48	111.71	4.91	119.44	119.66	5.26
65.57	65.80	2.89	76.71	76.94	3.38	88.53	88.75	3.90	111.71	111.94	4.92	119.66	119.89	5.27
65.80	66.03	2.90	76.94	77.16	3.39	88.75	88.98	3.91	111.94	112.16	4.93	119.89	120.12	5.28
66.03	66.25	2.91	77.16	77.39	3.40	88.98	89.21	3.92	112.16	112.39	4.94	120.12	120.35	5.29
66.25	66.48	2.92	77.39	77.62	3.41	89.21	89.44	3.93	112.39	112.62	4.95	120.35	120.57	5.30
66.48	66.71	2.93	77.62	77.85	3.42	94.89	95.12	4.18	112.62	112.85	4.96	120.57	120.80	5.31
66.71	66.94	2.94	77.85	78.07	3.43	95.12	95.35	4.19	112.85	113.07	4.97	120.80	121.03	5.32
66.94	67.16	2.95	78.07	78.30	3.44	95.35	95.57	4.20	113.07	113.30	4.98	121.03	121.25	5.33
67.16	67.39	2.96	78.30	78.53	3.45	95.57	95.80	4.21	113.30	113.53	4.99	121.25	121.48	5.34
67.39	67.62	2.97	78.53	78.75	3.46	95.80	96.03	4.22	113.53	113.75	5.00	121.48	121.71	5.35
67.62	67.85	2.98	83.53	83.75	3.68	96.03	96.25	4.23	113.75	113.98	5.01	149.66	149.89	6.59
67.85	68.07	2.99	83.75	83.98	3.69	96.25	96.48	4.24	113.98	114.21	5.02	149.89	150.12	6.60
68.07	68.30	3.00	83.98	84.21	3.70	96.48	96.71	4.25	114.21	114.44	5.03	150.12	150.35	6.61
68.30	68.53	3.01	84.21	84.44	3.71	96.71	96.94	4.26	114.44	114.66	5.04	150.35	150.57	6.62
68.53	68.75	3.02	84.44	84.66	3.72	96.94	97.16	4.27	114.66	114.89	5.05	150.57	150.80	6.63
68.75	68.98	3.03	84.66	84.89	3.73	97.16	97.39	4.28	114.89	115.12	5.06	150.80	151.03	6.64

Section of social security and hospital insurance tax table

WAGE-BRACKET INCOME TAX WITHHOLDING TABLES

Single PERSONS *Weekly* PAYROLL PERIOD

Wages are: At least	Wages are: Less than	0	1	2	3	4	5	6	7	8	9	10 or more
		Amount of income tax to be withheld										
$64.....	$66.....	$ 9.90	$ 7.60	$ 5.30	$ 3.10	$ 1.00						
66.....	68.....	10.30	8.00	5.70	3.40	1.30						
68.....	70.....	10.60	8.30	6.00	3.70	1.60						
70.....	72.....	10.90	8.60	6.40	4.10	1.90						
72.....	74.....	11.30	9.00	6.70	4.40	2.20	$ .30					
74.....	76.....	11.60	9.30	7.00	4.80	2.50	.50					
76.....	78.....	12.00	9.70	7.40	5.10	2.80	.80					
78.....	80.....	12.30	10.00	7.70	5.40	3.10	1.10					
80.....	82.....	12.60	10.30	8.10	5.80	3.50	1.40					
82.....	84.....	13.00	10.70	8.40	6.10	3.80	1.70					
84.....	86.....	13.30	11.00	8.70	6.50	4.20	2.00	$ .10				
86.....	88.....	13.70	11.40	9.10	6.80	4.50	2.30	.30				
88.....	90.....	14.10	11.70	9.40	7.10	4.80	2.60	.60				
90.....	92.....	14.50	12.00	9.80	7.50	5.20	2.90	.90				
92.....	94.....	14.90	12.40	10.10	7.80	5.50	3.20	1.20				
94.....	96.....	15.30	12.70	10.40	8.20	5.90	3.60	1.50				
96.....	98.....	15.70	13.10	10.80	8.50	6.20	3.90	1.80				
98.....	100.....	16.10	13.40	11.10	8.80	6.50	4.30	2.10	$ .10			
100.....	105.....	16.80	14.10	11.70	9.40	7.10	4.80	2.60	.60			
105.....	110.....	17.80	15.10	12.60	10.30	8.00	5.70	3.40	1.30			
110.....	115.....	18.80	16.10	13.40	11.10	8.80	6.50	4.30	2.10	$ .10		
115.....	120.....	19.80	17.10	14.40	12.00	9.70	7.40	5.10	2.80	.80		
120.....	125.....	20.80	18.10	15.40	12.80	10.50	8.20	6.00	3.70	1.50		
125.....	130.....	21.80	19.10	16.40	13.80	11.40	9.10	6.80	4.50	2.30	$ .40	
130.....	135.....	22.80	20.10	17.40	14.80	12.20	9.90	7.70	5.40	3.10	1.10	

(Column headings 0 through 10 or more: Number of withholding exemptions claimed)

Section of weekly income tax withholding table for single persons

EARNINGS RECORD FOR QUARTER ENDING June 30, 1967

MARITAL STATUS M TIME CARD NO. 20

Tupper (LAST NAME) Roy (FIRST) A. (MIDDLE INITIAL)

EXEMPTIONS 3 SOC. SEC. NO. 194-08-0862

POSITION Shipping Clerk

Week No.	Week Ended	Total Earnings	FICA Tax	Income Tax	Other		Total Deductions	Net Pay	Accumulated Earnings
								FORWARDED	1262.40
1	4/8	96.00	4.22	7.70	B	2.00	13.92	82.08	1358.40
2	4/15	96.00	4.22	7.70			11.92	84.08	1454.40
3	4/22	110.40	4.86	10.00			14.86	95.54	1564.80
4	4/29	96.00	4.22	7.70			11.92	84.08	1660.80
5	5/6	96.00	4.22	7.70	B	2.00	13.92	82.08	1756.80
6	5/13	96.00	4.22	7.70			11.92	84.08	1852.80
7	5/20	76.80	3.38	4.70			8.08	68.72	1929.60
8	5/27	96.00	4.22	7.70			11.92	84.08	2025.60
9	6/3	96.00	4.22	7.70	B	2.00	13.92	82.08	2121.60
10	6/10	110.40	4.86	10.00			14.86	95.54	2232.00
11	6/17	110.40	4.86	10.00			14.86	95.54	2342.40
12	6/24	106.80	4.70	9.30			14.00	92.80	2449.20
13	7/1	96.00	4.22	7.70	B	2.00	13.92	82.80	2545.20
QUARTERLY TOTALS		1282.80	56.42	105.60	B	8.00	170.02	1112.78	

(Column headings FICA Tax, Income Tax, Other and Total: Deductions)

Employee's earnings record

WAGE-BRACKET INCOME TAX WITHHOLDING TABLES

***Married* PERSONS *Weekly* PAYROLL PERIOD**

Wages are		Number of withholding exemptions claimed										
At least	Less than	0	1	2	3	4	5	6	7	8	9	10 or more
		Amount of income tax to be withheld										
$62....	$64....	$ 8.70	$ 6.70	$ 4.60	$ 2.60	$ .70						
64....	66....	9.00	7.00	4.90	2.90	1.00						
66....	68....	9.30	7.30	5.20	3.20	1.30						
68....	70....	9.60	7.60	5.50	3.50	1.60						
70....	72....	9.90	7.90	5.80	3.80	1.90						
72....	74....	10.20	8.20	6.10	4.10	2.10	$ .30					
74....	76....	10.50	8.50	6.40	4.40	2.40	.50					
76....	78....	10.80	8.80	6.70	4.70	2.70	.80					
78....	80....	11.10	9.10	7.00	5.00	3.00	1.10					
80....	82....	11.40	9.40	7.30	5.30	3.30	1.40					
82....	84....	11.70	9.70	7.60	5.60	3.60	1.70					
84....	86....	12.00	10.00	7.90	5.90	3.90	1.90	$ .10				
86....	88....	12.30	10.30	8.20	6.20	4.20	2.20	.30				
88....	90....	12.70	10.60	8.50	6.50	4.50	2.50	.60				
90....	92....	13.00	10.90	8.80	6.80	4.80	2.80	.90				
92....	94....	13.30	11.20	9.10	7.10	5.10	3.10	1.20				
94....	96....	13.70	11.50	9.40	7.40	5.40	3.40	1.50				
96....	98....	14.00	11.80	9.70	7.70	5.70	3.70	1.70				
98....	100....	14.40	12.10	10.00	8.00	6.00	4.00	2.00	$ .10			
100....	105....	15.00	12.70	10.60	8.50	6.50	4.50	2.50	.60			
105....	110....	15.80	13.50	11.30	9.30	7.30	5.30	3.20	1.30			
110....	115....	16.70	14.40	12.10	10.00	8.00	6.00	4.00	2.00	$ .10		
115....	120....	17.50	15.20	12.90	10.80	8.80	6.80	4.70	2.70	.80		
120....	125....	18.40	16.10	13.80	11.50	9.50	7.50	5.50	3.50	1.50		
125....	130....	19.20	16.90	14.60	12.30	10.30	8.30	6.20	4.20	2.20	$ .40	
130....	135....	20.10	17.80	15.50	13.20	11.00	9.00	7.00	5.00	3.00	1.10	
135....	140....	20.90	18.60	16.30	14.00	11.80	9.80	7.70	5.70	3.70	1.80	
140....	145....	21.80	19.50	17.20	14.90	12.60	10.50	8.50	6.50	4.50	2.50	$ .60
145....	150....	22.60	20.30	18.00	15.70	13.50	11.30	9.20	7.20	5.20	3.20	1.30
150....	160....	23.90	21.60	19.30	17.00	14.70	12.40	10.40	8.30	6.30	4.30	2.30
160....	170....	25.60	23.30	21.00	18.70	16.40	14.10	11.90	9.80	7.80	5.80	3.80

Section of weekly income tax withholding tables for married persons

Mr. Tupper's name is entered at the top of his earnings record, together with his payroll number and his social security number.

The amount columns of the employee's earnings record, except for the Accumulated Earnings column, are the same as the amount columns of the payroll register. The amounts opposite each employee's name on the payroll register are transferred to the corresponding columns of the employee's earnings record. The payroll register illustrated on page 445 is for the week ended June 24, the twelfth week in the second quarter. Mr. Tupper's earnings and deductions for that week are, therefore, entered on Line 12 of his employee's earnings record.

The Accumulated Earnings column shows the earnings for Mr. Tupper since the first of the year. The first entry in this column, $1,262.40, is the total amount of his earnings brought forward from his earnings record for the first quarter. The amounts in the Accumulated Earnings column supply an up-to-date reference for seeing when an employee's earnings have reached an amount beyond which certain payroll taxes do not apply. For example, employers do not have to pay state and federal unemployment taxes on the wages of an employee after his earnings for a year reach $3,000. Neither is the employee nor the employer required to pay any FICA tax after an employee's earnings for a year have reached $6,600.

The Quarterly Totals line provides space for the totals for the quarter. The form for the final quarter in the year also provides space for entering the totals for the year. These totals are needed in filing reports with the government on both a quarterly and an annual basis.

The law requires that the employee's earnings record be kept on file for a period of at least four years. This requirement is made in order to give the government time to check back on records of payments to employees and to audit the reports of employers.

PAYING THE PAYROLL

Paying the payroll by check

The Atlas Paper Company pays its employees weekly by check. It uses a special payroll check form that has a detachable stub on which are recorded the amounts deducted. The employee detaches the stub and keeps it as his record of deductions and cash received.

The payroll checks are drawn against a special payroll bank account. Each pay period a check for the total amount of the net pay is drawn on the regular checking account in favor of the payroll account. This check is deposited in a separate bank account against which the payroll checks are drawn. On June 26 the Atlas Paper Company drew a check for $1,351.98, deposited it in its payroll account, and then prepared the payroll checks.

The check for Mr. Tupper for the week ended June 24 appears below. The information for the check is taken directly from the payroll register.

PERIOD ENDING	EARNINGS			DEDUCTIONS						NET PAY	
	REG.	O.T.	TOTAL	FICA	INC. TAX WITH.	GROUP INS.	HOSP. CARE	OTHER	TOTAL	AMOUNT	CHECK NO.
6-24-67	106.80		106.80	4.70	9.30				14.00	92.80	655

No. 655

WESTSIDE BANK

76-2056
1041

ATLAS PAPER COMPANY
PAYROLL ACCOUNT

Lincoln, Nebraska, June 26, 1967

PAY TO THE ORDER OF Roy A. Tupper $92.80

The sum of $92 and 80 cts DOLLARS

Mark T. Perry
Treasurer

⑆1041⑈2056⑆ 136 32338⑈

Payroll check

Paying the payroll in cash

Some firms pay their employees in cash. This practice is usually followed when the employees find it difficult to get to a bank to have their checks cashed. When the payroll is to be paid in cash, the payroll clerk must obtain the cash from the bank in the proper denominations so that he will have the necessary change when he inserts the money in the pay envelopes. In order to have the necessary change, he prepares a payroll change sheet similar to the one at the right.

Each employee's number and the amount due him are entered in the first two columns of the payroll change sheet. Then, the bills and the coins required for the employee's pay envelope are listed in the columns at the right. For example, Employee No. 1 has $77.50 due him. To pay this amount, the payroll clerk needs three $20 bills, one $10 bill, one $5 bill, two $1 bills, and one 50-cent piece.

PAYROLL CHANGE SHEET

DATE Oct. 20, 1967

EMPLOYEE NO.	AMOUNT DUE	$20	$10	$5	$1	50¢	25¢	10¢	5¢	1¢
1	77 50	3	1	1	2	1				
2	84 26	4			4		1			1
3	84 88	4			4	1	1	1		3
4	61 21	3			1			2		1
75	67 06	3		1	2				1	1
76	78 61	3	1	1	3	1		1		1
77	57 33	2	1	1	2		1		1	3
78	84 12	4			4			1		2
TOTAL	4696 12	212	21	21	88	72	32	47	65	117

Payroll change sheet

After the payroll change sheet is completed, all the columns are totaled and a payroll requisition form is prepared. This form shows the number of each denomination desired and the amount of each denomination. The total of the amounts must equal the total of the payroll shown on the payroll change sheet. A typical payroll requisition form is shown at the left.

PAYROLL REQUISITION

DENOMINATION	NUMBER OF EACH DENOMINATION	AMOUNT
$20.00	212	4240 00
10.00	21	210 00
5.00	21	105 00
1.00	88	88 00
.50	72	36 00
.25	32	8 00
.10	47	4 70
.05	65	3 25
.01	117	1 17
TOTAL PAYROLL		4696 12

Payroll requisition

A check for the total amount of the payroll is then drawn. This check and the payroll requisition form are given to the bank teller, who gives the payroll clerk the number of each denomination needed. The payroll clerk places the money in the employees' pay envelopes.

Payroll receipt

When payrolls are paid in cash, a payroll receipt may be prepared in duplicate for each employee. The receipt contains a summary of the earnings record showing the employee's name, his gross earnings, an itemized list of the deductions, and the net amount he receives. When the employee receives his pay envelope, he signs one copy of the payroll receipt, which the business keeps. He retains the other copy as his record of earnings and deductions. An illustration of a payroll receipt is shown below.

PAYROLL RECEIPT

Name Theodore M. Seitz Payroll No. 11 So. Sec. No. 408-06-7186

For Period Ended Feb. 11, 1967 Date of Payment Feb. 13, 1967

HOURS		GROSS EARNINGS	DEDUCTIONS				NET PAY
REGULAR	OVERTIME		FICA TAX	INCOME TAX WITHHELD	OTHER	TOTAL	
40	5	114 75	5 05	10 00	GI 3 50	18 55	96 20

OTHER DEDUCTIONS:

CC – Community Chest
GI – Group Insurance
HC – Hospital Care
B – U. S. Savings Bonds
UD – Union Dues

Theodore M. Seitz
SIGNATURE

Payroll receipt showing the earnings, deductions, and net pay of an employee who is paid in cash

This payroll receipt shows that for the week ended February 11, Theodore M. Seitz had gross earnings of $114.75. The total deductions of $18.55 were: $5.05 for FICA taxes, $10.00 for income taxes withheld, and $3.50 for group insurance.

AUTOMATED PAYROLL ACCOUNTING

In Chapter 21 the bookkeeping machine was described and it was shown how this machine applies the write-it-once principle in preparing several records at one time. By means of the bookkeeping machine, all the payroll records may be prepared at the same time.

The payroll data are taken from the time cards or other time records and entered in the bookkeeping machine. All essential payroll records are prepared in the same posting operation. The illustration on the next page shows a payroll check, a statement of earnings and deductions, the employee's earnings record, the payroll journal (payroll register), and the check register. All of these records are prepared simultaneously on the bookkeeping machine. The same bookkeeping machine can be used to prepare the periodical tax reports that must be filed with the state and federal government.

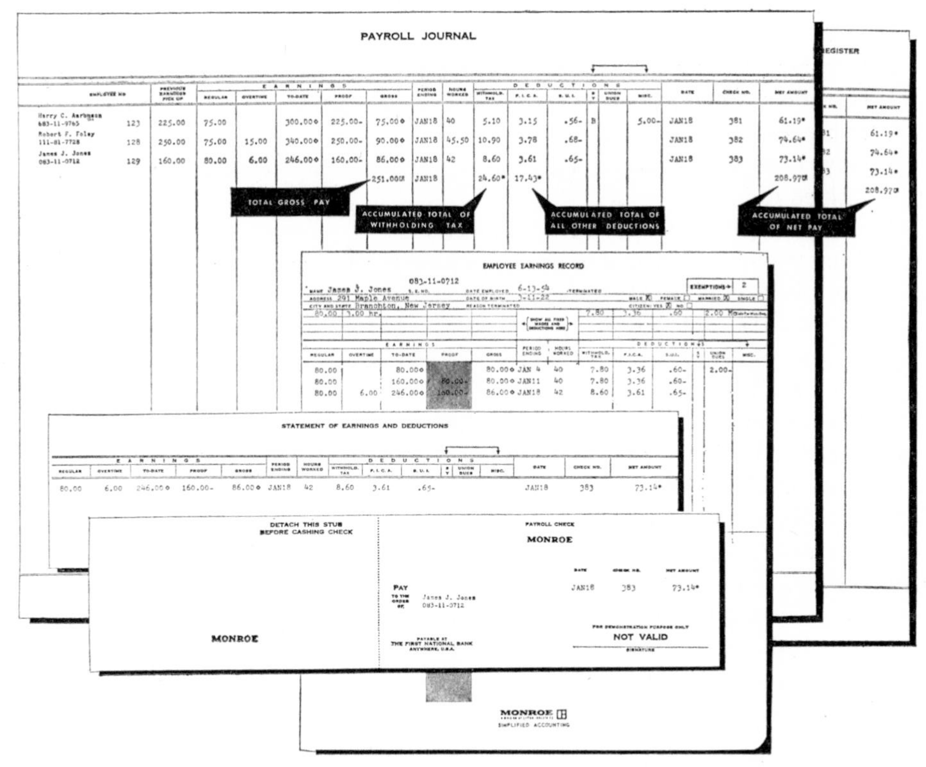

Monroe International, Inc.

Payroll check, statement of earnings and deductions, employee's earnings record, payroll journal, and check register prepared simultaneously in one automatic operation on the bookkeeping machine

Organizations with many employees often use punched-card equipment for payroll work. These firms have found that the use of automated equipment makes it possible to prepare all payroll records in a small fraction of the time formerly required. For example, a card-punch operator records in punched cards all the data shown on the time cards. The punched cards are "fed" into a calculator, which makes the calculations. A tabulator prepares the payroll register, the employee's earnings record, and the individual payroll checks. Payroll work that formerly required days to do by hand can now be done in a few hours by machine.

Increasing Your Business Vocabulary

What is the meaning of each of the following:

- a payroll
- b exemption
- c medicare
- d social security taxes
- e FICA tax
- f FUTA tax
- g state unemployment tax
- h employee's earnings record

Study Questions

1. Why are accurate payroll records necessary?
2. How does an employer collect for the federal government the income taxes of his employees?
3. How does an employer know how many exemptions each employee is entitled to?
4. How is a social security card obtained?
5. What are the principal types of information recorded on the time card illustrated on page 443?
6. On what day did Roy A. Tupper work overtime according to his time card on page 443?
7. What are the six steps commonly followed in determining each employee's earnings and the amount to be paid him?
8. What are the principal types of information recorded in the payroll register illustrated on page 445?
9. How is the amount of income taxes withheld from employees' wages determined?
10. On the employee's earnings record illustrated on page 448, what is the Accumulated Earnings column used for?
11. How is the payroll change sheet illustrated on page 451 prepared and used?
12. What payroll records may be prepared at the same time by the write-it-once principle on a bookkeeping machine?

Cases for Business Decision

CASE 1

The Bell Department Store is now paying its 85 employees in cash every two weeks. The head bookkeeper has recently talked with a representative of a business forms manufacturing company, who has recommended that the store pay its employees by check. The bookkeeper, too, feels that this would be a desirable change in the payroll accounting system. What factors should the bookkeeper investigate before making a recommendation to management that the present system of paying employees be changed?

CASE 2

The Dale Company, a small manufacturer of electronic parts, has been experiencing a rapid growth in the sale of its products. As a result, the company is planning to add 15 workers to its payroll. Presently the company does not use a time clock for recording the hours worked by its 25 employees. Each employee records by hand the hours worked on a time card that he gives to the bookkeeper at the end of the week.

As the bookkeeper for the Dale Company, you feel that a time clock should be installed and you are now commencing to prepare a report to the president of the company in which you recommend the purchase of a time clock. What advantages of using a time clock can you list in your report?

CASE 3

The Barker Company requires each employee to sign a payroll receipt, similar to the one illustrated on page 452, each time wages are paid. The Miles Company, on the other hand, does not require employees to sign payroll receipts. What difference in payroll procedures might make payroll receipts desirable for one company but not for the other?

Application Problems

PROBLEM 25-1 | Applying for a social security account number

If the workbook correlating with this textbook is not available, this problem may be omitted.

Instructions: Fill in the application for a social security account number given in the workbook. Use your own personal data. Compare your application with the illustration on page 442.

PROBLEM 25-2 | Using payroll time cards

If the workbook correlating with this textbook is not available, complete Appendix Problem 25-A instead of this problem.

Instructions: 1. Complete the time cards given in the workbook.

2. Record the time cards in a payroll register similar to the one on page 445 of the textbook. The date of payment is May 18.

3. Prepare a payroll change sheet similar to the one on page 451.

4. Prepare a payroll requisition form similar to the one on page 451.

PROBLEM 25-3 | Preparing an employee's earnings record

The total earnings of Lucille Edwards for the 13 weeks in the quarterly period July through September of the current year are given below, together with the deductions for hospital care.

Week Ended	Total Earnings	Deductions	Week Ended	Total Earnings	Deductions
7/6	$85.00	$6.50	8/24	$85.00	
7/13	86.00		8/31	87.00	
7/20	87.00		9/7	86.00	$6.50
7/27	85.00		9/14	85.00	
8/3	87.00	6.50	9/21	86.00	
8/10	86.00		9/28	87.00	
8/17	87.00				

Instructions: Prepare an employee's earnings record, similar to the one on page 448, for Lucille Edwards for the third quarter of the current year. Additional data needed to complete the record are as follows:

(a) Miss Edwards' time card number is 57.
(b) Miss Edwards' social security number is 268-05-9847.
(c) Miss Edwards' position is that of secretary.
(d) Miss Edwards' cumulative earnings for the first two quarters of the current year amount to $2,489.80.
(e) In addition to her deductions for hospital care, the following deductions for taxes should be made:
   (1) A deduction of 4.4% of her total earnings each week is to be made for FICA taxes. Use the social security wage tax table on page 447 for calculating the FICA tax on each week's total earnings.
   (2) A deduction is to be made from her total earnings each week for her income tax withheld. Miss Edwards claims only one withholding exemption for herself. Use the weekly wage-bracket withholding table on page 448 to obtain each of her weekly income tax deductions.

PROBLEM 25-4 Preparing a payroll

Lorraine Products pays its employees by check. For each pay period the bookkeeper prepares a payroll register showing the total earnings, the deductions, and the net pay of each employee.

A part of the payroll register for the week ended January 13 of the current year, showing the number, the name, the marital status, the number of exemptions, the total earnings, and other deductions of each employee, is given below.

PAYROLL REGISTER

WEEK ENDED January 13, 19-- DATE OF PAYMENT

No.	Employee's Name	Marital Status	No. of Exemptions	Total Earnings	Deductions			
					FICA Tax	Income Tax	Other	
1	Wm S. Barnes	M	5	107 00			B	2 00
8	John Bennett	S	1	96 00				
3	Steven Cohn	S	1	88 00				
10	Ida M. Cooke	M	2	76 00			CC	50
7	Jean DeMaris	S	1	66 00			B	1 00
5	R. S. Fromm	M	2	95 00			CC	1 50
9	Ruth Hensley	S	1	65 00				
4	Sandra Klein	S	1	76 00				
2	Mary Macke	S	1	88 00				
6	C. F. Sullivan	M	4	108 00			B	2 00

OTHER DEDUCTIONS: CC — COMMUNITY CHEST, B — BONDS

Instructions: 1. Prepare a payroll register similar to the one illustrated on page 445. The date of payment is January 15. Payroll checks beginning with the one for Mr. Barnes on Line 1, are numbered consecutively. Mr. Barnes' payroll check is No. 208.

2. Use the wage tax table on page 447 to find the deduction of 4.4% of each employee's total earnings for FICA taxes. Use the wage-bracket withholding tables on pages 448 and 449 to find the income tax deduction for each employee.

3. Prepare a check for the total amount of the net pay. Make the check payable to "Payroll Account" and sign your name as treasurer of the company. This check will be deposited in a separate bank account against which all payroll checks will be drawn.

4. Prepare a payroll check for Employee No. 1, William S. Barnes. Sign your name as treasurer of the company.

Optional Problems

★ SUPPLEMENTARY PROBLEM 25-S

Preparing a payroll

A part of a payroll register for the week ended April 7 of the current year, showing the number, the name, the marital status, the number of exemptions, the total earnings, and other deductions of each employee, is given below.

PAYROLL REGISTER

WEEK ENDED April 7, 19-- DATE OF PAYMENT

No.	Employee's Name	Marital Status	No. of Exemptions	Total Earnings	Deductions: FICA Tax	Deductions: Income Tax	Deductions: Other
11	Laura Cain	S	1	65 50			B 1 00
2	Jean Dewey	S	1	75 00			
4	Clement Eckler	M	4	107 00			HC 1 90
14	J. G. Flagg	M	3	95 00			
15	Esther Hawkins	M	2	67 50			
6	Walter Kern	M	3	108 50			HC 1 60
9	Mary Z. Lehmann	M	2	86 25			
10	Harriet Nyer	S	1	68 00			B 1 00
1	Betty Pringle	S	1	67 00			
13	Ethel L. Sargent	M	2	86 50			B 2 50
5	George Spaulding	M	3	95 60			HC 1 90
8	Paul Todd	M	4	106 75			HC 1 90
3	Ruth Vance	S	1	75 50			
12	Betty Lee Walden	S	1	67 25			B 1 00
7	C. L. Yates	M	2	88 33			

OTHER DEDUCTIONS: HC — HOSPITAL CARE, B — BONDS

Instructions: 1. Prepare a payroll register similar to the one illustrated on page 445. The date of payment is April 10.

2. Use the wage tax table on page 447 to find the deduction of 4.4% of each employee's total earnings for FICA taxes. Use the wage-bracket withholding tables on pages 448 and 449 to find the income tax deduction for each employee.

3. Prepare a payroll change sheet similar to the one illustrated on page 451.

4. Prepare a payroll requisition form similar to the one illustrated on page 451.

★BONUS PROBLEM 25-B

Computing piecework wages

Introductory remarks. Production workers in factories are frequently paid on the basis of the number of units they produce. This is called the piecework incentive wage plan. Most piecework wage plans include a guaranteed hourly rate to employees regardless of the number of units they produce. This guaranteed hourly rate is called the base rate.

Time and motion study engineers usually determine the standard time required for producing a single unit. For example, if time studies determine that 6 minutes is the standard time required to produce a unit, then the standard rate for one hour would be 10 units (60 minutes ÷ 6 minutes = 10 units per hour). If the worker's base pay is $1.80 per hour, the piece rate is 18¢ ($1.80 ÷ 10 units = 18¢ per unit). Therefore, if the worker produces 10 or less units per hour, he is paid only $1.80 per hour, his base pay. But for every unit in excess of 10 that he produces each hour, he is paid 18¢ in addition to his base pay.

The Billings Manufacturing Company has a crew of three men working in the welding department and a crew of three men working in the assembly department. Standard production for the welding department is 12 units per hour per man. Standard production for the assembly department is 8 units per hour per man. Each of the men in both departments worked 8 hours a day during the first week in July. Payroll records for the week ended July 6 show:

No.	Worker	Marital Status	No. of Exemptions	Guaranteed Hourly Rate	Units Produced					Weekly Total
					M	Tu	W	Th	F	
	Welding Dept.:									
W6	Charles Bramel....	S	1	$2.40	96	98	96	100	96	486
W14	James Dietz......	M	2	2.40	90	93	95	96	90	464
W12	William Welsh....	M	4	2.40	106	105	115	106	103	535
	Assembly Dept.:									
A3	John Eilers.......	M	3	1.80	68	66	66	71	73	344
A12	Carl Gorrell......	S	1	1.80	70	70	68	68	70	346
A16	Edward Jory......	M	2	1.80	65	67	65	68	70	335

A piecework incentive of 20¢ per unit is in operation for the welding department and 22.5¢ per unit is in operation for the assembly department.

Instructions: 1. Prepare a payroll register similar to the one illustrated on page 445. The date of payment is July 8.

2. Use the wage tax table on page 447 to find the deduction of 4.4% of each employee's total earnings for FICA taxes. Use the wage-bracket withholding tables on pages 448 and 449 to find the income tax deduction for each employee. None of the employees had "Other" deductions.

3. Prepare a payroll change sheet similar to the one illustrated on page 451.

4. Prepare a payroll requisition form similar to the one illustrated on page 451.

CHAPTER 26 PAYROLL ACCOUNTS, TAXES, AND REPORTS

The payroll information for each pay period is summarized in the payroll register. The payroll register becomes the bookkeeper's source document for journalizing the payroll information for each pay period.

RECORDING THE PAYROLL IN THE PAYROLL REGISTER

The payroll register of the Atlas Paper Company for the week ended June 24 is shown below.

PAYROLL REGISTER

WEEK ENDED June 24, 1967 DATE OF PAYMENT June 26, 1967

NO.	EMPLOYEE'S NAME	MARITAL STATUS	NO. OF EXEMPTIONS	TOTAL EARNINGS	DEDUCTIONS					NET PAY	
					FICA TAX	INCOME TAX	OTHER		TOTAL	AMOUNT	CK.NO.
1	John T. Archer	M	2	96.00	4.22	9.70			13.92	82.08	643
4	Charles Austin	S	1	120.00	5.28	18.10	CC	1.50	24.88	95.12	644
2	Richard Brett	M	3	116.50	5.13	10.80	CC	.50	16.43	100.07	645
6	Howard M. Caldwell	S	1	74.40	3.27	9.30			12.57	61.83	646
19	Phillip Dalton	M	4	110.80	4.88	8.00	CC	.50	13.38	97.42	647
7	Paul Maxon	M	3	120.00	5.28	11.50			16.78	103.22	648
16	Harry Nixon	M	2	89.00	3.92	8.50			12.42	76.58	649
8	William S. Parker	M	2	150.00	6.60	19.30	B	2.00	27.90	122.10	650
5	Howard Price	M	2	89.00	3.92	8.50			12.42	76.58	651
18	James Randolph	S	1	65.00	2.86	7.60	B	2.00	12.46	52.54	652
9	Allen J. Ross	M	3	96.00	4.22	7.70			11.92	84.08	653
11	Henry Stahl	S	1	116.50	5.13	17.10	B CC	4.00 1.00	27.23	89.27	654
20	Roy A. Tupper	M	3	106.80	4.70	9.30			14.00	92.80	655
10	Walter Wick	M	3	120.00	5.28	11.50			16.78	103.22	656
3	Russell Williams	M	2	62.00	2.73	4.60			7.33	54.67	657
17	Mary Zisk	S	1	75.00	3.30	9.30	B	2.00	14.60	60.40	658
	Totals			1607.00	70.72	170.80	CC B	3.50 10.00	255.02	1351.98	

OTHER DEDUCTIONS: CC—COMMUNITY CHEST: GI—GROUP INSURANCE: HC—HOSPITAL CARE: B—U.S. SAVINGS BONDS: UD—UNION DUES

Payroll register

Analyzing the debits and the credits in the payroll register

The total of the Total Earnings column, $1,607.00, is the salary expense for the period. Salary Expense is debited for this amount.

The total of the FICA Tax column, $70.72, is the amount withheld from the salaries of employees for FICA taxes. Until this amount is paid to the government, it is a liability of the business. To record this liability, FICA Taxes Payable is credited for $70.72.

The total of the Income Tax column, $170.80, is the amount withheld from salaries of employees for income taxes. Until this amount is paid to the government, it is a liability of the business. To record this liability, Employees Income Taxes Payable is credited for $170.80.

The $3.50 total of the Other column is the amount withheld from salaries to apply on the pledges that employees have made to the annual Community Chest drive. The total of $10.00 in this column is the amount withheld from the salaries of employees who wish to have U. S. Savings Bonds purchased for them. Until these respective amounts have been paid by the employer, they are liabilities of the business. To record these liabilities, Community Chest Donations Payable is credited for $3.50 and U. S. Savings Bonds Payable is credited for $10.00.

The total of the Net Pay Amount column, $1,351.98, is the amount of cash paid to employees. To record the decrease in the balance of the asset Cash, the cash account is credited for this amount.

The debits and the credits based on the column totals of the payroll register are summarized in the T accounts shown below.

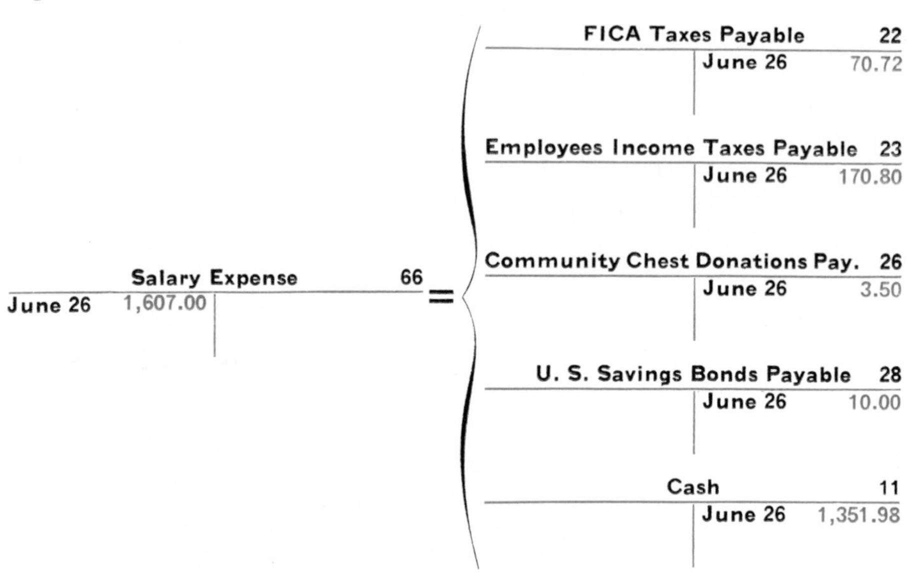

Recording the payroll entry in the combination journal

The payroll check was issued on June 26. The entry made in the combination journal to record the totals of the June 24 payroll register is shown on the next page.

The amount of the Salary Expense, $1,607.00, is entered in the General Debit column. The credit to Cash, $1,351.98, is entered in the Cash Credit column. The amounts of the two tax liabilities and the two "Other" liabilities are entered in the General Credit column.

PAGE 12 COMBINATION JOURNAL

	CASH DEBIT (1)	CASH CREDIT (2)	CK. NO.	DATE	ACCOUNT TITLE	POST. REF.	GENERAL DEBIT (3)	GENERAL CREDIT (4)	
11		1351 98	659	26	Salary Expense		1607 00		11
12					FICA Taxes Payable			70 72	12
13					Employees Income Taxes Pay.			170 80	13
14					Community Chest Donations Pay.			3 50	14
15					U.S. Savings Bonds Payable			10 00	15
16									16
17									17
18									18

Entry to record the payroll

Liability accounts for payroll withholdings

After the payroll entry of June 26 is posted, the four liability accounts for payroll withholdings appear as follows:

FICA Taxes Payable — ACCOUNT NO. 22

DATE	ITEMS	POST. REF.	DEBIT	CREDIT	BALANCE DEBIT	BALANCE CREDIT
26		12		70 72		592 38

Employees Income Taxes Payable — ACCOUNT NO. 23

DATE	ITEMS	POST. REF.	DEBIT	CREDIT	BALANCE DEBIT	BALANCE CREDIT
26		12		170 80		835 50

Community Chest Donations Payable — ACCOUNT NO. 26

DATE	ITEMS	POST. REF.	DEBIT	CREDIT	BALANCE DEBIT	BALANCE CREDIT
26		12		3 50		47 80

U. S. Savings Bonds Payable — ACCOUNT NO. 28

DATE	ITEMS	POST. REF.	DEBIT	CREDIT	BALANCE DEBIT	BALANCE CREDIT
26		12		10 00		97 50

The credits in the two tax liability accounts, $70.72 in FICA Taxes Payable and $170.80 in Employees Income Taxes Payable, represent liabilities of the business to the government for taxes withheld from employees' earnings.

The credit of $3.50 in Community Chest Donations Payable represents a liability of the business to pay to the local Community Chest the donations that employees authorized be withheld from their earnings. The credit of $10.00 in U. S. Savings Bonds Payable represents a liability of the business for the purchase of U. S. Savings Bonds for certain of its employees.

THE EMPLOYER'S PAYROLL TAXES

Employers must pay to the government the taxes they withhold from their employees' earnings. Most employers must also pay several payroll taxes of their own. These employer payroll taxes are expenses of the business.

The employer's FICA tax

The FICA taxes levied against the employer are computed at the same rate and on the same earnings used in computing the FICA tax on employees.

The Atlas Paper Company withheld $70.72 in FICA taxes from the pay of its employees for the pay period ended June 24, 1967. The amount, $70.72, was obtained by totaling the FICA Tax column on the payroll register. The employer's FICA tax is calculated by multiplying the total of the Total Earnings column by the tax rate. Thus, for the pay period ended June 24, the employer's FICA tax is $70.71 ($1,607.00 x 4.4%.)

> Sometimes there is a difference of a few cents between the total of the FICA taxes deducted from the employees' earnings and the employer's FICA tax. This difference is caused by the rounding of fractional cents when making the calculations. The tax imposed on the employees is based on the amount earned by each employee during the pay period, while the tax imposed on the employer is based on the total wages paid to all employees during the pay period.

The expense of FICA taxes to the Atlas Paper Company, $70.71, is recorded by a journal entry debiting Payroll Tax Expense and crediting FICA Taxes Payable, as illustrated in the combined entry on page 463.

The employer's state unemployment tax

Under the provisions of the federal and the state unemployment insurance laws, employers are required to pay taxes that are used for the payment of unemployment compensation. The taxes for unemployment purposes are based on the amount of the salaries and, in most states, are levied on the employers only.

Under the state unemployment compensation laws, employers are required to pay contributions into state unemployment compensation funds at a basic rate of 2.7% of the taxable wages. The taxable wages for unemployment taxes in most states consists of the first $3,000 earned by each employee. No employee on the Atlas Paper Company's payroll of June 24 had yet earned $3,000 in 1967. Thus, the state unemployment tax was 2.7% of the total earnings, $1,607.00, or $43.39. The recording of the expense for state unemployment taxes is included in the combined entry shown below. This entry shows a debit to Payroll Tax Expense and a credit to State Unemployment Taxes Payable.

The employer's federal unemployment tax

Employers are also required to pay an unemployment tax to the federal government. The tax consists of .4% of the first $3,000 earned by each employee.

The federal unemployment tax on the total wages of $1,607.00 paid by the Atlas Paper Company was .4% of this amount, or $6.43. The recording of this expense for federal unemployment taxes is included in the combined entry shown below. This entry shows a debit to Payroll Tax Expense and a credit to Federal Unemployment Taxes Payable.

Recording the employer's payroll taxes

The Atlas Paper Company's payroll taxes for the payroll period ended June 24, 1967, amounted to: FICA taxes, $70.71; state unemployment taxes, $43.39; and federal unemployment taxes, $6.43. The bookkeeper of the Atlas Paper Company recorded these three expenses in a combined entry as follows:

PAGE 12 COMBINATION JOURNAL

	1	2					3	4	
	CASH		CK. NO.	DATE	ACCOUNT TITLE	POST. REF.	GENERAL		
	DEBIT	CREDIT					DEBIT	CREDIT	
16				26	Payroll Tax Expense		120 53		16
17					FICA Taxes Payable			70 71	17
18					State Unemploy. Taxes Pay.			43 39	18
19					Fed. Unemploy. Taxes Pay.			6 43	19
20									20
21									21
22									22

Combined entry for employer's payroll taxes

Payroll Tax Expense is debited for $120.53 to record the total of the employer's payroll tax expense. The three credits in this combined entry record the three different liabilities resulting from the January 24 payroll as follows: FICA Taxes Payable, $70.71; State Unemployment Taxes Payable, $43.39; Federal Unemployment Taxes Payable, $6.43.

The use of one tax expense account for recording all of the employer's payroll taxes is a common practice. If a breakdown is ever needed of the amounts of the different payroll taxes, the amounts can be obtained from the payroll tax liability accounts.

Some businesses use a separate expense account for each kind of employer's payroll tax. When this is done, the single account, Payroll Tax Expense, is replaced with expense accounts such as FICA Taxes, State Unemployment Taxes, and Federal Unemployment Taxes.

Posting the entry for employer's payroll taxes

After the entry for the employer's payroll taxes is posted, the four accounts involved appear as follows:

FICA Taxes Payable ACCOUNT NO. 22

DATE	ITEMS	POST. REF.	DEBIT	CREDIT	BALANCE DEBIT	BALANCE CREDIT
26		12		70 72		592 38
26		12		70 71		663 09

State Unemployment Taxes Payable ACCOUNT NO. 24

DATE	ITEMS	POST. REF.	DEBIT	CREDIT	BALANCE DEBIT	BALANCE CREDIT
26		12		43 39		524 70

Federal Unemployment Taxes Payable ACCOUNT NO. 25

DATE	ITEMS	POST. REF.	DEBIT	CREDIT	BALANCE DEBIT	BALANCE CREDIT
26		12		6 43		103 60

Payroll Tax Expense ACCOUNT NO. 64

DATE	ITEMS	POST. REF.	DEBIT	CREDIT	BALANCE DEBIT	BALANCE CREDIT
26		12	120 53		484 72	

The debit of $120.53 to Payroll Tax Expense is the total employer's payroll tax expense for the week ended June 24. Offsetting this $120.53 debit are credits totaling $120.53 in the three liability accounts as follows: FICA Taxes Payable, $70.71; State Unemployment Taxes Payable, $43.39; Federal Unemployment Taxes Payable, $6.43.

Note that the FICA taxes payable account has two credits. The first credit, $70.72, is the employer's liability for the amount of FICA taxes withheld from the employees' wages for the week ended June 24. This amount was posted from the entry that recorded the payroll. The second credit, $70.71, is the employer's FICA tax. This amount was posted from the journal entry that recorded the employer's liability for his share of the FICA tax.

PAYING THE WITHHOLDING TAXES AND THE PAYROLL TAXES

At the end of each quarter of the year, every employer must pay to the government the amount of the income tax and FICA taxes withheld and the FICA taxes for which he is liable. If the total of these taxes for any month (except the third month of the quarter) exceeds $100.00, the employer is required to deposit these amounts in a bank authorized to accept the payment or in the Federal Reserve Bank that serves his district. Special rules apply for handling such taxes if the employees are household or agricultural workers.

Paying the liability for employees' income taxes and for FICA taxes

After payment of the last payroll in the second quarter, the liability account Employees Income Taxes Payable had a credit balance of $835.50 and the liability account FICA Taxes Payable had a credit balance of $663.10. On July 29 the Atlas Paper Company issued Check No. 712 for $1,498.60 in payment of these two liabilities. The entry to record this payment was as follows:

PAGE 14 COMBINATION JOURNAL

	1	2					3	4	
	CASH						GENERAL		
	DEBIT	CREDIT	CK. NO.	DATE	ACCOUNT TITLE	POST. REF.	DEBIT	CREDIT	
10		1498 60	712	29	Employees Income Taxes Pay.		835 50		10
11					FICA Taxes Payable		663 10		11
12									12
13									13
14									14
15									15
16									16

Entry to record payment of liability for employees' income taxes and for FICA taxes

The liability accounts Employees Income Taxes Payable and FICA Taxes Payable are debited to record the decreases in these liabilities. The cash account is credited to record the decrease in the asset Cash.

Paying the liability for state unemployment taxes

State requirements vary for reporting and paying the state unemployment taxes. In general, however, employers are required to pay these taxes during the month following each calendar quarter.

On July 31, the Atlas Paper Company paid its liability for the state unemployment taxes for the quarter ended June 30. The amount of this liability, $524.70, was obtained by adding the weekly credits in the account State Unemployment Taxes Payable. The entry to record this payment was as follows:

PAGE 14 — COMBINATION JOURNAL

	1	2					3	4	
	CASH		CK. NO.	DATE	ACCOUNT TITLE	POST. REF.	GENERAL		
	DEBIT	CREDIT					DEBIT	CREDIT	
23		524 70	734	31	State Unemployment Taxes Pay.		524 70		23
24									24
25									25

Entry to record payment of liability for state unemployment taxes

This payment covered the state unemployment taxes based on the payrolls of April, May, and June.

Paying the liability for federal unemployment taxes

The federal unemployment taxes are payable annually on or before January 31 of the following year.

The federal unemployment taxes are paid by the Atlas Paper Company after the close of the year. On December 31 the balance of the account Federal Unemployment Taxes Payable was $192.00. On January 24 of the following year, a check for this amount was sent to the District Director of Internal Revenue. To record the payment of the liability, the following entry was made:

PAGE 23 — COMBINATION JOURNAL

	1	2					3	4	
	CASH		CK. NO.	DATE	ACCOUNT TITLE	POST. REF.	GENERAL		
	DEBIT	CREDIT					DEBIT	CREDIT	
18		192 00	1835	24	Fed. Unemployment Taxes Pay.		192 00		18
19									19
20									20

Entry to record payment of liability for federal unemployment taxes

This payment covered the federal unemployment taxes based on the payrolls for 1967.

Employer's annual report to employees of taxes withheld

Each employer who is required to withhold income taxes and FICA taxes from employees' wages must furnish each of his employees annually a statement in duplicate showing the total earnings of the employee and the amounts withheld for taxes. This statement is made on Form W-2, which is furnished by the District Director of Internal Revenue.

The employee's copy of Form W-2 prepared by the Atlas Paper Company for Roy A. Tupper for the year 1967 is illustrated below.

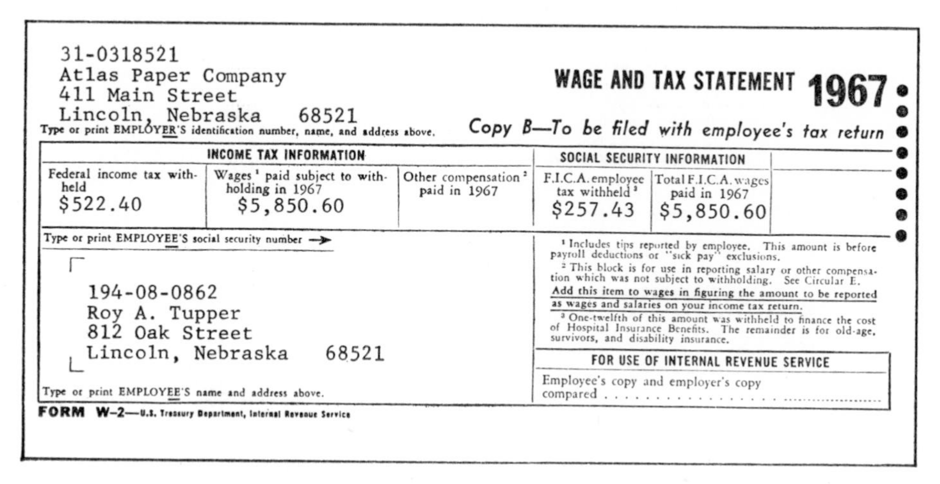

31-0318521
Atlas Paper Company
411 Main Street
Lincoln, Nebraska 68521
Type or print EMPLOYER'S identification number, name, and address above.

WAGE AND TAX STATEMENT 1967

Copy B—To be filed with employee's tax return

INCOME TAX INFORMATION			SOCIAL SECURITY INFORMATION	
Federal income tax withheld	Wages [1] paid subject to withholding in 1967	Other compensation [2] paid in 1967	F.I.C.A. employee tax withheld [3]	Total F.I.C.A. wages paid in 1967
$522.40	$5,850.60		$257.43	$5,850.60

Type or print EMPLOYEE'S social security number →

194-08-0862
Roy A. Tupper
812 Oak Street
Lincoln, Nebraska 68521

Type or print EMPLOYEE'S name and address above.

[1] Includes tips reported by employee. This amount is before payroll deductions or "sick pay" exclusions.

[2] This block is for use in reporting salary or other compensation which was not subject to withholding. See Circular E. Add this item to wages in figuring the amount to be reported as wages and salaries on your income tax return.

[3] One-twelfth of this amount was withheld to finance the cost of Hospital Insurance Benefits. The remainder is for old-age, survivors, and disability insurance.

FOR USE OF INTERNAL REVENUE SERVICE
Employee's copy and employer's copy compared . . . .

FORM W-2—U.S. Treasury Department, Internal Revenue Service

Wage and Tax Statement, Form W-2, given to the employee for taxes withheld

When the employee files his income tax return, he must attach the original of the W-2 form to his income tax return. An employee should receive a W-2 form from each employer for whom he worked during the taxable year.

The employer's quarterly federal tax return

Each employer who withholds income taxes and FICA taxes from employees' wages must file with the Internal Revenue Service on Form 941 a quarterly report of such withholdings. Form 941 prepared by the Atlas Paper Company for the calendar quarter ended June 30, 1967, is illustrated on page 468.

This quarterly report must be made on or before the last day of the month following the close of each calendar quarter. When the sum of the income taxes and the FICA taxes withheld is less than $100.00 for each of the first two months in a quarter, the employer is permitted to retain these withholdings until he files his quarterly report. When the sum of the income taxes and the FICA taxes withheld exceeds $100.00 for the first or the second month of a quarter, the employer is required to deposit that month's withholdings in an authorized bank. Then, when the quarterly report is submitted, the employer pays the balance of the withholdings that are due and attaches copies of the receipts of the previous deposits.

The employees' earnings records that were discussed in Chapter 25 and illustrated on page 448 are of considerable help in preparing Form 941.

FORM 941 **EMPLOYER'S QUARTERLY FEDERAL TAX RETURN**
U.S. Treasury Department—Internal Revenue Service

FEDERAL INCOME TAX WITHHELD FROM WAGES	1. AMOUNT OF INCOME TAX WITHHELD (If not required write "None")	2,172.30	
	2. ADJUSTMENT FOR PRECEDING QUARTERS OF CALENDAR YEAR	0	
	3. ADJUSTED TOTAL OF INCOME TAX WITHHELD →		2,172.30
FEDERAL INSURANCE CONTRIBUTIONS ACT TAXES	4a. TAXABLE WAGES PAID (From Item 21) $20,891.00 ×8.8% $	1,838.41	
	4b. TAXABLE TIPS REPORTED (Item 22) $ 0 ×4.4% $	0	
	5. TOTAL F.I.C.A. TAXES (Item 4a plus Item 4b) →		1,838.41
	6. ADJUSTMENT (See instructions)		0
	7. ADJUSTED TOTAL OF F.I.C.A. TAXES →		1,838.41
TOTALS	8. TOTAL TAXES (Item 3 plus Item 7)		4,010.71
	9. TOTAL OF ENCLOSED DEPOSITARY RECEIPTS (From Schedule B, other side)		2,697.21
	10. BALANCE DUE (Item 8 minus Item 9) PAY TO "INTERNAL REVENUE SERVICE"		1,313.50

Under penalties of perjury, I declare that I have examined this return, including accompanying schedules and statements, and to the best of my knowledge and belief it is true, correct, and complete.

Date 7-28-67 Signature *George Lind* Title Owner (Owner, President, Partner, Member, etc.)

If not liable for returns in succeeding quarters write "FINAL" here .... Complete items 11–13 on reverse.

BE SURE TO ENCLOSE REMITTANCE, DEPOSITARY RECEIPTS, AND SCHEDULE A WITH THIS RETURN.

T
P
D
I
T

Employer's name, address, identification number, and calendar quarter. (If not correctly printed please change)

Name (as distinguished from trade name) Atlas Paper Company
Date quarter ended June 30, 1967
Trade name, if any
Identification No. 31-0318521
Address and Postal ZIP code 411 Main Street, Lincoln, Nebraska 68521

If form is not preaddressed, check type of employer—
☒ Sole owner ☐ Partnership
☐ Corporation ☐ Other (specify)

Entries must be made both above and below this line

Name (as distinguished from trade name) Atlas Paper Company
Date quarter ended June 30, 1967
Trade name, if any
Identification No. 31-0318521
Address and Postal ZIP code 411 Main Street, Lincoln, Nebraska 68521

U.S. TREASURY DEPARTMENT
District Director of Internal Revenue
OFFICIAL BUSINESS
POSTAGE AND FEES PAID

POSTMASTER: If undeliverable treat in accordance with Section 355.56 of Postal Manual.

SCHEDULE A—QUARTERLY REPORT OF WAGES TAXABLE UNDER THE FEDERAL INSURANCE CONTRIBUTIONS ACT (FOR SOCIAL SECURITY)
IF WAGES WERE NOT TAXABLE UNDER THE F.I.C.A. MAKE NO ENTRIES BELOW

14. (First quarter only) Number of employees (except household) employed in the pay period including March 12th. 16
15. Total pages of this return, including this page and any pages of Form 941a. 1
16. Total number of employees listed. 16

List for each employee, except agricultural employees, the WAGES taxable under the Federal Insurance Contributions Act (for Social Security) which were paid during the quarter. If you pay an employee more than $6,600 in a calendar year, report ONLY THE FIRST $6,600 of such wages. In the case of "Tip Income" see instructions.

SAVE TIME AND MONEY—If your report shows each employee's name and number *exactly* as they appear on his Social Security card it will not be necessary to write back to you to ask for the correct information

17. EMPLOYEE'S SOCIAL SECURITY ACCOUNT NUMBER (If number is unknown, see Circular E) 000 00 0000	18. NAME OF EMPLOYEE (Please type or print)	19. TAXABLE F.I.C.A. WAGES Paid to Employee in Quarter (Before deductions) Dollars Cents	20. TAXABLE TIPS REPORTED (See instructions on page 4) Dollars Cents
143 05 3871	John T. Archer	1,248.00	
463 04 1224	Charles Austin	1,560.00	
194 08 0862	Roy A. Tupper	1,282.80	
211 12 4333	Walter Wick	1,560.00	
144 03 8998	Russell Williams	806.00	
343 08 1555	Mary Zisk	973.50	

If you need more space for listing employees, use Schedule A continuation sheets, Form 941a.
Totals of wages and tips reported in columns 19 and 20 on this page → 20,891.00

21. TOTAL WAGES TAXABLE UNDER F.I.C.A. PAID DURING QUARTER (Total of column 19 on this page and continuation sheets.) Enter here and in Item 4a above.......... $20,891.00

22. TOTAL TIPS REPORTED UNDER F.I.C.A. DURING QUARTER (Total of column 20 on this page and continuation sheets.) Enter here and in Item 4b above → $ 0

FILE THIS RETURN WITH YOUR DISTRICT DIRECTOR OF INTERNAL REVENUE. (Form 941) Page 1

Employer's Quarterly Federal Tax Return, Form 941 — Page 1

The employer's annual reconciliation report of income taxes withheld

Form W-3, Reconciliation of Income Taxes Withheld from Wages, provides for a comparison of the total income taxes withheld as reported on all W-2 forms and the total amount of income tax withheld as reported on the four quarterly tax returns, Form 941. The reconciliation form must be filed with the employer's last quarterly report each year. Along with this reconciliation report must be sent copies of all W-2 forms (Wage and Tax Statement) furnished to employees.

The reconciliation of quarterly returns prepared by the Atlas Paper Company for 1967 on Form W-3 is illustrated below.

Form W-3
U.S. Treasury Department
Internal Revenue Service

RECONCILIATION OF INCOME TAX WITHHELD AND TRANSMITTAL OF WAGE AND TAX STATEMENTS (FORMS W-2) 1967

Type or Print Employer's Name and Address as it appears on Forms 941 or 943

Name (as distinguished from trade name): Atlas Paper Company
Employer Identification No. (from Form 941 or 943): 31-0318521
Trade name (if any):
COPY FOR DISTRICT DIRECTOR
Street address: 411 Main Street
1. Number of Forms W-2 (Copy A), Wage and Tax Statements, attached: 16
City, State, and ZIP code: Lincoln, Nebraska 68521

2. Total income tax withheld from wages reported on Forms W-2 .... $ 9,011.50
3. Total "Uncollected Employee Tax on Tips" reported on Forms W-2 .... $ 0
4. Adjusted total of income tax withheld from wages as reported on Form 941 for Quarter ended:
a. Mar. 31 $ 2,180.40 b. June 30 2,172.30
c. Sept. 30 2,280.00 d. Dec. 31 2,378.80
5. Total of amounts shown on lines 4a through 4d (if different from total on line 2 attach explanation) .... $ 9,011.50

Under penalties of perjury, I declare that I have examined this return, including accompanying schedules and statements, and to the best of my knowledge and belief it is true, correct, and complete.

Date 1-29-68 Signature *George Lind* Title Owner
(Owner, President, Partner, Member, etc.)

Reconciliation of Income Tax Withheld from Wages, Form W-3

Study Questions

1. What is the source document for journalizing the payroll information for each payroll period?
2. The total earnings of the employees for the week ended June 24, 1967, as shown in the payroll register on page 459, amounted to $1,607.00. The total amount paid the employees was $1,351.98. What causes the difference between these two amounts?
3. What entry was made in the combination journal on page 461 to record the amounts withheld from the employees' wages and the payment of the payroll?
4. What use does the government make of the unemployment taxes that it collects?
5. What combined entry was made in the combination journal on page 463 to record the employer's three payroll taxes?
6. Why does the FICA taxes payable account on page 464 show two credit entries on the same date?
7. When is an employer required to deposit withholdings in an authorized bank?

8. How frequently must employers pay their federal unemployment taxes?
9. What two payroll tax liabilities are paid with one check and recorded as a combined entry?
10. What entry was made in the combination journal on page 466 to record the payment of the liability for state unemployment taxes?
11. What entry was made in the combination journal on page 466 to record the payment of the liability for federal unemployment taxes?
12. What statement is the employer required to furnish each employee at the end of the year? What does this statement show?
13. When the sum of the FICA taxes and income taxes withheld is less than $100.00 each month, how long may an employer retain these withholdings?

Cases for Business Decision

CASE 1

The Trippett Company is required to pay taxes under the Federal Insurance Contributions Act and the Federal Unemployment Tax Act. The company is also subject to a state unemployment tax of 2.7%. The general manager of the company has estimated that the total payroll for 1967 which will be subject to the FICA tax is $40,000.00. It is estimated that 50 percent of the total payroll for 1967 will be subject to federal and state unemployment taxes. The general manager has asked you, the bookkeeper, the following questions:

(a) What is the estimated total amount of social security tax expense the company will be required to pay in 1967?
(b) What percentage of the estimated payroll will the company be required to pay in social security tax expense in 1967?

CASE 2

The Sherman Canning Company has a weekly payroll of $5,000, with the following deductions:

Employees income taxes, $460.00
FICA taxes, $220.03
Hospital Care premiums, $49.60
Union dues, $28.50

The company's liabilities for payroll taxes are as follows:

FICA taxes, 4.4%
State unemployment taxes, 2.7%
Federal unemployment taxes, .4%

What entry should the bookkeeper make in the combination journal to record (a) the payment of the payroll and the amounts withheld, and (b) the liability of the company for payroll taxes?

Application Problems

PROBLEM 26-1 | Recording payrolls and payroll taxes

The totals of the payroll register of the Madison Television Service for the week ended May 24 are given below:

No.	Employee's Name	Marital Status	No. of Exemp-tions	Total Earnings	Deductions				Net Pay	
					FICA Tax	Income Tax	Other	Total	Amount	Check No.
	Totals...			840 00	36 96	78 00		114 96	725 04	

The employer's liabilities for payroll taxes include the following:

FICA taxes.. 4.4%
State unemployment taxes.................................. 2.7%
Federal unemployment taxes.............................. .4%

Instructions: 1. Record the payroll and the withholdings on page 38 of a combination journal. The payroll was paid by Check No. 842 on May 27 of the current year.

2. Record the employer's share of the payroll taxes in the combination journal.

PROBLEM 26-2 | Recording payroll transactions

Henry G. Thorpe, owner of a stationery store, completed the payroll transactions given below.

Feb. 28. Issued Check No. 34 for $1,187.80 in payment of the monthly payroll of $1,400.00 less a deduction of $150.60 for income taxes and a deduction of $61.60 for FICA taxes.

28. Recorded the employer's payroll taxes at the following rates: FICA taxes, 4.4%; state unemployment taxes, 2.7%; federal unemployment taxes, .4%.

Mar. 10. Issued Check No. 43 for $273.80 in payment of the liabilities for payroll taxes and taxes withheld as follows: income taxes, $150.60; FICA taxes, $123.20.

31. Issued Check No. 56 for $1,145.58 in payment of the monthly payroll of $1,350.00 less a deduction of $145.00 for income taxes and a deduction of $59.42 for FICA taxes.

31. Recorded the employer's payroll taxes at the same rates as in February.

Apr. 10. Issued Check No. 69 for $263.82 in payment of the liabilities for payroll taxes and taxes withheld as follows: income taxes, $145.00; FICA taxes, $118.82.

10. Issued Check No. 70 for $111.35 in payment of the liability for state unemployment taxes.

Instructions: Record the transactions on page 15 of a combination journal. Use the current year in the date.

PROBLEM 26-3 | Recording and posting payroll transactions

The Howell Electrical Shop completed the payroll transactions given below during the period January 1 to April 10. The Howell Electrical Shop is liable for payroll taxes at the following rates: FICA taxes, 4.4%; state unemployment taxes, 2.7%; and federal unemployment taxes, .4%. It is also liable for the purchase of U. S. Savings Bonds as the accumulated withholdings for each particular employee reaches the necessary amount.

Instructions: 1. Open the accounts given below and record the balances as of January 1 of the current year.

Acct. No.	*Account Title*	*Credit Balance*
22	FICA Taxes Payable	$156.25
23	Employees Income Taxes Payable	280.00
24	State Unemployment Taxes Payable	195.75
25	Federal Unemployment Taxes Payable	230.40
26	U.S. Savings Bonds Payable	146.50
64	Payroll Tax Expense	——
65	Salary Expense	——

Instructions: 2. Record the following selected transactions on page 26 of a combination journal.

3. After each transaction is journalized, post the items recorded in the General Debit and General Credit columns.

Jan. 10. Issued Check No. 15 for $436.25 in payment of the liabilities for employees income taxes and FICA taxes.
10. Issued Check No. 16 for $195.75 in payment of the liability for state unemployment taxes.
10. Issued Check No. 17 for $230.40 in payment of the liability for federal unemployment taxes.
31. Issued Check No. 29 for $1,995.90 in payment of the monthly payroll of $2,400.00 less deductions of $250.50 for income taxes, $105.60 for FICA taxes, and $48.00 for U. S. Savings Bonds deductions.
31. Recorded the employer's payroll tax liabilities.

Feb. 2. Issued Check No. 31 for $75.00 to purchase U. S. Savings Bonds (4 at $18.75) for employees.
10. Issued Check No. 38 for $461.70 in payment of the liabilities for employees income taxes and FICA taxes.
28. Issued Check No. 61 for $1,910.77 in payment of the monthly payroll of $2,300.00 less deductions of $240.00 for income taxes, $101.23 for FICA taxes and $48.00 for U. S. Savings Bonds deductions.
28. Recorded the employer's payroll tax liabilities.

Mar. 1. Issued Check No. 66 for $37.50 to purchase U. S. Savings Bonds (2 at $18.75) for employees.
10. Issued Check No. 74 for $442.43 in payment of the liabilities for employees income taxes and FICA taxes.
31. Issued Check No. 88 for $2,167.58 in payment of the monthly payroll of $2,600.00 less deductions of $270.00 for income taxes, $114.42 for FICA taxes, and $48.00 for U. S. Savings Bonds deductions.
31. Recorded the employer's payroll tax liabilities.

Apr. 2. Issued Check No. 92 for $56.25 to purchase U. S. Savings Bonds (3 at $18.75) for employees.
10. Issued Check No. 97 for $498.82 in payment of the liabilities for employees income taxes and FICA taxes.
10. Issued Check No. 98 for $197.10 in payment of the liability for state unemployment taxes.

PROJECT 3 BOOKKEEPING CYCLE USING THE COMBINATION JOURNAL

King Wholesale Toys

John P. King owns and operates King Wholesale Toys. The bookkeeping records for the company include:

1. A combination journal with the same column headings as the one illustrated on pages 406 and 407.

2. A general ledger with balance-column ruling similar to the one illustrated on page 412.

3. An accounts receivable ledger with balance-column ruling similar to the one illustrated on page 219.

4. An accounts payable ledger with balance-column ruling similar to the one illustrated on page 174.

Opening accounts in the ledger

Instructions: The chart of accounts for King Wholesale Toys is given on the next page.

1. Open an account in the general ledger for each of the accounts in the chart of accounts, using the account numbers given. If the workbook is not used, allow six lines in each account in the general ledger.

2. The balances of the general ledger accounts are listed at the top of page 475. Record the balances in the general ledger, using as the date December 1 of the current year. As you copy these balances, write the word "Balance" in the Items column of each account and place a check mark (√) in the Post. Ref. column.

KING WHOLESALE TOYS

CHART OF ACCOUNTS

(1) ASSETS	Acct. No.
Cash	11
Petty Cash	12
Accounts Receivable	13
Merchandise Inventory	14
Supplies	15
Prepaid Insurance	16

(2) LIABILITIES	
Accounts Payable	21
FICA Taxes Payable	22
Employees Income Taxes Payable	23
State Unemployment Taxes Payable	24
Federal Unemployment Taxes Payable	25
Hospital Care Premiums Payable	26

(3) PROPRIETORSHIP	
John P. King, Capital	31
John P. King, Drawing	32
Income and Expense Summary	33

(4) INCOME	Acct. No.
Sales	41
Sales Returns and Allowances	41.1
Sales Discount	41.2

(5) COST OF MERCHANDISE	
Purchases	51
Purchases Returns and Allowances	51.1
Purchases Discount	51.2

(6) EXPENSES	
Hospitalization Insurance Expense	61
Insurance Expense	62
Miscellaneous Expense	63
Payroll Tax Expense	64
Rent Expense	65
Salary Expense	66
Supplies Expense	67

Account Title	*Debit Balance*	*Credit Balance*
Cash	$ 6,786.00	
Petty Cash	50.00	
Accounts Receivable	2,610.50	
Merchandise Inventory	18,564.90	
Supplies	1,825.80	
Prepaid Insurance	680.00	
Accounts Payable		$ 3,045.80
FICA Taxes Payable		142.96
Employees Income Taxes Payable		163.60
State Unemployment Taxes Payable		87.52
Federal Unemployment Taxes Payable		77.76
Hospital Care Premiums Payable		65.60
John P. King, Capital		27,826.90
John P. King, Drawing	6,500.00	
Sales		78,694.10
Sales Returns and Allowances	649.90	
Sales Discount	390.00	
Purchases	47,686.30	
Purchases Returns and Allowances		669.60
Purchases Discount		950.90
Hospitalization Insurance Expense	275.00	
Miscellaneous Expense	2,094.70	
Payroll Tax Expense	1,421.64	
Rent Expense	2,750.00	
Salary Expense	19,440.00	

Instructions: 3. Open the following accounts in the accounts receivable ledger and record the balance to be collected from each customer. As you copy these balances in the accounts receivable ledger, write the word "Balance" in the Items column of each account and place a check mark (√) in the Post. Ref. column. Use the date December 1 of the current year. If the workbook is not used, allow four lines for each customer's account.

Customer	*Debit Balance*
Allen Toys, 5 Main Street, Lincoln, Nebraska 68502	$530.60
Morgan Toy Shop, 506 University, Lincoln, Nebraska 68502	641.25
Spencer Stores, Box 46, Waverly, Nebraska 68462	419.60
Stuart Hobby Shop, 419 North Street, Lincoln, Nebraska 68504	602.15
Thompson Famous Toys, 107 N. Dill, Seward, Nebraska 68434	416.90

Instructions: 4. Open the following accounts in the accounts payable ledger and record the balance owed to each creditor. As you copy these balances in the accounts payable ledger, write the word "Balance" in the Items column of each account and place a check mark (√) in the Post.

Ref. column. Use the date December 1 of the current year. If the workbook is not used, allow four lines for each creditor's account.

Creditor	*Credit Balance*
Clayton Toys, 355 Fremont Street, Toledo, Ohio 43617......	$ 962.00
Damone & Sons, 2611 Vine Street, Cincinnati, Ohio 45225...	698.20
Lily Company, 32 Walnut Street, Lincoln, Nebraska 68502...	310.60
Nelson Company, 4315 Center Street, Omaha, Nebraska 68101	1,075.00

Recording transactions for December

Instructions: 5. Record on page 48 of a combination journal the following transactions completed by King Wholesale Toys during the month of December of the current year.

Dec. 1. Record the cash on hand, $6,786.00, in a memorandum entry.

1. Issued Check No. 202 for $250.00 for the December rent.

1. Issued a credit memorandum for $45.00 to Stuart Hobby Shop for merchandise returned.

3. Received a check for $519.99 from Allen Toys in payment of our invoice of November 26 for $530.60 less a 2% discount of $10.61.

5. Issued Check No. 203 for $1,064.25 to Nelson Company in payment of their invoice of November 26 for $1,075.00 less a 1% discount of $10.75.

8. Received a check for $546.01 from Stuart Hobby Shop and gave the company credit for the amount plus a 2% discount of $11.14.

9. Damone & Sons allowed us credit for $54.00 for damaged merchandise purchased from that company.

10. Issued Check No. 204 for $306.56 in payment of the liabilities for payroll taxes and taxes withheld as follows: income taxes, $163.60; FICA taxes, $142.96.

11. Purchased merchandise on account from Lily Company, $263.40.

11. Issued Check No. 205 for $65.60 in payment of the liabilities for hospital care premiums withheld from employees' wages and for the employer's share in the cost of the hospitalization program during November.

King Wholesale Toys participates in a group hospitalization plan under which the company pays a portion of each employee's monthly premium. When the payment of each payroll is recorded, the amount of the premiums deducted from the employees' wages is credited to Hospital Care Premiums Payable. When the payroll expenses of the employer are recorded, the amount of his contribution to the hospital insurance program is debited to Hospitalization Insurance Expense and credited to Hospital Care Premiums Payable. The amount withheld from the employees' wages and the employer's share are paid the following month to the local Hospital Care agency.

11. Sold merchandise on account to Thompson Famous Toys, $201.50.
12. Issued Check No. 206 for $723.52 in payment of the semimonthly payroll of $870.00 less the following deductions:

FICA taxes	$38.28
Employees income taxes	87.90
Hospital Care premiums	20.30

12. Recorded the employer's payroll taxes and his share of the hospitalization insurance costs for the December 12 payroll as follows:

FICA taxes	$38.28
State unemployment taxes	23.49
Federal unemployment taxes	3.48
Hospitalization insurance expense	12.50

In one combined entry, debit Payroll Tax Expense for the total of the three payroll taxes. Debit Hospitalization Insurance Expense for the employer's share of the hospitalization insurance costs. Credit each of the three payroll tax liability accounts and the Hospital Care Premiums Payable account.

12. Purchased merchandise on account from Clayton Toys, $841.70.
12. Issued Check No. 207 for $300.00 to John P. King, the owner, for personal use.
16. Issued Check No. 208 for $30.15 for the telephone bill.
16. Sold merchandise on account to Spencer Stores, $363.75.
16. The cash sales for December 1 to 16 were $4,491.50.

    Post from the combination journal to the accounts receivable ledger and the accounts payable ledger.
17. Issued Check No. 209 for $50.14 for the electricity bill.
17. Received a check for $416.90 from Thompson Famous Toys in payment on account.
18. Issued Check No. 210 for $310.60 to Lily Company in payment on account.
19. Received a check for $197.47 from Thompson Famous Toys in payment of our invoice of December 11 less a 2% discount of $4.03.
22. Issued Check No. 211 for $824.87 to Clayton Toys in payment of their invoice of December 12 less a 2% discount of $16.83.
22. Sold merchandise on account to Spencer Stores, $417.00.
22. Issued Check No. 212 for $644.20 to Damone & Sons on account.
23. Received a check for $776.07 from Spencer Stores in payment on account of $783.35 less a 2% discount of $7.28 on our invoice of December 16.
23. Sold merchandise on account to Allen Toys, $325.00.
26. Purchased merchandise on account from Nelson Company, $250.00.
26. Purchased merchandise on account from Clayton Toys, $175.00.
29. Nelson Company allowed us credit for $25.00 for shipment of wrong merchandise to us.

30. Issued Check No. 213 for $300.00 to John P. King, the owner, for personal use.
30. Issued Check No. 214 for $30.87 to replenish the petty cash fund. The petty cash vouchers were sorted and the petty cash payments for December were as follows:

Supplies	$12.75
Miscellaneous Expense	18.12

31. Issued Check No. 215 for $766.02 in payment of the semimonthly payroll of $920.00 less the following deductions:

FICA taxes	$40.48
Employees income taxes	93.20
Hospital Care premiums	20.30

31. Recorded the employer's payroll taxes and his share of the hospitalization insurance costs for the December 31 payroll as follows:

FICA taxes	$40.48
State unemployment taxes	24.84
Federal unemployment taxes	3.68
Hospitalization insurance expense	12.50

31. The cash sales for December 17 to 31 were $4,965.00.

Post from the combination journal to the accounts receivable ledger and the accounts payable ledger.

Work at the end of the fiscal year

Instructions: 6. Foot all columns of the combination journal and prove the equality of debits and credits. Prove cash. The cash on hand and in the bank is $13,032.16. Total and rule the journal.

7. Post each amount in the two General columns of the combination journal. Post the totals of the special columns.

8. Prepare a schedule of accounts receivable and a schedule of accounts payable.

9. Prepare an eight-column work sheet. Additional data for the adjustments are:

Merchandise inventory, December 31, $21,371.00
Supplies inventory, December 31, $187.40
Value of insurance policies, December 31, $230.00

10. Prepare an income statement, a capital statement, and a balance sheet for the year ended December 31.

11. Record the adjusting entries and the closing entries in the combination journal. Post these entries to the general ledger.

Since accounts with balance-column ruling are used in the general ledger, there is no need to rule and balance the accounts. When an account is closed as the result of posting a closing entry, draw a short line in the Debit Balance column and in the Credit Balance column.

12. Prepare a post-closing trial balance.

CASH REGISTER

A popular business machine that is used to record sales transactions is the cash register.

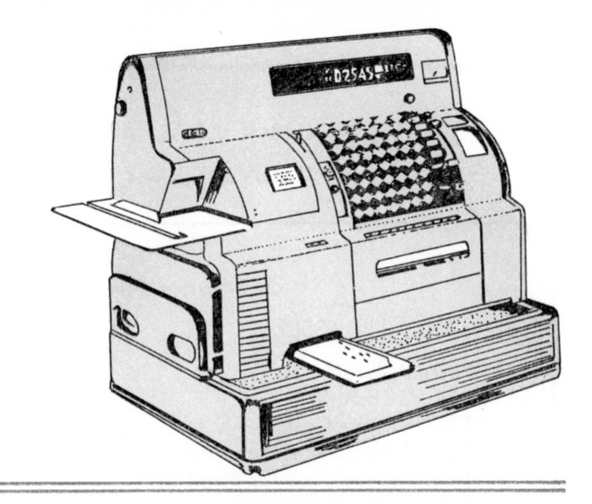

ACCOUNTS FOR SPECIAL TRANSACTIONS

Special bookkeeping transactions require special accounts.

Loss on Fixed Assets	
xxx	

Office Equipment	
xxx	

Gain on Fixed Assets	
	xxx

Notes Receivable	
xxx	

Interest Receivable	
xxx	

Interest Income	
	xxx

Allowance for Bad Debts	
	xxx

Bad Debts Expense	
xxx	

Accumulated Depreciation-Office Equipment	
	xxx

Depreciation Expense-Office Equipment	
xxx	

Delivery Equipment	
xxx	

Accumulated Depreciation-Delivery Equipment	
	xxx

Depreciation Expense-Delivery Equipment	
xxx	

Notes Payable	
	xxx

Interest Payable	
	xxx

Interest Expense	
xxx	

Sales Taxes Payable	
	xxx

Cash Short and Over	
	xxx

HARVEY AUTO PARTS
CHART OF ACCOUNTS

Balance Sheet Accounts

(1) ASSETS

11 *Current Assets*
- 111 Cash
- 112 Petty Cash
- 113 Accounts Receivable
- 113.1 Allowance for Bad Debts
- 114 Merchandise Inventory
- 115 Supplies
- 116 Prepaid Insurance

12 *Fixed Assets*
- 121 Delivery Equipment
- 121.1 Accumulated Depreciation — Delivery Equipment
- 122 Office Equipment
- 122.1 Accumulated Depreciation — Office Equipment

(2) LIABILITIES

21 *Current Liabilities*
- 211 Accounts Payable
- 212 FICA Taxes Payable
- 213 Employees Income Taxes Payable
- 214 State Unemployment Taxes Payable
- 215 Federal Unemployment Taxes Payable

(3) PROPRIETORSHIP

- 311 R. L. Harvey, Capital
- 312 R. L. Harvey, Drawing
- 313 Income and Expense Summary

Income Statement Accounts

(4) OPERATING INCOME

- 411 Sales
- 411.1 Sales Returns and Allowances
- 411.2 Sales Discount

(5) COST OF MERCHANDISE

- 511 Purchases
- 511.1 Purchases Returns and Allowances
- 511.2 Purchases Discount

(6) OPERATING EXPENSES

- 611 Bad Debts Expense
- 612 Delivery Expense
- 613 Depreciation Expense — Delivery Equipment
- 614 Depreciation Expense — Office Equipment
- 615 Insurance Expense
- 616 Miscellaneous Expense
- 617 Payroll Tax Expense
- 618 Rent Expense
- 619 Salary Expense
- 620 Supplies Expense

(7) OTHER INCOME

- 711 Gain on Fixed Assets

(8) OTHER EXPENSES

- 811 Loss on Fixed Assets
- 812 Cash Short and Over

The Chart of Accounts for Harvey Auto Parts is illustrated above for ready reference in your study of Chapters 27 through 30 in Part 5 of this book.

CHAPTER 27 FIXED ASSETS AND DEPRECIATION

Cash and other assets that will be turned into cash or consumed relatively soon in the operation of a business are called *current assets.* Examples of current assets are cash, accounts receivable, merchandise inventory, supplies, and prepaid insurance.

Assets that will be used for a number of years in the operation of a business are known as *fixed assets.* Examples of fixed assets are office equipment, delivery equipment, store equipment, buildings, and land. Some businesses use the term *plant assets* to describe fixed assets.

Fixed assets such as typewriters, desks, display cases, tables, machinery, and delivery trucks are commonly called *equipment.* Some businesses record the cost of all equipment in one asset account with the title Equipment. Other businesses prefer to record the various kinds of equipment in separate accounts. Examples of separate equipment accounts are Delivery Equipment, Office Equipment, and Store Equipment.

RECORDING THE PURCHASE OF FIXED ASSETS

Fixed assets may be bought either for cash or on credit. When a fixed asset is purchased, it is recorded at the cost price.

Harvey Auto Parts sells automobile parts and supplies to individuals and to automobile repair shops. On July 3, 1967, Harvey Auto Parts bought a new cash register for $1,000.00 in cash. The entry for this transaction is made in the combination journal. Mr. Harvey has a separate account for office equipment. The asset account, Office Equipment, is debited for the cost of the cash register and Cash is credited. After the entry is posted, the office equipment account appears as shown below.

Office Equipment — ACCOUNT NO. 122

DATE		ITEMS	POST. REF.	DEBIT	CREDIT	BALANCE DEBIT	BALANCE CREDIT
1967 Jan.	1	Balance	✓			3860 00	
July	3		4	1000 00		4860 00	

The January 1 balance in the office equipment account is the original cost of equipment that Harvey Auto Parts had on hand January 1. The debit balance of the office equipment account will always show the original cost of all office equipment owned.

Note that the account number of the office equipment account is 122. Many businesses, especially those with a large number of accounts, find it desirable to use account numbers with three or four digits. Each business numbers its accounts according to its particular needs. The chart of accounts for Harvey Auto Parts is shown on page 480.

WHAT IS DEPRECIATION?

A bicycle that cost $50.00 one Christmas is not worth $50.00 the following Christmas. Similarly, in a business a fixed asset, such as a cash register, bought in July for $1,000.00, is not worth $1,000.00 at the end of the year. Fixed assets such as office equipment decrease in value because of wear and because better models become available. The decrease in the value of a fixed asset because of wear and the passage of time is called *depreciation*. Land, because of its permanent nature, is a fixed asset that is not subject to depreciation.

The amount by which a fixed asset depreciates is an expense of the business. The amount of depreciation expense should be recorded each fiscal period. If depreciation expense is not recorded, the income statement will not contain all the expenses of the business. This will cause the net income to be reported higher than it should be.

Income tax laws allow a business to deduct depreciation as an expense in determining net income. If depreciation expenses are not included on the income tax reports, the business will pay more income taxes than it should.

DETERMINING THE AMOUNT OF DEPRECIATION EXPENSE

When a business buys a fixed asset, the business expects to use it for a number of years. When a fixed asset ceases to be useful or when it seems desirable to replace it, the asset may be traded in, sold, or discarded.

Original cost, scrap value, and estimated life

Before a bookkeeper can record the depreciation expense of a fixed asset, he must know how to calculate that expense. In order to calculate depreciation expense, the bookkeeper must know:

1. The original cost of the fixed asset.
2. The amount the business estimates it will receive at the time of disposing of the asset.
3. The estimated life of usefulness.

Original cost of the fixed asset. The original cost of the fixed asset is obtained from the seller's invoice. The cost is the amount that is debited to the proper fixed asset account at the time the fixed asset is bought. The cost of the new cash register bought by Mr. Harvey is $1,000.00.

Estimated scrap value. The amount that the owner of a fixed asset expects to receive at the time of disposing of the asset is called the *estimated scrap value.* The estimated scrap value is sometimes known as the *trade-in value* or the *salvage value.* The total estimated depreciation of a fixed asset is the original cost of the asset minus its estimated scrap value.

Mr. Harvey estimates that when his new cash register has served its useful life, it will have a scrap value of $250.00. Thus, Mr. Harvey determines the amount of the fixed asset he can depreciate as follows:

Original cost	$1,000.00
Less estimated scrap value	250.00
Total amount to be depreciated	$ 750.00

Estimated life of usefulness. Income tax laws require that the amount of depreciation expense of fixed assets be distributed over the expected number of years the assets will be used by the business. When a fixed asset is bought, it is not possible to know how long it will be useful to the business. Therefore, it is necessary to estimate the number of years of its usefulness.

The Internal Revenue Service issues guidelines that give the estimated life of many common fixed assets for different types of business. From these guidelines Mr. Harvey determined that for a business of his type, the estimated life of a cash register is ten years.

Calculating depreciation expenses for a fiscal period

The cash register that Mr. Harvey purchased on July 3, 1967, for $1,000.00 is estimated to have a scrap value of $250.00 and a useful life of ten years. Mr. Harvey calculates the depreciation expense on the cash register for *each year* as shown below:

Original cost	$1,000.00
Less estimated scrap value	250.00
Amount to be depreciated	$ 750.00

$$\frac{\$750.00 \text{ (amount to be depreciated)}}{10 \text{ (estimated life of usefulness)}} = \$75.00, \text{ the annual depreciation expense}$$

Since one half of the year had passed when Mr. Harvey purchased the cash register, only one half of the annual depreciation expense, or $37.50, is charged against the year 1967.

Charging an *equal* amount of depreciation expense for a fixed asset each year of the estimated life of the asset is called the *straight-line method of depreciation.* There are several other methods of charging depreciation expense, but the straight-line method is widely used because it is simple to use.

Book value of a fixed asset

The original cost of a fixed asset minus the total amount of recorded depreciation of the asset is called the *book value.* When Mr. Harvey bought the cash register on July 3, 1967, he debited the office equipment account for $1,000.00. The following table shows Mr. Harvey's estimate of depreciation expense and the book value of the cash register for the years he plans to use it.

Cash Register	Recorded Depreciation for Each Year	Total Recorded Depreciation	Book Value
Cost at time of purchase, July 3, 1967			$1,000.00
Last half of fiscal year ending 12/31/67	$37.50	$ 37.50	962.50
Fiscal year ending 12/31/68	75.00	112.50	887.50
Fiscal year ending 12/31/69	75.00	187.50	812.50
Fiscal year ending 12/31/70	75.00	262.50	737.50
Fiscal year ending 12/31/71	75.00	337.50	662.50
Fiscal year ending 12/31/72	75.00	412.50	587.50
Fiscal year ending 12/31/73	75.00	487.50	512.50
Fiscal year ending 12/31/74	75.00	562.50	437.50
Fiscal year ending 12/31/75	75.00	637.50	362.50
Fiscal year ending 12/31/76	75.00	712.50	287.50
First half of fiscal year ending 12/31/77	37.50	750.00	250.00

The book value of the cash register at the end of the first half of 1977 is $250.00. This amount is the scrap value that Mr. Harvey estimates he will be able to receive when he disposes of this asset.

FIXED ASSET RECORDS

In order for a business to determine the total amount of depreciation expense to be charged each fiscal period, the business should keep accurate records of fixed assets. The bookkeeping form on which a business records the data needed to determine the amount of depreciation on each fixed asset is called a *fixed asset record.*

The fixed asset record on which Mr. Harvey recorded the necessary data relating to the cash register through the year ended December 31, 1969, is shown on the next page.

FIXED ASSET RECORD — ACCOUNT NO. 122

ITEM Cash register — GENERAL LEDGER ACCOUNT Office Equipment

SERIAL NO. 498726 — DESCRIPTION American Cash Register

FROM WHOM PURCHASED Cole Equipment Company, Dayton, Ohio

ESTIMATED LIFE 10 years — ESTIMATED SCRAP OR TRADE-IN VALUE $250 — DEPRECIATION PER YEAR $75

DATE			EXPLANATION	ASSET			ACCUMULATED DEPRECIATION			BOOK VALUE
MO.	DAY	YR.		DR.	CR.	BAL.	DR.	CR.	BAL.	
7	3	67		1,000		1,000				1,000.00
12	31	67						37.50	37.50	962.50
12	31	68						75.00	112.50	887.50
12	31	69						75.00	187.50	812.50

Fixed asset record

At the time the cash register was bought, Mr. Harvey recorded: (1) a complete description of the machine, including its serial number; (2) the date it was bought; (3) the cost; (4) the estimated life; (5) the estimated scrap value, and; (6) the annual amount of depreciation. When the cost of the cash register was recorded, the amount was also extended to the Book Value column. At the end of the first fiscal period, December 31, 1967, the cash register had been owned for one-half year. Therefore, the amount of the depreciation expense for the half-year, $37.50, was recorded in the Accumulated Depreciation column. Since there was no previous depreciation on the cash register, the amount, $37.50, was deducted from the book value at the beginning of the fiscal period. This gave a new book value of $962.50 for the year ended December 31, 1967.

At the close of each fiscal period, each fixed asset record is brought up-to-date by recording the depreciation for that period and by calculating the book value.

DETERMINING DEPRECIATION FOR THE FISCAL PERIOD

At the end of each fiscal period, the bookkeeper for Harvey Auto Parts refers to each of the fixed asset records. He calculates the amount of depreciation on each asset and finds the total depreciation for all items.

According to the fixed asset records, the total depreciation of office equipment for the fiscal period ended December 31, 1967, is $327.40. This means that during the fiscal period the office equipment decreased in value an estimated amount of $327.40.

The depreciation expense account

The amount of depreciation on fixed assets is an operating expense of the business. The estimated amount of the depreciation of each asset is debited to the proper depreciation expense account at the end of each fiscal period. For example, the estimated amount of depreciation on office equipment is debited to Depreciation Expense — Office Equipment. The estimated amount of depreciation on delivery equipment is debited to Depreciation Expense — Delivery Equipment.

The accumulated depreciation account

The balance of a fixed asset account should always show the original cost of the asset owned by the business. Therefore, the amount of depreciation should not be credited to a fixed asset account. Fixed asset accounts are credited only when the assets are disposed of.

The account to which the estimated amount of depreciation is credited is called *Accumulated Depreciation*, followed by the name of the fixed asset account. For example, the estimated amount of depreciation on office equipment is credited to Accumulated Depreciation — Office Equipment. The amount of depreciation on delivery equipment is credited to Accumulated Depreciation — Delivery Equipment.

Allowance for Depreciation or Reserve for Depreciation are sometimes used as account titles instead of Accumulated Depreciation.

The debit balance of each fixed asset account continues to show the original cost of the asset on hand. The credit balance in the accumulated depreciation account shows the estimated decrease in the value of the asset because of depreciation. The difference between the balance of the fixed asset account and the balance of its related accumulated depreciation account is the book value of the asset.

At the beginning of the fiscal period, on January 1, 1967, the accounts Office Equipment and Accumulated Depreciation — Office Equipment of Harvey Auto Parts appear as shown on the next page.

The book value of the office equipment as of January 1, 1967, is found by subtracting the credit balance of the related accumulated depreciation account, $1,447.50, from the debit balance of the office equipment account, $3,860.00. The difference is $2,412.50, which is the book value of the total office equipment. The book value of each type of fixed asset is found in the same manner.

Office Equipment — ACCOUNT NO. 122

DATE		ITEMS	POST. REF.	DEBIT	CREDIT	BALANCE DEBIT	BALANCE CREDIT
1967 Jan.	1	Balance	✓			3,860.00	

Accumulated Depreciation–Office Equipment — ACCOUNT NO. 122.1

DATE		ITEMS	POST. REF.	DEBIT	CREDIT	BALANCE DEBIT	BALANCE CREDIT
1967 Jan.	1	Balance	✓				1,447.50

Valuation accounts

An account that is used in calculating the book value of the asset to which it is related is called a *valuation account.* Accumulated Depreciation—Office Equipment is a valuation account because it is used to determine the book value of the related account Office Equipment. The balance of a valuation account is always a credit balance because it is a deduction from the balance of the related asset account. A valuation account is also called a *minus asset account.*

A minus asset account is numbered the same as the asset account to which it is related, except the account number of the minus asset account is followed by a decimal point and a number. In the general ledger of Harvey Auto Parts, the account number of Office Equipment is 122. The account number of Accumulated Depreciation — Office Equipment is 122.1.

ADJUSTMENT FOR DEPRECIATION ON THE WORK SHEET

At the end of the fiscal period, December 31, 1967, the bookkeeper for Harvey Auto Parts refers to each of the fixed asset records and calculates the amount of depreciation expense for each asset. Next, he totals the amount of depreciation expense for each type of fixed asset — Delivery Equipment and Office Equipment. According to the fixed asset records, the total depreciation for the year for each type of asset is:

Depreciation on Delivery Equipment.......	$1,500.00
Depreciation on Office Equipment.........	327.40

Harvey Auto Parts
Work Sheet
For Year Ended December 31, 1967

	Account Titles	Acct. No.	1 Trial Balance Debit	2 Trial Balance Credit	3 Adjustments Debit	4 Adjustments Credit	5 Income Statement Debit	6 Income Statement Credit	7 Balance Sheet Debit	8 Balance Sheet Credit	
8	Delivery Equipment	121	821000						821000		8
9	Accum. Depr.-Delivery Equipment	121.1		187500		(f) 150000				337500	9
10	Office Equipment	122	486000						486000		10
11	Accum. Depr.-Office Equipment	122.1		144750		(g) 32740				177490	11
28	Depreciation Expense-Del. Equip.	613			(f) 150000		150000				28
29	Depreciation Expense-Office Equip.	614			(g) 32740		32740				29
34	Salary Expense	619	3175000				3175000				34
35	Supplies Expense	620			(d) 120800		120800				35
38			18608000	18608000	8042060	8042060	13627250	14734960	7934055	6826345	38
39	Net Income						1107710			1107710	39
40							14734960	14734960	7934055	7934055	40

Work sheet with adjustments for depreciation

At the end of the fiscal year on December 31, Mr. Harvey's bookkeeper makes an adjustment for the depreciation of fixed assets in the Adjustments columns of the work sheet. The partial work sheet is illustrated on the opposite page.

The amount of the depreciation for each type of fixed asset is an expense. In the Adjustments Debit column of the work sheet, each amount of depreciation is debited to the proper depreciation expense account. Each amount of depreciation expense is extended into the Income Statement Debit column. For example, as shown in the Adjustments Debit column on the partial work sheet, the total depreciation on delivery equipment, $1,500.00, is debited to the account Depreciation Expense — Delivery Equipment. This amount, like the other expenses, is extended into the Income Statement Debit column.

In the Trial Balance columns of the work sheet, the credit balance of each accumulated depreciation account represents the sum of amounts credited to this account in previous fiscal periods. In the Adjustments columns, each accumulated depreciation account is credited to record the additional decrease in the value of the fixed asset as a result of the depreciation during the period. The credit to each accumulated depreciation account is added to the credit balance of the account, and the total is extended to the Balance Sheet Credit column.

For example, in the Trial Balance Credit column of the work sheet, Accumulated Depreciation — Delivery Equipment has a credit balance of $1,875.00, the sum of amounts credited to this account in previous fiscal periods. In the Adjustments Credit column, Accumulated Depreciation — Delivery Equipment is credited for $1,500.00 to record the decrease in the value of delivery equipment as a result of the depreciation during the period. The credit of $1,500.00 to Accumulated Depreciation — Delivery Equipment is added to the credit balance of $1,875.00, and the total, $3,375.00, is extended to the Balance Sheet Credit column of the work sheet. This credit balance in the accumulated depreciation account will be deducted from the debit balance of the delivery equipment account when the balance sheet is prepared.

JOURNALIZING AND POSTING THE ADJUSTING ENTRIES

Harvey Auto Parts uses a combination journal in which to record the adjusting entries at the end of each fiscal period. The adjusting entries are made from the Adjustments columns of the work sheet. The adjusting entries to record the depreciation on fixed assets are shown on the next page.

PAGE 14 COMBINATION JOURNAL

	Cash Debit (1)	Cash Credit (2)	Ck. No.	Date	Account Title	Post. Ref.	General Debit (3)	General Credit (4)	
31				31	Depr. Expense - Del. Equip.		1500 00		31
32					Accum. Depr. - Del. Equip.			1500 00	32
33				31	Depr. Expense - Office Equip.		327 40		33
34					Accum. Depr. - Office Equip.			327 40	34
35									35

Adjusting entries to record depreciation

When the adjusting entries are posted, the fixed asset accounts, the accumulated depreciation accounts, and the depreciation expense accounts appear as shown below.

Delivery Equipment — ACCOUNT NO. 121

Date		Items	Post. Ref.	Debit	Credit	Balance Debit	Balance Credit
1967 Jan.	1	Balance	✓				8210 00

Accumulated Depreciation - Delivery Equipment — ACCOUNT NO. 121.1

Date		Items	Post. Ref.	Debit	Credit	Balance Debit	Balance Credit
1967 Jan.	1	Balance	✓				1875 00
Dec.	31		14		1500 00		3375 00

Office Equipment — ACCOUNT NO. 122

Date		Items	Post. Ref.	Debit	Credit	Balance Debit	Balance Credit
1967 Jan.	1	Balance	✓			3860 00	
July	3		4	1000 00		4860 00	

Accumulated Depreciation - Office Equipment — ACCOUNT NO. 122.1

Date		Items	Post. Ref.	Debit	Credit	Balance Debit	Balance Credit
1967 Jan.	1	Balance	✓				1447 50
Dec.	31		14		327 40		1774 90

Depreciation Expense - Delivery Equipment — ACCOUNT NO. 613

Date		Items	Post. Ref.	Debit	Credit	Balance Debit	Balance Credit
1967 Dec.	31		14	1500 00		1500 00	

Depreciation Expense - Office Equipment — ACCOUNT NO. 614

Date		Items	Post. Ref.	Debit	Credit	Balance Debit	Balance Credit
1967 Dec.	31		14	327 40		327 40	

REPORTING FIXED ASSETS AND DEPRECIATION ON FINANCIAL STATEMENTS

The income statement

When the bookkeeper prepares an income statement, he lists the balance of each depreciation expense account in the Operating Expenses section. The income statement for Harvey Auto Parts for the fiscal period ended December 31, 1967, is shown below.

Harvey Auto Parts
Income Statement
For Year Ended December 31, 1967

Income:			
Sales			103230 00
Less: Sales Returns and Allowances		797 50	
Sales Discount		1840 40	2637 90
Net Sales			100592 10
Cost of Merchandise Sold:			
Merchandise Inventory, Jan. 1, 1967		34737 15	
Purchases	54987 80		
Less: Purchases Returns and Allow. 1,050.20			
Purchases Discount 1,028.40	2078 60		
Net Purchases		52909 20	
Total Cost of Merchandise Available for Sale		87646 35	
Less Merchandise Inventory, Dec. 31, 1967		42041 00	
Cost of Merchandise Sold			45605 35
Gross Profit on Sales			54986 75
Operating Expenses:			
Delivery Expense		1465 10	
Depreciation Expense – Delivery Equipment		1500 00	
Depreciation Expense – Office Equipment		327 40	
Insurance Expense		1222 48	
Miscellaneous Expense		1055 20	
Payroll Tax Expense		2381 47	
Rent Expense		3000 00	
Salary Expense		31750 00	
Supplies Expense		1208 00	
Total Operating Expenses			43909 65
Net Income			11077 10

Income statement showing depreciation expense

The balance sheet

When the bookkeeper prepares a balance sheet, he shows for each type of fixed asset: (a) the original cost; (b) the decrease in value because of depreciation; and (c) the book value. See the balance sheet for Harvey Auto Parts on the next page.

In the Fixed Assets section of the balance sheet, the original cost of each type of fixed asset is shown in the first amount column. The accumulated depreciation of each type of fixed asset is written immediately under the original cost of the asset and is subtracted. The difference between the two amounts is the book value and is written in the second amount column. The book values are totaled and the sum is written in the third amount column.

Harvey Auto Parts
Balance Sheet
December 31, 1967

Assets			
Current Assets:			
Cash		6450 65	
Petty Cash		100 00	
Accounts Receivable		4623 90	
Merchandise Inventory		42041 00	
Supplies		575 00	
Prepaid Insurance		480 00	
Total Current Assets			54270 55
Fixed Assets:			
Delivery Equipment	8210 00		
Less Accum. Depr.-Delivery Equipment	3375 00	4835 00	
Office Equipment	4860 00		
Less Accum. Depr.-Office Equipment	1774 90	3085 10	
Total Fixed Assets			7920 10
Total Assets			62190 65
Liabilities			
Current Liabilities:			
Accounts Payable		6736 10	
FICA Taxes Payable		264 00	
Employees Income Taxes Payable		430 50	
State Unemployment Taxes Payable		253 10	
Federal Unemployment Taxes Payable		127 00	
Total Current Liabilities			7810 70
Proprietorship			
R. L. Harvey, Capital			54379 95
Total Liabilities and Proprietorship			62190 65

Balance sheet showing fixed assets and accumulated depreciation

Classifying assets on the balance sheet. When a business owns both current and fixed assets, it is customary to list them on the balance sheet under the headings "Current Assets" and "Fixed Assets." Anyone examining the balance sheet can then easily determine whether the current assets will provide sufficient cash to pay the liabilities of the business. Also, one can determine whether too much or too little has been invested in fixed assets for the successful operation of the business.

The correct order for listing current assets is to start with Cash and to follow with the other current asset accounts in the order in which they could most readily be converted into cash. The order of listing fixed assets is not so uniform in practice. One common order is to list those with the shortest life first.

A business having several fixed assets might prefer to list them on the balance sheet in a compact fashion as shown below.

TOWN INDUSTRIES, INC.
Balance Sheet
June 30, 1967

Assets				
Total Current Assets				$46,500.00
	Cost	Accumulated Depreciation	Book Value	
Fixed Assets:				
Delivery Equipment	$ 6,850.70	$ 2,640.00	$ 4,210.70	
Office Equipment	3,280.00	973.50	2,306.50	
Factory Equipment	29,742.20	16,557.12	13,185.08	
Buildings	60,000.00	20,000.00	40,000.00	
Land	8,000.00	. . .	8,000.00	
Total Fixed Assets	$107,872.90	$40,170.62		$67,702.28

Section of a balance sheet showing five fixed assets in compact form

Classifying liabilities on the balance sheet. Liabilities that will be due within a relatively short time, usually within a year, are called *current liabilities.* Examples of current liability accounts are: Accounts Payable, FICA Taxes Payable, Employees Income Taxes Payable, State Unemployment Taxes Payable, and Federal Unemployment Taxes Payable.

Liabilities that are not due for a number of years in the normal operation of the business are called *long-term liabilities.* An example of a long-term liability is Mortgage Payable. Sometimes long-term liabilities are called *fixed liabilities.*

Liabilities are commonly arranged on the balance sheet according to the order in which they fall due. All the liabilities of Harvey Auto Parts are current liabilities. Each liability is listed on the balance sheet, shown on page 492, under the heading "Current Liabilities" since all of these liabilities fall due within a year.

Increasing Your Business Vocabulary

What is the meaning of each of the following:

a current assets
b fixed assets
c equipment
d depreciation
e estimated scrap value
f straight-line method of depreciation
g book value
h fixed asset record
i valuation account
j current liabilities
k long-term liabilities

Study Questions

1. Why are most fixed assets worth less than their purchase price after they have been used for a fiscal period?
2. If the expense of using a fixed asset is not recorded, how will this affect the total expenses of the business? How will this omission affect the net income for the period?
3. What three things must a bookkeeper know about a fixed asset in order to calculate its depreciation expense?
4. On the fixed asset record on page 485, how is the book value calculated at the end of each fiscal period?
5. Why is the amount of depreciation on a fixed asset credited to an accumulated depreciation account rather than to the fixed asset account?
6. Why is the accumulated depreciation account called a valuation account or a minus asset account?
7. On the partial work sheet on page 488, what accounts are debited and credited in making the adjustments for the estimated depreciation on delivery equipment?
8. What is the correct order for listing assets on the balance sheet? For listing liabilities on the balance sheet?

Cases for Business Decision

CASE 1

The Oakland Supply Company needs a truck about three days each week to make deliveries to its customers. A truck that will handle the deliveries costs $3,200.00. It is estimated that the truck would have a useful life of five years and a trade-in value of $1,200.00 at the end of five years.

One member of the company suggests that it would be less expensive to rent a truck than to own one. Another member suggests that the least expensive method of making deliveries would be to use the services of a delivery truck company.

Before a decision can be made about which delivery plan to use, what information must be obtained?

CASE 2

Mr. Stone, the proprietor of a small business, maintains that since he makes no actual cash payments for depreciation, he is not entitled to record depreciation as an expense. What is wrong with Mr. Stone's point of view?

Drills for Understanding

DRILL 27-A Calculating depreciation

Instructions: For each of the following fixed assets, find the amount of annual depreciation.

Fixed Asset	*Original Cost*	*Estimated Scrap Value*	*Estimated Life*
1	$ 2,400.00	$ 400.00	4 years
2	600.00	100.00	5 years
3	300.00	none	3 years
4	6,720.00	1,500.00	20 years
5	26,400.00	2,400.00	8 years
6	12,800.00	800.00	16 years

DRILL 27-B Finding book value

Instructions: For each of the following items of equipment, find as of December 31, 1967, (a) the total amount of estimated depreciation, and (b) the book value.

Fixed Asset	*Date of Purchase*	*Original Cost*	*Estimated Scrap Value*	*Estimated Life*
1	Dec. 31, 1962	$ 800.00	$ 50.00	5 years
2	July 1, 1963	4,360.00	300.00	10 years
3	Jan. 3, 1964	975.00	150.00	20 years
4	Nov. 1, 1964	150.00	20.00	4 years
5	Jan. 2, 1965	738.50	none	10 years
6	Dec. 1, 1966	300.00	60.00	8 years

Application Problems

PROBLEM 27-1 | Calculating and recording depreciation

B. T. Amstutz purchased the following items of office equipment during the first two years he was in business:

Office Equipment	*Date of Purchase*	*Original Cost*	*Estimated Scrap Value*	*Estimated Life*
1	Jan. 3, 1966	$ 440.00	$ 10.00	10 years
2	July 1, 1966	80.00	none	4 years
3	Mar. 1, 1967	72.00	none	5 years
4	July 2, 1967	470.00	none	10 years
5	Nov. 1, 1967	960.00	60.00	5 years
6	Dec. 1, 1967	1,600.40	200.00	10 years

Instructions: 1. Record on page 12 of a combination journal the adjusting entry for the total depreciation expense for the year ended December 31, 1966.

2. Record the adjusting entry for the total depreciation expense for the year ended December 31, 1967.

PROBLEM 27-2 | Work at the end of the fiscal period

The account numbers, titles, and balances in the general ledger of V. R. Prince, a dealer in building materials, on June 30 of the current year are as follows:

111 Cash, $1,300.20
112 Accounts Receivable, $319.97
113 Merchandise Inventory, $5,326.98
114 Supplies, $170.00
115 Prepaid Insurance, $223.65
121 Delivery Equipment, $11,800.00
121.1 Accumulated Depreciation — Delivery Equipment, $3,600.00
122 Office Equipment, $2,750.00
122.1 Accumulated Depreciation — Office Equipment, $420.00
211 Accounts Payable, $2,267.20
212 FICA Taxes Payable, $105.60
213 Employees Income Taxes Payable, $148.30
214 State Unemployment Taxes Payable, $113.40
215 Federal Unemployment Taxes Payable, $31.20
311 V. R. Prince, Capital, $15,122.20
312 V. R. Prince, Drawing, $1,320.00 (Dr.)
313 Income and Expense Summary, (no balance)
411 Sales, $30,956.80
411.1 Sales Returns and Allowances, $160.30
511 Purchases, $16,067.40
511.1 Purchases Returns and Allowances, $170.50
611 Delivery Expense, $622.25
612 Depreciation Expense — Delivery Equipment, (no balance)
613 Depreciation Expense — Office Equipment, (no balance)
614 Insurance Expense, (no balance)
615 Miscellaneous Expense, $278.25
616 Payroll Tax Expense, $596.20
617 Salary Expense, $12,000.00
618 Supplies Expense, (no balance)

The additional data needed at the end of the annual fiscal period are: merchandise inventory, $10,238.65; supplies inventory, $58.45; value of insurance policies, $128.25; annual depreciation of delivery equipment, $750.00; annual depreciation of office equipment, $200.00.

Instructions: 1. Prepare an eight-column work sheet for the annual fiscal period ended June 30 of the current year.

2. Prepare an income statement, a capital statement, and a balance sheet from the work sheet.

3. Record the adjusting and closing entries on page 20 of a combination journal.

Optional Problems

★ SUPPLEMENTARY PROBLEM 27-S

Calculating depreciation, recording depreciation, and finding book value

Martha Vine purchased the following items of store equipment during the first two years that she was in business:

Store Equipment	*Date of Purchase*	*Original Cost*	*Estimated Scrap Value*	*Estimated Life*
1	Jan. 3, 1966	$ 240.00	$ 20.00	10 years
2	July 1, 1966	300.00	none	10 years
3	Apr. 2, 1967	640.00	100.00	5 years
4	Sept. 1, 1967	4,844.00	500.00	10 years
5	Nov. 1, 1967	72.00	none	8 years
6	Dec. 1, 1967	472.40	50.00	5 years

Instructions: 1. Record on page 18 of a combination journal the adjusting entry for the total depreciation expense for the year ended December 31, 1966.

2. Record the adjusting entry for the total depreciation expense for the year ended December 31, 1967.

3. Find the book value as of December 31, 1967, of each item of equipment.

★BONUS PROBLEM 27-B

Declining-balance method of depreciation

Federal income tax regulations permit a businessman to use the straight-line method of depreciation described in this chapter. The regulations also allow a businessman to use the *declining-balance method of depreciation.* Under the declining-balance method, the depreciation rate is twice the rate used under the straight-line method. The estimated scrap value is not considered in determining the depreciation rate under the declining-balance method. The rate is applied to the book value of the fixed assets at the beginning of each fiscal period.

For example, a new machine is purchased on January 2, 1968, for $2,000.00 and its estimated life is ten years. Under the straight-line method, the estimated life of ten years is equivalent to an annual depreciation rate of 10%. Under the declining-balance method, the annual depreciation rate is 20%. Thus, for the first year, the amount of depreciation is 20% of $2,000.00, or $400.00. At the beginning of the second year, the book value of the machine is $1,600.00. The depreciation for the second year is 20% of $1,600.00, or $320.00. At the beginning of the third year, the book value is $1,280.00. The depreciation for the third year is 20% of $1,280.00, or $256.00. At the end of the estimated period of usefulness of the machine, it is assumed that its book value approximates its estimated scrap value.

Instructions: The Old Towne Company purchases a new machine on January 4 of the current year. The machine costs $800.00 and has an estimated life of 5 years. Determine the amount of depreciation each year for the five-year period by using the declining-balance method.

CHAPTER 28 DISPOSING OF FIXED ASSETS

Fixed assets, such as a cash register, a delivery truck, or a desk, cannot be used forever. The assets may wear out or the business may replace them with newer models. When a fixed asset is no longer useful to a business, the asset may be disposed of by: (1) selling it; (2) discarding it as worthless; or (3) trading it in on a new asset.

GAIN OR LOSS ON DISPOSAL OF FIXED ASSETS

The book value of a fixed asset is only an estimate of its actual value. The actual value of a fixed asset can be determined only when the fixed asset is disposed of. If the actual value of a fixed asset is *more* than its book value, the assets of the business have increased and the records of the business need to be corrected to show this increase. For example, a fixed asset that has a book value of $80.00 is sold for $100.00. The difference between the book value and the actual value is $20.00. This amount, $20.00, is the amount of the increase in the value of this fixed asset. The amount of increase in value that occurs when a fixed asset is disposed of is known as *gain on fixed assets.*

If the actual value of a fixed asset is *less* than its book value, the assets of the business have decreased and the records of the business need to be corrected to show this decrease. For example, a fixed asset that has a book value of $80.00 is sold for $50.00. The difference between the book value and the actual value is $30.00. This amount, $30.00, is the amount of the decrease in the value of this fixed asset. The amount of decrease in value that occurs when a fixed asset is disposed of is known as *loss on fixed assets.*

Gains or losses on the sale and discarding of fixed assets must be shown as separate items on income tax returns. Accounts must therefore be maintained in the ledger in which to record the gains or the losses on fixed assets. An income account with the title *Gain on Fixed Assets* is used to record gains. An expense account with the title *Loss on Fixed Assets* is used to record losses.

GAIN ON SALE OF A FIXED ASSET

July 6, 1968. Harvey Auto Parts receives $100.00 from the sale of a typewriter purchased January 10, 1964.

The fixed asset record for the typewriter is shown below.

FIXED ASSET RECORD — ACCOUNT NO. 122

ITEM Typewriter — GENERAL LEDGER ACCOUNT Office Equipment

SERIAL NO. KL30763-4 — DESCRIPTION Regal

FROM WHOM PURCHASED Cole Equipment Company, Dayton, Ohio

ESTIMATED LIFE 5 years — ESTIMATED SCRAP OR TRADE-IN VALUE $60 — DEPRECIATION PER YEAR $40

DATE			EXPLANATION	ASSET			ACCUMULATED DEPRECIATION			BOOK VALUE
MO.	DAY	YR.		DR.	CR.	BAL.	DR.	CR.	BAL.	
1	10	64		260		260				260
12	31	64						40	40	220
12	31	65						40	80	180
12	31	66						40	120	140
12	31	67						40	160	100

Recording depreciation for part of a fiscal period

The typewriter was sold on July 6, 1968. It is therefore necessary to make a journal entry to record the depreciation on the typewriter for the six-month period, January 1, 1968, to July 6, 1968. The depreciation to be recorded is one half of the annual depreciation, or $20.00.

The journal entry to record the depreciation on the typewriter for six months is shown below.

PAGE 24 — COMBINATION JOURNAL

	1 CASH DEBIT	2 CASH CREDIT	CK. NO.	DATE	ACCOUNT TITLE	POST. REF.	3 GENERAL DEBIT	4 GENERAL CREDIT	
1				1968 July 6	Depr. Expense—Office Equip.		20 00		1
2					Accum. Depr.—Office Equip.			20 00	2
3									3
4									4

When a fixed asset is disposed of during a fiscal period, the time of depreciation is usually computed to the nearest number of months. Thus, an asset disposed of during the first half of a month need not have any depreciation expense charged to it for that month. A fixed asset disposed of during the last half of a month would have a full month's depreciation expense recorded.

After the journal entry is made, the fixed asset record is brought up-to-date by recording the depreciation for the half year, $20.00. The fixed asset record then shows a total accumulated depreciation of $180.00. The amount of the accumulated depreciation, $180.00, is subtracted from the cost of the typewriter, $260.00, to find the book value of $80.00 on July 6.

Recording the gain on the sale of a fixed asset

The typewriter was sold for $100.00, which is $20.00 more than the book value. Thus, the assets of the business increased $20.00. The analysis of this transaction is shown in the T accounts at the right.

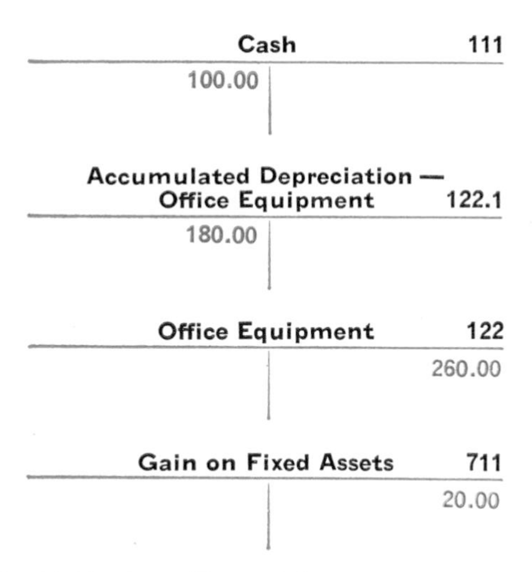

Cash is debited for $100.00 to show the increase in the balance of this account.

Accumulated Depreciation — Office Equipment is debited for $180.00 to show the decrease in the balance of this account. At the end of each fiscal period and at the time of selling the typewriter, the accumulated depreciation account was credited for the amount of depreciation applying to the typewriter.

When the typewriter was bought in 1964, the office equipment account was debited to record the original cost, $260.00. Office Equipment is now credited for $260.00 to show the decrease in the balance of this account. The credit of $260.00 cancels the debit and shows that this amount of office equipment is no longer owned.

Gain on Fixed Assets is credited for $20.00 to show that the typewriter was sold for $20.00 more than its book value.

> When the amount received from the sale of a fixed asset is more than its book value, it is evident that too much depreciation expense has been recorded in previous fiscal periods. This means that in previous fiscal periods, the net income has been understated. The Internal Revenue Service requires that this adjustment of net income be corrected. The gain on fixed assets account is used to show this additional income.

The journal entry to record the sale of the typewriter is shown below.

PAGE 24 COMBINATION JOURNAL

	1 Cash Debit	2 Cash Credit	Ck. No.	Date	Account Title	Post. Ref.	3 General Debit	4 General Credit	
3	100 00			6	Accum. Depr.-Office Equip.		180 00		3
4					Office Equipment			260 00	4
5					Gain on Fixed Assets			20 00	5
6									6

LOSS ON SALE OF A FIXED ASSET

October 3, 1968. Harvey Auto Parts receives $30.00 from the sale of a delivery trailer purchased January 6, 1963.

The fixed asset record for the delivery trailer is shown below.

FIXED ASSET RECORD — ACCOUNT NO. 121

ITEM Delivery trailer — GENERAL LEDGER ACCOUNT Delivery Equipment

SERIAL NO. TM-2076-A — DESCRIPTION Tully-Mason Two-Wheel

FROM WHOM PURCHASED Toms Trucks, Hamilton, Ohio

ESTIMATED LIFE 6 years — ESTIMATED SCRAP OR TRADE-IN VALUE $50 — DEPRECIATION PER YEAR $40

DATE			EXPLANATION	ASSET			ACCUMULATED DEPRECIATION			BOOK VALUE
MO.	DAY	YR.		DR.	CR.	BAL.	DR.	CR.	BAL.	
1	6	63		290		290				290
12	31	63						40	40	250
12	31	64						40	80	210
12	31	65						40	120	170
12	31	66						40	160	130
12	31	67						40	200	90

Recording depreciation for part of a fiscal period

Since the trailer was sold on October 3, 1968, it is necessary to make a journal entry to record the depreciation on the trailer for the 9-month period, January 1, 1968, to October 3, 1968. Nine months is three fourths of a year. Therefore, the depreciation to be recorded is three fourths of the annual depreciation, or $30.00.

The journal entry to record the depreciation on the trailer for three fourths of a year is shown below.

PAGE 28 — COMBINATION JOURNAL

	Cash Debit (1)	Cash Credit (2)	CK. NO.	DATE	ACCOUNT TITLE	POST. REF.	General Debit (3)	General Credit (4)	
1				1968 Oct. 3	Depr. Expense—Del. Equip.		30 00		1
2					Accum. Depr.—Del. Equip.			30 00	2
3									3
4									4
5									5

The fixed asset record is brought up-to-date by recording the depreciation of $30.00 for three fourths of a year. The fixed asset record then shows a total accumulated depreciation of $230.00. The amount of the accumulated depreciation, $230.00, is subtracted from the cost of the trailer, $290.00, to find the book value of $60.00 on October 3.

Recording the loss on the sale of a fixed asset

The trailer was sold for $30.00 less than its book value. Thus, the assets of the business decreased $30.00. The analysis of this transaction is shown in T-accounts at the right.

Cash is debited for $30.00 to show the increase in the balance of this account.

Accumulated Depreciation — Delivery Equipment is debited for $230.00 to show the decrease in the balance of this account. At the end of each fiscal period and at the time of selling the trailer, the accumulated depreciation account was credited for the amount of depreciation applying to the trailer.

Loss on Fixed Assets is debited for $30.00 to show that the trailer was sold for $30.00 less than its book value.

Cash	111
30.00	

Accumulated Depreciation — Delivery Equipment	121.1
230.00	

Loss on Fixed Assets	811
30.00	

Delivery Equipment	121
	290.00

In previous fiscal periods, an insufficient amount of depreciation expense was shown on the income tax returns. This resulted in the payment of a higher income tax than was necessary. Now that the asset has been sold, the income tax regulations permit this entry.

When the trailer was bought in 1963, the delivery equipment account was debited to record the original cost, $290.00. Delivery Equipment is now credited for $290.00 to show the decrease in the balance of the delivery equipment account. The credit of $290.00 cancels the debit and shows that this amount of delivery equipment is no longer owned.

The journal entry to record the sale of the trailer is shown below.

PAGE 28 COMBINATION JOURNAL

	1	2					3	4	
	CASH						GENERAL		
	DEBIT	CREDIT	CK. NO.	DATE	ACCOUNT TITLE	POST. REF.	DEBIT	CREDIT	
3	3000			3	Accum. Depr.-Del. Equip.		23000		3
4					Loss on Fixed Assets		3000		4
5					Delivery Equipment			29000	5
6									6
7									7
8									8

DISCARDING A FIXED ASSET

If a fixed asset is of no further use to the business and cannot be sold or traded, then the fixed asset is discarded. If a fixed asset has no book value, the fixed asset account is credited for the amount of the original cost of the item being discarded. At the same time, the accumulated depreciation account is debited for the amount of the total accumulated depreciation of the item being discarded. If the fixed asset has a book value at the time it is discarded, the business incurs a loss.

Discarding a fixed asset that has no book value

December 20, 1968. Harvey Auto Parts discards an office desk that cost $120.00 on January 10, 1959.

After the additional depreciation on this desk for 1968 is recorded, the fixed asset record shows that the desk has no book value. The analysis of this transaction to record the discarding of a fixed asset that has no book value is shown in the T-accounts at the right.

Accumulated Depreciation — Office Equipment	122.1
120.00	

Office Equipment	122
	120.00

Accumulated Depreciation — Office Equipment is debited for $120.00 to show the decrease in the balance of this account. At the end of each fiscal period and at the time of discarding the desk, the accumulated depreciation account was credited for the amount of depreciation applying to the desk.

When the desk was purchased in 1959, the office equipment account was debited to record the original cost, $120.00. Office Equipment is now credited for $120.00 to record the decrease in the balance of the office equipment account. The credit of $120.00 cancels the debit and shows that this amount of office equipment is no longer owned.

The journal entry to record the discarding of the desk is shown below.

PAGE 32 COMBINATION JOURNAL

	1	2						3	4	
	CASH		CK. NO.	DATE		ACCOUNT TITLE	POST. REF.	GENERAL		
	DEBIT	CREDIT						DEBIT	CREDIT	
1				1968 Dec.	20	Accum. Depr.–Office Equip.		120 00		1
2						Office Equipment			120 00	2
3										3
4										4
5										5
6										6
7										7

Discarding a fixed asset that has a book value

January 7, 1968. Harvey Auto Parts discards a file cabinet that cost $60.00 on January 19, 1961.

An examination of the fixed asset record of the file cabinet shows that the amount of accumulated depreciation on this asset is $35.00. The record also shows that the book value of the file cabinet on January 1, 1968, is $25.00. Since the file cabinet that is discarded has a book value of $25.00, Harvey Auto Parts incurs a loss of $25.00. The analysis of this transaction to record the discarding of a fixed asset that has a book value is shown in T-accounts at the right.

Accumulated Depreciation — Office Equipment is debited for $35.00 to show the decrease in the balance of this account. At the end of each fiscal period, the accumulated depreciation account was credited for the amount of depreciation applying to the cabinet.

Loss on Fixed Assets is debited for $25.00 to record the loss that resulted from discarding an asset that has a book value.

Accumulated Depreciation — Office Equipment	122.1
35.00	

Loss on Fixed Assets	811
25.00	

Office Equipment	122
	60.00

Office Equipment is credited for $60.00 to show the decrease in the balance of this asset account. When the file cabinet was purchased in 1961, the office equipment account was debited to record the original cost, $60.00. The credit of $60.00 cancels the debit and shows that this amount of office equipment is no longer owned.

TRADING IN A FIXED ASSET

A common business practice is to trade in a used asset for another similar asset. For example, a used delivery truck may be traded in on a new one. According to income tax regulations, a loss or a gain is not allowed when one fixed asset of a business is traded in for another similar fixed asset. The new asset is recorded at an amount equal to the sum of the cash actually paid plus the book value of the asset traded in.

April 26, 1968. Harvey Auto Parts buys a new truck. The payment for the new truck consists of Check No. 862 for $2,200.00 plus the trade-in of the old truck that has a book value of $1,000.00.

The fixed asset record of the old delivery truck immediately before the trade-in transaction, shows the following information:

FIXED ASSET RECORD — ACCOUNT NO. 121

ITEM Delivery truck — GENERAL LEDGER ACCOUNT Delivery Equipment

SERIAL NO. GT465008 — DESCRIPTION Almo Side Panel

FROM WHOM PURCHASED Almo Motors, Dayton, Ohio

ESTIMATED LIFE 4 years — ESTIMATED SCRAP OR TRADE-IN VALUE $600 — DEPRECIATION PER YEAR $600

DATE			EXPLANATION	ASSET			ACCUMULATED DEPRECIATION			BOOK VALUE
MO.	DAY	YR.		DR.	CR.	BAL.	DR.	CR.	BAL.	
1	5	65		3,000		3,000				3,000
12	31	65						600	600	2,400
12	31	66						600	1,200	1,800
12	31	67						600	1,800	1,200

Recording depreciation for part of a fiscal period

Since the delivery truck was traded in on April 26, it is necessary to make a journal entry to record the depreciation on the truck for the four-month period, January 1, 1968, to April 26, 1968. Since four months is one third of a year, the amount of depreciation to be recorded is one third of the annual depreciation, $600.00, or $200.00 for the four months.

The journal entry to record the depreciation on the delivery truck for one third of a year is shown below.

COMBINATION JOURNAL — PAGE 21

	1	2					3	4	
	CASH						GENERAL		
	DEBIT	CREDIT	CK. NO.	DATE	ACCOUNT TITLE	POST. REF.	DEBIT	CREDIT	
1				1968 Apr. 26	Depr. Expense—Del. Equip.		20000		1
2					Accum. Depr.—Del. Equip.			20000	2
3									3
4									4
5									5
6									6
7									7

The fixed asset record is brought up-to-date by recording the depreciation for one third of a year. The fixed asset record then shows a total accumulated depreciation of $2,000.00. The amount of the accumulated depreciation, $2,000.00, is subtracted from the cost of the delivery truck, $3,000.00, to find the book value of $1,000.00 on April 26.

Recording the trading in of a fixed asset

The amount at which the new truck is recorded on the books is found as follows:

Book value of the old truck traded in.	$1,000.00
Cash payment made to complete the purchase of the new truck.	$2,200.00
Amount at which the new truck is to be recorded. . . .	$3,200.00

An analysis of this transaction to record the trading in of a fixed asset is shown in T-accounts at the right.

Delivery Equipment	121
3,200.00	3,000.00

Accumulated Depreciation — Delivery Equipment	121.1
2,000.00	

Cash	111
	2,200.00

Delivery Equipment is debited for $3,200.00, the amount at which the new truck is to be recorded.

Accumulated Depreciation — Delivery Equipment is debited for $2,000.00 to show the decrease in the balance of this account. At the end of each fiscal period and at the time of the trade-in, the accumulated depreciation account was credited for the amount of depreciation applying to the old truck.

Delivery Equipment is credited for $3,000.00 to show the decrease in the balance of this account as the result of trading in the old truck. When the old truck was bought in 1965, the delivery equipment account was debited to record the original cost, $3,000.00. The credit of $3,000.00 cancels the debit and shows that this amount of delivery equipment is no longer owned.

Cash is credited for $2,200.00 to show the decrease in the balance of this account.

The journal entry to record this trade-in transaction is shown below.

PAGE 21 COMBINATION JOURNAL

	1 Cash Debit	2 Cash Credit	Ck. No.	Date	Account Title	Post. Ref.	3 General Debit	4 General Credit	
3		220000		26	Delivery Equipment		320000		3
4					Accum. Depr.–Del. Equip.		200000		4
5					Delivery Equipment			300000	5
6									6
7									7

OTHER INCOME AND OTHER EXPENSE ON THE INCOME STATEMENT

When a business has income and expenses that are not considered to be part of the regular operation of the business, such nonoperating income and expense items are classified separately on the income statement. The income statement of Harvey Auto Parts on the next page includes the nonoperating income account Gain on Fixed Assets and the nonoperating expense account Loss on Fixed Assets. How this income statement differs from previously illustrated statements is discussed in the following paragraphs.

Line 1

The more complete title *Income from Sales* is used instead of *Income* in order to distinguish sales income from other income reported on Line 28.

Line 27

The gross profit on sales minus the operating expenses is called *net income from operations*. The term *net income from operations* is used to distinguish between net income that came entirely from the regular operation of the business and net income that did not.

Lines 28 and 29

Harvey Auto Parts is not in business to make a profit on the sale of its fixed assets. A gain on the disposal of a fixed asset is not, therefore, considered to be part of the regular operating income of business. Gain on Fixed Assets is listed separately on the income statement under the heading *Other Income*.

Lines 30 and 31

A business will sometimes have an expense that is not an operating expense of the business. The expense account, Loss on Fixed Assets, is an example of a nonoperating expense. It is listed under the heading *Other Expense*.

Lines 32 and 33

The amount by which the Other Income exceeds the Other Expense is labeled *Net Addition* and is added to the Net Income from Operations. The sum is the *Net Income* of the business for the period.

When the Other Income during a fiscal period is less than the Other Expense, the difference is entitled *Net Subtraction*. This amount is then subtracted from the Net Income from Operations. The final lines of an income statement showing Other Income less than Other Expense are illustrated on page 510.

Harvey Auto Parts
Income Statement
For Month Ended July 31, 1968

1	Income from Sales:			
2	Sales			10300 00
3	Less: Sales Returns and Allowances		86 40	
4	Sales Discount		122 80	209 20
5	Net Sales			10090 80
6	Cost of Merchandise Sold:			
7	Merchandise Inventory, July 1, 1968		37600 00	
8	Purchases	2800 00		
9	Less: Purchases Returns and Allowances 160.00			
10	Purchases Discount 60.00	220 00		
11	Net Purchases		2580 00	
12	Cost of Merchandise Available for Sale		40180 00	
13	Less Merchandise Inventory, July 31, 1968		36070 00	
14	Cost of Merchandise Sold			4110 00
15	Gross Profit on Sales			5980 80
16	Operating Expenses			
17	Delivery Expense		172 00	
18	Depreciation Expense - Delivery Equipment		125 00	
19	Depreciation Expense - Office Equipment		30 00	
20	Insurance Expense		90 00	
21	Miscellaneous Expense		94 00	
22	Payroll Tax Expense		1206 50	
23	Rent Expense		250 00	
24	Salary Expense		2750 00	
25	Supplies Expense		60 00	
26	Total Operating Expenses			4777 50
27	Net Income from Operations			1203 30
28	Other Income:			
29	Gain on Fixed Assets		230 00	
30	Other Expense:			
31	Loss on Fixed Assets		156 00	
32	Net Addition			74 00
33	Net Income			1277 30

Income statement showing Other Income and Other Expense

Net Income from Operations..................			1,728	33
Other Income:				
Gain on Fixed Assets........................	116	50		
Other Expense:				
Loss on Fixed Assets........................	245	00		
Net Subtraction..............................			128	50
Net Income...................................			1,599	83

Portion of income statement showing Other Income less than Other Expense

Closing the accounts that are classified as other income and other expenses

The accounts that are classified as other income and other expense are closed into Income and Expense Summary in the same manner and at the same time that the operating income and operating expense accounts are closed.

Increasing Your Business Vocabulary

What is the meaning of each of the following:

a gain on fixed assets
b loss on fixed assets
c net income from operations

Study Questions

1. What are three ways of disposing of a fixed asset?
2. Why is it desirable to have separate ledger accounts to show the total gains or the total losses from the sale of fixed assets?
3. To what record does the bookkeeper refer to get the information he needs to determine whether a gain or a loss occurs when a fixed asset is disposed of?
4. When a fixed asset is disposed of during a fiscal period, what entry must be made to bring the depreciation expense account and the accumulated depreciation account up-to-date?
5. What determines the amount that should be debited to the accumulated depreciation account when a fixed asset is sold?
6. What determines the amount that should be credited to an equipment account when an asset is sold?
7. When cash and an old fixed asset are given in payment of a new asset, for what amount is the new asset recorded on the books?
8. Under what heading on the income statement is Gain on Fixed Assets listed?
9. Under what heading on the income statement is Loss on Fixed Assets listed?
10. Into what account are the balances of the accounts Gain on Fixed Assets and Loss on Fixed Assets closed at the end of each fiscal period?

Cases for Business Decision

CASE 1

Mr. Colvin finds that when he disposes of fixed assets, his records often show a gain. What decision could Mr. Colvin make about his depreciation rates that would help eliminate these gains?

CASE 2

The Porter Accounting firm had an adding machine stolen from its office. The original cost of the machine was $310.00. The accumulated depreciation is $90.00. What account titles do you recommend be used to record this loss?

CASE 3

When B. J. Cavan reported to his bookkeeper the discarding of a worthless file cabinet, the fixed asset record showed that the file cabinet no longer had any book value. Mr. Cavan told his bookkeeper that since all possible depreciation expense had been recorded and no loss on the fixed asset had been incurred, no further bookkeeping entry was necessary. Evaluate the advice given by Mr. Cavan to his bookkeeper.

CASE 4

A new adding machine that cost $160.00 was purchased by Mohr and Stark, partners in a lumber business. Mr. Mohr thought they should estimate its useful life at 10 years, while Mr. Stark thought that 12 years would be a better estimate. Finally, Mr. Mohr stated, "Whether we decide on 10 years or 12 years makes little difference in the long run. The total expense to the business will be $160.00 in either case." Evaluate Mr. Mohr's statement. Do you agree with him?

Application Problems

PROBLEM 28-1 | **Discarding fixed assets**

J. L. Yost, a certified public accountant, discarded as worthless the following items of office equipment:

Items	*Date of Purchase*	*Original Cost*	*Estimated Scrap Value*	*Estimated Life*	*Date of Disposal*
#1	Jan. 2, 1964	$400	$ 25	5 years	Jan. 7, 1968
#2	June 2, 1964	242	50	4 years	Mar. 7, 1968
#3	July 5, 1962	600	210	10 years	Jan. 7, 1968
#4	Apr. 28, 1961	200	None	5 years	Mar. 18, 1968

Instructions: 1. Calculate the book value and the amount of loss, if any, for each fixed asset.

2. Make the journal entries necessary to record depreciation for 1968 to the date of disposal of the assets. Calculate depreciation to the nearest month.

3. Make the journal entries necessary to record the discarding of each item of office equipment.

PROBLEM 28-2 | Selling fixed assets

Mary Dexter, owner of a food shop, sold the following items of equipment on December 1, 1968:

Item	*Purchase Price*	*Book Value Dec. 1, 1968*	*Cash Received from Sale of Fixed Asset*
Cash register	$480	$90	$120
Display counter	320	80	40

Instructions: Make the journal entries necessary to record the sale of these fixed assets.

PROBLEM 28-3 | Trading in fixed assets

Assume that, instead of selling the items in Problem 28-2 for cash, Miss Dexter traded them in on December 1, 1968, for new items of equipment as follows:

(a) A new cash register for the old cash register plus $460 in cash.

(b) A new display counter for the old counter plus $400 in cash.

Instructions: Make the journal entries necessary to record the trade-in of these fixed assets.

Optional Problems

⋆SUPPLEMENTARY PROBLEM 28-S

Purchase and disposition of fixed assets

Instructions: 1. Open the following accounts in the ledger of Lloyd Harvey and record the balances as of January 1 of the current year.

Account No.	*Account Title*	*Account Balance*
121	Delivery Equipment	$5,100.00
121.1	Accumulated Depreciation — Delivery Equipment	2,550.00
122	Office Equipment	1,260.00
122.1	Accumulated Depreciation — Office Equipment	720.00
614	Depreciation Expense — Delivery Equipment	———
615	Depreciation Expense — Office Equipment	———
712	Gain on Fixed Assets	———
812	Loss on Fixed Assets	———

Instructions: 2. Record on page 38 of a combination journal the following transactions selected from those completed during the current year.

Jan. 2. Issued Check No. 389 for $380.00 for cash purchase of office equipment.

Jan. 3. Discarded office equipment for which there was no further use and which could not be sold. The office equipment cost $160.00 and had a book value of $20.00 at the time it was discarded.

Jan. 10. Bought a new delivery truck for $2,500.00 cash (Check No. 397) and the old truck. The old truck cost $2,800.00 and had a book value of $1,050.00 at the time of the trade-in.

Jan. 12. Sold old office equipment for cash, $40.00. The equipment cost $90.00 and had a book value of $30.00 when it was sold.

June 30. Sold a truck for $950.00. The truck had been purchased two years ago on January 2 for $2,300.00. The amount of depreciation is $400.00 a year. Accumulated depreciation for that amount was recorded at the end of the two previous years.
(a) Record the depreciation for the current year to June 30.
(b) Record the sale of the truck.

June 30. Bought a new bookkeeping machine for $850.00 cash (Check No. 624) and the old machine that cost $960.00. The estimated life of the old machine was 10 years. The estimated trade-in value was $150.00. Accumulated depreciation recorded on the old machine from time of purchase until January 1 of the current year amounts to $324.00.
(a) Record the depreciation for the current year to June 30.
(b) Record the purchase of the new machine and the trade-in of the old one.

Instructions: 3. Post all amounts in the General columns.

4. Make the necessary adjusting entries to record depreciation for the year ended December 31, based on the following data: Depreciation Expense — Delivery Equipment, $650.00; Depreciation Expense — Office Equipment, $77.00.

5. Post the adjusting entries.

★ BONUS PROBLEM 28-B

Purchase and disposition of fixed assets

Instructions: 1. Open the following accounts in the ledger of J. Polk, using the account numbers indicated: Delivery Equipment, 121; Accumulated Depreciation — Delivery Equipment, 121.1; Office Machines, 122; Accumulated Depreciation — Office Machines, 122.1; Depreciation Expense — Delivery Equipment, 614; Depreciation Expense — Office Machines, 615; Gain on Fixed Assets, 712; Loss on Fixed Assets, 812.

2. Record on page 56 of a combination journal the following selected transactions:

Jan. 3, 1968. Purchased a used delivery truck for cash, $2,100.00. (Check No. 64.) The estimated life of the truck is 2 years and the estimated trade-in value is $200.00.

Jan. 6, 1968. Purchased a used adding machine for cash, $60.00 (Check No. 69.) The estimated life of the adding machine is 5 years and there is no estimated trade-in value.

Dec. 31, 1968. Made adjusting entries to record depreciation for the year.

Dec. 31, 1968. Made an entry to close the depreciation expense accounts.

Instructions: 3. Post the foregoing entries to the accounts that you opened in the ledger. As you do not have a complete ledger, you need not post to the account Income and Expense Summary.

4. Record in the combination journal the following selected transactions:

Jan. 10, 1969. Discarded adding machine purchased January 6, 1968. It was broken and could not be sold.

Jan. 11, 1969. Purchased new adding machine for cash, $640.00. (Check No. 73.) The estimated life of the adding machine is 10 years and the estimated trade-in value is $50.00.

July 2, 1969. Sold truck that was purchased January 3, 1968, for cash, $700.00.
(a) Record the depreciation for the current year to July 2.
(b) Record the sale of the truck.

July 3, 1969. Bought a new delivery truck for cash, $4,000. (Check No. 192.) The estimated life of the truck is 5 years and the estimated trade-in value is $700.00.

Dec. 28, 1969. Traded in truck bought on July 3 for a new model. The cost of the new truck was the book value of the old truck plus $600.00 in cash. (Check No. 246.)
(a) Record the depreciation from July 3 to December 28 of the current year.
(b) Record the purchase of the new truck and the trade-in of the old.

Dec. 31, 1969. Made adjusting entry to record for the year the depreciation expense that had not previously been recorded.

Dec. 31, 1969. Made an entry to close the income account.

Dec. 31, 1969. Made an entry to close the expense accounts.

Instructions: 5. Post the foregoing entries to the accounts that you opened in the ledger. As you do not have a complete ledger, you need not post to the account Income and Expense Summary.

6. Prepare the Fixed Assets section of J. Polk's balance sheet for December 31, 1969.

CHAPTER 29 BAD DEBTS AND VALUATION OF ACCOUNTS RECEIVABLE

Harvey Auto Parts sells merchandise for cash and on account. Most of its sales on account are made to individual automobile owners. The sales on account to individuals include such items as air conditioners, transistor radios, tires, and batteries.

Before Harvey Auto Parts extends credit, it obtains information about the credit standing of the prospective charge customer. Retailers usually obtain the credit rating of a prospective charge customer from a local credit bureau. Wholesalers and manufacturers may obtain this information from the financial reports submitted by the prospective customer and from national credit agencies such as Dun & Bradstreet.

> Dun & Bradstreet, Inc., publishes a credit-rating book containing information about the financial condition of business houses throughout the United States. This reference book is available to businesses subscribing for it.

VALUATION OF ACCOUNTS RECEIVABLE

When a business sells merchandise or services on credit, a portion of the accounts receivable usually proves to be uncollectible. Accounts receivable that cannot be collected are called *bad debts.* Because of the failure to collect the accounts receivable, the business incurs an operating expense from its loss on bad debts.

An account receivable does not become a bad debt until it is known to be uncollectible. Sometimes this is several months or even a year or more after the date the sale was made. During the time that this account receivable which proved to be uncollectible is carried on the books, the value of Accounts Receivable is overstated. Furthermore, the expense resulting from selling goods to a customer who did not pay is not recorded. It is desirable, therefore, for a business to estimate the amount of its uncollectible accounts. After this is done, an adjusting entry is made. One purpose of the adjusting entry is to prevent the value of Accounts Receivable from being overstated on the balance sheet. Another purpose is to include the estimated Bad Debts Expense on the income statement.

Aging Accounts Receivable

Many business firms base their estimate of uncollectible accounts on an analysis of the accounts receivable at the end of the fiscal period. Analyzing accounts receivable according to their age is called *aging accounts receivable*. The balance of each customer's account is classified according to the age of the outstanding balance.

Harvey Auto Parts lists those accounts that are more than six months past due and totals the account balances. Past experience shows what percentage of these past-due accounts will become uncollectible. Past experience of Harvey Auto Parts shows that $571.20 of the past-due accounts will prove to be uncollectible.

The accounts receivable account of Harvey Auto Parts as of December 31, 1968, is shown below. The account balance, $8,800.00, is the amount due from customers as of December 31, 1968. If Harvey Auto Parts lists the value of Accounts Receivable as $8,800.00, the value of this asset will be overstated by $571.20. The company must therefore find the book value of the accounts receivable account in order to estimate the value accurately.

Accounts Receivable — ACCOUNT NO. 113

DATE		ITEMS	POST. REF.	DEBIT	CREDIT	BALANCE DEBIT	BALANCE CREDIT
1968 Dec.	1	Balance	✓			7600 72	
	31		32	6400 51		14001 23	
	31		32		5201 23	8800 00	

Book value of Accounts Receivable

The book value of Accounts Receivable is the balance of the account less the amount estimated to be uncollectible. Mr. Harvey calculates the book value of Accounts Receivable on December 31, 1968, as follows:

Accounts Receivable	$8,800.00
Less amount estimated to be uncollectible	571.20
Book value of Accounts Receivable	$8,228.80

ESTABLISHING THE ALLOWANCE FOR BAD DEBTS

Even though Mr. Harvey estimates that $571.20 of the accounts receivable will not be collected, he is not certain which of his customers will fail to pay. He could record the estimated loss by debiting an expense account. But without knowing which customers will not pay, he cannot credit certain customers' accounts. Likewise, he cannot credit the accounts receivable account in the general ledger because the balance of that account has to equal the sum of the balances of the customers' accounts. He therefore makes an adjusting entry and credits the estimated amount of the bad debts to an account with the title *Allowance for Bad Debts.* The estimated loss from bad debts is one of the expenses of operating his business. He debits this amount to an expense account with the title *Bad Debts Expense.*

The titles Allowance for Uncollectible Accounts and Allowance for Doubtful Accounts are sometimes used instead of Allowance for Bad Debts. Until recent years the valuation account was often titled "Reserve for Bad Debts." Today, however, the American Institute of Certified Public Accountants recommends the term *allowance* be used in preference to the term *reserve* in the account title.

Analyzing the adjustment for estimated bad debts

In order to record the estimated bad debts so that the expense is charged to the fiscal period in which the expense is incurred, an adjusting entry is made in the journal. For the fiscal period ending December 31, 1968, Mr. Harvey's aging of the accounts receivable shows that $571.20 of the accounts receivable is estimated to be uncollectible.

The adjustment for estimated bad debts is analyzed in T accounts below.

Bad Debts Expense is debited for $571.20, the amount estimated to be lost during the fiscal period because of some customers who will fail to pay the amounts due.

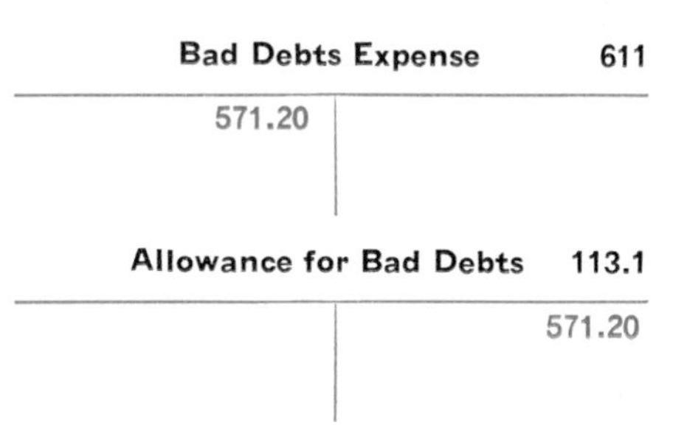

Allowance for Bad Debts is a valuation account. This valuation account, often called a minus asset, shows the amount to be deducted from the balance of the accounts receivable account. The allowance for bad debts account is credited for $571.20 to show an increase in the account balance. This account balance is the estimated amount of uncollectible accounts.

Adjustment for estimated bad debts on the work sheet

The December 31, 1968, work sheet for Harvey Auto Parts with the adjustment for estimated bad debts is shown on pages 518 and 519. The adjustment is shown on Lines 4 and 26.

Harvey Auto Parts
Work Sheet
For Year Ended December 31, 1968

	ACCOUNT TITLES	ACCT. NO.	1 TRIAL BALANCE DEBIT	2 TRIAL BALANCE CREDIT	3 ADJUSTMENTS DEBIT	4 ADJUSTMENTS CREDIT	5 INCOME STATEMENT DEBIT	6 INCOME STATEMENT CREDIT	7 BALANCE SHEET DEBIT	8 BALANCE SHEET CREDIT	
1	Cash	111	6130 20						6130 20		1
2	Petty Cash	112	100 00						100 00		2
3	Accounts Receivable	113	8800 00						8800 00		3
4	Allowance for Bad Debts	113.1				(a) 571 20					4
5	Merchandise Inventory	114	35205 50		(c) 38470 00	(b) 35205 50			38470 00		5
6	Supplies	115	690 00			(d) 455 00			235 00		6
7	Prepaid Insurance	116	754 00			(e) 530 00			224 00		7
8	Delivery Equipment	121	8440 00						8440 00		8
9	Accum. Depr.--Delivery Equip.	121.1		975 00		(f) 1720 00				2695 00	9
10	Office Equipment	122	5800 00						5800 00		10
11	Accum. Depr.--Office Equipment	122.1		1048 00		(g) 487 60				1535 60	11
12	Accounts Payable	211		4637 10						4637 10	12
13	FICA Taxes Payable	212		298 00						298 00	13
14	Employees Income Taxes Payable	213		515 30						515 30	14
15	State Unempl. Taxes Payable	214		269 40						269 40	15
16	Federal Unempl. Taxes Payable	215		138 00						138 00	16
17	R. L. Harvey, Capital	311		54379 95						54379 95	17
18	R. L. Harvey, Drawing	312	9000 00						9000 00		18
19	Income and Expense Summary	313			(b) 35205 50	(c) 38470 00	35205 50	38470 00			19
20	Sales	411		108320 50				108320 50			20
21	Sales Returns and Allowances	411.1	942 80				942 80				21
22	Sales Discount	411.2	1906 40				1906 40				22

Line	Account	Acct. No.	Trial Balance Dr.	Trial Balance Cr.	Adjustments Dr.	Adjustments Cr.	Income Statement Dr.	Income Statement Cr.	Balance Sheet Dr.	Balance Sheet Cr.	Line
23	Purchases	511	50870 00				50870 00				23
24	Purchases Returns and Allow.	511.1		1246 20				1246 20			24
25	Purchases Discount	511.2		1411 70				1411 70			25
26	Bad Debts Expense	611			(a) 571 20		571 20				26
27	Delivery Expense	612	1625 40				1625 40				27
28	Depreciation Expense--Del. Equip.	613	180 00		(f) 1720 00		1900 00				28
29	Depreciation Expense--Office Equip.	614	65 00		(g) 487 60		552 60				29
30	Insurance Expense	615			(e) 530 00		530 00				30
31	Miscellaneous Expense	616	2403 75				2403 75				31
32	Payroll Tax Expense	617	2612 10				2612 10				32
33	Rent Expense	618	3000 00				3000 00				33
34	Salary Expense	619	34828 00				34828 00				34
35	Supplies Expense	620			(d) 455 00		455 00				35
36	Gain on Fixed Assets	711		370 00				370 00			36
37	Loss on Fixed Assets	811	256 00				256 00				37
38			173609 15	173609 15	77439 30	77439 30	137658 75	149818 40	77199 20	65039 55	38
39	Net Income						12159 65			12159 65	39
40							149818 40	149818 40	77199 20	77199 20	40
41											41
42											42
43											43
44											44
45											45
46											46
47											47
48											48
49											49

Work sheet with adjustment for bad debts

Debit part of adjustment. On Line 26, Bad Debts Expense is debited for \$571.20 in the Adjustments Debit column. The amount is extended to the Income Statement Debit column because all expenses are recorded as debits in this column.

Credit part of adjustment. On Line 4, Allowance for Bad Debts is credited for \$571.20 in the Adjustments Credit column. This amount is extended to the Balance Sheet Credit column because it is a deduction from the accounts receivable account on the balance sheet.

Journalizing and posting the adjustment for estimated bad debts

The data needed to journalize the adjustment for estimated bad debts are obtained from the Adjustments columns of the work sheet. This adjusting entry is shown below.

PAGE 32 COMBINATION JOURNAL

	1 CASH DEBIT	2 CASH CREDIT	CK. NO.	DATE	ACCOUNT TITLE	POST. REF.	3 GENERAL DEBIT	4 GENERAL CREDIT	
26				31	Bad Debts Expense		571 20		26
27					Allowance for Bad Debts			571 20	27
28									28
29									29
30									30
31									31
32									32
33									33
34									34
35									35

Adjusting entry for estimated bad debts

When the adjusting entry is posted, the accounts receivable account, the allowance for bad debts account, and the bad debts expense account appear as shown on the next page.

The debit balance of the accounts receivable account, \$8,800.00, shows the total amount due from charge customers. The allowance for bad debts account has a credit balance of \$571.20, which is the estimated amount of uncollectible accounts as determined by aging the accounts receivable. The account number 113.1 shows that the allowance for bad debts account is a valuation account for account number 113. The balance of this valuation account is subtracted from the balance of asset account number 113 to obtain the book value of accounts receivable. The bad debts expense account has a debit balance of \$571.20, which is the estimated amount of loss on bad debts that is to be charged as an expense for the fiscal period.

Accounts Receivable — ACCOUNT NO. 113

DATE		ITEMS	POST. REF.	DEBIT	CREDIT	BALANCE DEBIT	BALANCE CREDIT
1968 Dec.	1	Balance	✓			7600 72	
	31		32	6400 51		14001 23	
	31		32		5201 23	8800 00	

Allowance for Bad Debts — ACCOUNT NO. 113.1

DATE		ITEMS	POST. REF.	DEBIT	CREDIT	BALANCE DEBIT	BALANCE CREDIT
1968 Dec.	31		32		571 20		571 20

Bad Debts Expense — ACCOUNT NO. 611

DATE		ITEMS	POST. REF.	DEBIT	CREDIT	BALANCE DEBIT	BALANCE CREDIT
1968 Dec.	31		32	571 20		571 20	

General ledger accounts after the adjusting entry for estimated bad debts is posted

SHOWING BAD DEBTS EXPENSE AND ALLOWANCE FOR BAD DEBTS ON THE FINANCIAL STATEMENTS

Bad debts expense on the income statement

When Harvey Auto Parts prepares its income statement from the work sheet of December 31, 1968, the account Bad Debts Expense is listed in the Operating Expenses section as shown on the income statement on the next page.

Allowance for bad debts on the balance sheet

When Mr. Harvey prepares his balance sheet from the work sheet of December 31, 1968, he indicates (1) the total accounts receivable, (2) the allowance for bad debts, and (3) the book value of accounts receivable as shown on page 523.

The total amount due from customers, $8,800.00, is written in the first column on the line with Accounts Receivable. "Less Allowance for Bad Debts" is written on the next line, slightly indented under Accounts Receivable. The amount, $571.20, is written below $8,800.00. A single

Harvey Auto Parts
Income Statement
For Year Ended December 31, 1968

Income from Sales:			
Sales			108320.50
Less: Sales Returns and Allowances		942.80	
Sales Discount		1906.40	2849.20
Net Sales			105471.30
Cost of Merchandise Sold:			
Merchandise Inventory, January 1, 1968		35205.50	
Purchases	50870.00		
Less: Purchases Returns and Allow. 1,246.20			
Purchases Discount 1411.70	2657.90		
Net Purchases		48212.10	
Total Cost of Merchandise Available for Sale		83417.60	
Less Merchandise Inventory, December 31, 1968		38470.00	
Cost of Merchandise Sold			44947.60
Gross Profit on Sales			60523.70
Operating Expenses:			
Bad Debts Expense		571.20	
Delivery Expense		1625.40	
Depreciation Expense—Delivery Equipment		1900.00	
Depreciation Expense—Office Equipment		552.60	
Insurance Expense		530.00	
Miscellaneous Expense		2403.75	
Payroll Tax Expense		2612.10	
Rent Expense		3000.00	
Salary Expense		34828.00	
Supplies Expense		455.00	
Total Operating Expenses			48478.05
Net Income from Operations:			12045.65
Other Income:			
Gain on Fixed Assets		370.00	
Other Expenses:			
Loss on Fixed Assets		256.00	
Net Addition			114.00
Net Income			12159.65

Bad debts expense on the income statement

line is ruled and the difference between the two amounts, $8,228.80, is written in the second amount column on the same line as the allowance amount. This is the book value of Accounts Receivable on December 31, 1968.

Harvey Auto Parts
Balance Sheet
December 31, 1968

Assets			
Current Assets:			
Cash		6130 20	
Petty Cash		100 00	
Accounts Receivable	8800 00		
Less Allowance for Bad Debts	571 20	8228 80	
Merchandise Inventory		38470 00	
Supplies		235 00	
Prepaid Insurance		224 00	
Total Current Assets			53388 00
Fixed Assets:			
Delivery Equipment	8440 00		
Less Accum. Depr.–Delivery Equipment	2695 00	5745 00	
Office Equipment	5800 00		
Less Accum. Depr.–Office Equipment	1535 60	4264 40	
Total Fixed Assets			10009 40
Total Assets			63397 40
Liabilities			
Current Liabilities:			
Accounts Payable		4637 10	
FICA Taxes Payable		298 00	
Employees Income Taxes Payable		515 30	
State Unemployment Taxes Payable		269 40	
Federal Unemployment Taxes Payable		138 00	
Total Current Liabilities			5857 80
Proprietorship			
R. L. Harvey, Capital			57539 60
Total Liabilities and Proprietorship			63397 40

Allowance for bad debts on the balance sheet

WRITING OFF UNCOLLECTIBLE ACCOUNTS

Canceling the balance of a customer's account because the customer will not or cannot pay the amount due is called *writing off an account*. As soon as it is decided that a customer's account is uncollectible, a journal entry is made to write off his account. Whenever a customer's account is credited in the accounts receivable ledger, the controlling account in the general ledger, Accounts Receivable, must also be credited for the same amount.

On January 3, 1969, Harvey Auto Parts decides that J. R. West's account balance of $48.00 is uncollectible. The analysis of the journal entry to write off this account is shown in T-account form at the right.

Allowance for Bad Debts is debited for $48.00 to reduce the balance of this account.

Accounts Receivable is credited for $48.00 to reduce the amount due from customers.

J. R. West's account in the accounts receivable ledger is credited for $48.00 to cancel the debit balance of his account.

GENERAL LEDGER

Allowance for Bad Debts 113.1

Debit	Credit
48.00	

Accounts Receivable 113

Debit	Credit
	48.00

ACCOUNTS RECEIVABLE LEDGER

J. R. West

Debit	Credit
	48.00

Recording the journal entry to write off an account

The entry to write off the account balance of J. R. West is shown at the bottom of this page and the following page.

Posting the journal entry to write off an account

When the journal entry to write off the account is posted, the allowance for bad debts account in the general ledger appears as follows:

Allowance for Bad Debts — ACCOUNT NO. 113.1

DATE		ITEMS	POST. REF.	DEBIT	CREDIT	BALANCE DEBIT	BALANCE CREDIT
1968 Dec.	31		32		571 20		571 20
1969 Jan.	3		34	48 00			523 20

Allowance for bad debts account in the general ledger after the entry writing off a bad debt is posted

PAGE 34 — COMBINATION JOURNAL

	1 CASH DEBIT	2 CASH CREDIT	CK. NO.	DATE	ACCOUNT TITLE	POST. REF.	3 GENERAL DEBIT	4 GENERAL CREDIT	
16				12	Allowance for Bad Debts	113.1	48 00		16
17					J. R. West	✓			17
18									18

Entry to write off an uncollectible

The corresponding credit to Accounts Receivable in the general ledger will be posted as a part of the column total at the end of the month.

When the credit to J. R. West's account in the accounts receivable ledger is posted, his account appears as follows:

NAME *J. R. West*
ADDRESS *504 Main Street, Dayton, Ohio 45409*

DATE		ITEMS	POST. REF.	DEBIT	CREDIT	DEBIT BALANCE
1968 May	15		30	48 00		48 00
1969 Jan.	3	*Written off*	34		48 00	—

Customer's account in the accounts receivable ledger after the entry writing off the account as a bad debt is posted

The posting of $48.00 to the customer's account cancels the balance of his account. The balance of the accounts receivable account in the general ledger will be reduced by the same amount, $48.00, when the total of the Accounts Receivable Credit column of the journal is posted.

OTHER METHODS OF ESTIMATING UNCOLLECTIBLE ACCOUNTS

Some businesses prefer to estimate the amount of uncollectible accounts by taking a percentage of the *net* sales for the fiscal period. Some other businesses prefer to estimate the amount of uncollectible accounts by taking a percentage of the total *charge* sales for the fiscal period.

Estimating uncollectible accounts on the basis of net sales

Mr. Conway, a wholesale hardware merchant, has found from past records and experience that his uncollectible accounts usually amount to about ½% (.005) of his net sales for a fiscal period. Mr. Conway's net sales for the quarterly fiscal period ended December 31, 1968, were

FOR MONTH OF *January* 19*69* PAGE *34*

	5	6	7	8	9	10	11	12	
	ACCOUNTS PAYABLE DEBIT	ACCOUNTS PAYABLE CREDIT	PURCHASES DISCOUNT CREDIT	ACCOUNTS RECEIVABLE DEBIT	ACCOUNTS RECEIVABLE CREDIT	SALES DISCOUNT DEBIT	PURCHASES DEBIT	SALES CREDIT	
16									16
17					48 00				17
18									18

account when an allowance account is used

$22,064.00. He therefore estimates that $110.32 ($22,064.00 × .005 = $110.32) of his Accounts Receivable would be bad debts expense for this period.

In order for Mr. Conway to determine the book value of his accounts receivable on December 31, it is necessary to subtract the estimated amount of uncollectible accounts from the balance of the accounts receivable account. The following calculation shows this:

Accounts Receivable	$5,515.77
Less amount estimated to be uncollectible	110.32
Book value of accounts receivable	$5,405.45

Estimating uncollectible accounts on the basis of charge sales

Some businesses find that they can secure their best estimate of bad debts expense by taking a percentage of their total *charge* sales for the period. For example, the Rockford Company knows from past experience that about one percent of its total charge sales will be uncollectible. If, for a fiscal period, the total charge sales amount to $300,000.00, the estimated bad debts expense for that period would be $3,000.00 ($300,000.00 × .01 = $3,000.00).

DIRECT WRITE-OFF OF UNCOLLECTIBLE ACCOUNTS

Some small businesses with relatively few uncollectible accounts record the bad debts expense at the time a debt is known to be worthless. This is done by debiting Bad Debts Expense and crediting Accounts Receivable and the customer's account for the amount of the debt.

Recording the bad debts expense at the time a customer's account is decided to be uncollectible is known as the *direct write-off of uncollectible accounts.*

The direct write-off method is simple and acceptable. In some cases, however, the method may fail to charge the expense to the period in which the debt was incurred. Thus, for that period the value of Accounts Receivable is overstated on the balance sheet.

Increasing Your Business Vocabulary

What is the meaning of each of the following:

a bad debts
b aging accounts receivable
c writing off an account
d direct write-off of uncollectible accounts

Study Questions

1. When does an account receivable become a bad debt?
2. Why is it desirable for a business to estimate the amount of its uncollectible accounts?
3. How is the book value of Accounts Receivable calculated?
4. Why is the amount of estimated uncollectible accounts receivable credited to Allowance for Bad Debts rather than to Accounts Receivable?
5. Why is the allowance for bad debts account called a valuation account?
6. In what section of the income statement on page 522 is Bad Debts Expense listed?
7. When is a customer's account written off?
8. What entry was made in the combination journal on pages 524 and 525 to write off the customer's account?
9. Why is the allowance for bad debts account debited when a customer's account is written off?
10. What three methods of estimating uncollectible accounts are presented in this chapter?
11. When the direct write-off of an uncollectible account is used, what entry is made to record the bad debt?

Case for Business Decision

CASE 1

D. B. Graff and Son operate a garage. No Allowance for Bad Debts is included on the balance sheet. No Bad Debts Expense is included on the income statement. How do these omissions affect (a) the total value of the assets on the balance sheet and (b) the net income or the net loss on the income statement?

Drill for Understanding

DRILL 29-A | Computing bad debts expense

The bookkeeping records of three furniture stores show the following summary information for the fiscal period ending December 31:

Furniture Store	*Total Net Sales*	*Total Charge Sales*	*Balance in Accounts Receivable Account*
#1	$27,890.00	$10,811.90	$1,045.00
#2	46,777.40	22,350.50	9,864.50
#3	37,890.10	19,211.20	6,160.00

Instructions: Compute the bad debts expense on December 31 for each of these stores under the following conditions:

a Store #1 estimates its bad debts will amount to ¼% (.0025) of its total *net sales*.

b Store #2 uses 2% of its total *charge sales* as its estimate of bad debts.

c Store #3 uses 3% of the *balance* in its accounts receivable account as its estimate of bad debts.

Application Problems

PROBLEM 29-1 | Recording transactions with bad debts expense

Elmer Eikens, proprietor of Eikens Store, records his transactions in a combination journal. In his general ledger he maintains accounts for Bad Debts Expense and Allowance for Bad Debts. At the beginning of the current year, the credit balance of the allowance for bad debts account was $126.36.

In this problem you are given transactions taken from those completed by the store during the year. The selected transactions cover only uncollectible accounts, bad debts expense, and allowance for bad debts.

Instructions: 1. Record all the necessary entries for the following transactions on page 22 of a combination journal.

Feb. 3. Decided that the past-due account of Al Issler, $49.80, was uncollectible. Wrote off his account as a bad debt.

Mar. 31. (End of first quarterly fiscal period.) Increased the allowance for bad debts by making the necessary adjusting entry. The estimated bad debts expense for each quarterly fiscal period is 1½% of the total charge sales. The charge sales for the quarterly fiscal period ended March 31 were $9,764.20.

May 15. Vernon Robey, a charge customer, became insolvent. Wrote off his account of $25.00 as a bad debt.

June 30. The charge sales for the second quarterly fiscal period ended June 30 were $8,262.15. Increased the allowance for bad debts 1½% of that amount.

Aug. 11. Decided that the past-due account of Helen Menke, $120.25, was uncollectible. Wrote off her account as a bad debt.

Sept. 30. The charge sales for the third quarterly fiscal period ended September 30 were $7,960.36. Increased the allowance for bad debts 1½% of that amount.

Dec. 31. Decided that the past-due accounts of the following charge customers are uncollectible:

J. T. Rankin, $60.56, Anna Vaughn, $25.40, Frank Snow, $53.00

Wrote them off as bad debts in one combined entry, debiting Allowance for Bad Debts for the total.

Dec. 31. The charge sales for the fourth quarterly fiscal period ended December 31 were $10,482.50. Increased the allowance for bad debts 1½% of that amount.

Instructions: 2. Foot, prove, and record the totals in the combination journal.

PROBLEM 29-2 | Work at the end of the fiscal period

If you are not using the workbook correlating with this textbook, complete Appendix Problem 29-A instead of this problem.

The ledger accounts of Wirtz Lumber Co., C. B. Wirtz, proprietor, are given in the workbook.

Instructions: 1. Prove cash. The cash on hand and in the bank on December 31 is $7,087.22.

2. Prepare an eight-column work sheet for the annual fiscal period ended December 31 of the current year, using the following additional data as of December 31:

Additional allowance for bad debts, ½% of net sales
Merchandise inventory, $15,478.90
Supplies inventory, $195.88
Value of insurance policies, $320.00
Annual depreciation on equipment, $215.50

3. Prepare an income statement, a capital statement, and a balance sheet.

4. Record the adjusting entries and the closing entries.

5. Post the adjusting entries and the closing entries.

6. Prepare a post-closing trial balance.

Optional Problems

★SUPPLEMENTARY PROBLEM 29-S

Recording transactions with bad debts expense

L. R. Kruse, a candy manufacturer, records his transactions in a combination journal. In his general ledger he maintains accounts for Bad Debts Expense and Allowance for Bad Debts. At the beginning of the current year, the balance of the allowance for bad debts account was $138.65.

In this problem you are given transactions taken from those completed by Mr. Kruse during the year. The selected transactions cover only uncollectible accounts, bad debts expense, and allowance for bad debts.

Instructions: 1. Record all the necessary entries for the following transactions on page 52 of a combination journal:

Feb. 18. Decided that the past-due account of Jeff Thomas, $54.25, was uncollectible. Wrote off his account as a bad debt.

Mar. 31. (End of first quarterly fiscal period.) Increased the allowance for bad debts by making the necessary adjusting entry. The estimated bad debts expense for each quarterly fiscal period was ½% (.005) of the total net sales. The net sales for the quarterly fiscal period ended March 31 were $12,427.10.

Apr. 9. R. D. Peck, a charge customer, became insolvent. Wrote off his account of $76.90 as a bad debt.

June 30. The net sales for the second quarterly fiscal period ended June 30 were $14,840.20. Increased the allowance for bad debts ½% (.005) of that amount.

July 23. Decided that the past-due account of Mabel King, $88.40, was uncollectible. Wrote off her account as a bad debt.

Sept. 30. The net sales for the third quarterly fiscal period ended September 30 were $13,660.90. Increased the allowance for bad debts ½% (.005) of that amount.

Dec. 31. Decided that the past-due accounts of the following charge customers were uncollectible:

Alan T. Schell, $26.80
Paul D. Haney, $80.00
Dale Bock, $45.95

Wrote them off as bad debts in one combined entry, debiting Allowance for Bad Debts for the total.

Dec. 31. The net sales for the fourth quarterly fiscal period ended December 31 were $15,260.80. Increased the allowance for bad debts ½%, (.005) of that amount.

Instructions: 2. Foot, prove, and record the totals in the combination journal.

★BONUS PROBLEM 29-B

Recording the collection of accounts previously written off

Introductory remarks: Occasionally a customer's account that has been written off as a bad debt is later collected. When this occurs, the customer's account is first reinstated by an entry debiting Accounts Receivable and the customer's account and crediting Allowance for Bad Debts. Next, a second entry debiting Cash and crediting Accounts Receivable and the customer's account is made. These two entries provide a complete record of the transactions.

When the old debt is not being collected in full and there is no indication that it will be collected in full, only the actual amount being collected should be used in each of the transactions given below.

Instructions: 1. During 1968 David Glenn completed the following transactions involving bad debts. Record these transactions on page 12 of a combination journal.

Mar. 7. Wrote off account of Henry Lewis, $40.00, as uncollectible.

May 23. Received 30% of the $345.00 balance owed by Paul Newkirk, bankrupt, and wrote off the remainder as uncollectible.

June 6. Received $20.00 from Elsa Tyler in full payment of her account which was written off on February 8, 1967, as uncollectible.

June 20. Wrote off account of Ted Krane, $124.80, as uncollectible.

Sept. 26. Received $35.00 from the receiver in bankruptcy for Randall James in final settlement of his account. His account totaled $60.00 when it was written off on March 29, 1967.

Dec. 12. Received $20.00 from Henry Lewis along with a written promise to pay the balance of his account written off on March 7, 1968.

Instructions: 2. Foot, prove, and record the totals in the combination journal.

CHAPTER 30 A CASH REGISTER BOOKKEEPING SYSTEM

The kinds of sales analyses to be made and the number of sales often determine the type of system a retail store uses to record its sales. Stores that wish to make a complete analysis of all sales use cash registers that record all the needed data at the time of each sale. A machine that is used to record sales transactions is called a *cash register.*

Cash registers are available that will do the following: (1) record the amount of sale and indicate whether it is a cash sale or a charge sale; (2) compute the amount of change, if any, due the customer; (3) indicate the type of merchandise sold; (4) produce a receipt for the customer; (5) keep a record of each transaction on a paper tape inside the machine; and (6) produce a by-product punched paper tape or special tape that data processing equipment can read and summarize in the form of sales journals, inventory records, and accounts receivable.

Stores with a large volume of sales use cash registers that produce output records that can be processed on automatic equipment. These special cash registers make it possible for the data processing equipment to analyze sales by types of merchandise, to keep inventory records up-to-date, and to keep customers' accounts posted and up-to-date.

RECORDING TRANSACTIONS ON A CASH REGISTER

Mr. Harvey of Harvey Auto Parts uses a cash register to record the following kinds of transactions: (1) sales by types of merchandise sold; (2) cash sales; (3) charge sales; (4) cash received on account; and (5) cash paid out for miscellaneous transactions.

Harvey Auto Parts sells auto parts, accessories, tires, and batteries. The store is a self-service store with a checkout counter attended by a cashier. After a customer selects his merchandise, he takes it to the checkout counter where the cashier records the sales on the cash register. The cash register used by Mr. Harvey's cashier is shown on the following page. The cashier operates the register by pressing the necessary keys and the motor bar.

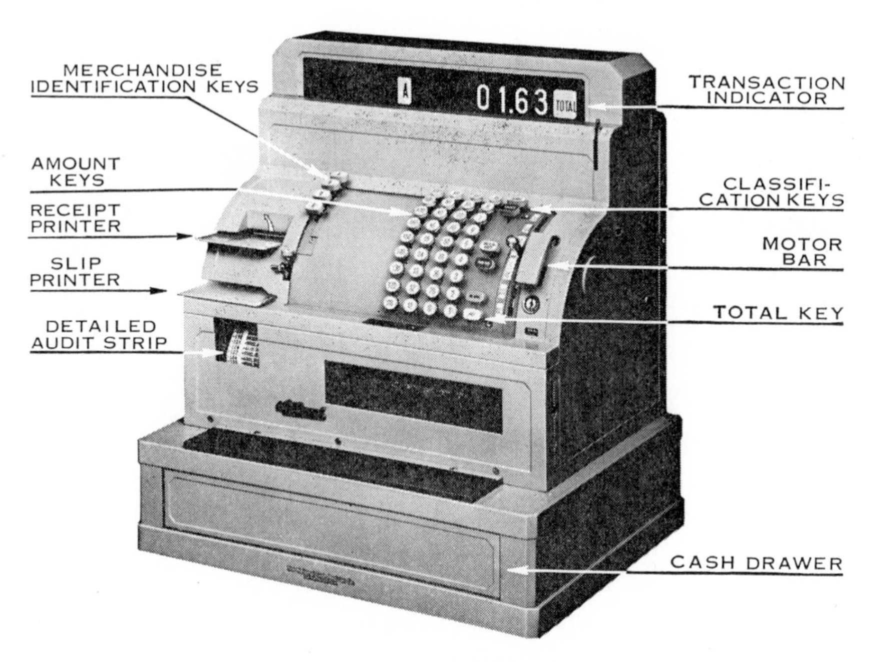

A cash register

The cash register records each transaction on a paper tape inside the machine, supplies a receipt for the customer, and provides a conveniently organized cash drawer.

Mr. Harvey has a petty cash fund of $100.00. This money is kept in the office safe. A definite amount, $20.00, is taken from the petty cash fund at the beginning of each day and is placed in the cash register for use in making change. At the end of the day, this amount, $20.00, is taken out of the cash register and returned to the safe.

Operating the cash register

A diagram of the key arrangement of Mr. Harvey's cash register is shown on the next page.

The keys on a cash register are arranged in three groups. The Merchandise Identification keys at the extreme left, lettered A, B, C, and D, are used to identify auto parts, accessories, tires, and batteries, respectively. The Amount keys are used to record the amount of each transaction. The Classification keys are used to record the nature of each transaction.

When the motor bar is pressed, the complete transaction is shown in the transaction indicator at the top of the register. The amount is printed on the paper tape inside the machine, with the appropriate letter to show what kind of merchandise was sold. At the same time, the cash drawer opens so that the amount received can be placed in it.

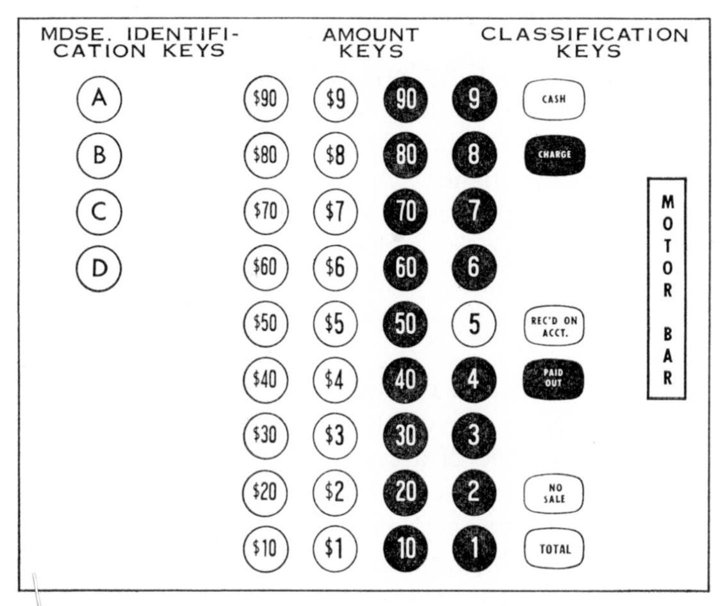

Key arrangement on a cash register

When several items are sold to a customer, the amount of each item and the merchandise identification of each item are recorded. The register operates like an adding machine in totaling the various items of the sale.

When the motor bar is operated, a receipt is automatically printed and pushed out of the machine at the point marked "Receipt Printer." The receipt is given to the customer as proof that the transaction is properly recorded.

Recording a cash sale

The transaction indicator in the illustration of the cash register on page 532 shows that $1.63 was the amount of the sale. When this sale was made, the cashier pressed the A key to indicate an auto part was sold. He depressed the following amount keys: $1, 60¢, 3¢; and the Cash key. Lastly, he pressed the motor bar.

Receipt for a cash sale

The –001 before the amount on the receipt shown at the right is the operation number of the cash register. The letters "CaA" after the amount indicate that cash (Ca) was received from the sale of auto parts (A).

Recording a charge sale

On January 2, Mr. J. B. Cory buys auto accessories on account amounting to \$9.15. The cashier at the checkout counter prepares the sales slip illustrated at the right. An original and a carbon copy are made. The cashier inserts both copies of the sales slip in the slip printer of the cash register and records the charge sale on the register.

JAN 2 -002 $0,009.15 ChB

JAN 2 -002 $0,009.15 ChB

HARVEY AUTO PARTS
136 Main Street
Dayton, Ohio 45421

893 Date Jan. 2, 1968

Mr. J. B. Cory
4221 Mt. Vernon Ave.
Dayton, Ohio 45405

Quan.	Description	Price	Amt.
1	side-view mirror	6 50	6 50
1	wrench set	2 65	2 65
			9 15

Printed figures at top of slip indicate amount paid or charged.

Sales slip in duplicate for a charge sale

To record the transaction on the cash register, the cashier presses the B key to indicate the sale of accessories; the following amount keys: \$9, 10¢, and 5¢; the Charge key; and finally the motor bar. A permanent record of the charge sale is made on the paper tape inside the cash register. The cash register also prints the operation number, the amount, and the merchandise identification on both copies of the sales slip.

The original copy of the sales slip is given to Mr. Cory. The duplicate copy is kept as the source document for the combination journal entry.

Recording cash payments

On January 2, Mr. A. L. Trent returns a side-view mirror for a cash refund of \$5.35. Each time the cashier makes a cash payment from the cash register he prepares a paid-out slip and records the payment on the cash register.

The paid-out slip shown at the right is prepared by the cashier. After the slip is prepared, the cashier inserts it into the slip printer of the cash register. He then presses the amount keys and the Paid-Out key. When he presses the motor bar, the machine prints the date, the transaction number, and the amount paid out at the top of the slip. The same information is printed on the register tape.

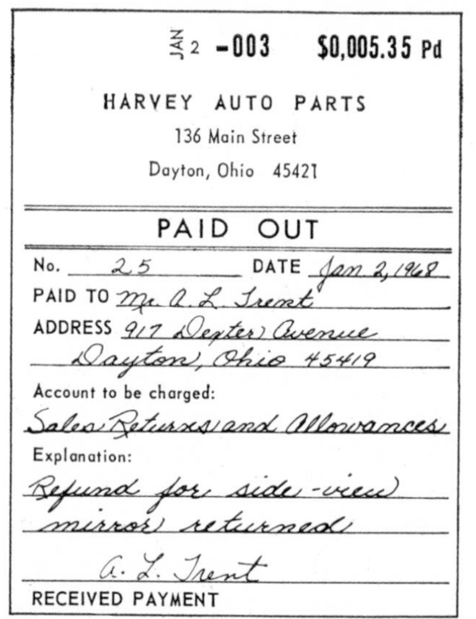
JAN 2 -003 $0,005.35 Pd

HARVEY AUTO PARTS
136 Main Street
Dayton, Ohio 45421

PAID OUT

No. 25 DATE Jan 2, 1968
PAID TO Mr. A. L. Trent
ADDRESS 917 Dexter Avenue
Dayton, Ohio 45419
Account to be charged:
Sales Returns and Allowances
Explanation:
Refund for side-view mirror returned
A. L. Trent
RECEIVED PAYMENT

Paid-out slip

Recording "no sale" transactions

A customer gives the cashier a dollar bill and asks for change to make a pay telephone call. To open the cash drawer, the cashier presses the No Sale key and the motor bar.

Recording cash received on account

On January 2, Mr. Harvey's cashier receives $30.00 from Mr. A. M. Thorpe to apply on his account. The cashier prepares a sales slip in duplicate for the cash received as shown at the right. Both slips are inserted in the slip printer of the cash register. He presses the amount keys, the Rec'd on Acct. key, and the motor bar. The cash register prints the date, the transaction number, and the amount with the letters "Rc" at the top of each slip. The cash register also records this information on the tape inside the machine.

JAN 2 -005 $0,030.00 Rc

HARVEY AUTO PARTS
136 Main Street
Dayton, Ohio 45421

899

Date Jan. 2, 1968

Mr. A. M. Thorpe
1345 Riverside Drive
Dayton, Ohio 45429

Quan.	Description	Price	Amt.
	Received on account		30 00

Printed figures at top of slip indicate amount paid or charged.

Sales slip for cash received on account

The original copy of the sales slip is given to Mr. Thorpe. The carbon copy is kept as the source document for the combination journal entry.

Recording sales returns and allowances for charge sales

On January 3, Mr. J. B. Cory, a charge customer, returned a $2.65 wrench set because it was defective. The cashier prepares a sales slip in duplicate as shown at the right. The cashier inserts both copies into the slip printer of the cash register and presses the amount keys, the No Sale key, and the motor bar. The cash register prints the date, the operation number, and the amount with the letters "NS" at the top of each slip.

The original copy of the sales slip is given to Mr. Cory. The carbon copy is the source document for an entry in the combination journal. This entry is illustrated on Lines 12 and 13 of the combination journal on pages 540 and 541.

JAN 3 -134 $0,002.65 NS

HARVEY AUTO PARTS
136 Main Street
Dayton, Ohio 45421

903

Date Jan. 3, 1968

Mr. J. B. Cory
4221 Mt. Vernon Avenue
Dayton, Ohio 45405

Quan.	Description	Price	Amt.
	Credit for one wrench set returned	2 65	2 65

Printed figures at top of slip indicate amount paid or charged.

Sales slip for a sales return

CASH REGISTER DETAILED AUDIT STRIP

A paper tape on which all transactions entered in the cash register are automatically printed is known as the *detailed audit strip.* A part of the detailed audit strip showing the first five transactions completed by the cashier of Harvey Auto Parts is illustrated at the right.

The detailed audit strip is read from the bottom to the top. The detailed audit strip shows the following:

1. The date of each transaction.
2. The cash register operation number.
3. The amount of each transaction.
4. The nature of each transaction.

On the detailed audit strip shown at the right, *CaA* indicates a cash sale of auto parts; *ChB*, a charge sale of accessories; *Pd*, an amount paid out; *NS*, no sale; and *Rc*, an amount received on account.

JAN 2	-005	$0,030.00	Rc
JAN 2	-004	$0,000.00	NS
JAN 2	-003	$0,005.35	Pd
JAN 2	-002	$0,009.15	ChB
JAN 2	-001	$0,001.63	CaA

Section of detailed audit strip showing individual transactions

Obtaining cash register totals

The cash register accumulates the total for each of the following types of transactions: (1) cash sales, (2) charge sales, (3) cash received on account, (4) cash paid out, and (5) sales by type of merchandise sold.

At the end of each day, the cashier presses each Merchandise Identification key, the Total key, and the motor bar. The cash register prints these totals on the tape inside the machine. The cashier then presses each Classification key, the Total key, and the motor bar. The cash register prints these totals on the tape inside the machine. When these totals are printed, the cash register is automatically cleared so that none of the amounts will be added to the transactions for the following day.

Analyzing the detailed audit strip

The section of the detailed audit strip of Harvey Auto Parts listing the totals at the end of the day, January 2, is shown at the right. The date and the cash register operation number are printed on the strip each time the cash register is operated. Reading from the bottom to the top of the tape, the amounts and the symbols have the following meanings:

JAN 2	-120	$0,346.40	GT
JAN 2	-119	$0,005.35	Pd
JAN 2	-118	$0,138.50	Rc
JAN 2	-117	$0,060.20	Ch
JAN 2	-116	$0,207.90	Ca
JAN 2	-115	$0,063.30	D
JAN 2	-114	$0,034.00	C
JAN 2	-113	$0,050.80	B
JAN 2	-112	$0,120.00	A

Section of detailed audit strip showing totals

Operation No.	*Amount*	*Symbol*	*Description*
112	$120.00	A	Auto parts sales
113	50.80	B	Accessory sales
114	34.00	C	Tire sales
115	63.30	D	Battery sales
116	207.90	Ca	Cash sales
117	60.20	Ch	Charge sales
118	138.50	Rc	Received on account
119	5.35	Pd	Paid out
120	346.40	GT	Grand total

The detailed audit strip is used by the bookkeeper for recording some of the journal entries shown on pages 540 and 541.

The charge sales, $60.20, plus the cash sales, $207.90, amount to $268.10. This total is the same as the total of the four amounts of sales of the different types of merchandise.

The amount received from cash sales, $207.90, plus the cash received from customers on account, $138.50, equals $346.40. This is the amount of the Grand Total of cash received as shown on the detailed audit strip.

PROVING CASH WITH THE CASH REGISTER TOTALS

After the cash register is cleared and the total of each type of transaction is printed on the detailed audit strip, the strip is removed from the machine. The $20.00 change is taken out of the cash register and returned to the petty cash fund in the office safe. The money remaining in the cash drawer is counted and entered on a daily balance slip similar to the one shown at the right. The total of each denomination of coin, the total paper money, and the total checks are listed in the spaces provided. The sum of all these items, $341.05, is the total cash in the drawer. To this amount is added the cash paid out, $5.35. The total, $346.40, is the total cash received. The total cash received as shown by the symbol GT on the detailed audit strip is then entered on the daily balance slip. As the two amounts are the same, $346.40, the record of all the transactions in the cash register is considered to be correct.

DAILY BALANCE SLIP

Denominations	Dollars	Cts.
Pennies		10
Nickels	2	75
Dimes	9	40
Quarters	8	50
Halves	4	50
Silver Dollars	—	
Paper Money	168	00
Checks	147	80
Total Cash in Drawer	341	05
Add Cash Paid Out	5	35
Total Cash Received	346	40
Total Cash Received on Detailed Audit Strip	346	40
Cash Short		
Cash Over		
No. of Paid-Out Slips	1	
No. of Charge Sales Slips	3	
No. of Rc. on A/c Slips	4	

Cashier L. W. Moore Date 1/2/68

Cash proof on daily balance slip

Cash short and over

If the sum of the cash on hand at the end of the day plus the cash paid out during the day is less than the grand total recorded by the cash register, the cash is said to be *short*. If the sum of the cash on hand at the end of the day plus the cash paid out during the day is greater than the grand total recorded by the cash register, the cash is said to be *over*.

Whether the cash is short or over, the error is caused by mistakes in recording transactions on the cash register or by mistakes in making change. If the error is large, the cashier should examine the detailed audit strip and try to recall the transaction that was recorded improperly or the transaction where a mistake was made in making change. If the error is small, usually no attempt is made to find the reason for it.

The daily balance slip for January 3 shows that the total cash received was $199.35. According to the detailed audit strip, the amount received was $198.85. The difference of 50¢ is recorded as cash over as shown on the daily balance slip.

DAILY BALANCE SLIP

Denominations	Dollars	Cts.
Pennies		35
Nickels	1	15
Dimes	6	80
Quarters	4	50
Halves	12	00
Silver Dollars	—	
Paper Money	126	00
Checks	45	00
Total Cash in Drawer	195	80
Add Cash Paid Out	3	55
Total Cash Received	199	35
Total Cash Received on Detailed Audit Strip	198	85
Cash Short		
Cash Over		50
No. of Paid-Out Slips	4	
No. of Charge Sales Slips	7	
No. of Rc. on A/c Slips	3	

Cashier O.V. Greene Date 1/3/68

Daily balance slip showing cash over

Cash short and over voucher

If "cash is over," the amount over is taken from the register and is placed with the petty cash. A cash short and over voucher is filled out and is placed with the petty cash as a receipt for the amount placed in the fund.

If "cash is short," the amount is made up from the petty cash fund. A cash short and over voucher is filled out and is placed with the petty cash fund as a receipt for the amount taken out of the fund.

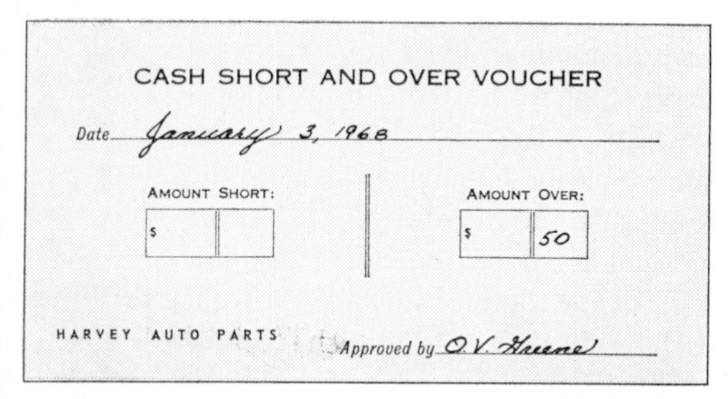
CASH SHORT AND OVER VOUCHER

Date January 3, 1968

AMOUNT SHORT: $

AMOUNT OVER: $ 50

HARVEY AUTO PARTS Approved by O.V. Greene

Cash short and over voucher showing cash over

Paid-out slips and the petty cash fund

Harvey Auto Parts deposits all cash receipts in the bank. All large payments are made by check. Small cash payments, such as the $5.35 refund on a cash sale to Mr. Trent on January 2, are made from the cash register. A paid-out slip is prepared for each of these transactions, and the amount is recorded by pressing the Paid-Out key of the cash register. The paid-out slips are kept in the cash register.

At the end of the day, the paid-out slips are placed with the petty cash fund in the office safe, and an amount of cash equal to the total of the paid-out slips is taken from the fund. The cash taken from the petty cash fund is combined with the cash in the cash register. The sum of these two amounts is proved with the grand total figure on the detailed audit strip (GT). This procedure makes it possible to deposit in the bank an amount equal to the total cash receipts for the day.

The petty cash fund, then, is used for three purposes:

1. To supply the cash register with an adequate amount of change at the beginning of the day.
2. To adjust the amount of cash short or over each day.
3. To replace the paid-out slips in the cash register with cash.

Replenishing the petty cash fund

When the petty cash fund is to be replenished, the paid-out slips and the cash short and over vouchers are sorted and stacked. Each stack represents a specific account in the general ledger. The *total* of the paid-out slips in each stack is used in making the journal entry to replenish the fund.

On January 31, Mr. Harvey sorts the paid-out slips and the cash short and over vouchers. Each stack of vouchers represents an account title as shown below:

Sales Returns and Allowances		$32.40
Miscellaneous Expense		21.40
Salary Expense		11.50
Cash Short	1.60	
Less Cash Over	.40	
Net Cash Short		1.20
Total		$66.50

Since the total of all the paid-out slips plus the net cash shortage for the month is $66.50, a check is drawn for that amount. The check is cashed and the money is placed in the petty cash fund. The fund then has $100.00, the amount of the petty cash account balance in the general ledger. The entry to record the replenishment of the petty cash fund is shown on the next page. All debits are recorded in the General Debit column, as special columns are not provided for any of these accounts.

PAGE 37 COMBINATION JOURNAL

	1 Cash Debit	2 Cash Credit	Ck. No.	Date	Account Title	Post. Ref.	3 General Debit	4 General Credit	
30		6650	1021	31	Sales Returns & Allowances		3240		30
31					Miscellaneous Expense		2140		31
32					Salary Expense		1150		32
33					Cash Short and Over		120		33
34									34
35									35

Left-hand page of combination journal showing entry to replenish petty cash

Each time the petty cash fund is replenished, the account Cash Short and Over is debited if cash short exceeds cash over. If cash over exceeds cash short, Cash Short and Over is credited. In the entry on Line 33 of the combination journal above, the total cash short for the period is larger than the total cash over.

If at the end of the fiscal period the cash short and over account has a debit balance, it is listed on the income statement in the "Other Expenses" section. If the cash short and over account has a credit balance, it is listed on the income statement in the "Other Income" section.

PAGE 35 COMBINATION JOURNAL

	1 Cash Debit	2 Cash Credit	Ck. No.	Date	Account Title	Post. Ref.	3 General Debit	4 General Credit	
1				1968 Jan. 2	Balance on hand, $6,820.40	✓			1
2	20790			2	✓	✓			2
3				2	J. B. Cory				3
4					Robert T. Mathis				4
5					O. C. Bentz				5
6	13850			2	A. M. Thorpe				6
7					William Parker				7
8		535		2	Sales Returns + Allowances		535		8
9	36015			3	✓	✓			9
10				3	Amos R. Zane				10
11	7845			3	Merrill Cars				11
12				3	Sales Returns + Allowances		265		12
13					J. B. Cory				13
14									14
15									15
16									16
17									17
18									18
19									19

Combination journal

USING THE COMBINATION JOURNAL IN A CASH REGISTER BOOKKEEPING SYSTEM

Recording transactions in a combination journal

The transactions of Harvey Auto Parts for January 2 and 3 are recorded in the combination journal shown below.

Analyzing the entries in the combination journal

Line 1. The cash balance of $6,820.40 is recorded in the Account Title column as a memorandum entry.

Line 2. The detailed audit strip on page 536 shows that cash sales for January 2 are $207.90. Cash is debited in the Cash Debit column for $207.90 and Sales is credited in the Sales Credit column for the same amount. A check mark is placed in the Account Title column. A check mark is also placed in the Post Ref. column to show that the individual amounts on this line are not to be posted. These amounts are posted as a part of the total of these columns.

Lines 3–5. The detailed audit strip on page 536 shows that sales on account for the day are $60.20. The carbon copy of the sales slip is the

FOR MONTH OF *January* 19 *68* PAGE *35*

	5	6	7	8	9	10	11	12	
	ACCOUNTS PAYABLE		PURCHASES DISCOUNT CREDIT	ACCOUNTS RECEIVABLE		SALES DISCOUNT DEBIT	PURCHASES DEBIT	SALES CREDIT	
	DEBIT	CREDIT		DEBIT	CREDIT				
1									1
2								207 90	2
3				9 15					3
4				28 05					4
5				23 00				60 20	5
6					30 00				6
7					108 50				7
8									8
9								360 15	9
10				147 90				147 90	10
11					78 45				11
12									12
13					2 65				13
14									14
15									15
16									16
17									17
18									18
19									19

of Harvey Auto Parts

source document for recording the amount sold on account to each customer. The name of each charge customer is written in the Account Title column. The amount of each charge sale is written in the Accounts Receivable Debit column. Sales is credited in the Sales Credit column for the total charge sales as shown on the detailed audit strip.

Prior to making this entry, the copies of the sales slips are totaled to make sure that this total is in agreement with the total shown on the cash register strip.

Lines 6 and 7. The detailed audit strip on page 536 shows that $138.50 was received from customers on account. Cash is debited for $138.50 in the Cash Debit column. The name of each charge customer from whom cash was received is written in the Account Title column. The amount received on account from each customer is written in the Accounts Receivable Credit column.

Prior to making this entry, the copies of the sales slips for cash received on account are totaled to make sure that this total is in agreement with the total shown on the cash register strip.

The detailed audit strip on page 536 shows a cash payment of $5.35 The copy of the paid-out slip indicates that this amount is a refund on a cash sale made to Mr. Trent on January 2. Thus, there is no need to record the customer's name in the Account Title column. The amount of the cash refund is debited to Sales Returns and Allowances when the petty cash fund is replenished on January 31.

Lines 8 and 9. To record the debit resulting from the purchases return, the name of the creditor, Ace Tool Company, is written in the Account Title column and the amount, $10.50, is written in the Accounts Payable Debit column. To record the credit, the account title, Purchases Returns and Allowances, is written in the Account Title column in the indented position. The amount of the credit is entered in the General Credit column.

The information needed to record this purchases return is obtained from the credit memorandum received from Ace Tool Company.

Lines 10–12. The cash sales, sales on account, and cash received on account for January 3 are recorded in the same manner as the January 2 transactions.

Lines 13 and 14. To record the debit resulting from the return by J. B. Cory, the account title, Sales Returns and Allowances, is written in the Account Title column and the amount, $2.65, is entered in the General Debit column. To record the credit, the name of the customer, J. B. Cory, is written in the Account Title column in the indented position. The amount of the credit is entered in the Accounts Receivable Credit column.

AUTOMATING ACCOUNTS RECEIVABLE IN A CASH REGISTER BOOKKEEPING SYSTEM

Recent years have brought about a tremendous growth in the retail industry. With each phase of growth there has been a demand for improved cash register systems that will provide management with accurate data quickly and economically.

In one type of automated cash register system, a credit card is used to record the customer's account number on the cash register tape at the time of the sales transaction. The rectangular holes in the customer's credit card shown below are his account number. The credit card is inserted into

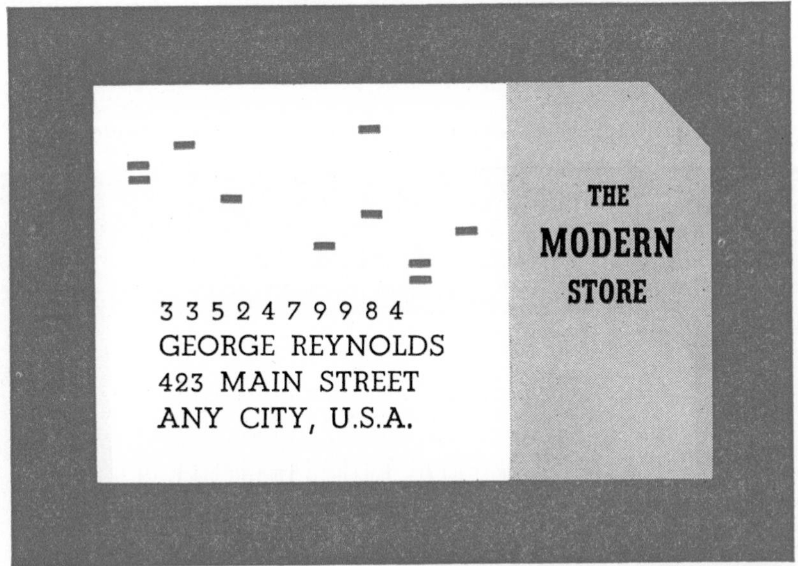

The National Cash Register Company

Customer's credit card

the credit card reader of the cash register and the account number is automatically "read" and printed when the charge key is depressed. The account number is printed on the cash register tape in a special kind of type, called *optical type*. Optical type numbers and letters are automatically "read" or scanned by special data processing equipment. The cash register also prints on the tape the register number, the date of the sale, the transaction number, control symbols, classification and/or department number, and the amount of sale. Each of these items of information is identified on the strip of tape shown on the next page.

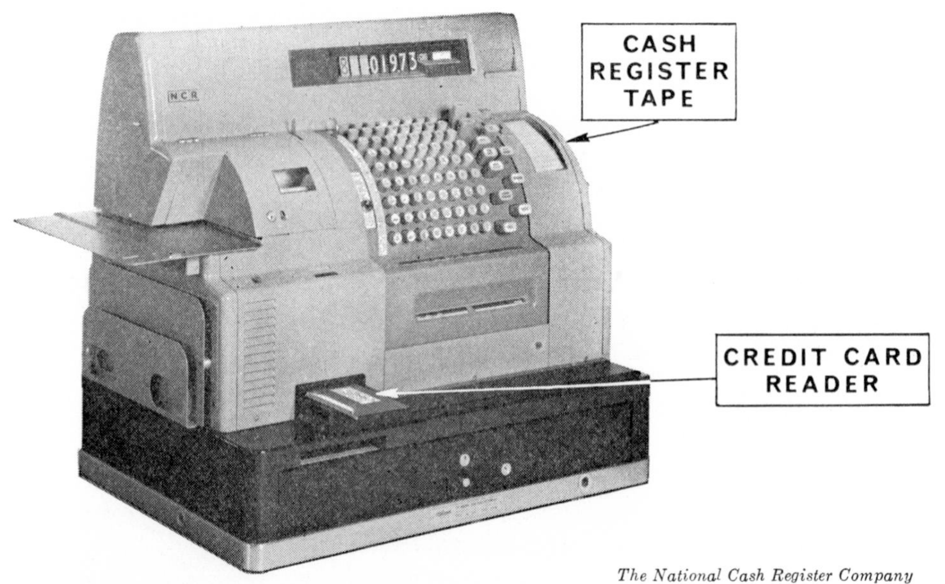

The National Cash Register Company

Cash register with credit card inserted in credit card reader

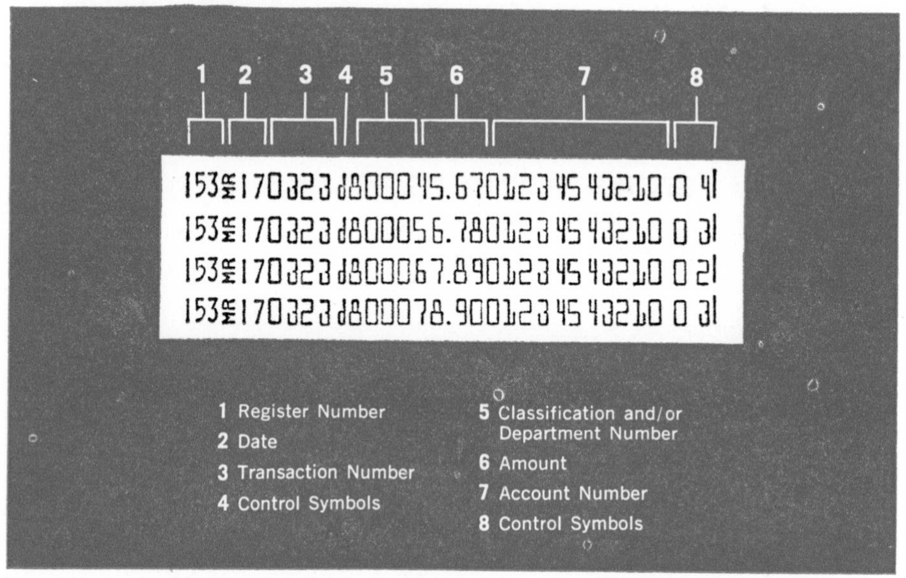

The National Cash Register Company

Data printed in optical type on a cash register tape

At the end of each day all the sales slips are sorted by type of transaction. The amounts are added to check against the control totals printed on the tape. A cashier's report is filled out to determine the amount of cash short or cash over. The cash register tape is sent to the data processing department where the optically printed symbols are "read" into a computer. Using the customer's account number, the computer searches through the accounts receivable file that is stored on magnetic tape. The computer posts to the customer's account the information recorded on the cash register tape.

The data stored on the magnetic tapes are later used in automatically processing and printing customer statements. Some computer systems are capable of printing 5,000 customer statements per hour. The stored data are also periodically "read out" of the computer to provide management with:

1. An up-to-date accounts receivable ledger.
2. An aging of the accounts receivable accounts to show past-due accounts.
3. An analysis of daily sales by type of sale.
4. A listing of daily sales and returns by department and classification.
5. An inventory control report showing the amount of goods each department is open to buy with respect to its budgeted purchases for the period.

Increasing Your Business Vocabulary

a cash register

b detailed audit strip

Study Questions

1. What kinds of operations may be performed by cash registers?
2. What is the meaning of the number 001 on the receipt for a cash sale shown on page 533?
3. When a charge sale is recorded on the cash register, why is a duplicate copy of the sales slip prepared?
4. What is the meaning of each of the following letters on the detailed audit strip shown on page 536: Rc, NS, Pd, ChB, and CaA?
5. How is a sales return for a charge sale recorded in a cash register bookkeeping system?
6. What is the source document that is used for recording the cash register totals in the journal?
7. How is cash on hand proved each day when a cash register bookkeeping system is used?
8. What are the three purposes of a petty cash fund in a cash register bookkeeping system?
9. If the cash short and over account has a debit balance at the end of the fiscal period, in what section of the income statement is the amount of the shortage listed?
10. If the cash short and over account has a credit balance at the end of the fiscal period, in what section of the income statement is the amount of cash over listed?

Case for Business Decision

CASE 1

The sales of the Akron Department Store have increased from $2½ million in 1957 to over $8½ million in 1967. The store is still using the cash register system that was installed in 1957. What are some of the decisions that management should consider in order to modernize its cash register system?

Application Problems

PROBLEM 30-1 | Proving cash

If you are not using the workbook correlating with this textbook, complete Appendix Problem 30-A instead of this problem.

Instructions: 1. Fill in the daily balance slip given in the workbook and prove cash. The count of cash in the cash register, the detailed audit strip totals, and the cash register papers for February 20 are given in the workbook.

2. Fill in the cash short and over voucher in the workbook for the cash shortage for the day.

PROBLEM 30-2 | Replenishing petty cash

If you are not using the workbook correlating with this textbook, complete Appendix Problem 30-B instead of this problem.

On September 30 of the current year, the end of a monthly fiscal period, the petty cash fund of the Kruger Grocery Store contains the petty cash paid-out slips and the cash short and over vouchers given in the workbook.

Instructions: 1. Detach the cash short and over vouchers and the petty cash paid-out slips and separate them along the perforated lines.

2. Sort the cash short and over vouchers and the petty cash paid-out slips into the following groups:

(a) Cash short.
(b) Cash over.
(c) Delivery expense.
(d) Miscellaneous expense.
(e) Sales returns and allowances.
(f) Supplies.

3. Find the net amount by which cash is short or over.

4. Find the total amount in each group of petty cash paid-out slips.

5. Record the entry to replenish the petty cash fund (Check No. 328).

PROBLEM 30-3 | Recording transactions from business papers

If you are not using the workbook correlating with this textbook, complete Appendix Problem 30-C instead of this problem.

Lee Ivey, who operates an electrical appliance store, records his transactions in a combination journal like the one on pages 540 and 541. On June 27 of the current year, he finds that page 63 of his combination journal is filled.

Instructions: 1. Forward the following column totals on June 27 to new page 64 of Mr. Ivey's combination journal:

Cash Debit, $4,216.32
Cash Credit, $3,487.70
General Debit, $792.00
General Credit, $34.85
Accounts Payable Debit, $6,950.12
Accounts Payable Credit, $5,713.28
Purchases Discount Credit, $56.22
Accounts Receivable Debit, $314.20
Accounts Receivable Credit, $309.30
Sales Discount Debit, $134.20
Purchases Debit, $4,896.85
Sales Credit, $7,702.34

Instructions: 2. Record in the combination journal the following transactions completed by Mr. Ivey on June 27 to 30. The business papers referred to are numbered and given in consecutive order in the workbook.

June 27. (Business Paper 1.) Issued Check No. 406 in payment of the telephone bill.

27. (Business Paper 2.) Received a credit memorandum from Link Appliances for returned merchandise.

27. (Business Paper 3.) Recorded the cash register totals for the day as shown on the detailed audit strip. The copies of the sales slips show the following:
Charge Sales: Henry Brandt, $10.00. *Cash Received on Account:* T. F. Fair, $25.00.

The name of each charge customer is written in the Account Title column and the amount of each charge sale is written in the Accounts Receivable Debit column. The total amount of charge sales is recorded in the Sales Credit column.

The name of each charge customer from whom cash is received is written in the Account Title column and the amount received from each customer is written in the Accounts Receivable Credit column. The total amount of cash received on account is recorded in the Cash Debit column.

28. (Business Paper 4.) Recorded the cash register totals for the day as shown on the detailed audit strip. The copies of the sales slips show the following:
    Charge Sales: M. O. Tyler, $10.90; Herman Craft, $7.00. *Cash Received on Account:* Martha Vine, $40.00; Ruth Bramble, $5.75.
30. (Business Paper 5.) Purchased merchandise on account from Gappen Manufacturing Company.
30. Issued Check No. 407 for $561.45 in payment of the semimonthly payroll of $675.00 less a deduction of $85.20 for employees income taxes payable and a deduction of $28.35 for FICA taxes payable.
30. Recorded the employer's liability of $28.35 for FICA taxes, $18.23 for state unemployment taxes, and $2.70 for federal unemployment taxes.
30. (Business Paper 6.) Issued Check No. 408 in payment of Willis & Sons invoice of June 21 less discount. This invoice was previously recorded as a debit to Purchases and a credit to Accounts Payable.
30. (Business Paper 7.) Issued Check No. 409 for $91.30 to replenish the petty cash fund.
30. (Business Paper 8.) Recorded the cash register totals for the day as shown on the detailed audit strip. The copies of the sales slips show the following:
    Charge Sales: P. R. Mather, $10.25. *Cash Received on Account:* Arthur Byer, $3.20.

Instructions: 3. Foot, prove, and rule the combination journal.

CHAPTER 31 SALES TAXES AND OTHER SALES AND PURCHASES TRANSACTIONS

An important source of income for city and state governments is the taxes that are collected on retail sales. A tax levied on a sale is called a *sales tax*. Sales tax rates are usually stated as a percentage of sales. The kinds of goods taxed and the tax rates vary from city to city and from state to state. At regular intervals, the retailer is required to pay the amount of sales taxes he has collected to the proper government unit.

SALES TAX RECORDS

Every business that collects sales taxes from its customers must keep accurate records of the amount of taxes collected. The sales tax records must show the following:

1. Total cash sales and total charge sales on which taxes are collected.
2. Total amount of sales taxes due the government.

Recording sales taxes on charge sales

Crane Paper Products sells paper, envelopes, mailing bags, and shipping cartons. The company operates in a state where the sales tax rate is 4%. When the company sells merchandise on which there is a tax, the customer is charged for the amount of the sale plus the sales tax.

October 2, 1968. Sold merchandise on account to Henry Marks, $100.00, plus sales tax of $4.00. Invoice No. 461.

Accounts Receivable is debited for $104.00, the amount of the invoice plus the sales tax of $4.00, to show the increase in the balance of this asset account.

Sales is credited for $100.00 to show the increase in the balance of the sales income account.

Sales Taxes Payable is credited for $4.00 to show the increase in the balance of this liability account. The amount of sales tax charged each customer is a liability because Crane Paper Products owes this amount to the state government.

GENERAL LEDGER

Accounts Receivable	115
104.00	

Sales	411
	100.00

Sales Taxes Payable	217
	4.00

Henry Marks' account in the accounts receivable ledger is debited for $104.00 to show the increase in the balance of this asset account.

ACCOUNTS RECEIVABLE LEDGER

Henry Marks

104.00	

The columnar sales journal used by Crane Paper Products is shown below. It contains a special column in which to record the amount of sales taxes charged to each customer.

SALES JOURNAL — PAGE 16

	DATE		SALE NO.	ACCOUNT DEBITED	POST. REF.	1 ACCOUNTS RECEIVABLE DEBIT	2 SALES CREDIT	3 SALES TAXES PAYABLE CREDIT	
1	1968 Oct.	2	461	Henry Marks	✓	104 00	100 00	4 00	1
2		2	462	J. R. Jolson	✓	79 46	76 40	3 06	2
3		2	463	M. L. Watts	✓	96 51	92 80	3 71	3
29		30	489	Frank Cody	✓	222 87	214 30	8 57	29
30		31	490	Henry Marks	✓	166 40 8549 32	160 00 8220 50	6 40 328 82	30
31		31		Totals		8549 32	8220 50	328 82	31
32						(115)	(411)	(217)	32
33									33
34									34
35									35
36									36
37									37

Columnar sales journal

The entry on Line 1 of the sales journal records the sale on account to Henry Marks. Accounts Receivable in the general ledger and the customer's account in the subsidiary ledger are debited for $104.00, the amount of the sales invoice plus the sales tax. Sales is credited for $100.00, the amount of the sale. Sales Taxes Payable is credited for $4.00, the amount of sales taxes on this sale.

Posting the columnar sales journal

The individual amounts in the Accounts Receivable Debit column are posted daily to the accounts receivable ledger so that each customer's account is always up-to-date. Check marks in the Post. Ref. column are used to indicate posting to the accounts receivable ledger accounts.

After the equality of debits and credits has been verified, the totals of the special columns are posted to the general ledger accounts named in the headings of the columns. As each total is posted, the account number is placed in parentheses below the total.

Recording sales taxes on cash sales

> *October 2, 1968. Received cash, $312.00, from cash sales of $300.00 and sales taxes of $12.00.*

On October 2, 1968, the cash register detailed audit strip of Crane Paper Products shows the following information:

Total cash sales..	$300.00
Sales taxes (4%)...	12.00
Total cash received from customers.......................	$312.00

The use of a special tax key on the cash register is especially helpful in businesses that sell both taxable and nontaxable merchandise. But when the sales tax applies to all merchandise sold by a business, the total of the selling price plus the sales tax may be recorded on the cash register in a single amount. When this practice is followed, the total cash sales figure at the end of the day would also include the sales taxes collected.

The detailed audit strip is the source document for making the entries in the cash receipts journal. The analysis of the journal entry to record the total cash sales and the taxes collected is shown in T accounts at the right.

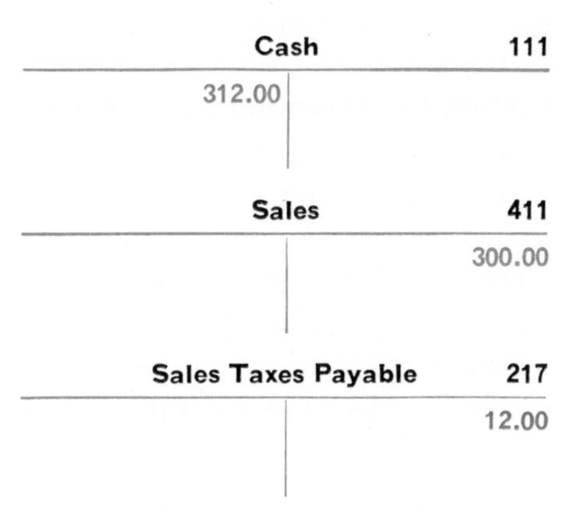

Cash is debited for $312.00, the total amount of cash received, to show the increase in the balance of this asset account.

Sales is credited for $300.00 to show the increase in the balance of this income account.

Sales Taxes Payable is credited for $12.00 to show the increase in the balance of this liability account. The amount of sales tax collected from cash customers is a liability because Crane Paper Products owes this amount to the state government.

The entry in the cash receipts journal to record the total cash sales on October 2 is shown on the next page.

Line 2 of the cash receipts journal shows the total cash sales for October 2. Cash is debited in the Cash Debit column for $312.00. Sales is credited in the Sales Credit column for the total sales for the day, $300.00. Sales Taxes Payable is credited in the Sales Taxes Payable Credit column for $12.00. A check mark is placed in the Account Credited column and in the Post. Ref. column.

CASH RECEIPTS JOURNAL — PAGE 18

	DATE		ACCOUNT CREDITED	POST. REF.	1 GENERAL CREDIT	2 SALES CREDIT	3 SALES TAXES PAYABLE CREDIT	4 ACCOUNTS RECEIVABLE CREDIT	5 CASH DEBIT	
1	1968 Oct.	1	Balance on hand #4,238.50	✓						1
2		2	✓	✓		300 00	12 00		312 00	2
3		2	A. M. Deal	✓				416 40	416 40	3
4		2	Office Equipment	122	40 00				40 00	4
30		30	✓	✓		290 30	11 61		301 91	30
31		31	✓	✓		186 40	7 46		193 86	31
					280 60	9250 30	371 21	4282 49	14184 60	
32		31	Totals		280 60	9250 30	371 21	4282 49	14184 60	32
33					(✓)	(411)	(217)	(115)	(111)	33
34										34
35										35
36										36
37										37
38										38

Columnar cash receipts journal

The entry on Line 3 of the cash receipts journal records the receipt of cash from a charge customer. Cash is debited and Accounts Receivable and the customer's account are credited for $416.40. The sales taxes on this sale were recorded in the sales journal when the invoice was recorded.

Posting the columnar cash receipts journal

Amounts in the Accounts Receivable Credit column are posted to the customers' accounts daily. Amounts in the General Credit column are posted frequently to avoid too much work at the end of the month.

After cash has been proved and the equality of debits and credits has been verified, the totals of the special columns are posted to the accounts named in the headings of the columns. As each total is posted, the account number is placed in parentheses below the total.

PAYING SALES TAXES COLLECTED

Sales taxes collected by the seller must be paid directly to the proper government unit. In many states the sales taxes collected on cash sales and from charge customers are paid to the state each month. In other states, the payment of sales taxes is made quarterly.

October 31, 1968. Issued Check No. 899 to the State Tax Commission for $1,955.46 in payment of sales taxes.

The analysis of this transaction is shown in T accounts on the next page.

The payment of this liability, $1,955.46, is recorded as a debit to Sales Taxes Payable to show a decrease in the balance of this liability account.

Sales Taxes Payable	217
1,955.46	

Cash is credited for the amount of the taxes paid, $1,955.46, to show a decrease in the balance of this asset account.

Cash	111
	1,955.46

Recording the payment of sales taxes

Crane Paper Products uses a columnar cash payments journal to record all cash payments. Since the company pays its sales taxes quarterly, a special column for sales taxes payable is not needed.

The entry to record the payment of sales taxes to the State Tax Commission is shown on Line 29 of the illustration below. Sales Taxes Payable is written in the Account Debited column and the amount, $1,955.46, is recorded in the General Debit column. Cash is credited for $1,955.46 in the Cash Credit column.

CASH PAYMENTS JOURNAL PAGE 10

	DATE	CK. NO.	ACCOUNT DEBITED	POST. REF.	1 GENERAL DEBIT	2 ACCOUNTS PAYABLE DEBIT	3 SALARY EXPENSE DEBIT	4 FICA TAXES PAY. CREDIT	5 EMPLOYEES INCOME TAXES PAY. CREDIT	6 PURCHASES DISCOUNT CREDIT	7 CASH CREDIT	
1	1968 Oct. 1	871	Rent Expense	619	275 00						275 00	1
2	2	872	Miscellaneous Expense	617	40 00						40 00	2
3	2	873	J. R. Towne	✓		332 00				6 64	325 36	3
29	31	899	Sales Taxes Payable	217	1955 46						1955 46	29
30	31	900	✓	✓			760 60	33 47	106 48		620 65	30
31	31	901	Supplies	117	8 60							31
32			Advertising Expense	611	3 75							32
33			Miscellaneous Expense	617	26 45						38 80	33
					4852 52	10123 60	1442 40	45 08	122 40	143 20	16107 84	
34	31		Totals		4852 52	10123 60	1442 40	45 08	122 40	143 20	16107 84	34
35					(✓)	(213)	(619)	(214)	(215)	(511.2)	(111)	35
36												36
37												37
38												38
39												39
40												40

Columnar cash payments journal

Posting the columnar cash payments journal

Amounts in the Accounts Payable Debit column are posted to the creditors' accounts daily. Amounts in the General Debit column are posted frequently to avoid too much work at the end of the month.

Cash is proved and the equality of debits and credits is verified. The totals of the special columns are posted to the accounts named in the headings of the columns. As each total is posted, the account number is placed in parentheses below the total.

A GENERAL JOURNAL WITH SPECIAL AMOUNT COLUMNS

To make it easier to record and post miscellaneous transactions with customers and creditors, Crane Paper Products uses a four-column general journal as shown below.

GENERAL JOURNAL PAGE

	1	2				3	4	
	ACCOUNTS PAYABLE DEBIT	GENERAL DEBIT	DATE	ACCOUNT TITLE	POST. REF.	GENERAL CREDIT	ACCOUNTS RECEIVABLE CREDIT	
1								1
2								2
3								3
4								4
5								5
6								6

A four-column general journal

The differences between this four-column general journal and the general journal in Chapter 16 are: (1) this journal has two additional amount columns. One is headed Accounts Payable Debit and the other is headed Accounts Receivable Credit, and (2) the two debit amount columns are at the left of the Account Title column and the two credit columns are at the right. The special columns make it possible to debit Accounts Payable or to credit Accounts Receivable without having to write the names of these general ledger accounts in the Account Title column.

Recording sales taxes on sales returns and allowances

October 15, 1968. Issued Credit Memorandum No. 18 to Henry Marks for $50.00 worth of merchandise he returned.

In the charge sale to Mr. Marks on October 2, his account was debited for $104.00. This was the amount of the invoice, $100.00, plus $4.00 sales taxes. In this transaction Mr. Marks is entitled to a credit of $50.00 plus a credit of $2.00 for sales taxes. The analysis of this transaction is shown in T accounts on the next page.

Sales Returns and Allowances is debited for the amount of the return, $50.00, to show an increase in the balance of this account.

Sales Taxes Payable is debited for $2.00 to reduce this liability by the amount of the sales tax on the merchandise returned.

Accounts Receivable in the general ledger and Henry Marks' account in the accounts receivable ledger are each credited for $52.00 to show the reduction in the balance of these asset accounts.

The journal entry to record this transaction is shown below.

GENERAL LEDGER

Sales Returns and Allowances 411.1	
50.00	

Sales Taxes Payable 217	
2.00	

Accounts Receivable 115	
	52.00

ACCOUNTS RECEIVABLE LEDGER

Henry Marks	
	52.00

GENERAL JOURNAL PAGE 10

	1	2				3	4	
	ACCOUNTS PAYABLE DEBIT	GENERAL DEBIT	DATE	ACCOUNT TITLE	POST. REF.	GENERAL CREDIT	ACCOUNTS RECEIVABLE CREDIT	
1		50 00	1968 Oct. 15	Sales Returns and Allowances				1
2		2 00		Sales Taxes Payable				2
3				Henry Marks			52 00	3
4				Credit Memo No. 18.				4
5								5
6								6
7								7
8								8
9								9
10								10
11								11
12								12
13								13
14								14
15								15

Sales Returns and Allowances is debited for $50.00 in the General Debit column. Sales Taxes Payable is debited for $2.00 in the General Debit column. Henry Marks is credited for $52.00 in the Accounts Receivable Credit column.

Recording a purchases return

October 18, 1968. Received a credit memorandum from Wilson and Hope for $75.00 for defective merchandise returned to them.

The journal entry to record this transaction is shown on the next page.

GENERAL JOURNAL PAGE 10

	1 Accounts Payable Debit	2 General Debit	Date	Account Title	Post. Ref.	3 General Credit	4 Accounts Receivable Credit	
5	75 00		18	Wilson and Hope				5
6				Purchases Returns and Allowances		75 00		6
7				Credit Memo No. 344.				7
8								8
9								9
10								10

Accounts Payable is debited for $75.00 in the Accounts Payable Debit column. The name of the creditor, Wilson and Hope, is written in the Account Title column. Purchases Returns and Allowances is credited for $75.00 in the General Credit column.

Recording the writing off of a bad debt

October 22, 1968. Received notice that a customer, J. L. Miller, who owes us $68.40, is bankrupt.

Since Mr. Miller is bankrupt, he is unable to pay his account. It is therefore necessary to write off his account. The journal entry to record the writing off of his account is shown below.

GENERAL JOURNAL PAGE 10

	1 Accounts Payable Debit	2 General Debit	Date	Account Title	Post. Ref.	3 General Credit	4 Accounts Receivable Credit	
8		68 40	22	Allowance for Bad Debts	115.1			8
9				J. L. Miller	✓		68 40	9
10				To write off uncollectible				10
11				account.				11
12								12
13								13
14								14
15								15

Allowance for Bad Debts is debited for $68.40 in the General Debit column. The name of the customer, J. L. Miller, is written in the Account Title column. Accounts Receivable is credited for $68.40 in the Accounts Receivable Credit column.

Recording a correcting entry

October 23, 1968. Received a letter from J. R. Jolson stating that he was overcharged $79.46.

An examination of the posting of the sales journal on October 2 shows that the account of J. R. Jolson was debited for $79.46 when, instead, the account of J. R. Olson should have been debited.

The journal entry to correct this error is shown below.

GENERAL JOURNAL — PAGE 10

	1	2				3	4	
	ACCOUNTS PAYABLE DEBIT	GENERAL DEBIT	DATE	ACCOUNT TITLE	POST. REF.	GENERAL CREDIT	ACCOUNTS RECEIVABLE CREDIT	
12		7946	23	J. R. Olson	✓			12
13				J. R. Jolson	✓	7946		13
14				To correct errors in				14
15				posting sales invoice				15
16				No. 714.				16
17								17
18								18
19								19

The debit of $79.46 to J. R. Olson in the General Debit column charges his account for this sale. The credit of $79.46 to J. R. Jolson in the General Credit column removes the charge from his account which was made in error. The correcting entry is recorded in the General columns only because the accounts receivable account in the general ledger is not affected.

Posting the four-column general journal

The individual amounts in the Accounts Payable Debit column and in the Accounts Receivable Credit column are posted daily to the appropriate accounts in the accounts payable ledger and the accounts receivable ledger. A check mark is placed in the Post. Ref. column of the general journal to indicate the completion of the posting.

The individual amounts in the General columns that affect accounts in the general ledger are posted to the proper accounts in the general ledger. The account number is written in the Post. Ref. column of the general journal to indicate the completion of the posting.

Posting the totals of the four-column general journal

The totals of the four-column general journal at the end of October, 1968, are shown below.

GENERAL JOURNAL — PAGE 10

	1	2				3	4	
	ACCOUNTS PAYABLE DEBIT	GENERAL DEBIT	DATE	ACCOUNT TITLE	POST. REF.	GENERAL CREDIT	ACCOUNTS RECEIVABLE CREDIT	
39	79600 79600	132564 132564	31	Totals		112956 112956	99208 99208	39
40	(213)	(✓)				(✓)	(115)	40

Before the totals are posted, the equality of debits and credits is verified. The sum of the two debit amounts equals the sum of the two credit amounts. The work is therefore considered correct.

The total of the Accounts Payable Debit column is posted as a debit to Accounts Payable. The number of the accounts payable account is written in parentheses (213) below the total. The total of the Accounts Receivable Credit column is posted as a credit to Accounts Receivable. The number of the accounts receivable account is written in parentheses (115) below the total.

The individual amounts in the General Debit and the General Credit columns were posted to the accounts named in the Account Title column. A check mark is placed in parentheses (√) below each of these two totals to show these totals are not to be posted.

USING SALES INVOICES AS A SALES JOURNAL

Some businesses use the duplicate copies of their sales invoices as their sales journal. When this is done, each sales invoice is posted directly to the proper customer's account in the accounts receivable ledger. (See page 223.) The number of the sales invoice is placed in the posting reference column of the customer's account to show the source of the entry. A check mark is placed at the right of the customer's name on the sales invoice to show the invoice was posted. Invoices are filed in numeric order after posting.

At the end of the month, the amounts on the invoices are totaled on an adding machine. If the business collects a sales tax, three different totals must be secured: (1) the total amount of all invoices, (2) the total sale price on all invoices, and (3) the total sales tax on all invoices. These totals are the basis for a journal entry debiting Accounts Receivable and crediting Sales and Sales Taxes Payable. For example, if the adding machine tape shows the grand total of all invoices to be $865.20, the total sales prices to be $840.00, and the total sales taxes to be $25.20, the following entry would be recorded in the general journal:

GENERAL JOURNAL — PAGE 16

	1	2				3	4	
	ACCOUNTS PAYABLE DEBIT	GENERAL DEBIT	DATE	ACCOUNT TITLE	POST. REF.	GENERAL CREDIT	ACCOUNTS RECEIVABLE CREDIT	
33		865 20	31	Accounts Receivable				33
34				Sales		840 00		34
35				Sales Taxes Payable		25 20		35
36				Total invoices for the				36
37				month.				37

Entry to record total monthly sales on account when sales invoices serve as a sales journal

Increasing Your Business Vocabulary

What is the meaning of the following:

a sales tax

Study Questions

1. How are sales tax rates usually expressed?
2. What kinds of records must be kept by a business that collects sales taxes?
3. Why do sales taxes collected from customers become a liability of the seller?
4. In the entry on Line 3 of the cash receipts journal on page 552, why is there no amount recorded in the Sales Taxes Payable Credit column?
5. What was the amount of the check written to pay employees in the transaction on Line 30 of the cash payments journal on page 553?
6. What are the advantages of having Accounts Payable and Accounts Receivable columns in the general journal?
7. Why is Sales Taxes Payable debited when a customer returns merchandise for credit?
8. Explain the procedure followed when sales invoices are used as the sales journal.

Cases for Business Decision

CASE 1

Crane Paper Products writes the names of accounts in the Account Title columns of its various journals. The Chapman Paper Company uses account numbers instead of account titles in the Account Title columns of its journals. What are the advantages and the disadvantages of each plan?

CASE 2

Crane Paper Products uses special journals instead of a combination journal. What decisions must the company make in determining whether a combination journal would be more suitable than special journals for its entries?

Drill for Understanding

DRILL 31-A | The effect of sales tax transactions on accounts

Instructions: 1. Open the following accounts in T-account form:

(a) *General Ledger:* Cash, Accounts Receivable, Sales Taxes Payable, Sales. (Allow eight lines for each account.)

(b) *Accounts Receivable Ledger:* T. Abel, F. Forbes. (Allow three lines for each account.)

2. Use T accounts to analyze the effect of the following transactions. In addition to the sales price listed in each of these transactions, there is a sales tax of 4% on each sale.

(a) Sold merchandise for cash, $30.00.
(b) Sold merchandise on account to T. Abel, $22.00.
(c) Sold merchandise on account to F. Forbes, $18.00.
(d) Sold merchandise for cash, $430.00.
(e) Received payment in full for T. Abel's account.
(f) Sold merchandise on account to F. Forbes, $160.00.
(g) Sold merchandise for cash, $210.00.
(h) Received payment in full for F. Forbes account.
(i) Sold merchandise on account to T. Abel, $370.00.
(j) Issued a check to the state in full payment of all sales taxes payable.

Instructions: 3. Prove the equality of the debits and the credits in the general ledger by taking a trial balance.

Application Problem

PROBLEM 31-1 | Recording transactions in columnar sales and cash receipts journals

Instructions: 1. Record the following transactions completed by Adler Radio Store during January of the current year in a sales journal (page 12) and a cash receipts journal (page 10) like those illustrated in this chapter. Begin numbering the sales invoices with No. 41.

Transactions

Jan. 1. Record the cash balance of $2,240.60 in the cash receipts journal as a memorandum entry.
2. Received a check for $80.00 from Fred Oakes on account.
3. Sold merchandise on account to J. R. Falls, $42.00; sales tax, $1.68.
5. Sold merchandise on account to T. R. Reed, $70.00; sales tax, $2.80.
5. Cash sales January 2 to 5, $600.00; sales taxes, $24.00.

Jan. 9. Received a check for $150.00 from J. C. Klein on account.
12. Cash sales January 7 to 12, $750.00; sales tax, $30.00.
16. Received cash, $7.50, for office supplies sold to accommodate a fellow merchant. (Sales taxes are not collected in this state on an accommodation sale.)
17. Sold merchandise on account to J. C. Klein, $160.00; sales tax, $6.40.
18. Received a check for $100.00 from T. R. Reed on account.
19. Cash sales January 14 to 19, $680.00; sales taxes, $27.20.
24. Received a check for $116.00 from R. C. Aker on account.
26. Cash sales January 21 to 26, $800.00; sales taxes, $32.00.
28. Received a check for $21.84 from J. R. Falls in payment of our invoice of January 3 for $43.68 less a credit of $21.84 granted on January 19 for merchandise returned.
29. Sold merchandise on account to B. L. Barry, $220.00; sales tax, $8.80.
31. Received a check for $50.00 from T. R. Reed on account.
31. Sold merchandise on account to T. R. Reed, $80.00; sales tax, $3.20.
31. Cash sales January 28 to 31, $250.00; sales taxes, $10.00.

Instructions: 2. Foot, prove, total, and rule both journals.

Optional Problems

★SUPPLEMENTARY PROBLEM 31-S

Recording transactions in columnar cash payments and general journals

Instructions: 1. Record the following transactions completed by Beacon Sales Company during January of the current year in a cash payments journal (page 64) and a general journal (page 48) like those illustrated in this chapter.

Transactions

Jan. 2. Issued Check No. 401 for $100.00 to establish a petty cash fund.
2. Issued Check No. 402 for $200.00 for January rent.
4. Issued Check No. 403 for $392.00 to Larkin Company in payment of their invoice of December 26 for $400.00 less $8.00 discount.
8. Issued Check No. 404 for $2,596.00 in payment of the liability of $1,540.00 for employees income taxes payable and the liability of $1,056.00 for FICA taxes payable for the previous month.
8. Issued Check No. 405 for $858.00 in payment of the state unemployment taxes payable for the previous quarter.
8. Issued Check No. 406 for $342.00 in payment of the federal unemployment taxes payable for the previous year.
10. Wrote off the account of Jerry Thomas, $36.00, as a bad debt.

Jan. 12. Issued Check No. 407 for $4,955.40 in payment of the biweekly payroll of $6,000.00 less a deduction of $780.60 for employees income taxes payable and a deduction of $264.00 for FICA taxes payable.

12. Recorded the employer's liability of $264.00 for FICA taxes, $162.00 for state unemployment taxes, and $24.00 for federal unemployment taxes.

15. Issued Check No. 408 for $10,480.00 in payment of the sales taxes payable for the previous quarterly period.

15. Issued Check No. 409 for $170.00 to Joseph Marr in payment of his invoice of December 15.

18. Received a credit memorandum for $32.50 from Olsen Company for merchandise returned to them.

19. Issued Credit Memorandum No. 742 for $21.84 to R. L. Orr for merchandise returned that had been part of the invoice of January 3, $21.00, and sales tax on the return, 84¢.

22. Issued Check No. 410 for $80.50 for electricity bill. (Debit Utilities Expense.)

23. Issued Credit Memorandum No. 743 for $7.28 to O. B. Reed for an allowance granted because of defective merchandise shipped to him as part of the invoice of January 17, $7.00, and sales tax on the allowance, 28¢.

26. Issued Check No. 411 for $712.95 to Olsen Company in payment of their invoice of January 16 for $760.00 less the $32.50 credit of January 18 and less $14.55 discount.

26. Issued Check No. 412 for $4,955.40 in payment of the biweekly payroll of $6,000.00 less the same deductions as on January 12.

26. Recorded the employer's liability for social security taxes, which were the same as on January 12.

29. Discovered that a December 29 sale of merchandise on account for $180.50, including sales tax, to R. L. Orr had been posted incorrectly to the account of F. W. Orr.

30. Issued Check No. 413 for $372.79 to Marks & Company in payment of their invoice of January 20 for $380.40 less $7.61 discount.

31. Issued Check No. 414 for $64.40 to replenish petty cash. The expenditures were as follows: Supplies, $14.20; Delivery Expense, $20.50; Miscellaneous Expense, $16.00; Sales Returns and Allowances, $11.80; Sales Taxes Payable, $1.90.

Instructions: 2. Foot, prove, total, and rule both journals.

★ BONUS PROBLEM 31-B

Recording transactions in columnar special journals

Instructions: 1. Record the following transactions completed by Milton Company during March of the current year in a sales journal (page 42), a cash receipts journal (page 28), a cash payments journal (page 20), and a general journal (page 39) like those illustrated in this chapter.

2. Use account numbers in the Account Title column of each journal for all *general ledger accounts* instead of writing the account titles. Use the account numbers given in the chart of accounts on page 480 and the additional account, Sales Taxes Payable, Account Number 216.

3. The amount of sales taxes is *not* included in the sales-on-account transactions. Be sure to compute the tax and add the tax to the amount of each invoice. The tax rate in this state is 3%.

4. Begin numbering the checks with Number 401.

5. Begin numbering the sales invoices with Number 264.

Transactions

Mar. 1. Recorded the cash balance of $4,400.10 with a memorandum entry.
1. Issued check for $300.00 for the March rent.
1. Sold merchandise on account to D. A. Hoke, $740.00.
2. Sold merchandise on account to F. J. Olsen, $120.60.
2. Received a check for $160.00 from Henry Voss on account.
2. Issued check for $656.60 in payment of the biweekly payroll of $800.00 less a deduction of $108.20 for employees income taxes payable and a deduction of $35.20 for FICA taxes payable.
2. Cash sales for March 1 and 2 were $640.50; sales taxes, $19.22; total, $659.72.
4. Wrote off the account of R. A. Rolf, $44.00, as a bad debt.
5. Issued check for $842.80 to Polson Sales Company in payment of their invoice of Feb. 28 for $860.00 less $17.20 discount.
7. Sold merchandise on account to D. A. Hoke, $460.00.
8. Issued check for $31.75 in payment of the telephone bill.
9. Cash sales for the week were $2,120.00; sales taxes, $63.60; total, $2,183.60.
11. Sold wrapping supplies for cash to accommodate a customer, $5.50. (There is no sales tax on such a transaction in this state.)
13. Issued Credit Memorandum No. 38 for $20.60 to D. A. Hoke for merchandise returned that had been part of the invoice of March 1, $20.00, and sales tax on the return, 60¢.
14. Received $750.00 from D. L. Thomas on account.
15. Issued check for $570.00 for a new calculating machine.

Mar. 16. Issued check for $761.80 in payment of the biweekly payroll of $925.00 less a deduction of $122.50 for employees income taxes payable and a deduction of $40.70 for FICA taxes payable.

16. Cash sales for the week were $2,830.00; sales taxes, $84.90; total, $2,914.90.

18. Received a credit memorandum for $12.75 from Polson Sales Co. for an allowance on defective merchandise.

19. Sold merchandise on account to F. J. Olsen, $924.00.

20. Received a check for $741.60 from D. A. Hoke for balance due on our invoice of March 1, less our credit memorandum No. 38 of March 13.

21. Issued check for $225.40 to Perry Corporation in payment of invoice of March 12 for $230.00 less $4.60 discount.

23. Cash sales for the week were $2,910.00; sales taxes, $87.30; total, $2,997.30.

26. Received a check for $500.00 from F. J. Olsen on account.

27. Sold merchandise on account to D. L. Thomas, $220.00.

28. Received a credit memorandum for $28.30 from Akers & Co. for merchandise returned.

29. Issued check for $840.50 for delivery service for the month.

30. Issued check for $761.80 in payment of the biweekly payroll of $925.00 less a deduction of $122.50 for employees income taxes payable and a deduction of $40.70 for FICA taxes payable.

30. Recorded the employer's liability, for the three payrolls paid this month: $116.60 for FICA taxes, $71.55 for state unemployment taxes, and $10.60 for federal unemployment taxes.

30. Issued check for $62.95 to replenish petty cash. The expenditures were as follows: Supplies, $36.00; Delivery Expense, $12.00; Sales Returns and Allowances, $14.20; Sales Taxes Payable, 75¢.

30. Cash sales for the week were $2,100.00; sales taxes, $63.00; total, $2,163.00.

Instructions: 2. Foot, prove, total, and rule all journals.

CHAPTER 32 NOTES AND INTEREST

PROMISSORY NOTES

An unconditional written promise to pay a certain sum of money at a definite time that is signed by the person or persons agreeing to make payment is known as a *promissory note*. A promissory note is frequently referred to simply as a *note*. One form of promissory note is shown in the illustration below.

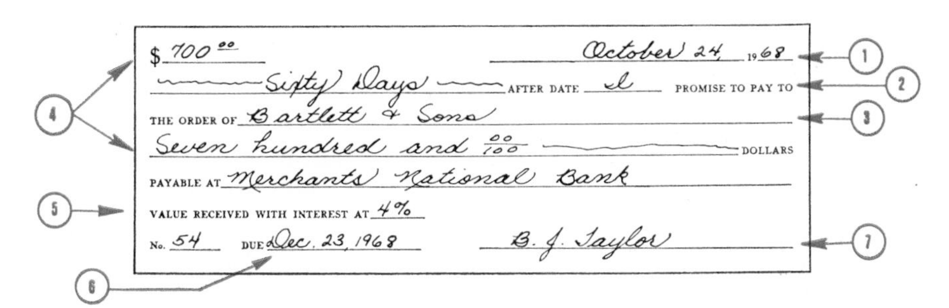
$ 700.00 October 24, 1968
Sixty Days AFTER DATE I PROMISE TO PAY TO
THE ORDER OF Bartlett & Sons
Seven hundred and 00/100 DOLLARS
PAYABLE AT Merchants National Bank
VALUE RECEIVED WITH INTEREST AT 4%
No. 54 DUE Dec. 23, 1968 B. J. Taylor

A promissory note

Analyzing a promissory note

The following table defines the terms used in connection with promissory notes. (See the illustration above.)

Terms	*Definitions*	*The Illustration*
① Date	The day on which the note is issued.	October 24, 1968
② Time	The days or months from the date of issue until the note is to be paid.	60 days
③ Payee	The one to whom a note is payable.	Bartlett & Sons
④ Principal	The amount the borrower promises to pay — the face of the note.	$700.00
⑤ Interest rate	The rate paid for the use of the money.	4%
⑥ Maturity date	The date on which the note is due.	December 23, 1968
⑦ Maker	The one who signs the note and thus promises to make payment.	B. J. Taylor

Use of promissory notes

When a person borrows at a bank, the bank requires the borrower to sign a note. Notes are sometimes given to creditors when the buyer wants credit beyond the usual time for which credit is given.

Notes have an advantage over oral promises and open accounts because, like checks, notes can be endorsed and transferred. Notes can also be useful in a court of law as evidence of a debt.

INTEREST

Interest-bearing and non-interest bearing notes

Most promissory notes require the payment of interest. Promissory notes that require interest payments are known as *interest-bearing notes.* Promissory notes that do not require the payment of interest are known as *non-interest-bearing notes.*

Interest is stated as a percentage of the principal. The percentage of the principal of a note that is paid for the use of the money is known as the *interest rate.* Interest at 6% means that 6 cents will be paid for the use of each dollar borrowed for a full year. The interest on $100.00 for a full year at 6% is $6.00.

When a note runs for a fraction of a year, the amount of interest is found by multiplying this fraction by the interest for a full year. For example, if the time of a note is 6 months, which is one half of a year, the amount of interest would be one half the amount that would be paid for a full year. The interest on $100.00 for a half-year at 6% is $3.00.

Computing interest using interest tables

Whenever a business has many calculations dealing with interest, it commonly uses an interest table. Interest tables may be purchased at an office supply store or may be obtained from some banks. The illustration at the right shows an interest table for 6% on a monthly basis. Interest tables are available for most interest rates on both a monthly and a daily basis.

INTEREST TABLE
6% for $1.00 on a Monthly Basis

Number of Months	Amount of Interest
1	.005
2	.01
3	.015
4	.02
5	.025
6	.03
7	.035
8	.04
9	.045
10	.05
11	.055
12	.06

A business has a 6% interest-bearing note for $500.00 that is to run for three months. The interest is computed as follows:

1. Follow down in the month column of the interest table to the figure 3. The amount column on this line shows .015, which is the amount of interest for $1 for three months.

2. Multiply \$500.00 by .015. The result is \$7.50, the interest on \$500.00 for three months.

Computing interest without interest tables

To compute the interest on a given amount for one year, the principal is multiplied by the interest rate. For example, a business has a 5% interest-bearing note for \$300.00 that is to run for one year. The interest is computed as follows:

$$\$300.00 \times .05 = \$15.00$$

To calculate the amount of interest for a period of less than one year, the following formula is used:

Principal × Rate × Fraction of Year = Amount of Interest

For example, to find the interest on \$600.00 for 4 months at 5%, the following computation is made:

Principal × Rate × Fraction of Year = Amount of Interest

$$\$600.00 \times .05 \times \frac{4}{12} = \frac{\$120.00}{12} = \$10.00$$

For convenience in calculating, 360 days are commonly used as the number of days in a year. To find the interest on \$400.00 for 90 days at 4% the following computation is made:

$$\$400.00 \times .04 \times \frac{90}{360} = \frac{\$1,440.00}{360} = \$4.00$$

Instead of multiplying the numbers and dividing by 360, the cancellation method can be used, as follows:

$$\$400.00 \times \overset{.01}{\cancel{.04}} \times \frac{\cancel{90}}{\underset{4}{\cancel{360}}} = \$4.00$$

NOTES PAYABLE

Notes that a business gives creditors, in which the business promises to pay, are known as *notes payable.* Notes payable are classified as *current liabilities* of the business.

A business that frequently issues notes may find it desirable to keep a special record showing the details of each note. The book in which notes payable are recorded in detail is called a *notes payable register.* When a notes payable register is used, the notes are recorded in the register in the order of the dates on which the notes are issued. The information recorded in a notes payable register includes: the number of the note; to whom the note is payable; where the note is payable; the date of the note; the time, the principal, the interest rate; and the date paid.

Several common uses of notes payable are illustrated in the following transactions.

Issuing a note payable for an extension of time

When a business is unable to pay for a purchase on account when it is due, the business may ask for an extension of time. Usually when a request for more time is made, the business offers to issue an interest-bearing note payable.

March 24, 1968. Issued a six-month, 6% note payable for $478.00 to the Herberg Furniture Company for an extension of time on an overdue account.

In this transaction, the balance of the liability account Accounts Payable is decreased. The balance of the creditor's account, Herberg Furniture Company, in the accounts payable ledger is also decreased. The balance of the liability account Notes Payable is increased. Accounts Payable is debited for $478.00; the creditor's account, Herberg Furniture Company, is debited for $478.00; and Notes Payable is credited for $478.00.

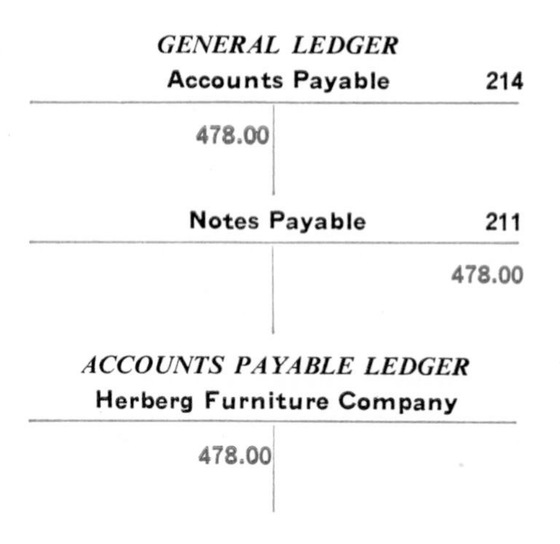

This transaction is recorded in the four-column general journal as shown below.

GENERAL JOURNAL — PAGE 22

	1 Accounts Payable Debit	2 General Debit	Date	Account Title	Post. Ref.	3 General Credit	4 Accounts Receivable Credit	
4	478 00		24	Herberg Furniture Company				4
5				Notes Payable		478 00		5
6				Note Pay. No. 54				6
7								7
8								8
9								9

Entry to record the issuance of a note payable for an extension of time

Borrowing from a bank

April 1, 1968. Issued a one-year, 6% note payable for $1,000.00 to the First Citizens State Bank. Interest payable semiannually.

The carbon copy of the note is the source document for analyzing and recording the transaction. In this transaction, the balance of the asset account Cash is increased and the balance of the liability account Notes Payable is increased. Cash is debited for $1,000.00. Notes Payable is credited for $1,000.00. No entry is made for the interest until a later date when the payment of interest is made.

Cash	111
1,000.00	

Notes Payable	211
	1,000.00

This transaction is recorded in the cash receipts journal as shown below.

CASH RECEIPTS JOURNAL — PAGE 33

	DATE	ACCOUNT CREDITED	POST. REF.	1 GENERAL CREDIT	2 SALES CREDIT	3 SALES TAXES PAYABLE CREDIT	4 ACCOUNTS RECEIVABLE CREDIT	5 CASH DEBIT	
22	1	Notes Payable		1000 00				1000 00	22
23									23
24									24
25									25
26									26
27									27
28									28
29									29
30									30
31									31

Entry to record cash received from a note payable

Buying office equipment with a note payable

April 2, 1968. Issued a one-year, 6% note payable for $750.00 to the Kent Office Equipment Company for the purchase of office equipment. Interest is payable at maturity.

In this transaction the balance of the asset account Office Equipment is increased and the balance of the liability account Notes Payable is increased. Office Equipment is debited for $750.00 and Notes Payable is credited for $750.00.

Office Equipment	123
750.00	

Notes Payable	211
	750.00

This transaction is recorded in the four-column general journal as shown on the next page.

GENERAL JOURNAL — PAGE 23

	1 ACCOUNTS PAYABLE DEBIT	2 GENERAL DEBIT	DATE	ACCOUNT TITLE	POST. REF.	3 GENERAL CREDIT	4 ACCOUNTS RECEIVABLE CREDIT	
14		750 00	2	Office Equipment				14
15				Notes Payable		750 00		15
16				Note Pay. No. 59 to				16
17				Kent Furniture Co.				17
18								18
19								19
20								20

Entry to record the purchase of office equipment with a note payable

Paying the interest on a note payable

When cash is paid for interest, the amount of the payment is debited to an expense account with the title *Interest Expense* and is credited to Cash.

October 1, 1968. *Issued Check No. 108 in payment of the semiannual interest of $30.00 now due on the note payable given to the First Citizens State Bank on April 1.*

In this transaction the balance of the interest expense account is increased and the balance of the cash account is decreased. Interest Expense is debited for $30.00 and Cash is credited for $30.00.

This transaction is recorded in the cash payments journal as shown below.

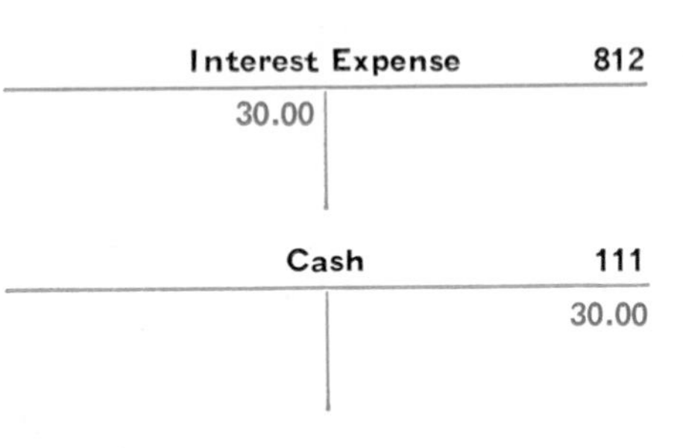

CASH PAYMENTS JOURNAL — PAGE 46

	DATE	CK. NO.	ACCOUNT DEBITED	POST. REF.	1 GENERAL DEBIT	2 ACCOUNTS PAYABLE DEBIT	3 SALARY EXPENSE DEBIT	4 FICA TAXES PAY. CREDIT	5 EMPLOYEES INCOME TAXES PAY. CREDIT	6 PURCHASES DISCOUNT CREDIT	7 CASH CREDIT	
8	1	108	Interest Expense		30 00						30 00	8
9												9
10												10
11												11
12												12
13												13
14												14
15												15
16												16
17												17

Entry to record payment of interest

Paying the principal and interest at maturity

October 15, 1968. *Issued Check No. 157 for $2,060.00 to the Jet Manufacturing Company in payment of the principal of $2,000.00 and the interest of $60.00.*

In this transaction the balance of the liability account Notes Payable is decreased; the balance of Interest Expense is increased; and the balance of the asset Cash is decreased. Notes Payable is debited for $2,000.00. Interest Expense is debited for $60.00. Cash is credited for $2,060.00.

This transaction is recorded in the cash payments journal below.

Notes Payable	211
2,000.00	

Interest Expense	812
60.00	

Cash	111
	2,060.00

CASH PAYMENTS JOURNAL PAGE 47

	Date	Ck. No.	Account Debited	Post. Ref.	1 General Debit	2 Accounts Payable Debit	3 Salary Expense Debit	4 FICA Taxes Pay. Credit	5 Employees Income Taxes Pay. Credit	6 Purchases Discount Credit	7 Cash Credit	
32	15		Notes Payable		2000 00							32
33		157	Interest Expense		60 00						2060 00	33
34												34
35												35
36												36
37												37
38												38

Entry to record the payment of principal and interest

Note that two lines in the cash payments journal are required to record the two debits and the one credit in this transaction. Note also that the sum of the two debit amounts is equal to the credit amount.

Bank discount

Some banks require the borrower to pay all the interest in advance at the time that a note is signed. Interest collected in advance by a bank is referred to as *bank discount*. The amount received for a note after the bank has deducted the bank discount is called the *proceeds*. When interest on a note is taken in advance, the note is said to be *discounted*.

There are two methods of recording the discounting of a non-interest-bearing note:

1. The bank may deduct the bank discount and credit the checking account of the borrower with the amount of the proceeds only.
2. The borrower may choose to have the principal of the note credited to his checking account and then write a check for bank discount.

Method No. 2 is used in this textbook for the following reasons. When a check is written for the amount of the bank discount and the principal of the note is the deposit, the advantages are: (a) the amount credited to the notes payable account in the cash receipts journal is the same as the principal of the note; (b) *all* entries in the cash payments journal are accounted for by checks and check numbers; (c) at the end of the month the bank statement of deposits agrees with the cash receipts in the cash receipts journal, and (d) at the end of the month the reconciliation of the bank statement with the two cash journals is more easily and quickly completed.

April 26, 1968. Discounted at the First Citizens State Bank our one-year, non-interest-bearing note payable for $2,000.00. Discount rate is 6%. Issued Check No. 73 for the amount of the bank discount, $120.00.

The source documents for this transaction are the copy of the note payable issued and the stub of the check.

Entry for the issuance of the note payable. The first part of the transaction is the issuance of a non-interest-bearing note payable that is to be discounted. In this part of the transaction, the balance of the asset account Cash is increased $2,000.00 and the balance of the liability account Notes Payable is increased $2,000.00. The cash account in the general ledger is debited for $2,000.00 and the notes payable account is credited for $2,000.00. The recording of this transaction is similar to the entry on Line 22 of the cash receipts journal on page 569.

Cash	111
2,000.00	

Notes Payable	211
	2,000.00

Entry for the payment of the bank discount. The second part of this transaction is the issuance of a check to cover the bank discount of $120.00. The balance of the interest expense account is increased $120.00 and the balance of the cash account is decreased the same amount. The interest expense account is debited for the amount of the bank discount, $120.00. The cash account is credited for the amount of the check, $120.00.

Interest Expense	812
120.00	

Cash	111
	120.00

The entry to record this payment is shown on the next page.

CASH PAYMENTS JOURNAL — PAGE 49

	DATE	CK. NO.	ACCOUNT DEBITED	POST. REF.	1 GENERAL DEBIT	2 ACCOUNTS PAYABLE DEBIT	3 SALARY EXPENSE DEBIT	4 FICA TAXES PAY. CREDIT	5 EMPLOYEES INCOME TAXES PAY. CREDIT	6 PURCHASES DISCOUNT CREDIT	7 CASH CREDIT	
8	26	73	Interest Expense		120 00						120 00	8
9												9
10												10
11												11
12												12

Entry to record the payment of bank discount by check

NOTES RECEIVABLE

Notes that a business accepts, for which it will later receive cash, are known as *notes receivable.* Notes receivable are classified as *current assets* of the business.

A business that frequently receives notes may find it desirable to keep a special record showing the details of each note. The book in which notes receivable are recorded in detail is called a *notes receivable register.* When a notes receivable register is used, the notes are recorded in the order of the dates on which the notes are received. The information recorded for each note receivable is similar to that recorded for a note payable.

Receiving a note receivable from a customer

When a customer is unable to pay his account on the due date, he may request additional time. A business may accept a note from a charge customer as a means of granting an extension of time for the payment of his account. The note does not pay the amount the customer owes, but it does change the form of the asset from an account receivable to a note receivable.

May 13, 1968. Received a six-month, 6% note receivable for $300.00 from Ernest Walters on account.

In this transaction the balance of the asset account Notes Receivable is increased and the balance of the asset account Accounts Receivable is decreased. The balance of the customer's account, Ernest Walters, in the accounts receivable ledger, is also decreased. Notes Receivable is debited for $300.00; Accounts Receivable is credited for $300.00; and the customer's account, Ernest Walters, is credited for $300.00.

GENERAL LEDGER

Notes Receivable	113
300.00	

Accounts Receivable	115
	300.00

ACCOUNTS RECEIVABLE LEDGER

Ernest Walters	
	300.00

It should be noted that whenever the balance of a customer's account in the accounts receivable ledger is decreased, the balance of the controlling account in the general ledger, Accounts Receivable, is decreased the same amount.

This transaction is recorded in the four-column general journal below.

GENERAL JOURNAL — PAGE 26

	1 Accounts Payable Debit	2 General Debit	Date	Account Title	Post. Ref.	3 General Credit	4 Accounts Receivable Credit	
7		300 00	13	Notes Receivable				7
8				Ernest Walters			300 00	8
9				Note Rec. No. 65.				9
10								10
11								11

Entry to record a note received on account

Collecting a note receivable and interest at maturity

When cash is received for interest, the amount received is debited to Cash and credited to an income account with the title *Interest Income.*

> October 1, 1968. *Received a check for $515.00 from Henry Saunders in settlement of his note and interest. Face of the note is $500.00.*

In this transaction the balance of the asset account Cash is increased; the balance of the asset account Notes Receivable is decreased; and the balance of Interest Income is increased. Cash is debited for $515.00; Notes Receivable is credited for $500.00; and Interest Income is credited for $15.00.

This transaction is recorded in the cash receipts journal below.

Cash 111	
515.00	

Notes Receivable 113	
	500.00

Interest Income 712	
	15.00

CASH RECEIPTS JOURNAL — PAGE 41

	Date	Account Credited	Post. Ref.	1 General Credit	2 Sales Credit	3 Sales Taxes Payable Credit	4 Accounts Receivable Credit	5 Cash Debit	
28	1	Notes Receivable		500 00					28
29		Interest Income		15 00				515 00	29
30									30
31									31
32									32

Entry to record the collection of principal and interest

Dishonored note receivable

A note that the maker refuses to pay, or is unable to pay, when it is due is called a *dishonored note*. The balance of the notes receivable account should show only the amount of those notes that probably will be collected. An amount of a dishonored note should therefore be removed from the notes receivable account. The amount of such a note is debited to the customer's account so that the account will show the total amount owed by the customer, including the amount of the dishonored note. This information may be important if the customer requests credit in the future.

March 29, 1968. L. C. Spence dishonors his note receivable for $300.00.

In this transaction the balances of the accounts receivable account in the general ledger and the customer's account in the accounts receivable ledger are increased $300.00. The balance of the notes receivable account is decreased $300.00. Accounts Receivable and the customer's account are each debited for $300.00 and Notes Receivable is credited for the same amount.

This transaction is recorded in the general journal as shown below.

GENERAL LEDGER

Accounts Receivable 115

Debit	Credit
300.00	

Notes Receivable 113

Debit	Credit
	300.00

ACCOUNTS RECEIVABLE LEDGER

L. C. Spence

Debit	Credit
300.00	

GENERAL JOURNAL PAGE 21

	1	2				3	4	
	ACCOUNTS PAYABLE DEBIT	GENERAL DEBIT	DATE	ACCOUNT TITLE	POST. REF.	GENERAL CREDIT	ACCOUNTS RECEIVABLE CREDIT	
9		300 00	29	Accounts Receivable/L.C. Spence	✓			9
10				Notes Receivable		300 00		10
11				To charge the L.C. Spence				11
12				account for dishonored				12
13				Note Rec. No. 64.				13
14								14
15								15
16								16
17								17

Entry to record a dishonored note receivable

If it is later decided that collection cannot be obtained from Mr. Spence, the balance of the account will be written off as a bad debt. At that time Allowance for Bad Debts will be debited and Accounts Receivable and L. C. Spence's account will be credited.

REPORTING THE RESULTS OF NOTES TRANSACTIONS

Classification of the two interest accounts in the general ledger

Interest Income does not result from the normal operation of a merchandising business. Therefore, it is reported as Other Income on the income statement. The account Interest Income is placed in the Other Income division of the general ledger.

Interest Expense is not an operating expense of a merchandising business. Therefore, it is reported as Other Expense on the income statement. The account Interest Expense is placed in the Other Expense division of the general ledger.

Interest accounts on the work sheet

The balance of Interest Income is always a credit balance. The balance of the interest income account always appears in the Trial Balance Credit column of the work sheet. The balance of the interest income account is extended into the Income Statement Credit column of the work sheet.

The balance of Interest Expense is always a debit balance. The balance of the interest expense account always appears in the Trial Balance Debit column of the work sheet. The balance of the interest expense account is extended into the Income Statement Debit column.

The balances of the two interest accounts are shown on the partial work sheet below.

			1	2	5	6
	ACCOUNT TITLES	ACCT. NO.	TRIAL BALANCE DEBIT	TRIAL BALANCE CREDIT	INCOME STATEMENT DEBIT	INCOME STATEMENT CREDIT
35	Salary Expense	619	10267 50		10267 50	
36	Supplies Expense	620			559 57	
37	Gain on Fixed Assets	711				
38	Interest Income	712		127 14		127 14
39	Loss on Fixed Assets	811	76 80		76 80	
40	Interest Expense	812	443 58		443 58	
41			142229 74	142229 74	55087 55	63597 34
42	Net Income				8509 79	
43					63597 34	63597 34

Interest Income and Interest Expense on the work sheet

Interest income and interest expense on the income statement

The work sheet is the source of data for preparing the income statement. The placement of the two interest accounts is shown on the partial income statement on the next page.

B. J. Taylor
Income Statement
For Year Ended December 31, 1968

Income from Sales:			
Sales			36168 43
...			
Salary Expense		10267 50	
Supplies Expense		559 57	
Total Operating Expenses			27265 40
Net Income from Operations			8903 03
Other Income			
Interest Income		127 14	
Other Expenses:			
Loss on Fixed Assets	76 80		
Interest Expense	443 58		
Total Other Expenses		520 38	
Net Subtraction			393 24
Net Income			8509 79

Interest Income and Interest Expense on the income statement

When the total amount of the Other Expenses section of the income statement exceeds the total amount of the Other Income section, the difference is labeled *Net Subtraction.* The amount of Net Subtraction is deducted from the amount of Net Income from Operations to obtain the amount of the Net Income.

Increasing Your Business Vocabulary

What is the meaning of each of the following:

a promissory note
b date of a note
c time of a note
d payee of a note
e principal of a note
f interest rate
g maturity date of a note
h maker of a note
i interest-bearing notes
j non-interest-bearing notes
k notes payable
l notes payable register
m bank discount
n proceeds
o notes receivable
p notes receivable register
q dishonored note

Study Questions

1. What are the two common uses of promissory notes?
2. What does "interest at 6%" mean?
3. What is the basic formula for calculating interest for less than a year when an interest table is not available?
4. What is the account classification of notes payable?
5. What accounts are debited and credited when money is borrowed from a bank on an interest-bearing note payable?
6. What accounts are debited and credited when an interest-bearing note payable is given for the purchase of office equipment?
7. What accounts are debited and credited when only the interest on a note payable is paid?
8. What accounts are debited and credited when a non-interest-bearing note payable is discounted at the bank and the payee issues a check for the amount of the discount?
9. What is the account classification of notes receivable?
10. What accounts are debited and credited when a note is accepted from a customer as extension of time on his account?
11. What accounts are debited and credited when a note receivable and interest are collected at maturity?
12. What accounts are debited and credited when a customer refuses to pay his note receivable?
13. Into what column of the work sheet is the balance of each of the following accounts extended: (a) Interest Income, (b) Interest Expense?
14. Under what heading on the income statement is each of the following accounts listed? (a) Interest Income, (b) Interest Expense?

Cases for Business Decision

CASE 1

Albert T. Cliff, a retail grocer, maintains a cash balance in his bank account sufficient to pay all his bills when they become due. Hank Blosser, another retail grocer, finds it necessary to borrow money from his bank at frequent intervals in order to pay his bills on time. Both merchants have an equal volume of sales. Which merchant is likely to receive a smaller net profit from his business? Why?

CASE 2

Henry Sisley, a dealer in farm equipment, receives a large number of notes. He has the Farmer's National Bank collect all his notes for him. What special columns would you advise Mr. Sisley to add to his cash receipts journal?

Drills for Understanding

DRILL 32-A Computing the maturity date and the interest

The Knodel Equipment Company holds five promissory notes that contain the following information:

No. of Note	Date of Note	Time	Interest Rate	Principal
411	March 1	1 month	6%	$200
412	March 1	60 days	5½%	400
413	March 12	6 months	5%	900
414	May 23	75 days	5¼%	500
415	August 4	30 days	4%	300

Instructions: Find for each of the notes above (a) the maturity date and (b) the interest.

DRILL 32-B Computing the discount and the proceeds

During the current year the Eagle Manufacturing Company discounts five of its own notes. Each note is discounted on the date of the note.

No. of Note	Date of Note	Date of Maturity	Discount Rate	Principal
21	January 1	January 31	6%	300
22	March 4	May 3	5%	600
23	March 15	April 29	4½%	2,000
24	May 28	August 26	6%	470
25	November 5	December 20	5¾%	300

Instructions: Find for each of the notes above (a) the number of days for which the note was discounted, (b) the amount of the discount, and (c) the proceeds.

Application Problem

PROBLEM 32-1 | Recording notes and interest

The transactions given below were selected from those completed by Steve Marsh, a used-car dealer, during the months of April, May, and June of the current year.

Instructions: 1. Record the following transactions, using a cash receipts journal (page 13), a cash payments journal (page 8), and a general journal (page 4) similar to those illustrated in this chapter.

Transactions

Apr. 1. Received Note Receivable No. 21 for $300.00 from Ruth Hyatt on account.
4. Issued Note Payable No. 15 for $2,500.00 to Triangle Motors for an extension of time on account.
8. Received Note Receivable No. 22 for $595.00 from Gene Waring on account.
15. Issued Note Payable No. 16 for $3,600.00 to the Billman Company for an extension of time on account.
26. Discounted at the First National Bank our Note Payable No. 17 for $1,000.00. The bank credited our checking account for the principal. Issued Check No. 87 for $10.00 in payment of the interest charged in advance.

May 6. Discounted at the First National Bank our Note Payable No. 18 for $5,000.00. The bank credited our checking account for the principal. Issued Check No. 95 for $20.83 in payment of the interest charged in advance.
8. Received a check for $595.00 from Gene Waring in payment of non-interest-bearing Note Receivable No. 22 for $595.00.
13. Received Note Receivable No. 23 for $300.00 from Walter Geier on account.
15. Issued Check No. 108 for $3,618.00 to the Billman Company in payment of Note Payable No. 16 for $3,600.00 plus $18.00 interest.
31. Received notice from the bank that Ruth Hyatt had refused to pay non-interest-bearing Note Receivable No. 21 for $300.00 when it became due on May 30. Charged the note to the account of the maker.

June 3. Issued Check No. 156 for $2,525.00 to Triangle Motors in payment of Note Payable No. 15 for $2,500.00 plus $25.00 interest.
5. Issued Check No. 161 for $5,000.00 to the First National Bank in payment of Note Payable No. 18 for $5,000.00.
11. Received a check for $301.25 from Walter Geier in payment of Note Receivable No. 23 for $300.00 plus $1.25 interest.
19. Received Note Receivable No. 24 for $1,750.00 from Darrell Lehman on account.
25. Issued Check No. 188 for $1,000.00 to the First National Bank in payment of Note Payable No. 17 for $1,000.00.

Instructions: 2. Foot and prove the columnar special journals.

Optional Problems

★ SUPPLEMENTARY PROBLEM 32-S

Calculating and recording interest and bank discount

The transactions given below were completed by A. N. Levy, a dealer in farm implements, during October of the current year.

Instructions: 1. Record the following transactions in a cash receipts journal (page 40) and a cash payments journal (page 32) similar to those illustrated in this chapter.

Transactions

Oct. 3. Issued Check No. 172 to O'Donnell Implement Co. in full payment of a 60-day, 5% interest-bearing note due today (Note Payable No. 41). Face of note, $600.00.

7. Discounted at the Farmers Bank our 30-day, non-interest-bearing note (Note Payable No. 45). Face of note, $400.00. Rate of discount, 6%. Our checking account was credited for the principal. Issued Check No. 175 for $2.00 in payment of the interest charged in advance.

8. Received a check from Lester Clum in payment of the principal and interest on a 20-day, 5% interest-bearing note due today (Note Receivable No. 78). Face of note, $240.00.

10. Issued Check No. 178 to the City National Bank in payment of the principal and interest on a 90-day, 4% interest-bearing note due today (Note Payable No. 36). Face of note, $1,000.00.

15. Discounted at the Farmers Bank our 90-day, non-interest-bearing note (Note Payable No. 46). Face of note, $1,500.00. Rate of discount, 6%. Our checking account was credited for the principal. Issued Check No. 179 for $22.50 in payment of the interest charged in advance.

17. Received a check from Paul Mersch in full settlement of his 180-day, 6% interest-bearing note due today (Note Receivable No. 61). Face of note, $500.00.

18. Issued Check No. 186 to Behr Manufacturing Co. in full payment of the principal and interest on a 60-day, 3% interest-bearing note due today (Note Payable No. 42). Face of note, $648.50.

24. Discounted at the Farmers Bank our 20-day, non-interest-bearing note (Note Payable No. 47). Face of note, $600.00. Rate of discount, 6%. Our checking account was credited for the principal. Issued Check No. 190 for $2.00 in payment of the interest charged in advance.

25. Received a check from George Elmore in payment of the principal and interest on a 30-day, 5% interest-bearing note due today (Note Receivable No. 79). Face of note, $540.80.

28. Issued Check No. 195 to Harvester Corporation in full payment of the principal and interest on a 90-day, 4% interest-bearing note due today (Note Payable No. 38). Face of note, $800.00.

28. Received a check from Barry Guy in full settlement of his 90-day, 6% interest-bearing note due today (Note Receivable No. 72). Face of note, $485.00.

Instructions: 2. Foot and prove the columnar special journals.

★BONUS PROBLEM 32-B

Calculating and recording interest and bank discount

Instructions: 1. Record the following selected transactions completed by R. Craig Lockwood during the current fiscal year. Use a cash receipts journal (page 60), a cash payments journal (page 46), and a general journal (page 32) similar to those illustrated in this chapter.

Transactions

Jan. 2. Received from Randall Roberts a 90-day, 6% note (Note Receivable No. 84) for $400.00 dated December 28, on account.

8. Received from Doyle Smith a 30-day, 6% note (Note Receivable No. 85) for $300.00, dated January 7, on account.

24. Issued a 30-day, 6% note (Note Payable No. 1) for $750.00 to Samson Company for an extension of time on account.

Feb. 6. Received a check from Doyle Smith in payment of the principal and the interest on Note Receivable No. 85 due today.

23. Issued Check No. 63 to Samson Company in payment of the principal and the interest on Note Payable No. 1 due today.

Mar. 5. Issued a 90-day, 5% note (Note Payable No. 2) for $2,500.00 to Thayer Company for an extension of time on account.

11. Purchased office equipment from the Lang Company for $2,000.00 Issued Check No. 88 for $500.00 and a 60-day, 4% note (Note Payable No. 3) for $1,500.00. (Record the entire transaction in the general journal and the payment in the cash payments journal. Insert check marks where necessary so that duplicate posting will be avoided.)

29. Received notice from the bank that Randall Roberts dishonored Note Receivable No. 84 when it became due on March 28. Charged the principal and the interest to Roberts' account.

May 6. Discounted at the Lincoln National Bank our 30-day, non-interest-bearing note (Note Payable No. 4). Face of note, $900.00, rate of discount, 6%. Our checking account was credited for the principal. Issued Check No. 94 in payment of the interest charged in advance.

10. Issued Check No. 103 to the Lang Company in payment of the principal and the interest on Note Payable No. 3 due today.

June 3. Issued Check No. 146 to Thayer Company in payment of the principal and the interest on Note Payable No. 2 due today.

5. Issued Check No. 151 to the Lincoln National Bank in payment of Note Payable No. 4 due today.

Oct. 15. Received a check for 50% of the $406.00 balance owed by Randall Roberts (see March 29 transaction). Wrote off the remainder of the account as uncollectible. (Record the cash receipt in the cash receipts journal in the usual manner. Record the write-off of the remainder of the account in the general journal.)

Instructions: 2. Foot and prove the columnar special journals.

CHAPTER 33 | ACCRUED INCOME AND ACCRUED EXPENSES

ACCRUED INCOME

At the end of each fiscal period, many businesses find that they have incomes that have been earned during the fiscal period but have not been recorded. A common example is interest income that has been earned but which cannot be collected until the due date in the next fiscal period. If the business has many notes receivable, the interest earned but not collected may be a sizable sum.

Income earned in one fiscal period but collected in a later fiscal period is called *accrued income.* At the end of each fiscal period, all accrued income should be recorded as an adjusting entry *before* the financial reports are prepared. Without this adjusting entry, the financial reports will not be accurate.

Need for recording accrued income

The Simpson Company has a note receivable in the amount of $1,000.00, with interest at 6% due November 1, 1968, and May 1, 1969. Cash was received for the interest income due on November 1, 1968, and the transaction was recorded. At the end of the 1968 fiscal year, there are two months' additional interest income earned ($10.00) but not collected. Interest earned but not collected is called *accrued interest income.*

The accrued interest income accumulated to December 31, 1968, will not be received until the next interest due date, May 1, 1969. However, the amount of the accrued interest income should be included on the financial reports of 1968. If an adjusting entry for the accrued interest income is not recorded and posted:

1. The 1968 total income and the net income will be understated on the 1968 income statement.
2. The total assets and the proprietorship as of December 31, 1968, will be understated on the 1968 balance sheet.
3. The 1969 total income and the net income will be overstated on the 1969 income statement.

Simpson
Work
For Year Ended

	1	2
ACCOUNT TITLES	ACCT. NO.	TRIAL BALANCE DEBIT	TRIAL BALANCE CREDIT

	ACCOUNT TITLES	ACCT. NO.	TRIAL BALANCE DEBIT	TRIAL BALANCE CREDIT
4	Interest Receivable	114		
44	Interest Income	712		67 00

Accrued interest income

Recording accrued interest income

The bookkeeper for the Simpson Company records the accrued interest income on December 31, 1968, as follows:

Step 1

Make the adjustment for accrued interest income in the Adjustments columns of the work sheet.

a Debit Interest Receivable, a current asset, for $10.00 and credit Interest Income for $10.00.

b Extend the debit balance of the interest receivable account, $10.00, to the Balance Sheet Debit column.

c Extend the sum of the interest income credit balance in the Trial Balance Credit column, $67.00, and the credit amount in the Adjustments Credit column, $10.00, to the Income Statement Credit column, $77.00.

Step 2

Record an adjusting entry in the general journal for accrued interest income, $10.00. Use the information written in the two Adjustments columns of the work sheet.

GENERAL JOURNAL PAGE 42

	1 ACCOUNTS PAYABLE DEBIT	2 GENERAL DEBIT	DATE	ACCOUNT TITLE	POST. REF.	3 GENERAL CREDIT	4 ACCOUNTS RECEIVABLE CREDIT	
11		10 00	31	Interest Receivable				11
12				Interest Income		10 00		12
13								13
14								14

Adjusting entry for accrued interest income

Company
Sheet
December 31, 1968

Adjustments Debit (3)	Adjustments Credit (4)	Income Statement Debit (5)	Income Statement Credit (6)	Balance Sheet Debit (7)	Balance Sheet Credit (8)	
(g) 1000				1000		4
	(g) 1000		7700			44

on the work sheet

Step 3

Post the adjusting entry for accrued interest income to the two accounts in the general ledger, Interest Receivable and Interest Income.

Interest Receivable — ACCOUNT NO. 114

Date	Items	Post. Ref.	Debit	Credit	Balance Debit	Balance Credit
1968 Dec. 31		J42	1000		1000	

Interest Income — ACCOUNT NO. 712

Date	Items	Post. Ref.	Debit	Credit	Balance Debit	Balance Credit
1968 Dec. 1		✓				6700
31		J42		1000		7700

Accounts affected by accrued interest income

Step 4

List the balance of the interest receivable account, $10.00, in the Current Assets section of the balance sheet.

Assets			
Current Assets			
Cash		5612 00	
Petty Cash		150 00	
Notes Receivable		1000 00	
Interest Receivable		10 00	
Accounts Receivable	4615 00		
Less Allowance for Bad Debts	531 00	4084 00	

Interest Receivable on the balance sheet

Step 5

List the balance of the interest income account, $77.00, in the Other Income section of the income statement.

Other Income:			
Gain on Fixed Assets	120 60		
Interest Income	77 00		
Total Other Income		197 60	
Other Expenses:			
Loss on Fixed Assets	152 00		
Interest Expense	170 00		
Total Other Expenses		322 00	
Net Subtraction			124 40
Net Income			22571 00

Other Income section of the income statement

Step 6

Close the balance of the interest income account, $77.00, into the Income and Expense Summary account.

a Debit Interest Income for $77.00 in the combined entry that closes all accounts having credit balances in the Income Statement Credit column (except the Income and Expense Summary Credit balance).

b Credit Income and Expense Summary for the total of all the accounts having credit balances in the Income Statement Credit column (except the Income and Expense Summary Credit balance).

GENERAL JOURNAL PAGE 42

	1 ACCOUNTS PAYABLE DEBIT	2 GENERAL DEBIT	DATE	ACCOUNT TITLE	POST. REF.	3 GENERAL CREDIT	4 ACCOUNTS RECEIVABLE CREDIT	
21				Closing Entries				21
22		71347 00	31	Sales				22
23		1076 00		Purchases Returns & Allowances				23
24		2480 00		Purchases Discount				24
25		120 60		Gain on Fixed Assets				25
26		77 00		Interest Income				26
27				Income & Expense Summary		75100 60		27
28								28
29								29
30								30

Closing entry for interest income account

Need for readjusting the interest receivable and the interest income accounts

When the Simpson Company has many notes receivable, there are many times during the fiscal period that cash is collected for interest income. Each time interest is collected during the year, it is inconvenient for the bookkeeper to refer back to previous entries to determine: (a) how much interest income was earned during the previous fiscal period and should now be credited to Interest Receivable, and (b) how much interest income was earned during the current fiscal period and should be credited to Interest Income. All this labor on each interest income transaction can be eliminated by transferring the balance of the interest receivable account as a debit to the interest income account.

The interest receivable and the interest income accounts are readjusted with a simple readjusting entry at the *beginning* of the fiscal period. A journal entry made at the beginning of a new fiscal period to readjust an adjusting entry made at the end of the preceding fiscal period is called a *reversing entry.*

After the reversing entry for interest income has been recorded and posted, every interest income transaction throughout the year is handled by simply debiting cash and crediting interest income for the full amount of cash received. Through the use of reversing entries for accrued income, it is not necessary to refer to the ledger and do extra calculating every time there is an interest income transaction.

Reversing entry for accrued interest income

The reversing entry for accrued interest income transfers the debit balance of the interest receivable account as a debit to the interest income account as shown on the next page.

GENERAL JOURNAL — PAGE 43

	1 ACCOUNTS PAYABLE DEBIT	2 GENERAL DEBIT	DATE		ACCOUNT TITLE	POST. REF.	3 GENERAL CREDIT	4 ACCOUNTS RECEIVABLE CREDIT	
1					Reversing Entries				1
2		10 00	1969 Jan.	2	Interest Income				2
3					Interest Receivable		10 00		3
4									4
5									5

Reversing entry for accrued interest income

The readjusting entry above is called a reversing entry because it is the reverse of the original adjusting entry. Compare this reversing entry with the adjusting entry on page 584 that is being readjusted.

Posting the reversing entry for accrued interest income

After the reversing entry above is posted, the two accounts in the general ledger, Interest Receivable and Interest Income, appear as follows:

Interest Receivable — ACCOUNT NO. 114

DATE		ITEMS	POST. REF.	DEBIT	CREDIT	BALANCE DEBIT	BALANCE CREDIT
1968 Dec.	31		J42	10 00		10 00	
1969 Jan.	2		J43		10 00	———	———

Interest Income — ACCOUNT NO. 712

DATE		ITEMS	POST. REF.	DEBIT	CREDIT	BALANCE DEBIT	BALANCE CREDIT
1968 Dec.	1		✓				67 00
	31		J42		10 00		77 00
	31		J42	77 00		———	———
1969 Jan.	2		J43	10 00		10 00	

Accounts after posting the reversing entry for accrued interest income

Effect of posting the reversing entry for accrued interest income

The interest receivable account shown above has a zero balance at the beginning of the new 1969 fiscal period. The interest receivable account will not receive any entries until it is needed for an adjusting entry for accrued interest income at the end of the 1969 fiscal period. The interest receivable account is needed for only one day each year, just long enough to prepare complete financial reports.

The interest income account illustrated on page 588 is debited at the beginning of the new 1969 fiscal period for the amount of interest income that belongs to the 1968 fiscal period but which will be collected in 1969. During 1969 the interest income account will be credited each time cash is received for interest income. At the end of the 1969 fiscal period, the credit balance will show the amount of interest income that belongs to the 1969 fiscal period. Then, at the end of the 1969 fiscal period there will be new accrued interest income, earned in 1969 but not collected in 1969. The accrued interest income on December 31, 1969, will be recorded in the same manner as the accrued interest income on December 31, 1968.

ACCRUED EXPENSES

At the end of each fiscal period, many businesses find that there are expenses that have been accumulating each day. Since these expenses have not been paid, they have not been recorded. A common example of such an accumulating expense is the interest expense that is not due until the next fiscal period. An expense that is incurred in one fiscal period but not paid during that period is called an *accrued expense.* Examples of accrued expenses are accrued interest expense and accrued salary expense.

Need for recording accrued interest expense

The income statement at the close of each fiscal period should show all the expenses for the period even though some have not been paid. Also, since accrued expenses are liabilities, they should appear on the balance sheet.

The Simpson Company owes a $3,000.00 note payable, with interest at 6%. The interest is payable September 1, 1968, and March 1, 1969. The ledger shows that the interest expense due on this note payable on September 1 was paid and recorded. However, at the end of the 1968 fiscal period, four months' interest expense on this note payable has accumulated that has not been paid and therefore has not been recorded. Interest incurred but not paid is called *accrued interest expense.*

The accrued interest expense from September 1 through December 31, $60.00, will not be paid until March 1, 1969, but this is really 1968 interest expense and should be included in the 1968 financial reports. The same steps used in recording accrued interest income are used in recording accrued interest expense.

			Simpson Work For Year Ended	
			1	2
	ACCOUNT TITLES	ACCT. NO.	TRIAL BALANCE DEBIT	CREDIT
15	Interest Payable	212		
46	Interest Expense	812	110 00	

Accrued interest expense

Recording accrued interest expense

The bookkeeper for the Simpson Company records the accrued interest expense on December 31, 1968, as follows:

Step 1

Make the adjustment for accrued interest expense in the Adjustments columns of the work sheet.

a Debit Interest Expense for $60.00, and credit Interest Payable for $60.00.

b Extend the credit balance of the interest payable account, $60.00, to the Balance Sheet Credit column.

c Extend the sum of the interest expense debit balance in the Trial Balance Debit column, $110.00, and the debit amount in the Adjustments Debit column, $60.00, to the Income Statement Debit column, $170.00.

Step 2

Record an adjusting entry in the general journal for accrued interest expense, $60.00. Use the information written in the two Adjustments columns of the work sheet.

GENERAL JOURNAL — PAGE 42

	1	2				3	4	
	ACCOUNTS PAYABLE DEBIT	GENERAL DEBIT	DATE	ACCOUNT TITLE	POST. REF.	GENERAL CREDIT	ACCOUNTS RECEIVABLE CREDIT	
13		60 00	31	Interest Expense				13
14				Interest Payable		60 00		14
15								15
16								16

Adjusting entry for accrued interest expense

Company Sheet December 31, 1968							
3	4	5	6	7	8		
ADJUSTMENTS		INCOME STATEMENT		BALANCE SHEET			
DEBIT	CREDIT	DEBIT	CREDIT	DEBIT	CREDIT		
	(h) 6000				6000	15	
(h) 6000		17000				46	

on the work sheet

Step 3

Post the adjusting entry for accrued interest expense to the two accounts in the general ledger, Interest Payable and Interest Expense.

Interest Payable ACCOUNT NO. 212

DATE		ITEMS	POST. REF.	DEBIT	CREDIT	BALANCE DEBIT	BALANCE CREDIT
1968 Dec.	31		J42		60 00		60 00

Interest Expense ACCOUNT NO. 812

DATE		ITEMS	POST. REF.	DEBIT	CREDIT	BALANCE DEBIT	BALANCE CREDIT
1968 Dec.	1	Balance	✓			110 00	
	31		J42	60 00		170 00	

Accounts affected by accrued interest expense

Step 4

List the balance of the interest payable account, $60.00, in the Current Liabilities section of the balance sheet. Obtain this information from the work sheet.

Liabilities		
Current Liabilities		
Notes Payable	3000 00	
Interest Payable	60 00	
Salaries Payable	240 00	
Accounts Payable	3233 00	

Partial Current Liabilities section of balance sheet

Step 5

List the balance of the interest expense account, $170.00, in the Other Expenses section of the income statement.

Other Income:			
Gain on Fixed Assets	120 60		
Interest Income	77 00		
Total Other Income		197 60	
Other Expenses:			
Loss on Fixed Assets	152 00		
Interest Expense	170 00		
Total Other Expenses		322 00	
Net Deduction			124 40
Net Income			22,571 00

Other Income and Other Expenses section of the income statement

Step 6

Close the balance of the interest expense account, $170.00, into the Income and Expense Summary account.

a Debit Income and Expense Summary for the total of all the accounts having debit balances in the Income Statement Debit column (except the Income and Expense Summary debit balance).

b Credit Interest Expense for $170.00, in the combined entry that closes all accounts having debit balances in the Income Statement Debit column (except the Income and Expense Summary debit balance).

GENERAL JOURNAL PAGE 42

	1 Accounts Payable Debit	2 General Debit	Date	Account Title	Post. Ref.	3 General Credit	4 Accounts Receivable Credit	
29		59,139 00	31	Income and Expense Summary				29
30				Sales Returns and Allowances		1,755 84		30
31				Sales Discount		1,530 00		31
46				Loss on Fixed Assets		152 00		46
47				Interest Expense		170 00		47
48								48
49								49
50								50

Closing entry for interest expense account

Need for readjusting the interest payable and the interest expense accounts

Each time interest is paid during the year, it is inconvenient for the bookkeeper to refer back to previous entries and split the debit amount between (a) interest expense and (b) interest payable. All this extra labor on each interest expense transaction is eliminated if the interest payable account is readjusted by having its credit balance transferred as a credit of the interest expense account.

As in the case of accrued interest income, the interest payable account and the interest expense account are readjusted on the first day of the new fiscal period through a reversing entry.

Reversing entry for accrued interest expense

The reversing entry for accrued interest expense transfers the credit balance of the interest payable account as a credit to the interest expense account as follows:

GENERAL JOURNAL — PAGE 43

	1 Accounts Payable Debit	2 General Debit	Date	Account Title	Post. Ref.	3 General Credit	4 Accounts Receivable Credit	
4		60 00	2	Interest Payable				4
5				Interest Expense		60 00		5
6								6

Reversing entry for accrued interest expense

Posting the reversing entry for accrued interest expense

After the reversing entry for accrued interest expense is posted, the two accounts in the general ledger, Interest Payable and Interest Expense, appear as follows:

Interest Payable — ACCOUNT NO. 212

Date	Items	Post. Ref.	Debit	Credit	Balance Debit	Balance Credit
1968 Dec. 31		J42		60 00		60 00
1969 Jan. 2		J43	60 00		—	—

Interest Expense — ACCOUNT NO. 812

Date	Items	Post. Ref.	Debit	Credit	Balance Debit	Balance Credit
1968 Dec. 1	Balance	✓			110 00	
31		J42	60 00		170 00	
31		J42		170 00	—	—
1969 Jan. 2		J43		60 00		60 00

Accounts after posting reversing entry for accrued interest expense

Effect of posting the reversing entry for accrued interest expense

The interest payable account on page 593 has a zero balance at the beginning of the new 1969 fiscal period. Like the interest receivable account, the interest payable account will not receive any entries until it is needed for an adjusting entry for accrued interest expense at the end of the 1969 fiscal period. Like the interest receivable account, the interest payable account is needed for only one day each year, just long enough to prepare complete financial reports.

The interest expense account illustrated on page 593 is credited at the beginning of the new 1969 fiscal period for the amount of interest expense that belongs to the 1968 fiscal period. This amount will be paid in 1969.

During 1969 the interest expense account will be debited each time cash is paid for interest expense. At the end of the 1969 fiscal period, the debit balance will show the amount of interest expense that belongs to the 1969 fiscal period. Then, at the end of the 1969 fiscal period there will be new accrued interest expense, accumulated in 1969 but not paid in 1969. The new accrued interest expense on December 31, 1969, will be handled in the same manner as the accrued interest expense on December 31, 1968.

Accrued salary expense

The Simpson Company pays all employees every Friday. At the end of the fiscal period, Tuesday, December 31, 1968, two fifths of the weekly payroll for the week ending January 3, 1969, is owed to employees as shown on the calendar at the right. The amount owed for salaries earned by em- employees but not paid at the end of the 1968 fiscal period should show as a liability on the December 31, 1968, balance sheet. The amount of the salary expense accrued but not paid should show on the income statement for 1968. All of this requires an adjusting entry for two days' accrued salary expense.

1968			DECEMBER			1968
S	M	T	W	T	F	S
1	2	3	4	5	6	7
8	9	10	11	12	13	14
15	16	17	18	19	20	21
22	23	24	25	26	27	28
29	30	31 ← End of 1968 fiscal period				
1969			JANUARY			1969
Start of 1969 fiscal period →			1	2	3	4

Adjusting entry for accrued salary expense

The accumulated payroll of the Simpson Company for the last two days in 1968, Monday, December 30, and Tuesday, December 31, is $240.00. At the end of the 1968 fiscal period, the bookkeeper makes an adjusting entry from the adjustment previously made on the work sheet on December 31. This adjusting entry is shown at the top of the next page.

GENERAL JOURNAL PAGE 42

	1 ACCOUNTS PAYABLE DEBIT	2 GENERAL DEBIT	DATE	ACCOUNT TITLE	POST. REF.	3 GENERAL CREDIT	4 ACCOUNTS RECEIVABLE CREDIT	
15		240 00	31	Salary Expense				15
16				Salaries Payable		240 00		16
17								17
18								18
19								19

Adjusting entry for accrued salary expense

In the adjusting entry for accrued salary expense, the salary expense account is debited for $240.00 so that the debit to this account will include the salary expense for 1968 that is accrued but not paid. This amount is added to the other 52 debits recorded during the year. Only in this manner will the income statement show the actual salary expense for the 1968 fiscal year.

The salaries payable account is credited for $240.00 so that the liability section of the 1968 balance sheet will show all the liabilities as of December 31, 1968.

Posting the adjusting entry for accrued salary expense

After the adjusting entry for accrued salary expense is posted, the two accounts in the general ledger, Salaries Payable and Salary Expense, appear as follows:

Salaries Payable — ACCOUNT NO. 213

DATE	ITEMS	POST. REF.	DEBIT	CREDIT	BALANCE DEBIT	BALANCE CREDIT
1968 Dec. 31		J42		240 00		240 00

Salary Expense — ACCOUNT NO. 619

DATE	ITEMS	POST. REF.	DEBIT	CREDIT	BALANCE DEBIT	BALANCE CREDIT
1968 Dec. 1	Balance	✓			28,127 00	
31		CP12	2,557 00		30,684 00	
31		J42	240 00		30,924 00	

Accounts after posting the adjusting entry for accrued salary expense

The credit balance of the Salaries Payable account, $240.00, shows the total amount owed for all salaries that have been earned but not paid at the end of the 1968 fiscal year. The debit balance of the Salary Expense account, $30,924.00, shows the total salary expense for the 1968 fiscal year. This balance includes the total salaries paid in cash during the year plus the additional accrued salary expense for the last two days of the 1968 fiscal period.

Like the balance of the interest payable account, the balance of the salaries payable account is listed in the Current Liabilities section of the balance sheet. The balance of the salary expense account is listed in the Operating Expenses section of the income statement. The balance of the salary expense account is closed into the income and expense summary account as part of the same combined entry in which the balance of the interest expense account is closed.

Need for readjusting the salary expense account

When the Simpson Company makes the entry for the next payroll on January 3, 1969, the entire amount will be debited to Salary Expense in the same manner as the payment of each payroll in 1968. But the salaries for only the first three days of January should be shown as an expense for the fiscal year 1969. This result can be obtained by recording a reversing entry at the beginning of the 1969 fiscal period.

Reversing entry for accrued salary expense

On January 2, 1969, the following entry is made to readjust the salary expense account:

GENERAL JOURNAL — PAGE 43

	1 Accounts Payable Debit	2 General Debit	Date	Account Title	Post. Ref.	3 General Credit	4 Accounts Receivable Credit	
6		240 00	2	Salaries Payable				6
7				Salary Expense		240 00		7
8								8
9								9
10								10
11								11
12								12
13								13
14								14

Reversing entry for accrued salary expense

Through this entry Salaries Payable is debited for $240.00, the amount of the accrued salary expense for the preceding fiscal period, the year 1968. Salary Expense is credited for the same amount. This reversing entry is exactly the opposite of the adjusting entry for accrued salary expense recorded on December 31, 1968.

Increasing Your Business Vocabulary

What is the meaning of each of the following:

a accrued income

b accrued interest income

c reversing entry

d accrued expense

e accrued interest expense

Study Questions

1. What is the effect upon the financial statements of a business if an adjusting entry for accrued interest income is not recorded and posted?
2. What entry is made in the general journal to record the adjusting entry for accrued interest income?
3. Under what heading on the income statement is the balance of the interest income account listed?
4. Under what heading on the balance sheet is the balance of the interest receivable account listed?
5. Why are the interest receivable and the interest income accounts readjusted at the beginning of a new fiscal period?
6. After the reversing entry for interest income has been recorded and posted, how is each interest income transaction handled throughout the year?
7. Why is there a need for recording accrued interest expense at the close of each fiscal period?
8. What entry is made in the general journal to record the adjusting entry for accrued interest expense?
9. Under what heading on the balance sheet is the balance of the interest payable account listed?
10. Why is it necessary to readjust the interest payable and the interest expense accounts at the beginning of each new fiscal period?
11. Why is there a need for recording accrued salary expense at the close of each fiscal period?
12. What reversing entry is made in the general journal to readjust the salary expense account?

Cases for Business Decision

CASE 1

At the end of the fiscal period, the bookkeeper for the Diamond Safe Company failed to record $200.00 arising from accrued interest income. What effect does this omission have (a) on the income statement and (b) on the balance sheet?

CASE 2

After Vance P. Drew closed his books on March 31, his ledger included two liability accounts, Salaries Payable and Interest Payable. All the salaries payable will be paid within three days after the beginning of the next fiscal period. The interest payable has accrued on five notes that will come due on different dates during the next period. For which of these two liabilities will a reversing entry be more beneficial?

Application Problems

PROBLEM 33-1 **Adjusting, closing, and reversing entries for accrued income and accrued expenses**

The following selected accounts from the ledger of Carl Zeiss contain the balances shown below on December 31 of the current year:

Acct. No.	*Account Title*	*Account Balance* Debit	Credit
114	Interest Receivable	——	——
212	Interest Payable	——	——
213	Salaries Payable	——	——
313	Income and Expense Summary	——	——
619	Salary Expense	$6,370.00	——
712	Interest Income	——	$212.00
812	Interest Expense	87.50	——

On December 31, accrued interest income on a note receivable is $19.50; accrued salaries are $121.00; and accrued interest on the two notes payable outstanding amounts to $43.60.

Instructions: 1. Open the general ledger accounts listed above and record the balances.

2. Record on page 34 of a columnar general journal as of December 31 the adjusting entries for the accrued income and the accrued expenses.

3. Post the adjusting entries to the ledger accounts.

4. Record in the columnar general journal the entries to close the interest income account and the salary expense and interest expense accounts.

5. Post the closing entries.

6. Record the reversing entries on January 2 of the new year.

7. Post the reversing entries to the ledger accounts.

PROBLEM 33-2 | Work at the end of the fiscal period

The account numbers, titles, and balances in the general ledger of Carriage Trade, a dress shop owned and operated by Helen DeMaris, on December 31 of the current year are given below and on the next page.

Acct. No.	*Account Title*	*Account Balance* *Debit*	*Credit*
111	Cash	$6,036.28	——
112	Petty Cash	75.00	——
113	Notes Receivable	500.00	——
114	Interest Receivable	——	——
115	Accounts Receivable	4,615.40	——
115.1	Allowance for Bad Debts	——	$ 168.15
116	Merchandise Inventory	10,648.82	——
117	Supplies	810.55	——
118	Prepaid Insurance	636.00	——
121	Equipment	2,137.50	——
121.1	Accumulated Depreciation — Equipment	——	613.49
122	Building	10,000.00	——
122.1	Accumulated Depreciation — Building	——	1,250.00
211	Notes Payable	——	2,000.00
212	Interest Payable	——	——
213	Salaries Payable	——	——
214	Accounts Payable	——	3,233.75
215	Employees Income Taxes Payable	——	191.40
216	FICA Taxes Payable	——	93.78
217	State Unemployment Taxes Payable	——	40.50
218	Federal Unemployment Taxes Payable	——	47.36
219	Sales Taxes Payable	——	137.04
311	Helen DeMaris, Capital	——	14,957.00
312	Helen DeMaris, Drawing	3,600.00	——
313	Income and Expense Summary		——
411	Sales	——	70,157.88
411.1	Sales Returns and Allowances	566.40	——
511	Purchases	41,898.71	——
511.1	Purchases Returns and Allowances	——	436.00
511.2	Purchases Discount	——	802.30

Acct. No.	*Account Title*	*Account Balance Debit*	*Credit*
611	Advertising Expense	1,875.00	——
612	Bad Debts Expense	——	——
613	Delivery Expense	1,710.60	——
614	Depreciation Expense — Building	——	——
615	Depreciation Expense — Equipment	——	——
616	Insurance Expense	——	——
617	Miscellaneous Expense	579.58	——
618	Payroll Tax Expense	392.20	——
619	Salary Expense	5,920.00	——
620	Supplies Expense	——	——
621	Utilities Expense	1,953.27	——
711	Interest Income	——	15.00
811	Interest Expense	172.14	——
812	Cash Short and Over	16.20	——

The additional data needed at the end of the period are:

Accrued interest income, $7.50
Additional allowance for bad debts, 1% of total charge sales of $36,330.20.
Merchandise inventory, December 31, $8,633.75
Supplies inventory, $254.12
Value of insurance policies, $136.00
Annual amount of estimated depreciation of equipment, $155.30
Annual amount of estimated depreciation of building, $500.00
Accrued interest expense, $20.00
Accrued salary expense, $148.50

Instructions: 1. Prepare an eight-column work sheet for the annual fiscal period ended December 31 of the current year.

2. Prepare an income statement, a capital statement, and a balance sheet.

3. Record the adjusting entries and the closing entries in a columnar general journal.

4. Record the reversing entries for the accruals as of January 2 of next year in a columnar general journal.

Optional Problems

★SUPPLEMENTARY PROBLEM 33-S

Adjusting, closing, and reversing entries for accrued income and accrued expenses

The following selected accounts from the ledger of Marvin Penn contain the balances shown below on December 31 of the current fiscal year before adjusting entries are made:

Acct. No.	*Account Title*	*Account Balance Debit*	*Account Balance Credit*
113	Interest Receivable	——	——
115	Prepaid Insurance	$ 360.00	——
212	Interest Payable	——	——
214	Salaries Payable	——	——
313	Income and Expense Summary	——	——
612	Insurance Expense	——	——
618	Salary Expense	12,635.00	——
711	Interest Income	——	$48.00
811	Interest Expense	110.00	——

Adjustment information at December 31 includes the following:

(a) Accrued interest has been earned on a 90-day, 5% note for $150.00 dated November 15.

(b) The $360.00 in the prepaid insurance account was the premium paid on July 1 covering a two-year period.

(c) Accrued salaries payable are $218.00.

(d) Accrued interest is payable on a 120-day, 6% note for $2,000.00 dated December 1.

Instructions: 1. Open the ledger accounts and record the balances.

2. Record on page 12 of a columnar general journal as of December 31 the adjusting entries for the accrued income and the prepaid expenses and the accrued expenses. Post to the ledger accounts.

3. Record the entries to close the income account and the expense accounts. Post the closing entries to the ledger accounts.

4. Record and post the reversing entries on January 2 of the new year.

* BONUS PROBLEM 33-B

Adjusting, closing, and reversing entries for accrued expenses and accrued income

The following selected accounts from the ledger of Neal Turpin contain the balances shown below on December 31 of the current fiscal year before adjusting entries are made:

Acct. No.	*Account Title*	*Account Balance Debit*	*Credit*
114	Interest Receivable	——	——
115	Rent Receivable	——	——
214	Salaries Payable	——	——
313	Income and Expense Summary	——	——
618	Salary Expense	$24,312.00	——
711	Interest Income	——	——
712	Rent Income	——	$1,000.00

Adjustment information at December 31 includes the following:

(a) Accrued interest has been earned on a 60-day, 6% note for $4,000.00 dated November 16.

(b) Accrued rent receivable amounts to $200.00.

(c) Accrued salaries payable are $187.00.

Instructions: 1. Open the ledger accounts and record the balances.

2. Record on page 19 of a columnar general journal as of December 31 the adjusting entries for the accrued income and for the accrued expenses. Post to the ledger accounts available.

3. Record the entries to close the income accounts and the expense account. Post to the ledger accounts.

4. Record and post the reversing entries on January 2 of the new year.

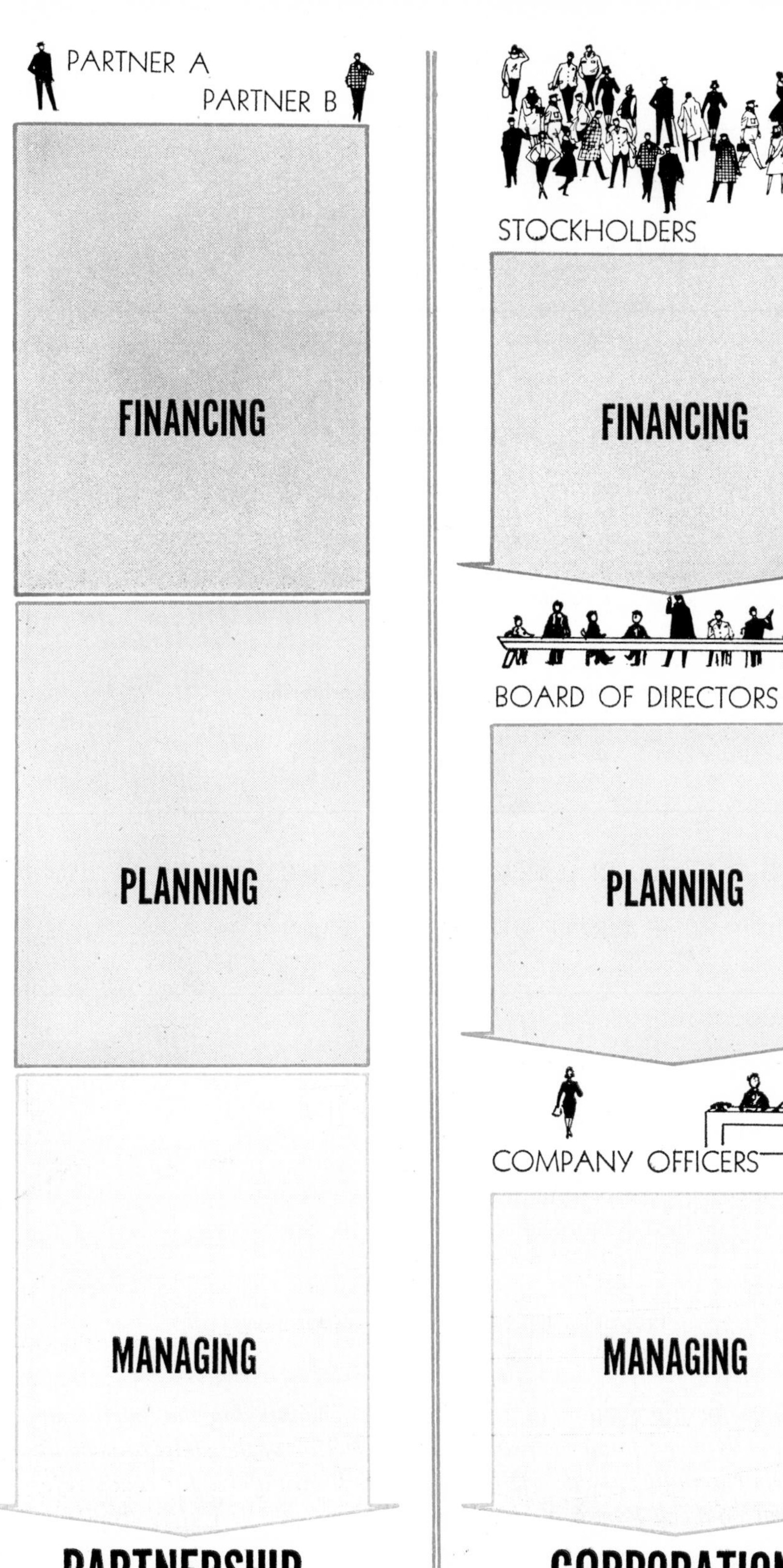
PARTNER A
PARTNER B
FINANCING
PLANNING
MANAGING
PARTNERSHIP
STOCKHOLDERS
FINANCING
BOARD OF DIRECTORS
PLANNING
COMPANY OFFICERS
MANAGING
CORPORATION

ELLIS AND SIMS

CHART OF ACCOUNTS

(3) PROPRIETORSHIP

311 R. L. Ellis, Capital
312 R. L. Ellis, Drawing
313 T. S. Sims, Capital
314 T. S. Sims, Drawing
315 Income and Expense Summary

Proprietorship accounts of a partnership

HENDRY MANUFACTURING COMPANY

CHART OF ACCOUNTS

(3) PROPRIETORSHIP

311 Capital Stock
312 Retained Earnings
313 Income and Expense Summary

Proprietorship accounts of a corporation

The proprietorship section of the chart of accounts for the partnership discussed in Chapter 34 and the proprietorship section of the chart of accounts for the corporation discussed in Chapter 35 are shown above for ready reference in your study of Part 6 of this book.

CHAPTER 34 PARTNERSHIPS

Some businesses, in order to be successful, require more money and different management skills than a single proprietor is able to furnish. In such cases, two or more persons may become the owners of a business and combine their assets and their abilities.

The form of business organization in which two or more persons combine their property or their skills and agree to share in the profits or the losses is a *partnership*. Each member of a partnership is known as a *partner*. Partnerships are common in retail stores, in personal service businesses, and among professional people such as doctors, lawyers, and accountants.

FORMING A PARTNERSHIP

Organizing a partnership

A partnership is formed by the completion of a contract between the partners. This contract may be oral. However, it is desirable to have the contract in writing. A written contract avoids any misunderstandings that might arise from an oral agreement. The written agreement by which a partnership is formed is called the *articles of copartnership*.

The articles of copartnership usually include:

1. The names of the partners, and the duties and rights of each.
2. The name, location, and kind of business.
3. The amount to be invested by each partner, and the agreed values of items invested other than cash.
4. The amount of salaries to be paid each partner and the extent of withdrawals that each is permitted.
5. How income and losses are to be shared.
6. Provisions for dissolving the partnership.

The illustration on the next page shows the information usually included in the articles of copartnership.

ARTICLES OF COPARTNERSHIP

THIS CONTRACT, made and entered into on the first day of November, 1968, by and between Phillip D. Berry, of Great Falls, Montana, and Robert S. Neal, of the same city and state.

WITNESSETH: That the said parties have this day formed a copartnership for the purpose of engaging in and conducting a wholesale drug supply business in the city of Great Falls under the following stipulations, which are a part of this contract:

FIRST: The said copartnership is to continue for a term of ten years from November 1, 1968.

SECOND: The business is to be conducted under the firm name of Acme Drug Supply Company, at 123 Main Street, Great Falls, Montana 59401.

THIRD: The investments are as follows: Phillip D. Berry, cash, $30,000; Robert S. Neal, cash, $30,000. These invested assets are partnership property in which the equity of each partner is the same.

FOURTH: Each partner is to devote his entire time and attention to the business and to engage in no other business enterprise without the written consent of the other partner.

FIFTH: During the operation of this partnership, neither partner is to become surety or bondsman for anyone without the written consent of the other partner.

SIXTH: Each partner is to receive a salary of $7,200 a year, payable $600 in cash on the last business day of each month. At the end of each annual fiscal period, the net income or the net loss shown by the income statement, after the salaries of the two partners have been allowed, is to be shared as follows: Phillip D. Berry, 60 percent; Robert S. Neal, 40 percent.

SEVENTH: Neither partner is to withdraw assets in excess of his salary, any part of the assets invested, or assets in anticipation of net income to be earned, without the written consent of the other partner.

EIGHTH: In case of the death or the legal disability of either partner, the other partner is to continue the operations of the business until the close of the annual fiscal period on the following December 31. At that time the continuing partner is to be given an option to buy the interest of the deceased or incapacitated partner at not more than 10 percent above the value of the deceased or incapacitated partner's proprietary interest as shown by the balance of his capital account after the books are closed on December 31. It is agreed that this purchase price is to be paid one half in cash and the balance in four equal installments payable quarterly.

NINTH: At the conclusion of this contract, unless it is mutually agreed to continue the operation of the business under a new contract, the assets of the partnership, after the liabilities are paid, are to be divided in proportion to the net credit to each partner's capital account on that date.

IN WITNESS WHEREOF, the parties aforesaid have hereunto set their hands and affixed their seals on the day and year above written.

Phillip D. Berry (Seal)

Robert S. Neal (Seal)

Articles of copartnership

Partnership accounts

Because two or more persons share in the ownership of a partnership, separate capital accounts are kept for each partner. Just as the capital account of a single proprietor shows his ownership in a business, so the capital account of each partner shows the value of each partner's share in the ownership of the business. If the partnership agreement permits withdrawals of cash or merchandise by the partners, a separate drawing account is kept for each partner.

There is little difference between the bookkeeping work for a partnership and that for a single proprietorship. The major difference is in the handling of the capital accounts and the drawing accounts.

Forming a partnership with cash investments

The opening entries of a partnership are similar to those of a single proprietorship. Ordinarily a separate entry is made to record the investment of each partner.

The illustration on the preceding page shows the articles of copartnership drawn up by P. D. Berry and R. S. Neal when they formed a partnership to begin a wholesale drug supply business on November 1. Each partner invested $30,000.00 in cash. To record the investment of each partner, the following entries were made in the columnar cash receipts journal:

CASH RECEIPTS JOURNAL — PAGE 1

	DATE		ACCOUNT CREDITED	POST. REF.	1 GENERAL CREDIT	2 SALES CREDIT	3 SALES TAXES PAYABLE CREDIT	4 ACCOUNTS RECEIVABLE CREDIT	5 CASH DEBIT	
1	1968 Nov.	1	P. D. Berry, Capital		30000 00				30000 00	1
2		1	R. S. Neal, Capital		30000 00				30000 00	2
3										3
4										4
5										5

Initial cash investments of a partnership recorded in a cash receipts journal

Converting a single proprietorship into a partnership

An established business operated by one owner may be converted into a partnership by a merger with another business or by the investment of cash or other assets by another person.

When a single proprietorship is converted into a partnership, it may be agreed that the books of the original business are to be continued. It is only necessary then to record the investment of the new partner. This may be done by debiting the asset accounts for the assets invested, crediting the liability accounts for the liabilities assumed, and crediting the new partner's capital account for the net amount of his investment.

In some cases when a single proprietorship is converted into a partnership, a new set of books may be opened. For example, R. L. Ellis operates a supply business. On January 2 he forms a partnership with T. S. Sims. Mr. Ellis invests the assets of his business, and the partnership assumes the liabilities of his business. Mr. Sim's invests $20,000.00 in cash.

The new partnership, Ellis and Sims, decides to open a new set of books. The investment of each partner is recorded with an opening entry in the columnar general journal. The two opening entries as they appear in the columnar general journal on January 2, 1968, are shown below.

GENERAL JOURNAL — PAGE 1

	1 ACCOUNTS PAYABLE DEBIT	2 GENERAL DEBIT	DATE		ACCOUNT TITLE	POST. REF.	3 GENERAL CREDIT	4 ACCOUNTS RECEIVABLE CREDIT	
1		800 00	1968 Jan.	2	Cash				1
2		3425 00			Accounts Receivable				2
3		20925 00			Merchandise Inventory				3
4		450 00			Supplies				4
5		5300 00			Equipment				5
6					Accounts Payable		900 00		6
7					R. L. Ellis, Capital		30000 00		7
8					Investment.				8
9		20000 00		2	Cash				9
10					T. S. Sims, Capital		20000 00		10
11					Investment.				11
12									12
13									13
14									14
15									15

Opening entries for a partnership recorded in a columnar general journal

The cash investments of the partners are not recorded in the cash receipts journal, as the amount of the cash is posted directly from the general journal. The amount of cash is, however, recorded as a memorandum entry on the first line of the cash receipts journal as a balance for future use in proving cash. The cash receipts journal of Ellis and Sims with the memorandum entry showing the beginning cash balance is illustrated below.

CASH RECEIPTS JOURNAL — PAGE 1

	DATE		ACCOUNT CREDITED	POST. REF.	1 GENERAL CREDIT	2 SALES CREDIT	3 SALES TAXES PAYABLE CREDIT	4 ACCOUNTS RECEIVABLE CREDIT	5 CASH DEBIT	
1	1968 Jan.	2	Balance on hand $20,800.00	✓						1
2										2
3										3
4										4
5										5
6										6
7										7

Beginning cash balance of a partnership recorded in a cash receipts journal

Partners' salaries

In the partnership of Ellis and Sims, Mr. Ellis has been operating a supply business for several years. Mr. Sims is a young man with no experience in the supply business. The articles of copartnership therefore provide that Mr. Ellis is to receive a monthly salary of $750.00 and Mr. Sims, a monthly salary of $500.00.

The federal income tax form filed by a partnership provides for reporting the payments of partners' salaries as an expense of the business. The partnership of Ellis and Sims therefore debits the payment of salaries to the partners to an account entitled *Partners Salaries.* At the end of the fiscal period this account, together with other expense accounts, is closed into Income and Expense Summary.

Partners are not considered to be employees of the business. For this reason, some accountants prefer to handle the salaries of partners as withdrawals by debiting the partners' drawing accounts the same as other withdrawals of cash or merchandise. Regardless of whether drawing accounts or an expense account is used, salary payments to partners are not subject to withholding for income taxes or FICA taxes. For tax purposes, each partner is treated as a self-employed person. Each partner's share of the net income from the business is subject to income tax and social security self-employment tax and is so reported on the individual's income tax return.

FINANCIAL STATEMENTS OF A PARTNERSHIP

Income statement of a partnership

The income statement of a partnership is similar to that of a single proprietorship. The income statement prepared for the Ellis and Sims partnership on December 31, 1968, is illustrated on the next page.

Division of net income or net loss among partners

Partnership net income or net loss may be divided in any way desired by the partners. The method of division is usually stated in the articles of copartnership. Some common ways by which partners agree to share the net income or the net loss are: (a) equally; (b) according to a certain ratio; (c) according to the ratio of their investments; and (d) by allowing interest on the partners' investments before sharing in the net income or net loss.

If the partnership agreement does not state how the income or loss is to be divided, it is assumed by law that the income or loss is to be shared equally.

The salary agreement for the partnership of Ellis and Sims provides for the difference in business experience between the two partners; $750.00 per month to Mr. Ellis as compared with $500.00 per month for Mr. Sims. But there is also a difference in the amount of capital that each partner has

Ellis and Sims
Income Statement
For Year Ended December 31, 1968

Income from Sales:			
Sales			$98,984.95
Less: Sales Returns and Allowances . .		$ 715.50	
Sales Discount		460.60	1,176.10
Net Sales			$97,808.85
Cost of Merchandise Sold:			
Merchandise Inventory, Jan. 2, 1968 . .		$20,925.00	
Purchases	$70,280.80		
Less: Purchases Ret.& Allow. $ 811.80			
Purchases Discount 1,011.50	1,823.30		
Net Purchases		68,457.50	
Total Cost of Mdse. Available for Sale		$89,382.50	
Less Mdse. Inventory, Dec. 31, 1968 . .		24,141.00	
Cost of Merchandise Sold.			65,241.50
Gross Profit on Sales.			$32,567.35
Operating Expenses:			
Bad Debts Expense		$ 167.47	
Delivery Expense		1,711.80	
Depreciation Expense.		975.00	
Insurance Expense		248.00	
Miscellaneous Expense		830.70	
Partners Salaries		15,000.00	
Payroll Tax Expense		479.22	
Property Taxes		615.20	
Salary Expense		7,061.75	
Supplies Expense.		366.60	
Total Operating Expenses.			27,455.74
Net Income from Operations			$ 5,111.61
Other Income:			
Interest Income		$ 63.10	
Other Expenses:			
Interest Expense.		443.61	
Net Deduction.			380.51
Net Income			$4,731.10

Income statement of a partnership

invested in the partnership. To provide for this difference, the articles of copartnership also state that the net income or the net loss is to be divided according to the ratio of each partner's investment to the total investment.

Mr. Ellis' investment of $30,000.00 is three fifths of the total investment of $50,000.00. Mr. Sims' investment of $20,000.00 is two fifths of the total investment. In dividing the net income or the net loss, Mr. Ellis will therefore receive three fifths and Mr. Sims will receive two fifths.

The net income for the partnership of Ellis and Sims, as shown on the income statement on page 610, is $4,731.10. The partners' shares of this net income are figured as follows:

R. L. Ellis: $\frac{\$30,000}{\$50,000}$ or 3/5 of $4,731.10 = $2,838.66

T. S. Sims: $\frac{\$20,000}{\$50,000}$ or 2/5 of $4,731.10 = $1,892.44

Total net income........................$4,731.10

Statement showing distribution of net income

After the distribution of net income is calculated, a separate statement that shows the details of the distribution is prepared for the two partners. On December 31, the end of the fiscal year, a distribution of net income statement is prepared as follows:

Ellis and Sims
Distribution of Net Income Statement
For Year Ended December 31, 1968

R. L. Ellis:	
3/5 of net income.	$2,838.66
T. S. Sims:	
2/5 of net income.	$1,892.44
Net Income.	$4,731.10

Distribution of net income statement

Balance sheet of a partnership

The balance sheet of Ellis and Sims on December 31, 1968, is shown on page 612. Note that this balance sheet is similar to that of a single proprietorship except that it shows each partner's present capital as of the date of the balance sheet.

Capital statement of a partnership

The balance sheet of the partnership of Ellis and Sims shows the present capital of each partner at the end of the fiscal period, but it does not show

Ellis and Sims
Balance Sheet
December 31, 1968

Assets			
Current Assets:			
Cash		$ 4,292.89	
Petty Cash		50.00	
Notes Receivable		2,400.00	
Accounts Receivable	$ 5,581.57		
Less Allowance for Bad Debts	167.47	5,414.10	
Merchandise Inventory		24,141.00	
Supplies		1,559.48	
Prepaid Insurance		666.00	
Total Current Assets			$38,523.47
Fixed Assets:			
Equipment	$ 5,300.00		
Less Accumulated Depreciation--Equip.	795.00	$ 4,505.00	
Building	$ 9,000.00		
Less Accumulated Depreciation--Bldg.	180.00	8,820.00	
Land		6,000.00	
Total Fixed Assets			19,325.00
Total Assets			$57,848.47

Liabilities		
Current Liabilities:		
Notes Payable	$ 1,600.00	
Interest Payable	32.00	
Accounts Payable	1,562.12	
Salaries Payable	125.60	
Employees Income Taxes Payable	176.75	
FICA Taxes Payable	74.73	
State Unemployment Taxes Payable	21.92	
Federal Unemployment Taxes Payable	24.25	
Total Current Liabilities		$ 3,617.37
Proprietorship		
R. L. Ellis, Capital	$32,488.66	
T. S. Sims, Capital	21,742.44	
Total Proprietorship		54,231.10
Total Liabilities and Proprietorship		$57,848.47

Balance sheet of a partnership

the details of the changes during the fiscal period. Each partner may have this detailed information by preparing a capital statement such as the one shown below.

Ellis and Sims
Capital Statement
For Year Ended December 31, 1968

R. L. Ellis:			
Capital, January 2, 1968		$30,000.00	
Share of Net Income.	$2,838.66		
Less Withdrawals.	350.00		
Net Increase in Capital.		2,488.66	
Present Capital, December 31, 1968			$32,488.66
T. S. Sims:			
Capital, January 2, 1968		$20,000.00	
Share of Net Income.	$1,892.44		
Less Withdrawals.	150.00		
Net Increase in Capital.		1,742.44	
Present Capital, December 31, 1968			21,742.44
Total Proprietorship, December 31, 1968			$54,231.10

Capital statement of a partnership

Note that the salaries paid the partners are not shown on the capital statement, as they were recorded as expenses of the partnership. The statement does show that R. L. Ellis withdrew $350.00 and T. S. Sims withdrew $150.00. These amounts represent withdrawals of cash or merchandise and were recorded as debits in the partners' drawing accounts.

ADJUSTING AND CLOSING ENTRIES FOR A PARTNERSHIP

Adjusting entries

The adjusting entries for a partnership are similar to those for a single proprietorship. The Adjustments columns of the work sheet are used as the basis for the adjusting entries. The adjusting entries are recorded in the general journal.

Closing entries

With the exception of the entries needed to close the income and expense summary account, the closing entries for a partnership are similar to those for a single proprietorship. All closing entries are made from the information given on the work sheet, except that the amount to be credited to each partner's capital account when the income and expense summary account is closed is obtained from the distribution of net income statement. The entries to close the income and expense summary account and the drawing accounts of Ellis and Sims are given on the next page.

GENERAL JOURNAL PAGE 3

	1 Accounts Payable Debit	2 General Debit	Date	Account Title	Post. Ref.	3 General Credit	4 Accounts Receivable Credit	
24		4731 10	31	Income and Expense Summary				24
25				R. L. Ellis, Capital		2838 66		25
26				T. S. Sims, Capital		1892 44		26
27		350 00	31	R. L. Ellis, Capital				27
28				R. L. Ellis, Drawing		350 00		28
29		150 00	31	T. S. Sims, Capital				29
30				T. S. Sims, Drawing		150 00		30
31								31
32								32
33								33
34								34

Closing entries for a partnership recorded in a columnar general journal

Increasing Your Business Vocabulary

What is the meaning of each of the following:

a partnership b partner c articles of copartnership

Study Questions

1. Why might a single proprietor consider changing his business to a partnership?
2. In what kind of businesses are partnerships commonly found?
3. Why should the partnership agreement be in writing?
4. What are the principal provisions of the partnership agreement on page 606?
5. What is the difference between the bookkeeping work for a partnership and that for a single proprietorship?
6. What account is debited to record the payment of partners' salaries?
7. Name some common ways by which partners agree to share the net income or the net loss of their business.
8. How is the amount of income or loss divided when the partnership agreement does not state the method of division?
9. What information does the distribution of net income statement show?
10. How does the balance sheet of a partnership differ from that of a single proprietorship?
11. What information does the capital statement show?
12. How do the closing entries for a partnership differ from the closing entries of a single proprietorship?

Cases for Business Decision

CASE 1

Bill Macklin owns and operates a garage in the center of a large city. The garage is used only for storage. Many of Mr. Macklin's customers have asked that their cars be repaired while stored during the day or night. Mr. Macklin decides to install a repair department. Cliff Vaughn, an able mechanic, is available to take charge of the new repair department. He is willing to consider the position either as a partner or as an employee. Indicate some of the possible advantages and disadvantages to Mr. Macklin of admitting Mr. Vaughn as a partner.

CASE 2

For the past 35 years Herb Pennington has operated a large mercantile store. He has decided to offer a partnership to Ben Case, a young man without capital and without much store experience. How may the partnership profits be divided so as to recognize (a) differences in business experience and (b) differences in investment?

Application Problems

PROBLEM 34-1 Opening entries for cash investment in a partnership

On March 1 of the current year, Thomas Shannon and John Harmon form a partnership to begin a family billiards business. Each partner invests $7,500.00 in cash.

Instructions: Record the opening entry for each partner on page 1 of a columnar cash receipts journal.

PROBLEM 34-2 Opening entries for investment of cash and other assets in a partnership

On July 1 of the current year, Harold Hamilton and Ted Holden form a partnership for the purpose of continuing a retail music store that Mr. Hamilton has been operating. The partnership, Hamilton & Holden, takes over the assets of Mr. Hamilton's business and assumes his liabilities. Mr. Holden invests cash equal to Mr. Hamilton's proprietorship. The balance sheet of Harold Hamilton appears on the next page.

Harold Hamilton
Balance Sheet
June 30, 19—

Assets			*Liabilities*		
Cash	3,361	75	Notes Payable	3,000	00
Notes Receivable	560	00	Accounts Payable	1,763	09
Accounts Receivable	2,126	75	Total Liabilities	4,763	09
Merchandise Inventory	7,930	57			
Supplies	388	62			
Equipment	2,395	40	*Proprietorship*		
			Harold Hamilton, Cap.	12,000	00
Total Assets	16,763	09	Total Liab. and Prop.	16,763	09

Instructions: 1. Record the opening entry for each partner on page 1 of a columnar general journal.

2. Record the memorandum entry to show the total cash balance on page 1 of a columnar cash receipts journal.

PROBLEM 34-3 | Distribution of the net income of a partnership

J. Roth, L. Sayers, and M. Tyler are partners in the retail clothing business of Roth, Sayers, & Tyler. The partners invested in the business $16,000.00, $14,000.00, and $10,000.00 respectively. According to the partnership agreement, the net income is to be divided in the ratio of their initial investments.

At the end of the annual fiscal period on December 31 of the current year, the income statement shows that the net income for the year, after the payment of partners' salaries, amounts to $6,000.00.

Instructions: 1. Prepare a distribution of net income statement.

2. Prepare a capital statement. The debit balances of the partners' drawing accounts on December 31 were: Roth, $250.00; Sayers, $100.00; Tyler, $120.00.

PROBLEM 34-4 | Work at the end of the fiscal period

The account numbers, titles, and balances in the general ledger of Judd & Peck, partners in a household furnishings business, on December 31 of the current year are given on the next page.

Acct. No.	*Account Title*	*Account Balance* Debit	*Account Balance* Credit
111	Cash	$ 2,439.18	——
112	Petty Cash	50.00	——
113	Accounts Receivable	5,505.66	——
113.1	Allowance for Bad Debts	——	$ 287.50
114	Merchandise Inventory	17,461.49	——
115	Supplies	293.60	——
116	Prepaid Insurance	240.00	——
121	Equipment	2,365.10	——
121.1	Accumulated Depreciation — Equipment	——	581.80
211	Notes Payable	——	1,000.00
212	Interest Payable	——	——
213	Accounts Payable	——	1,649.10
214	Salaries Payable	——	——
215	Employees Income Taxes Payable	——	120.60
216	FICA Taxes Payable	——	65.25
217	State Unemployment Taxes Payable	——	24.30
218	Federal Unemployment Taxes Payable	——	14.40
311	J. A. Judd, Capital	——	15,000.00
312	J. A. Judd, Drawing	361.40	——
313	C. R. Peck, Capital	——	10,000.00
314	C. R. Peck, Drawing	116.15	——
315	Income and Expense Summary	——	——
411	Sales	——	60,618.31
411.1	Sales Returns and Allowances	396.14	——
511	Purchases	41,060.63	——
511.1	Purchases Returns and Allowances	——	185.00
511.2	Purchases Discount	——	432.82
611	Bad Debts Expense	——	——
612	Delivery Expense	1,380.48	——
613	Depreciation Expense — Equipment	——	——
614	Insurance Expense	——	——
615	Miscellaneous Expense	629.75	——
616	Partners Salaries	12,000.00	——
617	Payroll Tax Expense	270.00	——
618	Rent Expense	1,800.00	——
619	Salary Expense	3,600.00	——
620	Supplies Expense	——	——
711	Interest Income	——	9.00
811	Interest Expense	18.50	——

Instructions: 1. Prepare an eight-column work sheet for the annual fiscal period ended December 31 of the current year. The additional data needed at the end of the annual fiscal period are:

Additional allowance for bad debts, 1% of charge sales of $20,731.16
Merchandise inventory, $20,723.40
Supplies inventory, $48.23
Value of insurance policies, $60.00
Annual amount of estimated depreciation of equipment, $118.26
Accrued interest expense, $5.00
Accrued salary expense, $75.00

2. Prepare an income statement.

3. Prepare a capital statement. The net income is to be distributed in proportion to the partners' investments as shown by their capital account balances.

4. Prepare a balance sheet.

5. Record the adjusting entries and the closing entries.

CHAPTER 35 CORPORATIONS AND COOPERATIVES

THE CORPORATE FORM OF BUSINESS ORGANIZATION

A form of business organization that has the legal right to act as one person but that may be owned by many is known as a *corporation*. Almost all large business enterprises are organized as corporations. Most corporations are authorized by state governments. Some corporations, such as national banks, are authorized by the federal government.

Ownership of a corporation

The ownership of a corporation is divided into units known as *shares*. All the shares of a corporation are referred to as *capital stock*. The owner of one or more shares of the capital stock is known as a *stockholder*. A stockholder is also called a *shareholder* or a *shareowner*. The evidence of each stockholder's ownership in the corporation is a certificate known as a *stock certificate*. A typical stock certificate is illustrated on page 620.

Advantages of the corporate form of business organization

The corporate form of business organization has many advantages over the single proprietorship and the partnership. Some of these advantages are:

1. The amount of capital of a corporation is limited only by (a) its ability to sell the authorized amount of stock and (b) its ability to borrow. This characteristic of a corporation makes it possible for many corporations to become very large enterprises. The amount of capital available in a single proprietorship or in a partnership is limited by the wealth of the owners plus their ability to secure loans.

2. A stockholder is not personally liable for any of the debts of the corporation. The creditors of a corporation can claim only the assets of the corporation itself. The most a stockholder can lose is the amount that he has invested in the corporation. In a single proprietorship or in a partnership, each owner may lose not only his entire investment in the business but also his personal assets if they are needed to pay the claims of creditors.

No. 1

100 Shares

Hendry Manufacturing Company

INCORPORATED UNDER THE LAWS OF THE STATE OF DELAWARE

AUTHORIZED CAPITAL STOCK 2,000 SHARES PAR VALUE $100 PER SHARE

This Certifies That ----------------James W. Sommers---------------- is the owner of ---------------One Hundred----------------- Shares of the Capital Stock of Hendry Manufacturing Company transferable only on the books of the Corporation by the holder hereof in person or by Attorney upon surrender of this Certificate properly endorsed.

In Witness Whereof, the said Corporation has caused this Certificate to be signed by its duly authorized officers and its Corporate Seal to be hereunto affixed this ninth day of July A.D. 1968

David G. Goodman
TREASURER

Charles B. Coe
PRESIDENT

SHARES --100-- EACH

Stock certificate

3. The length of life of the corporation may be for a specific number of years or it may be perpetual. The corporation is not terminated by the death of any stockholder. A single proprietorship or a partnership is dissolved immediately by the death of the owner or a partner.

4. In a corporation each stockholder may sell any part or all of his ownership in the corporation. A change in stock ownership does not dissolve the corporation. In a partnership, a partner may not sell any part of his interest in the business without the consent of all the other partners. When a partner sells or transfers any part of his ownership, the partnership is dissolved.

FORMING A CORPORATION

Securing a charter

Corporations are organized through the authority provided by state and federal laws. The laws grant the right to incorporate a business and prescribe the method of incorporation. Most states require that three or more individuals provide the assets with which to organize the corporation.

The incorporators must make written application to the proper state or federal officials. A written application to the state for permission to incorporate is known as a *certificate of incorporation.*

The certificate of incorporation usually contains: (1) the name under which the business is to be operated; (2) the location of the principal office of the corporation; (3) the purpose of the proposed corporation; (4) the amount of the capital stock, the kind of stock, and the number of shares; (5) the amount of capital with which the corporation will commence business; (6) the names and the addresses of the incorporators; and (7) the period for which the corporation is formed.

On July 1, 1968, Charles B. Coe, David G. Goodman, Gordon W. Riley, and James W. Sommers decide to organize a corporation to manufacture and sell motorcycles. They prepare a certificate of incorporation and file it with the Secretary of State of the state in which the corporation is to be formed. This certificate of incorporation is shown on page 622. The Secretary of State furnishes a certified copy of the certificate of incorporation to the organizers. This copy is recorded in the office of the recorder of the county in which the business is located. The certified copy of the certificate of incorporation is referred to as a *charter*.

Capital stock

The fourth paragraph of the charter illustrated on page 622 shows that the Hendry Manufacturing Company is authorized to issue capital stock in the amount of $200,000.00. The total amount of stock that a corporation is permitted to issue is known as the *authorized capital stock*.

According to the fourth paragraph of the charter, the total authorized capital stock of the Hendry Manufacturing Company is divided into 2,000 shares, each share having a face value of $100.00. The face value of each share as stated on the stock certificate is called *par value*. Shares of stock that do not have a value stated on the certificate are called *no-par-value stock*. The charter of a corporation that has no-par-value stock states the number of shares of stock that may be issued.

A corporation may issue two kinds of stock. Stock issued by a corporation that gives the holder preference as to earnings or other preferences is called *preferred stock*. Stock issued by a corporation that does not give the holder special preferences is known as *common stock*.

Stock subscriptions

Before application can be made for a charter, the organizers of a corporation must have written promises from the incorporators to buy stock. Persons who promise to buy stock to organize a corporation are known as *subscribers*.

CERTIFICATE OF INCORPORATION

of

HENDRY MANUFACTURING COMPANY, INC.

FIRST: The name of the corporation is Hendry Manufacturing Company, Inc.

SECOND: The principal office of said corporation is located at 105 West Tenth Street, in the City of Wilmington, County of New Castle, Delaware.

THIRD: The nature of the business, or objects or purposes to be transacted, promoted, or carried on are to engage in the business of manufacturing and selling motorcycles and all business incidental to such manufacture and sale.

FOURTH: The total number of shares of stock that the corporation shall have authority to issue is Two Thousand (2,000) and the par value of each of such shares is One Hundred Dollars ($100), amounting in the aggregate to Two Hundred Thousand Dollars ($200,000).

FIFTH: The amount of capital with which the corporation will commence business is Sixty-five Thousand Dollars ($65,000).

SIXTH: The names and the places of residence of the incorporators are as follows:

Charles B. Coe........1527 Vineyard Place, Dover, Delaware
David G. Goodman......3466 Trimble Avenue, Wilmington, Delaware
Gordon W. Riley.......17 Beechcrest Road, Newport, Delaware
James W. Sommers......351 Park Avenue, New York, New York

SEVENTH: The corporation is to have perpetual existence.

WE, THE UNDERSIGNED, being each of the incorporators hereinbefore named for the purpose of forming a corporation to do business both within and without the State of Delaware, being Chapter 65 of the Revised Code of Delaware, and the acts amendatory thereof and supplemental thereto, do make this certificate, hereby declaring and certifying that the facts herein stated are true, and accordingly have hereunto set our hands and seals this first day of July, A. D. 1968.

In the presence of:

Carl Berra
Kenneth Robesky

Charles B. Coe (SEAL)
David G. Goodman (SEAL)
Gordon W. Riley (SEAL)
James W. Sommers (SEAL)

State of Delaware) ss.:
County of New Castle)

BE IT REMEMBERED, that on this first day of July, A. D. 1968, personally came before me, Matthew J. Moore, a Notary Public for the State of Delaware, all of the parties to the foregoing certificate of incorporation, known to me personally to be such, and severally acknowledged the said certificate to be the act and deed of the signers respectively and that the facts therein stated are truly set forth.

GIVEN under my hand and seal of office the day and year aforesaid.

Matthew J. Moore
Notary Public

Certificate of incorporation

The Hendry Manufacturing Company has 650 shares of stock subscribed before the charter is granted. Mr. Coe subscribed for 200 shares, Mr. Goodman for 200 shares, Mr. Riley for 150 shares, and Mr. Sommers for 100 shares. The subscription price of each share is $100.00. As soon as the subscriptions are paid, the corporation will have $65,000.00 in cash with which to begin operations.

Management of a corporation

Most corporations have many stockholders. The stockholders attend an annual meeting to elect a group of persons to manage the business. Each stockholder owning common stock is usually entitled to one vote for each share of common stock that he owns.

The group of persons elected by the stockholders to manage the business of a corporation is known as the *board of directors*. The board of directors controls the general policies of the corporation and elects the officers. The corporate officers carry on the business of the corporation. The officers are responsible to the board of directors, and the board of directors is responsible to the stockholders.

Opening entry for a corporation

The opening entry for a proprietorship consists of debits to assets, credits to liabilities, and a credit to the proprietor's capital account. The opening entry for a partnership consists of debits to assets, credits to liabilities, and credits to the capital account of each partner. The opening entry for a corporation follows the same pattern as that for a single proprietor or for a partnership — assets are debited, liabilities are credited, and an account called Capital Stock is credited for the amount of the proprietorship.

The entry below illustrates the opening entry of a corporation where cash is the only asset and there are no liabilities.

CASH RECEIPTS JOURNAL PAGE 1

	DATE		ACCOUNT CREDITED	POST. REF.	GENERAL CREDIT (1)	SALES CREDIT (2)	SALES TAXES PAYABLE CREDIT (3)	ACCOUNTS RECEIVABLE CREDIT (4)	CASH DEBIT (5)	
1	1968 July	10	Capital Stock		6500000				6500000	1
2										2
3										3
4										4
5										5
6										6
7										7
8										8
9										9
10										10
11										11
12										12

Entry to record the sale of capital stock

Analyzing the opening entry

The certificate of incorporation of the Hendry Manufacturing Company provides that the corporation will begin business with $65,000.00. Therefore, on the day the charter is received, the four incorporators purchase for cash 650 shares of stock for $65,000.00. A stock certificate is issued to each subscriber to show the number of shares of stock he owns.

To record the receipt of cash by the corporation, an entry is made in the cash receipts journal as shown on page 623. Cash is debited for $65,000.00 in the Cash Dr. column. Capital Stock is credited for $65,000.00 in the General Cr. column.

> Individual accounts for each stockholder are not maintained in the general ledger. The entire amount of stock issued is shown as a credit in the account Capital Stock.

EXPANDING A CORPORATION

Purchasing a going business

The Hendry Manufacturing Company decides on July 11 to purchase the partnership of Frank & Wallace, owned by Roy A. Frank and Samuel G. Wallace. These two partners agree to accept shares of stock in the corporation as payment for their partnership.

The balance sheet of the partnership shows that the difference between the assets and the liabilities amounts to $30,000.00. At $100 a share, the corporation will issue 300 shares to Frank & Wallace. The entry in the general journal to record this transaction is illustrated below.

GENERAL JOURNAL — PAGE 1

	1	2				3	4	
	ACCOUNTS PAYABLE DEBIT	GENERAL DEBIT	DATE	ACCOUNT TITLE	POST. REF.	GENERAL CREDIT	ACCOUNTS RECEIVABLE CREDIT	
1		8,584.38	1968 July 11	Cash				1
2		4,000.00		Notes Receivable				2
3		5,175.62		Accounts Receivable				3
4		10,650.00		Merchandise Inventory				4
5		121.50		Supplies				5
6		250.00		Prepaid Insurance				6
7		5,000.00		Equipment				7
8				Notes Payable		2,500.00		8
9				Accounts Payable		1,281.50		9
10				Capital Stock		30,000.00		10
11				Purchase of the				11
12				business of Frank &				12
13				Wallace.				13
14								14
15								15

Entry to record the purchase of a going business

Analyzing the entry for the purchase of a going business

Each asset purchased is debited in the General Dr. column for the amount shown on the balance sheet of the Frank & Wallace partnership. The two liabilities taken over, Notes Payable and Accounts Payable, are credited in the General Cr. column for the amounts shown on the balance sheet. Capital Stock is credited for the amount of the difference between the total assets and the total liabilities of the partnership.

RECORDING AND REPORTING CORPORATE INCOME AND CAPITAL

The board of directors of a corporation has the responsibility for furnishing financial reports to the stockholders so that they may be kept informed of business operations. The financial reports are prepared from information on the work sheet.

The work sheet of a corporation

A partial work sheet of the Hendry Manufacturing Company for the fiscal period ended December 31, 1968, is shown on page 626. On this work sheet, the account titles that differ from those previously presented are the titles that relate to the proprietorship accounts and to federal income taxes. The two accounts that relate to proprietorship are Capital Stock and Retained Earnings. The two accounts that relate to federal income taxes are Federal Income Taxes Payable and Federal Income Taxes.

In the trial balance on the work sheet, the capital stock account shows a credit balance of $95,000.00. This is the amount of capital stock issued. Since this is the first work sheet of the Hendry Manufacturing Company, there is no balance in the retained earnings account in the trial balance. The accounts that relate to federal income taxes have no account balances in the trial balance because income taxes for the current year have not yet been recorded.

Before the financial reports are prepared, it is necessary to adjust certain accounts to reflect the end-of-period condition of the accounts. Only the calculation of and the adjustment for the federal income tax will be discussed. The other adjustments are not discussed because they are the same as those made on previous work sheets.

Calculating the federal income tax. The federal income tax paid by a corporation is not considered an operating expense of the business. The tax is considered a division of the net income between the corporation and the federal government.

Hendry Manufacturing Company
Work Sheet
For Year Ended December 31, 1968

	Account Titles	Acct. No.	1 Trial Balance Debit	2 Trial Balance Credit	3 Adjustments Debit	4 Adjustments Credit	5 Income Statement Debit	6 Income Statement Credit	7 Balance Sheet Debit	8 Balance Sheet Credit	
1	Cash	111	1978050						1978050		1
2	Petty Cash	112	10000						10000		2
3	Accounts Receivable	113	582000						582000		3
4	Allowance for Bad Debts	113.1				(a) 31000				31000	4
17	Interest Payable	212				(g) 2000				2000	17
18	Accounts Payable	213		246010						246010	18
19	FICA Taxes Payable	214		17420						17420	19
20	Employees Income Taxes Pay.	215		31040						31040	20
21	State Unempl. Taxes Pay.	216		12600						12600	21
22	Federal Unempl. Taxes Pay.	217		8950						8950	22
23	Federal Income Taxes Pay.	218				(h) 118462				118462	23
24	Capital Stock	311		9500000						9500000	24
25	Retained Earnings	312									25
26	Income and Expense Summary	313			(b) 1477590	(c) 1263510	1477590	1263510			26
46	Office Supplies Expense	624			(e) 16200		16200				46
47	Payroll Tax Expense	625	179530				179530				47
48	Rent Expense	626	210000				210000				48
49	Salary Expense	627	2308090				2308090				49
50	Interest Expense	811	70000		(g) 2000		72000				50
51	Federal Income Taxes	812			(h) 118462		1303217 8 118462	1357064 0			51
52			21002470	21002470	4320720	4320720	13150640	13570640	10544520	10124520	52
53	Net Income After Taxes						420000			420000	53
54							13570640	13570640	10544520	10544520	54
55											55

Partial work sheet of a corporation

To calculate the amount of federal income tax, the following steps are taken:

Step 1

Complete all adjustments on the work sheet and extend all amounts needed on the income statement to the Income Statement Debit and Credit columns.

Step 2

Foot the Income Statement columns and find the difference between the two footings. The amount of this difference is the net income before taxes. The computations for the Hendry Manufacturing Company are as follows:

Total of Income Statement Credit column...........	$135,706.40
Total of Income Statement Debit column............	130,321.78
Net income before taxes..........................	$ 5,384.62

Step 3

Determine the amount of the federal income tax from the tax rate tables furnished by the federal government. For the Hendry Manufacturing Company, this amount is $1,184.62.

Adjustment for the federal income tax. The steps in making the adjustment for the federal income tax on the work sheet are:

Step 1

Record the adjustment for the federal income tax in the Adjustments column of the work sheet. Federal Income Taxes is debited and Federal Income Taxes Payable is credited.

> Federal Income Taxes, an expense account, is located in the Other Expenses division of the general ledger. Federal Income Taxes Payable, a liability account, is located in the Liabilities division of the general ledger.

Step 2

Extend the amount of the federal income tax to the Income Statement Debit column. Also, extend the amount of the federal income taxes payable to the Balance Sheet Credit column.

Balancing the Income Statement columns. The Income Statement columns are totaled and the totals are written as shown in the illustration. The total of the Income Statement Credit column is $4,200.00 more than the total of the Debit column. This amount, $4,200.00, is written in the Income Statement Debit column. "Net Income After Taxes" is written on the same line as the amount. The two columns are then totaled and ruled as shown in the illustration.

Extending net income after taxes and balancing the Balance Sheet columns. All balance sheet items in the Trial Balance columns and the Adjustments columns of the work sheet are extended to the Balance Sheet Debit and Credit columns and the columns are totaled. The amount of the net income after taxes, $4,200.00, represents the increase in proprietorship of the Hendry Manufacturing Company. This amount is therefore extended to the Balance Sheet Credit column of the work sheet. The columns are then totaled and ruled as shown in the illustration.

The income statement of a corporation

The income statement prepared for the Hendry Manufacturing Company for the fiscal period ended December 31, 1968, is partially illustrated below. This statement is prepared from the Income Statement columns of the work sheet. The income statement is similar to those previously prepared, except for the federal income tax calculations at the bottom of the statement. To show this calculation on the income statement, the net income is found before the deduction of federal income taxes. Second, the federal income taxes are deducted. Finally, the net income after federal income taxes is shown. Those using the income statement often find that they can judge the progress of the business more easily when the net income both before and after federal income taxes is shown.

Hendry Manufacturing Company
Income Statement
For Year Ended December 31, 1968

Income from Sales:		
Sales	$120,216.40	
Less Sales Returns and Allowances	696.40	
Net Sales		$119,520.00
Total Operating Expenses		18,916.26
Net Income from Operations		$ 6,084.62
Other Expense:		
Interest Expense		700.00
Net Income Before Deducting Federal Income Taxes		$ 5,384.62
Less Federal Income Taxes		1,184.62
Net Income After Deducting Federal Income Taxes		$ 4,200.00

Income statement of a corporation

The balance sheet of a corporation

The only difference between the balance sheet of a corporation and the balance sheet of a single proprietorship or a partnership is in the proprietorship section. The proprietorship section of the balance sheet prepared for the Hendry Manufacturing Company on December 31, 1968, is shown below.

Proprietorship		
Capital Stock.................	$95,000.00	
Retained Earnings.............	4,200.00	
Total Proprietorship..........		99,200.00
Total Liabilities and Prop....		$125,400.00

Proprietorship section of a corporate balance sheet

The amount earned by a corporation and not yet distributed to stockholders is known as *retained earnings*. Other terms used instead of retained earnings are *earned surplus*, *earnings retained in the business*, *retained income*, and *accumulated earnings*. If costs and expenses exceed income, there is a net loss. The amount of the net loss is called a *deficit*.

The amount of net income earned by the Hendry Manufacturing Company and not yet distributed to the stockholders, $4,200.00, is listed on the December 31, 1968, balance sheet under the title *Retained Earnings*. This amount is added to the amount of the capital stock to give the total proprietorship of the corporation, $99,200.00.

Adjusting and closing entries for a corporation

In order that the ledger of the corporation will show the same information as the balance sheet, adjusting entries are made in the general journal from the information on the work sheet. With the exception of the adjusting entry for federal income taxes, the adjusting entries for a corporation are the same as those for a single proprietorship or a partnership.

The closing entries for the income, the cost, and the expense accounts of a corporation are the same as those of a single proprietorship or a partnership. Since there are no separate capital and drawing accounts for each owner in a corporation, the amount of the net income of the corporation is credited to Retained Earnings. The retained earnings account summarizes the changes in the proprietorship of the corporation resulting from the operations of the corporation.

The balance of the income and expense summary account is closed into the retained earnings account with an entry in the general journal as shown on the next page.

GENERAL JOURNAL — PAGE 14

	1 Accounts Payable Debit	2 General Debit	Date	Account Title	Post. Ref.	3 General Credit	4 Accounts Receivable Credit	
26		420000	31	Income and Expense Summary				26
27				Retained Earnings		420000		27
28								28
29								29
30								30
31								31

Entry to close the income and expense summary account

Post-closing trial balance

A post-closing trial balance is taken after the closing entries are posted. If no errors have been made in posting, the account balances on the post-closing trial balance will be the same as those shown on the balance sheet.

Reversing entries for a corporation

Reversing entries are made to transfer the balances of all accrued payable accounts and all accrued receivable accounts to the appropriate expense and income accounts. Thus, during the next fiscal period the payment of each expense can be debited to the appropriate expense account. The receipt of each income can be credited to the appropriate income account.

The Hendry Manufacturing Company has only one reversing entry. This entry transfers the credit balance of the liability account, Interest Payable, to the credit side of the expense account, Interest Expense, as shown below.

GENERAL JOURNAL — PAGE 15

	1 Accounts Payable Debit	2 General Debit	Date	Account Title	Post. Ref.	3 General Credit	4 Accounts Receivable Credit	
1				Reversing Entry				1
2		2000	1969 Jan. 2	Interest Payable				2
3				Interest Expense		2000		3
4								4
5								5
6								6
7								7
8								8

Reversing entry for a corporation

After this reversing entry is posted, the work at the end of the fiscal period is complete and the books of the corporation are ready for a new fiscal period.

DECLARING AND PAYING DIVIDENDS

Declaring dividends

The balance of the retained earnings account represents income of the corporation that really belongs to the stockholders of the corporation. However, the stockholders may not receive this income or any part of it except by formal action of the board of directors. The board of directors usually maintains a credit balance in the retained earnings account as a source of dividends in less prosperous years. The board of directors may also decide to keep part of the retained earnings for the future expansion of the business. When the board of directors meets, it decides whether it is advisable to distribute all or part of the earnings to the stockholders.

When the board of directors votes to distribute a definite amount of the retained earnings to the stockholders on a specific date, the board is said to have *declared a dividend.* The amount of retained earnings distributed to stockholders is called a *dividend.* The amount of the dividend is usually expressed in terms of a certain amount per share.

On January 6, 1969, the board of directors of the Hendry Manufacturing Company declares a dividend of $3.00 per share on the 950 shares of stock that have been issued. The dividend is to be paid on January 21. This action of the board of directors transfers $2,850.00 from the retained earnings account to a liability account with the title *Dividends Payable.* The account Dividends Payable is a liability account that shows the total amount of dividends owed to all stockholders.

The entry in the general journal to record the declaration of the dividend on January 6 is as follows:

GENERAL JOURNAL — PAGE 15

	1	2				3	4	
	ACCOUNTS PAYABLE DEBIT	GENERAL DEBIT	DATE	ACCOUNT TITLE	POST. REF.	GENERAL CREDIT	ACCOUNTS RECEIVABLE CREDIT	
18		2850 00	6	Retained Earnings				18
19				Dividends Payable		2850 00		19
20				To record Dividend				20
21				No. 1 of $3 a share.				21
22								22
23								23
24								24
25								25
26								26
27								27

Entry to record the declaration of a dividend

Paying dividends

On January 21 a check is mailed to each of the stockholders for the amount of the dividend due him. An entry is made in the cash payments journal to record the total payment of the dividend. Dividends Payable is debited for the total amount paid to all stockholders and Cash is credited for the same amount. The entry in the cash payments journal appears as follows:

CASH PAYMENTS JOURNAL — PAGE 10

	DATE	CK. NO.	ACCOUNT DEBITED	POST. REF.	GENERAL DEBIT (1)	ACCOUNTS PAYABLE DEBIT (2)	SALARY EXPENSE DEBIT (3)	FICA TAXES PAY. CREDIT (4)	EMPLOYEES INCOME TAXES PAY. CREDIT (5)	PURCHASES DISCOUNT CREDIT (6)	CASH CREDIT (7)	
12	21	23-28	Dividends Payable		2850 00						2850 00	12
13												13
14												14
15												15
16												16
17												17
18												18

Entry to record the payment of a dividend

THE COOPERATIVE FORM OF BUSINESS ORGANIZATION

A business that is owned by its customers is known as a *cooperative.* One of the chief differences between a cooperative enterprise and a private corporation is in the matter of voting rights. In a cooperative, each member has only one vote regardless of the number of shares of the cooperative that he owns. In a private corporation that issues only common stock, each stockholder of the corporation has one vote for each share of stock that he owns. It is possible, therefore, for a few large stockholders of a corporation to have the majority of the votes at each annual meeting.

The net income of a cooperative is distributed to its members in two ways: (a) according to the amount of purchases made by each member and (b) according to the amount of the investment of each member. The percentage of net income of a cooperative distributed to each member according to the total amount of his purchases is known as a *participation dividend.* The percentage of net income of a cooperative distributed to each member according to the amount of his investment is known as a *dividend on capital stock.*

During the fiscal year ended June 30, Richard Warner, a member of the Palmyra Consumers' Cooperative, bought merchandise totaling $2,500.00. On July 1 the board of directors of the cooperative declares a participation dividend of 2%. Mr. Warner, therefore, receives a participation dividend of $50.00. Mr. Warner owns shares of capital stock in the cooperative that cost him $500.00. The board of directors of the cooperative declares a dividend on the capital stock of 4%. Mr. Warner's dividend on capital stock is, therefore, $20.00.

Increasing Your Business Vocabulary

What is the meaning of each of the following:

a corporation
b shares
c capital stock
d stockholder
e stock certificate
f certificate of incorporation
g charter
h authorized capital stock
i par value
j no-par-value stock
k preferred stock
l common stock
m subscribers
n board of directors
o retained earnings
p deficit
q declared a dividend
r dividend
s cooperative
t participation dividend
u dividend on capital stock

Study Questions

1. What are four advantages that the corporate form of organization has over the single proprietorship?
2. What limits the amount of capital that a corporation may have?
3. What is the total liability of each stockholder for the debts of a corporation?
4. What is the total liability of each partner for the debts of a partnership?
5. According to its charter, how long does a corporation continue to exist?
6. When does a partnership cease to exist?
7. What seven items of information are usually included in a certificate of incorporation?
8. What accounts are debited and credited in the cash receipts journal on page 623 to open the books of the corporation when all the stock was sold for cash?
9. What groups of accounts are debited and credited in the general journal on page 624 to record the purchase of the partnership's assets and liabilities?
10. How does the income statement of a corporation differ from the income statement of a single proprietorship?

11. How does the proprietorship section of the balance sheet of a corporation differ from the proprietorship section of the balance sheet of a partnership?

12. What accounts are debited and credited in the general journal on page 631 to record the declaration of a dividend?

13. What accounts are debited and credited in the cash payments journal on page 632 to record the payment of a dividend?

14. How do the voting rights of the members of a cooperative differ from the voting rights of the common stockholders of a corporation?

15. In what two ways is the net income of a cooperative distributed to its members?

Cases for Business Decision

CASE 1

Corporation A has closed its fiscal year with a net income equal to 10% of its total outstanding stock. Partnership B has closed its fiscal year with a net income equal to 10% of its proprietorship. You have $25,000.00 to invest in one of the two business enterprises. What factors would you want to consider before making your decision?

CASE 2

You are a member of the board of directors of a corporation that has only common stock. At the end of the current fiscal year, the balance of the retained earnings account is equal to 8% of the capital stock. One member of the board of directors proposes that the board vote to declare a dividend of 8% on the common stock. Another member of the board proposes that a dividend of only 4% be declared. Which proposal will you decide to support? Why?

Application Problems

PROBLEM 35-1 | Opening entry to incorporate a going concern

On July 1 of the current year a charter was granted to Johnson & Company authorizing a capital stock of $80,000.00, consisting of 800 shares (par value $100.00).

This corporation has agreed to take over the hardware business owned by the partnership Madden & Shaw. On July 10 the corporation took over the assets and the liabilities of the partnership as shown in the balance sheet at the top of the next page.

Madden & Shaw Balance Sheet June 30, 19––					
Assets			*Liabilities*		
Cash..................	1,364	60	Notes Payable..........	2,500	00
Accounts Receivable.....	6,624	85	Accounts Payable.......	4,486	85
Merchandise Inventory...	35,487	15	Total Liabilities.........	6,986	85
Supplies...............	910	25	*Proprietorship*		
Equipment.............	12,600	00	W. J. Madden, Capital......30,000.00		
			E. R. Shaw, Capital......20,000.00		
			Total Proprietorship.....	50,000	00
Total Assets............	56,986	85	Total Liab. & Prop......	56,986	85

On July 15, 300 shares of stock were issued to Mr. Madden and 200 shares of stock were issued to Mr. Shaw for their equities in the partnership.

Instructions: Record the opening entry on page 1 of a general journal.

PROBLEM 35-2 | Declaring and paying a dividend

Instructions: Record on page 16 of a general journal the following entries of the current year for the Roberts Company.

June 30. The credit balance of the income and expense summary account, $14,800.00, was transferred to the retained earnings account.

July 10. A dividend of $4 a share was declared on the 3,000 shares of common stock outstanding.

July 31. The dividend declared on July 10 was paid.

PROBLEM 35-3 | End-of-period work for a corporation

The account balances in the ledger of Brigham & Company for the fiscal year ended December 31 of the current year are listed on the next page.

Instructions: 1. Prepare a work sheet for Brigham & Company for the fiscal year ended December 31. Additional data needed for completing the work sheet are given below the account balances on the next page.

2. Prepare the income statement for Brigham & Company. Use as your model the partial income statement shown on page 628.

3. Prepare the balance sheet for Brigham & Company. Add the net income after taxes for the current fiscal period to the balance of the retained earnings account. Use as your model for the proprietorship section the illustration on page 629.

4. Record the adjusting entries on page 64 of a general journal.

5. Record the closing entries.

BRIGHAM & COMPANY

Acct. No.	*Account Title*	*Account Balance* Debit	Credit
111	Cash	$ 8,320.60	——
112	Accounts Receivable	9,141.25	——
112.1	Allowance for Bad Debts	——	$ 629.16
113	Merchandise Inventory	44,736.78	——
114	Supplies	1,710.54	——
115	Prepaid Insurance	1,070.00	——
116	Equipment	7,800.00	——
116.1	Accumulated Depreciation — Equipment	——	660.00
211	Accounts Payable	——	5,232.75
212	FICA Taxes Payable	——	105.04
213	Employees Income Taxes Payable	——	302.15
214	State Unemployment Taxes Payable	——	97.74
215	Federal Unemployment Taxes Payable	——	49.80
216	Federal Income Taxes Payable	——	——
311	Capital Stock	——	40,000.00
312	Retained Earnings	——	5,692.46
313	Income & Expense Summary	——	——
411	Sales	——	174,612.40
411.1	Sales Returns & Allowances	540.13	——
511	Purchases	135,530.00	——
511.1	Purchases Returns & Allowances	——	487.00
511.2	Purchases Discount	——	948.50
611	Advertising Expense	1,750.00	——
612	Bad Debts Expense	——	——
613	Delivery Expense	1,600.00	——
614	Depreciation Expense — Equipment	——	——
615	Insurance Expense	——	——
616	Miscellaneous Expense	1,008.00	——
617	Payroll Tax Expense	914.50	——
618	Rent Expense	2,160.00	——
619	Salary Expense	12,460.00	——
620	Supplies Expense	——	——
811	Loss on Fixed Assets	75.20	——
812	Federal Income Taxes	——	——

Additional Data Needed for Completing Work Sheet

Additional allowance for bad debts, ¼% of *net* sales

Merchandise inventory, December 31, $35,602.50

Supplies inventory, December 31, $420.70

Value of insurance policies, December 31, $850.00

Annual depreciation on equipment, $700.00

Federal income taxes for the year, 25% of net income before taxes

APPENDIX PROBLEMS

CHAPTER 1

APPENDIX PROBLEM 1-A — Balance sheet for a motion picture theater

The following are the assets and the liabilities of the Strand Theater, of which Joseph Listro is the proprietor:

Assets		Liabilities	
Cash	$ 1,285.00	Monarch Films, Inc.	$ 412.00
Furniture	1,800.00	Valley Light and Power Company	74.00
Equipment	4,825.00		
Building	8,000.00	Valley National Bank	2,500.00
Land	3,500.00		

Instructions: Prepare a balance sheet for the Strand Theater dated August 31 of the current year.

APPENDIX PROBLEM 1-B — Balance sheet for a farm

The following are the assets and the liabilities of Raymond Mills, the owner of a small farm:

Assets		Liabilities	
Cash	$ 240.00	Farmers National Bank	$ 3,800.00
Livestock	870.00	Lloyd's Feed Company	$ 40.00
Machinery and Equipment	3,111.00	Triangle Grain Store	185.00
Buildings	8,500.00		
Land	11,200.00		

Instructions: Prepare a balance sheet for Raymond Mills dated June 30 of the current year.

CHAPTER 2

APPENDIX PROBLEM 2-A — Balance sheet and opening entry for a repair shop

Larry Shell is the owner and operator of the Bicycle Repair Shop with the following business assets: Cash, $812.50; Parts, $310.00; Office Equipment, $355.00; and Shop Equipment, $1,125.50. The shop also has the following liabilities: Hadley Wholesale Company, $425.00; and Indian Tire Company, $86.00.

Instructions: 1. Prepare a balance sheet dated September 1 of the current year.

2. Record the opening entry on page 1 in a general journal.

CHAPTER 3

APPENDIX PROBLEM 3-A — Recording and posting the opening entry for an attorney

The balance sheet of Walter Brandt, Attorney, on April 30 of the current year is shown below.

Walter Brandt, Attorney
Balance Sheet
April 30, 19--

Assets			Liabilities		
Cash	812	80	Legal Book Company	47	25
Supplies	73	50	Samson Furniture Company	540	00
Law Library	510	00			
Office Furniture	1,112	00	Total Liabilities	587	25
Office Equipment	685	20	**Proprietorship**		
			Walter Brandt, Capital	2,606	25
Total Assets	3,193	50	Total Liab. and Prop.	3,193	50

Instructions: 1. Record the opening entry on page 1 of a general journal. Use May 1 of the current year as the date.

2. Open accounts in a ledger for all the account titles listed on the balance sheet. Allow one fourth of a page in your ledger for each account. Number the accounts as follows: asset accounts, 11 to 15; liability accounts, 21 and 22; and the proprietor's capital account, 31.

3. Post the opening entry.

CHAPTER 4

APPENDIX PROBLEM 4-A — Analyzing transactions into their debit and credit parts

Howard Lipton, a doctor, decides to sell some of his old equipment and replace it with new equipment. His ledger contains the following balance sheet accounts:

Cash	Automobile
Medical Supplies	Atkins Equipment Company (creditor)
Medical Equipment	Dayville Furniture Company (creditor)
Office Equipment	Howard Lipton, Capital

During the first week in May of the current year, Dr. Lipton completed the selected transactions given on the next page.

Instructions: Use a pair of T accounts to analyze each of the transactions listed below. Analyze each transaction into its debit and credit parts as follows:

(a) Write the account title and the debit amount in the first T account.

(b) Write the account title and the credit amount in the second T account.

The analysis of Transaction No. 1 is given at the right.

Cash	
23.00	

Office Equipment	
	23.00

Transaction Number — *Transactions*

1. Received cash, $23.00, from sale of old waiting room chairs.
2. Received cash, $40.00, from sale of old operating room table.
3. Paid cash, $480.00, to Atkins Equipment Company in payment of amount owed.
4. Received cash, $78.00, from sale of old waiting room sofa.
5. Paid cash, $63.00, for drugs and other medical supplies.
6. Received cash, $40.00, from sale of old office desk.
7. Received cash, $15.00, from sale of old medical supplies cabinet.
8. Paid cash, $200.00, to Dayville Furniture Company in part payment of amount owed.
9. Received cash, $60.00, from sale of old waiting room table and magazine rack.
10. Paid cash, $460.00, for new typewriter and adding machine.
11. Paid cash, $120.00, for new filing cabinets.
12. Paid cash, $200.00, for new waiting room chairs.

CHAPTER 5

APPENDIX PROBLEM 5-A | Analyzing transactions into their debit and credit parts

Tim Parker owns and operates the Blue Grass Swim Club. His income is obtained from two sources — annual membership dues and daily swim fees. The account titles that he uses for these two kinds of income are Membership Dues and Swim Fees, as shown in the chart of accounts below.

CHART OF ACCOUNTS

Assets	Income
11 Cash	41 Membership Dues
12 Office Furniture and Equipment	42 Swim Fees
13 Pool Equipment	
Liabilities	**Expenses**
21 Calvert Chemical Company	51 Electricity Expense
22 Nolan Equipment Company	52 Miscellaneous Expense
Proprietorship	53 Pool Maintenance Expense
31 Tim Parker, Capital	54 Water Expense

Instructions: Use a pair of T accounts to analyze each of the selected transactions listed below. Analyze each transaction into its debit and credit parts as follows:

(a) Write the account title and the debit amount in the first T account.

(b) Write the account title and the credit amount in the second T account.

The analysis of Transaction No. 1 is given at the right.

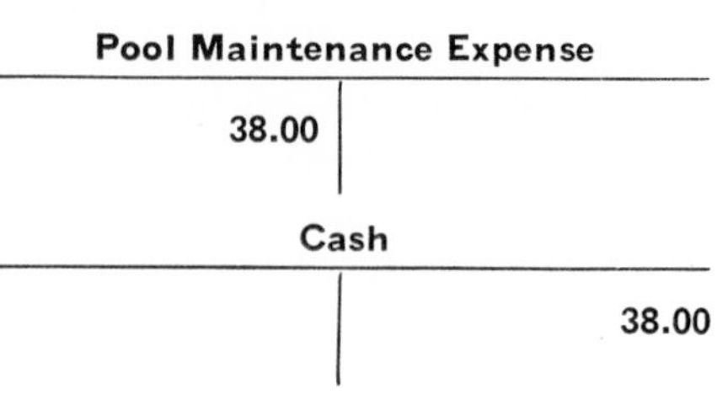

Transaction Number — *Transactions*

1. Paid cash, $38.00, for chlorine tablets.
2. Received cash, $575.00, from membership dues.
3. Paid cash, $16.00, for pool treatment solution.
4. Received cash, $30.00, from swim fees.
5. Received cash, $345.00, from membership dues.
6. Paid cash $27.00, to Calvert Chemical Company in payment of account.
7. Received cash, $260.00, from sale of old pump and filter.
8. Paid cash $1,500.00, for new circulating pump and filter.
9. Paid cash, $29.00, for electric bill.
10. Received cash, $40.00, from swim fees.
11. Paid cash, $88.00, for two-drawer office file.
12. Received cash, $500.00, from Mr. Parker as additional investment in the business.
13. Paid cash, $47.00, for water bill.
14. Paid cash, $25.00, for advertisement in weekly newspaper. (Miscellaneous Expense)
15. Paid cash, $85.00, for the installation of a new diving board.
16. Received cash, $1,150.00, from membership dues.
17. Received cash, $7.00, from sale of old office desk.
18. Paid cash, $220.00, for new office desk.
19. Paid cash, $65.00, for reclining pool chairs.
20. Paid cash, $55.00, to Nolan Equipment Company in payment of account.

CHAPTER 6

APPENDIX PROBLEM 6-A | Journalizing cash transactions of a shoe repair shop

Peter Bartel owns and operates Bartel's Shoe Repair Shop. The title he uses for his income account is Sales.

Instructions: 1. Record on page 12 of a five-column cash journal the selected transactions given on the next page. Use as your model the five-column cash journal illustrated on page 67. Use the current year in recording the date. In journalizing these transactions, use the following account titles:

Cash
Shop Equipment
Shop Supplies
Paulson Leather Works
Shafer Boot Shop
Peter Bartel, Capital
Sales
Advertising Expense
Fuel Expense
Maintenance Expense
Miscellaneous Expense
Rent Expense
Wages Expense

Transactions

June 1. Paid cash, $75.00, for June rent. (Check No. 311)
2. Paid cash, $23.75, for a month's supply of nails and leather. (Check No. 312)
3. Paid cash, $20.50, for maintenance of shop equipment. (Check No. 313)
4. Paid cash, $45.00, to Shafer Boot Shop in full payment of amount owed. (Check No. 314)
6. Paid cash, $25.75, for fuel oil. (Check No. 315)
7. Paid cash, $60.00, for wages of shop employee. (Check No. 316)
9. Paid cash, $5.00, for advertising. (Check No. 317)
11. Paid cash, $3.45, for water bill. (Check No. 318) (Miscellaneous Expense)
12. Paid cash, $75.00, for purchase of shop equipment. (Check No. 319)
14. Total receipts from cash sales for the first half of June amounted to $396.35. (Receipt Nos. 818–936)
14. Paid cash, $60.00, for wages of shop employee. (Check No. 320)
16. Received cash, $10.00, for sale of used shop equipment. (Receipt No. 937)
18. Paid cash, $10.50, to part-time errand boy. (Check No. 321) (Wages Expense)
21. Paid cash, $60.00, for wages of shop employee. (Check No. 322)
24. Paid cash, $56.80, to Paulson Leather Works in part payment of amount owed. (Check No. 323)
25. Paid cash, $5.20, for telephone bill. (Check No. 324) (Miscellaneous Expense)
26. Paid cash, $9.00, for advertising. (Check No. 325)
28. Paid cash, $60.00, for wages of shop employee. (Check No. 326)
29. Paid cash, $14.90, for electricity bill. (Check No. 327) (Miscellaneous Expense)
30. Total receipts from cash sales for the last half of June amounted to $416.85. (Receipt Nos. 938–1077)

Instructions: 2. Foot, prove, and rule the journal.

CHAPTER 7

APPENDIX PROBLEM 7-A | Journalizing and posting the transactions of a doctor

The chart of accounts for Dr. F. L. Nichols is given below.

Instructions: 1. Open the twelve accounts in the ledger that will be needed for this problem. Place six accounts on each page of your ledger.

Dr. F. L. Nichols
Chart of Accounts

(1) ASSETS	Acct. No.	(4) INCOME	Acct. No.
Cash	11	Fees Income	41
Automobile	12		
Office Equipment	13	**(5) EXPENSES**	
Office Supplies	14	Automobile Expense	51
		Miscellaneous Expense	52
(2) LIABILITIES		Rent Expense	53
Allington Company	21	Stationery Expense	54
Baker Garage	22		
(3) PROPRIETORSHIP			
F. L. Nichols, Capital	31		

Instructions: 2. Copy the following account balances in the proper accounts of your ledger, using November 1 of the current year as the date.

Assets (Debit Balances)		Liabilities and Proprietorship (Credit Balances)	
Cash	$ 1,540.50	Allington Company	$ 550.00
Automobile	3,000.00	Baker Garage	72.50
Office Equipment	6,225.00	F. L. Nichols, Capital	11,193.00
Office Supplies	1,050.00		

Instructions: 3. Record the transactions given below in a five-column cash journal. Use as your model the five-column cash journal illustrated on page 96, but use page 11 as the page number for your journal. Number all checks, beginning with No. 201. Number all receipts, beginning with No. 89.

Transactions

Nov. 1. Paid cash, $225.00, for rent.
2. Received cash, $150.00, for professional fees.
3. Paid cash, $19.00, for stationery.
5. Paid cash, $83.00, for office equipment.
7. Paid cash, $72.50, to Baker Garage.
9. Received cash, $45.00, from the sale of old office equipment.
11. Received cash, $185.00, for professional fees.
13. Paid cash, $200.00, to Allington Company.
15. Paid cash, $8.45, for stamps. (Miscellaneous Expense)
16. Paid cash, $9.50, for gas and oil.
17. Received cash, $230.00, for professional fees.
18. Paid cash, $11.50, for stationery.
20. Paid cash, $48.45, for office supplies.
23. Received cash, $290.00, for professional fees.
25. Paid cash, $8.40, for gas and oil.
27. Received cash, $345.00, for professional fees.
30. Paid cash, $16.25, for telephone service for the month. (Miscellaneous Expense)
30. Paid cash, $15.10, for electricity for the month. (Miscellaneous Expense)
30. Received cash, $265.00, for professional fees.

Instructions: 4. Post the individual amounts in the General Debit and the General Credit columns to the accounts in the ledger.

5. Place a check mark in the Post. Ref. column for each entry crediting Fees Income to show that these entries are not posted individually.

6. Foot each amount column with small pencil figures.

7. Prove the equality of debits and credits in your cash journal.

8. Prove cash. The cash balance is $2,333.35. All cash receipts have been deposited.

9. Total and rule your cash journal.

10. Post the totals of the three special columns. Place a check mark under the General Debit and General Credit columns to indicate that these totals are not to be posted.

CHAPTER 8

APPENDIX PROBLEM 8-A | Trial balance for a personal service business

Mr. Richard Judd is the proprietor and manager of the Judd Parcel Service. The balances in the accounts in Mr. Judd's ledger on June 30 of the current year are as follows:

Account	No.	Debit	Credit
Cash	11	1,280.85	
Delivery Equipment	12	6,357.00	
Office Equipment	13	822.00	
Edgar Gas & Oil Co.	21		1,320.00
Marathon Motors	22		182.50
Richard Judd, Capital	31		5,486.06
Service Fees	41		4,328.50
Heating Expense	51	273.20	
Labor Expense	52	1,327.00	
Miscellaneous Expense	53	263.40	
Rent Expense	54	307.00	
Truck Expense	55	686.61	

Instructions: Prepare a trial balance dated June 30 of the current year.

APPENDIX PROBLEM 8-B | Trial balance for a dentist

The footings in the ledger accounts of Dr. Theodore Paullin on October 31 of the current year are as follows:

Account Numbers	*Account Titles*	*Debit Footings*	*Credit Footings*
11	Cash	$1,501.90	$ 800.60
12	Equipment	3,950.00	
13	Office Furniture	1,455.00	
21	Athens Equipment Company	250.00	675.90
22	Colby Medical Supply Company	75.90	75.90
31	Theodore Paullin, Capital		4,657.85
41	Dental Fees		1,504.00
51	Miscellaneous Expense	66.45	
52	Rent Expense	140.00	
53	Salary Expense	275.00	

Instructions: 1. Prove cash. The bank balance according to the checkbook on October 31 of the current year is $701.30. All cash receipts have been deposited.

2. Prepare a trial balance dated October 31 of the current year.

CHAPTER 9

APPENDIX PROBLEM 9-A | Work sheet for an advertising agency

The account balances in the ledger of the Angevine Advertising Agency on March 31, the end of the first quarterly fiscal period of the current year, are as follows:

Cash....................	$1,813.00	J. R. Angevine, Capital....	$2,500.00
Automobile..............	2,230.00	Advertising Commissions..	4,279.00
Office Supplies...........	64.00	Automobile Expense......	164.80
Office Furniture..........	867.50	Electricity Expense........	42.00
Office Machines..........	610.20	Miscellaneous Expense....	38.20
Richard Howes (creditor)..	18.80	Rent Expense............	330.00
Samson Company (creditor)	71.00	Salary Expense...........	910.00
Tri-County Printers (creditor)..............	248.50	Telephone Expense.......	36.60
		Water Expense...........	11.00

Instructions: Prepare a six-column work sheet for the Angevine Advertising Agency dated March 31 of the current year. Use the account titles and account balances given above.

CHAPTER 10

APPENDIX PROBLEM 10-A | Financial reports for a theater

The work sheet for the Oakley Theater for the month of June of the current year is given below.

Oakley Theater
Work Sheet
For Month Ended June 30, 19--

Account Titles	Trial Balance		Income Statement		Balance Sheet	
	Debit	Credit	Debit	Credit	Debit	Credit
Cash....................	2,873 50				2,873 50	
Air Conditioning Equip...	3,375 00				3,375 00	
Projection Equipment.....	8,900 00				8,900 00	
Sound Equipment..........	878 50				878 50	
Acme Films, Inc..........		50 00				50 00
Denver Studios...........		114 00				114 00
Monarch Films............		28 00				28 00
Pacific Sound Service....		60 00				60 00
Star Supply Company......		34 25				34 25
David Harris, Capital....		14,931 00				14,931 00
Admissions Income........		2,304 00		2,304 00		
Advertising Expense.....	130 00		130 00			
Electricity Expense......	105 75		105 75			
Film Rental Expense......	925 00		925 00			
Maintenance Expense......	64 00		64 00			
Projection Expense.......	33 00		33 00			
Rent Expense.............	200 00		200 00			
Water Expense............	36 50		36 50			
	17,521 25	17,521 25	1,494 25	2,304 00	16,027 00	15,217 25
Net Income...............			809 75			809 75
			2,304 00	2,304 00	16,027 00	16,027 00

Instructions: 1. Prepare an income statement.

2. Prepare a balance sheet.

CHAPTER 11

APPENDIX PROBLEM 11-A | Closing entries for a theater

A work sheet for the Oakley Theater is given in Appendix Problem 10-A.

Instructions: Record the closing entries in a two-column general journal.

CHAPTER 12

APPENDIX PROBLEM 12-A | Recording purchases on account of a book store

The following purchases of merchandise on account were made by the Donnor Book Store during October of the current year:

Oct. 3.	MacLean Supplies Company	$215.00
7.	Palmer Paper Company	184.00
10.	Marty Book Company	315.00
12.	Allison Book Store, Inc.	225.00
12.	MacLean Supplies Company	189.00
17.	Marty Book Company	311.00
21.	Allison Book Store, Inc.	133.00
25.	Marty Book Company	228.00
25.	Watson Card Company	87.00
28.	MacLean Supplies Company	236.00
29.	Allison Book Store, Inc.	201.00

Instructions: 1. Record each purchase on page 12 of a purchases journal similar to the one on page 170.

2. Total and rule the purchases journal.

The purchases journal prepared in this problem will be used in Appendix Problem 12-B.

APPENDIX PROBLEM 12-B | Posting from the purchases journal to two ledgers

The Donnor Book Store has the following accounts in the accounts payable ledger:

Creditor	*Account Balance on October 1 of Current Year*
Allison Book Store, Inc., 300 Main Street Toledo, Ohio 43605	$128.00
MacLean Supplies Company, 100 North Bittersweet Muncie, Indiana 47304	——

Creditor	*Account Balance on October 1 of Current Year*
Marty Book Company, 106 Central Avenue Duluth, Minnesota 55807	26.50
Palmer Paper Company, 1240 Market Street Toledo, Ohio 43602	514.00
Watson Card Company, 6800 Third Street Toledo, Ohio 43605	89.40

Instructions: 1. Open an account for each of the creditors listed above. Use an accounts payable ledger with balance-column ruling as shown on page 174. Allow four lines for each account. Record the balance of each account that has one.

2. Post the entries in the purchases journal prepared in Appendix Problem 12-A to the proper accounts in the accounts payable ledger.

3. Open the following two accounts in the general ledger. Allow four lines for each account. Record the balance of each account that has a balance.

Account Number	*Account Title*	*Account Balance on October 1 of Current Year*
21	Accounts Payable	$757.90
51	Purchases	——

4. Post the total of the purchases journal prepared in Appendix Problem 12-A to the two accounts in the general ledger.

CHAPTER 13

APPENDIX PROBLEM 13-A | Recording and posting purchases transactions and cash payments transactions

John Rice owns and operates the Old Mill China Shop. The transactions listed below were completed by the Old Mill China Shop during the month of June of the current year. All payments were made by check, beginning with No. 901.

Instructions: 1. Record the purchases transactions on page 7 of a purchases journal similar to the one shown on page 170.

2. Record the cash payments transactions on page 11 of a cash payments journal similar to the one shown on page 196.

June 1. Paid June rent, $150.00.
2. Purchased merchandise on account from Monticello China Company, $628.30.
6. Paid $413.60 to Monticello China Company on account.
7. Purchased merchandise on account from Lynn China Company, $764.30.

12. Paid $228.20 to Lynn China Company on account.
15. Paid $325.00 for semimonthly payroll.
16. Paid $278.20 to Clinton Pottery Company on account.
19. Purchased merchandise on account from Clinton Pottery Company, $380.40.
21. Paid June electric bill, $17.90.
22. Purchased merchandise on account from Marshall Potteries, $550.40.
22. Paid cash for the purchase of merchandise, $75.50.
23. Paid $258.00 to Marshall Potteries on account.
26. Paid June telephone bill, $14.52.
28. Paid $350.00 to Mr. Rice for withdrawal of cash for personal use.
30. Paid $325.00 for semimonthly payroll.

Instructions: 3. Total and rule the purchases journal.

4. Foot, prove, total, and rule the cash payments journal.

5. Open the following accounts in the general ledger. Record the balances as of June 1 of the current year. Allow four lines for each account.

Account Number	*Account Title*	*Account Balance on June 1 of Current Year*
11	Cash	$5,214.30
21	Accounts Payable	1,178.00
32	John Rice, Drawing	——
51	Purchases	——
62	Miscellaneous Expense	——
63	Rent Expense	——
64	Salary Expense	——

6. Open the following accounts for creditors in the accounts payable ledger. Allow four lines for each account. Record the balances for each account as of June 1 of the current year.

Creditor	*Account Balance on June 1 of Current Year*
Clinton Pottery Company, 1204 High Street N. Columbus, Ohio 43201	$278.20
Lynn China Company, 632 Miami Avenue Charleston, South Carolina 29406	228.20
Marshall Potteries, 5101 Caldwell Drive Zanesville, Ohio 43705	258.00
Monticello China Company, 5 State Avenue Albany, New York 12207	413.60

7. Post from the purchases journal and the cash payments journal to the general ledger and the accounts payable ledger.

8. Prepare a schedule of accounts payable.

CHAPTER 14

APPENDIX PROBLEM 14-A | Journalizing sales on account for a furniture store

The following sales of merchandise on account were made by T. B. Brunner, a retail furniture dealer, during August of the current year. The sales slips are to be numbered consecutively beginning with No. 80.

Date	*Customer*	*Amount of Sale*
Aug. 1.	M. E. Anderson	$267.30
7.	M & M Company	322.95
7.	B. J. Barnett	110.55
16.	W. S. Hall	152.30
17.	M & M Company	85.00
24.	W. S. Hall	51.25
28.	M. E. Anderson	109.66
31.	M & M Company	155.99

Instructions: 1. Record each of these transactions on page 8 of a sales journal similar to the one illustrated on page 214.

2. Total and rule the sales journal.

The sales journal prepared in this problem will be used in Appendix Problem 14-B.

APPENDIX PROBLEM 14-B | Posting from the sales journal to two ledgers

Instructions: 1. Open the following accounts for the customers of T. B. Brunner. Use the customer's account form shown on page 219 as a model. Allow five lines for each account. Record the balances as of August 1 of the current year.

Customer	*Account Balance on August 1 of Current Year*
M. E. Anderson, 125 Buena Vista, W. Santa Fe, New Mexico 87501	$205.80
B. J. Barnett, 905 Cortez Santa Fe, New Mexico 87502.	35.00
W. S. Hall, 204 Camina Cerrito Santa Fe, New Mexico 87501	470.80
M & M Company, 312 Seville Road Santa Fe, New Mexico 87502.	236.40

Instructions: 2. Post the entries from the sales journal prepared in Appendix Problem 14-A to the proper accounts in the accounts receivable ledger.

3. Open the following accounts in the general ledger and record the beginning balance if the account has one. Allow four lines for each account.

Account Number	*Account Title*	*Account Balance on August 1 of Current Year*
12	Accounts Receivable..................	$948.00
41	Sales..................................	——

Instructions: 4. Post the total of the sales journal prepared in Appendix Problem 14-A to the proper accounts in the general ledger.

CHAPTER 15

APPENDIX PROBLEM 15-A | Recording and posting sales and cash receipts

A. M. Swan, a retail jeweler, sells on account to the following customers. The amounts due him on November 30 of the current year are:

Customer	*Account Balance on November 30 of Current Year*
Daniel Cabot, 1472 Dreman Avenue Potrero, California 92063..................	$194.60
Susan Crane, 8584 Donegal San Diego, California 92120................	84.00
George Graham, 4345 Michigan Avenue San Diego, California 92120	129.00
M. E. Hedges, 2311 Lakewood Drive Los Angeles, California 90012..............	71.00
A. R. Kelley, 412 Salem Avenue San Bernardino, California 92415...........	56.50
Michael Murphy, 4340 Trenton Street Pasadena, California 91136	230.00

Instructions: 1. Open accounts in an accounts receivable ledger with balance-column ruling for the customers listed above. Allow five lines for each account. Record the balance in each account as of December 1 of the current year.

2. In a general ledger open the following accounts. Allow four lines for each account. Record the balance for each account as of December 1 of the current year.

Account No.	*Account Title*	*Account Balance*
11	Cash...	$1,398.40
12	Accounts Receivable..........................	765.10
13	Office Supplies..............................	299.70
41	Sales..	——

The cash receipts and sales transactions completed by Mr. Swan during December of the current year are given on the next page.

Instructions: 3. Record the cash balance, $1,398.40, with a memorandum entry.

4. Record the cash receipts transactions on page 15 of a cash receipts journal similar to the one illustrated on page 233.

5. Record the sales transactions on page 12 of a sales journal similar to the one illustrated on page 213. Number the sales consecutively beginning with No. 501.

Transactions

Dec. 1. Received $71.00 from M. E. Hedges on account.
4. Sold merchandise on account to A. R. Kelley, $99.00.
7. Received $56.50 from A. R. Kelley on account.
8. Sold merchandise on account to Daniel Cabot, $159.95.
8. Received $820.10 from cash sales.
11. Received $15.00 from the sale of office supplies to a neighboring merchant.

Office supplies are not part of the merchandise kept in stock for resale. For this reason, the sales account is not credited for this transaction. Instead, Office Supplies is credited.

12. Sold merchandise on account to Michael Murphy, $110.00.
14. Received $194.60 from Daniel Cabot on account.
15. Received $230.00 from Michael Murphy on account.
15. Received $412.90 from cash sales.
19. Sold merchandise on account to Susan Crane, $50.00.
21. Received $84.00 from Susan Crane on account.
22. Received $629.95 from cash sales.
26. Sold merchandise on account to George Graham, $125.95.
28. Received $129.00 from George Graham on account.
29. Received $585.30 from cash sales.

Instructions: 6. Post the entries from the sales journal and the cash receipts journal to the proper accounts.

7. Total and rule the sales journal. Post the total to the accounts receivable account and the sales account in the general ledger.

8. Foot, prove, total, and rule the cash receipts journal.

9. Post the totals of the special columns in the cash receipts journal.

10. Prepare a schedule of accounts receivable from the accounts in the accounts receivable ledger.

CHAPTER 16

APPENDIX PROBLEM 16-A | Recording miscellaneous entries

The following transactions are some of those completed by George Kruger during the month of November of the current year. Mr. Kruger uses a purchases journal, a sales journal, a cash receipts journal, a cash payments journal, and a general journal.

Instructions: 1. Select only those entries that should be made in a general journal and record them on page 19 of two-column journal paper.

2. For each of the transactions not recorded in the general journal, state:

a The journal in which the transaction would be recorded.

b The account or accounts that would be debited.

c The account or accounts that would be credited.

Transactions

Nov. 1. Paid $200.00 for November rent. Check No. 631.

3. Sold merchandise on account to Gerald Miller, $27.00. Sales Invoice No. 164.

4. Received $581.45 from cash sales for the period November 1 to 4.

6. L. A. Condon reported that he had been charged $51.30 for merchandise he had not purchased. A check of sales invoice No. 137 dated October 24 shows that the sale was made to J. P. Conden. Memo dated November 6.

7. Purchased merchandise on account from City Supply Company, $78.80.

7. Mr. Kruger discovered that a $25.00 purchase of supplies on account in October had been charged to the purchases account in error. Memo dated November 7.

10. Sold merchandise on account to George Hayes, $36.98. Sales Invoice No. 165.

10. Mr. Kruger bought supplies on account from City Supply Company for use in the business, $43.06. Invoice of November 9.

14. Paid $100.00 to Mr. Kruger for his personal use. Check No. 632.

15. Received $45.00 from Gerald Miller on account.

16. Mr. Kruger withdrew stock for his personal use, $87.50. Memo dated November 16.

17. Received $1,050.45 from cash sales for the period November 13 to 17.

17. Paid $55.00 for salary of part-time employee in the store. Check No. 633.

21. Paid $78.80 to City Supply Company on account. Check No. 634.

24. Received a personal check for $1,000.00 from the owner, Mr. Kruger, as an additional investment in the business.

28. Paid cash, $249.95, for a new counter for the store. Check No. 635.

30. Mr. Kruger discovered that a $16.00 cash sale of supplies to a customer had been recorded in the sales account in error. Memo dated November 30.

CHAPTER 17

APPENDIX PROBLEM 17-A | Reconciling a bank statement

On August 1 of the current year, the Balfour Hardware Store, owned and operated by William Balfour, received a bank statement for July. The following information was found after comparing the bank statement with the check stubs:

a The cash balance, July 31, as shown on the last check stub for July, was $2,378.20.

b The bank balance, July 31, as shown on the bank statement was $2,573.70.

c Two charge slips accompanying the bank statement show that the bank made the following charges against the account of the Balfour Hardware Store: Bank service charge, $3.20; charge for collecting a note, $1.50.

d The following checks were outstanding: No. 161, $38.10; No. 168, $49.50; No. 169, $112.60.

Instructions: Prepare a reconciliation of the bank statement for the Balfour Hardware Store.

CHAPTER 18

APPENDIX PROBLEM 18-A | Work sheet for a hardware store

Albert Wick owns and operates Wicks Hardware. On June 30 of the current year, the end of the fiscal period for one month, the accounts and their balances in the general ledger and the list of inventories are as follows:

Account Titles	*Acct. No.*	*Balance*	*Account Titles*	*Acct. No.*	*Balance*
Cash................	11	$ 2,967.20	Sales................	41	$16,870.60
Accounts Receivable..	12	7,350.80	Purchases	51	15,151.10
Merchandise Inventory	13	21,000.00	Delivery Expense.....	61	350.20
Supplies.............	14	460.20	Insurance Expense....	62	——
Prepaid Insurance	15	240.00	Miscellaneous Expense	63	90.60
Accounts Payable.....	21	6,210.00	Rent Expense........	64	400.00
Albert Wick, Capital..	31	26,610.20	Salary Expense.......	65	1,180.70
Albert Wick, Drawing.	32	500.00	Supplies Expense.....	66	——
Income & Expense Summary..........	33	——			

Inventories, June 30, 19—

Merchandise inventory..................	$22,104.00
Supplies inventory......................	365.20
Value of insurance policies	120.00

Instructions: Prepare an eight-column work sheet for Wicks Hardware. Use as your guide the eight-column work sheet illustrated on page 318.

CHAPTER 19

APPENDIX PROBLEM 19-A | Preparing financial reports

A work sheet for the Shroyer Drug Store is given on the following page.

Instructions: 1. Prepare an income statement from this work sheet.

2. Prepare a capital statement from this work sheet.

3. Prepare a balance sheet from this work sheet.

CHAPTER 20

APPENDIX PROBLEM 20-A | Work at the end of the fiscal period

On January 31 of the current year, the end of a monthly fiscal period, the account balances in the ledger of Eastern Electric Company and the list of inventories are as follows:

Account Titles	*Acct. No.*	*Balance*	*Account Titles*	*Acct. No.*	*Balance*
Cash	11	$ 3,550.40	Sales	41	$ 9,635.15
Accounts Receivable	12	2,011.45	Purchases	51	5,960.20
Merchandise Inventory	13	11,220.00	Delivery Expense	61	425.45
Supplies	14	594.00	Insurance Expense	62	——
Prepaid Insurance	15	510.00	Miscellaneous Expense	63	361.25
Accounts Payable	21	1,810.00	Rent Expense	64	400.00
James Burns, Capital	31	14,928.40	Salary Expense	65	980.80
James Burns, Drawing	32	360.00	Supplies Expense	66	——
Income and Expense Summary	33	——			

Inventories, January 31, 19—

Merchandise inventory	$12,090.40
Supplies inventory	336.40
Value of insurance policies	480.00

Instructions: 1. Prepare an eight-column work sheet.

2. Prepare an income statement.

3. Prepare a capital statement.

4. Prepare a balance sheet.

5. Record the adjusting and closing entries on page 8 of a general journal.

Shroyer Drug Store
Work Sheet
For Month Ended, April 30, 19—

Account Titles	Acct. No.	Trial Balance Debit	Trial Balance Credit	Adjustments Debit	Adjustments Credit	Income Statement Debit	Income Statement Credit	Balance Sheet Debit	Balance Sheet Credit
Cash	11	2360 20						2360 20	
Accounts Receivable	12	1040 85						1040 85	
Merchandise Inventory	13	4885 00		(b) 4145 00	(a) 4885 00			4145 00	
Supplies	14	434 90			(c) 104 00			330 90	
Prepaid Insurance	15	120 00			(d) 10 00			110 00	
Accounts Payable	21		910 65						910 65
Hubert Shroyer, Capital	31		6967 50						6967 50
Hubert Shroyer, Drawing	32	400 00						400 00	
Income & Expense Sum.	33			(a) 4885 00	(b) 4145 00	4885 00	4145 00		
Sales	41		4160 35				4160 35		
Purchases	51	1874 45				1874 45			
Delivery Expense	61	210 30				210 30			
Insurance Expense	62			(d) 10 00		10 00			
Miscellaneous Expense	63	62 80				62 80			
Rent Expense	64	300 00				300 00			
Salary Expense	65	350 00				350 00			
Supplies Expense	66			(c) 104 00		104 00			
		12038 50	12038 50	9144 00	9144 00	7796 55	8305 35	8386 95	7878 15
Net Income						508 80			508 80
						8305 35	8305 35	8386 95	8386 95

For Use in Appendix Problem 19-A

CHAPTER 21

APPENDIX PROBLEM 21-A | Interpreting data on punched cards

The punched cards shown on pages 656 to 658 are for charge sales made by the Holmes Equipment Company during the month of November, 1967. Cards numbered 1, 2, and 3 will be used in this problem.

Instructions: 1. On a sheet of paper prepare a form similar to the one shown below.

Card No.	Customer's Name	Customer's Number	Date	Stock No. of Item Sold	Quantity	Unit Price	Amount
1							
2							
3							

Instructions: 2. Use punched cards 1, 2, and 3 to record the data called for on the form above. The illustration of the punched card on page 381 will be helpful to you in reading the data punched in the cards.

1

CUSTOMER'S NAME | CUST. NO. | DATE | STOCK NO. | QUANTITY | UNIT PRICE | AMOUNT

00000000000000000000000000000000000000000000000000000000000000000000000000000000
1 2 3 4 5 6 7 8 9 10 11 12 13 14 15 16 17 18 19 20 21 22 23 24 25 26 27 28 29 30 31 32 33 34 35 36 37 38 39 40 41 42 43 44 45 46 47 48 49 50 51 52 53 54 55 56 57 58 59 60 61 62 63 64 65 66 67 68 69 70 71 72 73 74 75 76 77 78 79 80
11111111111111111111111111111111111111111111111111111111111111111111111111111111
22222222222222222222222222222222222222222222222222222222222222222222222222222222
33333333333333333333333333333333333333333333333333333333333333333333333333333333
44444444444444444444444444444444444444444444444444444444444444444444444444444444
55555555555555555555555555555555555555555555555555555555555555555555555555555555
66666666666666666666666666666666666666666666666666666666666666666666666666666666
77777777777777777777777777777777777777777777777777777777777777777777777777777777
88888888888888888888888888888888888888888888888888888888888888888888888888888888
99999999999999999999999999999999999999999999999999999999999999999999999999999999
1 2 3 4 5 6 7 8 9 10 11 12 13 14 15 16 17 18 19 20 21 22 23 24 25 26 27 28 29 30 31 32 33 34 35 36 37 38 39 40 41 42 43 44 45 46 47 48 49 50 51 52 53 54 55 56 57 58 59 60 61 62 63 64 65 66 67 68 69 70 71 72 73 74 75 76 77 78 79 80

2

CUSTOMER'S NAME | CUST. NO. | DATE | STOCK NO. | QUANTITY | UNIT PRICE | AMOUNT

00000000000000000000000000000000000000000000000000000000000000000000000000000000
1 2 3 4 5 6 7 8 9 10 11 12 13 14 15 16 17 18 19 20 21 22 23 24 25 26 27 28 29 30 31 32 33 34 35 36 37 38 39 40 41 42 43 44 45 46 47 48 49 50 51 52 53 54 55 56 57 58 59 60 61 62 63 64 65 66 67 68 69 70 71 72 73 74 75 76 77 78 79 80
11111111111111111111111111111111111111111111111111111111111111111111111111111111
22222222222222222222222222222222222222222222222222222222222222222222222222222222
33333333333333333333333333333333333333333333333333333333333333333333333333333333
44444444444444444444444444444444444444444444444444444444444444444444444444444444
55555555555555555555555555555555555555555555555555555555555555555555555555555555
66666666666666666666666666666666666666666666666666666666666666666666666666666666
77777777777777777777777777777777777777777777777777777777777777777777777777777777
88888888888888888888888888888888888888888888888888888888888888888888888888888888
99999999999999999999999999999999999999999999999999999999999999999999999999999999
1 2 3 4 5 6 7 8 9 10 11 12 13 14 15 16 17 18 19 20 21 22 23 24 25 26 27 28 29 30 31 32 33 34 35 36 37 38 39 40 41 42 43 44 45 46 47 48 49 50 51 52 53 54 55 56 57 58 59 60 61 62 63 64 65 66 67 68 69 70 71 72 73 74 75 76 77 78 79 80

3

CUSTOMER'S NAME | CUST. NO. | DATE | STOCK NO. | QUANTITY | UNIT PRICE | AMOUNT

00000000000000000000000000000000000000000000000000000000000000000000000000000000
1 2 3 4 5 6 7 8 9 10 11 12 13 14 15 16 17 18 19 20 21 22 23 24 25 26 27 28 29 30 31 32 33 34 35 36 37 38 39 40 41 42 43 44 45 46 47 48 49 50 51 52 53 54 55 56 57 58 59 60 61 62 63 64 65 66 67 68 69 70 71 72 73 74 75 76 77 78 79 80
11111111111111111111111111111111111111111111111111111111111111111111111111111111
22222222222222222222222222222222222222222222222222222222222222222222222222222222
33333333333333333333333333333333333333333333333333333333333333333333333333333333
44444444444444444444444444444444444444444444444444444444444444444444444444444444
55555555555555555555555555555555555555555555555555555555555555555555555555555555
66666666666666666666666666666666666666666666666666666666666666666666666666666666
77777777777777777777777777777777777777777777777777777777777777777777777777777777
88888888888888888888888888888888888888888888888888888888888888888888888888888888
99999999999999999999999999999999999999999999999999999999999999999999999999999999
1 2 3 4 5 6 7 8 9 10 11 12 13 14 15 16 17 18 19 20 21 22 23 24 25 26 27 28 29 30 31 32 33 34 35 36 37 38 39 40 41 42 43 44 45 46 47 48 49 50 51 52 53 54 55 56 57 58 59 60 61 62 63 64 65 66 67 68 69 70 71 72 73 74 75 76 77 78 79 80

For Use in Appendix Problems 21-A and 21-B

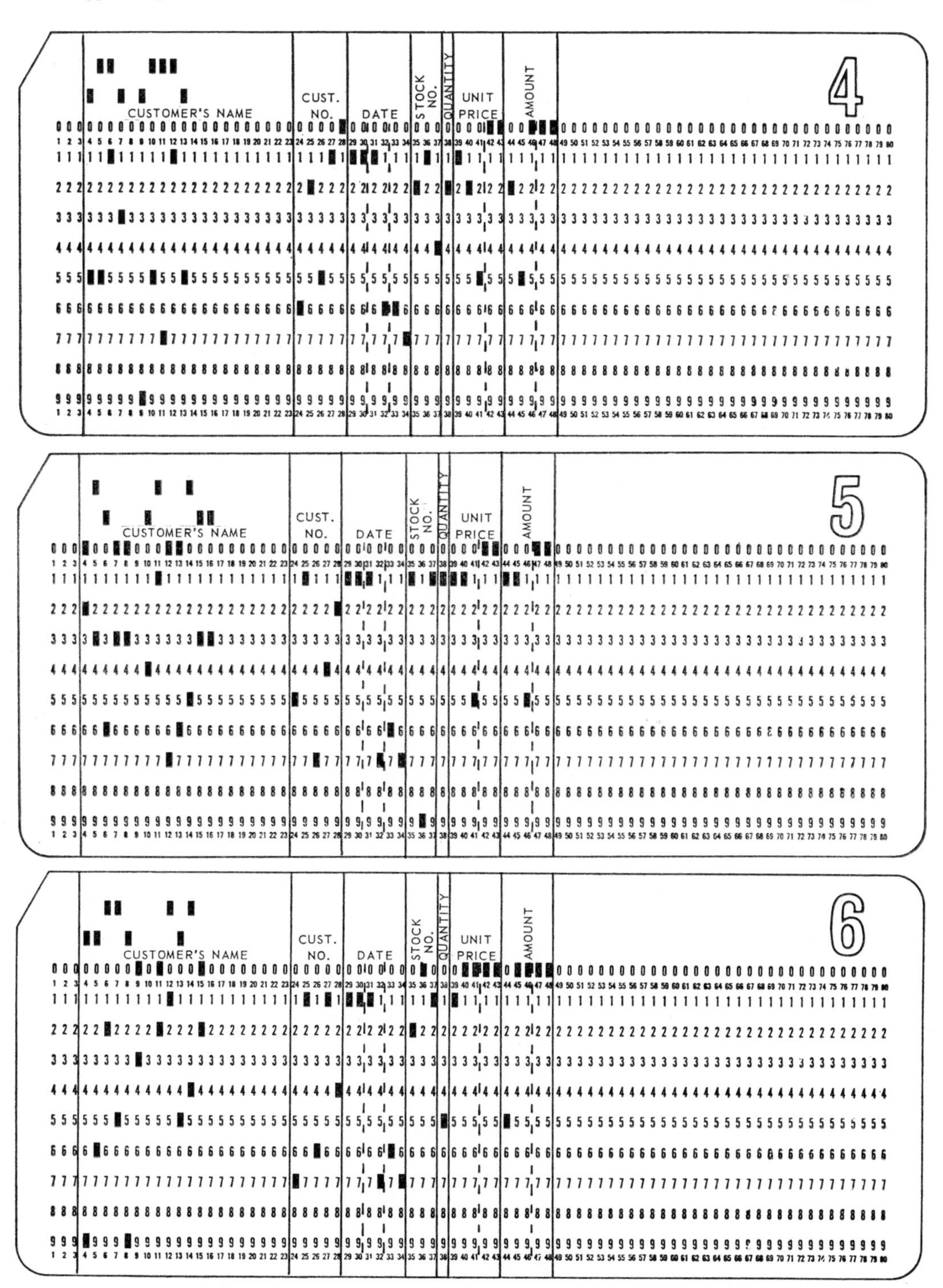

For Use in Appendix Problem 21-B

CUSTOMER'S NAME | CUST. NO. | DATE | STOCK NO. | QUANTITY | UNIT PRICE | AMOUNT

7

00000000000000000000000000000000000000000000000000000000000000000000000000000000
1 2 3 4 5 6 7 8 9 10 11 12 13 14 15 16 17 18 19 20 21 22 23 24 25 26 27 28 29 30 31 32 33 34 35 36 37 38 39 40 41 42 43 44 45 46 47 48 49 50 51 52 53 54 55 56 57 58 59 60 61 62 63 64 65 66 67 68 69 70 71 72 73 74 75 76 77 78 79 80
11111111111111111111111111111111111111111111111111111111111111111111111111111111
22222222222222222222222222222222222222222222222222222222222222222222222222222222
33333333333333333333333333333333333333333333333333333333333333333333333333333333
44444444444444444444444444444444444444444444444444444444444444444444444444444444
55555555555555555555555555555555555555555555555555555555555555555555555555555555
66666666666666666666666666666666666666666666666666666666666666666666666666666666
77777777777777777777777777777777777777777777777777777777777777777777777777777777
88888888888888888888888888888888888888888888888888888888888888888888888888888888
99999999999999999999999999999999999999999999999999999999999999999999999999999999
1 2 3 4 5 6 7 8 9 10 11 12 13 14 15 16 17 18 19 20 21 22 23 24 25 26 27 28 29 30 31 32 33 34 35 36 37 38 39 40 41 42 43 44 45 46 47 48 49 50 51 52 53 54 55 56 57 58 59 60 61 62 63 64 65 66 67 68 69 70 71 72 73 74 75 76 77 78 79 80

CUSTOMER'S NAME | CUST. NO. | DATE | STOCK NO. | QUANTITY | UNIT PRICE | AMOUNT

8

00000000000000000000000000000000000000000000000000000000000000000000000000000000
1 2 3 4 5 6 7 8 9 10 11 12 13 14 15 16 17 18 19 20 21 22 23 24 25 26 27 28 29 30 31 32 33 34 35 36 37 38 39 40 41 42 43 44 45 46 47 48 49 50 51 52 53 54 55 56 57 58 59 60 61 62 63 64 65 66 67 68 69 70 71 72 73 74 75 76 77 78 79 80
11111111111111111111111111111111111111111111111111111111111111111111111111111111
22222222222222222222222222222222222222222222222222222222222222222222222222222222
33333333333333333333333333333333333333333333333333333333333333333333333333333333
44444444444444444444444444444444444444444444444444444444444444444444444444444444
55555555555555555555555555555555555555555555555555555555555555555555555555555555
66666666666666666666666666666666666666666666666666666666666666666666666666666666
77777777777777777777777777777777777777777777777777777777777777777777777777777777
88888888888888888888888888888888888888888888888888888888888888888888888888888888
99999999999999999999999999999999999999999999999999999999999999999999999999999999
1 2 3 4 5 6 7 8 9 10 11 12 13 14 15 16 17 18 19 20 21 22 23 24 25 26 27 28 29 30 31 32 33 34 35 36 37 38 39 40 41 42 43 44 45 46 47 48 49 50 51 52 53 54 55 56 57 58 59 60 61 62 63 64 65 66 67 68 69 70 71 72 73 74 75 76 77 78 79 80

CUSTOMER'S NAME | CUST. NO. | DATE | STOCK NO. | QUANTITY | UNIT PRICE | AMOUNT

9

00000000000000000000000000000000000000000000000000000000000000000000000000000000
1 2 3 4 5 6 7 8 9 10 11 12 13 14 15 16 17 18 19 20 21 22 23 24 25 26 27 28 29 30 31 32 33 34 35 36 37 38 39 40 41 42 43 44 45 46 47 48 49 50 51 52 53 54 55 56 57 58 59 60 61 62 63 64 65 66 67 68 69 70 71 72 73 74 75 76 77 78 79 80
11111111111111111111111111111111111111111111111111111111111111111111111111111111
22222222222222222222222222222222222222222222222222222222222222222222222222222222
33333333333333333333333333333333333333333333333333333333333333333333333333333333
44444444444444444444444444444444444444444444444444444444444444444444444444444444
55555555555555555555555555555555555555555555555555555555555555555555555555555555
66666666666666666666666666666666666666666666666666666666666666666666666666666666
77777777777777777777777777777777777777777777777777777777777777777777777777777777
88888888888888888888888888888888888888888888888888888888888888888888888888888888
99999999999999999999999999999999999999999999999999999999999999999999999999999999
1 2 3 4 5 6 7 8 9 10 11 12 13 14 15 16 17 18 19 20 21 22 23 24 25 26 27 28 29 30 31 32 33 34 35 36 37 38 39 40 41 42 43 44 45 46 47 48 49 50 51 52 53 54 55 56 57 58 59 60 61 62 63 64 65 66 67 68 69 70 71 72 73 74 75 76 77 78 79 80

For Use in Appendix Problem 21-B

APPENDIX PROBLEM 21-B | Using punched cards to prepare sales reports

In this problem you will learn how data are tabulated from the information contained in punched cards. You will need the nine punched cards for the Holmes Equipment Company illustrated on pages 656 to 658.

Instructions: 1. On a sheet of paper prepare a form similar to the one shown below. Leave ten blank lines on which to record the data.

Total Sales by Customer			Total Sales by Stock Number	
1	2	3	4	5
Customer's Name	Customer's Number	Total Sales for November	Stock Number of Item Sold	Total Sales for Each Stock Number

Instructions: 2. On a separate sheet of paper, list each of the customers' names and customers' numbers contained in the nine punched cards. Arrange the customers' names in alphabetic order and record each customer's name and number in columns 1 and 2 of the form prepared in Instructions 1.

3. From the information in the punched cards, determine the total amount of sales for each customer. Write the amount of total sales for each customer in column 3 of the form.

4. On a separate sheet of paper list all the different stock numbers of items sold. Write the stock numbers in column 4 of the form, starting with the lowest stock number.

5. From the information in the punched cards, determine the total amount of sales for each stock number. Write this total amount in column 5.

6. Find the total of column 3 and of column 5. Compare the totals to see if they are the same. This provides you with a check that all the cards have been included in your tabulations. If the totals are not the same, the error or errors should be located and corrected.

7. From the information you have recorded on the form, answer the following questions:

a To which customer was the largest amount of sales on account made during November?

b For which item of merchandise was the largest amount of sales made during November?

CHAPTER 22

APPENDIX PROBLEM 22-A | Preparing a daily sales report from data in punched cards

The punched cards prepared from data about the sales on account for October 25, 1967, have been sorted automatically according to the stock number of the merchandise sold. The six cards illustrated on pages 661 and 662 represent the sale of a single item of merchandise, Stock No. 164. These cards are a portion of all those for the day's sales on account.

In this problem you are to use these punched cards to prepare a daily sales report. If data processing equipment were available, this report would be prepared on a tabulator.

Instructions: 1. On a form similar to the one shown below, record the data from each of the six punched cards.

Daily Sales Report

Merchandise Stock No.__________ **Date**________________

Customer's Account No.	Quantity	Amount

Instructions: 2. On the last line of the form, write the word "Total" in the Customer's Account No. column. Add the Quantity column and write the total on the same line with the word "Total." Add the Amount column and write the total on the same line with the word "Total."

CHAPTER 23

APPENDIX PROBLEM 23-A | Recording transactions in a combination journal

Mr. J. R. Weise, a retail florist, completed the transactions on page 663 during the month of May of the current year. The cash balance on May 1 was $3,780.00.

Instructions: 1. Record on page 8 of a combination journal like the model on pages 406 and 407 the cash balance with a memorandum entry.

2. Record the transactions completed from May 1 through May 26.

CUSTOMER'S NAME | CUST. ACCT. NO. | DATE | QUANTITY | STOCK NO. | UNIT PRICE | AMOUNT

1

0 0 0 0 0 0 0 0 0 0 0 0 0 0 0 0 0 0 0 0 0 0 0 0 0 0 0 0 0 0 0 0 0 0 0 0 0 0 0 0 0 0 0 0 0 0 0 0 0 0 0 0 0 0 0 0 0 0 0 0 0 0 0 0 0 0 0 0 0 0 0 0 0 0 0 0 0 0 0 0
1 2 3 4 5 6 7 8 9 10 11 12 13 14 15 16 17 18 19 20 21 22 23 24 25 26 27 28 29 30 31 32 33 34 35 36 37 38 39 40 41 42 43 44 45 46 47 48 49 50 51 52 53 54 55 56 57 58 59 60 61 62 63 64 65 66 67 68 69 70 71 72 73 74 75 76 77 78 79 80
1 1 1 1 1 1 1 1 1 1 1 1 1 1 1 1 1 1 1 1 1 1 1 1 1 1 1 1 1 1 1 1 1 1 1 1 1 1 1 1 1 1 1 1 1 1 1 1 1 1 1 1 1 1 1 1 1 1 1 1 1 1 1 1 1 1 1 1 1 1 1 1 1 1 1 1 1 1 1 1
2 2 2 2 2 2 2 2 2 2 2 2 2 2 2 2 2 2 2 2 2 2 2 2 2 2 2 2 2 2 2 2 2 2 2 2 2 2 2 2 2 2 2 2 2 2 2 2 2 2 2 2 2 2 2 2 2 2 2 2 2 2 2 2 2 2 2 2 2 2 2 2 2 2 2 2 2 2 2 2
3 3 3 3 3 3 3 3 3 3 3 3 3 3 3 3 3 3 3 3 3 3 3 3 3 3 3 3 3 3 3 3 3 3 3 3 3 3 3 3 3 3 3 3 3 3 3 3 3 3 3 3 3 3 3 3 3 3 3 3 3 3 3 3 3 3 3 3 3 3 3 3 3 3 3 3 3 3 3 3
4 4 4 4 4 4 4 4 4 4 4 4 4 4 4 4 4 4 4 4 4 4 4 4 4 4 4 4 4 4 4 4 4 4 4 4 4 4 4 4 4 4 4 4 4 4 4 4 4 4 4 4 4 4 4 4 4 4 4 4 4 4 4 4 4 4 4 4 4 4 4 4 4 4 4 4 4 4 4 4
5 5 5 5 5 5 5 5 5 5 5 5 5 5 5 5 5 5 5 5 5 5 5 5 5 5 5 5 5 5 5 5 5 5 5 5 5 5 5 5 5 5 5 5 5 5 5 5 5 5 5 5 5 5 5 5 5 5 5 5 5 5 5 5 5 5 5 5 5 5 5 5 5 5 5 5 5 5 5 5
6 6 6 6 6 6 6 6 6 6 6 6 6 6 6 6 6 6 6 6 6 6 6 6 6 6 6 6 6 6 6 6 6 6 6 6 6 6 6 6 6 6 6 6 6 6 6 6 6 6 6 6 6 6 6 6 6 6 6 6 6 6 6 6 6 6 6 6 6 6 6 6 6 6 6 6 6 6 6 6
7 7 7 7 7 7 7 7 7 7 7 7 7 7 7 7 7 7 7 7 7 7 7 7 7 7 7 7 7 7 7 7 7 7 7 7 7 7 7 7 7 7 7 7 7 7 7 7 7 7 7 7 7 7 7 7 7 7 7 7 7 7 7 7 7 7 7 7 7 7 7 7 7 7 7 7 7 7 7 7
8 8 8 8 8 8 8 8 8 8 8 8 8 8 8 8 8 8 8 8 8 8 8 8 8 8 8 8 8 8 8 8 8 8 8 8 8 8 8 8 8 8 8 8 8 8 8 8 8 8 8 8 8 8 8 8 8 8 8 8 8 8 8 8 8 8 8 8 8 8 8 8 8 8 8 8 8 8 8 8
9 9 9 9 9 9 9 9 9 9 9 9 9 9 9 9 9 9 9 9 9 9 9 9 9 9 9 9 9 9 9 9 9 9 9 9 9 9 9 9 9 9 9 9 9 9 9 9 9 9 9 9 9 9 9 9 9 9 9 9 9 9 9 9 9 9 9 9 9 9 9 9 9 9 9 9 9 9 9 9
1 2 3 4 5 6 7 8 9 10 11 12 13 14 15 16 17 18 19 20 21 22 23 24 25 26 27 28 29 30 31 32 33 34 35 36 37 38 39 40 41 42 43 44 45 46 47 48 49 50 51 52 53 54 55 56 57 58 59 60 61 62 63 64 65 66 67 68 69 70 71 72 73 74 75 76 77 78 79 80

CUSTOMER'S NAME | CUST. ACCT. NO. | DATE | QUANTITY | STOCK NO. | UNIT PRICE | AMOUNT

2

0 0 0 0 0 0 0 0 0 0 0 0 0 0 0 0 0 0 0 0 0 0 0 0 0 0 0 0 0 0 0 0 0 0 0 0 0 0 0 0 0 0 0 0 0 0 0 0 0 0 0 0 0 0 0 0 0 0 0 0 0 0 0 0 0 0 0 0 0 0 0 0 0 0 0 0 0 0 0 0
1 2 3 4 5 6 7 8 9 10 11 12 13 14 15 16 17 18 19 20 21 22 23 24 25 26 27 28 29 30 31 32 33 34 35 36 37 38 39 40 41 42 43 44 45 46 47 48 49 50 51 52 53 54 55 56 57 58 59 60 61 62 63 64 65 66 67 68 69 70 71 72 73 74 75 76 77 78 79 80
1 1 1 1 1 1 1 1 1 1 1 1 1 1 1 1 1 1 1 1 1 1 1 1 1 1 1 1 1 1 1 1 1 1 1 1 1 1 1 1 1 1 1 1 1 1 1 1 1 1 1 1 1 1 1 1 1 1 1 1 1 1 1 1 1 1 1 1 1 1 1 1 1 1 1 1 1 1 1 1
2 2 2 2 2 2 2 2 2 2 2 2 2 2 2 2 2 2 2 2 2 2 2 2 2 2 2 2 2 2 2 2 2 2 2 2 2 2 2 2 2 2 2 2 2 2 2 2 2 2 2 2 2 2 2 2 2 2 2 2 2 2 2 2 2 2 2 2 2 2 2 2 2 2 2 2 2 2 2 2
3 3 3 3 3 3 3 3 3 3 3 3 3 3 3 3 3 3 3 3 3 3 3 3 3 3 3 3 3 3 3 3 3 3 3 3 3 3 3 3 3 3 3 3 3 3 3 3 3 3 3 3 3 3 3 3 3 3 3 3 3 3 3 3 3 3 3 3 3 3 3 3 3 3 3 3 3 3 3 3
4 4 4 4 4 4 4 4 4 4 4 4 4 4 4 4 4 4 4 4 4 4 4 4 4 4 4 4 4 4 4 4 4 4 4 4 4 4 4 4 4 4 4 4 4 4 4 4 4 4 4 4 4 4 4 4 4 4 4 4 4 4 4 4 4 4 4 4 4 4 4 4 4 4 4 4 4 4 4 4
5 5 5 5 5 5 5 5 5 5 5 5 5 5 5 5 5 5 5 5 5 5 5 5 5 5 5 5 5 5 5 5 5 5 5 5 5 5 5 5 5 5 5 5 5 5 5 5 5 5 5 5 5 5 5 5 5 5 5 5 5 5 5 5 5 5 5 5 5 5 5 5 5 5 5 5 5 5 5 5
6 6 6 6 6 6 6 6 6 6 6 6 6 6 6 6 6 6 6 6 6 6 6 6 6 6 6 6 6 6 6 6 6 6 6 6 6 6 6 6 6 6 6 6 6 6 6 6 6 6 6 6 6 6 6 6 6 6 6 6 6 6 6 6 6 6 6 6 6 6 6 6 6 6 6 6 6 6 6 6
7 7 7 7 7 7 7 7 7 7 7 7 7 7 7 7 7 7 7 7 7 7 7 7 7 7 7 7 7 7 7 7 7 7 7 7 7 7 7 7 7 7 7 7 7 7 7 7 7 7 7 7 7 7 7 7 7 7 7 7 7 7 7 7 7 7 7 7 7 7 7 7 7 7 7 7 7 7 7 7
8 8 8 8 8 8 8 8 8 8 8 8 8 8 8 8 8 8 8 8 8 8 8 8 8 8 8 8 8 8 8 8 8 8 8 8 8 8 8 8 8 8 8 8 8 8 8 8 8 8 8 8 8 8 8 8 8 8 8 8 8 8 8 8 8 8 8 8 8 8 8 8 8 8 8 8 8 8 8 8
9 9 9 9 9 9 9 9 9 9 9 9 9 9 9 9 9 9 9 9 9 9 9 9 9 9 9 9 9 9 9 9 9 9 9 9 9 9 9 9 9 9 9 9 9 9 9 9 9 9 9 9 9 9 9 9 9 9 9 9 9 9 9 9 9 9 9 9 9 9 9 9 9 9 9 9 9 9 9 9
1 2 3 4 5 6 7 8 9 10 11 12 13 14 15 16 17 18 19 20 21 22 23 24 25 26 27 28 29 30 31 32 33 34 35 36 37 38 39 40 41 42 43 44 45 46 47 48 49 50 51 52 53 54 55 56 57 58 59 60 61 62 63 64 65 66 67 68 69 70 71 72 73 74 75 76 77 78 79 80

CUSTOMER'S NAME | CUST. ACCT. NO. | DATE | QUANTITY | STOCK NO. | UNIT PRICE | AMOUNT

3

0 0 0 0 0 0 0 0 0 0 0 0 0 0 0 0 0 0 0 0 0 0 0 0 0 0 0 0 0 0 0 0 0 0 0 0 0 0 0 0 0 0 0 0 0 0 0 0 0 0 0 0 0 0 0 0 0 0 0 0 0 0 0 0 0 0 0 0 0 0 0 0 0 0 0 0 0 0 0 0
1 2 3 4 5 6 7 8 9 10 11 12 13 14 15 16 17 18 19 20 21 22 23 24 25 26 27 28 29 30 31 32 33 34 35 36 37 38 39 40 41 42 43 44 45 46 47 48 49 50 51 52 53 54 55 56 57 58 59 60 61 62 63 64 65 66 67 68 69 70 71 72 73 74 75 76 77 78 79 80
1 1 1 1 1 1 1 1 1 1 1 1 1 1 1 1 1 1 1 1 1 1 1 1 1 1 1 1 1 1 1 1 1 1 1 1 1 1 1 1 1 1 1 1 1 1 1 1 1 1 1 1 1 1 1 1 1 1 1 1 1 1 1 1 1 1 1 1 1 1 1 1 1 1 1 1 1 1 1 1
2 2 2 2 2 2 2 2 2 2 2 2 2 2 2 2 2 2 2 2 2 2 2 2 2 2 2 2 2 2 2 2 2 2 2 2 2 2 2 2 2 2 2 2 2 2 2 2 2 2 2 2 2 2 2 2 2 2 2 2 2 2 2 2 2 2 2 2 2 2 2 2 2 2 2 2 2 2 2 2
3 3 3 3 3 3 3 3 3 3 3 3 3 3 3 3 3 3 3 3 3 3 3 3 3 3 3 3 3 3 3 3 3 3 3 3 3 3 3 3 3 3 3 3 3 3 3 3 3 3 3 3 3 3 3 3 3 3 3 3 3 3 3 3 3 3 3 3 3 3 3 3 3 3 3 3 3 3 3 3
4 4 4 4 4 4 4 4 4 4 4 4 4 4 4 4 4 4 4 4 4 4 4 4 4 4 4 4 4 4 4 4 4 4 4 4 4 4 4 4 4 4 4 4 4 4 4 4 4 4 4 4 4 4 4 4 4 4 4 4 4 4 4 4 4 4 4 4 4 4 4 4 4 4 4 4 4 4 4 4
5 5 5 5 5 5 5 5 5 5 5 5 5 5 5 5 5 5 5 5 5 5 5 5 5 5 5 5 5 5 5 5 5 5 5 5 5 5 5 5 5 5 5 5 5 5 5 5 5 5 5 5 5 5 5 5 5 5 5 5 5 5 5 5 5 5 5 5 5 5 5 5 5 5 5 5 5 5 5 5
6 6 6 6 6 6 6 6 6 6 6 6 6 6 6 6 6 6 6 6 6 6 6 6 6 6 6 6 6 6 6 6 6 6 6 6 6 6 6 6 6 6 6 6 6 6 6 6 6 6 6 6 6 6 6 6 6 6 6 6 6 6 6 6 6 6 6 6 6 6 6 6 6 6 6 6 6 6 6 6
7 7 7 7 7 7 7 7 7 7 7 7 7 7 7 7 7 7 7 7 7 7 7 7 7 7 7 7 7 7 7 7 7 7 7 7 7 7 7 7 7 7 7 7 7 7 7 7 7 7 7 7 7 7 7 7 7 7 7 7 7 7 7 7 7 7 7 7 7 7 7 7 7 7 7 7 7 7 7 7
8 8 8 8 8 8 8 8 8 8 8 8 8 8 8 8 8 8 8 8 8 8 8 8 8 8 8 8 8 8 8 8 8 8 8 8 8 8 8 8 8 8 8 8 8 8 8 8 8 8 8 8 8 8 8 8 8 8 8 8 8 8 8 8 8 8 8 8 8 8 8 8 8 8 8 8 8 8 8 8
9 9 9 9 9 9 9 9 9 9 9 9 9 9 9 9 9 9 9 9 9 9 9 9 9 9 9 9 9 9 9 9 9 9 9 9 9 9 9 9 9 9 9 9 9 9 9 9 9 9 9 9 9 9 9 9 9 9 9 9 9 9 9 9 9 9 9 9 9 9 9 9 9 9 9 9 9 9 9 9
1 2 3 4 5 6 7 8 9 10 11 12 13 14 15 16 17 18 19 20 21 22 23 24 25 26 27 28 29 30 31 32 33 34 35 36 37 38 39 40 41 42 43 44 45 46 47 48 49 50 51 52 53 54 55 56 57 58 59 60 61 62 63 64 65 66 67 68 69 70 71 72 73 74 75 76 77 78 79 80

For Use in Appendix Problem 22-A

CUSTOMER'S NAME | CUST. ACCT. NO. | DATE | QUANTITY | STOCK NO. | UNIT PRICE | AMOUNT

4

0 0 0 0 0 0 0 0 0 0 0 0 0 0 0 0 0 0 0 0 0 0 0 0 0 0 0 0 0 0 0 0 0 0 0 0 0 0 0 0 0 0 0 0 0 0 0 0 0 0 0 0 0 0 0 0 0 0 0 0 0 0 0 0 0 0 0 0 0 0 0 0 0 0 0 0 0 0 0 0
1 2 3 4 5 6 7 8 9 10 11 12 13 14 15 16 17 18 19 20 21 22 23 24 25 26 27 28 29 30 31 32 33 34 35 36 37 38 39 40 41 42 43 44 45 46 47 48 49 50 51 52 53 54 55 56 57 58 59 60 61 62 63 64 65 66 67 68 69 70 71 72 73 74 75 76 77 78 79 80
1 1 1 1 1 1 1 1 1 1 1 1 1 1 1 1 1 1 1 1 1 1 1 1 1 1 1 1 1 1 1 1 1 1 1 1 1 1 1 1 1 1 1 1 1 1 1 1 1 1 1 1 1 1 1 1 1 1 1 1 1 1 1 1 1 1 1 1 1 1 1 1 1 1 1 1 1 1 1 1
2 2 2 2 2 2 2 2 2 2 2 2 2 2 2 2 2 2 2 2 2 2 2 2 2 2 2 2 2 2 2 2 2 2 2 2 2 2 2 2 2 2 2 2 2 2 2 2 2 2 2 2 2 2 2 2 2 2 2 2 2 2 2 2 2 2 2 2 2 2 2 2 2 2 2 2 2 2 2 2
3 3 3 3 3 3 3 3 3 3 3 3 3 3 3 3 3 3 3 3 3 3 3 3 3 3 3 3 3 3 3 3 3 3 3 3 3 3 3 3 3 3 3 3 3 3 3 3 3 3 3 3 3 3 3 3 3 3 3 3 3 3 3 3 3 3 3 3 3 3 3 3 3 3 3 3 3 3 3 3
4 4 4 4 4 4 4 4 4 4 4 4 4 4 4 4 4 4 4 4 4 4 4 4 4 4 4 4 4 4 4 4 4 4 4 4 4 4 4 4 4 4 4 4 4 4 4 4 4 4 4 4 4 4 4 4 4 4 4 4 4 4 4 4 4 4 4 4 4 4 4 4 4 4 4 4 4 4 4 4
5 5 5 5 5 5 5 5 5 5 5 5 5 5 5 5 5 5 5 5 5 5 5 5 5 5 5 5 5 5 5 5 5 5 5 5 5 5 5 5 5 5 5 5 5 5 5 5 5 5 5 5 5 5 5 5 5 5 5 5 5 5 5 5 5 5 5 5 5 5 5 5 5 5 5 5 5 5 5 5
6 6 6 6 6 6 6 6 6 6 6 6 6 6 6 6 6 6 6 6 6 6 6 6 6 6 6 6 6 6 6 6 6 6 6 6 6 6 6 6 6 6 6 6 6 6 6 6 6 6 6 6 6 6 6 6 6 6 6 6 6 6 6 6 6 6 6 6 6 6 6 6 6 6 6 6 6 6 6 6
7 7 7 7 7 7 7 7 7 7 7 7 7 7 7 7 7 7 7 7 7 7 7 7 7 7 7 7 7 7 7 7 7 7 7 7 7 7 7 7 7 7 7 7 7 7 7 7 7 7 7 7 7 7 7 7 7 7 7 7 7 7 7 7 7 7 7 7 7 7 7 7 7 7 7 7 7 7 7 7
8 8 8 8 8 8 8 8 8 8 8 8 8 8 8 8 8 8 8 8 8 8 8 8 8 8 8 8 8 8 8 8 8 8 8 8 8 8 8 8 8 8 8 8 8 8 8 8 8 8 8 8 8 8 8 8 8 8 8 8 8 8 8 8 8 8 8 8 8 8 8 8 8 8 8 8 8 8 8 8
9 9 9 9 9 9 9 9 9 9 9 9 9 9 9 9 9 9 9 9 9 9 9 9 9 9 9 9 9 9 9 9 9 9 9 9 9 9 9 9 9 9 9 9 9 9 9 9 9 9 9 9 9 9 9 9 9 9 9 9 9 9 9 9 9 9 9 9 9 9 9 9 9 9 9 9 9 9 9 9
1 2 3 4 5 6 7 8 9 10 11 12 13 14 15 16 17 18 19 20 21 22 23 24 25 26 27 28 29 30 31 32 33 34 35 36 37 38 39 40 41 42 43 44 45 46 47 48 49 50 51 52 53 54 55 56 57 58 59 60 61 62 63 64 65 66 67 68 69 70 71 72 73 74 75 76 77 78 79 80

CUSTOMER'S NAME | CUST. ACCT. NO. | DATE | QUANTITY | STOCK NO. | UNIT PRICE | AMOUNT

5

0 0 0 0 0 0 0 0 0 0 0 0 0 0 0 0 0 0 0 0 0 0 0 0 0 0 0 0 0 0 0 0 0 0 0 0 0 0 0 0 0 0 0 0 0 0 0 0 0 0 0 0 0 0 0 0 0 0 0 0 0 0 0 0 0 0 0 0 0 0 0 0 0 0 0 0 0 0 0 0
1 2 3 4 5 6 7 8 9 10 11 12 13 14 15 16 17 18 19 20 21 22 23 24 25 26 27 28 29 30 31 32 33 34 35 36 37 38 39 40 41 42 43 44 45 46 47 48 49 50 51 52 53 54 55 56 57 58 59 60 61 62 63 64 65 66 67 68 69 70 71 72 73 74 75 76 77 78 79 80
1 1 1 1 1 1 1 1 1 1 1 1 1 1 1 1 1 1 1 1 1 1 1 1 1 1 1 1 1 1 1 1 1 1 1 1 1 1 1 1 1 1 1 1 1 1 1 1 1 1 1 1 1 1 1 1 1 1 1 1 1 1 1 1 1 1 1 1 1 1 1 1 1 1 1 1 1 1 1 1
2 2 2 2 2 2 2 2 2 2 2 2 2 2 2 2 2 2 2 2 2 2 2 2 2 2 2 2 2 2 2 2 2 2 2 2 2 2 2 2 2 2 2 2 2 2 2 2 2 2 2 2 2 2 2 2 2 2 2 2 2 2 2 2 2 2 2 2 2 2 2 2 2 2 2 2 2 2 2 2
3 3 3 3 3 3 3 3 3 3 3 3 3 3 3 3 3 3 3 3 3 3 3 3 3 3 3 3 3 3 3 3 3 3 3 3 3 3 3 3 3 3 3 3 3 3 3 3 3 3 3 3 3 3 3 3 3 3 3 3 3 3 3 3 3 3 3 3 3 3 3 3 3 3 3 3 3 3 3 3
4 4 4 4 4 4 4 4 4 4 4 4 4 4 4 4 4 4 4 4 4 4 4 4 4 4 4 4 4 4 4 4 4 4 4 4 4 4 4 4 4 4 4 4 4 4 4 4 4 4 4 4 4 4 4 4 4 4 4 4 4 4 4 4 4 4 4 4 4 4 4 4 4 4 4 4 4 4 4 4
5 5 5 5 5 5 5 5 5 5 5 5 5 5 5 5 5 5 5 5 5 5 5 5 5 5 5 5 5 5 5 5 5 5 5 5 5 5 5 5 5 5 5 5 5 5 5 5 5 5 5 5 5 5 5 5 5 5 5 5 5 5 5 5 5 5 5 5 5 5 5 5 5 5 5 5 5 5 5 5
6 6 6 6 6 6 6 6 6 6 6 6 6 6 6 6 6 6 6 6 6 6 6 6 6 6 6 6 6 6 6 6 6 6 6 6 6 6 6 6 6 6 6 6 6 6 6 6 6 6 6 6 6 6 6 6 6 6 6 6 6 6 6 6 6 6 6 6 6 6 6 6 6 6 6 6 6 6 6 6
7 7 7 7 7 7 7 7 7 7 7 7 7 7 7 7 7 7 7 7 7 7 7 7 7 7 7 7 7 7 7 7 7 7 7 7 7 7 7 7 7 7 7 7 7 7 7 7 7 7 7 7 7 7 7 7 7 7 7 7 7 7 7 7 7 7 7 7 7 7 7 7 7 7 7 7 7 7 7 7
8 8 8 8 8 8 8 8 8 8 8 8 8 8 8 8 8 8 8 8 8 8 8 8 8 8 8 8 8 8 8 8 8 8 8 8 8 8 8 8 8 8 8 8 8 8 8 8 8 8 8 8 8 8 8 8 8 8 8 8 8 8 8 8 8 8 8 8 8 8 8 8 8 8 8 8 8 8 8 8
9 9 9 9 9 9 9 9 9 9 9 9 9 9 9 9 9 9 9 9 9 9 9 9 9 9 9 9 9 9 9 9 9 9 9 9 9 9 9 9 9 9 9 9 9 9 9 9 9 9 9 9 9 9 9 9 9 9 9 9 9 9 9 9 9 9 9 9 9 9 9 9 9 9 9 9 9 9 9 9
1 2 3 4 5 6 7 8 9 10 11 12 13 14 15 16 17 18 19 20 21 22 23 24 25 26 27 28 29 30 31 32 33 34 35 36 37 38 39 40 41 42 43 44 45 46 47 48 49 50 51 52 53 54 55 56 57 58 59 60 61 62 63 64 65 66 67 68 69 70 71 72 73 74 75 76 77 78 79 80

CUSTOMER'S NAME | CUST. ACCT. NO. | DATE | QUANTITY | STOCK NO. | UNIT PRICE | AMOUNT

6

0 0 0 0 0 0 0 0 0 0 0 0 0 0 0 0 0 0 0 0 0 0 0 0 0 0 0 0 0 0 0 0 0 0 0 0 0 0 0 0 0 0 0 0 0 0 0 0 0 0 0 0 0 0 0 0 0 0 0 0 0 0 0 0 0 0 0 0 0 0 0 0 0 0 0 0 0 0 0 0
1 2 3 4 5 6 7 8 9 10 11 12 13 14 15 16 17 18 19 20 21 22 23 24 25 26 27 28 29 30 31 32 33 34 35 36 37 38 39 40 41 42 43 44 45 46 47 48 49 50 51 52 53 54 55 56 57 58 59 60 61 62 63 64 65 66 67 68 69 70 71 72 73 74 75 76 77 78 79 80
1 1 1 1 1 1 1 1 1 1 1 1 1 1 1 1 1 1 1 1 1 1 1 1 1 1 1 1 1 1 1 1 1 1 1 1 1 1 1 1 1 1 1 1 1 1 1 1 1 1 1 1 1 1 1 1 1 1 1 1 1 1 1 1 1 1 1 1 1 1 1 1 1 1 1 1 1 1 1 1
2 2 2 2 2 2 2 2 2 2 2 2 2 2 2 2 2 2 2 2 2 2 2 2 2 2 2 2 2 2 2 2 2 2 2 2 2 2 2 2 2 2 2 2 2 2 2 2 2 2 2 2 2 2 2 2 2 2 2 2 2 2 2 2 2 2 2 2 2 2 2 2 2 2 2 2 2 2 2 2
3 3 3 3 3 3 3 3 3 3 3 3 3 3 3 3 3 3 3 3 3 3 3 3 3 3 3 3 3 3 3 3 3 3 3 3 3 3 3 3 3 3 3 3 3 3 3 3 3 3 3 3 3 3 3 3 3 3 3 3 3 3 3 3 3 3 3 3 3 3 3 3 3 3 3 3 3 3 3 3
4 4 4 4 4 4 4 4 4 4 4 4 4 4 4 4 4 4 4 4 4 4 4 4 4 4 4 4 4 4 4 4 4 4 4 4 4 4 4 4 4 4 4 4 4 4 4 4 4 4 4 4 4 4 4 4 4 4 4 4 4 4 4 4 4 4 4 4 4 4 4 4 4 4 4 4 4 4 4 4
5 5 5 5 5 5 5 5 5 5 5 5 5 5 5 5 5 5 5 5 5 5 5 5 5 5 5 5 5 5 5 5 5 5 5 5 5 5 5 5 5 5 5 5 5 5 5 5 5 5 5 5 5 5 5 5 5 5 5 5 5 5 5 5 5 5 5 5 5 5 5 5 5 5 5 5 5 5 5 5
6 6 6 6 6 6 6 6 6 6 6 6 6 6 6 6 6 6 6 6 6 6 6 6 6 6 6 6 6 6 6 6 6 6 6 6 6 6 6 6 6 6 6 6 6 6 6 6 6 6 6 6 6 6 6 6 6 6 6 6 6 6 6 6 6 6 6 6 6 6 6 6 6 6 6 6 6 6 6 6
7 7 7 7 7 7 7 7 7 7 7 7 7 7 7 7 7 7 7 7 7 7 7 7 7 7 7 7 7 7 7 7 7 7 7 7 7 7 7 7 7 7 7 7 7 7 7 7 7 7 7 7 7 7 7 7 7 7 7 7 7 7 7 7 7 7 7 7 7 7 7 7 7 7 7 7 7 7 7 7
8 8 8 8 8 8 8 8 8 8 8 8 8 8 8 8 8 8 8 8 8 8 8 8 8 8 8 8 8 8 8 8 8 8 8 8 8 8 8 8 8 8 8 8 8 8 8 8 8 8 8 8 8 8 8 8 8 8 8 8 8 8 8 8 8 8 8 8 8 8 8 8 8 8 8 8 8 8 8 8
9 9 9 9 9 9 9 9 9 9 9 9 9 9 9 9 9 9 9 9 9 9 9 9 9 9 9 9 9 9 9 9 9 9 9 9 9 9 9 9 9 9 9 9 9 9 9 9 9 9 9 9 9 9 9 9 9 9 9 9 9 9 9 9 9 9 9 9 9 9 9 9 9 9 9 9 9 9 9 9
1 2 3 4 5 6 7 8 9 10 11 12 13 14 15 16 17 18 19 20 21 22 23 24 25 26 27 28 29 30 31 32 33 34 35 36 37 38 39 40 41 42 43 44 45 46 47 48 49 50 51 52 53 54 55 56 57 58 59 60 61 62 63 64 65 66 67 68 69 70 71 72 73 74 75 76 77 78 79 80

For Use in Appendix Problem 22-A

Transactions

May 1. Issued Check No. 123 for $50.00 to increase the balance of the petty cash fund.
1. Received $87.76 from Paul Smith on account.
2. Issued Check No. 124 for $150.00 for the May rent.
3. Sold merchandise on account to Jack Hendrix, $39.38.
3. Cash sales for May 1–3 were $206.80.
5. Purchased merchandise on account from Lamb & Sons, $251.36.
6. Issued Check No. 125 for $724.44 to Norton Mfg. Co. on account.
7. Received $113.50 from Thomas Kerl on account.
9. Issued Check No. 126 for $100.00 for a cash purchase of merchandise.
10. Cash sales for May 5–10 were $588.45.
12. Received $25.00 for an old display table. (Store Equipment)
13. Sold merchandise on account to Stephen Loescher, $110.75.
15. Issued Check No. 127 for $141.36 to Andrews Bros. on account.
16. Issued Check No. 128 for $300.00 to Mr. Weise for a withdrawal for personal use.
17. Cash sales for May 12–17 were $651.17.
19. Purchased merchandise on account from Dawson & Daily, $750.00.
21. Issued Check No. 129 for $40.00 for advertising. (Advertising Expense)
23. Sold merchandise on account to Robert Clippard, $50.00.
24. Cash sales for May 19–24 were $538.95.
26. Issued Check No. 130 for $76.98 for a cash purchase of merchandise.

Instructions: 3. Assume that on May 27 you have filled page 8 of your next combination journal. Total all columns and forward the totals to the next two pages of your combination journal. Then continue to record the transactions from May 27 to the end of the month.

27. Issued Check No. 131 for $500.40 to Boskin Company on account.
29. Issued Check No. 132 for $73.10 for gas and electricity bill for the month. (Utilities Expense)
31. Issued Check No. 133 for $38.45 for delivery expense.
31. Issued Check No. 134 for $625.00 for the payroll. (Salary Expense)
31. Issued Check No. 135 for $73.35 to replenish the petty cash fund. The petty cash payments were as follows: Supplies, $48.20; Advertising Expense, $7.50; Delivery Expense, $2.00; and Miscellaneous Expense, $15.65.
31. Cash sales for May 26–31 were $475.10.

Instructions: 4. Foot all columns of the combination journal and prove the equality of debits and credits in the journal.

5. Total and rule the combination journal.

CHAPTER 24

APPENDIX PROBLEM 24-A — Recording in a combination journal transactions related to sales and purchases

Instructions: 1. Record the following selected transactions, which were completed by Roger May during January of the current year, on page 15 of a combination journal similar to the one on pages 424 and 425. All sales shown in these transactions were made on account. The cash balance on January 2 was $1,230.50.

Transactions

Jan. 2. Purchased merchandise on account, $450.00, from Miller & Company.
3. Issued Check No. 114 for $90.00 for cash purchase of merchandise.
3. Issued Check No. 115 for $130.68 to Hill Toy Company in payment of their invoice of November 26 for $132.00 less a 1% discount of $1.32.
4. Received a check for $534.60 from Donald Sutton for our invoice of December 28 for $540.00 less a 1% discount of $5.40.
8. Received a credit memorandum for $15.00 from Miller & Company for defective merchandise returned to them.
9. Issued Check No. 116 for $391.05 to Miller & Company in payment of the balance of $395.00 on their invoice of December 20 less a 1% discount of $3.95.
The amount of the invoice of December 20 was $410.00, but a credit memorandum was received for $15.00 from Miller & Co. on January 8. The balance of the invoice to which the discount applied was $395.00.
10. Sold merchandise on account, $720.00, to G. F. Black.
12. Purchased merchandise on account, $956.00, from Pat Ault, Inc.
16. Issued a credit memorandum for $25.00 to G. F. Black for merchandise returned.
18. Sold merchandise on account, $519.50, to John McQueen.
19. Received a check for $688.05 from G. F. Black in payment of our invoice dated January 10 less a 1% discount of $6.95.
The amount of the invoice of January 10 was $720.00. A credit memorandum was given to G. F. Black for $25.00 on January 16. The balance of the invoice to which the discount was applied was $695.00.
23. Issued check No. 117 for $936.88 to Pat Ault, Inc., in payment of their invoice of January 12 less a 2% discount of $19.12.
25. Sold merchandise on account, $410.00, to Donald Sutton.
29. Received a credit memorandum for $18.00 from Gross Novelties, Inc., for merchandise returned to them.
30. Received a check for $514.30 from John McQueen in payment of invoice of January 18 with a 1% discount of $5.20.
31. Issued Check No. 118 for $47.40 to replenish petty cash fund. The summary of petty cash payments was as follows: Supplies, $7.40; Delivery Expense, $10.00; Miscellaneous Expense, $30.00.

Instructions: 2. Total the amounts in each column of the combination journal, prove the equality of debits and credits, and rule the journal.

CHAPTER 25

APPENDIX PROBLEM 25-A | Determination of earnings

The following table gives the hours worked and the hourly rate for ten employees. Each employee is paid his regular hourly rate for a maximum of 8 hours for Monday through Friday. If he works more than 8 hours on any of these five days, he receives time and a half for overtime. He also receives time and a half for Saturday.

Name	*Hours Worked*						*Hourly Rate*
	M	*Tu*	*W*	*Th*	*F*	*S*	
Henry A. Anthony	8	8	8	8	8	4	$1.90
Robert C. Bates	8	8	8	8	10		1.70
Marvin Fuhrman	8	10	8	8	8		1.80
Laurence Gibbs	8	8	8	8	8	3	1.60
William Jackson	8	8	8	0	8		2.10
Richard O'Neill	8	10	8	8	8		2.40
Raymond R. Rizzo	8	8	8	8	10		2.10
Frank O. Schaal	8	8	8	8	8	4	2.10
Martin Webster	8	8	8	8	8	2	2.00
David M. Zapp	8	10	8	8	8		2.20

Instructions: Determine the total earnings for the week for each employee and the total earnings for all employees.

CHAPTER 26

APPENDIX PROBLEM 26-A | Recording and posting payroll transactions

The Skaggs Print Shop completed the payroll transactions given below during the period January 1 to February 5. The Skaggs Print Shop is liable for payroll taxes at the following rates: FICA taxes, 4.4%; state unemployment taxes, 2.7%, and federal unemployment taxes, .4%. It is also liable for the purchase of U. S. Savings Bonds as the accumulated withholdings for each particular employee reaches the necessary amount.

Instructions: 1. Open the following accounts in the general ledger and record the balances as of January 1 of the current year. Allow ten lines for the FICA taxes payable account and five lines for each of the other accounts.

Acct. No.	*Account Title*	*Credit Balance*
22	FICA Taxes Payable..........................	$152.48
23	Employees Income Taxes Payable...............	253.60
24	State Unemployment Taxes Payable.............	210.75
25	Federal Unemployment Taxes Payable...........	121.60
26	U. S. Savings Bonds Payable..................	98.00
64	Payroll Tax Expense..........................	———
65	Salary Expense...............................	———

Instructions: 2. Record the following selected transactions on page 47 of a combination journal.

3. After each entry is journalized, post the items recorded in the General Debit and General Credit columns.

Transactions

Jan. 10. Issued Check No. 18 for $463.76 in payment of the weekly payroll of $610.00 less deductions of $83.40 for income taxes, $26.84 for FICA taxes, and $36.00 for U.S. Savings Bonds deductions.

10. Recorded the employer's payroll tax liabilities.

12. Issued Check No. 23 for $406.08 in payment of the liabilities for employees income taxes and FICA taxes for December.

12. Issued Check No. 24 for $210.75 in payment of the liability for state unemployment taxes for the last quarter of the previous year.

12. Issued Check No. 25 for $121.60 in payment of the liability for federal unemployment taxes.

12. Issued Check No. 26 for $93.75 to purchase five U.S. Savings Bonds for employees.

17. Issued Check No. 36 for $497.24 in payment of the weekly payroll of $640.00 less deductions of $90.60 for income taxes, $28.16 for FICA taxes, and $24.00 for U. S. Savings Bonds deductions.

17. Recorded the employer's payroll tax liabilities.

24. Issued Check No. 49 for $511.26 in payment of the weekly payroll of $660.00 less a deduction of $99.20 for income taxes, $29.04 for FICA taxes, and $20.50 for U. S. Savings Bonds deductions.

24. Recorded the employer's payroll tax liabilities.

31. Issued Check No. 61 for $558.86 in payment of the weekly payroll of $710.00 less a deduction of $99.40 for income taxes, $31.24 for FICA taxes, and $20.50 for U. S. Savings Bonds deductions.

31. Recorded the employer's payroll tax liabilities.

Feb. 1. Issued Check No. 63 for $37.50 to purchase U. S. Savings Bonds for employees.

5. Issued Check No. 70 for $603.16 in payment of the liabilities for employees income taxes and FICA taxes for January.

CHAPTER 27

APPENDIX PROBLEM 27-A | Calculating depreciation, recording depreciation, and finding book value

Dennis Nabors purchased the following items of equipment during the first six years he was in business:

Fixed Asset	*Date of Purchase*	*Original Cost*	*Estimated Life*	*Estimated Scrap Value*
1	January 4, 1962	$2,400	10 years	$200
2	June 30, 1962	250	5 years	None
3	January 6, 1963	6,000	10 years	800
4	September 6, 1963	60	4 years	None
5	April 1, 1965	3,300	8 years	500
6	December 3, 1967	72	4 years	None

Instructions: 1. Record on page 5 of a combination journal the adjusting entry for the total depreciation expense for (a) the year ended December 31, 1962, (b) the year ended December 31, 1963, and (c) the year ended December 31, 1967.

2. Find the book value as of December 31, 1967, of each item of equipment.

CHAPTER 28

APPENDIX PROBLEM 28-A | Purchase and disposition of equipment

Edgar Joseph, a retail shoe merchant, maintains in his general ledger accounts with Equipment, Accumulated Depreciation — Equipment, and Depreciation Expense — Equipment.

Instructions: 1. Record on page 16 of a combination journal the following transactions selected from those completed by Mr. Joseph during the current year.

Transactions

Jan. 2. Issued Check No. 110 for $430.00 for a new electric typewriter.

Mar. 31. Recorded the estimated depreciation of equipment for the quarter ended March 31, $184.60.

Apr. 1. Discarded two chairs for which there was no further use and which could not be sold. The chairs cost $60.00 and had a book value of $15.00 at the time they were discarded.

June 30. Recorded the estimated depreciation of equipment for the quarter ended June 30, $186.90.

July 1. Sold an old office desk for $15.00. The desk cost $80.00 and had a book value of $10.00 when it was sold.

Aug. 15. Issued Check No. 260 for $210.00 for new display shelves.

Sept. 30. Recorded the estimated depreciation of equipment for the quarter ended September 30, $188.40.

Oct. 1. Bought a new typewriter for $235.00 cash (Check No. 304) and an old typewriter. The old typewriter cost $185.00 and had a book value of $40.00 at the time of the trade-in.

Nov. 1. Sold an old adding machine for cash, $40.00. The adding machine cost $210.00 and had a book value of $60.00 after the depreciation was recorded on September 30. The depreciation rate is $3.00 a quarter.
(a) Record the depreciation for October.
(b) Record the sale of the adding machine.

Dec. 31. Recorded the estimated depreciation of equipment for the quarter ended December 31, $187.60.

Instructions: 2. Foot, prove, and record the totals in the combination journal.

CHAPTER 29

APPENDIX PROBLEM 29-A | Recording transactions with bad debts expense

The Sander Lumber Company maintains accounts with Bad Debts Expense and Allowance for Bad Debts. At the beginning of the current year, the balance of the allowance for bad debts account was $216.60.

In this exercise you are given transactions taken from those completed by the Sander Lumber Company during the current year. The transactions cover only uncollectible accounts, bad debts expense, and allowance for bad debts.

Instructions: 1. Record the following transactions on page 23 of a combination journal:

Transactions

Feb. 13. Decided that the past-due account of James Williams, $76.60, was uncollectible. Wrote off his account as a bad debt.

Mar. 27. Leroy Houck, a charge customer, became insolvent. Wrote off his account of $43.00 as a bad debt.

Mar. 31. (End of first quarterly fiscal period.) Increased the allowance for bad debts by making the necessary adjusting entry. The estimated bad debts expense for each quarterly fiscal period was 1¼% (.0125) of the total charge sales. The charge sales for the quarterly fiscal period ended March 31 were $11,650.00.

May 15. John Roth, a charge customer, became insolvent. Wrote off his account of $86.50.

June 30. The total charge sales for the second quarterly period ended June 30 were $9,990.80. Increased the allowance for bad debts 1¼% (.0125) of that amount.

Aug. 21. Decided that the past-due account of Herbert Strassell, $123.80, was uncollectible. Wrote off his account as a bad debt.

Sept. 30. The total charge sales for the third quarterly fiscal period ended September 30 were $10,060.75. Increased the allowance for bad debts 1¼% (.0125) of that amount.

Dec. 31. Decided that the past-due accounts of the following charge customers were uncollectible: Gus Darnell, $82.98; Ralph Fair, $160.30; R. I. Hobbs, $30.00. Wrote them off as bad debts in one combined entry, debiting Allowance for Bad Debts for the total.

Dec. 31. The total charge sales for the fourth quarterly fiscal period ended December 31 were $12,444.50. Increased the allowance for bad debts 1¼% (.0125) of that amount.

Instructions: 2. Foot, prove, and record the totals in the combination journal.

CHAPTER 30

APPENDIX PROBLEM 30-A | Proving cash

Instructions: 1. Make a daily balance slip like the one on page 537. Fill in this form and prove cash from the information given below.

At the close of business on May 2 of the current year, the count of cash in the cash register of Lynne's Gift Shop was as shown in the tabulation at the left below. The detailed audit strip totals for May 2 were as shown at the right below.

Pennies	$ .45
Nickles	3.55
Dimes	6.20
Quarters	13.25
Halves	16.00
Paper money	268.90
Check	35.00

–114	$0,354.60	GT
–113	$0,009.75	Pd
–112	$0.030.00	Rc
–111	$0,036.40	Ch
–110	$0,224.60	Ca

The cash register papers for May 2 were as follows:

(a) Sale on account to Mrs. Mae Jones, $12.80.
(b) Received on account from Miss Alma Carnes, $20.00.
(c) Paid out to Bill Tyler for delivering orders, $1.00.
(d) Sale on account to Mrs. Robert Hess, $10.00.
(e) Paid out to Mrs. B. T. Blair for merchandise returned, $5.30.
(f) Received on account from Mrs. Jay Price, $10.00.
(g) Sale on account to Mrs. Jesse Chapman, $13.60.
(h) Paid out to Greer Supply Co. for store supplies, $3.45.

Instructions: 2. Make a cash short and over voucher like the one on page 538. Fill in this voucher for the cash shortage for the day.

APPENDIX PROBLEM 30-B | Replenishing petty cash

On April 30 of the current year, the end of a monthly fiscal period, the petty cash fund of Tom's Toggery contained the following petty cash paid-out slips and cash short and over vouchers:

Paid-Out Slips			Cash Short and Over Vouchers		
No.	*Account*	*Amount*	*Date*	*Classification*	*Amount*
26	Miscellaneous Expense...	$1.85	Apr. 4	Over...............	$ .90
27	Supplies................	4.20	10	Short...............	.20
28	Sales Returns and Allow..	2.95	15	Short...............	.25
29	Miscellaneous Expense...	1.10	23	Over...............	.30
30	Delivery Expense........	1.80	29	Short...............	.60
31	Sales Returns and Allow..	2.70			
32	Miscellaneous Expense...	3.10			
33	Delivery Expense........	1.25			

Instructions: 1. Sort the paid-out slips according to the accounts to be charged and find the total amount in each group.

2. Find the net amount by which the cash is short or over.

3. Record on page 6 of a combination journal the entry to replenish the petty cash fund (Check No. 129).

APPENDIX PROBLEM 30-C | Recording transactions in a combination journal

J. C. Henry, who operates a retail shoe store, records his transactions in a combination journal like the one on pages 540 and 541. On April 27 of the current year, he finds that page 12 of his combination journal is filled.

Instructions: 1. Forward the following column totals on April 27 to new page 13 of Mr. Henry's combination journal:

Cash Debit, $4,265.68
Cash Credit, $2,458.90
General Debit, $394.10
General Credit, $41.50
Accounts Payable Debit, $2,677.31
Accounts Payable Credit, $3,876.29
Purchases Discount Credit, $34.26
Accounts Receivable Debit, $348.25
Accounts Receivable Credit, $287.50
Purchases Debit, $4,315.91
Sales Credit, $5,302.80

Instructions: 2. Record in the combination journal the following transactions completed by Mr. Henry on April 27 to 30:

Transactions

Apr. 27. Purchased merchandise on account from Zimmer Co., $251.50.

27. The cash register totals for the day were as follows:

Sales for cash, $241.36
Sales on account, $32.50 (A. B. Rhodes)
Received on account, $40.00 (Thomas K. Little)

Apr. 28. Issued Check No. 165 for $287.48 to Weber & Co. in payment of their invoice of June 19 for $312.48 less an 8% discount of $25.00.

28. Received a credit memorandum for $40.50 from Zimmer Co. for defective merchandise.

28. The cash register totals for the day were as follows:
    Sales for cash, $213.95
    Sales on account, $45.00 (J. P. Hyde, $18.50; Ann V. Meier, $26.50)
    Received on account, $34.50 (M. R. Clyde)

30. Issued Check No. 166 for $548.08 for the semimonthly payroll of $680.00 less a deduction of $102.00 for employees income taxes payable and a deduction of $29.92 for FICA taxes payable.

30. Recorded the employer's liability of $29.92 for FICA taxes, $18.36 for state unemployment taxes, and $2.72 for federal unemployment taxes.

30. Issued Check No. 167 for $150.00 to J. C. Henry for a personal withdrawal.

30. The cash register totals for the day were as follows:
    Sales for cash, $288.65
    Sales on account, $30.75 (A. B. Rhodes)
    Received on account, $50.60 (Walter Chase, $4.50; B. L. Kyle, $46.10)

30. Issued Check No. 168 for $37.80 to replenish the petty cash fund. The payments from this fund were as follows:
    Sales Returns and Allowances, $12.90
    Cash Short, $2.20
    Miscellaneous Expense, $22.70

Instructions: 3. Foot, prove, and rule the combination journal.

CHAPTER 31

APPENDIX PROBLEM 31-A | Recording transactions in columnar sales and cash receipts journals

Instructions: 1. Record the following transactions completed by the Shelly Company during May of the current year in a sales journal (page 40) and a cash receipts journal (page 28) like those illustrated in Chapter 31. Begin numbering the sales invoices with No. 61.

Transactions

May 1. Record the cash balance of $1,680.00 in the cash receipts journal as a memorandum entry.

1. Sold merchandise on account to J. T. Fox, $84.00; sales tax, $2.52.

3. Received a check for $160.80 from Fred Arden on account.

3. Sold merchandise on account to A. L. Edwards, $170.00; sales tax, $5.10.

3. Cash sales for May 1, 2, and 3 were $620.00; sales taxes, $18.60.

7. Sold merchandise on account to J. T. Fox, $74.00; sales tax, $2.22.

May 10. Cash sales for the week were $830.00; sales taxes, $24.90.
14. Received $78.00 from Fred Moore on account.
17. Cash sales for the week were $990.00; sales taxes, $29.70.
20. Sold merchandise on account to A. L. Edwards, $260.00; sales tax, $7.80.
21. Received a check for $65.92 from J. T. Fox for balance due on our invoice of May 1 less our credit memorandum No. 18 of May 13 for $20.60.
24. Cash sales for the week were $1,200.00; sales taxes $36.00.
27. Received a check for $180.00 from A. L. Edwards on account.
27. Sold merchandise on account to Ed Carey, $316.00; sales tax, $9.48.
30. Received cash, $6.00, for office supplies sold to accommodate a nearby merchant. (There is no sales tax on this kind of sale.)
30. Cash sales for the week were $1,260.00; sales taxes, $37.80.

Instructions: 2. Foot, prove, total, and rule both journals.

CHAPTER 32

APPENDIX PROBLEM 32-A | Calculating and recording interest and bank discount

The selected transactions given below were completed by Marvin Greene during part of the current fiscal year.

Instructions: 1. Record the following transactions in a cash receipts journal (page 33), a cash payments journal (page 26), and a general journal (page 12) similar to those illustrated in Chapter 32.

Transactions

Mar. 3. Issued our 30-day, 6% Note Payable No. 1 for $1,500.00 to the Macke Lumber Co. for an extension of time on account.
10. Received Note Receivable No. 12 for $600.00 at 5% for 60 days from Todd Hopkins on account.
16. Discounted at the First National Bank our 45-day, 6% Note Payable No. 2 for $1,000.00. The bank credited our checking account for the principal. Issued Check No. 90 for $7.50 in payment of the interest charged in advance.
21. Received a non-interest-bearing, 90-day Note Receivable No. 13 for $450.00 from Jeff Thornton on account.

Apr. 2. Issued Check No. 121 to the Macke Lumber Co. in full payment of principal and interest on Note Payable No. 1, dated March 3.
20. Discounted at the First National Bank our 40-day, 6% Note Payable No. 3 for $400.00. The bank credited our account for the principal. Issued Check No. 186 for $2.67 in payment of the interest charged in advance.

Apr. 30. Issued Check No. 216 to the First National Bank in full payment of our Note Payable No. 2, dated March 16 and due today.

May 9. Received a check from Todd Hopkins in full payment of principal and interest on Note Receivable No. 12, dated March 10 and due today.

10. Issued our 30-day, non-interest-bearing Note Payable No. 4 for $600.00 to the Dexter Lumber Co. for an extension of time on account.

30. Issued Check No. 296 to the First National Bank in full payment of our Note Payable No. 3, dated April 20 and due today.

June 9. Issued Check No. 318 to the Dexter Lumber Co. in full payment of our Note Payable No. 4, dated May 10 and due today.

19. Received notice from the bank that Jeff Thornton dishonored Note Receivable No. 13 when it became due today. Charged the note to the account of the maker.

Aug. 1. Decided that the past-due account of Jeff Thornton (see transactions of March 21 and June 19) was uncollectible. Wrote off his account as a bad debt.

Instructions: 2. Foot and prove the columnar special journals.

CHAPTER 33

APPENDIX PROBLEM 33-A | Adjusting and reversing entries for accrued income and accrued expenses

On December 31 of the current year, before the financial reports were prepared, the salary expense account of J. O. Cobb had a debit balance of $8,245.67. The interest income account had a credit balance of $194.00. The interest expense account had a debit balance of $68.45.

On December 31, accrued interest income on a note receivable was $24.50; accrued salaries were $186.00; and accrued interest on two notes payable amounted to $33.70.

Instructions: 1. Open the following general ledger accounts: Interest Receivable, Account No. 114; Interest Payable, Account No. 212; Salaries Payable, Account No. 213; Income and Expense Summary, Account No. 313; Salary Expense, Account No. 619; Interest Income, Account No. 712; and Interest Expense, Account No. 812. Record the balances in the income and expense accounts.

2. Record on page 10 of a columnar general journal as of December 31 of the current year the adjusting entries for the accrued income and the accrued expenses. Post to the ledger accounts.

3. Record in the columnar general journal the entries to close the interest income account and the salary expense and interest expense accounts. Post to the ledger accounts.

4. Record in the columnar general journal, as of January 2 of the next year, the reversing entries.

CHAPTER 34

APPENDIX PROBLEM 34-A — Distribution of the net income of a partnership

Ruth Hardy, Alice Canter, and Mildred Van Horn are partners in the Tiny Tot Dress Shop. The partners invested in the business $15,000.00, $10,000.00, and $8,000.00, respectively. According to the partnership agreement, the net income is to be divided as follows:

(1) Each partner is to receive an amount equal to 6% of her capital.

(2) The remainder of the net income or the net loss is to be distributed among the partners equally.

At the end of the annual fiscal period on December 31 of the current year, the income statement shows that the net income for the year, after the payment of partners' salaries, amounts to $6,000.00.

Instructions: 1. Prepare a distribution of net income statement.

2. Prepare a capital statement. The debit balances of the partners' drawing accounts on December 31 are: Hardy, $265.00; Canter, $320.00; Van Horn, $120.00.

APPENDIX PROBLEM 34-B — Opening entries and distribution of net income of a partnership

On January 2 of the current year William R. Kerr and Kenneth E. Roman, proprietors of separate retail groceries, formed a partnership. The partnership, Kerr and Roman, took over the assets of the two proprietors and assumed their liabilities. Mr. Roman invested enough additional cash in the partnership to make his proprietorship equal to that of Mr. Kerr. The balance sheets of Mr. Kerr and Mr. Roman at the time the partnership was formed are shown below and on the next page.

William R. Kerr
Balance Sheet
January 2, 19--

Assets			Liabilities		
Cash	2325	60	Notes Payable	1500	00
Notes Receivable	200	00	Accounts Payable	2317	30
Accounts Receivable	3312	40			
Merchandise Inventory	7821	80	Total Liabilities	3817	30
Supplies	157	50			
Equipment	3200	00	**Proprietorship**		
			W. R. Kerr, Capital	13200	00
Total Assets	17017	30	Total Liab. & Prop.	17017	30

Kenneth E. Roman
Balance Sheet
January 2, 19--

Assets			Liabilities		
Cash	1210	65	Accounts Payable	2711	25
Accounts Receivable	3279	40			
Merchandise Inventory	6104	10	**Proprietorship**		
Supplies	101	10	K.E. Roman, Capital	9895	80
Prepaid Insurance	36	80			
Equipment	1875	00			
Total Assets	12607	05	Total Liab. and Prop.	12607	05

Instructions: 1. Record the opening entry for each partner on page 1 of a columnar general journal.

According to the partnership agreement, the net income is to be divided as follows:

(1) Each partner is to receive an amount equal to 6% of his capital.

(2) The remainder of the net income or the net loss is to be distributed between the partners equally.

At the end of the first year in business, the December 31 income statement shows that the net income for the year, after the payment of partners' salaries, is $14,000.00.

Instructions: 2. Prepare a distribution of net income statement.

3. Prepare a capital statement. The debit balances of the partners' drawing accounts on December 31 are: Kerr, $550.00; Roman, $675.00.

CHAPTER 35

APPENDIX PROBLEM 35-A | Opening entry to incorporate a going concern

On March 1 of the current year a charter was granted to Pine & Ault, Inc., that authorized a capital stock of $50,000.00, consisting of 1,000 shares (par value $50.00). This corporation has agreed to take over the printing business owned by the partnership of Pine and Ault. On March 1 the corporation took over the assets and assumed the liabilities of the partnership as shown in the balance sheet on the next page.

Pine and Ault
Balance Sheet
February 28, 19--

Assets			Liabilities		
Cash	4721	85	Notes Payable	1875	00
Notes Receivable	900	00	Accounts Payable	2871	90
Accounts Receivable	4621	45			
Mdse. Inventory	6676	80	Total Liabilities	4746	90
Supplies	716	40			
Equipment	12110	40	**Proprietorship**		
			M. A. Pine, Capital	10000	00
			J. S. Ault, Capital	15000	00
Total Assets	29746	90	Total Liab. and Prop.	29746	90

On March 1, 200 shares of stock were issued to Mr. Pine and 300 shares were issued to Mr. Ault for their equities in the partnership.

Instructions: Record the opening entry on page 1 of a general journal.

APPENDIX PROBLEM 35-B | Balance sheet for a corporation

The Balance Sheet columns of the work sheet of Michael & Co. for the fiscal year ended December 31 of the current year are shown on the next page.

Instructions: Prepare the balance sheet for Michael & Co. Add the net income for the current fiscal period to the balance of the retained earnings account.

Account Titles	*Balance Sheet*			
	Debit		*Credit*	
Cash	7360	21		
Accounts Receivable	8187	25		
Allowance for Bad Debts			106	84
Merchandise Inventory	41639	87		
Supplies	872	45		
Equipment	6750	00		
Accumulated Depreciation — Equipment			562	50
Accounts Payable			6123	40
Taxes Payable			385	60
Capital Stock			50000	00
Retained Earnings			3731	29
	64809	78	60909	63
Net Income			3900	15
	64809	78	64809	78

APPENDIX PROBLEM 35-C | Work at the end of the fiscal period

The account balances in the general ledger of Robbins Corporation on March 31 of the current year are as follows:

Acct. No.	*Account Title*	*Account Balance* *Debit*	*Credit*
111	Cash	$16,819.80	—
112	Petty Cash	150.00	—
113	Accounts Receivable	10,112.64	—
113.1	Allowance for Bad Debts	—	$ 281.60
114	Merchandise Inventory	32,410.50	—
115	Supplies	2,380.75	—
116	Prepaid Insurance	1,401.80	—
117	Equipment	4,800.00	—
117.1	Accumulated Depreciation — Equipment	—	570.00
211	Notes Payable	—	2,000.00
212	Interest Payable	—	—
213	Accounts Payable	—	6,460.50
214	Salaries Payable	—	—
215	FICA Taxes Payable	—	132.70
216	Employees Income Taxes Payable	—	285.45
217	State Unemployment Taxes Payable	—	122.85
218	Federal Unemployment Taxes Payable	—	58.20
219	Federal Income Taxes Payable	—	—
311	Capital Stock	—	30,000.00
312	Retained Earnings	—	6,867.09
313	Income and Expense Summary	—	—
411	Sales	—	127,876.12
411.1	Sales Returns and Allowances	521.30	—
411.2	Sales Discount	1,194.10	—
511	Purchases	81,976.64	—
511.1	Purchases Returns and Allowances	—	561.57
511.2	Purchases Discount	—	2,295.65
611	Bad Debts Expense	—	—
612	Delivery Expense	2,610.20	—
613	Depreciation Expense — Equipment	—	—
614	Insurance Expense	—	—
615	Miscellaneous Expense	4,126.45	—
616	Payroll Tax Expense	941.25	—
617	Rent Expense	3,500.00	—
618	Salary Expense	14,550.00	—
619	Supplies Expense	—	—
811	Interest Expense	16.30	—
812	Federal Income Taxes	—	—

The additional data needed at the end of the annual fiscal period are: additional allowance for bad debts, ¼% of annual *net* sales; merchandise inventory, $34,816.33; supplies inventory, $876.30; prepaid insurance, $576.90; estimated depreciation for the year, $240.00; accrued salary expense, $262.00; accrued interest expense, $7.50; federal income taxes for the year, 25% of net income before taxes.

Instructions: 1. Prepare an eight-column work sheet for the annual fiscal period ended March 31 of the current year.

2. Prepare an income statement and a balance sheet from the work sheet.

3. Record the adjusting and closing entries in the general journal.

4. Record the reversing entries for the accruals in the general journal as of April 1 of the next period.

INDEX

B

D

E

H

I

J

K

L

M

N

O

P

R

S

T

U

V

W